The α-carbon diagram of sperm whale myoglobin shows [...] fferent amino acids are found for porpoise myoglobin. (α-carb[...] ard E. Dickerson, in H. Neurath [ed.], *The Proteins*, 2d ed., vol. [...] 1964.)

The amino acid sequences of sperm whale (blue boxes) [...] boxes) are compared. The fourteen differences are indicated by whit[...] oglobin sequence from Edmundson, 1965; porpoise myoglobin sequence from Bradshaw and Gurd, 1967.)

Matrix shows twelve codon possibilities involved in substitution of lysine for arginine at position 45. The single base substitutions of adenine (A) for guanine (G) are the most probable.

15	16	17	18	19	20	21	22	23	24	25	26
ala	lys	val	glu	ala	asp	val	ala	gly	his	gly	gln
gly	lys	val	glu	ala	asp	val	ala	gly	his	gly	gln

41	42	43	44	45	46	47	48	49	50	51	52
glu	lys	phe	asp	arg	phe	lys	his	leu	lys	thr	glu
glu	lys	phe	asp	lys	phe	lys	his	leu	lys	thr	glu

67	68	69	70	71	72	73	74	75	76	77	78
thr	val	leu	thr	ala	leu	gly	ala	ile	leu	lys	lys
thr	val	leu	thr	ala	leu	gly	gly	ile	leu	lys	lys

93	94	95	96	97	98	99	100	101	102	103	104
his	ala	thr	lys	his	lys	ile	pro	ile	lys	tyr	leu
his	ala	thr	lys	his	lys	ile	pro	ile	lys	tyr	leu

119	120	121	122	123	124	125	126	127	128	129	130
his	pro	gly	asn	phe	gly	ala	asp	ala	gln	gly	ala
his	pro	ala	glu	phe	gly	ala	asp	ala	gln	gly	ala

145	146	147	148	149	150	151	152	153
lys	tyr	lys	glu	leu	gly	tyr	gln	gly
lys	tyr	lys	glu	leu	gly	phe	his	gly

BASIC BIOLOGICAL CHEMISTRY

HENRY R. MAHLER
EUGENE H. CORDES

Department of Chemistry, Indiana University

HARPER & ROW, PUBLISHERS

New York, Evanston, and London

Basic Biological Chemistry

Contents

Preface

The warm reception accorded *Biological Chemistry,* our earlier effort in the realm of biochemistry textbooks, and the encouragement of our colleagues and publisher have provided the incentives for assembling this related volume: a book directed for the most part to a different audience, but one that retains the essential flavor of its predecessor. Experience has indicated that only students with very thorough training in both physical and organic chemistry can use *Biological Chemistry* to good advantage. Furthermore, that book is somewhat difficult to adapt for a one-semester course or for a longer course in which substantial amounts of material outside the scope of the text proper must be included. Even though students lacking comprehensive training in chemistry and short courses are common phenomena, we do not believe that either of these circumstances excuses a coverage of biological chemistry so superficial as to leave the student ill-prepared to deal with relevant problems. We have therefore attempted to adapt *Biological Chemistry* to meet these circumstances. Thus the *essential* differences between *Basic Biological Chemistry* and its parent are found neither in organization and content, nor direction—though some differences in these areas do exist—but in the method of approach to the subject matter. Qualitative statements replace mathematical ones wherever the latter might prove too difficult; emphasis has shifted slightly, away from the physical chemistry of macromolecules and kinetics and mechanism of enzymatic reactions, to metabolism and molecular biology; detailed compilations of experimental data have been avoided; and, finally, there is less use of actual experimental findings as a means of introducing students to new subject areas. On the whole, we hope that with these changes we can introduce the subject matter of *Biological Chemistry* to a new group of students and make it meaningful and understandable to them. Though depth-of-coverage did have to be sacrificed, to some extent, because of restrictions in both the length of the book and its intended audience, we must emphasize that the treatment of each topic remains thorough and reasonably sophisticated. Thus, graduates of courses employing this textbook, rather than the more detailed treatment of its predecessor, may speak of biochemical matters in slightly different terms, but their understanding of the field in general ought to be comparable.

In terms of organization and content, *Basic Biological Chemistry* is distinct from its parent in three principal respects: thermodynamics has been introduced a good deal earlier, a chapter on the chemistry of carbohydrates has been included, and the sections dealing with molecular biology have been broadly reorganized. Other changes are within the framework of the discussion indicated just above.

We owe particular thanks to Professors W. W. Cleland, J. H. Copenhaver, D. Fahrney, W. Terry Jenkins, Albert Light, and Walter Nelson for reading *Biological Chemistry* in its entirety and making line-by-line suggestions, as well as general comments, relevant to its adaptation for the present purpose. We have also profited from the frank comments of a number of reviewers and of others who have written on the same and related topics. Nevertheless, we have not always followed the advice so generously given and the final product must be judged our responsibility alone. Credit for whatever might prove to be right with this work ought to be shared with our advisors; criticism for whatever may prove to be wrong must be directed to no other than the authors. We are also indebted to Andrew Sinauer, our editor at Harper & Row, and to the excellent production and design staffs, especially to Gayle Jaeger for the elegant design of both this book and its predecessor, as well as to Irving Geis for the fine endpaper.

H.R.M.
E.H.C.

Some Symbols and Abbreviations Used in This Book

A	absorbance
D	translational diffusion coefficient
E	extinction
c	concentration in grams per cm^3
f	frictional coefficient
f/f_0	frictional ratio
F	Faraday constant
E	voltage
Fd	ferredoxin
fp	flavoprotein
DFP	diisopropylfluorophosphate
G	Gibbs free energy
g	force of gravity
H	enthalpy
$H_{(\lambda)}$	hypochromicity
$h_{(\lambda)}$	hyperchromicity
i_θ	scattered light intensity
I_θ	incident light intensity
K	equilibrium constant
K_a	acid dissociation constants
hr	hour
k	Boltzmann's constant
m	particle mass

M	molar
M	molecular weight
$M_{\min}$	minimum molecular weight
$\bar{M}_n$	number average molecular weight
$\bar{M}_w$	weight average molecular weight
$\bar{M}_z$	z-average molecular weight
K_s'	salting out constant
n	index of refraction
pK	negative logarithm of K
pI	isoelectric point
PMS	phenazine methosulfate
PRPP	5-phospho-1-pyrophosphoryl ribose
R	gas constant
R_G	radius of gyration
$[R]_\lambda$	reduced mean residue rotation
s	sedimentation constant (coefficient)
S	Svedberg unit
t_m	melting point in degrees C
T_m	melting point in degrees K
S	entropy
$\bar{Z}$	mean net charge
α_λ	rotation at wavelength λ
$[\alpha]_\lambda$	specific rotation
γ	activity coefficient
ϵ	molar extinction coefficient
$\Gamma/2$	ionic strength
η	viscosity
$[\eta]$	intrinsic viscosity
λ	wavelength
μ	ionic strength
$\bar{\nu}$	partial specific volume
ρ	solvent density
σ	transition width
$^\circ$	degrees Centigrade
Π	osmotic pressure

BASIC BIOLOGICAL CHEMISTRY

1 | History and Scope of Biochemistry

Biological chemistry is, for the most part, a science of the twentieth century. In the modern development of the subject, the scope of classical biochemistry has broadened so much that the lines of demarcation between it and other chemical and biological disciplines have become blurred. Indeed, it seems perfectly possible that in the not-so-distant future biochemistry as an independent field of specialization may either practically disappear or else engulf a good deal of what presently fits into the various classifications of chemistry and biology.

Research along the lines of modern biochemistry clearly goes back 200 years. During the latter half of the eighteenth century and throughout the nineteenth, a substantial effort was made to understand both the structural and the metabolic aspects of the life process, efforts that met with some success. Because of the inherent complexity of the problems under attack, a sophisticated appreciation of the chemicals and chemical reactions associated with living material had to wait for the development of other chemical disciplines, particularly of analytical and organic chemistry.

Early structural biochemistry is indissolubly linked with the development of organic chemistry. In fact the pioneering researches of the great Swedish chemist Karl Scheele (1742–1786) concerning the chemical composition of plant and animal tissues proved, eventually, to be the impetus required for this development of biochemistry. Scheele isolated a number of natural substances, including tartaric, lactic, uric, oxalic, citric, and malic acids as well as glycerol, several esters, and casein. With the development of techniques for quantitative elemental analysis in the laboratories of Jöns Berzelius and Justus Liebig during the early stages of the nineteenth century, the substances isolated by Scheele were found to contain carbon.

1

Efforts to synthesize carbon-containing, that is, organic, compounds followed. This was a development of more significance than might appear at first glance, for a belief termed *vitalism*, which maintained that organic compounds could be synthesized only through the agency of a vital force, supposed to be present only in living tissues, was widespread during this period. Although not many investigators realized it at the time, vitalism was rendered untenable by the synthesis of urea by Friedrich Wöhler (1800–1882) in 1828. This achievement was the unexpected result of attempts to prepare ammonium cyanates through the treatment of metal cyanates with ammonium salts. Wöhler's work was followed by the synthesis of acetic acid by Adolf Kolbe in 1844 and the synthesis of several organic compounds by Marcellin Berthelot in the 1850s. Vitalism was quietly laid to rest. Organic synthesis remains very much alive.

The structural chemistry of lipids received considerable attention in the nineteenth century through the work of Michel Chevreul (1786–1889). He demonstrated through studies on saponification, that fats were composed of fatty acids, of which he isolated several, and glycerol. Several others made modest contributions to structural biochemistry during this period. The most elegant and significant work in this field, however, came from the laboratory of the German chemist Emil Fischer (1852–1919). In the course of his studies, this remarkable man completely revolutionized research concerning the structures of carbohydrates, amino acids, and fats.

The nineteenth century also saw the initiation of work on the isolation and characterization of the high-molecular-weight materials so prominent in living matter. Of particular note is the work of Mulder, Liebig, Schützenberger, and others on the isolation of amino acids from protein hydrolysates and again that of Fischer, who deduced how these amino acids are linked in the intact protein. In 1868, F. Miescher discovered nucleic acid in the nuclei of pus cells obtained from discarded surgical bandages and initiated a series of investigations concerning the distribution and properties of the nucleic acids.

Certain facets of the metabolic aspect of biochemistry were also pursued prior to the twentieth century, usually as a result of attention focused on agricultural or medical problems. Of particular note are the basic studies of Antoine Lavoisier on respiration in the period 1779–1784. As a result of the calorimetric measurement of the heat evolved in combustion and respiration of living cells, Lavoisier concluded that respiration can be equated with combustion, slower but not essentially different from that of charcoal. These findings initiated extensive research into energy metabolism, and, as a result, the caloric values per gram of carbohydrate, fat, and protein were established early in the nineteenth century. During the same period the process of fermentation was recognized by Theodor Schwann as being of biological origin. Schwann clearly recognized yeast as a plant capable of converting sugar to alcohol and carbon dioxide. Many of the leading chemists of the day, including Berzelius, Wöhler, and Liebig, considered yeast to be nonliving and fermentation to be caused solely by oxygen.

Research on fermentation was subsequently pursued by several important chemists, the greatest of whom was Louis Pasteur. He identified several organisms that carried out various fermentations, including that leading to butyric acid, a type performed by organisms that function without oxygen. Thus Pasteur introduced the concept of aerobic and anaerobic organisms and their associated fermentations. These conclusions again aroused the ire of Liebig, who had failed to modulate his earlier feelings concerning these processes. These studies culminated in the demonstration of Eduard Buchner in 1897 of fermentation of sugars by a yeast extract. This observation permitted the subsequent identification of the individual reactions comprising the overall process and that of the enzymes that catalyzed each of them. It also expunged, quietly, yet once and for all, any traces of vitalism still remaining.

Other important developments of the nineteenth century included investigations of photosynthesis and carbon dioxide fixation in plants by Horace de Saussure, studies on the process of digestion by Lazaro Spallanzani, René de Réaumur, William Beaumont, and Claude Bernard, and the development of surgical techniques for the study of animal physiology and biochemistry. One of the most important conclusions derived from work in this era was that of the basic unity of biochemistry throughout nature. Although each species, of course, exhibits biochemical individuality, there proved to be striking similarities in the fashions in which widely differing life forms accomplished closely related tasks. This fact enormously simplifies the overall problem of the understanding of life processes.

With the advent of the twentieth century, biochemistry burst into full bloom. Important developments occurred rapidly on many fronts. From a medical standpoint, an understanding of human nutritional requirements is of great importance. The significance of unknown food factors was clearly recognized by Frederick Hopkins at Cambridge University and his associates, who developed the concept of deficiency diseases. Extensive series of feeding experiments utilizing synthetic diets followed in this country, principally under the direction of Babcook, McCollum, Osborne, Sherman, and Mendel. Pellagra, scurvy, rickets, and beriberi became widely recognized as such deficiency diseases, and the curative agents, vitamins, a term introduced by the Polish biochemist Funk, were isolated and subsequently characterized. The work of McCollum, Szent-Györgyi, Steenbock, and Elvehjem is of particular note.

The work of Buchner on cell-free systems capable of carrying out fermentations was energetically followed up in many laboratories, including those of Harden and Young, Embden, and Meyerhof, with the result that the complete biochemical pathway was eventually elucidated. The work of Warburg during this period resulted in the elucidation of the structure of certain cofactors required for the fermentation process. The beautiful work of Krebs on the oxidative metabolism of carbohydrates followed, as did important developments in other areas of intermediary metabolism, particularly in the laboratories of Green, Lynen, Leloir, Bloch, Kennedy, Krebs, Davis, and Shemin. The results of these investigations occupy a considerable portion of this book. Most of the remainder of these pages is devoted to results of studies concerning the properties of macromolecules, particularly proteins and nucleic acids.

Interest in the structure and biochemical properties of proteins was dramatically stimulated by the classic contribution of Sumner — the discovery in 1926 that biocatalysts, enzymes, are proteins. The phenomenon of catalysis was clearly recognized by Berzelius in 1835. At that time, he pointed out potato diastase, an enzyme that catalyzes the hydrolysis of starch, as an example of a biocatalyst and reasoned that all materials of living tissues are formed under the influence of catalytic action, a conclusion thoroughly vindicated by subsequent work. Following, and in some cases preceding, the recognition of biocatalysts, many such entities were isolated, purified to some extent, and the associated reactions investigated kinetically. This work, together with the development of the dynamic aspects of biochemistry indicated above, focused great attention on enzymes. Nevertheless, the chemical composition of these substances was completely unknown prior to Sumner's work. Early workers had suggested that enzymes were protein in nature, but the prevailing opinion in the early twentieth century was that enzymes belonged to none of the recognized classes of organic compounds. The revelation of Sumner was greeted with skepticism and derision, particularly by Willstätter and his students. Sumner's contention rested on his crystallization of the enzyme urease, and its chemical constitution and degradability by proteolytic enzymes, with resultant loss of enzymatic activity, of the crystalline material. Sumner was a persistent and tenacious man armed with a body of convincing evidence and did not capitulate to authority. Subsequent work on the purification of enzymes by Northrup and Kunitz corroborated the protein nature of enzymes and established Sumner as the father of modern enzymology. Invaluable work in this field has been accomplished by du Vigneaud, Sanger, Stein, Moore, Perutz, Kendrew, and Phillips. Concurrently, the work of Chargaff, Watson, Crick, and Wilkins led to the formulation of the structure of deoxynucleic acid, and this marked the beginning of the field of molecular biology.

SCOPE OF BIOCHEMISTRY

During the early part of the twentieth century, the central theme of biochemistry was the development of the field of intermediary metabolism, that is, the elucidation of the pathways for the synthesis and degradation of the constituents of living tissues. Although such studies continue to be important, they no longer dominate research activity in this field. At the present, biochemical research may be classified into nine major areas:

1. Intermediary metabolism
2. Physical chemistry of biological macromolecules, principally the proteins and nucleic acids
3. Organic chemistry of enzyme-catalyzed reactions
4. Protein and nucleic acid biosynthesis
5. Bioenergetics, particularly the mechanisms of formation of adenosine triphosphate in the processes of oxidative and photophosphorylation
6. Cellular control mechanisms
7. Cell ultrastructure
8. The molecular basis for genetic and developmental phenomena
9. The molecular basis for physiological phenomena, including nerve conduction, muscle contraction, vision, and transport across membranes.

LITERATURE OF BIOCHEMISTRY

The rapidity with which new and important developments in biochemistry occur makes a thorough understanding of the biochemical literature mandatory. A table of the most important review and research publications, and their customary abbreviations, follows.

Review Publications		
	Advances in Carbohydrate Chemistry	Advan. Carbohydrate Chem.
	Advances in Enzymology	Advan. Enzymol.
	Advances in Protein Chemistry	Advan. Protein Chem.
	Annals of the New York Academy of Sciences	Ann. N.Y. Acad. Sci.
	Annual Reports of the Chemical Society	Ann. Reps.
	Annual Review of Biochemistry	Ann. Rev. Biochem.
	Annual Review of Microbiology	Ann. Rev. Microbiol.
	Annual Review of Physiology	Ann. Rev. Physiol.
	Annual Review of Plant Physiology	Ann. Rev. Plant Physiol.
	Bacteriological Reviews	Bacteriol. Rev.
	Biochemical Journal	Biochem. J.
	Biochemical Society Symposia	Biochem. Soc. Symp.
	Biological Reviews	Biol. Rev.
	British Medical Bulletin	Brit. Med. Bull.
	Chemical Reviews	Chem. Rev.
	Cold Spring Harbor Symposia on Quantitative Biology	Cold Spring Harbor Symp. Quant. Biol.
	Essays in Biochemistry	Essays in Biochem.
	Harvey Lectures	Harvey Lectures
	Physiological Reviews	Physiol. Rev.
	Quarterly Review of Biology	Quart. Rev. Biol.
	Quarterly Reviews of the Chemical Society	Quart. Rev. (London)
	Vitamins and Hormones	Vitamins and Hormones

Research Publications		
	Acta Chemica Scandinavica	Acta Chem. Scand.
	American Journal of Physiology	Am. J. Physiol.
	Analytical Biochemistry	Anal. Biochem.
	Archives of Biochemistry and Biophysics (until 1951, Archives of Biochemistry)	Arch. Biochem. Biophys. (until 1951, Arch. Biochem.)
	Berichte der Deutschen Chemischen Gesellschaft	Chem. Ber.
	Biochemische Zeitschrift	Biochem. Z.
	Biochimica et Biophysica Acta	Biochim. Biophys. Acta
	Biochemical and Biophysical Research Communications	Biochem. Biophys. Res. Comm.
	Biochemistry	Biochemistry
	Biochemistry (Eng. trans. of Biokhimiya)	Biochemistry (U.S.S.R.) (English trans.)
	Biopolymers	Biopolymers
	Bulletin de la Société Chimie Biologique	Bull. Soc. Chim. Biol.
	Canadian Journal of Biochemistry	Can. J. Biochem.
	Comparative Biochemistry and Physiology	Comp. Biochem. Physiol.
	Comptes Rendus	Compt. Rend.
	Enzymologia	Enzymologia
	Federation Proceedings	Federation Proc.
	Helvetica Chimica Acta	Helv. Chim. Acta
	(Hoppe-Seyler's) Zeitschrift für Physiologische Chemie	Z. Physiol. Chem.
	Journal of the American Chemical Society	J. Am. Chem. Soc.
	Journal of Bacteriology	J. Bacteriol.
	Journal of Biological Chemistry	J. Biol. Chem.
	Journal of Cell Biology	J. Cell. Biol.
	Journal of Cellular Physiology	J. Cellular Physiol.
	Journal of Chromatography	J. Chromatog.
	Journal of Lipid Research	J. Lipid Res.
	Journal of Molecular Biology	J. Mol. Biol.
	Journal of Biochemistry, Tokyo	J. Biochem. (Tokyo)
	Journal of the Chemical Society	J. Chem. Soc.
	Journal of Experimental Medicine	J. Exp. Med.
	Journal of General Microbiology	J. Gen. Microbiol.
	Journal of General Physiology	J. Gen. Physiol.
	Journal of Immunology	J. Immunol.
	Journal of Neurochemistry	J. Neurochem.
	Journal of Nutrition	J. Nutr.
	Journal of Organic Chemistry	J. Org. Chem.
	Journal of Pharmacology and Experimental Therapeutics	J. Pharmacol. Exp. Therap.

Journal of Physical Chemistry	J. Phys. Chem.
Journal of Physiology	J. Physiol.
(Liebig's) Annalen der Chemie	Ann. Chem.
Nature	Nature
Naturwissenschaften	Naturwissenschaften
Plant Physiology	Plant Physiol.
Proceedings of the National Academy of Sciences	Proc. Nat. Acad. Sci. U.S.
Proceedings of the Royal Society	Proc. Roy. Soc. (London)
Proceedings of the Society for Experimental Biology and Medicine	Proc. Soc. Exp. Biol. Med.
Science	Science
Zeitschrift für Naturforschung	Z. Naturforsch.

ABBREVIATIONS OF BIOCHEMISTRY

Perhaps to a greater extent than in any other discipline, the language of biochemistry is expressed by abbreviations. The tables of accepted abbreviations indicated below are hardly comprehensive but will serve as an introduction to those which are most frequently encountered in the literature.

TABLE 1-1. Symbols for Monomeric Units in Macromolecules (or in Phosphorylated Compounds)

Symbol	Monomeric unit in macromolecule	Symbol	Monomeric unit in macromolecule
A, Ado	Adenosine	Hyl	Hydroxylysine
Ala	Alanine	Hyp	Hydroxyproline
Arg	Arginine	I, Ino	Inosine
Asp	Aspartic Acid	Ile	Isoleucine
Asp(NH$_2$), Asn	Asparagine	Leu	Leucine
C, Cyd	Cytidine	Lys	Lysine
Cys˙	Cystine (half)	Man	Mannose
Cys	Cysteine	Met	Methionine
de, d	(indicates "deoxy" in carbohydrates and nucleotides)	Nir	Ribosylnicotinamide
		Orn	Ornithine
f	(Suffix) furanose	*P*, p	Phosphate
Fru	Fructose	*p*	(Suffix) pyranose
Gal	Galactose	Phe	Phenylalanine
G, Glc†	Glucose	Pro	Proline
G, Guo†	Guanosine	Rib	Ribose
GlcA	Gluconic acid	Ser	Serine
GlcN	Glucosamine	Thr	Threonine
GlcNAc	*N*-acetylglucosamine	Trp	Tryptophan
GlcUA	Glucuronic acid	T, Thd	Ribosylthymine
Glu	Glutamic acid	Tyr	Tyrosine
Glu(NH$_2$), Gln	Glutamine	U, Urd	Uridine
Gly	Glycine	Val	Valine
His	Histidine	Xao	Xanthosine

˙ With vertical bond above or below "s."
† The one-letter symbol G must *not* be used if confusion between its two meanings can arise.

TABLE 1-2. Abbreviations for Semisystematic or Trivial Names

ACTH	Adrenocorticotropin, adrenocorticotropic hormone, or corticotropin
ADP	Adenosine 5′-diphosphate (pyro)
AMP	Adenosine 5′-phosphate
ATP	Adenosine 5′-triphosphate (pyro)
BAL	2,3-dimercaptopropanol
CDP	Cytidine 5′-diphosphate (pyro)

Abbreviations for Semisystematic or Trivial Names (*Continued*)

CM-cellulose	O-(carboxymethyl)cellulose
CMP	Cytidine 5′-phosphate
CoA (or CoASH)	Coenzyme A
CoASAc	Acetyl coenzyme A
CTP	Cytidine 5′-triphosphate (pyro)
DEAE-cellulose	O-(diethylaminoethyl) cellulose
DDT	1,1,1-trichloro-2, 2-bis(p-chlorophenyl)ethane
DFP	Di-isopropyl phosphorofluoridate
DNA	Deoxyribonucleic acid
DNP-	2,4-dinitrophenyl-
DOPA	3,4-dihydroxyphenylalanine
DPN*	Diphosphopyridine nucleotide
DPT	Diphosphothiamine (thiamine pyrophosphate, cocarboxylase)
EDTA	Ethylenediaminetetraacetate
FAD	Flavin-adenine dinucleotide
FDNB	1-fluoro-2,4-dinitrobenzene
FMN	Riboflavin 5′-phosphate
GDP	Guanosine 5′-diphosphate (pyro)
GMP	Guanosine 5′-phosphate
GSH	Glutathione
GSSG	Oxidized glutathione
GTP	Guanosine 5′-triphosphate (pyro)
Hb, HbCO, HbO$_2$	Hemoglobin, carbon monoxide hemoglobin, oxyhemoglobin
IDP	Inosine 5′-diphosphate (pyro)
IMP	Inosine 5′-phosphate
ITP	Inosine 5′-triphosphate (pyro)
Mb, MbCO, MbO$_2$	Myoglobin, carbon monoxide myoglobin, oxymyoglobin
MetHb, MetMb	Methemoglobin, metmyoglobin
MSH	Melanocyte-stimulating hormone
NAD	Nicotinamide-adenine dinucleotide (cozymase, Coenzyme I, diphosphopyridine nucleotide)
NADP	Nicotinamide-adenine dinucleotide phosphate (Coenzyme II, triphosphopyridine nucleotide)
NMN	Nicotinamide mononucleotide
P$_i$	Inorganic orthophosphate
PP$_i$	Inorganic pyrophosphate
RNA	Ribonucleic acid
TEAE-cellulose	O-(triethylaminoethyl)cellulose
TPN†	Triphosphopyridine nucleotide
Tris	Tris(hydroxymethyl)aminomethane (2-amino-2-hydroxymethylpropane-1,3-diol)
UDP	Uridine diphosphate (pyro)
UDPG	Uridine diphosphate glucose
UMP	Uridine monophosphate
UTP	Uridine triphosphate (pyro)

* Replaced by NAD.
† Replaced by NADP.

REFERENCES   Chittenden, R. H.: "The Development of Physiological Chemistry in the United States," Chemical Catalogue Company, Inc., New York, 1930.

Ihde, A. J.: "The Development of Modern Chemistry," Harper & Row, Publishers, Incorporated, New York, 1964.

Partington, J. R.: "A Short History of Chemistry," Harper & Row, Publishers, Incorporated, New York, 1960.

2 | Equilibria and Thermodynamics in Biochemical Transformations

An understanding of equilibria and thermodynamic behavior for reactions or systems of reactions is frequently a prerequisite to the full appreciation of biochemical processes. In this chapter, treatment of protonic and metal-ion equilibria and methods for calculation of changes in the basic thermodynamic functions — the Gibbs free energy G (or F), the enthalpy H, and the entropy S — are outlined. Several examples of biochemically important calculations are presented.

PROTONIC EQUILIBRIA

Many important biochemical phenomena are sensitive functions of the state of ionization of the molecular species concerned. These include rates of enzyme-catalyzed reactions, protein conformations and transconformations, ion-binding properties of proteins, electrophoretic and chromatographic behavior of small and large molecules, hemoglobin-mediated transport of oxygen, and so forth. At this point, techniques of dealing with typical protonic equilibria problems are discussed.

The pH Scale

It is frequently more convenient to express the "acidity" of aqueous solutions in terms of the negative logarithm of the hydrogen ion concentration, pH, rather than in terms of this quantity itself. If we ignore the difference between concentrations and activities (this usually involves an error of less than 0.1 pH unit), we may write $p\mathrm{H} \equiv -\log(\mathrm{H}^+)$. Thus a solution 0.1 M in a strong acid is characterized by a value of pH of 1, pure water by a value of 7, and a solution 0.1 M in a strong base by a value of 13. Values of pH are ordinarily measured with the aid of a commercial pH meter equipped with a glass electrode. Such measurements are accurate to ± 0.01 pH units if carried out carefully with an instrument of good quality. More accurate measurements usually require the use of electromotive-force cells, which do not involve a liquid junction.

Calculation of pH
in Systems of
Known Acid or
Base Strength
In the case of strong (i.e., completely dissociated) acids or bases in aqueous solution, values of pH for solutions containing known concentrations of acid or base may be arrived at immediately. Clearly, for the case of strong monobasic acids, $pH = -\log C$, and, for the case of strong bases, $pH = 14 - \log C$, in which C is the molar concentration of acid or base and 14 is the negative logarithm of the dissociation constant for water, $K_w = (H^+)(OH^-) = 10^{-14}$. The calculation is slightly more complicated for the case of a weakly dissociating acid (or base) in aqueous solution. Let K_a be the dissociation constant for a weak acid HA and C the total concentration of A-containing species; i.e.,

$C = (HA) + (A^-)$:

$$K_a = \frac{(H^+)(A^-)}{(HA)} \qquad (2\text{-}1)$$

The condition that the solution be electrically neutral overall requires the equality

$$(A^-) + (OH^-) = (H^+) \qquad (2\text{-}2)$$

Since the concentration of hydroxide ion in mildly acidic solutions is very small indeed, Eq. (2-2) can ordinarily be simplified to

$$(A^-) = (H^+) \qquad (2\text{-}3)$$

Inserting Eq. (2-3) into Eq. (2-1) yields

$$K_a = \frac{(H^+)^2}{C - (H^+)} \qquad (2\text{-}4)$$

This quadratic equation may be solved by the usual methods to give an explicit relationship between the hydrogen ion concentration, K_a, and C:

$$(H^+) = \tfrac{1}{2}[-K_a \pm (K_a^2 + 4K_aC)^{1/2}] \qquad (2\text{-}5)$$

Under most conditions, a somewhat simpler equation may be employed to yield the same information. This equation may be derived by returning to Eq. (2-4) and realizing that usually $C \gg (H^+)$. For example, a 0.1 M solution of acetic acid has $C = 0.1$ and $(H^+) \simeq 0.002$. Employing this assumption, solving Eq. (2-4) yields

$$(H^+)^2 = CK_a \qquad (2\text{-}6)$$

Taking logarithms, rearranging, and defining $-\log K \equiv pK_a$, we obtain

$$pH = \frac{pK_a - \log C}{2} \qquad (2\text{-}7)$$

Returning to the example of a solution of 0.1 M acetic acid, Eq. (2-5) yields a calculated pH of 2.878, and Eq. (2-7) yields a calculated pH of 2.875 (K_a for acetic acid is 1.76×10^{-5}, $pK_a = 4.75$). This calculation clearly indicates that, provided C is not too small, nor the acid too strong, Eq. (2-7) is quite adequate for calculation of pH values for most purposes. Clearly, similar equations may be derived for the case of solutions of weakly dissociating bases. The analogue of Eq. (2-7) for this case is

$$pH = \frac{14 + pK_a + \log C}{2} \tag{2-8}$$

in which pK_a refers to the conjugate acid of the added base.

Titration of
a Weak Acid with
a Strong Base *Henderson-Hasselbach Equation.* Values of pH for a solution of a weak acid to which a known amount of strong base, sodium or potassium hydroxide, for example, has been added may be arrived at by considerations similar to those employed above. The principal distinction lies in the fact that the equation of electrical neutrality must be rewritten so as to include the cation of the strong base. Thus, if we define C as before and X as the amount of strong base added, the equation of electrical neutrality is

$$(M^+) + (H^+) = (A^-) + (OH^-) \simeq (A^-) \tag{2-9}$$

Realizing that $(M^+) = X$, the expression for K_a becomes

$$K_a = \frac{(H^+)(A^-)}{(HA)} = \frac{(H^+)(H^+ + X)}{C - X - (H^+)} \tag{2-10}$$

Although this equation may be solved directly, it is convenient to realize that ordinarily $X, C \gg (H^+)$, in which case Eq. (2-10) simplifies to

$$K_a = \frac{(H^+)(X)}{C - X} \tag{2-11}$$

Taking logarithms, we obtain

$$pH = pK_a + \log \frac{X}{C - X} = pK_a + \log \frac{(\text{base})}{(\text{acid})} \tag{2-12}$$

the well-known and very useful *Henderson-Hasselbach equation.* In terms of this equation, it is easy to see that the pK_a is just that pH at which HA is present half

TABLE 2-1. Values of pK_a for the Dissociation of Some Important Acids

Acid	Conjugate base	pK_a
Acetic acid	Acetate	4.75
Chloroacetic acid	Chloroacetate	2.86
Trichloroacetic acid	Trichloroacetate	0.65
Propionic acid	Propionate	4.88
Lactic acid	Lactate	3.86
Pyruvic acid	Pyruvate	2.50
Acetoacetic acid	Acetoacetate	3.58
Malic acid	Malate monoanion	3.40
Malate monoanion	Malate dianion	5.20
Fumaric acid	Fumarate monoanion	3.03
Fumarate monoanion	Fumarate dianion	4.54
Citric acid	Citrate monoanion	3.09
Citrate monoanion	Citrate dianion	4.75
Citrate dianion	Citrate trianion	5.41
Ammonium ion	Ammonia	9.21
Methylammonium ion	Methylamine	10.62
Imidazolium ion	Imidazole	7.12
Tris (hydroxymethyl) methyl ammonium ion	Tris (hydroxymethyl) amino methane	8.10
H_3PO_4	$H_2PO_4^-$	Small
$H_2PO_4^-$	$HPO_4^=$	7.21
$HPO_4^=$	PO_4^{3-}	12.32

associated and half dissociated; that is, (base) = (acid). Clearly, values of pK_a yield quantitative information concerning acid strength, strong acids being characterized by small values of pK_a and vice versa. Values of pK_a for the common amino acids are presented in Table 3-1; other values of biochemical interest, in Table 2-1.

A plot of pH against equivalents of added hydroxide ion for the titration of acetic acid is shown in Fig. 2-1. Values of pK_a are frequently evaluated from the

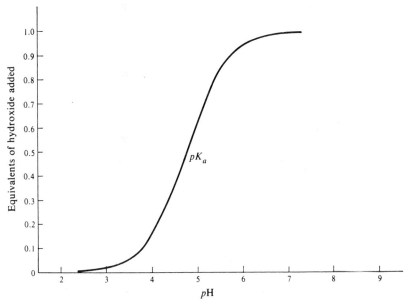

FIGURE 2-1.   The Titration of Acetic Acid.

midpoint of titration curves. At values of pH removed from the vicinity of the pK_a of acetic acid (4.75) the pH changes very rapidly with the addition of small amounts of base. However, near the pK_a the addition of base results in only modest alterations in pH; that is, solutions of acetic acid are *buffered* at values of pH near 4.75. Buffering is very important biochemically both in the sense that organisms must maintain reasonably constant values of pH in the intra- and intercellular milieu and in the sense that proper handling of biochemical materials in the laboratory requires the maintenance of constant pH. It is easy to demonstrate that buffering capacity is a maximum at a value of pH equal to the pK_a of the acid component of the buffering system. Defining dX/dpH as *buffering value* and α as (base)/[(acid) +(base)], it is clear that dX/dpH = constant $\times d\alpha/dp$H. Writing the Henderson-Hasselbach equation in terms of α, we obtain

$$dp\mathrm{H} = dpK_a + d\log\frac{\alpha}{1-\alpha} = \frac{1}{2.3}\,d\ln\frac{\alpha}{1-\alpha} = \frac{d\alpha}{2.3\alpha(1-\alpha)} \qquad (2\text{-}13)$$

from which we conclude

$$\frac{d\alpha}{dp\mathrm{H}} = 2.3\alpha(1-\alpha) \qquad \text{or} \qquad \frac{dX}{dp\mathrm{H}} = \text{constant}\cdot 2.3\alpha(1-\alpha) \qquad (2\text{-}14)$$

Because the product $\alpha(1 - \alpha)$ is a maximum for $\alpha = 0.5$, which corresponds to a value of pH equal to the pK_a, it follows directly that buffering capacity is a maximum at the pK_a. In practice, a given acid-base pair may usually be employed as a buffer in a pH range that extends from one pH unit below the associated pK_a to one pH unit above it.

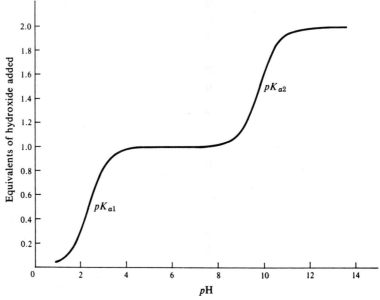

FIGURE 2-2.   The Titration of Glycine.

Dibasic Acids: Protonic Equilibria of Amino Acids. In Fig. 2-2, the titration curve for glycine is shown. This curve is characterized by two dissociations having values of pK_a of 2.35 and 9.78. Reference to Table 2-1 suggests that pK_{a1} (2.35) corresponds to the ionization of the glycine carboxyl group and that pK_{a2} (9.78) corresponds to the ionization of the glycine ammonium ion. Although such a description actually yields a very nearly correct picture of glycine ionization, it is oversimplified and may introduce appreciable errors in related cases. The actual ionization of the glycine molecule is represented by

$$\begin{array}{ccc}
 & \overset{+}{H_3N}\!-\!CH_2 \;\; CO_2^{-} & \\
 & \text{H}A & \\
\overset{+}{H_3N}\!-\!CH_2\!-\!CO_2H & & NH_2\!-\!CH_2\!-\!CO_2^{-} \\
\text{H}A\text{H} & & A \\
 & NH_2\!-\!CH_2\!-\!CO_2H & \\
 & A\text{H} &
\end{array} \tag{2-15}$$

The complete ionization pattern is described by four microscopic dissociation constants, k_a, k_b, k_c, and k_d, one for each of the four microscopic dissociations of the system. These are related by $k_a k_c = k_b k_d$. Thus if three of the microscopic constants are known, the fourth is uniquely defined. The observed macroscopic dissociation constants, K_1 and K_2, are clearly related to the microscopic constants, as indicated below:

$$K_1 = \frac{(H^+)[(HA) + (AH)]}{(HAH)} = k_a + k_b \tag{2-16}$$

$$K_2 = \frac{(H^+)(A)}{[(HA) + (AH)]} = \frac{k_c k_d}{k_c + k_d} \tag{2-17}$$

Thus the macroscopic constant K_1 includes contributions from loss of a proton from both the carboxyl and ammonium functions, and K_2 contains similar contributions. Because we have three independent microscopic constants and only two measurable macroscopic constants, the latter are insufficient to determine the former. However, the magnitude of k_b may be estimated from the dissociation constant of, for example, glycine ethyl ester, $K_a = 2 \times 10^{-8}$. Assuming that $k_b = K_a$ and employing Eqs. (2-16) and (2-17), we find that

$$k_a = K_1 - k_b = K_1 - K_a = 4.45 \times 10^{-3} - 2 \times 10^{-8} \simeq 4.45 \times 10^{-3}$$

$$k_b = K_a = 2 \times 10^{-8}$$

$$k_c = K_2 \frac{k_a + k_b}{k_a} \simeq K_2 \simeq 1.66 \times 10^{-10} \tag{2-18}$$

$$k_d = \frac{k_a k_c}{k_b} \simeq 3.70 \times 10^{-5}$$

Thus, for the case of glycine, K_1 is very nearly equal to k_a, and K_2 is very nearly equal to k_c, in accordance with the assignments of the macroscopic constants to the individual ionizations indicated above. Only in cases in which k_a and k_b or k_c and k_d are of comparable magnitudes are appreciable differences found between microscopic and macroscopic constants.

The ratio of k_a to k_b yields the pH-independent ratio of the concentrations of the zwitterionic and uncharged forms of the glycine molecule:

$$\frac{k_a}{k_b} = \frac{(HA)}{(AH)} = \frac{(Gly^\pm)}{(Gly^0)} = 223{,}000 \tag{2-19}$$

The magnitude of this ratio clearly indicates that, at all values of pH, the zwitterionic form of glycine predominates over the uncharged form (see page 39).

METAL-ION–LIGAND EQUILIBRIA

The association of protonic acids (Brønsted acids) with anionic or neutral bases may be regarded as a special case of the association of acids in general (Lewis and Brønsted acids) with bases in general. A very important additional special case is the association of metal ions with anionic and neutral ligands. These two cases are closely related, as may be appreciated from the fact that the hydrated proton and metal ions frequently compete for available binding sites in suitable bases, such as ammonia and imidazole.

Metal ions play a prominent role in biochemical phenomena, resulting, in part, from their association with both large and small molecules. In the former class are the metal-ion–nucleic acid complexes as well as a great many metal-ion–protein complexes, which fall into two general categories. In some cases, metal ions are an integral part of protein structure and cannot be removed without the concomitant destruction of the structure. Such proteins are termed *metalloproteins*. In addition there are a large number of reversible metal-ion–protein interactions known. Formation of such complexes usually results in the stabilization of a particular conformation of the protein moiety. The association of ATP with metal ions, which is absolutely required before this molecule can react in ATP-dependent enzymatic reactions, is a prominent example of the importance of interactions between metal ions and small organic molecules.

The principal difference in the handling of problems concerning metal-ion equilibria and protonic equilibria arises from the fact that metal ions generally interact with more than one basic site. Thus, metal-ion–ligand systems may be described by assuming the stepwise formation of complexes, $MA, MA_2, \ldots, MA_n$, in which M denotes the metal ion, A the ligand, and n the maximum number of ligands that may associate with M. We may then write a series of equilibrium constants, $K_1, K_2, \ldots, K_n$ for the successive addition of ligands to the metal ion (see page 15):

$$K_1 = \frac{(MA)}{(M)(A)}; \quad K_2 = \frac{(MA_2)}{(MA)(A)}; \quad \ldots; \quad K_n = \frac{(MA_n)}{(MA_{n-1})(A)} \tag{2-20}$$

Alternatively these systems may be described in terms of overall association constants, $\beta_1, \beta_2, \ldots, \beta_n$, in which $\beta_n = (MA_n)/(M)(A)^n$. These constants are related to the successive constants by $\beta_1 = K_1; \beta_2 = K_1 K_2; \beta_n = K_1 K_2 \ldots K_n$. Such constants may be measured conductometrically, spectrophotometrically, and by a variety of additional techniques.

Metal ions typically interact with either two ligands, in a linear array, four ligands, which are disposed about a central metal ion in either a planar or tetrahedral fashion, or six ligands, which are disposed about a central metal ion at the corners of an octahedron. The number of ligands complexed and the stereochemistry of the complex depends both on the nature of the metal ion and on the nature of the ligand.

In general, the successive association constants for complex formation — Eq. (2-20) — tend to decrease with increasing number of ligands. For example, the logarithms of the association constants that characterize the addition of one, two, three, and four molecules of imidazole to cupric ion are 4.36, 3.57, 2.85, and 2.06, respectively. Behavior of this type is usually quite marked in cases in which the basic form of the ligand carries a net charge (i.e., an oxygen anion), because the addition of successive ligands creates successively greater electrostatic repulsions between the ligands.

In Table 2-2, logarithms of association constants for the formation of 1 : 1 metal-ion–ligand complexes are presented. As may be judged from the data in this table, the stabilities of divalent metal-ion–ligand complexes increase in the order

Ca < Mg < Mn < Fe < Co < Ni < Cu > Zn

This order is substantially independent of the nature of the ligand.

As may also be recognized from the data in Table 2-2, the association constants for those ligands which contain more than one binding site are much greater than for those with monodentate ligands. Furthermore, association constants for bidentate ligands are greater than the sum of the two association constants for corresponding monodentate ligands. Thus glycine binds metal ions better than a mixture of acetic acid and ammonia. Cases in which the metal ion is bound to two or more

TABLE 2-2.   Logarithms of Formation Constants

Ligand	H^+	Mg^{+2}	Ca^{+2}	Mn^{+2}	Fe^{+2}	Co^{+2}	Ni^{+2}	Cu^{+2}	Zn^{+2}
Acetic acid	4.7	0.5	0.5	...	...	...	0.7	2.0	1.0
Oxalic acid	4.2	3.4	3.0	3.9	4.7	4.7	5.3	6.2	4.9
Ammonia K_1	9.3	...	−0.2	...	...	2.1	2.8	4.2	2.4
K_2	...	...	...	...	...	1.6	2.2	3.5	2.4
Ethylenediamine	10.1	...	...	2.7	4.3	5.9	7.7	10.6	5.7
Imidazole	7.0	...	0.1	1.7	...	2.4	3.3	4.3	2.6
Histidine	9.2	...	...	1.8	...	6.9	8.7	10.4	6.6
Glycine	9.7	3.4	1.4	3.4	...	5.2	6.2	8.6	5.5
Glutathione (sulfhydryl only)	8.9	...	...	1.9	...	3.7	4.0	...	5.0
Mercaptoacetic acid	10.6	...	...	4.4	5.5	5.8	7.0	...	7.8
Mercaptopropionic acid	10.4	...	...	...	...	...	5.2	...	6.8
2-Mercaptoethyl-amine	10.8	...	...	...	6.2	10.2	10.1	...	9.9
Cysteine	10.5	...	...	4.1	6.2	9.3	10.5	...	9.9

SOURCE: R. B. Martin, "Introduction to Biophysical Chemistry," p. 337, McGraw-Hill Book Company, Inc., New York, 1964.

donor atoms in a single ligand are said to exhibit *chelate* formation. All the amino acids, for example, are capable of chelating metal ions. Of particular interest are the cases of histidine and cysteine, in which a variety of chelate structures may be formed. These are indicated for the case of cysteine below:

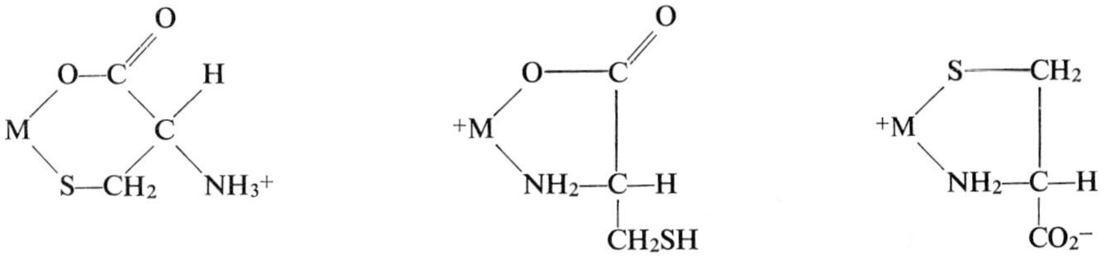

These amino acids bind metal ions more strongly than any others and are probably intimately involved in the formation of metal-ion–protein complexes.

FREE-ENERGY CHANGES: NON-OXIDATION-REDUCTION REACTIONS

The change in free energy of a chemical reaction is, for our purposes, the most important thermodynamic quantity. ΔG is a measure of the amount of *useful chemical energy* (energy other than pressure-volume work) that may be derived from a reaction. In addition, the sign and magnitude of ΔG indicate the extent to which a reaction proceeds. Reactions characterized by a large negative ΔG proceed nearly to completion; those characterized by a large positive ΔG occur only to a very limited extent (or, in the presence of products, go backwards) in the absence of an external driving force. It should be kept in mind that the magnitude of ΔG for a chemical reaction indicates only the extent to which it proceeds and the amount of energy available from it and does not necessarily provide information concerning the rate of the reaction. For many chemical reactions, factors stabilizing or destabilizing the starting material or product also stabilize or destabilize the transition state. For such cases, at least a rough correlation between ΔG and rate exists.

The relationship among the actual free-energy change in a chemical reaction ΔG, its standard free-energy change ΔG^0, and the reactant concentrations is given by

$$\Delta G = \Delta G^0 + RT \ln \frac{(C)^c (D)^d}{(A)^a (B)^b} \qquad (2\text{-}21)$$

At equilibrium, $\Delta G = 0$, and, therefore,

$$0 = \Delta G^0 + RT \ln \frac{(C_{eq})^c (D_{eq})^d}{(A_{eq})^a (B_{eq})^b}$$

since

$$K_{eq} = \frac{(C_{eq})^c (D_{eq})^d}{(A_{eq})^a (B_{eq})^b} \qquad (2\text{-}22)$$

$$\Delta G^0 = -RT \ln K_{eq}$$

in which K_{eq} is the *equilibrium constant* for the reaction. This equation provides the means for the experimental determination of the standard free-energy change of a reaction from the measured equilibrium constant. The actual free-energy change for a reaction occurring under any conditions may then be obtained with the help of Eq. (2-21). It is essential to note that the expression $(C)^c(D)^d/(A)^a(B)^b$ in Eq. (2-21) is not equal to the equilibrium constant except when $\Delta G = 0$. Hence, Eq. (2-21) may be abbreviated to read $\Delta G = \Delta G^0 + RT \ln (P)/(R)$, in which $(P)/(R)$ is the products-over-reactants ratio and becomes equal to K_{eq} at equilibrium, but must not be abbreviated to read $\Delta G = \Delta G^0 + RT \ln K$. If all reactants are present in their standard state, i.e., all activities equal to unity, or, in general, if the $(P)/(R)$ ratio is equal to unity, Eq. (2-21) reduces to

$$\Delta G = \Delta G^0 \qquad (2\text{-}23)$$

Thus, the standard free-energy change is a measure of the useful chemical work that may be obtained from the conversion of 1 mole of reactant to product under conditions in which the $(P)/(R)$ ratio is unity.

The calculation of standard free-energy changes from an equilibrium constant and Eq. (2-22) is deceptively nontrivial. In cases involving the loss or uptake of a proton, which are exceedingly common biochemically, there are three ways, all correct, of making such a calculation. The first equilibrium constant measured, that for the hydrolysis of ethyl acetate, was determined by Berthelot and St. Giles in 1863. This reaction provides a suitable case for the discussion of the three conventions employed to obtain standard free-energy changes.

Convention 1. The hydrolysis of ethyl acetate may be described by the equation

$$\underset{\|}{\overset{\text{O}}{CH_3C}}\!-\!OCH_2CH_3 + H_2O \rightleftharpoons CH_3CO_2H + CH_3CH_2OH \qquad (2\text{-}24)$$

with the associated equilibrium constant

$$K = \frac{(CH_3CO_2H)(CH_3CH_2OH)}{(CH_3CO_2CH_2CH_3)(H_2O)} = 0.33$$

the activity of water being taken as 55 M. It follows directly that at $25°$

$$\Delta G^0 = -RT \ln 0.33 = (-RT \ln 10) \log 0.33$$

$$= -2.3 \times 1.99 \times 298 \log 0.33 = 650 \text{ cal/mole}$$

Rather than include the concentration of water in the equilibrium expression for reactions occurring in aqueous solution, one generally takes, by convention, the activity of water as unity. If we reformulate the equilibrium expression for the hydrolysis of ethyl acetate, employing unit activity for water instead of 55 M, the equilibrium constant becomes $0.33 \times 55 = 18$, and the standard free-energy change at 25° becomes -1710 cal/mole:

$$\Delta G^0 = -RT \ln 18 = (-RT \ln 10) \log 18$$

$$\Delta G^0 = -1710 \text{ cal/mole}$$

Thus, by taking the activity of water as unity, we automatically make the standard free energy of hydrolysis more negative by $-RT \ln 55 = -2370$ cal/mole. We shall continue to employ unit activity for water in discussions of the other conventions below.

Convention 2. Under physiological conditions (*p*H 7), the product of ethyl acetate hydrolysis is largely acetate ion. Hence, an alternative formulation of ethyl acetate hydrolysis is given by

$$\overset{\displaystyle O}{\underset{\displaystyle \|}{CH_3C}}\!\!-\!\!OCH_2CH_3 + H_2O \rightleftharpoons CH_3CO_2{}^- + H^+ + CH_3CH_2OH \qquad (2\text{-}25)$$

with the associated equilibrium constant

$$K' = \frac{(CH_3CO_2{}^-)(H^+)(CH_3CH_2OH)}{(CH_3CO_2CH_2CH_3)} = 18 \times 1.76 \times 10^{-5} = 3.20 \times 10^{-4}$$

The value of K' is obtained from the value of K indicated above and the dissociation constant for acetic acid, $K_{diss} = (CH_3COO^-)(H^+)/(CH_3COOH) = 1.76 \times 10^{-5}$. Employing this formulation, the standard free-energy change for ethyl acetate hydrolysis is

$$\Delta G^0 = 1.3 \times 1.99 \times 298 \times \log 3.18 \times 10^{-4}$$

$$\Delta G^0 = +4900 \text{ cal/mole}$$

Convention 3. The two conventions above are both based on *p*H-independent equilibrium constants and yield *p*H-independent values for the standard free-energy change for this reaction. The calculated values may be employed, together with Eq. (2-21), to calculate the available free energy at any concentration of reactants and any *p*H by substituting into Eq. (2-21) the actual concentration of the indicated species present at that *p*H. Alternatively, the hydrolysis reaction may be formulated for a particular *p*H, usually *p*H 7, and in terms of the total concentration of each reactant:

$$\overset{\displaystyle O}{\underset{\displaystyle \|}{CH_3C}}OCH_2CH_3 + H_2O \rightleftharpoons \begin{pmatrix} CH_3CO_2{}^- \\ + \\ CH_3CO_2H \end{pmatrix} + CH_3CH_2OH + (H^+; \, p\text{H } 7) \qquad (2\text{-}26)$$

For this equation, the appropriate equilibrium constant is

$$K'' = \frac{[(CH_3CO_2H) + (CH_3CO_2{}^-)](CH_3CH_2OH)}{(CH_3CO_2CH_2CH_3)} = K' \times 10^7 = 3.20 \times 10^3$$

and the standard free-energy change, denoted by $\Delta G^{0\prime}$,

$\Delta G^{0\prime} = -2.3 \times 1.98 \times 298 \times \log 3.20 \times 10^3$

$\Delta G^{0\prime} = -4780$ cal/mole

To recapitulate, each of these conventions is correct and useful. The first two yield pH-independent standard free-energy changes and the last a pH-dependent standard free-energy change; that is, the last is directly useful only at the pH for which it is defined. In employing the first two conventions, the actual concentration of species present in acid-base equilibrium must be employed to calculate free-energy changes according to Eq. (2-21). With the third convention, total concentrations are employed. Convention 3 is probably the most generally useful procedure for biochemical problems. In the first place, biochemical reactions generally occur at or near pH 7. In the second place, the calculation of free-energy changes according to conventions 1 or 2 frequently requires the knowledge of the dissociation constants of the acids participating in the reaction. These are often unknown for compounds of biological interest. Finally, convention 1 is mildly displeasing on aesthetic grounds, because it frequently does not accurately represent the actual reaction taking place in solution.

Prior to taking leave of the hydrolysis of ethyl acetate, two additional points are of importance. First, the available free energy from this reaction is pH-dependent. Because, above pH 5, this reaction liberates one proton, the free-energy change for this reaction becomes more negative by $\Delta G = -2.3 \times 1.99 \times 298 \log 10 = -1364$ cal/mole per pH unit. We return to this point below. Second, the free-energy change for this reaction depends, not only on the relative concentrations of reactants and products, but on their absolute concentrations as well. As indicated above, $\Delta G^{0\prime}$ for all components present in their standard state at 25° is -4760 cal/mole. In contrast, if all components are present at 0.01 M (more accurately at activities of 0.01), $\Delta G'$ becomes -7560 cal/mole.

Another example follows. The standard free energy of the hydrolysis of adenosine triphosphate (ATP) to adenosine diphosphate (ADP) and inorganic phosphate,

$$H_2O + ATP \rightleftharpoons ADP + phosphate \tag{2-27}$$

an important biochemical reaction (see Chap. 8), has been evaluated indirectly from the measured equilibrium constant, K_{eq}, for the reaction catalyzed by glutamine synthetase:

$$Glutamate + NH_4^+ + ATP \rightleftharpoons glutamine + ADP + P_i + H_2O \tag{2-28}$$

Expressing K_{eq} in terms of convention 3, we obtain

$$K_{eq} = \frac{(glutamine)(\Sigma\ ADP)(\Sigma\ P_i)}{(glutamate)(NH_4^+)(\Sigma\ ATP)} = 1{,}200 \qquad pH\ 7\ and\ 37° \tag{2-29}$$

In the presence of magnesium ion, a requirement for biochemical ATP-dependent reactions, Eq. (2-29) must be reformulated as

$$K'_{eq} = \frac{(glutamine)(\Sigma\ Mg\ ADP)(\Sigma\ P_i)}{(glutamate)(NH_4^+)(\Sigma\ Mg\ ATP)} = 442 \tag{2-30}$$

to account for the complex formation between this metal ion and the polyphosphates. The overall glutamine synthetase reaction may be expressed as the sum of two reactions:

$$\Sigma \text{ Mg ATP} \rightleftharpoons \Sigma \text{ Mg ADP} + \Sigma P_i \qquad K_1', \Delta G_1^{0'} \qquad\qquad (2\text{-}31)$$

$$\text{Glutamate} + NH_4^+ \rightleftharpoons \text{glutamine} \qquad K_2', \Delta G_2^{0'} \qquad\qquad (2\text{-}32)$$

It follows directly that

$$K_{eq}' = K_1' \cdot K_2' \qquad \Delta G_{eq}^{0'} = \Delta G_1^{0'} + \Delta G_2^{0'} \qquad\qquad (2\text{-}33)$$

$\Delta G_1^{0'}$ can now be calculated by substituting the experimentally determined values for K_{eq}' — Eq. (2-30) — and K_2' — Eq. (2-32) — into Eq. (2-33). K_2' has been measured at 37° and pH 7 as equal to 2.5×10^{-3} M^{-1}. This value, plus the one given earlier for K_{eq}', allows the following calculation for $\Delta G_1^{0'}$, the free energy of hydrolysis of the magnesium chelate of ATP at 37° and pH 7:

$$\Delta G_2^{0'} = 1.98 \times 2.3 \times 310 \times \log 2.5 \times 10^{-3} = 3750 \text{ cal/mole}$$

$$\Delta G_{eq}^{0'} = 1.98 \times 2.3 \times 310 \times \log 442 = -3670 \text{ cal/mole}$$

$$\Delta G_1^{0'} = \Delta G_{eq}^{0'} - \Delta G_2^{0'} = -3670 - 3750 = -7420 \text{ cal/mole}$$

Consequently, the standard free-energy change for the hydrolysis of the magnesium chelate of ATP at 37° and pH 7 is slightly more negative than 7 kcal/mole. This value is in good agreement with estimates obtained by other means.

The actual available free energy from the hydrolysis of 1 mole of ATP under the intracellular conditions is considerably more negative than the standard free-energy change and is probably in the range of -10 to -12 kcal/mole.

The standard free-energy changes for the hydrolysis of a number of substances of biochemical interest are summarized in Table 2-3.

TABLE 2-3. Standard Free Energy of Hydrolysis at pH 7 for Several Compounds of Biochemical Importance

Substrate	$-\Delta G^{0'}$ (pH 7)
Acetyl oxygen esters	5,100
Acetyl thiol esters	7,700
Acetoacetyl-SCoA	10,500
Amino acid esters	8,400
Acetyl phosphate	10,500
Acetyl adenylate	13,300
Mg ATP (ADP, P_i)	7,400
Mg ATP (AMP, PP_i)	7,600
Ordinary phosphomonoesters	3,000
Ordinary phosphodiesters	6,000
Aldose-1-phosphates	5,000
Phosphocreatine	9,000 (pH 7.7)
Phosphoenolpyruvate	13,000
Peptides	500
Glutamine	3,400
Acetylimidazole	13,300
Glycosides	3,000
Dihemiacetals (sucrose)	6,570
S-Adenosyl methionine	10,000
Uridine diphosphoglucose	7,600

As noted above, the use of $\Delta G^{0'}$ values, which are based on total analytical concentrations at the pH at which they are measured and are, therefore, pH-dependent, is frequently preferred to the use of pH-independent ΔG^0 values. The problem thus arises of how to evaluate the variation of $\Delta G^{0'}$ values with pH. If H^+ is a reactant in an equation and the stoichiometry does not change in the pH range of interest — that is, no reactants ionize in this pH range, or if they do, they are on opposite sides of the equation with identical pK_a values — we can represent the reaction as

$$A + B = P + Q + nH^+ \tag{2-34}$$

For such a reaction at equilibrium

$$\Delta G^0 = -RT \ln \frac{(P)(Q)(H^+)^n}{(A)(B)} \tag{2-35}$$

or if

$$\Delta G^{0'} = -RT \ln \frac{(P)(Q)}{(A)(B)}$$

we get

$$\Delta G^0 = \Delta G^{0'} - RT \ln (H^+)^n$$

which can be rearranged to

$$\Delta G^{0'} = \Delta G^0 - n(RT \ln 10)pH \tag{2-36}$$

To correct $\Delta G^{0'}$ from one pH to another

$$\Delta G_2^{0'} = \Delta G_1^{0'} - n(RT \ln 10) \Delta pH \tag{2-37}$$

where $\Delta pH = pH_2 - pH_1$. If the H^+ in Eq. (2-34) were on the left side of the equation, the signs of the last terms would be positive in Eqs. (2-36) and (2-37). We thus see that for reactions with a single H^+ involved, $\Delta G^{0'}$ changes $RT \ln 10$ cal per mole per pH unit.

Although many reactions can be handled by the equations above, there are many common biochemicals that ionize in the neutral pH range, so that we must consider the energy involved in the ionization process. To evaluate these changes, one may employ Eq. (2-38), in which $K_1, K_2, \ldots, K_n$ are the successive proton dissociation constants for the compound in question:

$$\Delta G_{ion} = -RT \ln \left[1 + \frac{K_1}{H^+} + \left(\frac{K_1}{H^+}\right)\left(\frac{K_2}{H^+}\right) + \cdots + \left(\frac{K_1}{H^+}\right)\left(\frac{K_2}{H^+}\right) \times \left(\cdots\right)\left(\frac{K_n}{H^+}\right) \right] \tag{2-38}$$

This is the general equation for ΔG_{ion} at any pH.

As an example of the calculation of the variation of $\Delta G^{0'}$ with pH, we consider the case of ATP hydrolysis. Both ATP and ADP have strongly acidic ionizations, which we shall ignore. The dissociation constants of interest are those for the conversion of the ATP trianion to the ATP tetraanion, $K^{ATP} = 1.12 \times 10^{-7}$; for the conversion of the ADP dianion to the ADP trianion, $K^{ADP} = 2.09 \times 10^{-7}$; for the conversion of the phosphate monoanion to the phosphate dianion, $K^{P_1} = 1.51 \times 10^{-7}$; and for conversion of the phosphate dianion to the phosphate trianion,

$K^{P_2} = 3.16 \times 10^{-13}$. Substituting these values into Eq. (2-38) and thence into the equation that relates ΔG^0 of the reaction with the ΔG's of the ionization constants of the reactants, we obtain

$$\frac{\Delta G_{pH}^{0\prime} - \Delta G_7^{0\prime}}{RT} = \ln\left(\frac{1 + K^{ADP}/10^{-7}}{1 + K^{ADP}/(H^+)}\right)$$

$$+ \ln\left(\frac{1 + K^{P_1}/10^{-7} + K^{P_1}K^{P_2}/10^{-14}}{1 + K^{P_1}/(H^+) + K^{P_1}K^{P_2}/(H^+)^2}\right) - \ln\left(\frac{1 + K^{ATP}/10^{-7}}{1 + K^{ATP}/(H^+)}\right) \quad (2\text{-}39)$$

in which $(\Delta G_{pH}^{0\prime} - \Delta G_7^{0\prime})$ is the difference in $\Delta G^{0\prime}$ values at the pH in question and at pH 7. A plot of the quantity on the left side of Eq. (2-39) against pH is shown in Fig. 2-3. The $\Delta G^{0\prime}$ for ATP hydrolysis is seen to be nearly constant from

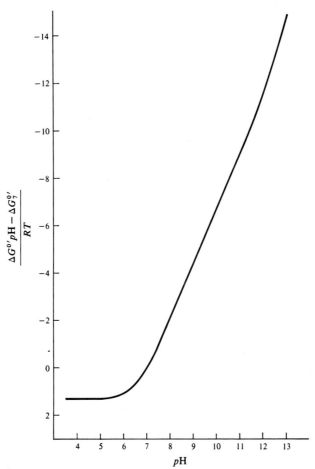

FIGURE 2-3. Variation in $\Delta G^{0\prime}$ for ATP Hydrolysis. As a Function of pH.

pH 4 to pH 6, to decrease linearly from pH 7 to pH 11, and to decrease more rapidly under more alkaline conditions.

FREE-ENERGY CHANGES: OXIDATION-REDUCTION REACTIONS

The calculation of free-energy changes for oxidation-reduction reactions requires a quantitative measure of the tendency of substances to donate or accept electrons. Such a quantitative measure is termed an *oxidation-reduction potential*.

The establishment of a scale of oxidation-reduction potentials requires the choice of a common standard, whose potential is arbitrarily set equal to zero, to which other potentials may be referred. This common standard is the hydrogen electrode, $\frac{1}{2}H_2 \rightarrow H^+ + e^-$, whose potential is taken as zero for a solution containing hydrogen ions at unit activity in equilibrium with hydrogen gas at 1 atm pressure. The oxidation-reduction potential of any electrode may then be conveniently measured relative to the hydrogen electrode by use of an apparatus depicted schematically in Fig. 2-4. Inert metallic electrodes are placed in both half-cells

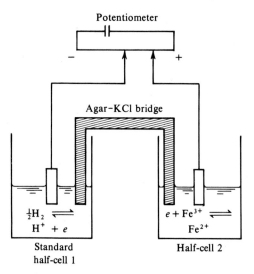

FIGURE 2-4.   A Schematic Representation of an Apparatus Suitable for the Determination of Oxidation-Reduction Potentials. — *J. Fruton and S. Simmonds, "General Biochemistry," page* 297, Wiley, New York, 1958.

and connected through a *potentiometer*, a device capable of measuring the potential difference between the two half-cells, ordinarily expressed in volts. The two half-cells are then connected by means of a salt bridge, which permits the migration of ions but prevents direct chemical reaction between the components of the individual half-cells. Electrons now tend to flow either into or out of the hydrogen electrode, depending on whether the alternate half-cell has a greater or lesser tendency than the reference electrode to donate electrons. The difference in oxidation-reduction potential between the two electrodes is then measured by determining, with the potentiometer, the voltage just necessary to prevent such an electron flow.

In quantitative terms, the difference between the oxidation-reduction potential of any electrode and the hydrogen electrode is given by

$$E = E_0 - \frac{RT}{nF} \ln \frac{\text{(reduced)}}{\text{(oxidized)}} \tag{2-40}$$

in which R is the gas constant; T the absolute temperature; F the faraday, equal to 23,000 cal/absolute volt equivalent; and n the number of electrons per gram equivalent transferred in the reaction. E is the observed potential difference measured in volts, and E_0 is the standard oxidation-reduction potential for the electrode in question. It is clear that, when the activity of the oxidized species is equal to that of the reduced species, the measured potential difference is equal to the standard oxidation-reduction potential. The variation of E with the percentage of oxidation is shown schematically in Fig. 2-5. Equation (2-40) is more conveniently written as

$$E = E_0 - \frac{2.3RT}{nF} \log \frac{\text{(red)}}{\text{(oxid)}} \tag{2-41}$$

At 30°, $2.3RT/nF$ has the value of 0.06 for $n = 1$ and 0.03 for $n = 2$.

Two conventions exist for the determination of the sign of oxidation-reduction potentials: one that assigns more negative potentials to systems that have an

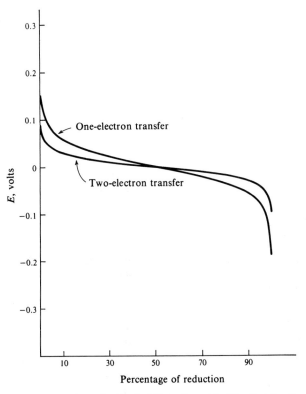

FIGURE 2-5. A Representation of a Typical Potentiometric Titration for Reactions Involving the Transfer of One and Two Electrons. E_0 is arbitrarily taken as zero volts.

increasing tendency to donate electrons (reduction potentials) and one that assigns more negative potentials to systems that have an increasing tendency to accept electrons (oxidation potentials). In accordance with the recommendation of the International Union of Pure and Applied Chemistry, the former convention is used in this book.

Just as it is frequently convenient to obtain standard free-energy changes for hydrolytic reactions for pH 7, it is often necessary to know standard oxidation-reduction potentials at this pH rather than at pH 0. Such electrode potentials are indicated by the symbol E_0'. Several electrode potentials of biochemical interest are collected in Table 2-4.

Oxidation-reduction reactions that involve the uptake or liberation of hydrogen ions are characterized by electrode potentials that are a function of pH. The

TABLE 2-4. Standard Reduction Potentials for Systems of Biochemical Importance

System	E_0' (pH 7), volts
Oxygen/water	0.815
Ferric/ferrous	0.77
Nitrate/nitrite	0.42
Ferricyanide/ferrocyanide	0.36
Oxygen/hydrogen peroxide	0.30
Cytochrome a; ferric/ferrous	0.29
Cytochrome c; ferric/ferrous	0.22
Crotonyl-SCoA/butyryl-SCoA	0.19
Methemoglobin/hemoglobin	0.17
Cytochrome b_2; ferric/ferrous	0.12
Ubiquinone; ox/red	0.10
Dehydroascorbate/ascorbate	0.08
Metmyoglobin/myoglobin	0.046
Fumarate/succinate	0.03
Methylene blue, ox/red	0.01
Yellow enzyme; $FMN/FMNH_2$	-0.122
Pyruvate + ammonium/alanine	-0.13
α-Ketoglutarate + ammonium/glutamate	-0.14
Oxaloacetate/malate	-0.17
Pyruvate/lactate	-0.19
Acetaldehyde/ethanol	-0.20
Riboflavin, ox/red	-0.21
Glutathione, ox/red	-0.23
Acetoacetate/β-hydroxybutyrate	-0.27
Lipoic acid, ox/red	-0.29
$NAD^+/NADH$	-0.32
Pyruvate/malate	-0.33
Uric acid/xanthine	-0.36
Carbon dioxide/formate	-0.42
H^+/H_2	-0.42
Acetate/acetaldehyde	-0.60
Succinate/α-ketoglutarate	-0.67
Acetate + carbon dioxide/pyruvate	-0.70

simplest such case is the hydrogen electrode itself. For this instance, because the standard potential for this electrode is zero,

$$E = \frac{RT}{F} \ln \frac{(H^+)}{P_{H_2}^{1/2}} \tag{2-42}$$

which reduces to

$$E = \frac{2.3RT}{F} \log (H^+) = 0.06 \log (H^+) = -0.06\,pH \tag{2-43}$$

because the standard hydrogen electrode is defined with respect to hydrogen gas at a pressure of unity. Thus at pH 7, the electrode potential for the hydrogen electrode is -0.420 volt.

A somewhat more complicated example is provided by the pH dependence of the potential for half-oxidation of anthraquinone-2,7-disulfonate:

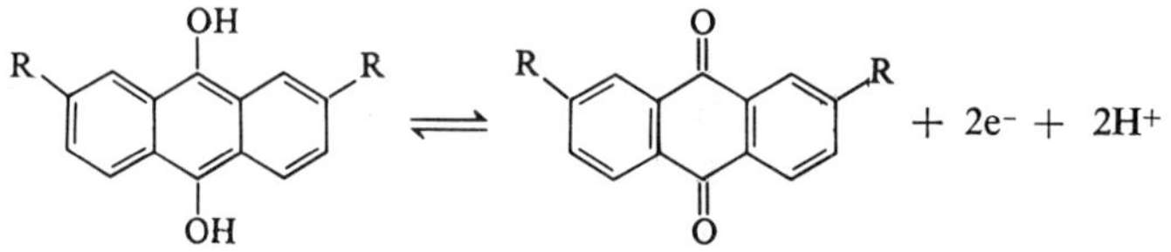

$$+ 2e^- + 2H^+ \tag{2-44}$$

Defining the two dissociation constants for the reduced species

$$K_1 = \frac{(H^+)(Hred^-)}{(H_2red)} \qquad K_2 = \frac{(H^+)(red^=)}{(Hred^-)}$$

and realizing that (total red) $= H_2red + Hred^- + red^=$, we can express (total red) in terms of H_2red and these equilibrium constants:

$$(\text{total red}) = (H_2red)\left[1 + \frac{K_1}{(H^+)} + \frac{K_1K_2}{(H^+)^2}\right] \tag{2-45}$$

Solving Eq. (2-45) for (H_2red) and substituting into the equation describing the electrode potential for this system

$$E = E_0 + \frac{RT}{nF}\ln\frac{(\text{oxid})(H^+)^2}{(H_2red)} \tag{2-46}$$

we obtain

$$E = E_0 + \frac{RT}{2F}\ln\frac{(\text{oxid})}{(\text{total red})} + \frac{RT}{2F}\ln[(H^+)^2 + K_1(H^+) + K_1K_2] \tag{2-47}$$

At low values of pH, $(H^+)^2$ is greater than $K_1(H^+)$ and K_1K_2, and Eq. (2-47) reduces to

$$E = E_0 + \frac{RT}{nF}\ln\frac{(\text{oxid})}{(\text{red})_T} + \frac{RT}{2F}\ln(H^+)^2 = E_0 + 0.03\log\frac{(\text{oxid})}{(\text{red})_T} - 0.06\,pH \tag{2-48}$$

Provided the ratio of concentrations of oxidized and reduced species is constant, the electrode potential for this reaction varies in a linear manner with pH, characterized by a slope of -0.06. Similar considerations indicate that under less acidic conditions in which $K_1(H^+) \gg (H^+)^2$ and K_1K_2, a linear dependence of E on pH is again observed, characterized by a slope of -0.03, and, finally, under basic conditions in which $K_1K_2 \gg (H^+)^2$ and $K_1(H^+)$, E becomes independent of pH. This behavior is indicated in Fig. 2-6.

In general for an oxidation reaction involving the release of a protons and the transfer of n electrons, the expression for the electrode potential

$$H_a red \rightleftharpoons oxid + aH^+ \qquad n \text{ electron transfer}$$

has the form

$$E = E_0 + \frac{RT}{nF}\ln\frac{(\text{oxid})}{(\text{red})_T} + \frac{RT}{nF}\ln(H^+)^a \tag{2-49}$$

Hence, the variation of electrode potential with pH is described by

$$\frac{\Delta E}{\Delta pH} = -0.06\frac{a}{n} \tag{2-50}$$

With these considerations in mind, we are now in a position to turn to the actual evaluation of free-energy changes for oxidation-reduction reactions. Because, once the standard free-energy change is known, Eq. (2-21) suffices to calculate the actual free-energy change under any given set of conditions, the problem is to evaluate

ΔG^0 from the standard oxidation-reduction potentials. The method for accomplishing this evaluation is developed in terms of the following example.

Consider the reversible oxidation-reduction reaction composed of

$$A_{red} + B_{ox} \rightleftharpoons B_{red} + A_{ox} \tag{2-51}$$

the two individual electrode reactions $A_{red} \rightleftharpoons A_{ox}$ and $B_{red} \rightleftharpoons B_{ox}$, which are characterized by standard oxidation-reduction potentials $E_0{}^A$ and $E_0{}^B$, respectively. At

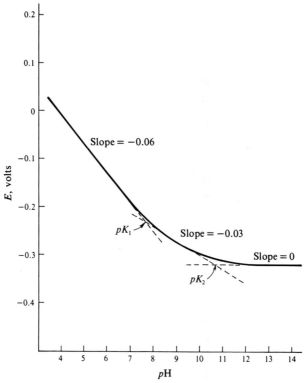

FIGURE 2-6.   The Dependence of the Electrode Potential for the Half Oxidation of Anthraquinone-2,7-disulfonate upon pH.

equilibrium, the electrode potential is clearly given by either of the following two expressions:

$$E = E_0{}^A - \frac{RT}{nF} \ln \frac{(A_r)}{(A_o)} \tag{2-52}$$

or

$$E = E_0{}^B - \frac{RT}{nF} \ln \frac{(B_r)}{(B_o)} \tag{2-53}$$

Hence, we may write

$$E_0{}^B - E_0{}^A = \frac{RT}{nF}\left[\ln \frac{(B_r)}{(B_o)} - \ln \frac{(A_r)}{(A_o)} \right] \tag{2-54}$$

and

$$\Delta E^0 = \frac{RT}{nF} \ln \frac{(A_o)(B_r)}{(A_r)(B_o)} = \frac{RT}{nF} \ln K \tag{2-55}$$

Remembering that $\Delta G^0 = -RT \ln K$, we have, finally,

$$\Delta G^0 = -nF\Delta E_0 \tag{2-56}$$

A typical biochemically important oxidation-reduction reaction is the conversion of β-hydroxybutyrate to acetoacetate, molecular oxygen serving as the ultimate oxidizing agent:

$$\underset{\underset{H}{\overset{|}{\underset{}{}}}}{\overset{\overset{OH}{|}}{CH_3-C-CH_2-CO_2^-}} + \tfrac{1}{2}O_2 \rightleftharpoons \overset{\overset{O}{\parallel}}{CH_3-C-CH_2CO_2^-} + H_2O \tag{2-57}$$

Reference to the values of E_0' in Table 2-4 indicates that the standard free-energy change for this reaction at pH 7 may be obtained as follows:

$$\Delta G^{0\prime} = -2 \times 23,000 \times [0.815 - (-0.293)]$$

$$= -46,000 \times (1.11) = -51,000 \text{ cal/mole}$$

STANDARD ENTHALPY AND ENTROPY CHANGES   The magnitude of the change in enthalpy or entropy for biochemical reactions is sometimes of considerable value for the understanding of the reaction. The standard enthalpy changes associated with reactions are usually evaluated from measurement of the equilibrium constant as a function of temperature and the *van't Hoff equation*:

$$\frac{d \ln K}{dT} = \frac{\Delta H^0}{RT^2} \tag{2-58}$$

Assuming that ΔH^0 is independent of temperature over the range of interest, this equation may be integrated to yield

$$\ln K = -\frac{\Delta H^0}{RT} + \text{constant} \tag{2-59}$$

A plot of log K against the reciprocal of the absolute temperature, provided the assumption of the temperature independence of ΔH^0 is correct, yields a straight line of slope $-\Delta H^0/2.3R$, from which ΔH^0 may be easily evaluated.

Once ΔG^0 and ΔH^0 for a reaction at a given temperature have been established, the standard entropy change ΔS^0 may be obtained immediately from the relationship $\Delta S^0 = (\Delta H^0 - \Delta G^0)/T$.

The use of enthalpy and entropy changes as aids in the understanding of biochemical reactions is illustrated by a consideration of studies on the temperature dependence of the denaturation of proteins. In Table 2-5, the derived thermodynamic parameters for denaturation of chymotrypsin, trypsin, and trypsin inhibitor are collected. The entropy changes are exceedingly large, the ΔS^0 values for most chemical reactions falling in the range $+10$ to -30 eu/mole, and emphasizes, in a dramatic fashion, the degree of structural organization of these proteins in the native state and the loss of this organization in the thermal denaturation process.

Values of ΔH^0 and ΔS^0 are also helpful in identifying the nature of acidic or

TABLE 2-5. Thermodynamics of Protein Denaturation

Enzyme	$\Delta H_d{}^0$	$\Delta S_d{}^0$	Ref.
Chymotrypsin (pH 3)	14.4	438	*
Trypsin inhibitor	57.3	180	†
Trypsin (pH 2)	68	213	‡

* M. Kunitz, *J. Gen. Physiol.*, **32**: 291 (1948).
† M. A. Eisenberg and G. W. Schwert, *J. Gen. Physiol.*, **34**: 583 (1951).
‡ M. L. Anson and A. E. Mirsky, *J. Gen. Physiol.*, **17**: 393 (1934).

basic residues required for enzymatic activity (see Chap. 7) and as an indication of the nature of the forces binding substrates or inhibitors to enzymes.

HIGH-ENERGY COMPOUNDS   The understanding of the essential role of molecules such as ATP as a driving force for a very large number of endergonic reactions has led to a classification of biochemical substances as *high-energy* or *low-energy* compounds. The alternate terms *energy-rich* and *energy-poor* are similarly employed. Molecules such as ATP, which are characterized by a large negative free energy of hydrolysis under physiological conditions are considered energy-rich, and molecules such as ordinary phosphate esters are considered energy-poor. This somewhat nebulous classification has introduced a fair amount of confusion into the biochemical literature, because these terms do not mean the same to all chemists. In this book, we use a definition suggested by Jencks: "An energy-rich compound may be defined as one whose reaction with a substance commonly present in the environment is accompanied by a large negative free energy change at physiological pH." Quantitatively, how does one ascertain if a particular compound falls into the energy-rich class?

There is no clear line of demarcation between the energy-rich and energy-poor classes. As an approximate guide, compounds exhibiting a free energy of hydrolysis at pH 7 more negative than 7 kcal/mole may be considered energy-rich. Because, as emphasized in the definition above, we are interested in free-energy changes at physiological pH, it is clear that, for hydrolysis and related reactions, only free-energy changes calculated according to convention 3 can be considered as a measure of the energy-rich nature of a compound.

Energy-rich compounds fall into several distinct groups, the most prominent of which are those derived from phosphate. The latter compounds fall into four categories: phosphoric acid anhydrides, phosphoric-carboxylic anhydrides, phosphoguanidines, and enol phosphates. In addition, thiol esters, amino acid esters, and dihydropyridines, among others, are all regarded as energy-rich.

Phosphoric Acid Anhydrides. As indicated above, the prime example of an energy-rich compound is the phosphoric acid anhydride ATP. Reference to Table 2-3 indicates that the hydrolysis of this substance to ADP and inorganic phosphate or to AMP and pyrophosphate is accompanied, in both cases, by the release of more than 7 kcal of free energy. Other phosphoric acid anhydrides exhibit similar standard free energies of hydrolysis at pH 7. The energy-rich nature of compounds of this type is most easily understood through consideration of the chemically more familiar, and directly related, case of acetic anhydride. The large negative free-energy change that accompanies the hydrolysis of acetic anhydride at pH 7 is principally the result of two factors. First, the electrophilic carbonyl carbon atom is stabilized by electron donation and destabilized by electron withdrawal. Because the acetyl group is a reasonably strong electron-withdrawing substituent, it tends to destabilize acetic anhydride with respect to the products of the hydrolysis reaction. This is easily grasped by considering the reactivities of acetyl chloride, acetic anhydride, acetyl phosphate, ethyl acetate, and acetamide. Although other factors are certainly involved, the order of reactivity of these derivatives of acetic acid decreases with the decreasing ability of the substituent on the carbonyl carbon to withdraw electrons. Second, the resonance energy of acetic anhydride, 29 kcal, is considerably less than 36 kcal, the resonance energy of two acetate anions, the hydrolysis products at *pH* 7. Consequently, acetic anhydride is unstable with respect to its hydrolysis products. The loss of resonance energy upon the formation of the anhydride results from the fact that the pi electrons of the oxygen atom linking the two carbonyl carbons cannot satisfy the electronic demand of both carbonyl functions simultaneously:

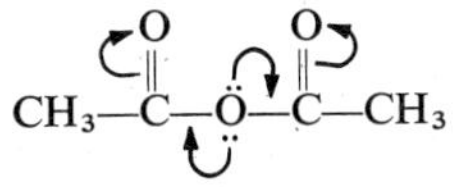

$$CH_3-C(=O)-O-C(=O)-CH_3$$

This situation has been termed *competing resonance*, because both carbonyl functions are competing for the electrons on a single oxygen. This competition is clearly relieved in the hydrolysis products. Similar considerations apply with equal validity to the hydrolysis of phosphoric anhydrides such as ATP, although the gain in resonance energy on hydrolysis is probably less important. In the latter case, an additional factor is also probably important. Because ATP and related substances exist as either the trianion or tetraanion at neutral *pH*, electrostatic repulsions, which are at least partially relieved in the products, may tend to destabilize polyphosphates with respect to the hydrolytic products.

Carboxylic-phosphoric Anhydrides. The biochemically most prominent acyl phosphates (carboxylic phosphoric anhydrides) are acetyl phosphate and amino acyl adenylates, which are characterized by standard free energies of hydrolysis at *pH* 7 of -10.5 kcal and -13.3 kcal, respectively (see Table 2-3). The factors that account for these free energies of hydrolysis are similar to those discussed above for acetic anhydride: the destabilizing influence of the electron-withdrawing phosphate group on the carbonyl function and the decreased resonance energy of the starting material relative to the hydrolysis products.

Phosphoguanidines. Creatine phosphate, which serves as an energy storehouse in the muscles, and arginine phosphate are important examples of naturally occurring phosphoguanidines:

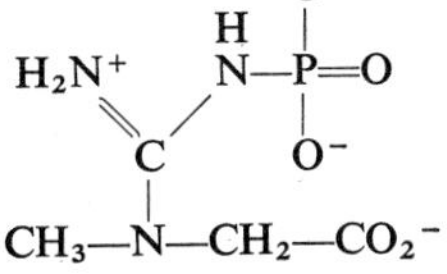

Creatine phosphate

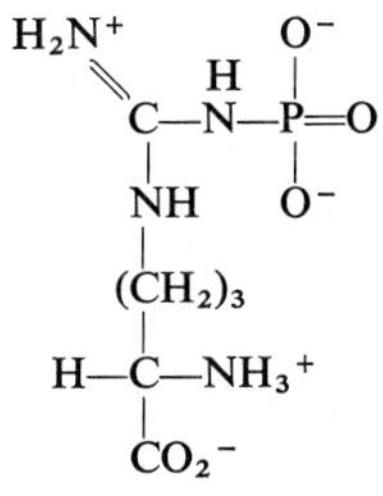

Arginine phosphate

The standard free energy of hydrolysis of such compounds at physiological pH is approximately -9 kcal (see Table 2-3). The energy-rich nature of such compounds is largely due to the inhibition of the normal resonance of the guanidinium ion. The guanidinium ion, or alkyl guanidinium ion, is a nearly symmetrical species with roughly equal contributions to its stability from each of the valence bond forms that may be written for it. The large resonance energy associated with this symmetrical species accounts for the very high basicity of the guanidines. The conversion of guanidines to guanidine phosphates destroys the symmetry of this molecule. In particular, the resonance form with the positive charge adjacent to the positively charged phosphorus atom is quite unfavorable:

$$\begin{array}{ccc} \overset{H}{\underset{|}{}}\ \overset{N^+H_2}{\underset{\|}{}} & & \overset{H}{\underset{|}{}}\ \overset{NH_2}{\underset{|}{}} \\ R\!-\!N\!-\!C & \leftrightarrow & R\!-\!N^+\!=\!C & \leftrightarrow & R\!-\!N\!-\!C \\ \diagdown NH_2 & & \diagdown NH_2 & & \diagdown N^+H_2 \end{array}$$

$$\text{Enol Phosphates.}$$

Enol Phosphates. Phosphoenol pyruvate, an important intermediate in the metabolism of carbohydrates, is characterized by such a large negative free energy of hydrolysis (13 kcal) that its reaction with ADP to form ATP and pyruvic acid proceeds very nearly to completion:

$$\overset{\displaystyle OPO_3^=}{\underset{\displaystyle CH_2\!=\!C\!-\!CO_2^-}{|}}$$

Phosphoenol pyruvate

Compounds of this general nature are excellent phosphorylating agents and have recently found wide application in the synthesis of organic phosphates. The energy-rich nature of phosphoenol pyruvate is the result of two factors. First, the enol of pyruvic acid, in which form the phosphate is constrained to exist, is less stable than the keto form, which is adopted by the hydrolysis product, by approximately 10 to 12 kcal/mole. Thus the conversion of the enol to the keto form provides a strong driving force for the hydrolysis reaction. Second, the hybridization of the O—P bond in phosphoenol pyruvate is sp_2. Such bonds are inherently less strong than sp_3 bonds, and, consequently, enol phosphates are less stable than ordinary phosphate esters. An additional example of behavior of this type is provided by the acyl cyanides, in which the bond to be cleaved is sp. Acyl cyanides are excellent acyl group donors.

Thiol Esters. Thiol esters, particularly those involving coenzyme A (see Chap. 8), play a very significant role in metabolism, particularly in acyl group transfer reactions. As indicated in Table 2-3, the standard free energy of hydrolysis under physiological conditions is approximately -8 kcal/mole. Thus thiol esters clearly fall into the category of high-energy compounds. The diminished resonance interaction between the pi electrons of the sulfur atom and the carbonyl group, compared with such interaction in ordinary oxygen esters or in carboxylate anions, provides a driving force for the hydrolysis reaction and accounts for the increased standard free energy of hydrolysis compared with oxygen esters (see page 19). Indeed, some studies have actually suggested that the sulfur atom, not only does not act as an effective electron donor to the carbonyl group, but may actually act as an electron acceptor:

$$R_1-\overset{\overset{\displaystyle O}{\|}}{C}-O-R_2 \ \leftrightarrow \ R_1-\overset{\overset{\displaystyle O^-}{|}}{C}=O^+-R_2$$

$$R_1-\overset{\overset{\displaystyle O}{\|}}{C}-S-R_2 \ \leftrightarrow \ \left[R_1-\overset{\overset{\displaystyle O^-}{|}}{C}=S^+-R \ \leftrightarrow \ R_1-\overset{\overset{\displaystyle O^+}{|}}{C}=S^--R \right]$$

Relatively poor

Amino Acid Esters. Amino acid esters, which are important intermediates in the biosynthesis of proteins, exhibit a standard free energy of hydrolysis comparable with that of ATP. It should be noted that the free energy of hydrolysis of glycine ethyl ester, for example, to the free acid is nearly the same as that for ethyl acetate. However, the high acidity of glycine, $pK_a = 2.3$, compared with that of acetic acid, $pK_a = 4.76$, results in the standard free energy of hydrolysis of the amino acid ester at pH 7 being greater than that of ethyl acetate by $298 \times 1.98 \times 2.3 \times \Delta pK_a = -3300$ cal/mole at $25°$. Although the division of ester hydrolysis at pH 7 into a hydrolysis reaction to the free acid and an ionization of the acid is convenient for the purposes of calculating free-energy changes, it is improper to regard the large free-energy changes accompanying the hydrolysis of esters of strongly acidic acids as resulting from a large ΔG term for the ionization. The free energy is a state function and does not depend on the course arbitrarily chosen for the reaction. The thermodynamic instability of amino acid esters is properly considered as resulting from destabilization of the ester by the strongly electron-withdrawing ammonium group.

REFERENCES

Clark, W. M.: "Topics in Physical Chemistry," Williams & Wilkins, Baltimore, 1948.

Edsall, J. T., and J. Wyman: "Biophysical Chemistry," Academic, New York, 1958.

Glasstone, S.: "Thermodynamics for Chemists," Van Nostrand, Princeton, N.J., 1947.

Gurd, F. R. N., and P. E. Wilcox: Complex Formation between Metallic Cations and Proteins, Peptides, and Amino Acids, *Advances Prot. Chem.*, **11**: 311 (1956).

Klotz, I. M.: "Chemical Thermodynamics," Prentice-Hall, Englewood Cliffs, N.J., 1950.

Laidler, K. J.: "The Chemical Kinetics of Enzyme Action," Oxford, Fair Lawn, N.J., 1958.

Lipmann, F.: Metabolic Generation and Utilization of Phosphate Bond Energy, *Advan. Enzymol.*, **1**: 99 (1941).

Rossini, F. D.: "Chemical Thermodynamics," Wiley, New York, 1950.

Rossotti, F. J. C., and H. Rossotti: "Determination of Stability Constants," McGraw-Hill, New York, 1961.

3 | Proteins: Classification, Properties, Purification

Proteins are ubiquitous components of all living tissues — animal, plant, and bacterial. They serve indispensable functions in cellular architecture, catalysis, metabolic regulation, and contractile processes and are an important weapon in the defense arsenal of many higher organisms. Indeed, proteins are intimately concerned with virtually all physiological events. It is apropos, then, that the name "protein" is derived from a Greek word meaning first.

Proteins are macromolecules and, like nearly all biological macromolecules, are polymers. There is no clear line of demarcation indicating how many monomeric units are required to make a protein. Arbitrarily, the lower boundary for the molecular weight of proteins is taken to be about 5,000; the term *polypeptide* is reserved for substances of lower molecular weight built from similar units. Many proteins commonly occurring in living material have molecular weights of several million. The chemistry of molecules of this size is necessarily very complex and is, at this stage in the development of macromolecular chemistry, not completely manageable. We begin with a brief discussion of the chemistry of the monomeric units of proteins, the α-amino acids, then consider their assembly into polymeric material, discuss some of the properties of the proteins, and finally indicate something about the isolation and purification of these materials from natural sources. In Chap. 4, a more detailed discussion of the structure of proteins is presented.

AMINO ACIDS:
STRUCTURAL UNITS
OF PROTEINS
Structures

The complete hydrolysis of proteins yields a mixture of about twenty *amino acids*. With two exceptions, these substances have a primary amino function and a carboxyl function joined to the same carbon atom; hence they are termed α-amino

32

acids and are derivatives of the general structure NH_2—CHR—COOH. The two exceptions, proline and hydroxyproline, are α-imino acids. The structures of the amino acids that are commonly found in the hydrolysates of proteins are shown in Table 3-1. These amino acids are classified into seven groups: those which have (1) aliphatic side chains, (2) hydroxylic side chains, (3) carboxylic side chains and their amides, (4) basic side chains, (5) aromatic side chains, (6) sulfur-containing side chains, and (7) the imino acids. In addition to those listed in Table 3-1, several other amino acids have been reported to be present in the hydrolysates of individual proteins. As these are distinctly isolated cases and are not apparently intimately concerned with either the structure or function of these proteins, they will not be considered further.

For the most part, proteins are constructed of linear, covalently bonded chains of amino acids. Because each position in such a chain may be occupied by any of about twenty distinct amino acids, the total number of structurally unique proteins containing, for example, 100 monomeric units is almost limitless (20^{100} in the present case). The reality of enormous structural variation in this group of polymers accounts, in part, for their broad spectrum of biological functions.

Many amino acids and their derivatives that are not constituents of proteins are, nevertheless, biochemically important. A brief compilation of some of the most prominent such substances, together with a few comments concerning their biochemical importance, is presented in Table 3-2.

Optical Activity   With the single exception of glycine, all amino acids obtained from proteins are optically active, since the α carbon of each is asymmetric. The absolute configuration of the amino acids has been related to that of L-glyceraldehyde. Without exception, amino acids obtained from protein digested in such a way that racemization does not occur are of the L- configuration. The stereochemical relationship of L-glyceraldehyde to L-alanine is depicted below:

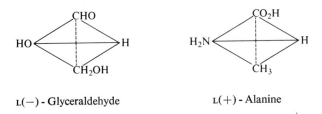

L(−) - Glyceraldehyde   L(+) - Alanine

It is worth emphasizing that the designations L- and D- refer, not to the direction of rotation of plane-polarized light, but to absolute configurations relative to those of glyceraldehyde.

The sign and magnitude of the optical rotation of the amino acids is, of course, a sensitive function of the nature of the side chain. In addition, as both the amino and carboxyl functions undergo protolytic reactions, the optical rotation is also a function of the pH of the solution in which it is measured.

In addition to the asymmetric center at the α-carbon atom, threonine, isoleucine, hydroxyproline, hydroxylysine, and cystine have a second asymmetric center. Thus, there exist, in the laboratory if not in nature, four diastereomers of these amino acids. These are designated L-, D-, L-allo-, and D-allo-. The configurations

TABLE 3-1. Amino Acids that Commonly Occur in Proteins

Name	Structure	Values of pK_a	pI	Remarks
I. Aliphatic amino acids				
1. Glycine (Gly)	$H_2N-CH_2-CO_2H$	2.34; 9.6	5.97	
2. Alanine (Ala)	CH₃ | $H_2N-CH-CO_2H$	2.35; 9.69	6.02	
3. Valine (Val)	CH₃ CH₃ \ / CH | $H_2N-CH-CO_2H$	2.32; 9.62	5.97	
4. Leucine (Leu)	CH₃ CH₃ \ / CH | CH₂ | $H_2N-CH-CO_2H$	2.36; 9.60	5.98	
5. Isoleucine (Ile)	CH₃ | CH₂ | CH—CH₃ | $H_2N-CH-CO_2H$	2.36; 9.68	6.02	Has two asymmetric carbon atoms
II. Hydroxyamino acids				
6. Serine (Ser)	CH₂OH | $H_2N-CH-CO_2H$	2.21; 9.15	5.68	
7. Threonine (Thr)	CH₃ | CH—OH | $NH_2-CH-CO_2H$	2.63; 10.43	6.53	Has two asymmetric carbon atoms

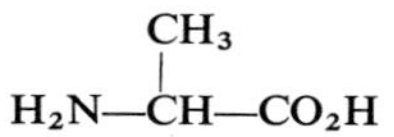

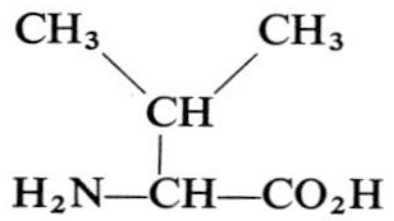

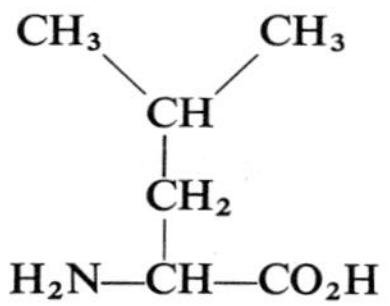

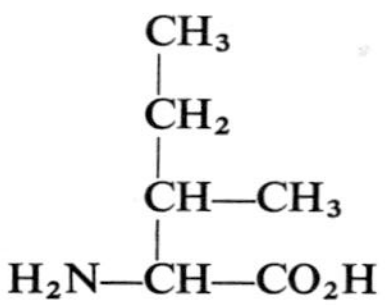

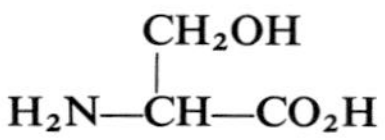

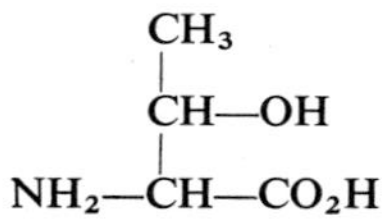

III. Dicarboxylic amino acids and their amides

	Structure	pK values	pI	Remarks
8. Aspartic acid (Asp)	$NH_2-CH-CO_2H$ | CH_2 | CO_2H	2.09 (α-carboxyl); 3.86 (β-carboxyl); 9.82	2.97	
9. Asparagine (AspNH$_2$) (or Asn)	$NH_2-CH-CO_2H$ | CH_2 | $CONH_2$	2.02; 8.8	5.41	
10. Glutamic acid (Glu)	$NH_2-CH-CO_2H$ | CH_2 | CH_2 | CO_2H	2.19 (α-carboxyl); 4.25 (γ-carboxyl); 9.67	3.22	
11. Glutamine (GluNH$_2$) (or Gln)	$NH_2-CH-CO_2H$ | CH_2 | CH_2 | $CONH_2$	2.17; 9.13	5.65	

IV. Amino acids having basic functions

	Structure	pK values	pI	Remarks
12. Lysine (Lys)	$NH_2-CH-CO_2H$ | $(CH_2)_4-NH_2$	2.18; 8.95 (α-amino); 10.53 (ε-amino)	9.74	
13. Hydroxylysine (Hyl)	$NH_2-CH-CO_2H$ | $(CH_2)_2$ | $CH-OH$ | CH_2-NH_2	2.13; 8.62 (α-amino); 9.67 (ε-amino)	9.15	Has two asymmetric carbon atoms; occurs only in collagen and gelatin

TABLE 3-1. Amino Acids that Commonly Occur in Proteins (*Continued*)

Name	Structure	Values of pK_a	pI	Remarks
14. Histidine (His)		1.82; 6.0 (imidazole); 9.17	7.58	
15. Arginine (Arg)		2.17; 9.04 (α-amino); 12.48 (guanidino)	10.76	
V. Aromatic amino acids (histidine included in category IV) 16. Phenylalanine (Phe)		1.83; 9.13	5.98	$\lambda_{max} = 259\ m\mu$ $\varepsilon_{259} = 2 \times 10^2$
17. Tyrosine (Tyr)		2.20; 9.11 (α-amino); 10.07 (phenolic hydroxyl)	5.65	$\lambda_{max} = 278\ m\mu$ $\varepsilon_{278} = 1.1 \times 10^3$

No.	Amino acid	pK_a values	pI	Notes
18.	Tryptophan (Trp)	2.38; 9.39	5.88	$\lambda_{max} = 279\ m\mu$ $\varepsilon_{279} = 5.2 \times 10^3$
19.	Thyroxine			Occurs only in the protein thyroglobulin (elaborated by the thyroid gland)
VI.	Sulfur-containing amino acids			
20.	Cysteine (CySH)	1.71; 8.33 (sulfhydryl); 10.78 (α-amino)	5.02	
21.	Cystine (CyS—SCy)	1.65; 2.26 (carboxyls); 7.85; 9.85 (aminos)	5.06	
22.	Methionine (Met)	2.28; 9.21	5.75	
VII.	Imino acids			
23.	Proline (Pro)	1.99; 10.60	6.10	
24.	Hydroxyproline (Hyp)	1.92; 9.73	5.83	Has two asymmetric carbon atoms; occurs only in collagen and gelatin

TABLE 3-2. Amino Acids and Derivatives of Biological Importance

Name	Structure	Occurrence, Function, etc.
1. β-Alanine	$NH_2-CH_2CH_2-COOH$	A component of the vitamin pantothenic acid and the derived coenzyme, coenzyme A; also occurs in the naturally occurring peptides carnosine and anserine
2. γ-Amino butyric acid	$NH_2-(CH_2)_3-COOH$	A constituent of plant tissue and of brain tissue in mammals and some amphibia and birds
3. Sarcosine	N-methyl glycine	An intermediate in the metabolism of one-carbon compounds; a constituent of the actinomycins, a group of potent antimetabolites
4. Betaine	N,N,N-trimethyl glycine	A constituent of plant and animal tissues; an intermediate in the metabolism of lipids
5. O-diazoacetylserine (azaserine)	$CH_2O-COCHN_2$ | $NH_2-CH-COOH$	Antimetabolite isolated from certain molds; inhibits the synthesis of nucleic acids
6. Homoserine	CH_2CH_2OH | $NH_2-CH-COOH$	An important intermediate in metabolism; occurs in plant and animal tissues
7. Ornithine	$(CH_2)_3-NH_2$ | $NH_2-CH-COOH$	An important intermediate in the biosynthesis of urea
8. Citrulline	$(CH_2)_3-NH-\overset{\overset{\textstyle O}{\|\|}}{C}-NH_2$ | $NH_2-CH-COOH$	An important intermediate in urea biosynthesis; the immediate precursor of arginine
9. Histamine	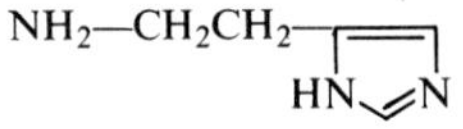 $NH_2-CH_2CH_2$ (imidazole ring, HN–N)	The decarboxylation product of histidine; a powerful vasodepressor
10. 5-Hydroxytryptamine (serotonin)	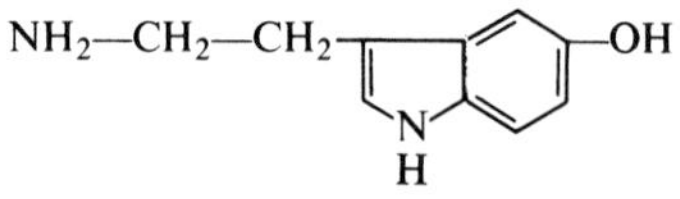 $NH_2-CH_2-CH_2$ (indole ring with OH, N–H)	A substance important in the transmission of nerve impulses
11. Epinephrine (adrenalin)	$\overset{\overset{\textstyle H}{\|}}{CH_3N}-CH_2-\overset{\overset{\textstyle}{}}{\underset{\underset{\textstyle OH}{\|}}{CH}}$ (benzene ring with two OH groups)	A derivative of tyrosine; an important hormone involved in many regulatory processes
12. Taurine	$NH_2-CH_2CH_2-SO_3H$	An oxidation product of cysteine metabolism; a component (in conjugation with a steroid) of bile salts
13. Penicillamine	$(CH_3)_2C-SH$ | $NH_2-CH-COOH$	A component of the antibiotic penicillin

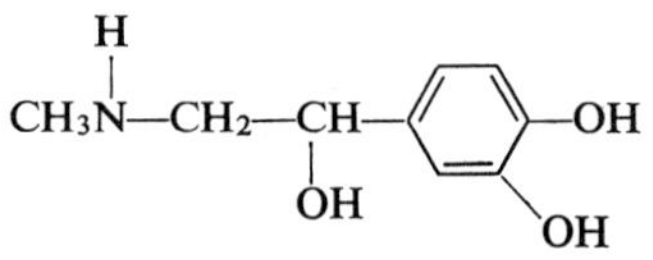

of threonine are indicated below:

$$
\begin{array}{cccc}
\text{COOH} & \text{COOH} & \text{COOH} & \text{COOH} \\
H_2N{-}C{-}H & H{-}C{-}NH_2 & H_2N{-}C{-}H & H{-}C{-}NH_2 \\
H{-}C{-}OH & HO{-}C{-}H & HO{-}C{-}H & H{-}C{-}OH \\
CH_3 & CH_3 & CH_3 & CH_3 \\
\text{L-Threonine} & \text{D-Threonine} & \text{L-Allothreonine} & \text{D-Allothreonine}
\end{array}
$$

Cystine is clearly a special case, because the two asymmetric centers are identical. In cases of this type, the configuration of one center may be the mirror image of the other, and the molecule is "internally compensated" and optically inactive. Such forms are termed *meso-* forms:

$$
\begin{array}{cc}
\begin{array}{cc}
\text{COOH} & \text{COOH} \\
H_2N{-}C{-}H\ H_2N{-}C{-}H \\
CH_2{-}S{-}S{-}CH_2 \\
\end{array} &
\begin{array}{cc}
\text{COOH} & \text{COOH} \\
H_2N{-}C{-}H\ \ \ H{-}C{-}NH_2 \\
CH_2{-}S{-}S{-}CH_2 \\
\end{array} \\
\text{L-Cystine} & \textit{Meso}\text{cystine}
\end{array}
$$

Although, as noted above, D-amino acids do not occur naturally in proteins, they are found widely distributed in living tissue. D-Amino acids are particularly abundant as constituents of bacterial cell walls. In addition they are found incorporated into the structures of many antibiotics, including bacitracin, gramicidin, and the actinomycins (see page 488).

Acid-Base Behavior   A reasonably detailed discussion of the protonic and metal-ion equilibria in which amino acids are involved was presented in Chap. 2. The following points are worth reviewing.

All amino acids have at least two groups that are involved in protolytic reactions in aqueous solution. The α-carboxyl group of amino acids is characterized by a value of pK_a (that pH at which the group under consideration is half associated and half dissociated) in the range of 2 to 3. The α-amino group, in contrast, is characterized by a pK_a (for the conjugate acid) near 10. Thus at pH values between about 4 and 9, the amino acid exists in a *dipolar ion* or *zwitterionic* form, the carboxyl group being dissociated and the amino group associated:

$$
\begin{array}{c}
R \\
H_3N^+{-}CH{-}COO^-
\end{array}
$$

Over this entire pH range, the amino acids bear little net charge, and at one pH, the isoelectric point pI (see page 65), bear no net charge. A little reflection will indicate that, for amino acids having no additional acidic or basic groups, the pI is midway between the two pK_a values; $pI = (pK_a^{NH_2} + pK_a^{CO_2H})/2$. The pK_a values and isoelectric points for protein amino acids are included in Table 3-1.

The side chains of several of the amino acids, including those of aspartic acid, glutamic acid, lysine, histidine, arginine, cysteine, and tyrosine, have appreciable acidic or basic properties. The appropriate values of pK_a are also included in Table 3-1. The isoelectric structures for these amino acids vary according to the basicity or acidity of the side-chain group. The predominant isoelectric structures of aspartic acid and lysine, determined from the pK_a data, are indicated below:

```
      COOH                NH₃⁺
       |                   |
      CH₂                (CH₂)₄
       |                   |
H—C—NH₃⁺             H—C—NH₂
       |                   |
      COO⁻                COO⁻
```

The isoelectric point for aspartic acid must be very nearly midway between the pK_a values for the α- and β-carboxyls. At this pH, 2.97, the amino function exists almost completely as the ammonium ion and the α-carboxyl largely as the carboxylate, the β-carboxyl being largely undissociated. Hence, aspartic acid at pH 2.97 has one positively charged group and one negatively charged group and is isoelectric. Similar considerations indicate that the isoelectric point for lysine must be midway between the pK_a values for the α-amino and ε-amino functions.

The dipolar-ion structures for amino acids suffice to account for many of their properties. These include (1) a relatively high solubility in water, (2) a relatively low solubility in organic solvents, (3) large dipole moments, and (4) high melting points. The last point may be attributed to substantial electrostatic attractions between the oppositely charged groups in the crystal lattice.

Chemical Reactions   All the amino acids have a series of reactions in common — those which occur at the amino or carboxyl functions, or both. In addition, if the amino acid contains a reactive side chain, it exhibits a series of specific reactions. Such specific reactions are of interest in two particular respects. First, reactions of those groups which result in the production of color are frequently useful for the detection and semiquantitative estimation of proteins and of the individual amino acids. These reactions will not be discussed in detail here, but a compilation of them is presented in Table 3-3. Second, reactions that occur at the side chains of amino acids are frequently of use in efforts to modify proteins chemically.

TABLE 3-3.   Reactions Useful for Detection and Semiquantitative Estimation of Amino Acids and Proteins

Name	Reactants	Amino acid detected	Color
Millon reaction	$HgNO_3$ in nitric acid with a trace of nitrous acid	Tyrosine	Red
Xanthoproteic reaction	Boiling concentrated nitric acid	Tyrosine, tryptophan, phenylalanine	Yellow
Glyoxylic acid reaction (Hopkins-Cole reaction)	Glyoxylic acid in conc H_2SO_4	Tryptophan	Purple
Ehrlich reaction	p-Dimethylaminobenzaldehyde in conc HCl	Tryptophan	Blue
Sakaguchi reaction	α-Naphthol and sodium hypochlorite	Arginine	Red
Nitroprusside reaction	Sodium nitroprusside in dil NH_3	Cysteine	Red
Sullivan reaction	Sodium 1,2 naphthoquinone-4-sulfonate and sodium hydrosulfite	Cysteine	Red
Pauly reaction	Diazotized sulfanilic acid in alkaline solution	Histidine, tyrosine	Red
Folin-Ciocalteu reaction	Phosphomolybdotungstic acid	Tyrosine	Blue

Many of the reactions at the amino or carboxyl group are quite familiar (alkylation, acylation, ester and amide formation) and need not be reiterated here. Instead we consider a few reactions that are of general utility in amino acid and protein chemistry.

Ninhydrin. The reaction of ninhydrin (triketohydrindene hydrate) with amino acids is of particular importance for the detection and quantitative estimation of the latter. Ninhydrin is a powerful oxidizing agent and elicits the oxidative deamination of the α-amino group, liberating ammonia, carbon dioxide, the corresponding aldehyde, and a reduced form of the ninhydrin:

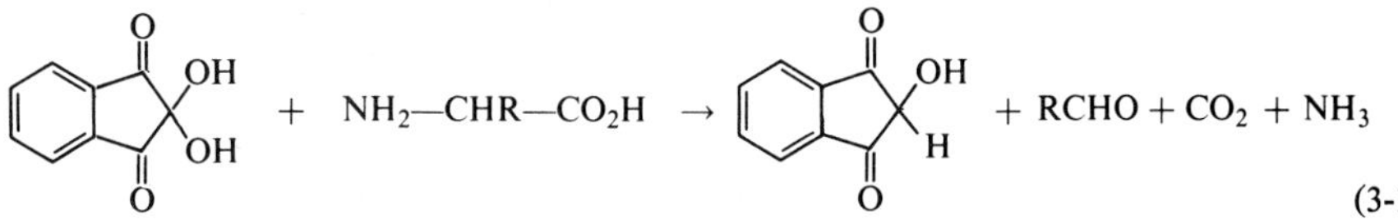

$$
\text{Ninhydrin} + NH_2-CHR-CO_2H \rightarrow \text{Hydrindantin} + RCHO + CO_2 + NH_3 \tag{3-1}
$$

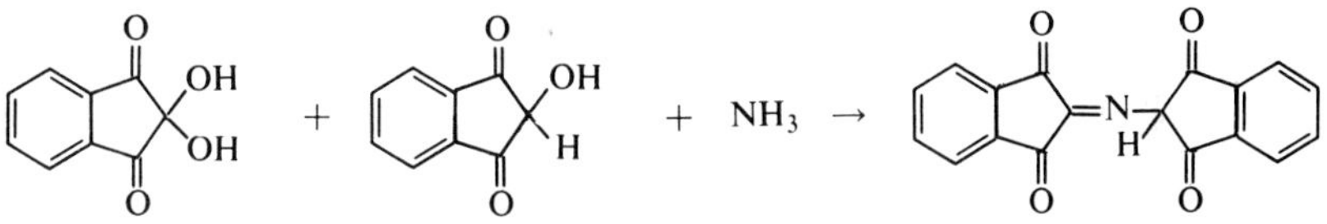

$$
+ \quad + \quad NH_3 \rightarrow \qquad \text{Purple} \tag{3-2}
$$

The ammonia then reacts with an additional mole of ninhydrin and the reduced ninhydrin to yield a purple substance that absorbs maximally near 570 mμ. Because this absorption is nearly a linear function of the amount of amino groups originally present, this reaction provides a convenient and quantitative colorimetric assay for amines. Although the ninhydrin reaction is quite general for primary amines, the evolution of carbon dioxide, which may be followed manometrically, is reasonably diagnostic for α-amino acids. In the cases of the imino acids, an alternate product that is bright yellow (absorption maximum near 440 mμ) is formed. Hence, the ninhydrin reaction serves to distinguish these substances from the bulk of the protein amino acids.

1-Fluoro-2,4-dinitrobenzene. The arylation of amino acids with 1-fluoro-2,4-dinitrobenzene (FDNB) is of great importance in structural protein chemistry (see page 80):

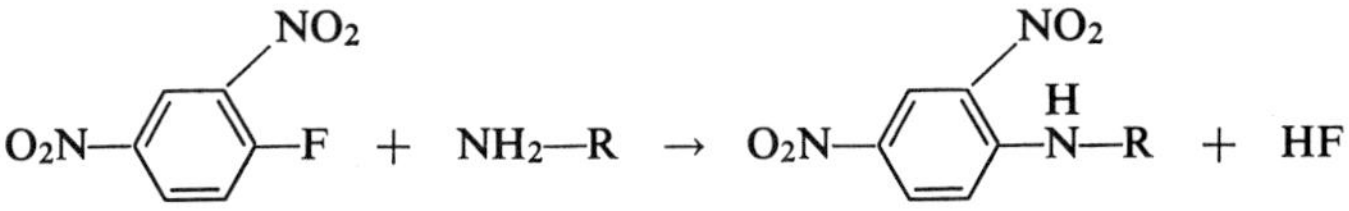

$$
O_2N-\!\!\!\bigcirc\!\!\!-F \ (NO_2) + NH_2-R \rightarrow O_2N-\!\!\!\bigcirc\!\!\!-\overset{H}{N}-R \ (NO_2) + HF \tag{3-3}
$$

The value of dinitrophenylation lies (1) in the quantitative production of yellow crystalline derivatives which are readily separated by chromatographic techniques and which may be quantitated spectrophotometrically and (2) in the resistance of the DNP–amino acid linkage to acid hydrolysis. The importance of the latter point for structural studies is discussed in Chap. 4.

Phenylisothiocyanate. Phenylisothiocyanate reacts readily with amino acids to yield the corresponding phenylthiohydantoic acids:

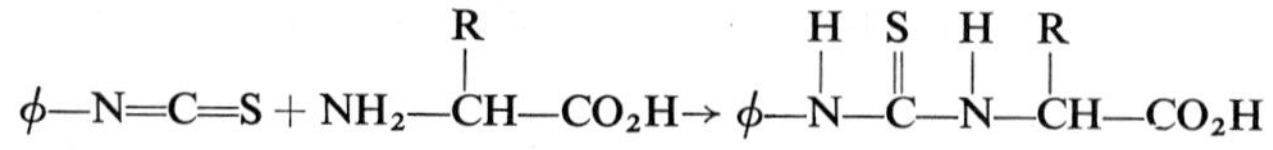

$$\phi—N{=}C{=}S + NH_2—\underset{R}{CH}—CO_2H \rightarrow \phi—\underset{H}{N}—\underset{S}{C}—\underset{H}{N}—\underset{R}{CH}—CO_2H \tag{3-4}$$

Phenylthiohydantoic acid

These products, on treatment with acid in nonhydroxylic solvents, cyclize, yielding the phenylthiohydantoins:

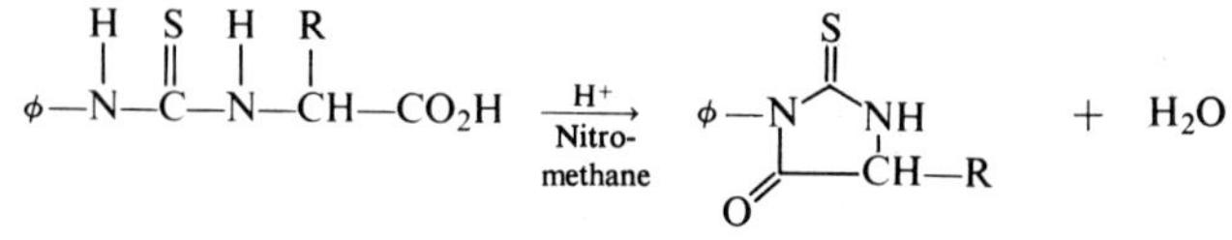

$$\phi—\underset{H}{N}—\underset{S}{C}—\underset{H}{N}—\underset{R}{CH}—CO_2H \xrightarrow[\substack{\text{Nitro-}\\\text{methane}}]{H^+} \phi—N \overset{S}{\underset{O}{\diagdown}} \begin{smallmatrix} NH \\ CH—R \end{smallmatrix} + H_2O \tag{3-5}$$

Phenylthiohydantoin

These amino acid derivatives are easily characterized and quantitated. This reaction, like that of FDNB, is quite useful in structural studies.

Phosgene. The reaction of phosgene with α-amino acids yields *N*-carboxy anhydrides (Leuchs anhydrides):

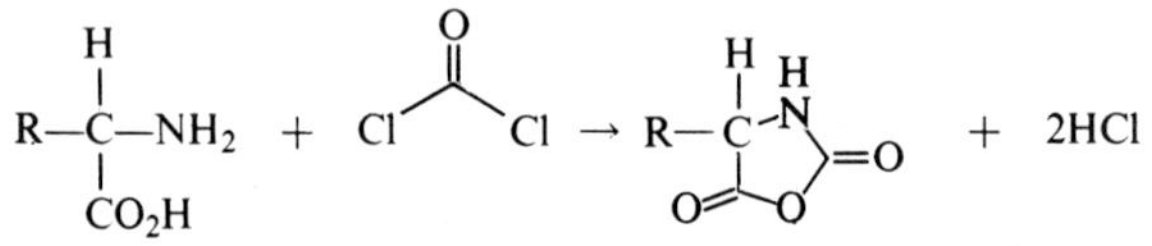

$$R—\underset{\substack{|\\CO_2H}}{\overset{\substack{H\\|}}{C}}—NH_2 + Cl—\overset{O}{\overset{\|}{C}}—Cl \rightarrow R—C{<}{=}O + 2HCl \tag{3-6}$$

These compounds react readily with nucleophilic reagents and are important intermediates in the synthesis of proteinlike polymers. A similar reaction occurs with carbon disulfide:

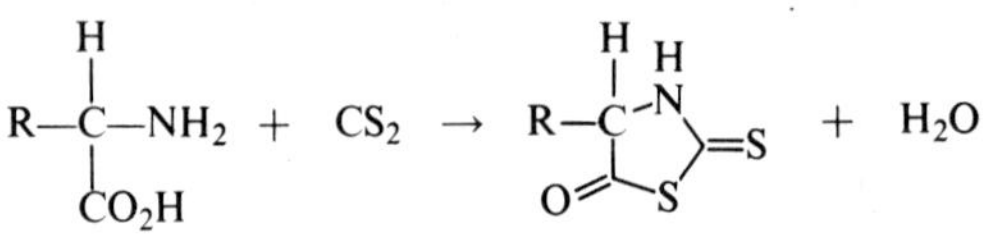

$$R—\underset{\substack{|\\CO_2H}}{\overset{\substack{H\\|}}{C}}—NH_2 + CS_2 \rightarrow R—C{<}{=}S + H_2O \tag{3-7}$$

THE
PEPTIDE
BOND

A very important structural feature of any polymer is the nature of the linkages that unite the monomeric units. In 1902, Hofmeister and Fischer independently suggested that proteins were assembled through the formation of secondary amide linkages between the α-carboxyl and α-amino functions of adjacent amino acids. Such bonds are commonly termed *peptide bonds*. The structures resulting from the formation of peptide bonds are termed *peptides*. The individual amino acids of peptides are termed *residues*. Thus a peptide containing two amino acid residues is a dipeptide, one containing three such residues is a tripeptide, and so forth. The structure of a typical tetrapeptide is indicated below:

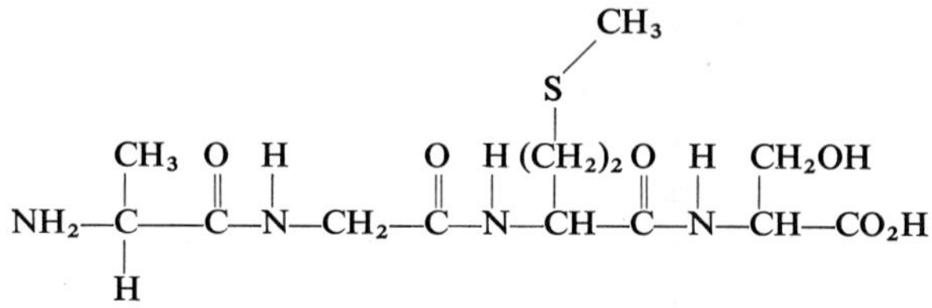

$$NH_2—\underset{\substack{|\\H}}{\overset{\substack{CH_3\\|}}{C}}—\overset{\substack{O\\\|}}{C}—\underset{\substack{|\\}}{\overset{\substack{H\\|}}{N}}—CH_2—\overset{\substack{O\\\|}}{C}—\underset{\substack{|\\}}{\overset{\substack{H (CH_2)_2\\|}}{N}}—CH—\overset{\substack{O\\\|}}{C}—\underset{\substack{|\\}}{\overset{\substack{H\\|}}{N}}—\underset{\substack{|\\CH_2OH}}{CH}—CO_2H$$

Peptides are usually written with the terminal amino group on the left and the terminal carboxyl group on the right. They are named as acyl derivatives of the C-terminal amino acid. Thus the tetrapeptide indicated above is alanylglycyl-methionylserine.

Evidence favoring the peptide bond as the basic structural feature of proteins is compelling. We summarize the principal lines of evidence requiring this conclusion below:

1. Proteins have relatively few titratable amino and carboxyl functions. Those which are found are accounted for in terms of the terminal residues and the side chains of aspartic acid, glutamic acid, arginine, and lysine. In the course of the hydrolysis of proteins, the titratable amino and carboxylic groups rapidly increase in number and do so in concert; that is, the rate of appearance of carboxyl groups is equal to that of amino groups. Thus, one carboxyl and one amino group appear to be involved in a peptide bond in the intact protein.

2. Analysis of incomplete protein hydrolysates reveals the presence of di- and tripeptides and other oligopeptides. The structures of these materials may be unambiguously established by comparison with synthetically prepared products.

3. Enzymes (proteins with catalytic activities) that degrade proteins specifically hydrolyze amide or closely related bonds, as revealed from studies on model compounds of known structure.

4. Biuret, whose structural formula is

$$\text{H}$$
$$NH_2CONCONH_2$$

and related materials containing peptide bonds give a purple color when treated with copper sulfate in alkaline solution (the biuret reaction). Proteins give a particularly strong biuret reaction, suggesting that a great many such bonds are present.

5. Proteins exhibit both infrared spectra and far ultraviolet spectra which are consistent with and give support for the presence of peptide bonds.

6. In the case of one protein, insulin, and several smaller polypeptides, the structures have been unambiguously established by total synthesis. In all cases, the amino acids were linked by peptide bonds.

7. Finally, the elegant X-ray diffraction studies of Perutz, Kendrew, and Phillips (see Chap. 4) have established the peptide bond as the inter-amino acid linkage for the proteins myoglobin, hemoglobin, and lysozyme.

Thus, the peptide-bond hypothesis must be regarded as firmly established. This conclusion is not intended to rule out the occasional presence of covalent bonds of other types. Clearly, closely related bonds might be formed involving the side-chain carboxyl and amino functions of aspartic acid and lysine, for example. Or interresidue ester bonds might be formed between glutamic acid and serine or threonine. Indeed, some examples of bonds other than amide linkages involving α-carboxyl and α-amino functions are known to occur in proteins. The common occurrence of such bonds is clearly ruled out by the considerations above.

What are the important properties of the peptide bond from the standpoint of protein structure? In this regard, two properties are dominant. First, the six atoms of the peptide group C_α—CO—NH—C_α, in which C_α refers to the α-carbon atoms of adjacent residues in the peptide chain, are coplanar. This coplanarity results from the substantial resonance energy stabilization derived from the maximum interaction of the lone electron pair on nitrogen with the pi electrons of the C=O. The C—N bond of the peptide group is about 1.32 A long, corresponding to about 50 per cent double-bond character. Second, the α-carbon atoms of the peptide group lie trans to the C—N. The configuration and dimensions of an extended

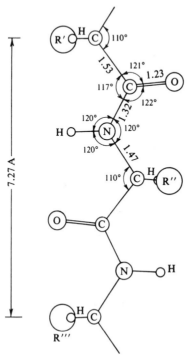

FIGURE 3-1.   Dimensions and Configuration of a Fully Extended Polypeptide Chain. — *L. Pauling, R. B. Corey, and H. R. Branson, Proc. Nat. Acad. Sci., U.S., 37: 205 (1951).*

polypeptide chain are shown in Fig. 3-1. As will be shown later, the coplanarity of the peptide group and the trans configuration of α-carbon atoms with respect to the C—N play a most important structural role in proteins.

PEPTIDE   Interest in the chemical synthesis of peptides stems principally from the use of
SYNTHESIS   such syntheses for (1) the unambiguous assignment of structures to naturally occurring peptides and (2) the production of chemical analogues of the naturally occurring peptides. Peptides of the latter class are of great interest in terms of aiding in the understanding of the relationships between chemical structure and biological function and for their potential medicinal value.

Basically, peptide synthesis consists of three steps. First, those amino and carboxyl groups which are not to participate in the reaction must be chemically blocked. Second, the free amino and carboxyl functions must be linked. Third, the blocking groups must be removed. In addition, if amino acids, such as cysteine, lysine, and aspartic acid, which contain side chains that may react during the condensation reaction, are involved in the synthesis, their side chains must be blocked as well. The qualifications of potential blocking agents that render them suitable for use in peptide synthesis include (1) their introduction should proceed quantitatively and without racemization of the amino acid; (2) the blocked amino acid must be stable to the conditions employed in the condensation reaction; (3) the group must be readily removed under conditions in which the peptide bond is stable and in which racemization of the peptide does not occur.

It may be readily appreciated that the synthesis of even simple peptides is a tedious process, involving many steps. Merrifield has recently devised a solid-state method of peptide synthesis that simplifies and shortens the procedures greatly. The key to this method is the covalent attachment of the carboxyl function of the C-terminal amino acid to a resin particle. The attached amino acid may then be reacted with an activated amino acid, yielding a blocked dipeptide attached to the resin that is purified simply by filtration. Removing the blocking group and collecting the resin particles completes one cycle of the synthesis. Following the attachment of all the required amino acids, the completed peptide is liberated from the resin particle and purified by electrophoresis. Employing this procedure, the nonapeptide bradykinin was synthesized in only eight days.

The methods just indicated permit the ordered synthesis of many peptides, including some of considerable size and complexity (insulin, molecular weight 6,000, is the largest molecule successfully synthesized by these means at present). In addition, the unordered synthesis of polypeptides is also of great value. Of particular importance is the synthesis of *homo-polypeptides*, such as polyglycine, polyserine, and polyglutamic acid. The use of these materials as aids in the understanding of protein structure is indicated in Chap. 4. Such polyamino acids are most conveniently synthesized from the N-carboxyanhydrides formed in the reaction of amino acids with phosgene. N-carboxyanhydrides of amino acids react readily with nucleophilic reagents, liberating carbon dioxide and forming a free amino group:

$$\text{(3-8)}$$

This amino group may then react with another molecule of N-carboxyanhydride, extending the chain and forming still another free amino group. Repetition of this process clearly yields polymers:

$$\text{(3-9)}$$

The degree of polymerization obtained in these reactions is a function of the nature and concentration of the reaction initiator (that molecule which performs the initial attack on the N-carboxyanhydride), solvent, and temperature. Thus the desired degree of polymerization may frequently be obtained within reasonably narrow limits by the proper choice of reaction conditions and initiator.

NATURALLY OCCURRING PEPTIDES

Nearly all living tissues appear to contain appreciable quantities of low-molecular-weight peptides. For example, glutathione (γ-L-glutamyl-L-cysteinylglycine) — see page 202 — is a constituent of most plant and animal tissues, carnosine (β-alanyl-L-histidine) and anserine (β-alanyl-1-methyl-L-histidine) are present in vertebrate muscle tissue:

$$\underset{\text{Carnosine}}{H_2N-CH_2-CH_2-\overset{\overset{\displaystyle O}{\|}}{C}-\underset{\underset{\displaystyle CH_2}{|}}{\overset{\overset{\displaystyle H}{|}}{N}}-CH-CO_2H}$$

$$\underset{\text{Anserine}}{H_2N-CH_2-CH_2-\overset{\overset{\displaystyle O}{\|}}{C}-\underset{\underset{\displaystyle CH_2}{|}}{\overset{\overset{\displaystyle H}{|}}{N}}-CH-CO_2H}$$

More interesting classes of peptides are those which exhibit well-known physiological or antibacterial activity.

The mammalian neurohypophysis elaborates several peptide hormones, including the nonapeptides oxytocin and vasopressin:

```
NH2                              NH2
|                                |
Cys—Tyr—Ile                      Cys—Tyr—Phe
|       |                        |       |
S       |                        S       |
|       |                        |       |
S       |                        S       |
|       |                        |       |
Cys—Asn—Gln                      Cys—Asn—Gln
|              O                 |              O
|              ‖                 |              ‖
Pro—Leu—Gly—C—NH2                Pro—Arg—Gly—C—NH2
    Beef oxytocin                   Beef vasopressin
```

Oxytocin elicits the contraction of smooth muscle and the ejection of milk in lactating females, and vasopressin elicits pressor and antidiuretic effects. The structure and chemical synthesis of these hormones were elegantly established in a classic series of investigations by du Vigneaud and his collaborators. Oxytocin and vasopressin are structurally related and differ only in the nature of the residues at positions 3 and 8. *Vasopressin* refers to a class of compounds in which the hormones performing the physiological role of vasopressin in a variety of mammals differ in the nature of the amino acid at position 8 and, occasionally, at position 3.

In addition to oxytocin and vasopressin, the neurohypophysis also liberates two polypeptide hormones that stimulate the pigment-forming activity of the melanocytes. Accordingly, these are termed α- and β-melanocyte-stimulating hormones. The β-melanocyte-stimulating hormone of several species has been characterized structurally and, like vasopressin, exhibits some species specificity. The structures of the hormones isolated from five species are shown in Fig. 3-2.

Human	Ala·Glu·Lys·Lys·Asp·Glu·Gly·Pro·Tyr·Arg·Met·Glu·His·Phe·Arg·Try·Gly·Ser·Pro·Pro·Lys·Asp
Monkey	Asp·Glu·Gly·Pro·Tyr·Arg·Met·Glu·His·Phe·Arg·Try·Gly·Ser·Pro·Pro·Lys·Asp
Horse	Asp·Glu·Gly·Pro·Tyr·Lys·Met·Glu·His·Phe·Arg·Try·Gly·Ser·Pro·Arg·Lys·Asp
Beef	Asp·Ser·Gly·Pro·Tyr·Lys·Met·Glu·His·Phe·Arg·Try·Gly·Ser·Pro·Pro·Lys·Asp
Pig	Asp·Glu·Gly·Pro·Tyr·Lys·Met·Glu·His·Phe·Arg·Try·Gly·Ser·Pro·Pro·Lys·Asp

FIGURE 3-2.   Amino Acid Sequences of β-Melanocyte-stimulating Hormone from Five Species. Amino acid substitutions among these species, as compared with the human, are indicated by the underlined residues. — *Abraham White et al.,* " *Principles of Biochemistry," 3d ed., page 902, McGraw-Hill, New York, 1964.*

The adenohypophysis secretes, among others, the adrenocorticotropic hormone (ACTH) that stimulates the growth and metabolic activity of the adrenal cortex. ACTH is a polypeptide consisting of 39 amino acid residues, the sequence of the first 24 of which being common to the hormone of all species investigated. The last 15 show several variations from species to species. The structure of human ACTH is indicated below:

Ser·Tyr·Ser·Met·Glu·His·Phe·Arg·Trp·Gly·Lys·Pro·Val·Gly·Lys·Lys·Arg·Arg·
Pro·Val·Lys·Val·Tyr·Pro·Asp·Ala·Gly·Glu·Asp·GluNH$_2$·Ser·Ala·Glu·Ala·
Phe·Pro·Leu·Glu·Phe

Human ACTH

One of the most interesting groups of biologically active peptides is derived from proteins, normally present in the plasma, that are themselves biologically inert. These include the angiotensins, bradykinin, and kallidin.

The *angiotensins* are a group of octapeptides that have pressor activity. The individual angiotensins are distinguished by the nature of the residue in position 5, which varies from species to species. These substances are derived from a plasma protein termed *angiotensinogen* by successive cleavage of particular peptide bonds by the proteolytic enzymes trypsin, renin, and converting enzyme (see Fig. 3-3).

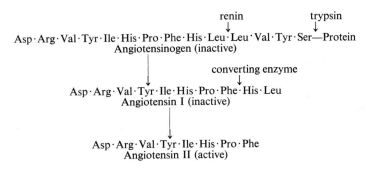

FIGURE 3-3.   Conversion of Angiotensinogen into the "Pressor" Peptide Angiotensin.

Bradykinin, a nonapeptide liberated upon treatment of plasma with trypsin or snake venom, is a potent smooth-muscle hypotensive agent. The structure of bradykinin is:

Arg·Pro·Pro·Gly·Phe·Ser·Pro·Phe·Arg

Bradykinin

Kallidin, a decapeptide with physiological properties similar to those of bradykinin, is liberated from a plasma protein termed *kallidinogen*:

Lys·Arg·Pro·Pro·Gly·Phe·Ser·Pro·Phe·Arg

Kallidin

The structure of this peptide differs from that of bradykinin only by the addition of one lysine residue to the *N*-terminal end of the peptide chain.

DETECTION
AND ESTIMATION
OF PROTEINS

The quantitative or semiquantitative estimation of protein concentration is a frequently encountered problem, one which, for example, arises continually in devising methods for the purification of a particular protein (see below). A number of color tests have been described that are due to the reaction of one or more of the amino acid side chains with an appropriate reagent (see Table 3-3). Unhydrolyzed proteins give these reactions as well, indicating that, in the intact protein, these side chains are not in covalent linkage. However, they are not generally useful for the quantitative estimation of proteins, because the frequency with which each of the side chains appears, and hence the strength of the reaction observed, varies from protein to protein. For example, the protamine salmine, which is composed of 85 per cent arginine by weight, gives a great deal more red color per gram of protein in the Sakaguchi reaction (see Table 3-3) than does the milk protein β-lactoglobulin, which contains less than 3 per cent arginine by weight.

A commonly employed method of protein estimation, measurement of the optical density of protein solutions, also suffers from this disadvantage. Most proteins exhibit ultraviolet-light absorption spectra with absorption maxima near 278 mμ. Reference to Table 3-1 indicates that tryptophan, tyrosine, and phenylalanine absorb light in this region of the spectrum, the absorption of the former two being stronger than that of the latter (see Fig. 3-4).

The absorption of monochromatic light by a dissolved substance may be conveniently described by the Beer-Lambert law:

$$\log \left(\frac{I_0}{I} \right) = \varepsilon c l \tag{3-10}$$

in which I_0 and I refer to the incident and transmitted light intensities respectively, ε is a proportionality constant called the *molar absorptivity* or *extinction coefficient*, c is concentration in moles per liter, and l is the length of the optical path in centimeters. The term $\log (I_0/I)$ is readily measured by means of a spectrophotometer and is usually called A, the *absorbance*, or E, the *extinction*. Measurements of A are usually made in optical cells of path length 1 cm; under these conditions, the Beer-Lambert law may be rewritten as

$$A \equiv E = \varepsilon c \tag{3-11}$$

where ε is then the absorbance of a 1 M solution of the material of interest at the chosen wavelength and has the dimensions liter/mole/cm = M^{-1}/cm. Clearly if ε is known, measurements of A yield concentrations directly. Because many values of ε are known or may be easily measured and because the determination of A is simple, this method is exceptionally widely employed for concentration determination.

The difficulty of this method for protein determination is, of course, the variability of the abundance of tyrosine and tryptophan, upon which values of ε for protein preparations depend, from protein to protein. This method is reasonably reliable if a heterogeneous mixture of proteins is to be analyzed and may be used to good advantage in dealing with relatively pure protein preparations whose extinction coefficients may be accurately measured (or calculated from the amino-acid composition, if known).

A more generally accurate, and correspondingly more tedious, method of protein determination is based on the quantitative estimation of protein nitrogen. Nearly all proteins are approximately 16 per cent nitrogen by weight. The analysis is accomplished by the conversion of the protein nitrogen to ammonia through digestion with concentrated sulfuric acid in the presence of copper sulfate, mercuric sulfate, or other suitable catalyst. The ammonia formed may be quantitated by removal from the digestion mixture through steam distillation followed by titration or the addition of Nessler's reagent (mercuric potassium iodide in aqueous sodium hydroxide), which permits ammonia to be determined colorimetrically.

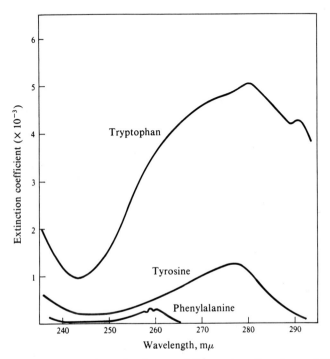

FIGURE 3-4.   The Ultraviolet Absorption Spectra of Tryptophan, Tyrosine, and Phenylalanine.

The biuret reaction (see Table 3-3) may also be used to quantitate protein concentration, because this reaction detects peptide bonds. These occur with approximately the same frequency per gram of material for most proteins.

Other methods employed for the estimation of protein include (1) measurement of refractive index, (2) measurement of turbidity following precipitation with trichloracetic acid, and (3) determination of dry weight — the basic method employed to standardize the more frequently employed techniques.

AMINO ACID ANALYSIS OF PROTEINS   The accurate determination of the amino acid composition of proteins is of great importance in their characterization and for an understanding of their structure. Such an analysis consists of two steps: hydrolysis of the protein to the constituent amino acids, followed by quantitative estimation of the hydrolysis products.

Protein Hydrolysis   The complete hydrolysis of proteins may be accomplished by the use of strong acid, strong base, or proteolytic enzymes as catalysts. The use of strong acid is ordinarily the method of choice. Constant boiling hydrochloric acid, about 6 N, is most frequently employed in evacuated sealed tubes at about 110° for periods ranging from 12 to 96 hr. Under these conditions, the peptide bonds are quantitatively hydrolyzed (relatively long periods of hydrolysis are required for the complete liberation of valine, leucine, and isoleucine), yielding the amino acid hydrochlorides. Tryptophan is completely destroyed in this process, and small losses of serine and threonine, which may be corrected for, are encountered. The amino acids are not racemized by acid hydrolysis under these conditions.

The complete hydrolysis of proteins may also be achieved by incubating them with 2 to 4 N sodium hydroxide at 100° for 4 to 8 hr. Such hydrolysis is of limited utility for routine analysis; it is useful for the estimation of tryptophan, the amino acid destroyed by acid hydrolysis.

The complete enzymatic hydrolysis of proteins is difficult, because most enzymes attack only specific types of linkages rapidly (see Chap. 7). Although of limited use for complete hydrolysis, enzymatic methods have been employed with great success for the partial hydrolysis of proteins, an important step for amino acid sequence determination (see Chap. 4).

Amino Acid Analysis

Following the complete hydrolysis of a protein, the analysis is completed by obtaining a quantitative analysis for each of the amino acids.

The separation of amino acids is most readily accomplished by employing *ion-exchange chromatography*. The column material of choice is a sulfonated polystyrene resin, a cation exchanger. The amino acid mixture is placed on the column at *p*H 3, conditions under which the individual amino acids are positively charged. The cationic amino acids displace some of the sodium ions from the $-SO_3^-Na^+$ form of the column and thus are bound to the column material by electrostatic forces. Clearly, those amino acids which are most basic are bound most tightly and those which are least basic are bound least tightly. The column is then developed by gradually increasing the *p*H and ionic strength of the buffers with which the column is washed. These conditions gradually cause neutralization of the positive charges on the amino acids and, in addition, weaken salt linkages. Thus, as the column is developed, the acidic amino acids, such as glutamic and aspartic acids, are removed readily from the resin, followed by the neutral amino acids, followed, finally, by the basic amino acids. This method serves to separate all the amino acids commonly found in proteins, because it depends on the adsorption of the amino acids to the resin material as well as on ion-exchange properties. The column material is sufficiently selective in its adsorption properties so that all the neutral amino acids, which cannot be separated on the basis of ion exchange, are eluted separately from the column. As the amino acids are eluted from the column, they are collected individually in an automatic fraction collector. Once separated, the individual amino acids are quantitated by reaction with ninhydrin and measurement of the resultant color intensity. Several automatic amino acid analyzers are commercially available. These instruments automatically separate the amino acids on an ion-exchange column, collect them, add ninhydrin, heat to develop the color, record the color intensity, and plot the intensity on a graph. A typical automatically recorded chromatographic analysis of an amino acid mixture is shown in Fig. 3-5. The identity of each amino acid is established on the basis of its position on the chromatogram and is estimated quantitatively on the basis of the area under each curve. This analysis is frequently accurate to within 2 per cent and may be routinely accomplished in a few hours. Needless to say, other cation-exchange resins and anion-exchange resins may also be employed for the separation of amino acids.

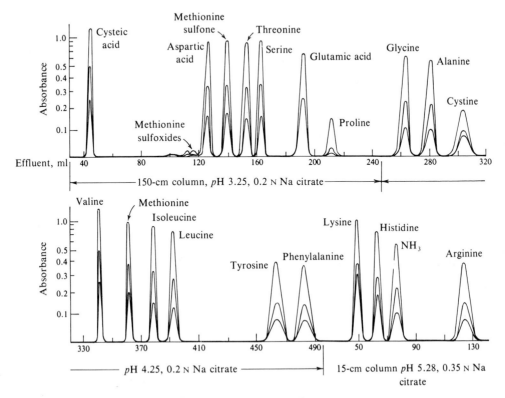

FIGURE 3-5. Automatically Recorded Chromatographic Analysis of a Synthetic Mixture of Amino Acids on a Sulfonated Polystyrene Resin. — *D. H. Spackman, W. H. Stein, and S. Moore, Anal. Chem., 30: 1190 (1958).*

Amino acid mixtures may also be separated by *paper chromatographic techniques*, a method of great historical significance. Paper chromatographic separations principally reflect differences in partition coefficients of the various amino acids between an organic and an aqueous phase. In practice, the development of a chromatogram with a single solvent system is not adequate for the complete separation of all the amino acids. Consequently one resorts to *two-dimensional* chromatography. In this technique, the chromatogram is developed in one direction with a first solvent system, rotated 90°, and developed a second time with a second solvent system. A typical two-dimensional chromatogram illustrating the separation of amino acids from a protein hydrolysate is presented in Fig. 3-6. The individual amino acids are located by treatment of the chromatogram with ninhydrin, the amino acids appearing as purple spots. These spots may be cut out and eluted. Measurement of the optical density of the eluate affords a quantitative evaluation of the quantity of amino acid present. This method is clearly somewhat more tedious, and less accurate, than automatic analysis employing column chromatography but is often more sensitive.

TABLE 3-4.   Amino Acid Composition of Proteins

(1) Grams of amino acid in 100 g of protein
(2) Moles of amino acid in 100,000 g of protein
nd = not determined

Protein	Insulin	Cytochrome c	Serum albumin		Glucagon		Hemoglobin α-chain	Hemoglobin β-chain	Histone		Collagen	
Source	Bovine	Horse heart	Human		Bovine		Human	Human	Calf thymus		Elastoidin (sharkfin)	
Molecular weight	5,733	12,100	68,000		3,647		15,120	15,860	15,500		nd	
Total N	nd	15.98	nd		17.45		nd	nd	17.4		18.2	
	(2)	(2)	(1)	(2)	(1)	(2)	(2)	(2)	(1)	(2)	(1)	(2)
Glycine	70.5	90.1	1.60	21.3	2.08	27.7	46.1	82.4	5.07	67.6	25.53	330.4
Alanine	44.8	43.0	nd	nd	2.68	30.1	139.0	95.0	9.68	108.8	11.39	128.0
Serine	53.0	0	3.70	35.2	11.60	110.5	71.4	29.6	4.92	46.9	4.43	42.2
Threonine	17.3	72.7	5.0	42.0	9.93	83.4	56.8	42.8	5.47	46.0	2.87	24.1
Proline	16.7	24.0	5.1	44.3	0	0	47.5	46.0	4.62	40.2	14.11	122.7
Hydroxyproline	0	0	0	0	0	0	0	0	0	0	9.68	73.9
Valine	71.0	17.3	7.7	65.8	3.22	27.5	86.7	112.5	5.79	49.5	2.02	17.3
Isoleucine	10.0	42.1	1.7	13.0	0	0	<0.06	<0.06	4.59	35.0	2.46	18.8
Leucine	101.0	43.0	11.9	90.8	7.42	56.6	121.0	115.0	8.18	62.4	2.50	19.1
Phenylalanine	49.8	26.4	7.8	47.3	9.42	57.1	46.4	50.2	2.79	16.9	2.45	14.8
Tyrosine	66.0	31.4	4.66	25.7	10.60	58.6	18.7	17.8	3.69	20.4	1.72	9.5
Tryptophan	0	8.3	0.19	0.9	5.71	28.0	5.9	11.1	0	0	0	0
Cystine/2	52.0	nd	5.58	46.5	0	0	6.1	12.3	0	0	0	1.8
Cysteine	nd	18.2	0.7	5.8	0	0	nd	nd	0	0	0.22	0
Methionine	0	nd	1.28	8.6	3.77	25.3	12.6	6.11	1.14	7.6	2.05	13.8
Aspartic acid	53.0	58.7	10.4	78.2	15.40	115.8	78.0	81.9	5.12	38.5	6.13	46.1
Glutamic acid	115.8	89.3	17.4	11.8	12.40	84.4	33.8	76.3	9.71	66.0	12.07	82.1
Amide-N	nd	70.2	0.88	62.9	1.60	114.3	33.3	62.6	0.71	50.7	0.56	40.8
Arginine	16.3	14.9	6.15	35.3	9.52	54.7	35.6	18.6	11.61	66.7	9.02	51.8
Histidine	34.5	21.5	3.50	22.6	3.81	24.5	65.8	56.0	2.48	16.0	0.70	4.5
Lysine	14.5	147.1	12.30	84.2	4.06	27.8	72.6	69.6	17.35	118.8	3.59	24.6
Hydroxylysine	0	0	0	0	0	0	0	0	0	0	1.17	7.1
Total	786.2	748.0		780.0	812.1		944.0	978.2		807.3		1,042.7

SOURCE: G. R. Tristram and R. H. Smith, in H. Neurath (ed.), "The Proteins," pp. 46–50, Academic Press, Inc., New York, 1963.

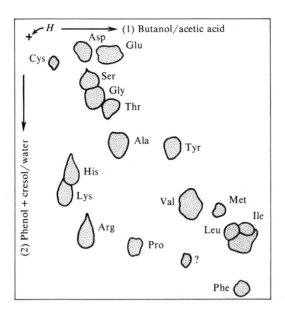

FIGURE 3-6.   A Two-dimensional Chromatogram of Amino Acids. — *F. Haurowitz, "The Chemistry and Function of Proteins," 2d ed., page 31, Academic Press, New York, 1963.*

Electrophoretic migration in an electric field, like ion-exchange methods, takes advantage of charge differences between the amino acids at appropriate values of pH. For example, if an amino acid mixture is placed on a suitable support, frequently paper saturated with an appropriate buffer in aqueous solution, and subjected to an electric field, glutamic and aspartic acid, at neutral pH, migrate toward the anode, and histidine, lysine, and arginine migrate toward the cathode, thus effecting separation. Amino acids may be detected and quantitated as in the case of paper chromatography. Chromatography and electrophoresis on paper are frequently combined — chromatography in one direction and electrophoresis in the other.

The amino acid analyses of several proteins, derived by one or more of the methods above, are collected in Table 3-4.

MOLECULAR-WEIGHT DETERMINATION FOR MACROMOLECULES

The amino acid composition and molecular weight are the basic pieces of information employed to characterize proteins. Obtaining reliable and reasonably accurate determinations of the molecular weight of macromolecules is not a trivial task. Methods ordinarily employed for molecular-weight determination on small molecules, notably boiling-point elevation, freezing-point depression, and vapor-pressure measurement, are of little or no use for macromolecules, owing to their size and instability. For example, to obtain a freezing-point depression in water of 0.1° with a protein of molecular weight of 100,000 would require a solution containing nearly $5\frac{1}{2}$ kg of protein per liter. One is, of course, considerably worse off employing measurements of alteration in vapor pressure or boiling point. The following discussion outlines the principal methods currently employed for the estimation of the molecular weight of proteins. Most of these methods are also applicable to similar determinations for macromolecules of other sorts.

Analytical Data   The metal-ion content, for cases in which there is any, or amino acid composition
of a protein may be employed to calculate *minimum molecular weights*. Such calculations are made on the assumption that each protein molecule contains only one
metal atom or one amino acid residue of the chosen type. If more than one such
constituent is present, the calculated molecular weight will be too small by a
factor equal to the number actually present. Quantitatively, we may write

$$M_{\min} = \frac{\text{constituent weight} \times 100}{\text{percentage of constituent}} \qquad\qquad (3\text{-}12)$$

Thus the knowledge that hemoglobin, an oxygen-transporting protein, contains
0.335 per cent iron by weight indicates a minimum molecular weight (55.85/0.335)
$\times$ 100 = 16,700 for this protein. Physical measurements of the type described below
demonstrate that the actual molecular weight is near 66,000. Hence each molecule
of hemoglobin must contain four atoms of iron. When attempting similar calculations employing amino acid composition data, one chooses, naturally, that amino
acid which appears least frequently in the protein. This method is principally
employed as a check on molecular-weight determinations obtained by physical
methods.

Electron   The electron microscope is an instrument capable of obtaining, for properly pre-
Microscopy   pared samples and under optimal conditions, an optical resolution of about 20 A.
Because most proteins are larger than 20 A in their shortest dimension, they may be
detected directly in the electron microscope and photographed. If one knows (1) the
number of particles in a given field under the electron microscope, (2) the volume
of solution from which it was originally derived, and (3) the dry weight of protein
per milliliter of the original solution, one can evidently calculate a value for the
molecular weight. Conditions 1 and 3 are readily satisfied, the former by counting
the number of particles in an electron micrograph and the latter by analytical
means discussed earlier in this chapter. The volume from which a particular field
is derived may be obtained by the prior addition of a known number of polystyrene
latex particles to the original solution. For example, suppose a solution containing
1 mg/ml of protein and 10^{13} latex particles/ml is examined under the electron
microscope and a field is observed to contain 10 latex particles and 100 protein
particles. A simple calculation reveals that each protein particle must weigh about
10^{-17} g, from which a molecular weight of about 6×10^6 is obtained. Of course,
several such fields must be examined in order to avoid serious uncertainties, owing
to statistical fluctuations in the number of particles that appear.

Electron microscopy, for sufficiently large molecules, also clearly yields information concerning particle shape. It must be borne in mind, however, that electron
microscopy requires desiccated preparations, precluding the examination of proteins in their normal hydrated state. Thus, uncertainties are introduced regarding
the relationship of protein shape and dimensions as seen by the electron microscope and those which exist in solution. Nevertheless, the electron microscope is a
potent tool in revealing particle shapes, and its utility should not be underestimated.
It has been of great value, for example, in the understanding of the morphology of
viruses. An electron micrograph of individual T2 bacteriophage particles is presented in Fig. 3-7.

Osmotic
Pressure

Among the colligative properties of matter, only osmotic pressure is of utility for the determination of macromolecular weight. The theory underlying measurement of osmotic pressure is straightforward. If, for example, a protein solution is separated from a protein-free buffer solution by a semipermeable membrane through which buffer components and solvent may pass but which is impermeable to protein, a nonequilibrium situation will exist. The chemical activity of water in the protein solution will be lower than that in the solution on the other side of the membrane; consequently water will tend to flow into the protein solution. The strength of this tendency is termed the *osmotic pressure* and may be conveniently measured by the amount of hydrostatic pressure just required to prevent

FIGURE 3-7.   An Electron Micrograph of T2 bacteriophage. — *Courtesy of The Virus Laboratory, University of California, Berkeley, California.*

the net transport of water across the membrane. Such measurements are accomplished with the aid of an osmometer, such as the one illustrated in Fig. 3-8.

For a two-component system, the osmotic pressure Π is related to the concentration by the van't Hoff law, which is more conveniently written, for our purpose, in terms of the molecular weight M and concentration c in grams per liter,

$$\lim_{c \to 0} \frac{\Pi}{RTc} = \frac{1}{M} \tag{3-13}$$

This equation provides the basis for the determination of molecular weight by osmotic-pressure measurement, because c, T, and Π are all susceptible to experimental determination. Because a limiting value of Π/RTc is required, osmotic-pressure measurements must be carried out at a variety of protein concentrations and the values carefully extrapolated to zero concentration. This is a fairly tedious procedure and constitutes one of the major drawbacks to this method. Alternatively the osmotic pressure may be expressed in terms of a power series in c:

$$\frac{\Pi}{RTc} = \frac{1}{M} + Bc + Cc^2 + \cdots \tag{3-14}$$

and the coefficients determined from measurements of Π as a function of c. Values of M may then be calculated without extrapolation to zero concentration.

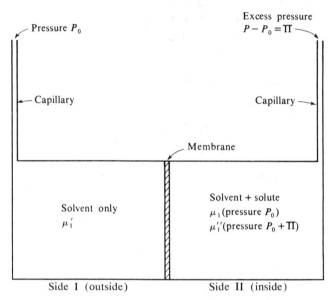

FIGURE 3-8.   Schematic Representation of an Osmotic-pressure Apparatus.—*C. Tanford, "Physical Chemistry of Macromolecules," Wiley, New York, 1961.*

In addition to the large amount of time required for an accurate molecular-weight determination, the principal drawbacks to this method include (1) the possibility of protein aggregation or precipitation during the time period, often extended, required to attain equilibrium, (2) the fact that the measurement is best made under conditions, frequently unknown, in which the protein carries no net charge (see below), and (3) the method yields no information regarding the purity of the sample. If the sample is heterogeneous, containing molecules of varying molecular weight, osmotic-pressure measurement yields *number-average* molecular weights defined as

$$\overline{M_n} = \frac{c_i}{\Sigma c_i/M_i} \tag{3-15}$$

in which c_i is the concentration of the ith component and M_i is its molecular weight. The number-average molecular weight tends to overemphasize the contribution made by molecules of relatively small size.

If the protein carries a net charge, osmotic-pressure measurement yields values of Π lower than those which may be attributed to the presence of protein alone. The basis of this phenomenon is termed the *Gibbs-Donnan effect*. Consider the situation in which the protein carries a net negative charge in a solution of sodium chloride. Denoting the two sides of the semipermeable membrane by the subscripts i and o, for inside and outside, and protein concentration by (P^-), we write

$$(Na^+)_i = (Cl^-)_i + (P^-)_i \qquad (3\text{-}16)$$

for solution i, and

$$(Na^+)_o = (Cl^-)_o \qquad (3\text{-}17)$$

for solution o, because electroneutrality must be maintained on both sides of the membrane. Because the negative charges of the protein are present on only one side of the membrane, the sodium and chloride ions distribute themselves unequally across the membrane. Such asymmetric distribution increases the observed value of the osmotic pressure. For the reaction

$$(Na^+)_o + (Cl^-)_o \rightleftharpoons (Na^+)_i + (Cl^-)_o \qquad (3\text{-}18)$$

at equilibrium (see page 15)

$$\Delta G = 0 = -RT \ln \frac{(Na^+)_i(Cl^-)_i}{(Na^+)_o(Cl^-)_o} \qquad (3\text{-}19)$$

Rewriting and solving, we find

$$(Na^+)_o(Cl^-)_o = (Na^+)_i(Cl^-)_i \qquad (3\text{-}20)$$

Now, employing Eqs. (3-16), (3-17), and (3-20), it is easy to show that

$$(Cl^-)_o = (Cl^-)_i \left[1 + \frac{(P^-)}{(Cl^-)_i} \right]^{1/2} \qquad (3\text{-}21)$$

Thus the extent of asymmetric distribution of a diffusible ion across the membrane is accentuated by a high concentration of protein salt and is minimized by a high ionic strength. Consequently, particularly if the pH at which the protein bears no net charge is not known, osmotic-pressure measurements with proteins or other charged macromolecules should be conducted in the presence of high salt concentrations. For many purposes a salt concentration of about 0.2 M is sufficient.

The comments above may, of course, be readily generalized for any protein charge and for electrolytes that are other than uni-univalent.

Sedimentation Velocity-Diffusion   The rapid development of techniques for the study of the behavior of macromolecules in intense gravitational fields continues to revolutionize methods for the molecular-weight determination for such substances. The first ultracentrifuge was constructed by Svedberg and his associates in 1925. The *ultracentrifuge* consists basically of a rotor, in which cells containing the material under investigation are placed, a refrigerated and evacuable chamber in which the rotor turns, a high-speed electrical motor, and an optical system suitable for measuring the concentration of protein, or other material, at each point in the cell throughout a run. A cross section through an electrically driven ultracentrifuge is shown in Fig. 3-9. Modern ultracentrifuges operate at speeds up to 70,000 revolutions/min, generating gravitational fields up to 500,000 times the force of gravity. Such intense forces rapidly sediment macromolecules and are sufficient to cause asymmetric distribution of low-molecular-weight materials, such as sucrose and cesium chloride, within the ultracentrifuge cell. The use of the ultracentrifuge lends itself to several independent

methods for the determination of molecular weight. We discuss the most important
of these below, beginning with the classical method — sedimentation-velocity
studies. Schachman, who has originated many of the important advances in the
technique of ultracentrifugation, has summarized recent developments in cell
design, optical systems, and other experimental, as well as theoretical, advances.

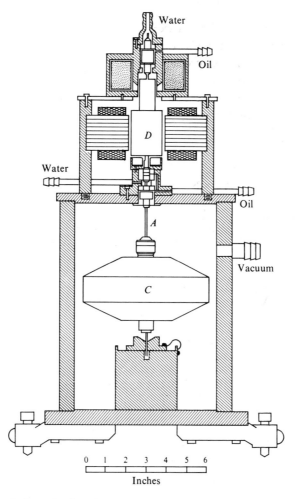

FIGURE 3-9. A Cross Section Through an Electrically Driven Ultracentrifuge; the rotor *(C)* is suspended
from a motor armature *(D)* by means of the flexible shaft *(A)*. — *C. Skarstrom and J. W. Beams,
Rev. Sci. Instr., 11: 398 (1940).*

The relationship between molecular weight M, the diffusion constant D, and the
partial specific volume of the protein $\bar{v}$ (the reciprocal of the protein density) is
given by

$$M = \frac{RT}{D(1 - \bar{v}\rho)}\left(1 + \frac{d(\ln \gamma)}{dc}\right) \cdot \frac{dx/dt}{\omega^2 x} \tag{3-22}$$

in which ω is the angular velocity of the rotor in radians per second, x is the distance
from the center of rotation to the sample, and γ is the activity coefficient of the

latter. Equation (3-22) is termed the *Svedberg equation*. The quantity in the equation that is determined with the aid of the ultracentrifuge is $(dx/dt)/\omega^2 x$, which is ordinarily termed the *sedimentation constant* and designated s. Equation (3-22) then assumes the form

$$M = \frac{RTs}{D(1-\bar{v}\rho)}\left[1 + \frac{d(\ln \gamma)}{dc}\right] \qquad \lim_{c \to 0} M = \frac{RTs}{D(1-\bar{v}\rho)} \qquad (3\text{-}23)$$

The units of s are reciprocal seconds; the basic unit, for convenience, is taken as 10^{-13} sec, which is termed *one Svedberg* (S). Employing these units, the sedimentation constants for most proteins fall in the range of 1 to 50 S.

The velocity dx/dt with which the protein sediments in the gravitational field is obtained by observing, photographically, the position of the maximum concentration of protein throughout the course of the run. A typical sedimentation pattern is shown in Fig. 3-10. These photographs were taken by employing the *Schlieren*

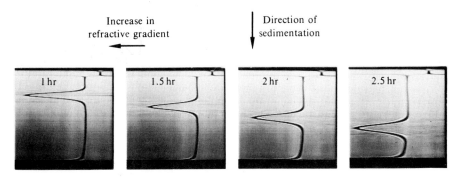

FIGURE 3-10. Sedimentation of Triose Phosphate Dehydrogenase. The set of four photographs was recorded by the refractive index method.

optical system, which measures the refractive-index gradient at each point in the cell. As the protein moves down the cell, the peak height diminishes and the peak width increases. This is a normal consequence of the diffusion of the protein molecules. Because ω is a known quantity and x may be measured directly from the photographs as a function of time, the determination of dx/dt suffices to determine s. Sedimentation constants are ideally obtained at a variety of protein concentrations and the values of s extrapolated to zero concentration, conditions in which the activity coefficient term becomes unity. In addition, it is customary to correct sedimentation constants to a standard state with reference to solvent viscosity taken as that of water at 20° (see page 126).

Sedimentation-velocity studies frequently provide information regarding the homogeneity of the protein preparation. Preparations that contain more than one component may exhibit several peaks in the ultracentrifuge or asymmetry in a single peak. The criterion for homogeneity in the ultracentrifuge, then, is a single sharp, symmetrical peak whose width is not greater than can be accounted for in terms of diffusion of the protein.

As indicated in Eq. (3-23), values for D and $\bar{v}$, as well as that for s, must be obtained for a molecular-weight determination. The partial specific volume is defined as the volume increase resulting from the addition of 1 g of protein to an infinite volume of water. Values of $\bar{v}$ are determined by density measurements in a pycnometer or may be calculated, approximately, from amino acid composition data. Typical values of $\bar{v}$ for proteins are in the range of 0.70 to 0.75 cm³/g. Because the density ρ of the solvent is usually near 1, the quantity $(1 - \bar{v}\rho)$ varies markedly with small changes in the value of $\bar{v}$. Consequently, accurate molecular-weight determination by the sedimentation velocity-diffusion method depends on an accurate determination of the partial specific volume. Regrettably, values for $\bar{v}$ are more frequently guessed than measured.

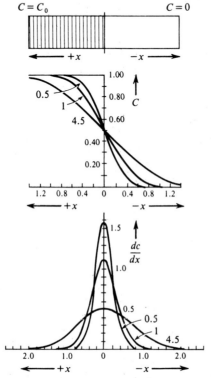

FIGURE 3-11.   Relationship between Concentration and Distance of Migration in a Diffusion Column. *Top:* graphical illustration of the diffusion column; *center:* relationship between concentration and distance of migration; *bottom:* relationship between concentration gradient and distance of migration. The curves as drawn refer to diffusion times of 0.5, 1 and 4.5 hr, respectively. The whole diagram should be rotated counter-clockwise about an angle of 90° in order to conform to the proper space directions. — *H. Neurath, Chem. Rev., 30: 357 (1942); by permission of the copyright owner, The American Chemical Society.*

The basic equation that describes the process of diffusion is due to Fick and is usually referred to as *Fick's first law of diffusion*:

$$\frac{ds}{dt} = -DA\left(\frac{\partial c}{\partial x}\right)_t \tag{3-24}$$

This equation states that the amount ds of a substance crossing a given area A in time dt is proportional to the concentration gradient $\partial c/\partial x$ across that area. The diffusion constant D, which is related to molecular size and shape, is the proportionality constant. Beginning with Eq. (3-24), it is possible to derive *Fick's second law of diffusion*, which is a more useful statement for the purpose of determining D:

$$\left(\frac{\partial c}{\partial t}\right)_x = D\left(\frac{\partial^2 c}{\partial x^2}\right)_t \tag{3-25}$$

For particular geometrical cases, Eq. (3-25) may be solved directly. For example, for diffusion from an infinitely long column of solution at concentration C_0 into an infinitely long column of pure solvent (in a container of uniform cross section), solution of Eq. (3-25) yields

$$\left(\frac{\partial c}{\partial t}\right)_x = \frac{C_0 x}{4\pi^{1/2}D^{1/2}t^{3/2}} \cdot e^{-x^2/4Dt} \tag{3-26}$$

Thus measurement of $(\partial c/\partial t)_x$ as a function of t and distance from the original boundary x provide the experimental information necessary for the determination of D. In Fig. 3-11, a diagrammatic representation of the results of a diffusion experiment is presented.

Provided the molecular weight is known, the diffusion constant may be employed to provide preliminary information concerning the shape of the protein in solution. The deviation of the quantity f/f_0, termed the *frictional ratio*, from unity is a measure of the asymmetry and hydration of the protein molecule:

$$\frac{f}{f_0} = \left(\frac{f}{f_0}\right)_{hydration}\left(\frac{f}{f_0}\right)_{asymm} \tag{3-27}$$

In Table 3-5, a compilation of molecular weights, diffusion constants, partial specific volumes, and frictional ratios for several proteins is presented.

TABLE 3-5. Molecular Weights, Diffusion Constants, Partial Specific Volumes, and Frictional Ratios for Several Proteins

Protein	M	$\bar{v}$	$D_{20,w}^0 \times 10^7$	f/f_0
Ribonuclease	13,683	0.728	11.9	1.14
Lysozyme	14,100	0.688	10.4	1.32
Chymotrypsinogen	23,200	0.721	9.5	1.20
β-Lactoglobulin	35,000	0.751	7.82	1.25
Ovalbumin	45,000	0.748	7.76	1.17
Serum albumin	65,000	0.734	5.94	1.35
Hemoglobin	68,000	0.749	6.9	1.14
Catalase	250,000	0.73	4.1	1.25
Urease	480,000	0.73	3.46	1.20
Tropomyosin	93,000	0.71	2.24	3.22
Fibrinogen	330,000	0.710	2.02	2.34
Collagen	345,000	0.695	0.69	6.8
Myosin	493,000	0.728	1.16	3.53

SOURCE: C. Tanford, "Physical Chemistry of Macromolecules," John Wiley & Sons, Inc., New York, 1961.

To recapitulate, measurement of the sedimentation and diffusion constants (1) permits the calculation of molecular weights, (2) may provide information regarding sample homogeneity, and (3) yields preliminary information concerning protein hydration and shape.

Sedimentation Equilibrium

An alternative approach to molecular-weight determinations utilizing the ultracentrifuge is the sedimentation-equilibrium technique. Employing low rotor speeds to avoid sedimentation of high-molecular-weight material on the bottom of the ultracentrifuge cell, the ultracentrifuge is operated until an equilibrium distribution of solute is achieved throughout the length of the cell. At equilibrium, there is no net migration of solute across any cross section of the cell; that is, the movement of the solute to the bottom of the cell due to the centrifugal force is exactly balanced by the movement of the solute to the top of the cell by diffusion down the concentration gradient. Quantitatively, we write

$$D\frac{dc}{dr} = c\,\frac{dx}{dt} \tag{3-28}$$

Employing Eq. (3-22) for the value of dx/dt and rearranging, we obtain

$$M = \frac{RT\left[1 + \dfrac{d(\ln\gamma)}{dc}\right]}{r\omega^2(1 - \bar{v}\rho)} \cdot \frac{1}{c}\frac{dc}{dr} \tag{3-29}$$

Because values for c and dc/dr are obtained from the experimental measurements, molecular weights may be calculated directly from Eq. (3-29) without recourse to the measurement of the diffusion constant. Values of M so obtained are extrapolated to infinite dilution, a condition in which, as noted above,

$$\left[1 + \frac{d(\ln\gamma)}{dc}\right]$$

approaches unity.

The principal drawback to the use of sedimentation equilibrium for molecular-weight determinations is the length of time required for the attainment of equilibrium. This may require several days or weeks of continuous operation of the ultracentrifuge, during which time aggregation or degradation of the protein sample may occur and aggravation of one's colleagues is certain to occur. This objection has been largely overcome by the development of cells with extremely short (0.1 mm) path lengths. With such cells, equilibrium may usually be achieved in, at most, a few hours.

Sedimentation-equilibrium methods provide information concerning the homogeneity of the protein preparation. If the system is polydisperse, these methods provide a *weight-average molecular weight* defined as

$$\overline{M}_w = \frac{\Sigma\, c_i M_i}{\Sigma\, c_i} \tag{3-30}$$

in which the c_i's refer to the concentration of the ith component and the M_i's to its molecular weight. Values of $\overline{M}_w$ overemphasize the contribution of heavy molecules to the average molecular weight. Polydispersity may be detected experimentally by nonlinearity of plots of ln c versus r^2.

Approach to Sedimentation Equilibrium (Archibald Method)

The potential simplicity of the sedimentation-equilibrium method for the determination of molecular weights prompted the development of methods to overcome the lengthy time period required by this method (prior to the development of short-path-length cells). Archibald, realizing that the equilibrium condition of no net flow across a boundary is always met at two places in the cell, the meniscus and the bottom, derived an approach-to-equilibrium method. Thus, in a fashion analogous to that used to arrive at Eq. (3-29), we may write

$$M_m = \frac{RT\left[1 + \dfrac{d(\ln \gamma)}{dc}\right]}{(1 - \bar{v}\rho)\omega^2} \cdot \frac{(dc/dr)_m}{c_m r_m} \tag{3-31}$$

and

$$M_b = \frac{RT\left[1 + \dfrac{d(\ln \gamma)}{dc}\right]}{(1 - \bar{v}\rho)\omega^2} \cdot \frac{(dc/dr)_b}{c_b r_b} \tag{3-32}$$

in which the subscripts m and b refer to the situation at the top and bottom of the cell respectively. The experimental parameters in Eqs. (3-31) and (3-32) may be evaluated from photographs obtained with the Schlieren or other optical system, soon after the initiation of the run. In general M_m and M_b are not identical, because, as a result of concentration differences, the activity coefficient terms are not identical.

If the system is polydisperse, weight-average molecular weights are obtained, and M_b is always greater than M_m. Some molecular weights obtained by the approach-to-equilibrium method are collected in Table 3-6.

TABLE 3-6. Molecular Weights of Selected Materials Obtained by Approach-to-equilibrium Method

Solute	Molecular weight
Sucrose (true molecular weight = 342.3)	341
Ribonuclease	13,700
β-Lactoglobulin	38,000
Ovalbumin	43,500
Serum albumin	68,000

SOURCE: C. Tanford, " Physical Chemistry of Macromolecules," John Wiley & Sons, Inc., New York, 1961.

Sedimentation Equilibrium in a Density Gradient

A gradient of density may be established in an ultracentrifuge cell by spinning a concentrated solution of a suitable low-molecular-weight material, usually cesium chloride or sucrose. A macromolecular species present in such a solution bands at a position in the cell where the density is equal to its own. Molecular weights may be obtained from the shape and width of such bands (see p. 126).

PROTEINS AS ELECTROLYTES

Many of the interesting and important properties of proteins derive from the fact that, under most conditions, they are multivalent electrolytes. The groups in proteins that are involved in acid-base equilibria are principally the side chains of glutamic and aspartic acid, lysine, histidine, arginine, cysteine, and tyrosine (see Table 3-1). The α-amino and α-carboxyl groups of the constituent amino acids are, for the most part, bound in peptide linkage and, hence, contribute little to the electrolyte character of proteins.

Titration   Titration curves for proteins are complex and difficult to interpret theoretically. This complexity is the result of two factors. First, there is ordinarily a large number of titratable groups present in each protein molecule; 50 to 60 such groups per 100,000 molecular weight is a typical figure. Second, the value of pK_a for each of the titratable groups of proteins may differ by one or more pH units from that for the simple amino acid (see Table 3-1). Thus, for example, if a protein contains 10 aspartic acid residues, each β-carboxyl is, in general, characterized by a distinct value of pK_a, and these might range from 3 to 6. Such variation in pK_a for groups present in proteins, or other charged macromolecules, may be ascribed to three factors: (1) electrostatic effects resulting from the ionization of other groups on the protein, (2) medium effects due to the proximity of hydrophobic residues, and (3) hydrogen bonding.

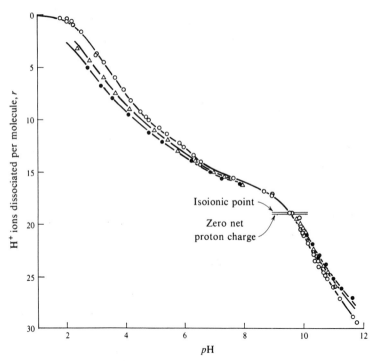

FIGURE 3-12.   Titration Data for Ribonuclease at 25°, ionic strengths 0.01 (●), 0.03 (△), and 0.15 (○). The figure shows the point of zero net charge (corresponding to r = 19) and also the isoionic pH at the particular concentration that was used. — *C. Tanford and J. D. Hauenstein, J. Am. Chem. Soc., 78: 5287 (1956); by permission of the copyright owner, The American Chemical Society.*

The titration curve for ribonuclease, a small, nearly spherical protein of known amino acid composition, is shown in Fig. 3-12. A comparison of the number of titratable groups in each pH region with the amino acid composition is presented in Table 3-7. Excellent agreement is found. Of particular interest is the behavior of the phenolic groups of tyrosine. Of the six present in ribonuclease, three dissociate normally with an intrinsic pK_a of 9.95. The other three dissociate only above pH 12 and are, hence, almost certainly buried in the interior of the protein in its native state and, therefore, not readily accessible to solvent. In accordance with this concept, titrations of these groups lead to irreversible effects on the structure of the protein as revealed by the fact that the back titration does not follow the same course as the forward one.

TABLE 3-7. Titratable Groups of Ribonuclease

Group	pK_{int} expected from data on small molecules	Number of sites from amino acid analysis	Data obtained from titration curve	
			Number of sites	pK_{int}
α-COOH	3.75	1	11 { (1)	
Side chain COOH	4.6	10	10	4.7
Imidazole	7.0	4	5 { 4	6.5
α-NH₂	7.8	1	(1)	7.8
Phenolic	9.6	6	16 { 6	9.95
Side chain NH₂	10.2	10	10	10.2
Guanidyl	>12	4	4	>12

SOURCE: C. Tanford and J. D. Hauenstein, *J. Am. Chem. Soc.*, **78**: 5287 (1956), by permission of the copyright owner, The American Chemical Society.

In general, one does not expect such good agreement between the amino acid composition and the number of titratable groups in each pH range as that illustrated in Table 3-7, particularly if extremes in acid and base concentrations are avoided. However, because most of the ionizable groups of proteins appear to be near the protein surface, fair agreement is usually found. Back titration of proteins is always essential to assure that irreversible structural alteration, revealing formerly hidden groups, has not occurred or to detect it if it has.

Isoelectric Point. In the course of the titration of a protein from the completely acidic to the completely basic form, at some pH the mean charge on the protein must be zero. This pH is termed the *isoelectric point*. Experimentally the isoelectric point is defined as that pH at which the protein does not migrate in an electric field (see the discussion below on electrophoresis). The isoelectric point may be calculated approximately from amino acid composition data. Because the electro-neutrality of proteins is affected by the presence of salts as a result of the capacity of proteins to bind ions and the alteration in pK_a due to ionic-strength effects, the isoelectric point is a function of the nature and concentration of the buffer and, in general, of any other solutes present. On the other hand, isoelectric points are not a function of protein concentration. The isoelectric points of most proteins are close to neutrality, reflecting their approximately equal content of acidic and basic residues. In some cases, however, distinctly different behavior is noted. For example, pepsin, an enzyme found in the stomach, where conditions are normally very acid, has an isoelectric point near 1, and protamines typically have isoelectric points near 12.

Isoionic Point. A protein solution that contains no ion other than ionic residues on the protein itself plus those derived from the dissociation of water is called an isoionic solution. They may be prepared by passing the protein solution through a column containing both anion and cation exchange resins (a mixed-bed resin) so that all ions other than hydroxyl and hydrogen are removed. Isoionic solutions may also be prepared by dialysis against distilled water (see below) for extended periods of time. This method is ordinarily less satisfactory than the use of mixed-bed resins. The pH of an isoionic protein solution is termed the *isoionic point* of that protein. Because electroneutrality requires that

$$(H^+) + (P)\bar{Z} = (OH^-) \tag{3-33}$$

an isoionic solution is not isoelectric unless the isoelectric point happens to be exactly pH 7. Equation 3-33, furthermore, indicates that the isoionic point is a function of protein concentration. Clearly, for sufficiently dilute solutions all proteins have their isoionic point at pH 7. However, at moderate protein concentrations, the isoionic point is an insensitive function of protein concentration and closely approximates the isoelectric point unless the latter is measured in the presence of strongly bound ions.

Interaction with Small Ions The binding of protons, discussed above, is one example of a general property of proteins, that is, their ability to interact with small ions. Such interactions are of considerable physiological importance. For example, many enzymes exhibit an absolute requirement for a divalent metal ion for the integrity of the catalytic process; ion transport in the blood is largely mediated by proteins, particularly by serum albumin, etc.

Experimentally, the degree of ion binding may be determined in several ways, the most popular being *equilibrium dialysis.* For this method one employs a bag fashioned from a material impermeable to protein but permeable to small ions, as in osmotic-pressure measurements. The protein solution is placed in this bag, which is, in turn, immersed in a solution containing the ion of interest. After permitting complete equilibration of the ion across the membrane, the concentration of diffusible ion is determined in the protein-free solution and, by subtraction, in the protein-containing solution. If these are equal, no binding can have occurred. If binding has occurred, the concentration of the diffusible ion in the protein solution must be greater than that outside, and the degree of disparity in concentration is a quantitative measure of the number of moles bound. In order to avoid Gibbs-Donnan effects, such experiments must be carried out either at the isoelectric point of the protein or at high ionic strengths. Other procedures useful for ion-binding studies include ultrafiltration, partition analysis, and, where applicable, absorption spectrophotometry.

The interaction of proteins with polyvalent metal ions is a particularly important case. The discussion of ion binding to amino acids presented in Chap. 2 is directly relevant to this topic.

In addition to ions, proteins also bind many small uncharged molecules, including steroids, hydrocarbons, long-chain alcohols, and, of course, water.

Solubility Properties The solubility of most proteins is a sensitive function of ionic strength, pH, and the concentration of organic solvents. We consider each of these variables in turn.

Ionic Strength. In Fig. 3-13, the solubility of isoelectric carboxyhemoglobin is shown as a function of the ionic strength for several salts. Ionic strength is defined as

$$\mu = \tfrac{1}{2} \Sigma \, c_i Z_i^2 \tag{3-34}$$

in which c_i is the concentration of the ith component and Z_i is its charge. From the data in this figure, it is clear that at low ionic strengths the protein is *salted in* and at high ionic strengths it is *salted out*. This behavior is typical of most proteins.

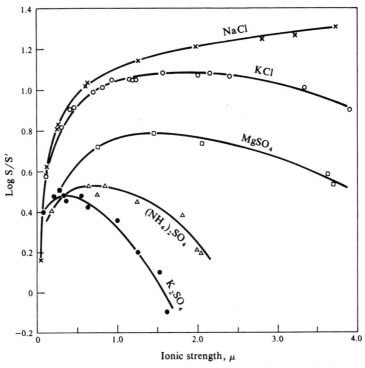

FIGURE 3-13.   Solubility of Isoelectric Carboxyhemoglobin as a Function of Ionic Strength and Ion Type. — *A. A. Green, J. Biol. Chem.*, **95**: 47 (1932). S and S's are solubilities in H_2O and salt solutions respectively.

From the Debye-Hückel theory, the activity coefficient for a given ion is related to the ionic strength by the expression

$$-\log \gamma = \frac{1.81 \times 10^6}{D^{3/2} T^{3/2}} Z_1 Z_2 \sqrt{\mu} \tag{3-35}$$

in which D is the dielectric constant of the medium and Z_1 and Z_2 are the charges on the ion and its counterion. Proteins, as multivalent electrolytes, behave in a fashion qualitatively similar to that predicted for simple ions by Eq. (3-35) at low salt concentrations; that is, increasing concentrations of salt stabilize (decrease the activity coefficient of) the charged groups on the protein, thereby increasing its solubility. The phenomenon of salting out, observed at higher ionic strengths, is probably the result of competition between the protein and the salt ions for the available water molecules for purposes of solvation. Thus, at sufficiently high concentrations of salt, insufficient molecules of water are available for the full solvation of the protein, and protein-protein interactions become more important than protein-water interactions; that is, precipitation occurs. In this region of salt concentration, protein solubility is often logarithmically related to ionic strength, as indicated in Eq. (3-36):

$$\log S = \beta' - K_s' \mu \tag{3-36}$$

In this equation, S is solubility in grams per liter, β' is the logarithm of the hypothetical solubility (not the actual solubility) at zero ionic strength, and K_s' is termed the *salting-out constant*.

The logarithm of the solubility of several proteins in ammonium sulfate solution that obey this relation is plotted against ionic strength in Fig. 3-14. Small changes in ionic strength are seen to cause large changes in protein solubility. This fact is

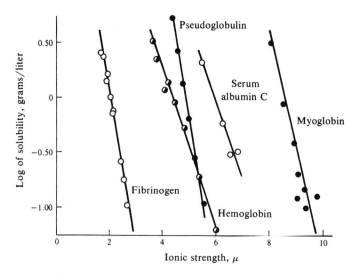

FIGURE 3-14. The Solubility of Proteins in Ammonium Sulfate Solutions. — *E. Cohn and J. T. Edsall, "Proteins, Amino Acids, and Peptides," Academic Press, New York, 1943.*

frequently taken advantage of for the purification of proteins (see below). K_s' is seen to depend only slightly on the nature of the protein but varies markedly with the nature of the salt (Fig. 3-13). In contrast, β' is very dependent on the nature of the protein.

pH. The solubilities of most proteins, when plotted against pH at constant ionic strength, exhibit U-shaped curves, with the minimum near the isoelectric point. Such behavior is illustrated for β-lactoglobulin in Fig. 3-15. Although the solubilities are markedly dependent on the ionic strength, the minimum occurs in each case near pH 5.2 to 5.4, the isoelectric point. This behavior may be rationalized on the basis that, at the isoelectric point, intermolecular electrostatic repulsions between solute molecules are at a minimum and crystal-lattice forces in the solid are at a maximum. For many proteins, the effect of pH on solubility is more complicated (one case even exhibits a double minimum), indicating that the naïve explanation presented above is not completely adequate.

Organic Solvents. Most organic solvents are good protein precipitants. Because increasing concentrations of acetone, for example, decrease the capacity of aqueous solvents to solubilize the charged groups of proteins, this phenomenon receives a ready explanation. Some organic solvents, which are characterized by relatively high dielectric constants, are, in contrast, rather good protein solvents. These include dimethyl sulfoxide, formamide, and dichloroacetic acid.

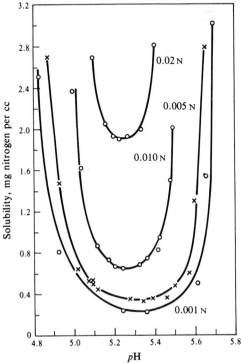

FIGURE 3-15.   Solubility of β-Lactoglobulin As a Function of pH at Four Different Concentrations of Sodium Chloride. — *S. Fox and J. S. Foster, "Introduction to Protein Chemistry," Wiley, New York, 1957.*

Electrophoresis   The movement of charged species under the influence of an external electric field is termed *electrophoresis.* The electrophoresis of proteins was introduced by Tiselius in 1937 and has been widely employed, for a variety of purposes, ever since. Because one of the more distinctive features of proteins is their difference in charge and because electrophoretic mobilities are principally a function of charge, electrophoresis is one of the best methods for the study of the composition of complex mixtures of proteins and for their separation. Two electrophoretic techniques are commonly employed in the study of proteins: the moving-boundary type and the zone type.

Moving-boundary Electrophoresis. A schematic representation of an apparatus for moving-boundary electrophoresis experiments is shown in Fig. 3-16. The apparatus is first partially filled with the protein solution, forming a sharp boundary between the two. Electrodes are then immersed in the buffer solution, and the entire apparatus is placed in a carefully thermostated bath for the maintenance of constant temperature and for the dissipation of heat generated by the apparatus. The run is initiated by turning on the current, and the progress of the run is followed with a suitable optical system. If several components are present and if their electrophoretic mobilities differ, several moving boundaries are observed. As an example of the type of data obtained, the electrophoretic pattern of the mixture of proteins contained in human plasma is shown in Fig. 3-17. Because the complete separation of the proteins is not achieved, this method is not well suited to the isolation of the individual components but is often of great value for the analysis of complex mixtures.

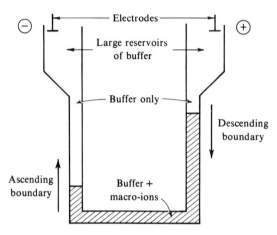

FIGURE 3-16.   Schematic Diagram of the Tiselius Cell for measuring electrophoretic mobility by the moving-boundary method. The macroions are assumed to have a positive charge; for negatively charged ions, the electrodes would be reversed. — C. Tanford, "Physical Chemistry of Macromolecules," Wiley, New York, 1961.

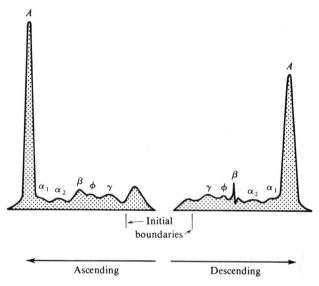

FIGURE 3-17.   The Electrophoretic Refractive Index Gradient Pattern for Normal Human Blood Plasma, measured at pH 8.6, where all the proteins are negatively charged; the peak labeled A represents serum albumin; α_1, α_2, β, and γ are mixtures of serum globulins, and ϕ represents fibrinogen. The two unlabeled peaks are the stationary peaks near the positions of the initial boundary. — R. A. Alberty, J. Chem. Educ., 25: 619 (1948); by permission of the copyright owner, The American Chemical Society.

Zone Electrophoresis. Zone electrophoresis is distinguished from moving-boundary electrophoresis principally in that the former involves the use of a support on which the material moves but in the latter the ions move freely in solution. Typical supports employed in zone electrophoresis include paper, cellulose, starch gels or blocks, polyurethane foam, and polyacrylamide gels. A typical zone electrophoresis apparatus is depicted schematically in Fig. 3-18.

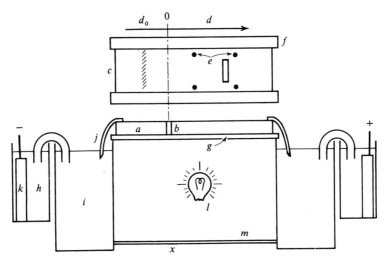

FIGURE 3-18.   Block Electrophoresis by Moving-zone Method. *(a)* Side view of starch block at time t_0; *(b)* initial zone; *(c)* top view of starch block after time t; *(d)* distance from origin to migrated zone; *(d_0)* distance from origin to substance with zero mobility (moved by solvent flow); *(e)* reference marker substances along each border; *(f)* strip used in molding block; *(g)* glass support; *(h)*, *(i)* two-chamber electrode vessel; *(j)* connecting bridge to block; *(k)* electrode; *(l)* lamp; *(m)* connecting tube to equalize levels in electrode vessels. — *R. Trautman, in M. Florkin and E. H. Stotz (eds.), "Comprehensive Biochemistry," vol. 7, page 134, Elsevier, New York, 1963.*

In zone electrophoresis, the material to be examined is initially applied to the support in a narrow band approximately midway between the buffer reservoirs in which the electrodes are immersed. As electrophoresis proceeds, each component migrates toward the cathode or anode, depending on its charge, at its characteristic rate. Thus at the termination of a run, each component is, ideally, clearly separated from the others. The support may then be divided into sections, and the individual components may be eluted separately. Thus, zone electrophoresis is useful both for the analysis of a multicomponent mixture and for the preparation of purified proteins from such a mixture. The choice of support in zone electrophoresis is largely dictated by the purpose of the experiment. If the resolution of the components is the primary objective, paper, starch, or, preferably, polyacrylamide gel is employed as support. If, on the other hand, the experiment is principally for preparative purposes, a starch block might well be employed, because rather large quantities of material may be readily applied to it. The extreme resolving power of zone electrophoresis on starch gel is illustrated in Fig. 3-19, for the case of the plasma proteins. Fully 18 separated components are readily detectable.

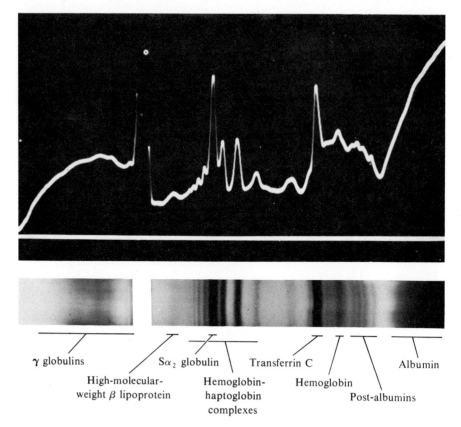

γ globulins   Sα₂ globulin   Transferrin C   Albumin

High-molecular-   Hemoglobin-   Hemoglobin
weight β lipoprotein   haptoglobin   Post-albumins
                          complexes

FIGURE 3-19.   The Possibility of Quantitative Serum Protein Analyses by Starch-gel Electrophoresis is illustrated in this figure. *(Bottom)* a photograph taken by transmitted light of a stained, unsliced 3-mm starch gel made transparent in glycerol; *(top)* a photograph of the corresponding trace appearing on the cathode-ray tube of an electronic analyzer. — *O. Smithies, Advan. Protein Chem.*, **14**: *65 (1959)*.

PURIFICATION
OF PROTEINS

The purification of proteins from natural sources is usually a formidable task. To begin with, the protein of interest may constitute only 0.1 per cent or less of the dry weight of the starting material, and much of the remainder of the material may be composed of other proteins some of whose properties probably closely resemble those of the desired product. In addition, many of the usual methods of purification of organic materials, such as distillation and solvent extraction, are not suitable for the purification of proteins, owing to their size and instability. It is difficult to imagine an organic chemist attempting to isolate a desired product from a reaction that went in only 0.1 per cent yield and produced several hundred side products. This is, nevertheless, the problem frequently faced by the biochemist who wishes to study the physical or biological properties of a particular protein.

The initial problem in protein purification is the choice, if indeed one has a choice, of a natural material from which isolation is to be attempted. The principal consideration in this matter is to find a source that is relatively rich in the desired protein. If the protein has a definite measurable biological activity, it is frequently possible to assay the protein in a variety of potential sources in crude mixtures and, on this basis, to select a favorable source. Because tissues vary widely in their content of particular proteins, an initial search of this type is usually very worthwhile. It is frequently also possible to increase the level of a protein by a suitable modification of the physiological environment, such as diet, culture conditions, etc.

Having discovered a suitable natural source, the next problem is to free the protein from the tissue. This may be done by exposing the tissue to ultrasonic irradiation, grinding it in a homogenizer, subjecting it to the action of a Waring blendor, or other related techniques. If the protein is bound to a particulate portion of the cell, the mitochondria for example, treatment with lipid solvents or detergents may be necessary to free it. In such cases it is advisable to isolate the particular fraction of the cell in which the protein occurs first, as an initial purification step (see Chap. 9).

Several precautions must be observed during the procedures necessary for the release of the protein from the tissue and during the subsequent fractionation steps. These include careful control of temperature, pH, and protein concentration. Other variables include ionic strength, the presence of heavy metals (removed by EDTA), and the redox potential (maintained at reducing levels by the addition of mercaptoethanol or dithiothreitol). Proteins are fragile molecules. In general, exposure to even moderate temperatures, for example, 37°, elicits their slow denaturation. Consequently, most protein-purification procedures should be carried out near the freezing point of the solvent in use. On the other hand, if the protein of interest happens to be unusually stable to heat, a brief heat treatment may serve to precipitate the bulk of the contaminating material, thus effecting a substantial purification. In addition to heat, proteins are sensitive to extremes of acid and base concentration. Hence protein purification should ordinarily be carried out in the presence of buffers that maintain the pH in the neighborhood of 7. Finally, protein concentration should always be maintained as high as reasonably possible, because many proteins tend to denature in dilute solution. Proteins, if they are enzymes, may often be protected by the presence of their substrates, which tend to confer additional stability on them.

Many fractionation methods are available for the purification of proteins. We discuss a few of these below.

Salt Precipitation. As indicated in Fig. 3-14, proteins vary markedly in their solubilities in concentrated salt solutions. Consequently, purification may be achieved by the addition, for example, of sufficient salt to precipitate some of the contaminating proteins, which may then be collected by centrifugation and discarded, a further addition precipitating the protein of interest but not all the remaining contaminating proteins. The protein of interest, together with other proteins that may have precipitated over the same concentration range, may then be collected. The salts most frequently employed for this purpose are ammonium sulfate and sodium sulfate; the former is usually preferable.

Isoelectric Precipitation. Because, as noted above, most proteins have a minimum solubility near their isoelectric point, suitable adjustment of the pH may result in the precipitation of the protein of interest, most of the contaminating proteins remaining in solution.

Precipitation with Organic Solvents. A variant of the methods above involves the use of organic solvents, particularly acetone, methanol, and ethanol, in attempts to precipitate certain proteins selectively from a mixture. These solvents often denature proteins easily, and the use of very low temperatures is advisable.

Ion-exchange Chromatography. Proteins, like amino acids, may frequently be purified by column chromatography on ion-exchange resins. Resins with hydrophilic backbones, usually cellulose, are the most satisfactory for this purpose. Two commonly used column materials for protein purification include DEAE-cellulose, an anion-exchange resin formed by linking diethylaminoethyl functions to a cellulose backbone, and CM-cellulose, a cation-exchange resin formed by linking carboxymethyl functions to a cellulose backbone. Such columns are developed by washing with buffers of increasing ionic strength or increasing or decreasing values of *p*H, as appropriate. Properly employed, the resolving power of these columns is great, and very substantial purifications may frequently be obtained through their use.

Adsorption Chromatography. The selective adsorption of proteins onto certain materials and the selective elution of proteins following adsorption may often be used as a purification procedure. Such chromatography may be performed either on a column or in slurries of the adsorbant. Frequently employed materials for the adsorption chromatography of proteins include calcium phosphate gel, alumina gel, diatomaceous earth (Celite), starch, and hydroxylapatite.

Electrophoresis. As mentioned above, the electrophoresis of protein mixtures by the zone method employing a high-capacity support, usually starch blocks, may effect excellent separations and permits near quantitative recovery of the protein of interest. Thus, zone electrophoresis is a good purification procedure.

Molecular Sieves. The use of molecular sieves, which sort out molecules according to size, may be adapted to protein purification. The most useful molecular sieves for work with proteins are certain polymeric carbohydrates and polyacrylamides that are available in a variety of pore sizes. These are commercially known as Sephadex and Biogel. Recently, diethylaminoethyl and carboxymethyl functions have been linked to Sephadex, so that a single run through a column may fractionate both on the basis of size and charge.

Crystallization. Provided that the use of other procedures has yielded a reasonably pure protein preparation, crystallization may sometimes be achieved. Repeated recrystallizations usually make significant contributions to the overall purity of the product. Proteins exhibit wide variations in their ease of crystallizability. Conditions for the crystallization of a given protein must be arrived at empirically. The careful control of *p*H, ionic strength, protein concentration, and temperature is essential.

The purification of proteins is frequently more an art than a science. The selection of methods for a particular case must be arrived at by trial and error. The evaluation of a particular procedure for inclusion in an overall purification scheme rests on two criteria: the degree of purification and the yield. Clearly a procedure that results in an overall purification of 100-fold but yields only 1 per cent of the product is of little use. The degree of purification is calculated by comparing the specific activities of the protein under study before and after each step. The specific activity is defined as the ratio of a convenient measure of the protein, enzymatic activity, for example, to the total amount of protein present. In Table 3-8, a hypothetical purification procedure is presented together with the specific activities, yields, and degrees of purification calculated for each step. A careful study of this table should result in a thorough understanding of the way in which the various quantities are derived.

TABLE 3-8.   Summary of a Hypothetical Protein-purification Procedure

Preparation	Volume, ml	Protein, mg/ml	Activity, arbitrary units/ml	Specific activity, units/ mg protein	Yield per cent (overall)	Fold purification (overall)
Crude extract	200	2.5	100	40	100	1
(NH₄)₂SO₄ precipitation	80	1.25	200	160	80	4
DEAE-cellulose chromatography	20	1.0	500	500	37.5	12.5
Preparative electrophoresis	5	1.0	1,500	1,500	37.5	37.5
Isoelectric precipitation	3	0.3	2,000	6,700	30	167
Crystallization	1	0.5	5,000	10,000	25	250

The purification of proteins employs several auxiliary procedures in addition to the fractionation methods discussed above. Two of these, dialysis and lyophilization, are of particular importance. The removal of salt from a protein solution by dialysis, the equilibration of a protein solution with a buffer solution across a protein-impermeable membrane, has been employed for many years. This procedure is of obvious importance, following, for example, a step involving protein precipitation with ammonium sulfate. Alternatively, desalting may be achieved by passing the protein solution through a suitable molecular sieve.

Lyophilization, freeze drying, is an important method of concentrating protein solutions or reducing them to dryness. In this procedure, the protein solution is frozen in an acetone–dry-ice bath and connected to a vacuum line. The rate of cooling due to the evaporation of the solvent from the frozen solution is sufficient to maintain the solution in the frozen state throughout the course of the concentration. Most proteins are not denatured by this procedure and may be stored in the dry state, in the cold, for long periods of time without deterioration of the sample. Frozen solutions are, in general, less stable. Pumping on a protein solution can result in extensive foaming, so that most of the protein ends up in the pump oil; furthermore, proteins are denatured on surfaces, and hence foaming must be avoided.

CRITERIA OF PURITY

One of the most difficult questions that arises in the course of purification of a protein is when to stop. That is, how does one know when a protein preparation is homogeneous? Several criteria are employed to answer this question. These are briefly discussed below.

Crystallinity. Small organic compounds that have been crystallized and recrystallized a few times may ordinarily be considered to be pure. Although this generalization was originally thought to apply to proteins as well, numerous examples of heterogeneous crystalline protein preparations have been identified. Consequently, although the crystallization of a protein is certainly a happy event, it cannot be considered an adequate criterion of the purity of the preparation.

Solubility Curves. One of the more satisfactory criteria for protein purity is the nature of its solubility curves. Solubility curves are constructed by carefully measuring the amount of protein in solution as a function of the amount of solid protein added to it. The ionic strength, the temperature, and the volume of the solution must, of course, be kept constant, and complete equilibration between the solid and solute phases must be reached. For a pure preparation, a plot of the amount of protein in solution against the amount of solid protein added yields, below the saturation point, a straight line of finite slope, breaks sharply at the saturation point, and above the saturation point, yields a line of slope zero. Solubility curves for a pure and an impure preparation of the proteolytic enzyme pepsin are shown in Fig. 3-20. The presence of impurities may alter the shape of the solu-

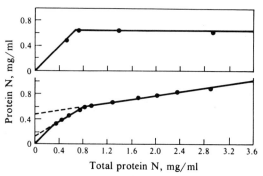

FIGURE 3-20.   Solubility Diagrams of Pure A Pepsin *(upper)* and of Crystalline Pepsin prepared from Cudahy pepsin *(lower)* in half-saturated magnesium sulfate in 0.05 M acetate buffer, pH 4.6 at 22°. Ordinates: protein N in solution; abscissae: total protein N in the mixture. —*John H. Northrop, Moses Kunitz, and Roger Moss Herriott, " Crystalline Enzymes," 2d ed., Columbia University Press, New York, 1948.*

bility curves from the ideal in a number of ways, depending on whether the impurity is more or less soluble than the protein and on its relative abundance. Even if this test is carefully applied, a 5 per cent impurity can be overlooked.

Ultracentrifuge Studies. The shape, width, and rate of spreading of the protein peak as it sediments in the ultracentrifuge can provide evidence concerning protein purity. Impurities are detected as distinct peaks, shoulders on the main peak, asymmetry of the main peak, or a peak width greater than that which may be accounted for in terms of the diffusion constant of the protein. Such studies are best carried out at a variety of values of pH and ionic strength.

Electrophoretic Studies. Homogeneity on electrophoresis, particularly employing starch or acrylamide gel as the supporting medium, at several values of pH is a good criterion of purity. As above, one should observe only a single symmetrical peak whose width is consistent with the diffusion constant.

Comparison of Molecular-weight Determinations. Independent determinations of the molecular weight by methods that yield number-average molecular weights for heterogeneous systems, such as osmotic pressure, and those which yield weight-average molecular weights for the same systems, such as light scattering, may be employed as a criterion of purity. Clearly, if the preparation is heterogeneous, distinct molecular weights are likely to be obtained for the two determinations.

Analytical Data. Amino acid composition data may be employed to detect impurities in protein preparations. For example, suppose such an analysis reveals that a particular protein contains 0.3 mole of histidine per mole of protein. One is entitled to conclude that the protein probably contains no histidine but that an impurity in the preparation does.

Detection of Impurities by Functional Tests. Minute amounts of impurities may frequently be detected if they have specific biological properties, such as enzymatic or hormonal activity. If a sample of protein is found to contain several such activities and if they are all due to a single protein, the ratio of their activities should remain unchanged throughout the course of the purification. If such ratios change as the enzyme is fractionated, the individual functional activities must be considered to belong to distinct proteins, and the protein of interest cannot be considered pure until the extraneous activities have been eliminated.

Homogeneity on Chromatography in Several Solvent Systems and with a Variety of Supports. None of the criteria of purity above are, in themselves, adequate to establish the homogeneity of protein preparations. Careful work requires that several independent criteria be employed and that, even if each provides a satisfactory result, carefully qualified conclusions be drawn.

REFERENCES   Cohn, E. J., and J. T. Edsall: "Proteins, Amino Acids, and Peptides as Ions and Dipolar Ions," Reinhold Publishing Corporation, New York, 1942.

Edsall, J. T., and J. Wyman: "Biophysical Chemistry," vol. 1, Academic Press Inc., New York, 1958.

Florkin, M., and E. Stotz (eds.): "Comprehensive Biochemistry," vols. 2, 3, 7, and 8, Elsevier Publishing Company, New York, 1963.

Fox, S. W., and J. F. Foster: "Introduction to Protein Chemistry," John Wiley & Sons, Inc., New York, 1957.

Fruton, J. S.: The Synthesis of Peptides, *Adv. Prot. Chem.*, **5**: 1 (1949).

Goodman, M., and G. W. Kenner: The Synthesis of Peptides, *Adv. Prot. Chem.*, **12**: 465 (1957).

Haurowitz, F.: "The Chemistry and Function of Proteins," Academic Press Inc., New York, 1963.

Hill, R. L.: Hydrolysis of Proteins, *Adv. Prot. Chem.*, **20**: 37 (1965).

Martin, R. B.: "Introduction to Biophysical Chemistry," McGraw-Hill Book Company, Inc., New York, 1964.

Meister, A.: "Biochemistry of the Amino Acids," Academic Press Inc., New York, 1965.

Neuberger, A.: Stereochemistry of Amino Acids, *Adv. Prot. Chem.*, **4**: 297 (1948).

Neurath, H. (ed.): "The Proteins," vols. 1 and 2, Academic Press Inc., New York, 1963.

——— and K. Bailey: "The Proteins," Academic Press Inc., New York, 1953.

Schachman, H. K.: The Ultracentrifuge: Problems and Prospects, *Biochemistry*, **2**: 887 (1963).

Sela, M., and E. Katchalski: Biological Properties of Poly-α-amino Acids, *Adv. Prot. Chem.*, **14**: 391 (1959).

Steiner, R. W.: "The Chemical Foundation of Molecular Biology," D. Van Nostrand Company, Inc., Princeton, N. J., 1965.

Tanford, C.: "Physical Chemistry of Macromolecules," John Wiley & Sons, Inc., New York, 1961.

Tristram, G. R., and R. H. Smith: Amino Acid Composition of Proteins, *Adv. Prot. Chem.*, **18**: 227 (1963).

4 | Structural Organization of Proteins

In Chap. 3, we outlined certain basic features of protein structure. They included structures for the constituent amino acids and a discussion of the covalent linkage, the peptide bond, through which they are linked in linear arrays. We now want to consider some of the structural characteristics of proteins in more detail, together with a description of the physical and chemical methods employed for their elucidation.

ORGANIZATIONAL LEVELS OF PROTEIN STRUCTURE

The complexity of the detailed structure of proteins is inherent in their size. Discussions of this topic are rendered a good deal more manageable, and perhaps more meaningful, by considering several levels of structural organization—primary, secondary, tertiary, and quaternary. They are distinguished by the nature of the interactions necessary for their maintenance. The *primary* structure of a protein is defined by its covalent bonding, that is, by the number and sequence of amino acid residues linked by peptide bonds. Thus the primary structure corresponds to the usual structural formula written for an organic compound. For small organic compounds, which have a relatively small number of conformations, such structural formulas tell most of the story, because the spatial relationships between atoms are approximately defined. Clearly, the situation is hardly so simple for molecules composed of one or more long flexible chains of molecular weights ranging up to 1 million and beyond. The number of possible conformations is staggering, and the introduction of higher orders of structural organization is obligatory.

Any ordering of the otherwise flexible peptide chains resulting from the formation of hydrogen bonds between the carbonyl oxygen and amide nitrogen atoms of the polypeptide backbone:

$$\begin{array}{c} \diagdown \\ \diagup \end{array} C{=}O \cdots H{-}N \begin{array}{c} \diagup \\ \diagdown \end{array}$$

is termed *secondary* structure. The formation of such hydrogen bonds may impose a variety of conformations on the polypeptide. These fall into two broad classes: *helical* structures and *sheet* structures.

It is also clear, for example, that a long helical segment of a polypeptide might itself assume a variety of conformations, owing to interactions between the side chains of the various amino acid residues. Such interactions might include hydrogen-bond formation, van der Waals interactions, charge transfer forces, salt linkages, and so forth. Protein structure that results from interactions between the residue side chains is termed *tertiary* structure. Such superfolding usually requires that long helical regions be broken up into shorter helical segments interspersed with segments of flexible random coils.

Finally, the intermolecular interactions between polypeptide chains — themselves generally folded or superfolded — can yield aggregates; they define *quaternary* structure. Aggregate or polymer formation depends on surface interactions between residue side chains as well as between exposed portions of the peptide backbone of separate monomeric polypeptides. Each of these organizational levels of protein structure will now be considered separately.

PRIMARY STRUCTURE OF PROTEINS   The determination of the sequence of amino acids along a polypeptide backbone is far from trivial. Indeed, the first successful determination was not completed until 1955, when F. Sanger and his associates at Cambridge succeeded in the determination of the complete primary structure of the polypeptide hormone insulin, molecular weight 6,000.

The elucidation of primary structure is a multistep process, consisting basically of (1) the determination of the number of independent polypeptide chains of the protein, (2) the cleavage of the interpeptide bonds and the separation of the individual chains, (3) the specific cleavage of each of the polypeptide chains of the native molecule into smaller chains of manageable size, (4) the sequence determination for each of the cleavage products, (5) fitting the individual segments into a unique sequence for each of the native chains, and (6) identifying the sites of linkage holding individual peptide chains together. Thus the molecule is degraded in an orderly fashion, the structure of the degradation products determined, and, employing this information, the structure of the native molecule deduced. Preliminary to performing this sequence of operations, the molecular weight and amino acid composition for the protein under consideration must be determined by the methods outlined in Chap. 3.

Determination of N- and C-terminal Amino Acids   Each peptide chain of a protein molecule, provided the chain is not circular or blocked at either end, has an N-terminal amino acid, bearing a free α-amino group, and a C-terminal amino acid, bearing a free α-carboxyl group. Thus the number of polypeptide chains may be determined from the analysis of the number of such residues. If a protein is found to contain one alanine, one lysine, and one serine each per mole of protein in N-terminal positions, the conclusion that three peptide chains are present is warranted.

The N-terminal amino acids are usually determined by one of four methods. First, the polypeptide may be arylated by treatment with 1-fluoro-2,4-dinitroben-zene — Eq. (3-3) — yielding the 2,4-dinitrophenyl derivative of the N-terminal residue. The complete hydrolysis of the protein, extraction of the DNP-amino acid into organic solvents, and chromatographic or other determination of the amino acid involved reveals the nature of the N terminus. Of course, other groups of the protein, i.e., the ε-amino group of lysine, also react with this reagent, but only one α-amino group, that of the N-terminal residue, is so modified. This method was developed by Sanger, and, in consequence, 1-fluoro-2,4-dinitrobenzene is frequently referred to as the *Sanger reagent*.

The second important reagent employed for the determination of N-terminal residues is phenylisothiocyanate (the *Edman reagent*). This reagent reacts with the free α-amino groups in dilute alkali to yield the phenylthiocarbamyl peptide — Eq. (3-4). The treatment of this product with acid, preferably but not necessarily in organic solvents, results in cyclization, producing the phenylthiohydantoin of the N-terminal amino acid, whose structure may be determined chromatographically, and forming a new N-terminal amino acid:

$$\phi-\overset{\overset{\displaystyle S}{\underset{\displaystyle \parallel}{C}}}{N}\overset{H}{\underset{}{}}\quad \overset{H}{\underset{}{N}}-CHR_1-\overset{\overset{\displaystyle O}{\underset{\displaystyle \parallel}{C}}}{}-\overset{H}{\underset{}{N}}-R_2 \xrightarrow{\ H^+\ } \quad \overset{\phi}{\underset{}{N}}\overset{\overset{\displaystyle S}{\underset{\displaystyle \parallel}{C}}}{\underset{}{}}\overset{}{NH} \quad C-C-H + NH_2-R_2 \tag{4-1}$$

An important development for the use of the Edman reagent has been introduced by Koningsberg and Hill, who have provided methods for the chromatographic separation of a purified sample of the degraded peptide. This permits the determination of the N terminus by subtractive methods; that is, amino acid analysis of the starting and degraded peptide identifies the nature of the amino acid split off. This makes the Edman reagent currently the most powerful weapon in the arsenal of those interested in determining amino acid sequences. The determination may be repeated and the next-to-N-terminal residue may be subsequently identified. In theory one might expect to work his way down the entire length of the peptide chain. Practical difficulties limit the use of this method to about five successive determinations (or a few more in the hands of careful and experienced technicians).

A third chemical reagent well suited to the determination of N-terminal residues is potassium cyanate. The treatment of peptides with this reagent in slightly alkaline solution results in carbamylation of amino functions:

$$NCO^- + NH_2-CHR_1-\overset{\overset{\displaystyle O}{\underset{\displaystyle \parallel}{C}}}{}-\overset{H}{\underset{}{N}}-R_2 \rightarrow NH_2\overset{\overset{\displaystyle O}{\underset{\displaystyle \parallel}{C}}}{}\overset{H}{\underset{}{N}}-CHR_1-\overset{\overset{\displaystyle O}{\underset{\displaystyle \parallel}{C}}}{}-\overset{H}{\underset{}{N}}-R_2 \tag{4-2}$$

Exposing of the carbamylated peptides to dilute acid at elevated temperatures results in the cleavage of the N-terminal residue from the chain with its cyclization to the hydantoin:

$$\underset{H_2N}{\overset{O}{\overset{\|}{C}}}\underset{N-CHR_1-\overset{O}{\overset{\|}{C}}-\overset{H}{\overset{|}{N}}-R_2}{\overset{H}{\overset{|}{N}}} \xrightarrow[100°]{H^+} \underset{O}{\overset{\overset{O}{\overset{\|}{C}}}{\underset{HN\quad NH}{\overset{}{C}}}} \underset{R_1}{\overset{}{C-H}} + R_2NH_2 \qquad (4\text{-}3)$$

These reactions are clearly closely related to those involved in the use of phenyl-isothiocyanate. The principal advantage of the cyanate procedure is the ease of separation and identification of the hydantoin by chromatography on ion-exchange resins.

Finally, the use of the *exopeptidase*, leucine aminopeptidase, is applicable to N-terminal amino acid determinations. This enzyme requires the presence of a free α-amino function for activity and, hence, splits only the N terminus from the polypeptide chain. As with the Edman reagent, cleavage of the N-terminal amino acid from the chain results in the unmasking of a new such residue. By following the kinetics of the release of amino acids from a polypeptide, information as to their sequence may be obtained. For example, for a peptide of structure $H_2N—A \cdot B \cdot C \cdot D \cdots$, A is liberated more rapidly than B, which is liberated more rapidly than C, and so forth. Leucine aminopeptidase, as the name implies, cleaves N-terminal leucine residues most rapidly but splits off all amino acids, although many only very slowly. Most of the difficulties and ambiguities experienced in the use of this technique are ascribable to this difference in the rate of release; e.g., if B above is a good substrate and A a poor one, A and B are released almost simultaneously.

Methods for the determination of the C-terminal residues are less satisfactory. In a fashion quite analogous to that described for leucine aminopeptidase, the enzyme carboxypeptidase (actually a class of closely related enzymes), which requires a free α-carboxyl function for activity, may be employed. An alternative method, due to Akabori, is the complete hydrazinolysis of the polypeptide. Hydrazine reacts at each of the peptide bonds, converting all the amino acids except the C-terminal one, whose carboxyl is not involved in peptide linkage, to the acyl hydrazines. The C-terminal amino acid may be separated and identified chromatographically. A less widely employed method involves the reduction of the C-terminal carboxyl to the corresponding alcohol through the use of appropriate hydride ion donors. Complete hydrolysis then yields the amino alcohol of the C-terminal residue, which may be isolated and identified.

Cleavage of Disulfide Bridges

Independent polypeptide chains comprising a protein molecule are frequently held together by the disulfide bridges of cystine residues. For proteins composed of a single chain, these bridges may bring together two quite distant points in terms of linear amino acid sequence. The hydrolysis of chains containing such disulfide linkages may lead to complex mixtures of peptides. In addition, the disulfide bridges are unstable to most hydrolytic conditions and, furthermore, readily undergo a number of rearrangement reactions. Consequently, prior to the initiation of sequence studies, the disulfide bridges are usually destroyed.

Two general methods are employed: oxidation and reduction. Oxidation of disulfides with performic acid, a technique employed in studies on both insulin and ribonuclease, yields the corresponding cysteic acid residues:

$$\begin{array}{c} | \\ S \\ | \\ S \\ | \end{array} \quad \xrightarrow[\text{H—C—O}_2\text{H}]{\overset{\text{O}}{\|}} \quad \begin{array}{c} | \\ SO_3^- \\ \\ SO_3^- \\ | \end{array} \qquad\qquad (4\text{-}4)$$

These residues are quite stable to hydrolytic and other procedures, and their polar character may be employed to advantage for the separation of peptides. Performic acid also converts methionine to the corresponding sulfone, a derivative happily less susceptible to air oxidation than methionine itself. The principal disadvantages in the use of performic acid are the destruction of tryptophan and the less than quantitative oxidation of the disulfide bridges.

Disulfides may be reduced to the sulfhydryl form by a variety of reagents, including mercaptoethanol, thioglycollate, and sodium borohydride:

$$\begin{array}{c} | \\ S \\ | \\ S \\ | \end{array} + 2HSCH_2CH_2OH \rightarrow \begin{array}{c} | \\ SH \\ \\ SH \\ | \end{array} + \begin{array}{c} S—CH_2CH_2OH \\ | \\ | \\ S—CH_2CH_2OH \end{array} \qquad (4\text{-}5)$$

Mercaptoethanol is the most suitable reagent for this purpose. Because the liberated sulfhydryl groups are quite reactive and susceptible to reoxidation to the disulfide, they are generally blocked before one proceeds further in the degradation of the peptide chain. Early studies employed iodoacetamide or iodoacetate, which alkylate the sulfhydryl groups. More recent experience indicates that acrylonitrile is a better reagent for this purpose. The cyanoethylation of protein sulfhydryl groups with acrylonitrile is quantitative and proceeds without detectable side reactions:

$$R—SH + CH_2{=}CH—CN \rightarrow R—S—CH_2CH_2CN \qquad (4\text{-}6)$$

The number of chains and disulfide bridges for several proteins are shown in Table 4-1.

Specific Cleavage of Polypeptides

The amino acid sequence determination of a long polypeptide requires that the polypeptide be specifically cleaved at a limited number of sites, yielding products containing several amino acids. The specificity of cleavage is important, in fact, crucial, to ensure that a limited number of peptides is obtained in reproducible fashion, each in sufficient quantity to permit its further investigation. For the specific cleavage of peptide chains, the proteolytic enzymes trypsin, chymotrypsin, and pepsin are frequently employed.

Each of these enzymes exhibits specificity for the types of peptide bond that it attacks. Trypsin catalyzes the hydrolysis of peptide bonds whose carbonyl function is donated by a basic amino acid, usually arginine or lysine. Pepsin and chymotrypsin prefer to catalyze the hydrolysis of peptide linkages involving the aromatic amino acids, particularly tryptophan, tyrosine, and phenylalanine. Among the proteolytic enzymes, trypsin is the most specific and, hence, the enzyme of choice for such studies. It is clear, however, that the use of a single perfectly specific enzyme does not suffice for the determination of the complete sequence. If, for example, trypsin cleavage of a polypeptide resulted in the production of five peptides, which comprise the entire length of the native chain, and if the sequence of amino acids within each of the five segments were established, one would still need to know the order in which the segments appeared in the native peptide. For this purpose other peptides must be obtained that overlap those initially obtained.

The principal advantage of the use of enzymatic hydrolysis, the specificity of the reaction in terms of the nature of the peptide bonds cleaved, also imposes a stringent limitation on the versatility of this method. Ideally one might well desire cleavage at a point not ordinarily susceptible to the action of trypsin, for example. Alternatively, one might wish to prevent cleavage at a susceptible site. Recent developments

TABLE 4-1. Molecular Weight, Number of Chains, and Number of Disulfide Bridges for Proteins

Protein	Molecular weight	Number of chains	Number of —S—S—bonds
Insulin	5,800	2	3
Ribonuclease	13,700	1	4
Lysozyme	14,400	1	5
Myoglobin	17,000	1	0
Papain	20,900	1	3
Trypsin	23,800	1	6
Chymotrypsin	24,500	3	5
Carboxypeptidase	34,300	1	0
Hexokinase	45,000	2	0
Taka-amylase	52,000	1	4
Bovine serum albumin	66,500	1	17
Yeast enolase	67,000	1	0
Hemoglobin	68,000	4	0
Alkaline phosphatase	80,000	2	4
Liver alcohol dehydrogenase	83,000	2	0
Hemerythrin	107,000	8	0
Glyceraldehyde-3P-dehydrogenase	140,000	4	0
Lactic dehydrogenase	140,000	4	0
Aldolase	142,000	3	0
Yeast alcohol dehydrogenase	150,000	4	0
γ-Globulin	160,000	4	25
Glutamic dehydrogenase	250,000	4	0
Myosin	620,000	3	0

SOURCE: H. K. Schachman, *Cold Spring Harbor Symp. Quant. Biol.*, **28**: 409 (1963).

have partially fulfilled these objectives. For example, the reaction of the ε-amino groups of lysine with ethyltrifluorothioacetate in mildly basic solution yields a blocked amino acid residue whose adjacent peptide bond is no longer susceptible to trypsin catalyzed hydrolysis:

$$R{-}NH_2 + CF_3{-}\overset{\overset{\displaystyle O}{\|}}{C}{-}S{-}CH_2CH_3 \rightarrow R{-}\overset{\overset{\displaystyle H}{}}{N}{-}\overset{\overset{\displaystyle O}{\|}}{C}{-}CF_3 + C_2H_5SH \tag{4-7}$$

Thus, the treatment of such a peptide with trypsin would lead to cleavage only at the arginyl residues. Following the removal of the blocking group under mildly alkaline conditions, trypsin catalyzes a subsequent cleavage at lysine residues. In a similar fashion, the alkylation of cysteine residues with β-halo ethylamines yields peptide linkages that are susceptible to trypsin-catalyzed hydrolysis:

$$R{-}SH + Br{-}CH_2CH_2{-}NH_2 \rightarrow R{-}S{-}CH_2CH_2{-}NH_2 + HBr \tag{4-8}$$

Hence the versatility and power of trypsin as a specific reagent for polypeptide cleavage is markedly increased, and overlapping peptides may be obtained by successive treatments of suitably modified substrates with the enzyme.

Sequences deduced from lower peptides

Gly·Ile·Val·Glu·Glu·CySO$_3$H·CySO$_3$H·Ala
Ser·Val·CySO$_3$H
Ser·Leu·Tyr·Glu·Leu·Glu·Asp·Tyr·CySO$_3$H
CySO$_3$H·Asp

Peptides from peptic hydrolysate

Gly·Ile·Val·Glu·Glu·CySO$_3$H·CySO$_3$H·Ala·Ser·Val·CySO$_3$H·Ser·Leu
Gly·Ile·Val·Glu·Glu·CySO$_3$H·CySO$_3$H·Ala·Ser·Val
Gly·Ile·Val·Glu
Tyr·Glu
Tyr·Glu·Leu
Tyr·Glu·Leu·Glu
Leu·Glu
Leu·Glu·Asp·Tyr·CySO$_3$H·Asp
Glu·Asp·Tyr·CySO$_3$H·Asp
Asp·Tyr·CySO$_3$H·Asp

Peptides from chymotryptic hydrolysate

Gly·Ile·Val·Glu·Glu·CySO$_3$H·CySO$_3$H·Ala·Ser·Val·CySO$_3$H·Ser·Leu·Tyr
Gly·Ile·Val·Glu·Glu·CySO$_3$H·CySO$_3$H·Ala·Ser·Val·CySO$_3$H
Ser·Leu·Tyr
Glu·Leu·Glu·Asp·Tyr
Glu·Leu·Glu·Asp·Tyr·CySO$_3$H·Asp

Structure of fraction A

Gly·Ile·Val·Glu·Glu·CySO$_3$H·CySO$_3$H·Ala·Ser·Val·CySO$_3$H·Ser·Leu·Tyr·Glu·Leu·Glu·Asp·Tyr·CySO$_3$H·Asp
 1   2   3   4   5   6   7   8   9   10   11   12   13   14   15   16   17   18   19   20   21

Bonds split by pepsin

Bonds split by chymotrypsin

↑ major sites of action of enzymes;   ↑ other bonds split by enzymes.

FIGURE 4-1.   The Structure of the A Chain of Oxidized Insulin. — *J. I. Harris and V. M. Ingram, in Alexander and Block (eds.), "The Composition, Structure, and Reactivity of Proteins," vol. 2, Pergamon, New York, 1960.*

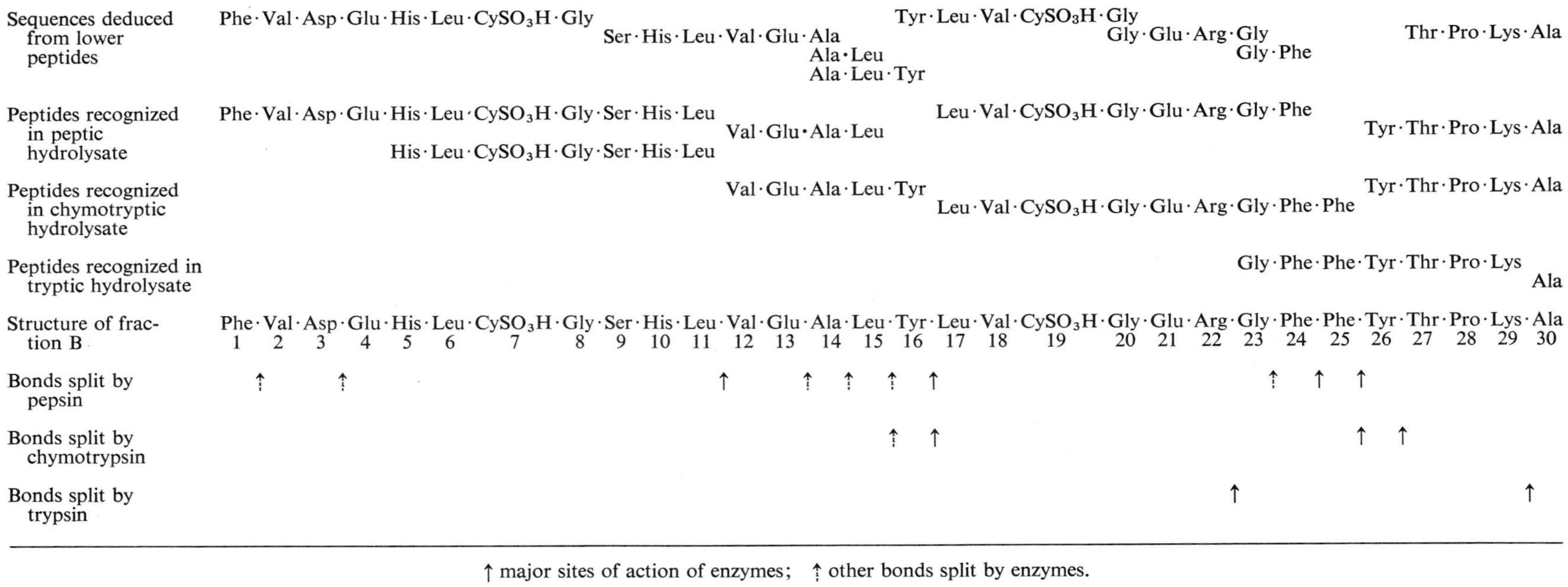

FIGURE 4-2. Structure of the B Chain of Oxidized Insulin

Sequences deduced from lower peptides	Phe·Val·Asp·Glu·His·Leu·CySO₃H·Gly Ser·His·Leu·Val·Glu·Ala Tyr·Leu·Val·CySO₃H·Gly Gly·Glu·Arg·Gly Thr·Pro·Lys·Ala
	Ala·Leu Ala·Leu·Tyr Gly·Phe
Peptides recognized in peptic hydrolysate	Phe·Val·Asp·Glu·His·Leu·CySO₃H·Gly·Ser·His·Leu Val·Glu·Ala·Leu Leu·Val·CySO₃H·Gly·Glu·Arg·Gly·Phe Tyr·Thr·Pro·Lys·Ala
	His·Leu·CySO₃H·Gly·Ser·His·Leu
Peptides recognized in chymotryptic hydrolysate	Val·Glu·Ala·Leu·Tyr Leu·Val·CySO₃H·Gly·Glu·Arg·Gly·Phe·Phe Tyr·Thr·Pro·Lys·Ala
Peptides recognized in tryptic hydrolysate	Gly·Phe·Phe·Tyr·Thr·Pro·Lys Ala

Structure of fraction B:

Phe·Val·Asp·Glu·His·Leu·CySO₃H·Gly·Ser·His·Leu·Val·Glu·Ala·Leu·Tyr·Leu·Val·CySO₃H·Gly·Glu·Arg·Gly·Phe·Phe·Tyr·Thr·Pro·Lys·Ala
1 2 3 4 5 6 7 8 9 10 11 12 13 14 15 16 17 18 19 20 21 22 23 24 25 26 27 28 29 30

Bonds split by pepsin

Bonds split by chymotrypsin

Bonds split by trypsin

↑ major sites of action of enzymes; ↑ other bonds split by enzymes.

FIGURE 4-2. The Structure of the B Chain of Oxidized Insulin. — J. I. Harris and V. M. Ingram, in Alexander and Block (eds.), "The Composition, Structure, and Reactivity of Proteins," vol. 2, Pergamon, New York, 1960.

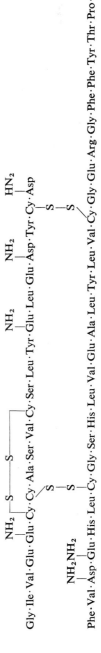

Gly·Ile·Val·Glu·Glu·Cy·Cy·Ala·Ser·Val·Cy·Ser·Leu·Tyr·Glu·Leu·Glu·Asp·Tyr·Cy·Asp

Phe·Val·Asp·Glu·His·Leu·Cy·Gly·Ser·His·Leu·Val·Glu·Ala·Leu·Tyr·Leu·Val·Cy·Gly·Glu·Arg·Gly·Phe·Phe·Tyr·Thr·Pro·Lys·Ala

FIGURE 4-3. The Covalent Structure of Bovine Insulin. — J. I. Harris and V. M. Ingram, in Alexander and Block (eds.), "The Composition, Structure, and Reactivity of Proteins," vol. 2, Pergamon, New York, 1960.

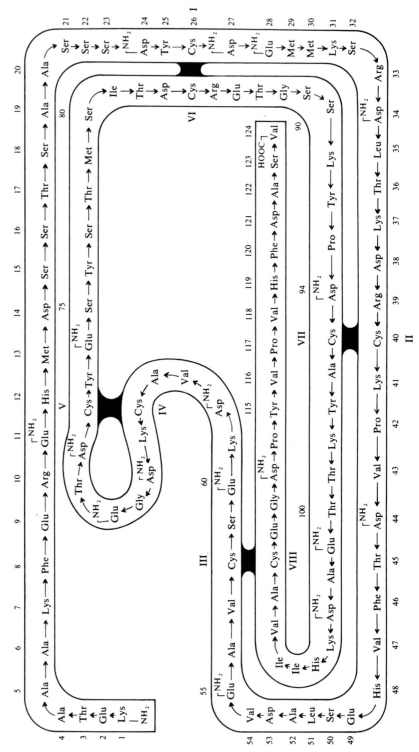

FIGURE 4-4.   The Covalent Structure of Ribonuclease. — D. G. Smyth, W. H. Stein, and S. Moore, J. Biol. Chem., 238: 227 (1963).

Sequence
Determination
of Short
Peptide Chains

Following specific cleavage of polypeptide chains and separation of the hydrolysis products chromatographically, the next task is the sequence determination for each of the degradation products. In general this is accomplished by (1) determination of the amino acid composition of each peptide, (2) determination of the N- and C-terminal residues, and (3) further degradations, if necessary. Clearly, for the case of tripeptides, knowledge of the composition and nature of the terminal residues suffices to establish the amino acid sequence uniquely. For longer peptides, use of the Edman reagent is of great value. Sequential analysis from the N-terminal end, if used in conjunction with knowledge of the amino acid composition and C terminus, may suffice to establish the sequence of peptides containing 8 to 10 amino acids. Similar experiments may be attempted, generally less successfully, with the use of leucine aminopeptidase and carboxypeptidase.

When all the sequences of the degradation products have been determined, together with those for a suitable number of overlapping peptides, the complete sequence of the native chain is established. This point is illustrated below. The final step is the localization of the disulfide bridges. This may be accomplished by the enzymatic cleavage of the protein with the disulfide groups intact. A limited amount of additional sequence work usually suffices to localize the groups involved in disulfide linkage.

Structure
of Insulin

Insulin is a polypeptide hormone concerned with the regulation of the rate of carbohydrate metabolism. The bovine hormone contains 51 amino acids arrayed in two chains, as evidenced by the presence of N-terminal glycine and phenylalanine. The chain terminating in glycine is termed the A chain and contains 21 amino acids. The chain terminating in phenylalanine is termed the B chain and contains 30 amino acids. Sanger and his group oxidized insulin with performic acid and separated the two chains chromatographically. Each chain was degraded both enzymatically and by acid hydrolysis. In Figs. 4-1 and 4-2, the major peptides obtained from the hydrolysis of each of the chains are shown together with the unique structures that were deduced. The sites of cleavage by trypsin, chymotrypsin, and pepsin, as indicated in these figures, conform in large part to expectations based on the known specificity of these enzymes toward synthetic materials. Cleavage at some additional sites was also found, particularly in the case of the pepsin-catalyzed hydrolyses. Note how the overlapping peptides obtained with the use of different hydrolytic techniques complement each other and permit an unambiguous assignment of the overall sequence. Each of the major peptides shown in Figs. 4-1 and 4-2 was sequenced by nonspecific hydrolysis with acid, determination of the sequences of the resultant di-, tri-, and tetrapeptides, and correlating this information into a unique sequence. As indicated above, this task is currently markedly simplified by use of the Edman reagent. The complete sequences of the A and B chains, together with the localization of the disulfide bridges and amide groups of aspartic and glutamic acids (these are destroyed by acidic hydrolysis), yielded the complete structure for insulin as shown in Fig. 4-3.

Structure of
Ribonuclease

The second major achievement in the establishment of amino acid sequences for proteins was the work of Hirs, Stein, Moore, and Anfinsen on ribonuclease. This single-chain enzyme, composed of 124 amino acids and containing four intrachain disulfide bridges, was approached in a manner similar to that employed for insulin: performic acid oxidation was followed by enzymatic hydrolysis. The principal

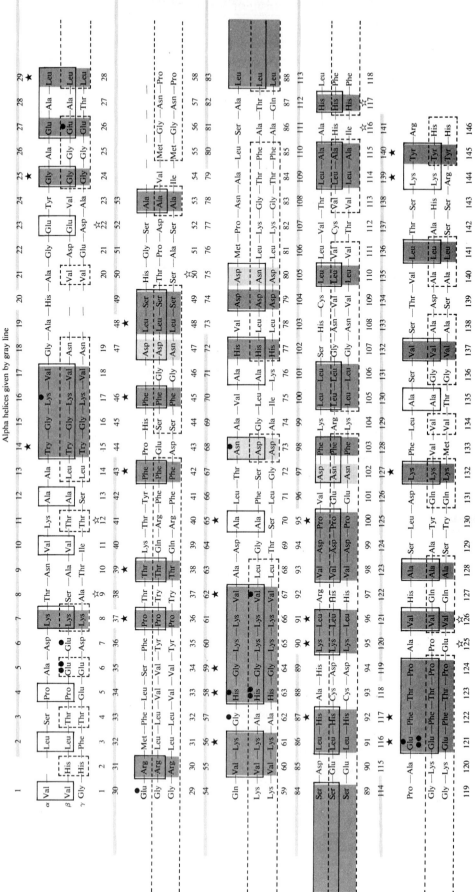

FIGURE 4-5. The Alpha, Beta, and Gamma Chains of Normal Human Hemoglobins. — *Copyright © 1963, by Frank W. Putnam. Prepared by Frank W. Putnam, Division of Biology, Indiana University.*

advances in techniques employed to establish the primary structure of this larger protein were (1) the use of ion-exchange resins for the quantitative separation of low-molecular-weight peptides and (2) the use of quantitative methods for the determination of amino acid composition of peptides. The complete structure for ribonuclease is shown in Fig. 4-4.

Primary Structure of Other Proteins

Following the spectacular successes with insulin and ribonuclease, the amino acid sequences of several additional proteins have been established. These include lysozyme, the coat protein of tobacco mosaic virus, chymotrypsinogen, trypsinogen, papain, myoglobin, hemoglobin, cytochrome *c*, clupeine, and additional proteins.

Generalizations

Work on amino acid sequence determination thus far permits the following generalizations to be drawn. First, the ordering of amino acids within polypeptide chains is random. All or nearly all possible dipeptide sequences have been found. Repeating sequences within the same molecule are not commonly observed. Second, proteins have unique structures; that is, ribonuclease, for example, is not a class of polypeptides whose individual members differ by a few random substitutions along the chain. These comments do not exclude the ordered replacement of certain amino acids in functionally similar molecules found, for instance, in different species (see below). Third, proteins are heterogeneous with respect to the number and type of disulfide bridges, although the number and arrangement of disulfide bridges is unique for a particular protein. Certain proteins have no disulfide bridges, others have either inter- or intrachain disulfides, and others have both types. Fourth, sequence studies have largely confirmed the specificity for proteolytic enzymes originally deduced from studies on low-molecular-weight peptides. Finally, these studies have confirmed our earlier conclusions that only amino acids of the L- configuration occur in proteins and that covalent linkages other than the peptide bond are rare.

Individuality of Proteins: Species Specificity and Mutational Alterations

As emphasized in Chap. 3, certain polypeptide hormones, i.e., vasopressin and β-MSH, that perform functionally identical tasks in different species may exhibit subtle differences in their primary structure. Such species specificity also exists for the case of proteins. For example, Sanger and his associates have sequenced insulins obtained from several mammalian sources. In each case, amino acid variations either within the disulfide loop of the A chain or at the carboxyl terminus of the B chain were found. Similarly, samples of cytochrome *c* isolated from a variety of species exhibit individuality in the nature of certain amino acids in a crucial peptide segment.

In addition to those arising from species specificity, alterations in protein structure are also found that derive from mutational events. Much of our knowledge concerning the dependence of protein structure on mutation results from the elegant work of Ingram, now at the Massachusetts Institute of Technology. Hemoglobin, as noted below in more detail, consists of two pairs of identical chains: the α and β chains (or α and γ chains in fetal hemoglobin). Ingram and his associates were able to demonstrate that normal hemoglobin and the hemoglobin of victims of sickle-cell anemia (Hb S), a genetically controlled disease, differ only in the substitution of a valine residue for a glutamic acid residue at a unique position in the β chain. Subsequently, a large number of abnormal hemoglobins have been studied, and many single amino acid replacements noted (Fig. 4-5).

Subtle differences in the primary structure of closely related proteins may often be readily detected by the technique of *fingerprinting*. Obtaining the fingerprint of a protein involves partial digestion by one or more proteolytic enzymes followed by determination of the pattern of the product peptides on electrophoresis or chromatography. Fingerprints for normal and sickle-cell hemoglobin are shown in Fig. 4-6. Close examination of these fingerprints indicates that, with the exception of one peptide, the patterns are identical. Hence, that structural unit which is genetically altered is pinpointed immediately, and the nature of the structural alteration may be defined without the necessity of sequencing the entire molecule. Indeed, in favorable cases, strong evidence for the nature of the amino acid substitution may be gained simply from comparison of the amino acid compositions of the corre-

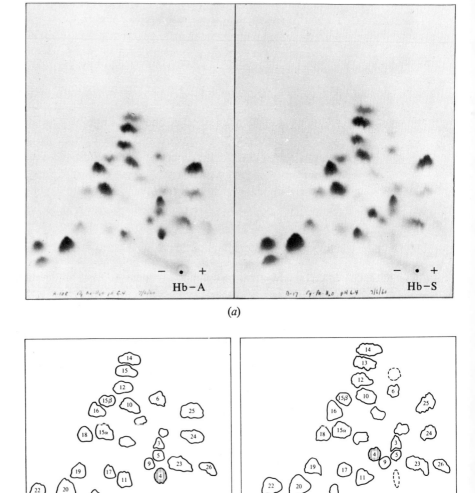

FIGURE 4-6.   Fingerprints of Trypsin Digest of Hemoglobins A and S. *(a)* Photograph of a pair of fingerprints. *(b)* Tracings of a pair of fingerprints showing the system for numbering peptide pairs. Dotted lines indicate peptides that become visible only after heating the chromatogram. — C. Baglioni, *Biochim. Biophys. Acta,* **48**: 392 (1961).

sponding peptides isolated from the two proteins. Definitive evidence for the substitution depends, of course, on obtaining the sequence of the peptides concerned.

SECONDARY
STRUCTURE
OF PROTEINS

Understanding of the secondary structure of proteins, that structure which is due to the formation of hydrogen bonds between the components of the peptide linkage itself, is largely due to the brilliant investigations of Pauling and Corey. From an extensive series of X-ray diffraction studies on crystalline low-molecular-weight amides, Pauling, Corey, and Branson established a set of criteria for formation of the most stable secondary structure. These requirements include (1) that the peptide group be planar and have bond lengths and angles identical to those found in crystals of simple secondary amides (see Fig. 3-1), (2) that every carbonyl oxygen and amide nitrogen be involved in hydrogen-bond formation, (3) that the hydrogen-bonded hydrogens lie close to a line joining the oxygen and nitrogen

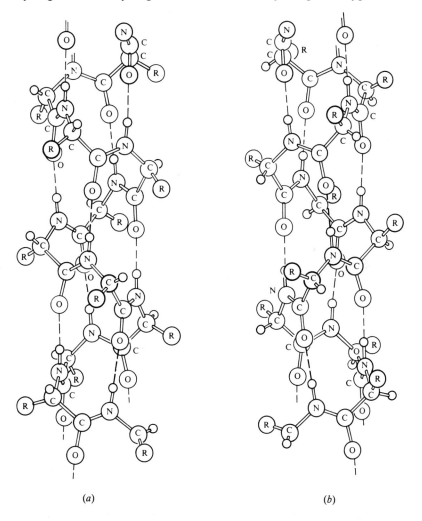

(a)   (b)

FIGURE 4-7.   Drawings of the Left-handed (a) and Right-handed (b) α-Helical Forms of a Polypeptide Chain Containing L-Amino Acids. The side chains, R, and hydrogen atoms attached to the α-carbons in the main chain have positions corresponding to the known configuration of L-amino acids. — B. W. Low and J. T. Edsall, in D. E. Green (ed.), "Currents in Biochemical Research," page 398, Interscience, New York, 1956.

atoms involved in formation of the bond, and (4) that the operation, in going from
one residue to the next (in terms, for example, of translation along or rotation
around a central axis), be the same for every residue. Acceptable structures that
meet these requirements fall into two general categories: helical structures derived
from formation of intramolecular hydrogen bonds and sheet structures derived from
formation of intermolecular hydrogen bonds.

Among the many possible helical structures considered by Pauling, Corey, and
others, only one fully meets all the specifications for maximum stability. This is
termed the α *helix* and is illustrated in Fig. 4-7. The α helix is characterized by a

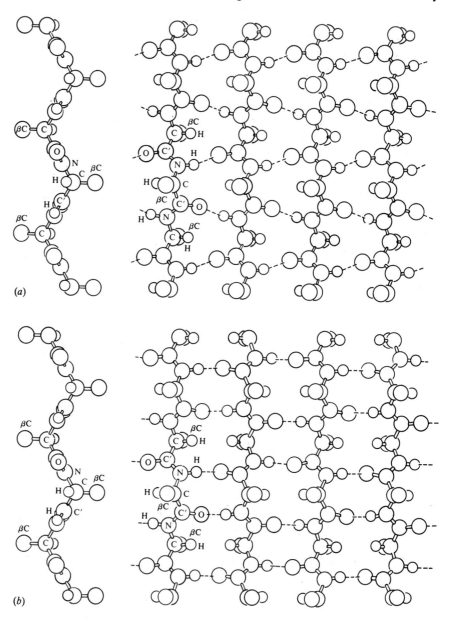

FIGURE 4-8.   Representation of the Parallel *(a)* and Antiparallel *(b)* Pleated Sheet Structures for Polypeptides. — *L. Pauling and R. B. Corey, Proc. Nat. Acad. Sci., U.S., 37: 729 (1951).*

translation along a central axis parallel to the long axis of the helix of 5.4A per turn. A complete turn is made for every 3.6 residues. Thus the translation per residue is near 1.5 A, and the rotation per residue is 100°. In striking support of the α helix as a structural feature of proteins are the results of earlier X-ray diffraction studies on certain proteins that revealed spacings of 5.4 and 1.5 A, precisely the values predicted for the α helix. Examination of Fig. 4-7 reveals that the hydrogen bonds formed between the components of the peptide linkages are nearly parallel to the long axis of the helix. The side chains of the amino acid residues bristle out from the helix. Each carbonyl oxygen and amide nitrogen is involved in hydrogen-bond formation; carbonyl oxygens are hydrogen-bonded to amide nitrogens three residues back in the peptide chain. Thus the repeating hydrogen-bonded unit may be visualized as follows:

$$
\begin{array}{c}
\overset{\textstyle O}{\underset{\textstyle \parallel}{}} \qquad\quad \overset{\textstyle H}{} \\[-2pt]
N\!-\!(C\!-\!CHR\!-\!N)_3\!-\!C \\[-2pt]
\underset{\textstyle H}{|} \;-\;-\;-\;-\;-\;-\;-\;-\; \overset{\textstyle \parallel}{O}
\end{array}
$$

Proteins that contain α-helical structure may be either globular or fibrous.

The sheet structures that result from formation of intermolecular hydrogen bonds are of two principal types, both consistent with the requirements of Pauling, Corey, and Branson. These are termed the *parallel* and *antiparallel pleated sheets* and are depicted in Fig. 4-8. As the names imply, the former structure is composed of a series of chains that are parallel in the sense of having all their N termini at the same end, and the latter structure has every other chain pointed in the opposite direction. In contrast to the α helix, the hydrogen bonds of the pleated-sheet structures are nearly perpendicular to the long axis of the polypeptide chain. Proteins that contain sheet structures are fibrous and are generally insoluble in aqueous solvents. In the following discussion, we are concerned principally with helical structures and the methods for their detection and estimation.

The Helical Content of Polypeptides   *Optical Rotatory Dispersion.* The helical content of a protein is an important parameter for its structural characterization. For example, paramyosin has a very large fraction (greater than 90 per cent) of its amino acids involved in α-helical structures, but β-lactoglobulin probably contains no α-helical structure at all. Most proteins have helical regions of varying length interspersed with regions of random coil. Estimation of helical content may be attempted by several means. The most widely employed method is based on the study of *optical rotatory dispersion* of model polypeptides. In Fig. 4-9, a schematic representation of the variation of optical rotation for the synthetic polypeptide poly-L-glutamate is given as a function of wavelength at pH 7 and pH 4. Such variation in rotatory power is termed optical rotatory dispersion. The curves at the two values of pH are clearly very different both in the region from 250 to 190 mμ and in that from 350 to 700 mμ. These differences are correlated with changes in the structure of the polypeptide: at pH 4, poly-L-glutamate is completely helical; at pH 7, it is a random coil. Since the helix is basically an asymmetric structure, it is not surprising that it contributes to rotatory power of polypeptides (as do the asymmetric amino acid residues). The important question is whether or not one can dissect out the contribution of the helix in a quantitative fashion. Attempts to do so can be made on the basis of the information derived from the two regions of the spectrum indicated above. In the long wavelength range, Moffitt and Yang have proposed the following empirical expression for the correlation of optical rotation of polypeptides with wavelength:

$$[R]_\lambda = a_0 \frac{\lambda_0{}^2}{\lambda^2 - \lambda_0{}^2} + b_0 \frac{\lambda_0{}^4}{(\lambda^2 - \lambda_0{}^2)^2} \tag{4-9}$$

in which $[R]_\lambda$ is a measure of the observed rotation (plus some correction terms), λ is the wavelength, and a_0, b_0, and $\lambda_0 = 212$ mμ are constants. The value of b_0 in this equation, which is obtained by graphical means, is a measure of helical content. It has been observed with a number of synthetic homopolypeptides that

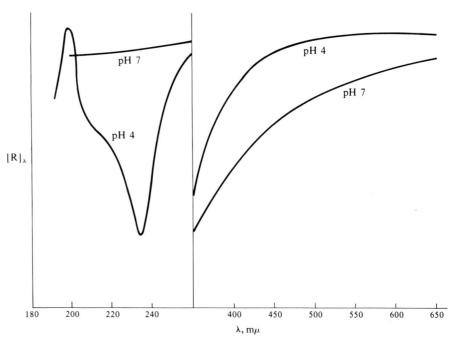

FIGURE 4-9. A schematic representation of the variation of optical rotation as a function of wavelength for the synthetic polypeptide poly-L-glutamic acid at pH 4 and 7. This molecule is helical at the former pH and exists as a random coil at the latter. Note that the value of the ordinate would change as the transition from the wavelength region above 300 mμ to that below this value is made since the rotational strengths are very much greater at lower wavelengths.

those which are helical have values of this parameter near -630 and those which exhibit no such structures have values near zero. Intermediate helical contents can be obtained from observed values of b_0 by interpolation.

   Use of b_0 values for the estimation of the extent of helicity in native proteins has been fairly successful, although the results are somewhat less pleasing than those obtained with synthetic polypeptides. Some proteins exhibit b_0 values a good deal more negative than -630. This is a result rather difficult to interpret in the light of the naïve discussion presented above. Uncertainties in the calculation of helical content from values of b_0 in the case of native proteins are introduced by (1) the lack of a theoretical basis for the Moffitt-Yang equation, (2) side-chain interactions that may influence rotatory power, (3) the possible presence of ordered structures other than the α helix or random coil, and (4) the possibility that a protein may contain segments of right-handed and segments of left-handed α helix. In the last case, contributions of helical regions of the opposite sense to the overall rotatory power would compensate each other, and the total helix content would be markedly underestimated.

Recent developments in instrumentation have made optical rotation measurements on solutions of polypeptides and proteins in the region of 185 to 240 mμ possible (though not routine). In this region of the ultraviolet spectrum, the optical rotatory dispersion curves of polypeptides exhibit several interesting features (see Fig. 4-9). The rotatory dispersion curves of α-helical polypeptides, i.e., poly-L-glutamate at pH 4, exhibit a minimum at 233 mμ, a crossover point (point of zero rotation) near 225 mμ, a shoulder at 215 to 220 mμ, a maximum at 198 mμ, and a second crossover point at 193 mμ. The rotational strengths at 233 and 198 mμ are conformation-dependent; that is, they provide quantitative information themselves relevant to the degree of helicity of polypeptides.

TERTIARY STRUCTURE OF PROTEINS It has been recognized for quite some time that most proteins, in their native state, exist as rather tight compact structures. This can be appreciated directly from a consideration of the hydrodynamic behavior of proteins. Consider, for example, the *intrinsic viscosities* of a number of macromolecules. The intrinsic viscosity is defined as

$$[\eta] = \frac{V}{m}\Lambda \qquad (4\text{-}10)$$

in which V is the volume of the particle, m is its mass, and Λ is a function of the axial ratio of the molecule and is equal to 2.5 for rigid spheres (a result due to Einstein) and increases with increasing axial ratio. In Table 4-2, values of the function $[\eta]$ are collected for several macromolecules that are grouped into three classes:

TABLE 4-2. Intrinsic Viscosities for Macromolecules

Compact globular particles	Molecular weight	$[\eta]$, cc/g	Randomly coiled chains	Molecular weight	$[\eta]$, cc/g	Rodlike particles	Molecular weight	$[\eta]$, cc/g
Polystyrene latex particles	10^9	2.4	Polystyrene in toluene	45,000	28	Fibrinogen	330,000	27
			Polystyrene in toluene	70,000	37	Collagen	345,000	1,150
Ribonuclease	13,700	3.3	Reduced ribonuclease	13,700	14.4	Myosin	620,000	230
Lysozyme	14,400	3.0	Oxidized ribonuclease	14,100	11.6			
Myoglobin	17,000	3.1	Oxidized ribonuclease in urea	14,100	13.9	DNA	5×10^6	5,000
β-Lactoglobulin	35,000	3.4						
Ovalbumin	44,000	4.0	Ovalbumin in urea	44,000	34	TMV	4×10^7	29
Serum albumin	65,000	3.7	Serum albumin in urea	66,000	22			
Hemoglobin	67,000	3.6	Reduced serum albumin in urea	66,000	53			
Liver alcohol dehydrogenase	83,000	4.0	Myosin in guanidine-hydrochloride	200,000	93			
Hemerythrin	107,000	3.6						
Aldolase	142,000	3.8						
			RNA	1.5×10^6	100			
Ribosomes (yeast)	3.5×10^6	5.0	Heat-denatured DNA	5×10^6	150			
Bushy stunt virus	8.9×10^6	4.0						

SOURCE: H. K. Schachman, *Cold Spring Harbor Symp. Quant. Biol.*, **28**: 409 (1963).

compact globular particles, randomly coiled chains, and rodlike structures. As predicted by Eq. 4-10, the values for most of the native globular proteins are independent of molecular weight. Intrinsic viscosities are dependent on molecular weight for molecules that are not spherical, but the variations in $[\eta]$ in Table 4-2 are principally the result of shape differences. Note particularly the marked increase in $[\eta]$ that occurs on unfolding the polypeptide chain by cleavage of disulfide bridges (ribonuclease, serum albumin) or by treatment with concentrated solutions of urea (ovalbumin, serum albumin). Finally, note the very large values of $[\eta]$ for molecules, such as collagen and DNA (discussed in Chap. 5), which have a helical secondary structure but which lack superfolding of the helix. Data of the type shown in Table 4-2 lead to the conclusion that most proteins exhibit such superfolding (tertiary structure).

In addition, the folded structures for proteins must be highly specific; that is, the polypeptide chain or chains do not merely collapse into a roughly spherical structure but undergo a precise series of folding operations, yielding a unique, or nearly unique, structure. This conclusion follows directly from the extreme sensitivity of the biological activity, i.e., enzymatic activity, of proteins to alterations in their tertiary structure (see below). In terms of the protein as a highly and specifically folded structure, we wish, first, to ascertain detailed information concerning the intimate details of such structures and, second, to account for such structures in terms of the nature of the forces responsible for their maintenance. Measurements of viscosities, frictional coefficients, and light scattering yield information concerning the general topography of macromolecules. A more sophisticated approach to the understanding of the tertiary structure of proteins is afforded by X-ray diffraction.

X-ray Diffraction
and Tertiary
Structure of
Proteins

X-ray diffraction is one of the most potent general methods for the determination of molecular structures. Its successes in unraveling complicated chemical structures are numerous (vitamin B_{12}, for example). It should be recognized that the classical uses of X-ray diffraction involved molecules much less complicated than even the simplest and smallest proteins. The brilliant work of Perutz and Kendrew, described below, has convincingly established that, at least in some cases, this method may be successfully applied to obtain detailed information about the latter class of molecules as well.

Determination of X-ray diffraction patterns of proteins requires crystalline preparations meeting special requirements. First, the crystals should be 1 mm long in their longest dimension; this is a good deal larger than most protein crystals prepared by conventional means. Second, the structure solutions from X-ray diffraction patterns require the use of a series of *isomorphous derivatives* as well as the native protein. These are formed by the introduction of one heavy atom, such as Hg, per unit cell into the crystal structure of the protein. It is essential that this introduction does not alter the size or symmetry of the unit cell nor the coordinates of the atoms within it. Formation of suitable heavy-atom derivatives of proteins is frequently the greatest stumbling block to the determination of three-dimensional structure for macromolecules by X-ray diffraction. Kendrew required four such derivatives for the myoglobin problem, and Perutz needed six for the solution of the hemoglobin structure.

A typical X-ray diffraction pattern, that for myoglobin, is indicated in Fig. 4-10.

The dark spots on the photographic plate, diffraction maxima, provide an indirect view of the protein structure. The diffraction pattern is actually a reciprocal view of the crystal; that is, the diffraction maxima near the center of the pattern correspond to long spacings and those near the periphery to short spacings within the crystal. The structure is deduced by measurements of the positions and intensity of the diffraction maxima for the native protein and a suitable number of isomorphous

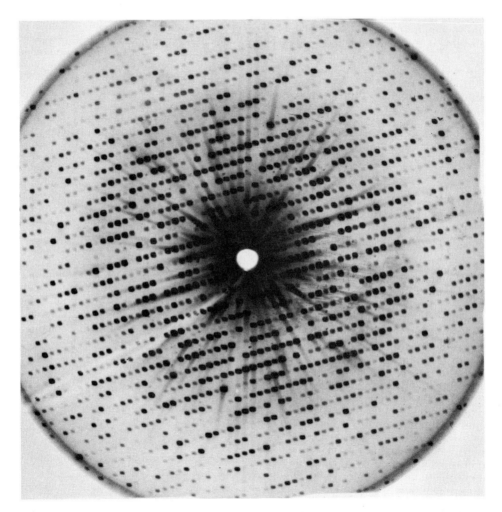

FIGURE 4-10.   Precession Diagram, Myoglobin. — *F. H. C. Crick and J. C. Kendrew, Advan. Protein Chem.,* **12**: *133 (1957).*

derivatives. To obtain a highly resolved structure, it is necessary to include measurements on a large number of maxima. For example, the work of Kendrew on the structure of myoglobin involved the use of more than 10,000 diffraction maxima. A resolution of about 1.5 A has been obtained. Such work is very complicated mathematically and requires the use of very high-speed electronic computers.

Structure of Myoglobin
Myoglobin is the oxygen-carrying protein of mammalian muscle. It consists of a single chain of 153 amino acid residues and 1 iron-containing heme group and has a molecular weight of 17,500. It is a somewhat atypical protein in two respects:

a relatively high content of α helix (77 per cent) and a complete lack of disulfide bridges or free sulfhydryl groups.

The X-ray diffraction studies of Kendrew and his associates on sperm-whale myoglobin have revealed the structural aspects of this molecule in intimate detail. Early work on this molecule involved the determination of a structure with a 6A resolution. At this resolution, the polypeptide chain was recognizable as a region of high electron density that was folded in a highly intricate fashion, yielding a rather compact structure. Determination of a refined structure with a resolution of 1.5 A permits most of the atoms in the molecule to be unambiguously located.

TABLE 4-3. Parameters Characterizing the Helical Segments of the Myoglobin Molecule

Helix	Number of residues	ϕ, radians	h, A/residue
A	16	1.73	1.50
B	16	1.69	1.47
D	7	1.73	1.45
E_1	10	1.74	1.52
E_2	10	1.71	1.49
F	9	1.70	1.46
G	19	1.75	1.53
H	24	1.73	1.49
α-helix	...	1.74	1.50

ϕ = axial rotation per residue.
h = axial translation per residue.
SOURCE: J. C. Kendrew, Enzyme Models and Enzyme Structure, *Brookhaven Symp. Biol.*, **15**: 215 (1963).

Such resolution, of course, permits the amino acid sequence to be determined directly from the X-ray diffraction data. Comparison of the sequence derived from X-ray data with that derived by classical chemical means yields concordant results.

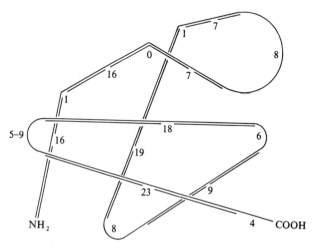

FIGURE 4-11. A Schematic Representation of Myoglobin. Double lines indicate segments of α-helical structure. Numbers indicate the length of each segment in residues. — *D. W. Green, in M. Florkin and E. H. Stotz (eds.),* "Comprehensive Biochemistry," *vol. 7, page 249, Elsevier, New York, 1963.*

In addition, knowledge of the structure at this resolution permits reliable calculations of interatomic distances from which a great deal of information concerning the interactions of residue side chains may be derived. We shall return to this point later.

In Fig. 4-11, a schematic picture of myoglobin is shown that traces out the course of the polypeptide chain and identifies the α-helical segments. The molecule is seen to consist of eight helical segments that are interrupted by regions of random coil. The latter regions occur, for the most part, at the corners of the molecule, where the polypeptide chain drastically alters direction. In Table 4-3, data concerning the length of the helical regions and the axial rotation and translation per residue are presented and compared with corresponding values deduced by Pauling and Corey for the α helix. These data offer striking proof for the existence of α-helical structures in myoglobin. A complete model of myoglobin is presented in Fig. 4-12.

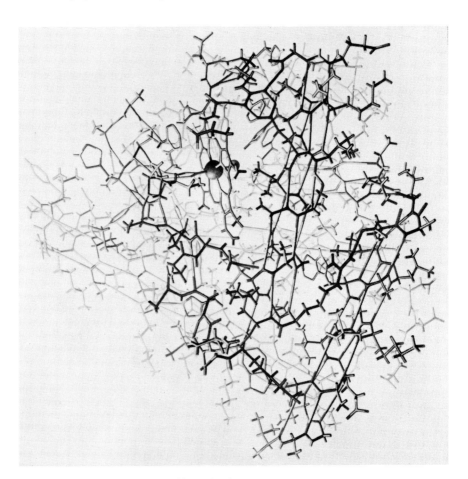

FIGURE 4-12.   A Model of the Complete Myoglobin Molecule.
— *Photo from painting by Irving Geis. J. C. Kendrew, Sci. Am., 205: 98–99 (1961).*

Kendrew has summarized the principal features of the myoglobin molecule, and we reiterate them at this point. (1) The molecule is compact and contains, at most, four molecules of water in its interior. (2) Nearly all the polar groups (Lys, Arg, Glu, Asp, His, Ser, Thr, Tyr, Trp) are on the surface of the molecule and, hence, exposed to solvent. (3) Bound water molecules are attached to all polar groups at the surface. (4) Apart from the water molecules bound to the polar groups, the liquid regions surrounding the crystal show no sign of ordering. (5) The interior of the molecule is composed of nonpolar residues. (6) The fifth coordination site of the iron atom in the tetrapyrrole prosthetic group is occupied by a histidine residue. The sixth such coordination site, on the other side of the tetrapyrrole structure, is probably occupied by a water molecule that is presumably displaced by O_2 when the myoglobin is converted to its oxygenated form.

The one nagging uncertainty concerning protein structures derived from X-ray diffraction measurements is whether the structure in the crystal is closely related to that for the protein in aqueous solution. A definitive answer to this question is not yet in hand. The best evidence to date that suggests that the crystal and solution structures are very closely related is provided by the work of Gurd and his associates, who have studied the reaction of a variety of residue side chains of myoglobin with alkylating agents. Those residue side chains which, according to the crystal structure, are exposed to solvent are found to react readily, and those which are buried in the interior of the crystal, and, hence, would not be expected to react, do not react. This work nicely confirms, then, that the general features of the myoglobin molecule must be similar in the crystal and in solution.

Structure of Hemoglobin   Hemoglobin, the oxygen-transporting pigment of mammalian serum, is a more complicated protein than myoglobin, although closely related to it structurally. Hemoglobin, molecular weight 65,000, consists of four chains that are identical in pairs. The two types of chains are known as the α and β chains. The approach to the structure of hemoglobin was quite similar to that for the case of myoglobin. Despite the fact that the hemoglobin work was actually initiated several years prior to that on myoglobin, the detailed structure of hemoglobin, owing to its greater complexity, is not quite so well understood as that of myoglobin. As work on the refinement of the hemoglobin structure is well under way, this is to be regarded as a temporary phenomenon. The work of Perutz and his colleagues on the detailed

FIGURE 4-13.   The Completed Model of a Single Molecule of Reduced Human Hemoglobin *(left)*, compared with the horse oxyhemoglobin model *(right)*. — *H. Muirhead and M. F. Perutz, Cold Spring Harbor Symp. Quant. Biol., **28**: 451 (1963).*

structure of hemoglobin has yielded many very significant results. Of particular importance are the findings (1) that the tertiary structure of the chains of hemoglobin are closely related to that of the myoglobin molecule and (2) that oxygenation of hemoglobin results in a marked alteration of structure. In regard to the latter point, models of oxygenated horse hemoglobin and reduced human hemoglobin are shown in Fig. 4-13. As may be appreciated qualitatively from this figure, oxygenation of hemoglobin results in a decrease in the distance between the β chains of about 7 A. This change in structure appears to be principally an alteration in the relative dispositions of the β chains without marked structural alterations in the β chains themselves.

Structure
of Lysozyme

Phillips and his associates, following the guidelines established in the myoglobin and hemoglobin work, have very recently established the crystal structure of hen egg-white lysozyme at a 2A resolution. This molecule is reasonably compact and roughly ellipsoidal. It consists of a single polypeptide chain of known primary sequence that is 129 residues long. The three-dimensional conformation of the polypeptide chain is constrained by the formation of four disulfide bridges. The main course of the backbone of lysozyme and the location of these disulfides is indicated schematically in Fig. 4-14. As may be readily appreciated from this

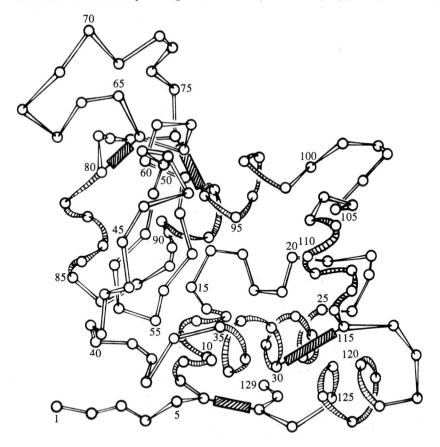

FIGURE 4-14. A Schematic Drawing of the Main Chain Conformation of Lysozyme. The shaded rectangles represent disulfide bridges, and the numbers refer to individual residues, counting from the N terminus. — *C. C. F. Blake, D. F. Koenig, G. A. Mair, A. C. T. North, D. C. Phillips, and V. C. Sarma, Nature, 206: 757 (1965).*

figure, the structure of lysozyme is exceptionally complicated, particularly in the region bounded by residues 35 and 80. Lysozyme contains somewhat less helical structure than myoglobin; a maximum of 42 per cent of the residues are so structured.

As in the case of myoglobin, all lysine and arginine side chains are exposed to the surrounding solvent. However, at least one serine and one glutamic acid appear to be shielded from solvent. Furthermore, several hydrophobic side chains are clearly on the molecular surface or actually protrude beyond this surface.

X-ray diffraction studies of the structure of several other molecules, including insulin, chymotrypsinogen, and carbonic anhydrase are in progress. Detailed structures for several additional proteins will soon be available.

FORCES INVOLVED IN MAINTENANCE OF SECONDARY AND TERTIARY STRUCTURES

Four types of interactions are considered principally responsible for the maintenance of the secondary and tertiary structures of proteins. These include interpeptide hydrogen bonds, side-chain hydrogen bonds, ionic bonds, and apolar or hydrophobic bonds (Fig. 4-15). It is certainly possible that interactions of other

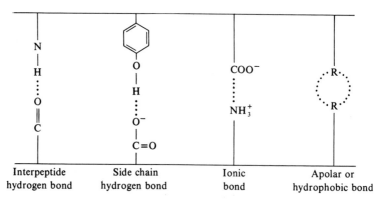

FIGURE 4-15. Intramolecular Noncovalent Bonds Responsible for Secondary and Tertiary Structures. — H. K. Schachman, *Cold Spring Harbor Symp. Quant. Biol.*, **28**: 409(1963).

types may contribute to the stability of the folded form of certain polypeptides, but little evidence concerning them is available at this time.

Apolar Bonds

The tendency of hydrocarbons or other nonpolar molecules to associate in aqueous solution is termed *apolar* (or hydrophobic) bond formation. There is a good deal of evidence that formation of apolar bonds is one of the most important, if not the most important, factors influencing the higher-order structures of proteins. Our most detailed information concerning the relative importance of apolar and polar interactions comes from the studies on myoglobin. Employing computer methods, Kendrew calculated the interatomic distances, pairwise, for all the atoms of myoglobin. Those atoms which were more than 2 and less than 3.1 A apart were considered to be involved in polar interactions, and those more than 3.1 and less than 4.1 A apart to be involved in apolar interactions. The number of interactions in the latter category exceeds those in the former by an order of magnitude. Thus, for myoglobin at least, the formation of apolar bonds appears to be of primary significance for formation of the compact structure of this molecule.

What is the driving force for the formation of apolar bonds? It is reasonable to suppose that exposed hydrophobic residues in the extended less highly structured form of the protein have an organizing effect on the surrounding water molecules. This organization restricts the rotational and translational freedom of the water molecules and hence is accompanied by a negative entropy change. Association of the hydrocarbonlike moieties in the interior of the native molecule thus tends to free this organized solvent shell. Thus, the driving force for formation of apolar bonds is largely the positive entropy change resulting from the liberation of solvent molecules organized about the apolar residues that accompanies the transfer of these residues from an aqueous to a nonaqueous environment.

Polar Interactions

As in the case of the apolar, our most detailed information concerning polar interactions in proteins is provided by the X-ray diffraction studies on myoglobin. These are summarized in Table 4-4. The most striking aspect of these data is the

TABLE 4-4. Polar Interactions in Myoglobin

Residue	Total number	Number in solvent or surface	Number "buried"	Bonding to other than solvent		Partners
				None, inter-molecular or weak intra-molecular	Strong intra-molecular	
Lys	19	19	0	16	3	Glu
Arg	4	4	0	2	1	Asp, propionyl Asp, Asp
Glu or Gln	19	19	0	12–13	2–3 1 1–3	Lys Lys, Trp Chain, own NH
Asp or Asn	8	8	0	3–4	3 1	Arg His
Ser	6	5	1	2	3 1	Chain CO, 4 back Chain NH
Thr	5	3	1–2	1–2	1 1 1	Chain CO, 4 back Chain CO, 3 back Chain NH
His	11	7–8	3	7–8	2 1	Chain CO, $Fe^{++}(H_2O)$ Asp
Trp	2	2	0	1	1	Glu
Tyr	3	3	0	2	1	Chain CO

SOURCE: F. M. Richards, *Ann. Rev. Biochem.*, **32**: 269 (1963).

fact that relatively few of the total possible strong polar interactions are realized. In most cases, the polar groups are bound to solvent. The preliminary conclusion appears to be warranted that, at least in the case of myoglobin, the protein molecule assumes a conformation in which a maximum number of the polar groups is exposed on the surface and that strong interresidue polar interactions occur only when allowed by restrictions imposed by a structure otherwise largely dictated by apolar interactions. It remains to be established whether this generalization is true for most other proteins as well.

As indicated above, most, if not all, proteins have a well-defined structure, in terms of both the sequence of amino acids and the folding of the polypeptide chain. The important question immediately arises as to the origin of the higher-order structures of proteins. The simplest possibility is that the three-dimensional structure of proteins is completely determined by the primary structure. This is equivalent to the statement that a protein assumes that conformation which is thermodynamically most stable under the existing conditions. Alternatively, it is possible that, at the time of its synthesis, a specific three-dimensional structure is imparted to the protein that persists after the release of the protein from the synthetic apparatus. This conformation need not be the thermodynamically most stable one; it is only required that the energy barrier for transconformation reactions be sufficiently high so that the occurrence of such processes is rare and their speed slow. Several lines of evidence, summarized below, strongly suggest that the former alternative is correct.

Perhaps the most convincing experiments suggesting that primary structure determines secondary and tertiary structures are those which demonstrate restoration of proteins to their native states following an initial loss of the native structure. For example, if the ribonuclease molecule is completely unfolded by reduction of the four disulfide bridges with mercaptoethanol in 8 M urea, reoxidation of the molecule under properly controlled conditions results in the recovery of 95 to 100 per cent of the molecules in the native conformation as judged by recovery of enzymatic activity and by comparison of physical properties. Such an experiment is illustrated diagrammatically in Fig. 4-16. Statistical calculations indicate that, if

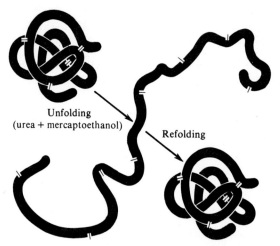

Unfolding
(urea + mercaptoethanol)

Refolding

FIGURE 4-16.   Model System for Studying the Conversion of a Linear Polypeptide Chain to a Folded Protein. A native protein, with intramolecular disulfide bonds, is reduced and unfolded with β-mercaptoethanol and 8 M urea. After removal of these reagents, the reduced protein is allowed to undergo spontaneous refolding and reoxidation. — C. J. Epstein, R. F. Goldberger, and C. B. Anfinsen, Cold Spring Harbor Symp. Quant. Biol., 28: 439 (1963).

reforming of the disulfide bridges were completely random, only about 1 per cent of the molecules would have assumed their native conformations. A collection of data of this type is presented in Table 4-5. In each case, with the exception of insulin, reformation of native structures greatly exceeds that expected on the basis of random recovery. These results do not imply that formation of disulfide bonds of proteins is an uncatalyzed process in vivo. Indeed, reformation of native structures from reduced proteins may be a good deal too slow to account for the rate of synthesis of biologically active proteins in the living cell. An enzymatic system has been identified in beef liver that accelerates the reactivation of reduced ribonuclease.

TABLE 4-5. Refolding of Disulfide-bond-containing Proteins (Following Reduction and Unfolding)

Protein	Disulfide bonds	Recovery of activity, per cent	Random recovery, per cent
Ribonuclease (bovine pancreatic)	4	95–100	ca. 1
Lysozyme (egg white)	4	50–80	ca. 1
Taka-amylase A (*Aspergillus oryzae*)	4	48	ca. 0.3
Trypsin (bovine):	6		ca. 0.01
CM-cellulose trypsin (insoluble)		4	
Poly-DL-alanyl trypsin (soluble)		8	
Insulin (bovine)	3	5–10	ca. 6.7
Alkaline phosphatase (*E. coli*)	2	80	ca. 33
Pepsinogen (swine)	3	50	ca. 6.7
Serum albumin (human)	17	50	?

SOURCE: C. J. Epstein, R. F. Goldberger, and C. B. Anfinsen, *Cold Spring Harbor Symp. Quant. Biol.*, **28**: 439 (1963).

The refolding experiments do establish that undirected reformation of disulfide bridges of reduced proteins largely yields structures that are identical to those of proteins isolated from living material. Because undirected reformation of tertiary structures very probably yields the thermodynamically most stable conformation, it follows that native proteins exist in the thermodynamically most stable conformation.

DENATURATION
OF PROTEINS

Transconformation reactions of proteins, including denaturation, have been the subject of intense interest to the protein chemist. The utility of such studies for understanding the structures of proteins and those forces which are responsible for these structures, the possible role of reactions of this type in enzymatic catalysis, and the challenge to the chemist inherent in reactions of great complexity account for this interest. Kauzmann has defined protein denaturation as a "process (or sequence of processes) in which the spatial arrangement of the polypeptide chains within the molecule is changed from that typical of the native protein to a more disordered arrangement." Broad as this definition is, clearly not all transconformations are included in it.

Perhaps the most perplexing problem concerning protein denaturation is how to measure it. In Table 4-6, an incomplete summary of the parameters whose variation may be taken as a measure of protein denaturation is presented. Clearly a very large number of experimental techniques is available, but it is imperative to realize that results of studies of denaturation are very frequently a function of the types of measurement that are made. Thus, a particular treatment of a protein may, for example, drastically alter its biological activity, even though exhaustive physical measurements reveal slight alterations in structure or no change at all.

Many agents typically elicit protein denaturation. These include heat, ultraviolet irradiation, organic solvents, urea, guanidinium chloride, LiBr, detergents, and extremes of pH. Denaturation by these factors may lead to very different denatured states. For example, complete denaturation by heat is frequently irreversible, but denaturation by urea is usually reversible; that is, removal of the urea regenerates the native state of the protein. Clearly the states of protein reversibly and irreversibly denatured must be substantially different.

TABLE 4-6. Methods for Investigating the Denaturation of Proteins

I. Shape properties of proteins	II. Short-range properties of proteins
A. Hydrodynamic properties	A. Thermodynamic properties
1. Frictional ratio	1. Energy and heat capacity
2. Viscosity increment	2. Solubility
3. Rotatory diffusion constant	B. Optical properties
B. Radiation scattering	1. Optical rotation and dispersion
1. Light scattering	2. Infrared absorption and dichroism
2. Small-angle X-ray scattering	3. Visible and ultraviolet absorption
C. Electron microscopy	4. Index of refraction
	C. Chemical properties
	1. Reactivity of groups
	2. H-D exchange
	3. Binding of small molecules
	4. Immunochemical properties
	5. Biological activity
	6. Electrophoresis

SOURCE: W. Kauzmann, *Adv. Protein Chem.*, **14**: 1 (1959).

Studies of the relative effectiveness of various chemicals as protein denaturants measure (provided the denaturation is of the reversible type) their effect on the equilibrium constant for interconversion of the native and denatured states. Thus, a given denaturant may function by destabilizing the native state, stabilizing the denatured state, or both. Employing the myoglobin molecule as a model, one may tentatively conclude that most of the polar groups are exposed to the solvent in both the native and denatured states but that the peptide backbone and nonpolar groups are largely isolated from solvent in the native state and exposed in the denatured state. Because the effects of the denaturant on the stability of the polar groups should be largely the same in the native and denatured states and because the peptide backbone and the nonpolar groups are largely isolated from the denaturant in the native state, it is reasonable to consider the denaturing ability of urea and related compounds as primarily reflecting stabilization of the exposed peptide backbone and nonpolar residues by the denaturant. Studies on the ability of various denaturants to solubilize the model compounds acetyl tetraglycine and CBZ-diglycinamide suggest that stabilization of both peptide linkages and nonpolar residues is important for denaturing activity.

The chemical basis of denaturing activity is ill-understood, despite the fact that it has been the subject of thorough investigation. In general, good denaturants have the structure indicated below, in which for X,

$$R{-}C{-}N{-}Y$$

$NH_2 > S > O$; for R, $NH_2 > CH_3S \sim CH_3O > S > O \sim H \sim CH_3$; and for Y, $H > NH_2 >$ anion. On this basis, urea ($X = O$, $R = NH_2$, $Y = H$), guanidinium salts ($X = NH_2$, $R = NH_2$, $Y = H$), and S-methylisothio-urea ($X = NH_2$, $R = CH_3S$, $Y = H$) would be expected to be excellent denaturants, as, indeed, they are.

QUATERNARY STRUCTURE OF PROTEINS

Many proteins are composed of several polypeptide chains, independent in the sense of not being covalently linked to one another. Hemoglobin is clearly such a protein, containing four chains and no disulfide bridges. Proteins in this class are said to contain quaternary structure. Each of the individual chains in turn has its own primary, secondary, and tertiary structure. A large number of proteins have been recognized as being composed of subunits. Indeed, it now appears that most, if not all, proteins with molecular weights greater than about 50,000 are composed of such subunits. The concept of subunit structures for proteins was initially enunciated by Soerenson and Svedberg in the 1930s, following which the idea fell into disrepute only to be resurrected in the last few years.

Multichain enzymes may usually be dissociated into the monomeric units by the same agents that typically cause protein denaturation. The association-dissociation behavior of several proteins has been studied; we focus attention here on two of the best understood cases: glutamic dehydrogenase and aldolase.

The glutamic dehydrogenase molecule exhibits three levels of structural organization at the quaternary level. As isolated, glutamic dehydrogenase has a molecular weight of 1.0 to 1.3×10^6 (sedimentation velocity and diffusion). Upon dissociation into subunits — which is promoted by NADPH, certain purine nucleotides, or simply by dilution of the enzyme — subunits of molecular weight 250,000 to 350,000 are obtained. Thus the fully associated molecule is probably a tetramer of the smaller units (a trimer structure cannot be definitely ruled out, however). This monomer-tetramer equilibrium is readily and fully reversible. Treatment of the 300,000-molecular-weight monomer with sodium lauryl sulfate, 6 M urea, or moderate concentrations of acid or base results in a further, and irreversible, dissociation into probably identical subunits of molecular weight 40,000.

Two important questions concerning the monomer-tetramer equilibrium deserve mention. The first of these deals with the catalytic activity of the subunits. Careful studies of Frieden on the extent of tetramer formation as a function of protein concentration reveal that, in the very dilute solutions in which glutamic dehydrogenase is assayed for enzymatic activity, this protein exists almost completely in the monomeric form. It follows directly that the monomeric units are enzymatically active. The 40,000-molecular-weight subunits are, in contrast, enzymatically inert. The second question concerns the fashion in which NADPH and, for example, guanylic acid inhibit association of the monomeric units. Studies, again from Frieden's laboratory, indicate that these substances associate with the monomers and, apparently, induce in them a conformational alteration preventing their association.

Treatment of aldolase, molecular weight 150,000, with acid (pH 2.9 or below) yields subunits of molecular weight 40,000. Hence the native aldolase molecule must be a tetramer. The monomers exhibit identical behavior in the ultracentrifuge and cannot be separated on electrophoresis. Furthermore, each has a C-terminal tyrosine. Hence, the subunits comprising the aldolase molecule appear to be identical or very nearly so. They are very asymmetric, being characterized by axial ratios of nearly 30 : 1. In contrast, the tetramer has an axial ratio of only 6 : 1. Hence, dissociation of the native molecule into monomers must be accompanied by their unfolding.

Structural
Basis for
Isozymes

Quaternary structure of proteins appears to be intimately related to and provides a structural basis for *isozymes*. Isozymes are enzymes that exist in more than one structural form in the same species. A particularly well-understood case, owing to the researches of Kaplan, Markert, and their associates, is that of lactic dehydro-

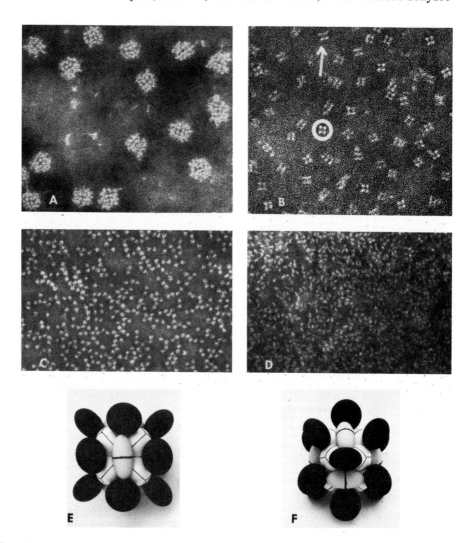

FIGURE 4-17.   *(a)* Electron micrograph of the *E. coli* pyruvate dehydrogenase complex negatively stained with phosphotungstate. ×200,000. *(b)* Electron micrograph of dihydrolipoyl transacetylase component. ×200,000. Two orientations of the transacetylase particle can be seen, corresponding to a view down a fourfold axis (circled) and a twofold axis (arrow) of a cube. *(c, d)* Electron micrographs of the pyruvate dehydrogenase and dihydrolipoyl dehydrogenase components, respectively. ×200,000. *(e, f)* Tentative model of the *E. coli* pyruvate dehydrongenase complex. The 12 molecules of pyruvate dehydrogenase (black oblate spheroids) and 6 molecules of dihydrolipoyl dehydrogenase (prolate spheroids) are aligned, respectively, on the 12 edges and on the 6 faces of the transacetylase cube. — *Courtesy of Dr. Lester J. Reed and Dr. R. M. Oliver of the University of Texas.*

genase. In the chicken, lactic dehydrogenase occurs in two principal forms: that characteristic of breast muscle and that characteristic of heart muscle (page 271). These two forms are distinguishable on the basis of amino acid composition and distinct physical, immunologic, and catalytic properties. The number of different lactic dehydrogenases in the chicken and in several other species is five. Three of these isozymes exhibit properties that are intermediate between those of muscle and heart types. For example, electrophoresis yields five distinct and equally spaced bands with the muscle and heart types at the extremes of the pattern. Furthermore, the amino acid compositions of the five isozymes show a regular variation from that characteristic of the muscle to that of the heart type. Likewise, the enzymatic and immunologic properties exhibit a similar gradation from one of the extreme types to the other.

The structure of lactic dehydrogenase provides a ready explanation for these results. Treatment with concentrated solutions of guanidinium chloride in the presence of mercaptoethanol converts lactic dehydrogenase into four subunits. If lactic dehydrogenase is a tetramer (and it almost certainly is), the assumption of two gene products (two types of subunit) accounts for the observed findings. Thus, designating one type of subunit as H (heart) and the other as M (muscle), five structurally distinct lactic dehydrogenases may be formed: HHHH, HHHM, HHMM, HMMM, and MMMM. This formulation clearly assumes that all the subunit sites in the tetramer are equivalent; otherwise one might have, for example, four molecules corresponding to the structure HHHM. Consideration of the lactic dehydrogenase isozymes as composed of varying amounts of each of two subunit types obviously accounts for the gradual variation in the properties of the isozymes between two extremes (the HHHH and MMMM molecules).

It remains to be established whether all cases of isozymes can be accounted for on the basis above. In cases such as that of lactic dehydrogenase, the term *hybrid enzymes* has been suggested as a reasonable alternative to isozymes.

Multienzyme Complexes

Formation of multienzyme complexes is closely related to formation of quaternary structure for proteins. Several multienzyme complexes are discussed in modest detail in later sections of this book. A particularly good example is the pyruvate dehydrogenase of *E. coli* (see page 277 and Fig. 4-17). This particle, of molecular weight 4,000,000, is composed of three types of enzymes, one of which, at least, is in turn composed of subunits. The complete particle contains a minimum of 88 separate polypeptides. This complex system is remarkably self-organizing and can be spontaneously formed by mixing the component parts. This reassociation proceeds in high yields.

REFERENCES

Crick, F. H. C., and J. C. Kendrew: X-ray Analysis and Protein Structure, *Adv. Prot. Chem.*, **12**: 133 (1957).

Florkin, M., and E. Stotz (eds.): "Comprehensive Biochemistry," vols. 2, 3, 7, and 8, Elsevier, New York, 1963.

Harrington, W. F., R. Josephs, and D. M. Segal: Physical Chemical Studies on Proteins and Polypeptides, *Ann. Rev. Biochem.*, **35**: 599 (1966).

Harris, J. I., and V. M. Ingram: Methods of Sequence Analysis in Proteins, in P. Alexander and R. J. Block (eds.) "Analytical Methods of Protein Chemistry," vol. 2, Pergamon Press, New York, 1960.

Hirs, C. H. W.: The Chemistry of Peptides and Proteins, *Ann. Rev. Biochem.*, **33**: 597 (1964).

Kauzmann, W.: Some Factors in the Interpretation of Protein Denaturation, *Adv. Protein Chem.*, **14**: 1 (1959).

Kendrew, J. C.: Side Chain Interactions in Myoglobin, *Brookhaven Symp.*, **15**: 216 (1962).

Klotz, I.: Non-covalent Bonds in Protein Structure, *Brookhaven Symp.*, **13**: 25 (1960).

Linderstrom-Lang, K. U., and J. A. Schellman: Protein Structure and Enzyme Activity, in P. Boyer, H. Lardy, and K. Myrbäck (eds.), "The Enzymes," vol. 1, Academic, New York, 1959.

Low, B. W.: The Use of X-ray Diffraction in the Determination of Protein Structure, *J. Polymer Sci.*, **49**: 153 (1961).

—— and J. T. Edsall: Aspects of Protein Structure, in D. E. Green (ed.), "Currents in Biochemical Research," Interscience, New York, 1956.

Martin, R. B.: "Introduction to Biophysical Chemistry," McGraw-Hill, New York, 1964.

Muirhead, H., and M. F. Perutz: Structure of Reduced Human Hemoglobin, *Cold Spring Harbor Symp. Quant. Biol.*, **28**: 451 (1963).

Neurath, H. (ed.): "The Proteins," vols. 1 and 2, Academic, New York, 1963.

Reithel, F.: The Dissociation and Association of Protein Structures, *Adv. Protein Chem.*, **18**: 124 (1963).

Richards, F. M.: Structure of Proteins, *Ann. Rev. Biochem.*, **32**: 269 (1963).

Sanger, F.: The Arrangement of Amino Acids in Proteins, *Adv. Protein Chem.*, **7**: 1 (1952).

—— The Structure of Insulin, in D. E. Green (ed.), "Currents in Biochemical Research," Interscience, New York, 1956.

Schachman, H.: Considerations on the Tertiary Structure of Proteins, *Cold Spring Harbor Symp. Quant. Biol.*, **28**: 409 (1963).

Schroeder, W. A.: The Hemoglobins, *Ann. Rev. Biochem.*, **32**: 301 (1963).

Steiner, R. F.: "The Chemical Foundations of Molecular Biology," Van Nostrand, Princeton, N.J., 1965.

Tanford, C.: "Physical Chemistry of Macromolecules," Wiley, New York, 1961.

Timasheff, S. N., and M. J. Gorbunoff: Conformation of Proteins, *Ann. Rev. Biochem.*, **36**: 13 (1967).

Urnes, P., and P. Doty: Optical Rotation and the Conformation of Polypeptides and Proteins, *Adv. Protein Chem.*, **16**: 401 (1961).

Witkop, B.: Methods for Cleavage and Modification of Proteins, *Adv. Protein Chem.*, **16**: 221 (1961).

5 | Nucleic Acids

The nucleic acids provide for some of the most essential functions in the economy of a living organism: the storage and transmission of its genetic make-up and the means by which this information is utilized in the synthesis of all cellular proteins and hence of all cellular constituents. We shall concern ourselves with these functions in Chaps. 18 to 20; here we consider some aspects of their chemistry.

GENERAL
CONSIDERATIONS

Nucleic acids, like proteins, are macromolecules. As a matter of fact, among them are the largest molecules known: there is now good reason to believe that in certain microorganisms all the deoxyribonucleic acid (DNA) is constituted into a single molecule with molecular weights ranging from 10^6 to 10^8 or even 10^9 or more. As the name indicates, nucleic acid molecules are strongly acidic, and at physiological pH they carry a high density of negative charge. For this reason they are found associated in the cell with various species of cations: frequently with basic proteins, such as histones or histonelike entities; sometimes with oligoamines, such as cadaverine — $[H_2N(CH_2)_5NH_2]$, putrescine — $[H_2N(CH_2)_4NH_2]$, spermidine — $[H_2N(CH_2)_4NH(CH_2)_3NH_2]$, or spermine — $[H_2N(CH_2)_3NH(CH_2)_4NH-(CH_2)_3NH_2]$, and, very commonly, with the alkaline earth cations, especially Mg^{+2}. In order to break the strong multiple electrostatic bonds that link the cationic protein to the anionic nucleic acid, a variety of methods have been employed. One of the most generally useful is to treat a buffered solution of the complex at neutrality with aqueous phenol, frequently in the presence of an added protein denaturant, such as sodium dodecyl (lauryl) sulfate or sodium salicylate, sometimes at elevated temperatures. The denatured protein is extracted into the phenol phase, and the nucleic acid remains behind in the aqueous layer, from which it can be precipitated in the cold by the addition of two to three volumes of ethanol.

Pure nucleic acids contain approximately 15 per cent nitrogen and 10 per cent phosphorus. They contain heterocyclic bases that cause a strong absorption in the ultraviolet, with a peak around 260 mμ (see below). Per gram atom of phosphorus they contain one molecule of a sugar: either D-ribose in ribonucleic acid (RNA) or 2-deoxy-D-ribose in deoxyribonucleic acid (DNA). These sugars can be identified and assayed quantitatively by characteristic color reactions: ribose by reaction with orcinol and $FeCl_3$ in HCl; deoxyribose by reaction with diphenylamine or indole in HCl.

They can also be distinguished readily by their susceptibility to digestion by specific nucleases (DNases versus RNases).

THE
MONOMERIC
UNITS

When nucleic acids are subjected to complete chemical hydrolysis, there are obtained, ideally, mixtures containing 1 mole of phosphate, 1 mole of sugar, and 1 mole of a mixture of heterocyclic bases. If the chemical hydrolysis is performed under milder conditions or by enzymatic means, we obtain either an equimolar mixture of nucleosides, which are the N-ribo (or deoxyribo) sides of the bases, or the corresponding set of nucleotides, which are sugar-phosphate esters of the latter. Nucleotides are the true monomeric units of the nucleic acids (see Fig. 5-1).

Bases

The bases found in nucleic acids are either pyrimidines or purines — the latter containing a fused pyrimidine-imidazole ring system (see Fig. 5-2). In DNA the common bases are the pyrimidines thymine (T) and cytosine (C) and the purines adenine (A) and guanine (G). Some 5-methylcytosine occurs occasionally, especially in the DNA from higher plants (e.g., wheat germ) and certain bacteria; 6-methylaminopurine is a minor constituent of the DNA of bacteria and bacterial viruses (bacteriophages); and uracil and 5-hydroxymethyluracil have been reported as occurring in certain bacteriophage DNAs. A particular class of bacteriophages, the so-called T-even phages of *Escherichia coli*, contains 5-hydroxymethylcytosine (sometimes linked to glucose residues in glycoside linkage) in place of cytosine. The structure of these bases is shown in Fig. 5-2.

Most RNAs also contain only four bases: the purines adenine and guanine and the pyrimidines uracil (not thymine, as in DNA) and cytosine. In some RNAs, especially the low-molecular-weight ("soluble") amino acid transfer RNA of the cytoplasm (see page 142), hypoxanthine and various methylated bases, such as thymine, 5-methylcytosine, 6-methylaminopurine (and its 6,6-dimethyl derivative), 1-methylguanine, and 2-methylamino-6-hydroxypurine (and its 2,2-dimethyl derivative), as well as dihydrouracil, hypoxanthine, thiouracil, and others (see Fig. 5-2), replace some of the normal constituents. The methylated bases in RNA, and in DNA as well, appear to be formed as a result of methylation of intact polymeric nucleic acids rather than of the component monomeric units. Certain bases (and their nucleosides and nucleotides) not usually occurring in nature have recently aroused interest as chemotherapeutic and mutagenic agents, because they prove to be readily incorporated into nucleic acids instead of the "natural" bases. Among them are the uracil analogues 2-thio-[1] and 5-fluorouracil, the thymine analogue 5-bromouracil, and the guanine analogues 8-azaguanine and 2,6-diaminopurine.

Other purine and pyrimidine bases also occur in living organisms without, however, being components of nucleic acids: among them are the pyrimidine orotic acid, an intermediate in pyrimidine biosynthesis (see page 439), hypoxanthine,[1] xanthine, and uric acid, which are catabolites of the purine bases. Their nucleotides, inosinic and xanthylic acid, on the other hand, are key intermediates in purine

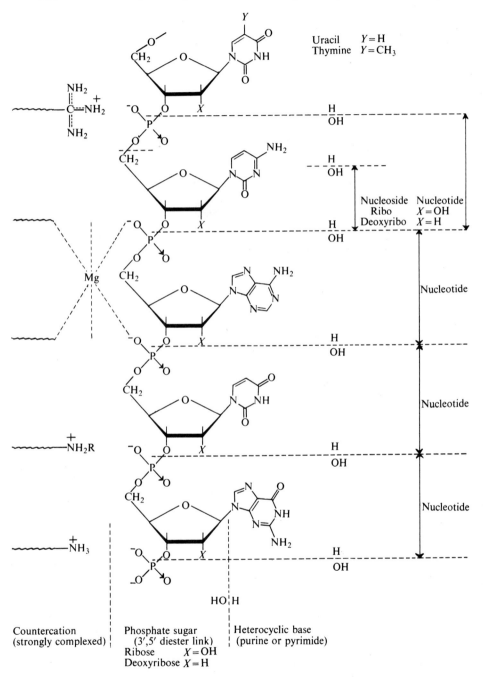

FIGURE 5-1.   A Random Segment of a Hypothetical Nucleoprotein Chain and Its Constituent Parts.

[1] As mentioned, this base is found in transfer RNA.

Pyrimidine (Chemical Abstracts numbering system;
an older convention used a system analogous to that
indicated for the pyrimidine portion of purine)

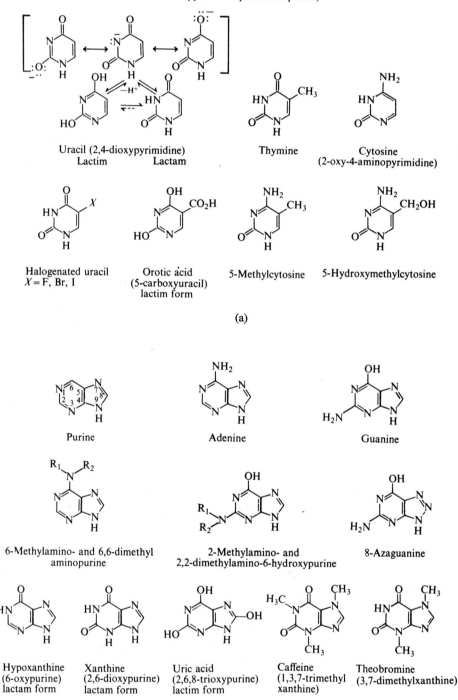

Uracil (2,4-dioxypyrimidine)
Lactim   Lactam

Thymine

Cytosine
(2-oxy-4-aminopyrimidine)

Halogenated uracil
X = F, Br, I

Orotic acid
(5-carboxyuracil)
lactim form

5-Methylcytosine

5-Hydroxymethylcytosine

(a)

Purine

Adenine

Guanine

6-Methylamino- and 6,6-dimethyl
aminopurine

2-Methylamino- and
2,2-dimethylamino-6-hydroxypurine

8-Azaguanine

Hypoxanthine
(6-oxypurine)
lactam form

Xanthine
(2,6-dioxypurine)
lactam form

Uric acid
(2,6,8-trioxypurine)
lactim form

Caffeine
(1,3,7-trimethyl
xanthine)

Theobromine
(3,7-dimethylxanthine)

(b)

FIGURE 5-2.   Structures of (a) Common Pyrimidines and (b) Common Purines (the preponderant tautomer
found in aqueous solution pH ∼ 7 is indicated).

biosynthesis (see page 433). The substituted oxygenated purines theophylline, theobromine, and caffeine are important constituents of plants.

Three sets of properties of the bases are of concern to us here: (1) they are all capable of lactam-lactim and enamine-ketimine tautomerism. The case of uracil is shown as an example. The predominant form is indicated in all cases (it predominates, not only in the bases, but in their more complex derivatives as well); yet the rarer tautomers may be of great importance in biology, as potential causes of mutation (cf. page 134). (2) The purines and pyrimidines are weak bases: typical pK_a values are for uracil $N^1 - 9.5$, for thymine $N^1 - 9.9$, and for guanine $(N^1-C^6-OH) - 9.5$; in addition we find for cytosine $NH_3^+ - 4.5$, for adenine $NH_3^+ - 4.2$, and for guanine $NH_3^+ - 3.2$. The third set of characteristic properties is their light absorption in the ultraviolet, which accounts for that of the nucleic acids (cf. below, page 132). Typical absorption spectra for the five most common bases are shown in Fig. 5-3.

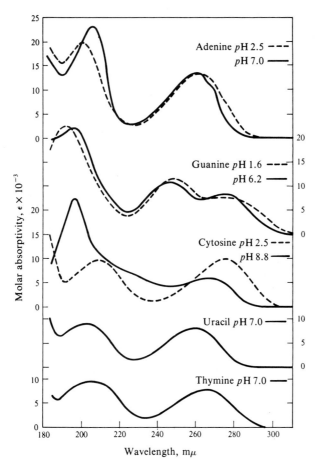

FIGURE 5-3. The Absorption Spectra of the Common Bases. — *D. Voet, W. B. Gratzer, R. A. Cox, and P. Doty, Biopolymers, 1: 193 (1963).*

Nucleosides   A nucleoside is an *N*-glycoside of a heterocyclic base. As indicated above, the two sugars of interest are D-ribose and D-2-deoxyribose; the glycosidic linkage is β from N^1 of pyrimidines and N^9 of purines, and the sugar is in the furanose configuration. Thus adenosine is 9-β-D-ribofuranosyladenine, deoxyadenosine is 9-β-D-2-deoxyribofuranosyladenine, guanosine is 9-β-D-ribofuranosylguanine, deoxyguanosine is 9-β-D-2-deoxyribofuranosylguanine, uridine is 1-β-D-ribofuranosyluracil, thymidine is 1-β-D-2-deoxyribofuranosylthymine, cytidine is 1-β-D-ribofuranosylcytosine, and deoxycytidine is 1-β-D-2-deoxyribofuranosylcytosine:

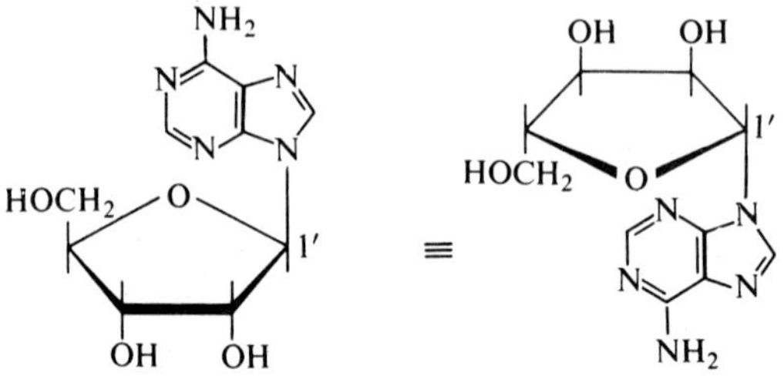

(A) Adenosine, 9-β-D-ribofuranosyladenine

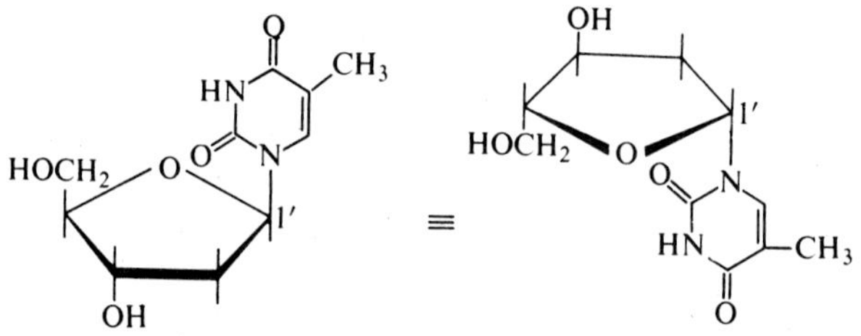

(T) Thymidine, 1-β-D-2-deoxyribofuranosylthymine

In addition to the unusual and methylated bases, certain RNAs, especially amino acid transfer RNA, also contain, in significant amounts, a second nucleoside of uracil called pseudouridine (ψ-uridine, ψU or ψ) with a *C*-glycoside bond:

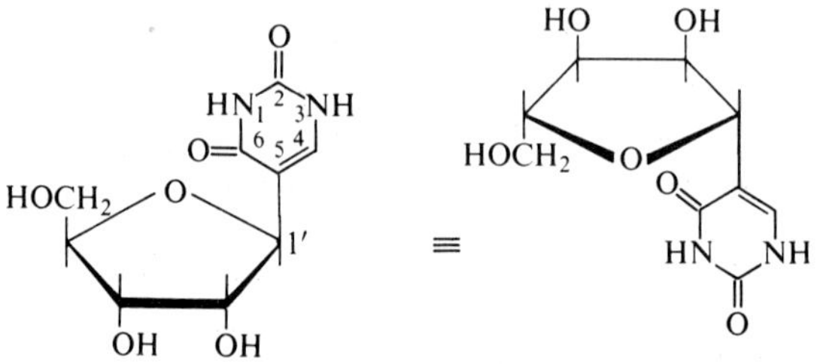

(ψ) Pseudouridine,
5-β-D-ribofuranosyluridine

Nucleotides   Nucleotides are the sugar-*O*-phosphate esters of the nucleosides and can be obtained by mild chemical or enzymatic hydrolysis of the nucleic acids. In the case of the ribonucleotides we might expect to find 2'- and 3'- as well as 5'-mononucleotides (or ribonucleoside-2'-, 3'-, or 5'-phosphates; the prime indicates esterification on the sugar moiety), but only the 3'- and 5'- isomers can exist in the deoxy- series. These compounds are indeed found in nature, not only as products or substrates of nucleic acid metabolism, but also, at least some of them, as constituents of nucleotide coenzymes (see Chap. 8). In addition the cyclical 2',3'-diphosphates of all the ribonucleotides are formed as hydrolytic products (see page 118), the cyclical 3',5'-phosphate of adenosine is an activator of phosphorylase and other enzymes (see page 266), and adenosine 2',5'-diphosphate and adenosine 3'-5'-diphosphate occur as parts of the coenzymes NADP and coenzyme A, respectively (see page 212). Nucleotides can also be regarded as monoesterified derivatives of phosphoric acids. They are, therefore, strong, dibasic acids with pK_a values of 1.0 and 6.0, owing to their phosphoric residue. Note that these ionizations are in addition to those ascribable to acid functions in their heterocyclic rings. The structure of some of these compounds is shown in Fig. 5-4.

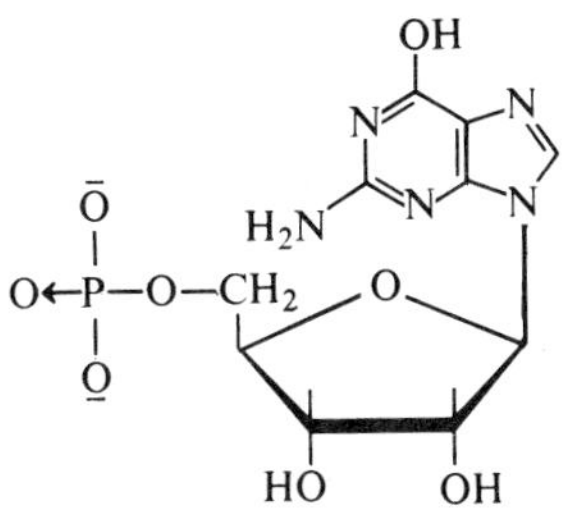

Guanosine-5′-phosphate
(9-β-D-Ribofuranosylguanine-5′-phosphate)
a 5′-ribonucleotide

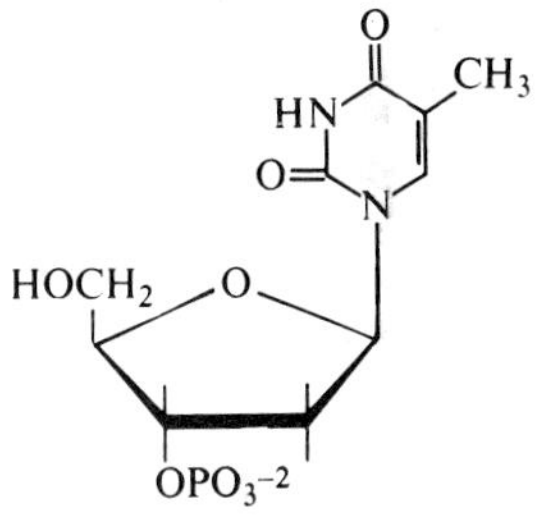

Thymidine-3′-phosphate
(1-β-D-Deoxyribofuranosylthymine-3′-phosphate
a 3′-deoxyribonucleotide

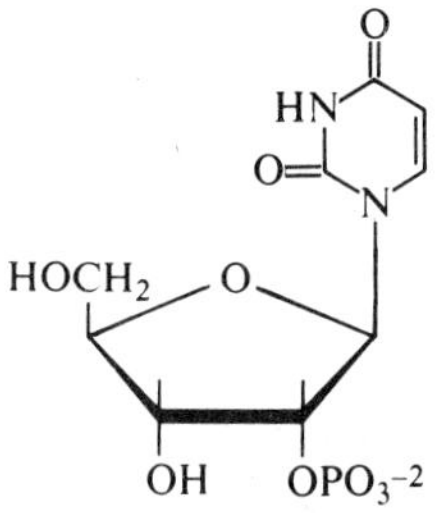

Uridine-2′-phosphate
(1-β-D-Ribofuranosyluracil-2′-phosphate)
a 2′-ribonucleotide

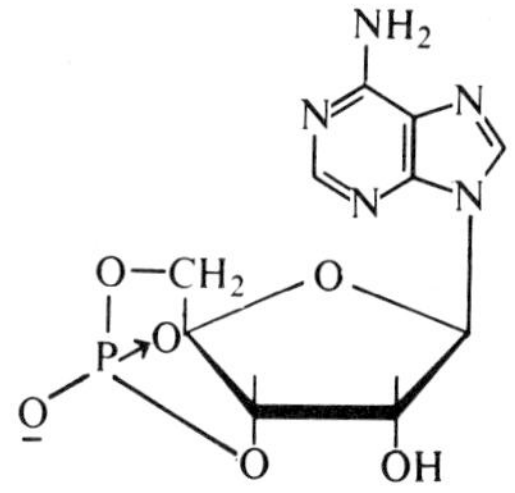

Adenosine-3′-5′ cyclic phosphate

FIGURE 5-4.   The Structures of Some Common Nucleotides (different bases are used as examples).

POLYNUCLEOTIDES
Primary Structure—
The Phosphodiester
Backbone

An overwhelming body of evidence suggests that the naturally occurring poly-nucleotides all have the same basic structure (see Fig. 5-1): a linear polymer in which successive monomeric nucleotide residues are linked to one another by the phosphate groups leading to 3′,5′-phosphodiester bridges between the pentoses of adjacent nucleoside units. Two shorthand notations have been employed to represent the structure of such linear polymers; the conventions implicit are self-evident:

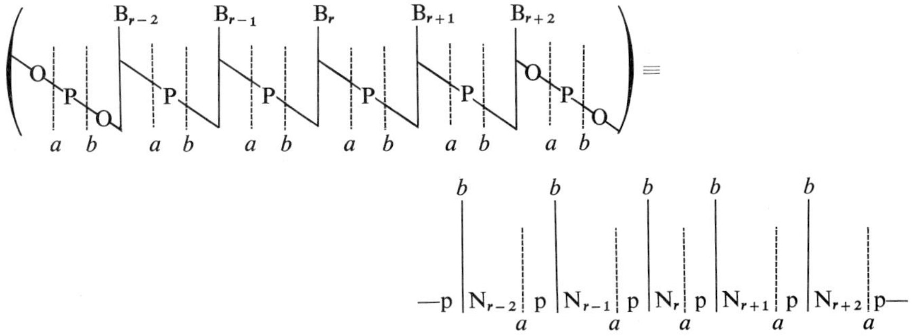

where B = A, C, G, U, or T, respectively; N are the corresponding nucleosides;

and a and b indicate points of attachment of P to O, $pN \equiv N$—5′—P and $Np \equiv N$—3′—P or N—2′—P.

Because two of the three ionizable hydroxyl groups in phosphoric acid are esterified when the residue is incorporated into a polynucleotide structure, the internal nucleotide units $(Np)_{n-2}$ exhibit only the primary phosphate ionization with $pK_a' \simeq 1$. Hence, as pointed out earlier, nucleic acids occur commonly as salts, neutralized by various cationic species.

Hydrolytic Procedures   Polyribonucleotides are degraded by alkali (0.1 or 1 N alkali metal hydroxides) at room temperature to yield n-2 mixed 2′- and 3′-ribonucleotides from the interior of the chain, a 2′- or 3′-phosphate of the head nucleotide (or nucleoside) and a nucleotide (or nucleoside) with a free 3′-OH at the tail. The cleavage of the phosphodiester linkages, therefore, occurs more or less at random, in the interior, in position b. The cyclic 2′,3′-phosphates are reaction intermediates, and attack on them by OH$^-$ brings about the cleavage of either of the C—O—P bonds with equal facility and hence produces a mixture of the 2′- and 3′-phosphates:

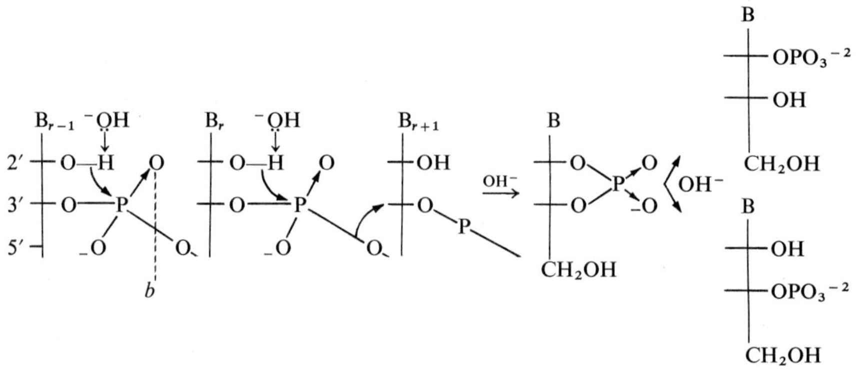

No such participation by the neighboring *cis*-2′-OH group is possible in the deoxy- series. These facts account for the alkali lability of polyribo- contrasted with the well-established stability of polydeoxyribonucleotides. In effect, degradation of this type (*b* cleavage) leads to the transfer of a phosphate residue from a 5′-nucleotide to its nearest neighbor on the left.

The enzyme ribonuclease (RNase) from bovine pancreas — a well-characterized protein whose complete structure has now been established (see page 87) — exhibits a similar mode of action and cleavage. It is an *endonuclease* attacking intranucleotide bonds, but the phosphate of the susceptible P—O bond must be attached to the 3′-OH of a pyrimidine nucleoside. The first step, i.e., the formation of cyclic phosphates from polynucleotides, appears to be reversible. The same type of cleavage *(b)* is also catalyzed by *phosphodiesterases* isolated from various plant sources (peas, tobacco leaves, and rye grass) all of which are, however, relatively nonspecific with respect to the nature of the bases forming part of the susceptible nucleotides. One enzyme from *Bacillus subtilis*, on the other hand, appears to have a specificity complementary to that of the pancreatic one: it preferentially catalyzes hydrolysis adjacent to purine 3′-phosphate residues. Even more specific enzymes have been isolated from the crude enzyme *Takadiastase*: ribonuclease T1 catalyzes the cleavage of internucleotide linkages adjacent to a

3'-guanylate residue exclusively; ribonuclease T2 effects only the cleavage adjacent to 3'-adenylate groups.

All the enzymes discussed so far appear to be specific for the ribo- series and to require free —OH groups in the 2'- position. A less demanding enzyme has been isolated from bovine spleen: this diesterase appears to be nonspecific with respect not only to the nature of the base, but also to the sugar moiety and attacks both polyribonucleotides and oligodeoxyribonucleotides. It is an *exonuclease* of type *b*, liberating nucleoside-3'-phosphates stepwise, starting preferentially at that head end which carries a free 5'-OH group.

An equally useful enzyme, but of opposite specificity, has been isolated in highly purified form from the venom of poisonous snakes (Russell's viper, rattlesnake, etc.). It, too, is an exonuclease relatively nonspecific with respect to bases and catalyzes the hydrolysis of both polyribo- and oligodeoxyribonucleotides. Its specificity is of type *a*, and it therefore liberates nucleoside-5'-phosphates in a stepwise manner, starting at the tail, where it requires a free 3'-OH group.

These various procedures useful for the elucidation of polyribonucleotide structure are summarized in Fig. 5-5, using a hypothetical decanucleotide. They have been successfully employed for the recently announced elucidation of the complete nucleotide sequence of transfer RNAs.

Polydeoxyribonucleotides are stable to the action of alkali but can be hydrolytically degraded by a variety of enzymatic procedures. A common type of deoxyribonuclease (DNase I) is the one isolated from bovine pancreas: it is a protein of molecular weight 61,500, an endonuclease requiring bivalent metal ions (usually Mg^{+2}), effective at neutral pH, and catalyzing random *a* cleavage of intranucleotide bonds preferentially between adjacent purines and pyrimidines. The products are oligonucleotides. Subsequent or simultaneous attack by purified snake-venom phosphodiesterase, freed of contaminating enzymes, then leads to almost quantitative liberation of the constituent deoxyribonucleoside-5'-phosphates.

If the complementary specificity, i.e., *b* cleavage, is desired, one makes use of DNases with an acidic pH optimum and no metal requirement, frequently called DNases II. Such enzymes have been isolated from mammalian (spleen, thymus) and bacterial sources (*Staphylococcus aureus*, formerly called *Micrococcus pyogenes* var. aureus). The products are oligonucleotides, which can then be further degraded by the phosphodiesterase from spleen to yield the desired deoxyribonucleoside-3'-phosphates. Particularly useful for a variety of studies are DNases, or phosphodiesterases in general, which can distinguish between polynucleotides in single-stranded and double-stranded conformation (cf. page 138). Pancreatic RNase is of this type: it rapidly hydrolyzes single- but not double-stranded regions in RNA, or RNA-DNA hybrid duplexes, and can therefore be used as a diagnostic reagent for the identification of such structures. Most ordinary DNases are not similarly conformation-specific. However, such rather special enzymes have been isolated both from microbial (*Escherichia coli* exonuclease 1) and mammalian sources, and under carefully controlled conditions the micrococcal DNase II also appears to behave in this manner.

Simultaneous exposure of deoxyribonucleotides to moderate heat and low pH ($\geq 60°$, pH ≤ 3) leads to an interesting reaction. Most features of the primary structure are retained (i.e., only relatively few scissions of the phosphodiester

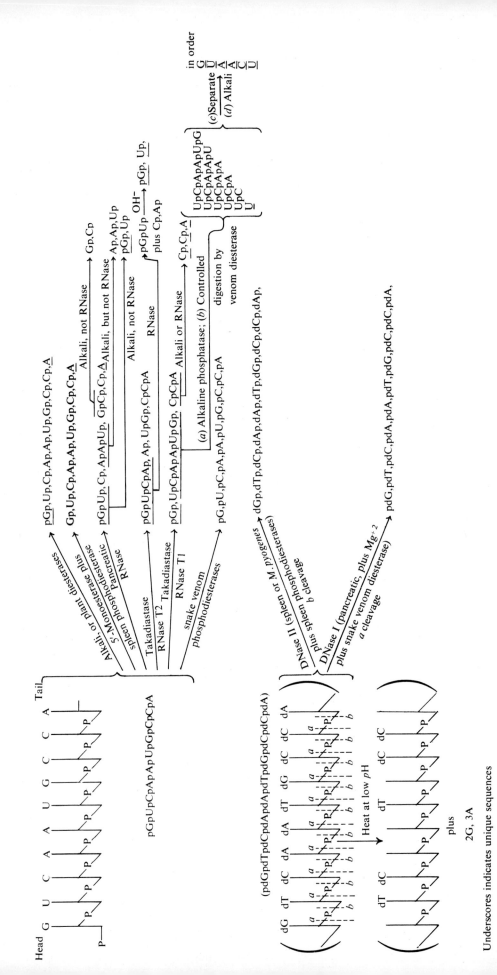

FIGURE 5-5. Hydrolytic Procedures for Polynucleotides. A decaribonucleotide and an analogous segment of a polydeoxyribonucleotide are shown.

backbone occur), but the sugar-purine bonds are cleaved specifically leading to the formation of *apurinic acids*. Similarly, treatment of DNA with hydrazine produces *apyrimidinic acids*.

**POLYDEOXYRIBO-
NUCLEOTIDES
Localization
and Function**

In all organisms except viruses and bacteria the cellular DNA is concentrated in their nuclei. Some DNA is also found in chloroplasts, mitochondria, and other large organelles, which are at least potentially self-reproducing. In bacteria the DNA appears to be present in a small number (one to three) of aggregates

TABLE 5-1. Base Composition of Various DNAs

ANIMALS AND PLANTS

Species	Organ	A	G	C^a	T	A/T	G/C	Pu/Py	$(A+T)/(G+C^b)$
Man	Thymus	30.9	19.9	19.8	29.4	1.05	1.00	1.04	1.52
Hen	Erythrocytes	28.8	20.5	21.5	29.2	1.02	0.95	0.97	1.38
Turtle	Erythrocytes	29.7	22.0	21.3	27.9	1.05	1.03	1.00	1.31
Herring	Sperm	27.8	22.5	20.7 (1.9)	27.5	...	...	...	1.23
Locusta migratoria (locust)	Whole	29.3	20.5	20.7 (0.2)	29.3	1.00	1.00	1.00	1.41
Paracentrotus lividus (sea urchin)	Sperm	32.8	17.7	17.3 (1.1)	32.1	...	...	...	1.85
Marine crabs	All tissues^c (minor component)	47.3	2.7	2.7	47.3	1.00	1.00	1.00	17.5
Wheat germ		27.3	22.7	22.8	27.1	...	...	...	1.19
Aspergillus niger (mold)		25.0	25.1	25.0	24.9	1.00	1.00	1.00	1.00
Saccharomyces cerevisiae (baker's yeast)	Whole cell	31.3	18.7	17.1	32.9	0.95	1.09	1.00	1.79
	Mitochondria	41.3	11.3	10.0	37.5	1.10	1.03	1.10	3.69
Euglena gracilis	Cell DNA	22.6	27.7	25.8^d	24.4	0.93	1.07	1.01	0.88
	Chloroplast	38.2	12.3	11.3	38.1	1.00	1.09	1.02	3.23
Chlamydomonas	Cell DNA	18.0	29.3	32.1	20.5	0.88	0.91	0.90	0.63
	Chloroplast	29.9	20.6	18.7	30.8	0.98	1.10	1.01	1.55

BACTERIA AND VIRUSES

Species	Organ	A	G	C^a	T	A/T	G/C	Pu/Py	$(A+T)/(G+C^b)$
Sarcina lutea		13.4	37.1	37.1	12.4	1.08	1.00	1.02	0.35
Brucella abortus		21.0	29.0	28.9	21.1	1.00	1.00	1.00	0.73
Escherichia coli W		24.7	26.0	25.7	23.6	1.04	1.01	1.02	0.93
Staphylococcus aureus SA-B		30.8	21.0	19.0	29.2	1.05	1.11	1.07	1.50
Clostridium perfringens		36.9	14.0	12.8	36.3	...	...	...	2.70
Coliphage T2		32.5^e	18.2	16.8^f	32.5	1.00	1.08	1.03	1.44
Coliphage T7		26.0	24.0	24.0	26.0	1.00	1.00	1.00	1.08
Coliphage φX174 (isolated virus)		24.6	24.1	18.5	32.7	0.75	1.30	0.95	1.34
Coliphage φX174 (replicative form)^g		26.3	22.3	22.3	26.4	1.00	1.00	1.00	1.18
B. megaterium phage α (virus)		28.4	22.1	22.3^e	27.4	1.04	0.98	1.02	1.25
Chain A		30.1	24.1	21.3	24.5	1.23	1.13	1.19	1.20
Chain B		24.0	19.9	24.2	32.1	0.75	0.82	0.79	1.23

^{a} Values for 5-methylcytosine are shown in parentheses.
^{b} Includes various substituted cytosines.
^{c} Approximately 0.3 of the DNA is of this type.
^{d} Contains 10 moles of 5-methylcytosine/100 moles cytosine.
^{e} Contains 5-hydroxymethyluracil.
^{f} Hydroxymethylcytosine completely replaces cytosine.
^{g} Isolated from phage-infected cells.

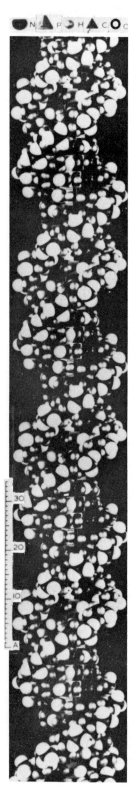

(nucleoids) in the interior of the cell but connected to its membrane, whereas in DNA-containing viruses it occupies the central region of their spherical or polyhedral head structures. Nuclei of animal cells contain on the order of 2 mg DNA per g of fresh tissue. This is equivalent to about 4 to 8×10^{-12} g (picogram) of DNA per nucleus. These values (for any one cell type) are quite invariant with the physiological state of the animal but are directly dependent on the multiplicity of chromosome units (ploidy) in the cell. Bacterial cells contain about one-thousandth of this amount, i.e., of the order of 4×10^{-3} picogram, and DNA-containing viruses (animal and bacterial) range all the way from 2×10^{-4} down to 2×10^{-6} picogram. For all these organisms there is now very strong evidence to suggest that DNA is the genetic material. Further discussion of this point is deferred to Chap. 19.

The base composition of a large variety of DNAs isolated from all types of organisms has been investigated intensively and thoroughly. The pioneering investigations of this kind which formed the chemical and analytical basis on which the imposing edifice of present-day *molecular biology* rests were carried out by E. Chargaff and his collaborators in the period 1950–1953. Some of the generalizations which emerged from these investigations and which have been amply confirmed subsequently may be stated as follows (see Table 5-1):

1. The base composition of its DNA is characteristic of the organism (species).

2. Different cells or tissues of the same organism have identical or at least closely similar base composition; the latter is unaffected by age, development, nutritional state, and all other physiological or environmental factors.

3. The actual base composition exhibits a wide variation from organism to organism (about 25 to 75 mole per cent G + C); this variation is much greater in bacteria than in higher organisms. It is most clearly expressed by the *dissymmetry ratio* $(A + T)/(G + C)$.

4. Closely related organisms exhibit similar base composition; this has been made part of a chemical taxonomy of bacteria.

5. All "normal" DNAs exhibit certain chemical regularities that are defined by *Chargaff's rules*;[1] viz., $A \equiv T$; $G \equiv C$; $A + G \equiv C + T$ (i.e., purine = pyrimidines); $A + C \equiv G + T$ (this used to be 6 amino = 6 keto with the old numbering system for pyrimidines).

6. Because $A + G + C + T = 1$, a corollary to generalization 5 states that any nucleic acid not exhibiting the regularities just described must contain certain unusual structural features (cf., for example, the case for the DNA from bacteriophage ϕX174, which has been shown to be an unusual *non-Watson-Crick DNA*).

On the basis of these items of information, plus new X-ray diffraction measurements obtained by Wilkins on the lithium salt of DNA, which showed the repeat distance to be 34 A and strong maximal reflections at 3.4 A, and the chemical data

---

[1] If the DNA contains unusual bases, such as substituted cytosines, then C in the identities stands for the sum of C plus all substituted cytosines, and T stands for uracil plus all substituted uracils (including thymine).

FIGURE 5-6.   The Structure of DNA in the B Configuration. *Left:* space filling model with van der Waals radii indicated; *right:* projection of the model. — *Courtesy of Professor M. H. F. Wilkins.*

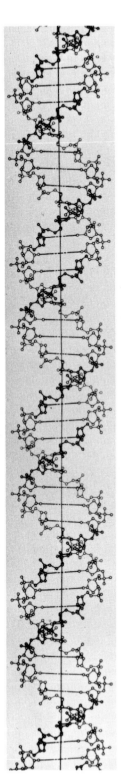

discussed in the last paragraph, Crick and Watson proposed their *new model for DNA* in 1953. It provided, for the first time, a means of expressing basic biological phenomena in precise structural chemical terms and has proved to be the starting point for the revolution in biological thinking during the past decade. For these contributions, Watson, Crick, and Wilkins received the Nobel Prize in 1962. This model has since been revised on the basis of more refined X-ray data by Wilkins and his collaborators, and its characteristic structural features are summarized in Figs. 5-6 and 5-7.

DNA in its B lattice configuration, which is the one stable at high (i.e., >66 per cent) relative humidity, consists of two right-handed helical polynucleotide chains of opposite polarity,[1] plectonemically coiled[2] around the same axis to form a double helix. The bases are on the inside of the helix in pairs arranged in such a fashion that a pyrimidine of one chain always pairs with a purine of the opposite strand, and vice versa. Only certain base pairs can be accommodated spatially; these allowed base pairs are A and T, and G and C (hydrogen-bonded, as shown in Fig. 5-7, with substituted C's replacing the latter, wherever they occur). These pairing rules require that the bases in the two chains are complementary so that the sequence of one chain is completely determined by the sequence in its partner. The nucleoside pairs in the interior of the helix measure approximately 11 A from C_1' to C_1', have the planes of their aromatic rings at right angles to the helix axis, and their apolar bulk stacked on top of one another, with a distance of 3.4 A between base pairs. The highly negatively charged phosphodiester backbone, conversely, faces outward, and its strongly polar groups can thus interact with the components of the aqueous environment. There are 10 bases per turn of the double helix, and because each turn has a height of 34 A, these features give the helix an exact 10-fold screw axis with the sense of the screw being right-handed. The helix has one shallow groove (approximately 12 A) and one deep one (approximately 22 A across). Electron micrographs, as well as other physical evidence summarized below, of many viral and even of certain bacterial DNAs indicate that these molecules consist of a double helix joined end to end in a closed loop.

Direct, experimental evidence for the Watson-Crick structure is of the following type:

1. The length of an unbranched double helix of any given molecular weight (M) and number of base pairs (N) having the required characteristics can be calculated; it is, e.g., 2.0 μ for the DNA of the small bacteriophage ϕX174 (in its double-stranded replicative form), 17.5 μ for that of bacteriophage λ, 63 μ for that of bacteriophage T2, and nearly 1,400 μ for that of *E. coli*. Direct measurement of such DNA preparations by radio-autography or electron microscopy has shown that they have indeed the dimensions postulated by the model. Examples of the type of picture obtained are shown in Fig. 5-8.

2. Evidence for complementariness plus the opposing polarity of the two strands comes from a study of nearest-neighbor frequencies (see page 482): opposite polarity generates a pattern different from that produced by strands of identical

---

[1] In chemical terms this means the internucleotide linkage in one strand is $3' \rightarrow 5'$ and in the other is $5' \rightarrow 3'$.

[2] This means the double helix cannot be separated into its constituent coils without unwinding.

polarity; e.g., TpG = CpA and GpA = TpC for antiparallel, but TpG = ApC and GpA = CpT for parallel chains. Experiments of Josse and Kornberg clearly indicate that the first alternative obtains (see page 483).

3. The structure predicts that the two strands, although complementary, need not have identical base compositions[1] and that it should, therefore, be possible to

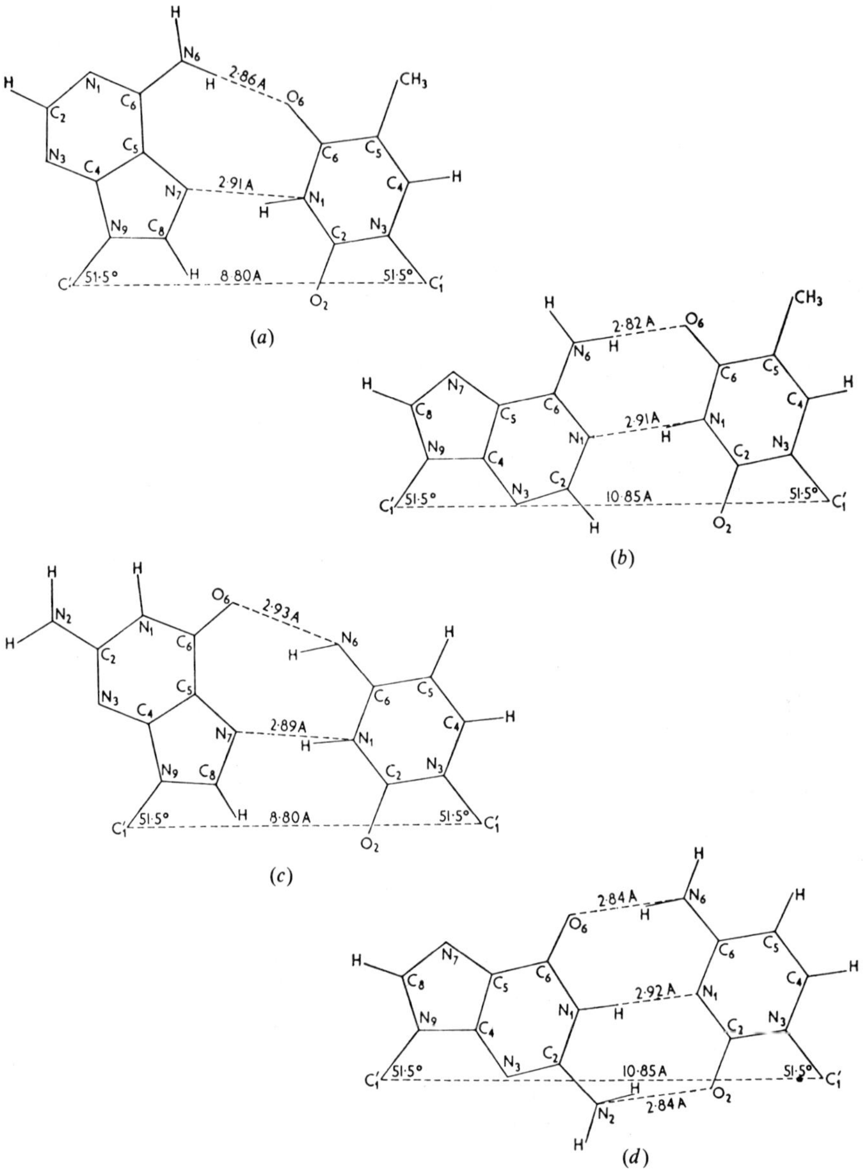

FIGURE 5-7.   Adenine-thymine hydrogen-bonded pairs: (a) found by Hoogsteen in a 1:1 complex of 3-N-methylthymine and 9-N-methyladenine; (b) postulated by Watson and Crick (current version refined by Arnott) for part of the structure of DNA. Guanine-cytosine pairs: (c) Hoogsteen type; (d) Watson-Crick type. — Courtesy of Dr. M. H. F. Wilkins and Dr. S. Arnott from J. Mol. Biol., 11, 391–402 (1965).

[1] The base pairs in the two orientations $A_1:T_2 \neq T_1:A_2$ and $G_1:C_2 \neq C_1:G_2$, where subscripts refer to the two chains.

separate the two chains either chemically or physically. This was accomplished first in the case of bacteriophage α (Table 5-1) and more recently for a number of other DNAs as well.

4. The chemical and physical properties of DNA in solution (cf. below) accord well with those predicted from the model.

FIGURE 5-8. Electronmicrographs of DNA from Bacteriophage $\lambda_c b_2 b_5$ and λ_c circles, naked preparations ("Beer technique"); the bar in the upper picture is 2 μ long. — *Courtesy Prof. C. A. Thomas, Jr. and Dr. L. McHattie.*

Noncomplementary and Other Unusual Polydeoxyribonucleotides

The first DNA that did not appear to obey Chargaff's rules was isolated from the small *E. coli* bacteriophage ϕX174. It has a molecular weight of 1.6×10^6 daltons and the base composition shown in Table 5-1. Its properties indicated that its conformation was quite different from that of most "normal" DNAs and resembled much more closely those characteristic of some RNAs; it is now known that this DNA is in fact single-stranded. It is of interest that, like some RNA viruses, it undergoes a transformation during its replication in vivo to a so-called *replicative form*, which contains the complementary strand and appears to be a circular supercoiled duplex helix.

When *E. coli* DNA polymerase is allowed to react with the nucleoside triphosphate pairs (dATP plus dTTP) or (dGTP plus dCTP), two unusual duplex polymers ensue. From the first pair is obtained an alternating copolymer duplex dAdT: dTdA, from the second a homopolymer duplex dG:dC. A natural DNA resembling the former (but containing a small proportion of G + C residues) has been isolated by Sueoka from various tissues of marine crabs. The polymerase acting on (dATP plus dTTP) with a rA:rU primer produces dA:dT.

Physical Chemistry of High-molecular-weight DNA in Solution

Sedimentation in Homogeneous Media. One of the most useful techniques for the study of substances of very high molecular weight is to observe their behavior in the ultracentrifuge. Runs are usually made at a high dilution of the polymer (to minimize aggregation and other concentration effects), under conditions in which it assumes its most stable conformation, i.e., in the presence of a counterion (usually a monovalent inorganic cation such as Na^+) at a relatively high ionic strength (>0.1 M) and at moderate speeds of the ultracentrifuge rotor. The low concentration ($\sim 10 \mu g/ml$) necessitates the use of ultraviolet optics. The rate of migration of the concentration boundary with time is then measured and substituted in Eq. (3-24). Usually the observed s is corrected to $s_{20, w}$, its value in a solvent with the density and viscosity of water at 20°, and is expressed in Svedberg units (S) equal to 10^{-13} sec:

$$s_{20, w} = \left[s_{obs} \left(\frac{\eta_t}{\eta_{20}} \right) \left(\frac{\eta}{\eta_0} \right) \right] \left(\frac{1 - \bar{v} \rho_{20, w}}{1 - \bar{v} \rho} \right) \simeq [\quad] \left(\frac{\rho_B - \rho_{20, w}}{\rho_B - \rho} \right) \tag{5-1}$$

where η_t and η_{20} are viscosities of water at t, the temperature of the run and at 20°, $\eta/\eta°$ is the viscosity of the solvent relative to that of water, $\rho_{20, w}$ and ρ are the densities of water at 20° and of the solvent at $t°$, respectively, and $\bar{v}$ is the partial specific volume of the solute. The latter is equal to $1/\rho_B$, where ρ_B is the buoyant density of the macromolecule in the system under investigation and is a function of composition (see below). On the average it is close to 0.55 for native double-stranded DNA and slightly lower for single-stranded polynucleotides; e.g., for TMV RNA it is 0.524, for microsomal RNA it is 0.53, and for tRNA a value of 0.48 has been reported. (For proteins, the values are close to 0.725.) The sedimentation coefficients so determined are dependent on the concentration of the DNA added.

In general the s values for a polymer of any given molecular weight increase the more rigid (i.e., less flexible) its conformation.

Centrifugation in Density Gradients. Convective disturbances and interactions between solute molecules are minimized or eliminated if centrifugation is carried out in the presence of a continuous gradient of a denser material. Two types of experiment can be performed here also: sedimentation-velocity experiments and equilibrium experiments.

For sedimentation runs the preferred medium is a buffered linear gradient of sucrose, often between 5 and 20 per cent, that can be generated in the centrifuge tube before the start of the run by means of simple mixing devices. An alternative is the use of self-forming gradients of CsCl. The material sedimenting in the gradient can be monitored continuously by means of the ultraviolet optical system of the analytical ultracentrifuge. Alternatively the preparative tube may simply be pierced at the bottom, or the fluid column extruded continuously through the top, and fractions of fluid collected, or monitored continuously, and the concentration of material measured by light absorption (UV at 260 mμ), chemical reactivity (deoxyribose content), biological activity, content of a selective radioactive label (P^{32}), etc.

A most convenient method is a comparison of the unknown with a standard of similar composition and known s value under identical conditions, preferably in the same tube. Such standards are now readily available, some even commercially; thus a number of enzymes can serve as protein standards (lysozyme — M = 17,200, $s_{20, w} = 2.15$ S; alcohol dehydrogenase from yeast — $M = 150,000$, $s_{20. w} = 7.6$ S; catalase — $M = 250,000$, $s_{20, w} = 11.35$ S). Transfer RNA from liver, yeast, or *E. coli* has an s value of 4.5 S, the two ribosomal RNAs from *E. coli* have s values of 16 and 23 S, respectively, and can be used as standards for RNA; the DNA from bacteriophages λ and T7 can be obtained relatively easily in an undegraded form with s values of 33.6 and 32.5 S, respectively, and are used as standards for "normal" DNA. Then the following simple relationship holds for any one pair of standard and unknown of identical $\bar{v}$:

$$s_{20,\,w} \text{ (unknown)} = s_{20,\,w} \text{ (standard)} \times R \qquad (5\text{-}2)$$

where $R = \left(\dfrac{\text{distance travelled from meniscus by unknown}}{\text{distance travelled from meniscus by standard}}\right)_{\bar{v}\,=\,\text{constant}}$

Equilibrium sedimentations of DNA in CsCl gradients were first studied by Meselson, Stahl, and Vinograd. Here a concentrated solution of a salt of high density (such as 7.7 M CsCl, concentrated Cs_2SO_4, or concentrated potassium tartrate) is spun in the ultracentrifuge, which leads, after establishment of sedimentation-diffusion equilibrium, to a continuous, stable, and linear gradient of the solute molecules with the most concentrated, densest region at the bottom of the tube.

If a dilute solution of a macromolecule, such as DNA, is placed in such a system, it forms, at equilibrium, a relatively narrow band centered at r_0, the density position corresponding to ρ_B, its own buoyant density under these conditions (see Fig. 5-9). If ρ_{std}, the density of a standard, is known (migration to r_{std}), then at 44,700 rpm and 25°,

$$\rho_B = \rho_{\text{std}} + 0.0092\,(r_0{}^2 - r_{\text{std}}{}^2)\ \text{g/cm}^3 \qquad (5\text{-}3)$$

The DNA of E. coli (50 per cent G + C) is a commonly used standard, with $\rho = 1.709$ g/cm^3. The density of double-stranded DNA solutions in concentrated CsCl is a linear function of the sum of the mole fractions X of G plus C. Quantitatively the relation is given by

$$\rho_B = 1.660 + 0.098\,(X_G + X_C) \qquad (5\text{-}4)$$

Single-stranded DNA, because of greater binding by the heavy Cs^+ ions, has a density approximately 0.016 g/cm^3 higher than the corresponding double-helical DNA. Because, under the same conditions, RNA has a buoyant density considerably higher still (~ 2.0), and proteins are considerably less dense, these components can be cleanly separated from DNA.

If the macromolecules in the density gradient at equilibrium are homogeneous, the distribution of their concentration about r_0 is Gaussian. Because large macromolecules diffuse less rapidly than small ones, they produce narrower bands. The variance σ^2 of the Gaussian distribution is given by

$$\sigma^2 = \frac{RT}{M_s(d\rho/dr)\bar{v}_s\omega^2 r_0} \qquad (5\text{-}5)$$

where the only quantity not defined previously is $d\rho/dr$, the density gradient, and the subscript s in M, the molecular weight, and in $\bar{v}$, the partial specific volume of the macrospecies, refers to their solvated forms actually present under the conditions of the experiment. Mixtures of macromolecules of identical buoyant density but differing in molecular weight form symmetrical but non-Gaussian bands. Therefore molecular weights can be calculated from band shapes in density equilibrium experiments.

Viscosity. Solutions of native DNA, because of the great size and asymmetry of the molecule, have a very high viscosity. This property, then, provides a means for a relatively easy, inexpensive, and convenient method for the characterization of the polymer from the point of view of its size, shape, and conformation.

The parameter to be determined is $[\eta]$, the *limiting viscosity number*, defined by

$$[\eta] = \lim_{c \to 0} \left[\frac{(\eta/\eta_0) - 1}{c} \right] \tag{5-6}$$

where c is the concentration of the polymer in grams per milliliter, η is the viscosity

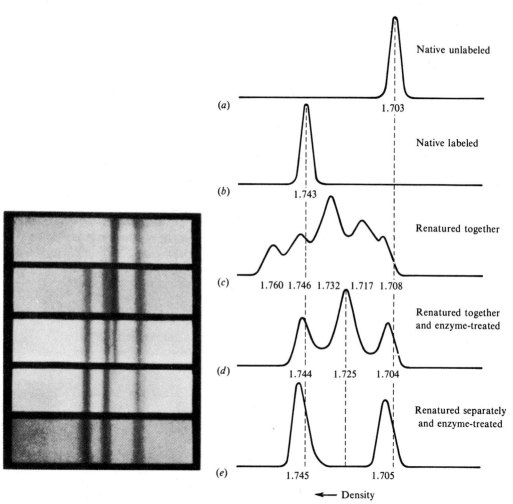

FIGURE 5-9.   Density Gradient Centrifugations in CsCl. *Left:* Ultraviolet absorption photographs of N^{14}–N^{15} labeled DNA showing different stages of the thermally induced separation into subunits. The band at the far right has been used as a standard and is DNA isolated from *D. pneumoniae*. The other band in the top photograph is the biologically formed hybrid DNA. The second photograph shows the stability of the hybrid to a 20-min exposure at 93.8°C. At 100°C the number of molecules separating increases rapidly with time of exposure, as shown in the next three photographs. The examples were heated in SSC at 30 μg/ml for 30 sec, 1 min, and 10 min, respectively. *Right:* The effect of *E. coli* phosphodiesterase on a heated and annealed mixture of heavy labeled and normal *B. subtilis* DNA. *(a)* and *(b)* Native samples; *(c)* mixed so that the final concentration of each was 5μg/ml and then heated and annealed; *(d)* the sample shown in *(c)* was dialyzed against 0.067 M glycine buffer and incubated with the *E. coli* phosphodiesterase; *(e)* heated and annealed separately, treated with the phosphodiesterase and then mixed. — *From C. L. Schildkraut, J. Marmur, and P. Doty, J. Mol. Biol. 3: 595 (1961).*

of the solution, and η_0 is the viscosity of the pure solvent. The fraction η/η_0 is frequently called the *viscosity ratio* or the *relative viscosity*, η_{rel}, and the quantity $[(\eta/\eta_0) - 1]$ is referred to as the *specific viscosity*, η_{sp}. When the concentration c is expressed in grams per deciliter, the parameter defined by Eq. (5-6) is usually called the *intrinsic viscosity*, which is therefore given in units of deciliters per gram.

Rotating cylinder viscometers can be operated under conditions virtually approaching zero shear rate. Easy degradation by hydrodynamic shear is one of the important properties of DNA of high molecular weight; as a matter of fact the large bacteriophage DNAs can be degraded with double-strand scission near the center of the molecule by simple pipetting of dilute solutions to produce half, quarter, and eighth molecules. If a capillary viscometer is to be used, care must be taken to extrapolate first to zero shear before performing an extrapolation to zero concentration.

Determination of Molecular Weight and Shape from Hydrodynamic Measurements. In polymer chemistry, different measurements can yield different types of average molecular weight if the solution in question is made up, as is most frequently the case, of a population of molecules differing somewhat in their properties. The three most common averages used are the weight-average molecular weight $\overline{M}_w$, the number-average molecular weight $\overline{M}_n$, and the z-average molecular weight $\overline{M}_z$, defined by

$$\overline{M}_n = \frac{n_1 M_1 + n_2 M_2 + n_3 M_3 + \cdots}{n_1 + n_2 + n_3 + \cdots} = \frac{\Sigma\, n_i M_i}{\Sigma\, n_i} \tag{5-7}$$

$$\overline{M}_w = \frac{c_1 M_1 + c_2 M_2 + c_3 M_3}{c_1 + c_2 + c_3} = \frac{\Sigma\, c_i M_i}{\Sigma\, c_i} = \frac{\Sigma\, n_i M_i^2}{\Sigma\, n_i M_i} \tag{5-8}$$

$$\overline{M}_z = \frac{\Sigma\, n_i M_i^3}{\Sigma\, n_i M_i^2} \tag{5-9}$$

In all these, n_i is the number of moles of species i (with molecular weight M_i) per unit volume. The weight concentration in grams per unit volume is $c_i = n_i M_i$. $\overline{M}_n$ is the most "democratic" measure: each molecule is counted once, regardless of weight; $\overline{M}_w$ and $\overline{M}_z$ give increased representation to the heaviest molecules — heaviest weight to the heavyweights, most of all in the z-average. $\overline{M}_n$ is obtained from a measure of colligative properties such as osmotic pressure or end-group analysis as well as from X-ray diffraction and electron micrography. $\overline{M}_w$ is the molecular-weight average obtained from light scattering, dielectric dispersion, fluorescence depolarization, or sedimentation measurements; viscosity measurements yield an average close to, but usually not identical with, $\overline{M}_w$.

For monodisperse systems, i.e., those containing one and only one species, all three molecular weights are identical. For others the ratio $\overline{M}_w/\overline{M}_n$ is a measure of their polydispersity. Fortunately in the field of nucleic acid chemistry viruses provide a source of remarkably monodisperse macromolecules of high M. As we have seen, in protein chemistry and other branches of polymer chemistry, M can be determined from s plus a measure of the shape of the molecule. An alternative method is to measure $[\eta]$ and to utilize an equation derived by Scheraga and Mandelkern:

$$M = \left[\frac{s[\eta]^{1/3} \eta_0 N 10^{-13}}{\beta(1 - \bar{v}\rho)} \right]^{3/2} \tag{5-10}$$

All terms have the usual meaning: s is the sedimentation coefficient corrected to the reference temperature and water, $[\eta]$ is the specific viscosity of the polymer in deciliters per gram, η_0 is the viscosity of solvent, N is Avogadro's number, $\bar{v}$ is the partial specific volume of the polymer, and ρ is the density of the solvent at the reference temperature t; β is a constant for any polymer, which is, however, a function of the shape (specifically the axial ratio) of the molecule. It varies from 2.12×10^6 for a sphere to 2.6×10^6 for a random, free-draining coil to 3.6×10^6 for a rigid rod of essentially infinite axial ratio.

Equation (5-10) adequately describes the behavior of single-stranded poly-nucleotides (most RNAs and completely denatured or single-stranded native DNAs) with a value of $\beta \simeq 2.25 \times 10^6$. For native double-stranded DNAs we use the empirical relations due to Eigner and Doty:

$$s^\circ_{20,\,w} \simeq 0.034 M^{0.405} \qquad \text{and} \qquad [\eta] \simeq 6.9 \times 10^{-4} M^{0.70} \tag{5-11}$$

Light Scattering. When a beam of light is allowed to impinge on solute molecules in dilute solution, it is scattered or diffracted in all directions, owing to secondary emission by oscillating dipoles induced in the solute molecules by the electric vector of the radiation. If the solute is a macromolecule, e.g., a nucleic acid, its dimension in at least one direction is greater than 0.05 times the wavelength of the incident light (usually a mercury arc that provides monochromatic radiation at 4,358 or 5,461 A). Under these circumstances the solute particles no longer act as point dipoles, but instead it is necessary to consider them as containing several different scattering centers. The consequence is that the amount of light scattered to and measured at angles different from that of the incident light is not equal, and the greatest scattering is in the forward direction (with $\theta = 0$), and the back-scattering ($\theta = 180°$) is least, owing to destructive interference. Advantage can be taken of these facts to determine, not only the $\overline{M}_w$, but also the molecular shape of macromolecules from one and the same type of measurement. Unfortunately the methodological difficulties (measurements at small angles, 10° or less are required) become most severe precisely in the region of M of greatest interest in DNA chemistry, i.e., for DNA of $\geq 3 \times 10^6$, unless special instruments are used, but for smaller DNA molecules, and for most species of RNA as well, the technique is of great power and precision. In any event the technique is valid only for macro-molecules for which $0.05 \times$ long dimension $< \lambda < 0.5 \times$ long dimension.

In practice one determines the scattered or diffracted intensity i_θ obtained by irradiating the solution with a beam of incident intensity I_0 and wavelength λ at different angles θ with a phototube placed at a distance r from the solution. One thus obtains the Rayleigh ratio $R = i_\theta r^2/I_0$ or, more commonly, the parameter R_θ defined by Eq. (5-12), which equals Rayleigh's ratio at $\theta = 0$:

$$R_\theta = \frac{r^2 i_\theta}{I_0(1 + \cos^2 \theta)} \tag{5-12}$$

In the limit when $\theta \to 0$, Eq. (5-13) describes the dependence of M on R_θ:

$$\left(\lim_{\theta \to 0} \frac{Kc}{R_\theta}\right)_{c\,=\,\text{const}} = \frac{1}{M} + 2Bc + 3Cc^2 + \cdots \tag{5-13}$$

where B and C are constants for the solute and K is an optical constant for the system.[1] On the other hand, it can be shown that, as $c \to 0$, Eq. (5-14) describes the dependence of Kc/R_θ on shape as measured by P_θ:

$$\left(\lim_{c \to 0} \frac{Kc}{R_\theta}\right)_{\theta = \text{const}} = \frac{1}{MP_\theta} = \frac{1}{M}\left(1 + \frac{h^2 R_G{}^2}{3} + \cdots\right) \tag{5-14a}$$

$$h = \frac{4\pi}{\lambda} \sin \frac{\theta}{2}$$

$$P_\theta{}^{-1} = \left(1 + \frac{h^2 R_G{}^2}{3} + \cdots\right) \tag{5-14b}$$

Light-scattering measurements provide a measure both of M, specifically of $\overline{M}_w$ — by Eq. (5-13) alone — and of shape, through use of the parameter R_G, the *radius of gyration* — by Eq. (5-14) plus Eq. (5-13) — since R_G is related to the dimensions of a macromolecule depending on its shape. Thus for spheres, rods, and random coils it equals $(\frac{3}{5})^{1/2} r$, $(\frac{1}{12})^{1/2} l$, and $(\frac{1}{6})^{1/2} <r^2>^{1/2}$, where r is the radius of the sphere, l the length of the rod, and $<r^2>^{1/2}$ the root-mean-square end-to-end distance of the coil. Quite generally the more flexible a polymer, the larger its R_G.

Direct Physical Methods. Perhaps the oldest and most straightforward method is examination in the electron microscope. Recently Kleinschmidt discovered that nucleic acid either liberated in situ by osmotic shock or after prior isolation could be spread and stabilized on water as a monomolecular film by means of complexation with a basic protein such as cytochrome c. An electromicrograph of the DNA of phages produced by Thomas and McHattie with this technique is shown as Fig. 5-8. Both its circular nature and its dimensions can be clearly seen; its observed length as well as its width are those demanded by the Watson-Crick hypothesis. A number of DNAs have been shown to exist as circles or closed loops. In the case of the molecules from the bacteriophages λ and T2, the change from linear to circular molecule has been shown to be freely reversible.

Another extremely useful set of techniques is that of *autoradiography* (sometimes also called radioautography). Two types of experiment have been performed. The first is similar to that used with a number of other structures or preparations and uses H^3, a soft-beta emitter, usually in the form of a tritiated thymidine, incorporated into the DNA, to generate an image in a suitably sensitive photographic emulsion. In the hands of Cairns this technique has provided a magnificent insight into the molecular dimensions of DNAs of viral and even bacterial sources and has given results that are neatly supplementary to those obtained with electron micrography and completely consistent with the model.

Another autographic technique was developed by Levinthal and Thomas. In this technique P^{32} at a high concentration is incorporated into the DNA of a bacteriophage. The virus particle or its DNA is then embedded in a sensitive emulsion, and after radioactive decay for a suitable length of time and photographic development, the number of β-ray tracks emanating from single-point sources (corresponding to the viral DNA) are measured. These patterns are essentially star-shaped, and the method has frequently been referred to as *star gazing*. Because every track

---

[1] Given by $[2\pi^2 n_0{}^2(n - n_0)^2]/\lambda_0{}^4 \overline{N}$, where n_0 is the refractive index of the solvent, n the refractive index of the solution, λ_0, the wavelength in a vacuum, and $\overline{N}$ the number of scattering centers per cubic centimeter.

represents the decay of a single P^{32} atom, the total phosphorus content of each point source (i.e., each viral DNA molecule) can be estimated from the number of tracks emanating from it, the exposure time, the known half-life of P^{32}, and the experimentally determined specific radioactivity of the virus used. The DNA of bacteriophage T2 had a molecular weight of 1.3×10^8 daltons, corresponding to the total DNA content of the virus; thus all its DNA could be regarded as being constituted by a single molecule.

Optical Properties of DNA in Solution

Hypochromism. In qualitative terms the light-absorbing properties of the nucleic acids can be understood in terms of the absorption spectra of the component nucleotides with one important proviso: its hypochromism, i.e., the fact that its actual absorption of ultraviolet light is less than would be predicted on the basis of a summation of the light absorption by its constituent nucleotide chromophores. Generally:

1. All DNAs regardless of base composition exhibit very similar extinction coefficients at 260 mμ.

2. Hypochromism is directly dependent on A + T content.

3. Hypochromism is in the order DNA > RNA, and double-stranded polymers > single-stranded polymers.

4. Even relatively structureless polymers, such as heat-denatured DNA or single-stranded homopolymers, exhibit considerable residual hypochromism. This phenomenon is closely related to the fact that oligonucleotides, even dinucleotides of appropriate structure, can produce hypochromism.

Hypochromism is of importance, not just as an exceedingly interesting optical phenomenon in its own right, but also as a particularly simple and convenient tool for the qualitative and quantitative measurement of orientation-disorientation processes in nucleic acid chemistry (such as denaturation, renaturation, the reversible formation of homopolymer complexes, formation of hybrid DNA-RNA helices, and establishment of genetic relationships between DNAs from different organisms or different cells from the same organism). All that is required is a spectrophotometer or other device capable of measuring light absorption in the vicinity of 260 mμ. In general all DNAs examined have an absorption maximum in the region of 256 to 265 mμ, a trough around 230 mμ, and a second peak in the far ultraviolet around 195 mμ. Per mole of P, ordinary double-stranded DNAs have an extinction coefficient between 6,100 and 6,900. This corresponds to 18.0 or 19.0 per mg DNA; for RNA the value is close to 23 per mg.

Optical Rotation. Ordered polynucleotides exhibit a relatively strong positive optical rotation (usually reported as $[\alpha]_D$ or as $[M_P]_D$, the "molar" rotation based on phosphate) that decreases as their degree of order decreases; the corresponding mixtures of nucleotides obtained after complete hydrolysis show only an insignificant rotation. For double-stranded DNA in aqueous solution $[\alpha]_D = +100$ to $150°$ (corresponding to $[M_P]_D$ of $\sim 40,000$); after treatments designed to disrupt its ordered structure $[\alpha]_D$ drops to small positive values or may even become negative, and for mononucleotide mixtures it is close to zero. Single-stranded polynucleotides of ordered conformation, on the other hand, show $[\alpha]_D$ in the range of 150 to 200, i.e., values at least as high as, and probably higher than, those of DNA, and di- and other small oligonucleotides exhibit extremely small rotations of the order of $\pm 10°$ or less. It is thus clear that the molecular dissymmetry introduced by arrang-

Chemical Reactions
of DNA in Solution

ing the polynucleotide in orderly but twisted stacks is responsible for the high rotations observed.

Reagents Capable of Reacting with Free Amino Groups. A reagent frequently employed in nucleic acid chemistry is formaldehyde; it can react with the free amino groups of cytosine, guanine, and adenine to form the corresponding hydroxymethyl derivatives (or perhaps, after dehydration, the Schiff bases). This change is accompanied by an alteration in the absorption spectrum, giving rise to a red shift and an increase in absorption at the peak wavelength, and can, therefore, be followed spectrophotometrically. All the bases in double-stranded helical DNA in its native conformation, and varying proportions in other ordered polynucleotides, are protected against this attack provided precautions are observed (neutral pH, low temperature, and low concentration) to minimize conformational alteration that can be brought about even in the absence of covalent-bond formation.

Another very useful reagent, especially in studies of mutagenesis in vitro, is nitrous acid: 0.05 to 1 M $NaNO_2$ in acetate buffers at pH 4.0 to 5.0. Under these conditions adenine is transformed to hypoxanthine, guanine to xanthine, and cytosine to uracil. The base-pairing properties (see Fig. 5-10) make a *transition* to the other pair likely in the course of the replication process in at least two of these cases.[1] Another common process, occurring at about one-fourth the rate of deamination, is one that leads (probably via the formation of a common intermediate, the diazonium salt of the amino bases, followed by N_2 elimination and simultaneous alkylation at susceptible sites) to the cross linking of the two chains by covalent bonds.

Similar cross links can be obtained by treating DNA with acid, with ultraviolet light at relatively high intensities, or with bifunctional alkylating agents, such as the nitrogen mustards:

$$ClCH_2CH_2NCH_2CH_2Cl$$
$$|$$
$$R$$

Cross linking by the last two agents occurs respectively between appropriately placed thymine or guanine pairs in the polymer. Cross-link formation also appears to contribute to the effect of the antibiotic Mitomycin C (which is first reduced to an active derivative in the cell) in preventing DNA synthesis in vivo. In principle covalent end-to-end linkage in circular DNAs is equivalent to cross linking: complete unwinding cannot take place. Therefore, circular double-stranded DNAs, such as the one from polyoma virus, share many of the properties of cross-linked DNA.

One of the most effective mutagens in vitro is hydroxylamine, NH_2OH. Unlike most of the other agents, it inactivates the biological functions of DNA only slowly at high concentrations (~ 1 M) and is highly specific in its mode of action: it reacts almost exclusively with cytosine (or 5-hydroxymethyl cytosine) to yield the corresponding uracil derivatives. The mutagenic effect is due to the *transition*

$$G\text{---}C \xrightarrow{\text{HONH}_2} G\text{---}U \rightarrow A\text{---}U \rightarrow A\text{---}T.$$

[1] $A\text{---}T \xrightarrow{\text{HNO}_2} I\text{---}T \rightarrow \underbrace{I\text{---}C \rightarrow G\text{---}C}_{\text{replication}}$ and $G\text{---}C \xrightarrow{\text{HNO}_2} G\text{---}U \rightarrow \underbrace{A\text{---}U \rightarrow A\text{---}T.}_{\text{replication}}$

ACIDIC	NEUTRAL	BASIC
($pH \sim 3$)	$pH \sim 7$)	($pH > 12$)

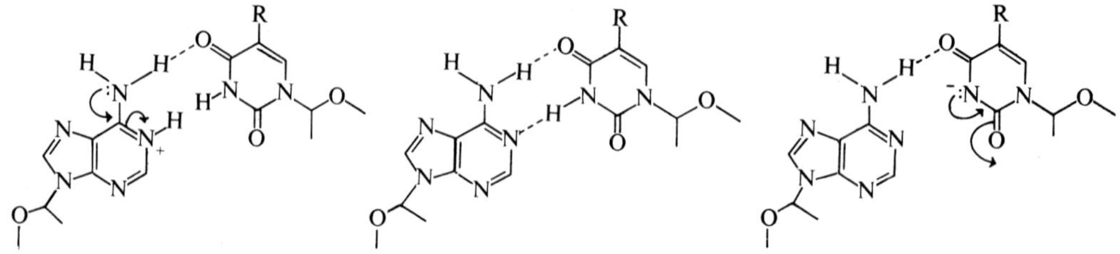

Adenine—thymine, uracil, bromuracil (common tautomer)

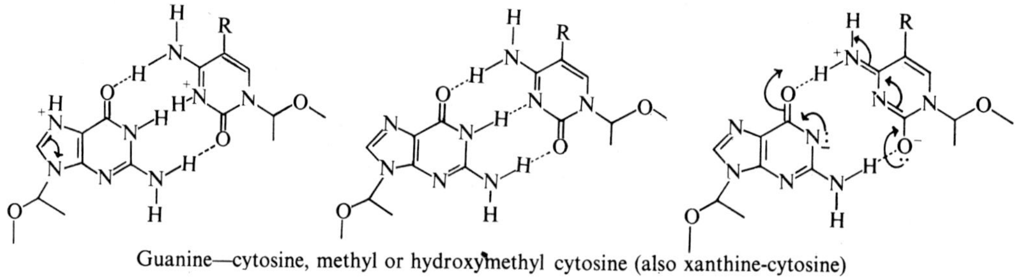

Guanine—cytosine, methyl or hydroxymethyl cytosine (also xanthine-cytosine)

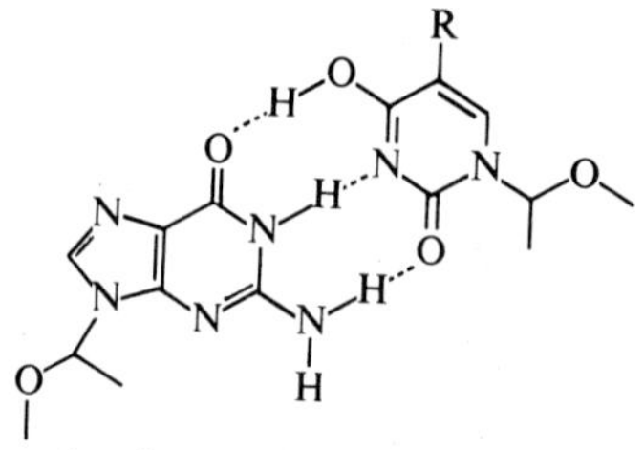

Guanine—thymine, uracil, bromuracil (rare tautomer)

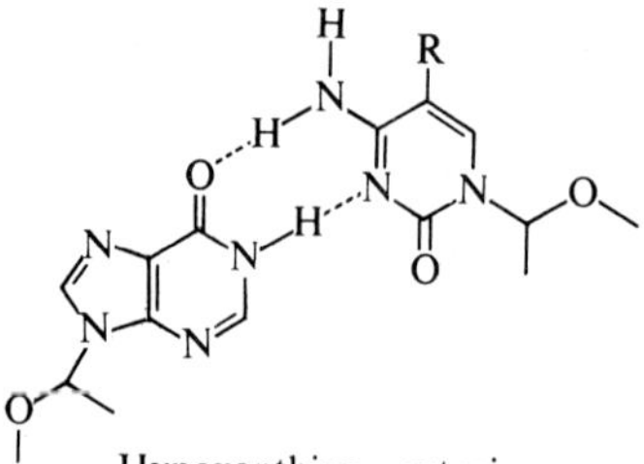

Hypoxanthine—cytosine

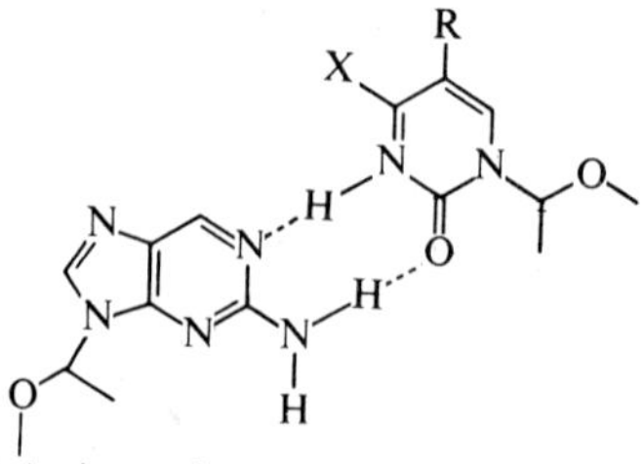

2-Aminopurine—cytosine or thymine

FIGURE 5-10. Base-pairing Properties Under Various Conditions.

Protonation and Deprotonation Reactions. The protonation of DNA in solution occurs at pH values that differ from those of either the free bases or the nucleotides in the same solvent. If the solution is neutral to start with, adenine and cytosine are protonated first (with pK_a values between 5 and 4), followed by guanine (with a $pK_a' \simeq 3$). A consideration of Fig. 5-10 indicates that the first set of protonations leaves base-pairing properties and helix dimensions virtually unchanged; on the contrary the monoprotonated $[A(H)^+ - T]$ and especially $[G-C(H)^+]$ pairs may actually afford greater stability. But on protonation of guanine we are faced with a powerful charge repulsion within one and the same base pair, which can only lead to profound, possibly irreversible, changes in structure occurring over a very narrow pH range. As might be expected, single-stranded DNAs are titrated at somewhat higher pH values. Conversely the removal of protons from guanine and thymine bases in DNA can be observed by titration with alkali. With double-stranded DNA this occurs over an exceedingly narrow pH range — between pH 11 and 12. On banding in CsCl there is an increase in ρ_B by a constant amount of 0.063 g/cm^3 over the neutral form. Single-stranded DNAs are titrated at a lower and less narrow pH range in the vicinity of 10 to 11. In CsCl this is accompanied by a rise in ρ_B of ~ 0.047.

Interactions with Small Molecules and Ions. Nucleic acids, as polyanions, must be accompanied by an appropriate number of cations in their vicinity in order to maintain electrical neutrality. The extent of binding of these ions can vary greatly, however. On the one hand alkali metal cations, such as Na$^+$ and Li$^+$, serve only to neutralize the negative charges on the phosphate residues electrostatically; this allows the nucleic acid to assume its most compact conformation. Divalent cations, such as the alkaline earths, certain transition metals (Co^{+2}, Mn^{+2}, Ni^{+2}, and Zn^{+2}), or organic diamines, which usually accompany DNA in vivo, show a different behavior: they are bound stoichiometrically, probably to the phosphate residues. Thus within this stoichiometric range they are far more effective than the monovalent ions (at the equivalence point 1 Mg^{+2} is equivalent to 10^2 to 10^3 Na$^+$) in affecting the conformation of the macromolecules. In addition relatively large organic molecules may exert other effects on DNA structure not duplicated by the inorganic ions.

Of great interest is the interaction of nucleic acids with certain polynuclear, aromatic planar cationic (basic) dyes of which the acridines (proflavine, acridine orange, etc.) are examples. Dyes of this type have long been used as biological stains capable of binding selectively to and thus rendering visible DNA or RNA (or rather double-stranded versus less highly organized polyanions) by virtue of their absorption or fluorescence. More recently they have come into prominence as highly selective mutagens, capable apparently of producing additions or deletions of single nucleotides in the course of DNA replication and of specific inhibition of this process (see page 464).

Denaturation

General Considerations. When solutions of DNA, originally at pH values around neutrality and in the presence of counterions of moderate ionic strength, are exposed to a variety of agents—such as increase in temperature, addition of hydrogen or hydroxyl ions, removal of the counterion, or the addition of a large variety of organic reagents (alcohols or glycols, amides, aliphatic and heterocyclic amines, substituted ureas, phenols, sulfoxides, etc.) or certain anions (CCl$_3$CO$_2{}^-$,

CNS^-, ClO_4^-) — they undergo a number of structural (conformational) changes, some reversible, some irreversible. These changes, by analogy with the somewhat similar processes in protein chemistry, discussed in the last chapter, have been termed *denaturation*, and the agents responsible have been called *denaturants* or *denaturing agents*. Any one of the hydrodynamic (i.e., s^0, $[\eta]$, R_G, etc.) or optical properties (h, $[\alpha]$, etc.) of the macromolecule can be used to follow the process qualitatively and, if only two states, *native* and *denatured*, need to be distinguished, quantitatively as well. Agents of various classes are frequently potentiating and mutually complementary — e.g., addition of various denaturing agents lowers the temperature at which denaturation takes place, as does a decrease in ionic strength; at an elevated temperature the concentration of denaturant required to give a

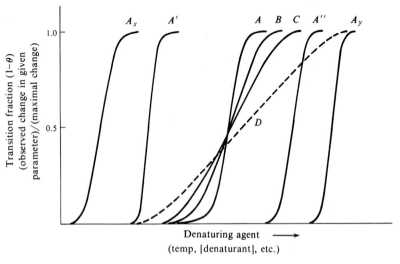

FIGURE 5-11.   Schematic Transition Profiles for Denaturation. Curve *A*: DNA (*a* per cent G + C) from a bacterial virus; *B*: DNA (*a* per cent G + C) from a bacterium: *C*: DNA (*a* per cent G + C) from a higher animal or plant; *A'*: DNA (*b* per cent G+C, $b \ll a$) from a bacterial virus, $M \simeq$ that of DNA in *A*; *A"*: DNA (*c* per cent G + C, $c > a$) from a bacterial virus, $M \simeq$ that of DNA in *A* or *A'*; A_x: same DNA as in *A* but in the presence of additional denaturing conditions or agents; A_y: same DNA as in *A* but in the presence of a stabilizing agent; *D*: single-stranded DNA.

desired degree of denaturation is lower than at room temperature, etc. Some of these factors are brought out in the simplified and schematic Fig. 5-11, as are some of the following additional points:

1. The transitions observed can be represented by simple sigmoids defined by two parameters: the position of their midpoint and the steepness of the slope at this point (or, by an equivalent parameter, the transition width). The steepness and the shape of these transitions are analogous to those observed in highly cooperative order-disorder phase transitions of crystallites or other polymers.

2. If the system under study involves just two components (i.e., if intermolecular heterogeneity is absent, and the only two species involved are the native and those denatured form(s) in equilibrium which are to be measured by the changes observed) and if the transition is reversible over a considerable region beyond the midpoint, one can regard the latter as that point at which,

statistically, 50 per cent of the molecules have been converted from the native to the denatured forms (i.e., some combination between the two extremes of all the molecules having been denatured to the extent of 50 per cent or half of the molecules denatured 100 per cent). That means for the transition DNA (native) $\rightleftharpoons$ DNA (denatured), with an equilibrium constant

$$K_{tr} = (1 - \theta) = \frac{[\text{denatured}]}{[\text{native}]} \equiv \frac{\text{fraction of base pairs in coiled regions}}{\text{fraction in helical regions}} \qquad (5\text{-}15)$$

this is the point at which $\Delta G_{tr} = 0$ and $\Delta H_{tr} = T_{1/2} \Delta S_{tr}$. If the transition measured is the thermal one, i.e., the independent variable is temperature, then it becomes analogous to the melting of a unidimensional crystallite, and the temperature at the transition midpoint $t_{1/2}$ (on the absolute scale $T_{1/2}$) is equivalent to a melting point t_m (or T_m).

3. The position of $T_{1/2}$ shows a direct, and frequently a linear, functional dependence on the composition of the DNA, increasing with increasing $(X_G + X_C)$. No such dependence obtains with respect to the transition width. The value of $T_{1/2}$ is relatively insensitive to the molecular weight of the polymer, although the width of the transition may increase as the molecular weight decreases. In the thermal transition in 0.2 M Na$^+$, $t_m = 69.3 + 0.41 \ (X_G + X_C)$, where 69.3 is, of course, the $t_{1/2}$ of a hypothetical polymer containing only (A + T). Both these parameters appear to be equally valid for natural DNAs and for enzymatically synthesized homopolymer duplexes.

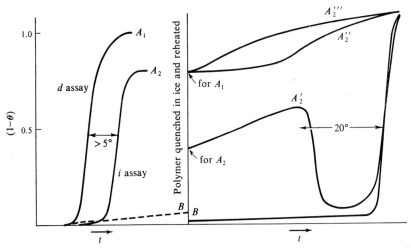

FIGURE 5-12.   Reversible and Irreversible Denaturation (schematic). Note that ionic strength at right is greater than at left.

4. Transition profiles have usually been determined in one of two ways (see Fig. 5-12): at the ambient conditions (temperature, pH, etc.) or after rapid return to some standard condition of temperature, pH, etc. (usually a temperature around 20°, a pH around 6 to 7, an ionic strength of 0.1 to 0.2, etc.). The former, curve A_1, called *d assay* by Geiduschek, measures the extent of the transition actually observed (i.e., the position of the equilibrium) at the moment of measurement; the latter, curve A_2, termed *i assay*, the extent of rapid thermodynamic

reversibility of the process obtaining under standard conditions. If the new value is identical with the one originally obtained under standard conditions, then the change has been prima facie reversible; if not, then some irreversible process must have intervened.

Nature of Stabilizing Forces. Contrary to earlier opinion it has recently become clear that hydrogen bonds, although of the utmost importance in controlling the form and specificity of the helix, make relatively little contribution, if any, to its stability. The preferred explanation for this, at first glance, somewhat surprising conclusion, is that there is really no very great change in hydrogen bonding in going from helix to coil; there simply is a substitution of base-solvent hydrogen bonds for base-base bonds, and although the former may be somewhat weaker than the latter individually, there will be more of them, because H_2O can act as both a hydrogen donor and acceptor. The main contributions to helix stability, then, are the forces that have variously been referred to as stacking or hydrophobic (apolar) forces, and very little is known about their nature or magnitude.

Native and Denatured Conformations. A number of different conformations have been identified in denaturation studies. On the one extreme we have, of course, the completely ordered perfectly double helical and complementary conformation I in Fig. 5-13. At the other extreme we find an essentially completely disordered conformation: two separated, completely flexible random coils with no extensive structure or order remaining (conformation V). This corresponds to the completely and "irreversibly" denatured form obtained at high temperatures or extremes of pH, etc., where, not only the d assay, but also the i assay has indicated the completion of the transition (curve A_2 in Fig. 5-12). On removal of the denaturing agent and return to standard conditions a certain amount of order is restored. Two possible conformations are indicated as III and VI in Fig. 5-13. This is the extent of order restored to single-stranded polynucleotides (either homogeneous DNA or RNA species — i.e., consider only strand A present). The denaturation profiles of such polymers, which are identical to those observed when an "irreversibly" denatured double-stranded polynucleotide is subject to a second cycle of denaturation, is given by curve A_2''' and A_2'' of Fig. 5-12 (A_2''' for minimal and A_2'' for relatively extensive complementariness inherent in the single strand). Conformations similar to IV, i.e., extensively disoriented coils still held together by very short complementary regions in register and identical to those present originally in the native form ("nuclei" or "sticky regions"), probably occur as intermediates in the course of most denaturation processes. Their existence explains the differences observed between so-called reversible and irreversible processes (that is the d versus i assay described above). For covalently cross-linked or circular DNA some regions always remain in register, and denaturation is reversible as long as the links remain intact (curve B in Fig. 5-12). Finally, intermediate forms, such as II, which contain both extensively ordered as well as disordered regions capable of instantaneous reversion to the completely ordered starting conformation, have been identified in denaturation brought about by heat, high pH, or certain organic solvents.

Irreversible Denaturation. The separation and recombination of complementary strands in double-stranded polynucleotides have been studied extensively in recent years. Under appropriate conditions the complete separation of the two complementary strands can be brought about; this process of strand disentanglement may be quite slow (of the order of minutes) and require relatively extreme conditions of temperature, pH, etc., well beyond the midpoint of the reversible transition (see Fig. 5-12). In order to bring about the reverse process of strand recombination several conditions must obtain:

1. The reaction must be thermodynamically favored; i.e., it must be allowed to take place in a region well below t_m at a relatively high ionic strength.

2. It must be favored kinetically as well. Strand recombination is second-order and, therefore, is favored by high concentrations of the nucleic acid. The strands

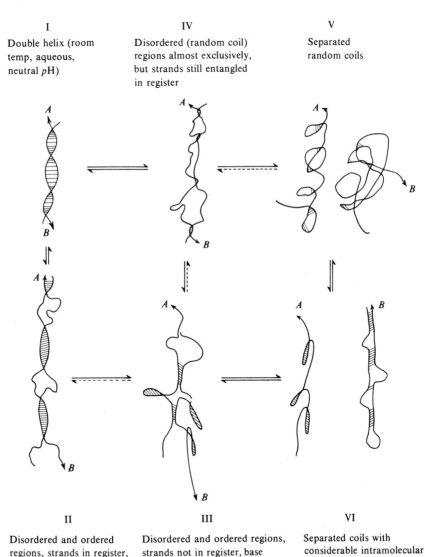

I

Double helix (room temp, aqueous, neutral pH)

IV

Disordered (random coil) regions almost exclusively, but strands still entangled in register

V

Separated random coils

II

Disordered and ordered regions, strands in register, ordered regions may no longer contain H bonds

III

Disordered and ordered regions, strands not in register, base pairs other than AT and GC possible, as is stacking without H bond formation

VI

Separated coils with considerable intramolecular helicity (two extreme cases shown)

FIGURE 5-13.   Hypothetical Conformations in Denaturation Processes.

must be able to approach closely; this again is favored by high ionic strength and the presence of specific counterions, such as Mg^{+2}, as well as an absence of charges in the bases, i.e., neutrality.

3. For complete re-formation of order all base pairs must be perfectly matched. This is easily accomplished in the case of homopolymers, i.e., the formation of dG : dC or rU : rA or dAT : dAT. But with a natural polynucleotide the probability is much greater that extensive mismatching will occur and only short, imperfectly matched regions will originally be present (structures similar to III in Fig. 5-13). In order for extensive reordering to take place, these imperfect regions must be ruptured; this will be reflected in a high free energy of activation, restrict the permissible temperatures to those just below the t_m, and require a relatively long period of time. The process just described has aptly been termed *annealing* (see Fig. 5-9c and d and Fig. 5-12, curve A_2').

4. Annealing and restoration of order are, therefore, favored by conditions that permit homologous matching segments to be sorted out and combined. For chains in free solution molecular homogeneity is the prime consideration, and renaturation is most easily accomplished with DNA from small viruses, somewhat less easily with that from large viruses, still less easily with that from bacteria, and least easily, if at all, with that from higher organisms. It also means that the process is favored if one of the strands can be immobilized, say in an agar gel or on hydroxylapatite columns, and the other is broken down to segments of relatively short length ($M \simeq 10^4$ to 10^5).

5. This process of *hybridization* can then be used to measure the extent of relatedness, not only between complementary DNA strands isolated from cells or organisms, but also between separated single DNA strands and various RNAs, because all cellular RNA appears to be synthesized on DNA templates[1] (see page 485). Hybridization between, for example, $N^{15}D$ and $N^{14}H$ strands from "heavy" and "light" DNAs present initially also provides the best evidence for the actual occurrence of the strand separation and recombination phenomena (see Fig. 5-9).

POLYRIBO-
NUCLEOTIDES
Localization
and Function

Ribonucleic acid (RNA) is found in almost all cell fractions. Quantitatively the most important contribution (usually about 50 to 60 per cent, rising in some cells to 80 per cent of the total) is made by ribonucleoprotein particles, called *ribosomes*, associated with each other in aggregates called *polysomes* or *ergosomes* (see page 229), which, in turn, may be attached to other cytologically distinct entities, such as the endoplasmic reticulum of highly specialized cells of higher forms of the cell membrane of microorganisms (see page 236). Ribosomelike particles are also frequently found in intimate association with the chromosomal or nuclear apparatus of the cell. Chromatin- (i.e., DNA) associated RNA appears to be of at least two types (some of the ribosomal RNA just described and "messenger," cf. below); in addition there appears to be a considerable quantity of RNA in the nucleolus. These various forms of nuclear RNA account for 10

[1] Identification and isolation of such hybrids is greatly aided by three characteristic properties: (1) their RNA component is relatively insensitive to pancreatic RNase; (2) they band in CsCl at densities intermediate between those of DNA and RNA; (3) they are retained by cellulose nitrate filters, but RNA is not.

to 20 per cent of the total RNA of the cell. RNA is also found in the soluble portion of the cytoplasm (i.e., that fraction which does not sediment after several hours at $140,000 \times g$); this fraction accounts for 10 to 20 per cent of the cellular RNA. Finally there are small amounts of RNA associated with the mitochondria of animal and plant tissues and the chloroplasts of plants. Functionally all these RNAs appear to be involved in one phase or another of protein synthesis, which is discussed in Chap. 21. The ribosomes provide the machinery by means of which the amino acids are polymerized to polypeptide chains. The template for this process is provided by a special form of RNA ("messenger" RNA) synthesized on and complementary to one of the two strands of the appropriate DNA segment, eventually transferred and attached to ribosomes. The amino acids, in turn, are brought to and arranged on this template by means of adapters provided by more than 20 different aminoacyl transfer RNAs, all contained within the soluble RNA mentioned above.

Another class of RNA is provided by a group of viruses. Three different types may be distinguished: small, spherical plant and bacterial viruses (such as the *E. coli* viruses f2 or MS2, and turnip yellow virus), yielding RNA molecules of $M = 1$ to 2×10^6; small rodlike viruses, such as tobacco mosaic virus, with an RNA of approximately the same size; and large animal viruses, such as Newcastle disease virus, containing larger RNA molecules.

Base Composition

The base composition of a variety of different RNAs falling into the various classes just described is summarized in Table 5-2. In general it will be seen that the striking complementariness found in DNA and described by Chargaff's rules is absent even in the viral RNAs, the only regularity remaining being the fact that $G + U \simeq A + C$. "Messenger" RNAs, especially if relatively large segments of the DNA have been transcribed, are frequently more DNA-like in their overall base composition. Yet, as we shall see, extensive second-order structure and helicity in the molecule prevents its proper function. Most ribosomal RNAs from microorganisms contain $\sim 52 \operatorname{mol}\%$ $G + C$ and most soluble RNAs $\sim 58 \operatorname{mol}\%$ $G + C$ regardless of the base composition of the DNA from the same cell.

Structures and Properties

Ribosomal and viral RNA may be discussed together, because we are dealing with molecules very similar in size and properties. These ribopolynucleotides appear to be single molecules, single-stranded, highly flexible, and deformable, and behave hydrodynamically as random coils (especially at low ionic strength or high temperature), with the consequences already discussed: a very pronounced and dramatic dependence of various optical and hydrodynamic properties on ionic strength, etc., and a closer concordance with the theoretical and experimental parameters given by other polyelectrolytes. Chemically the bonding of the various entities is similar to that found in DNA, i.e., a polynucleotide made up of a single unbranched chain with the monomeric units linked by 3′,5′-phosphodiester bonds. Because the 2′-OH position is free, the polynucleotides are cleaved by mild alkali; other reactions were discussed on page 133. The reactivity of the free amino groups to such agents as HNO_2 and HCHO is greater than it is in DNA (but less than in the free nucleotides), and not all residues appear to be equally reactive. The hypochromism is less, and denaturation transition profiles are considerably broader than those of double-stranded DNA, resembling those of single-stranded DNA. In general, the transition midpoints are still dependent on base composition in the same sense, but not so strongly as are those of DNA; almost all transitions are readily reversible. These and related observations suggest a structure for high-molecular-weight RNA in solution in media of high

TABLE 5-2.   Base Composition of Various RNAs

Species (DNA composition in parentheses)	Type	A	G	C	U	ψU*
Rat liver (42 per cent GC)	Nuclear	20.2	25.7	29.5	24.6	
	Nucleolar	16.3	33.0	29.9	20.7	
	Mitochondrial	17.8	31.8	28.4	20.9	
	Ribosomal	20.0	30.5	31.6	20.2	
	Soluble (largely transfer)*	20.9	30.9	28.5	20.4	3.8
	"Messenger"	23.8	28.3	27.4	20.5	
		26.5	20.1	24.0	29.4	
Yeast (36 per cent GC)	Ribosomal (average of two sets)	25.9	27.7	19.4	26.7	
	Soluble*†	18.5	29.2	28.4	20.0	
	"Messenger"	27.5	25.1	20.3	27.1	
Bacillus cereus (35 per cent GC)	Bulk ribosomes	25.2	31.7	21.9	21.2	
	Soluble*	20.5	31.1	28.0	18.8	1.6
Escherichia coli (50 per cent GC)	30S ribosomes	24.6	31.6	22.8	21.0	
	50S ribosomes	25.6	31.4	20.9	22.1	
	70S ribosomes	25.0	31.5	22.1	21.4	
	Soluble (average of three sets)	19.3	32.0	28.3	16.0	5.9
	"Messenger"	24.1	27.7	24.7	23.5	
Micrococcus lysodeikticus (72 per cent GC)	"Large" ribosomes	23.0	33.3	20.8	22.7	
	"Small" ribosomes	22.2	31.5	22.1	24.1	
	Soluble*	19.6	31.7	25.1	23.4	
Tobacco mosaic	Plant virus	29	26	19	27	
Turnip yellow	Plant virus	23	17	38	22	
Wound tumor	Plant virus	31.1	18.6	19.1	31.3	
Polio	Animal virus	29	24	22	25	
Reovirus	Animal virus	28.0	22.3	22.0	27.9	
F2 (MS2)	Bacterial virus	22	26	27	25	

* ψU, when not shown, has been included in the analysis for U. Soluble RNA also contains the methylated bases as well as ψU in much higher concentrations than any of the other types. In soluble RNA from rat liver, 25 per cent of U is replaced by ψU, 10 per cent by 5-methylcytosine, 8.1 per cent by 6-methylaminopurine, and approximately 3 per cent each by 1-methylguanine, 2-methyl-6-hydroxypurine, and 2,2-dimethyl-6-hydroxypurine.
† See Table 5-3.

ionic strength that allows for short helical regions containing stacks of hydrogen-bonded AU and GC pairs, interspersed with others where no such structures are possible or found.

Aminoacyl transfer RNAs are small polyribonucleotides of $M \simeq 25{,}000$ particularly suitable for chemical investigation. The structure of several has now been completely elucidated. Considering their small size — and the fact that they contain a relatively large proportion of the unusual bases, such as ψU, etc. — they exhibit a remarkably large degree of structure. This is especially true in the presence of Mg^{+2} — an ion absolutely essential for their function (see page 493) — when, unlike monovalent cations even at much higher concentration, not only the extent and the midpoint of the thermal transition, but also its width

TABLE 5-3.   Homologous Alignment of Base Sequences in Yeast Alanine, Serine, Tyrosine and Phenylalanine Transfer RNAs

	Ala	Ser	Tyr	Phe		Ala	Ser	Tyr	Phe
H_1	pG	pG	pC	pG	H_3'	G	Ψ'	Ψ'	Ψ'
	G	G	U	C		G	C	C	CMe
	G	C	C	G		G	U	U	U
	C	A	U	G		A	U	U	G
	G	A	C	A		G	U	G	G
	U	C	G	U					
	G	U	G	U	50	A	UOMe	A	A
						*G	G	G	G
a	*U	U	U	U		—	G	A	GMe
	GMe	G	A	A		—	G	—	—
						—	C	—	—
10	*G	G	GMe	GMe		—	U	—	—
H_2	*C	C	C	C	c	—	U(C)	—	—
	G	CAc	C	U		—	U	—	—
	C	G	A	C		—	G	—	—
						—	C	—	—
L_1	G	—	—	—		—	C	—	—
	U	—	—	—		—	C	—	—
	*A	A	A	A	60	UH₂	G	UH₂	U
	*G	G	G	G		*C	CMe	CMe	C
	*UH₂	UH₂	UH₂	UH₂					
	C	—	UH₂	UH₂		U	G	G	CMe
20	*G	GOMe	GOMe	G		C	C	G	U
	*G	G	G	G	H_4	C	A	G	G
	—	—	UH₂	—		G	G	C	U
	—	—	UH₂	—		*G	G	G	G
	UH₂	UH₂	UH₂	G					
	*A	A	A	A		*T	T	T	T
						*Ψ'	Ψ'	Ψ'	Ψ'
H_2'	G	A	A	G		*C	C	C	C
	C	G	G	A	L_3	*G	G(A)	G	G
	*G	G	G	G	70	*A	A	AMe	AMe
	*C	C	C	C		U	G(A)	C	U
						U	U	U	C
b 30	*GMe₂	GMe₂	GMe₂	GMe₂					
	C	A	C	C		*C	C	C	C
	U	A	A	C	H_4'	C	C	G	A
H_3	C	A	A	A		G	U	C	C
	C	G	G	G		G	G	C	A
	C	A	A	A		A	C	C	G
	U	Ψ'	C	COMe		C	A	C	A
	*U	U	U	U	80	U	G	C	A
	I	I	G	GOMe		C	U	G	U
L_2	G	G	Ψ'	A	H_1'	G	U	G	U
40	C	A	A	A		U	G	G	C
	IMe	Aisop	AMe₂	Y		C	U	A	G
	Ψ'	A	A	A		C	C	G	C
					d 86	A	G	A	A

C
C
A-OH

H_1, H_1' = first helical region
H_2, H_2' = second helical region, etc.
a, b, c, d, = connecting regions
L_1, L_2, L_3 = loops
* Denotes common residues
SOURCE: T. H. Jukes, with permission.

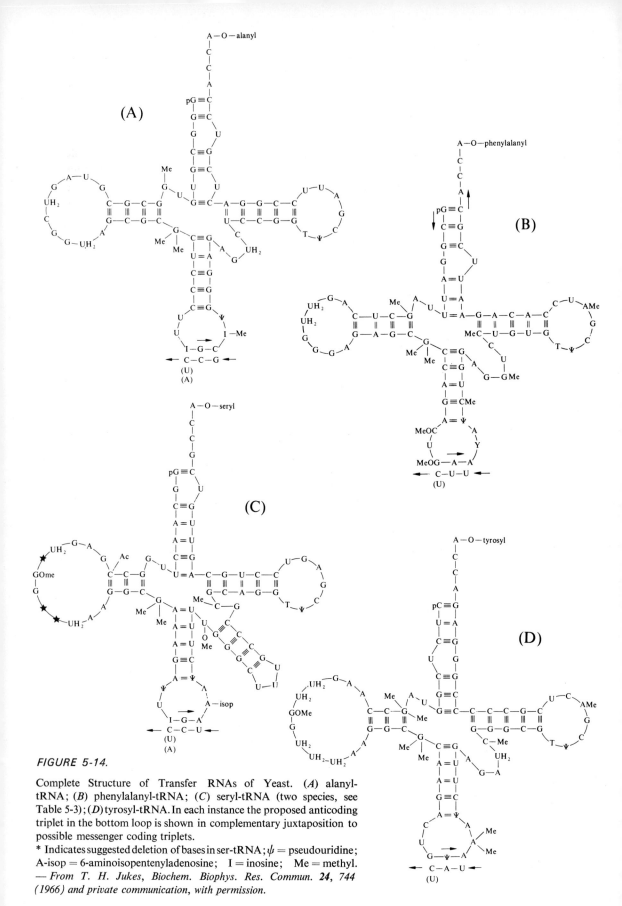

FIGURE 5-14.

Complete Structure of Transfer RNAs of Yeast. (*A*) alanyl-tRNA; (*B*) phenylalanyl-tRNA; (*C*) seryl-tRNA (two species, see Table 5-3); (*D*) tyrosyl-tRNA. In each instance the proposed anticoding triplet in the bottom loop is shown in complementary juxtaposition to possible messenger coding triplets.

* Indicates suggested deletion of bases in ser-tRNA; ψ = pseudouridine; A-isop = 6-aminoisopentenyladenosine; I = inosine; Me = methyl.

— *From T. H. Jukes, Biochem. Biophys. Res. Commun.* **24,** 744 *(1966) and private communication, with permission.*

(and hence its cooperativeness and the stacking energy) is affected profoundly. Under these conditions, also, large portions of the molecule become completely refractory to reaction with ribonuclease or formaldehyde. Figure 5-14 gives the complete primary and reasonable secondary structures of an alanine transfer RNA studied by Holley, a tyrosine transfer RNA studied by Madison in Holley's laboratory, two closely related serine transfer RNAs investigated by Zachau and his collaborators, and a phenylalanine transfer RNA studied by Khorana and his colleagues. All these molecular species were isolated from yeast. The two Ser-tRNAs are composed of 84 nucleotides each; the Phe-tRNA contains 76, the Ala-tRNA contains 77, and the Tyr-tRNA contains 78 nucleotides respectively. Nevertheless their structures appear closely related and, as suggested by T. H. Jukes, may have been derived, by mutational changes, from a common precursor. The similarities, homologies and differences among the four molecules are most clearly brought out by a consideration of Table 5-3. Observe the large number of rare and unusual bases and nucleosides — 9 in Ala-tRNA, 12 in Ser-tRNA, 12 in Phe-tRNA, and 15 in Tyr-tRNA. Besides pseudouridine (see page 116), inosine (I) (the nucleoside of hypoxanthine; see page 114), dihydrouridine (UH$_2$), and various N-mono- and dimethyl derivatives, there also occurs O-methyl compounds and 6-aminoisopentenyl adenosine. The structures of these derivatives are summarized in Fig. 5-15. Their function is discussed on page 493.

Synthetic Polyribonucleotides   The action of polynucleotide phosphorylase on nucleoside diphosphates, present singly or in appropriate combination, leads to homo- or heteropolymeric polyribonucleotides (see page 484) that have been of great utility as simpler models for RNA and DNA (see page 140). Especially useful have been the homopolymer pairs poly A plus poly U and poly I plus poly C, which form

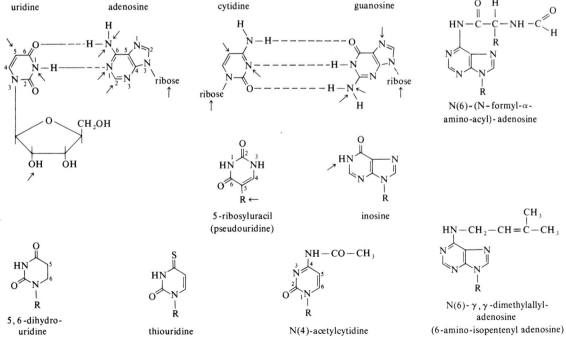

FIGURE 5-15.   The "unusual" bases and nucleosides in transfer RNA. Arrows (→) indicate positions susceptible to methyl substitution.

stoichiometric duplexes (rA:rU and rI:rC) in solution,[1] and the heteropoly-mers poly AGUC of various base ratios. The application of these and other polymers and oligomers in solving the coding problem is discussed in Chap. 19.

RNA polymerase (see page 485) with dG or dC as templates, and CTP or GTP as substrate, produces the duplexes dG:rC and dC:rG. DNA polymerase with rA:rU as primer and dATP plus dTTP as substrate forms dA:dT; the synthesis and formation of the polydeoxyribonucleotide duplexes dG : dC, dAdT, etc., was mentioned briefly on page 125.

NUCLEOPROTEINS
Nucleohistones

In general all animal and viral DNAs and RNA (with the possible exception of transfer RNA) occur in vivo in close association with protein. Of special interest are the histones, a family of exceedingly heterogeneous, basic proteins of rela-tively low molecular weight that appear to be strongly and stoichiometrically complexed to the DNA of all somatic cells of higher organisms, plants and animals alike. The histones may be dissociated from the DNA and subdivided into four main fractions by chromatography. Other techniques show that each of these fractions, which vary from the most lysine-rich fraction I to the most arginine-rich fraction IV is, in turn, made up of several species. X-ray diffraction has given some clues concerning secondary structure of both the isolated free histones and the protein and DNA in the nucleoprotein. Free histones appear to have a high helical content, probably of α helix, and this structure appears to be maintained and stabilized in the nucleohistone; the latter also appears to contain DNA in the same configuration (B helix) found in free solution. What is not clear is whether the protein helices are arranged in parallel with, or at right angles to, the DNA helices; if the latter were the case, one would have to con-ceive of a grid with several DNA molecules arranged in parallel and cross-linked by histone molecules.

Histones in association with DNA can affect the ability of the latter to specify (or be "transcribed" into) a complementary RNA in the reaction catalyzed by the DNA-dependent RNA polymerase in vitro (see page 485). Because this type of RNA can subsequently function as messenger in protein synthesis, such effects by histones constitute a control of protein synthesis at the transcriptional level (page 508).

In the mature sperm cells of some families of fishes, the DNA is associated, not with histones, but with other basic proteins called *protamines*. These prot-amines are very basic proteins, containing a high proportion of arginine and in this respect bear some resemblance to the arginine-rich histones. They are, however, proteins of smaller size, less heterogeneous in size and composition, and appear to be species specific. The replacement of histones by protamines in the course of spermatogenesis represents an interesting chapter in the chemical aspects of subcellular differentiation.

Viruses

An exceedingly interesting example of autonomous and homogeneous nucleo-proteins is provided by the viruses. These obligatory parasites are capable of

---

[1] Poly G has been more refractory; it is formed only with difficulty, associates with itself in solution, and the stable complex with poly C is the triplex G:C:G. Poly A at acid pH values (~ 4) associates with itself to form interrupted double helices. The duplex poly A: poly U consists of a double helix with structure parameters very similar to those of DNA.

vegetative existence and replication only inside the cells of their hosts (which, depending on virus species, may be bacteria, plants, or animals), fashioning and controlling the host's metabolism to their own purposes. In their ability to reproduce their own kind, to multiply, to be capable of mutation, and to exchange genetic material provided by more than one parent, they exhibit the most salient characteristics of living organisms. Yet they can be isolated, in pure, frequently crystalline forms, stored, examined, analyzed, and manipulated and, in short, treated as distinct chemical entities. Thus, although themselves forming part of living nature, they have also provided investigators with more easily comprehensible models or analogues for life processes characteristic of more complex forms.

Let us briefly consider the different classes of viruses and their hosts. Bacterial viruses (bacteriophages) are frequently fairly large. Their nucleic acid, usually regular double-stranded DNA, is contained in a crystalline head of polyhedral symmetry that is made up of many small ($M \sim 2 \times 10^4$) identical protein subunits. Frequently they also have a more or less flexible tail that serves as an attachment and injection organ. Because this tail assembly may itself be made up of many and diverse functional and structural components, the number of different proteins present in one and the same virus may, in certain instances, be quite large. Some of the smaller bacterial viruses contain unusual nucleic acid: in the case of viruses of the class of ϕX174 it is a relatively small single-stranded circular DNA; in that of the class of MS2, a single-stranded RNA molecule. In this respect and in the icosahedral symmetry of their protein shell or *capsid* they resemble the smaller plant or animal viruses. In these viruses, the capsid (a "surface crystal") is made up of symmetrical clusters of structural polypeptide subunits. These clusters form the morphological units of which the capsid is composed; they can be clearly seen in electron micrographs and are called *capsomeres*. The smallest viruses contain 60 structural units clustered into 12 capsomeres.

The plant viruses all contain RNA and are of two main types. The first type is helical, as exemplified by tobacco mosaic virus (TMV), in which the capsid is made up of many (2,100) identical structural units of $M = 18,000$ arranged in helical fashion around a central core, 40 A in diameter, containing a fully extended RNA molecule. Thus the RNA is encased in a sheath or tubing of protein producing a rodlike virus about 3,000 A long and 150 A across. Incidentally, such rods, identical in all respects to the parent virus, have been constituted in vitro by mixing together isolated highly purified TMV RNA and homogeneous TMV protein (of which the complete primary structure is now known). The helical type of structural arrangement is, therefore, capable of formation by straightforward aggregation of the components, produces the maximal amount of surface area exposed and of nucleic acid–protein interaction, and probably necessitates complete disassembly prior to or in the course of the infection process.

The other type of stable and symmetrical arrangement is found in the icosahedral viruses and is exemplified by bushy stunt virus. The shell of this virus is made up of about 60 capsomeres containing $\sim$200 structural units arranged in an isometric capsid, like one of the geodesic domes designed by Buckminster Fuller, only 200 A in diameter. This arrangement must result from a more complex process than simple aggregation, exposes the minimum of surface area to the environment, and probably requires that not all the nucleic acid can be in contact with the protein shell, which, however, need not be disassembled in order for the genetic material to be expelled.

Animal viruses may contain either RNA or DNA; in the former case they frequently reproduce in the cytoplasm, in the latter in the nuclei of the host cell. Of the small RNA viruses, those producing poliomyelitis and the Cocksackie viruses are simple polyhedral nucleoproteins, similar to the plant viruses described. Others, such as those responsible for various forms of encephalitis and for influenza, contain RNA of about the same small molecular weight but are themselves much larger though still polyhedral, owing, in part, to the inclusion of other components, such as lipids or polysaccharides, respectively. One of the most intriguing groups of animal viruses is that of the Reoviruses, which contain double-stranded helical, complementary RNA of high molecular weight, which, therefore, resembles ordinary DNA in many of its chemical, structural, and functional aspects. In plants a group of viruses with very similar properties with regard to morphology, size (capsids about 700 A in diameter, containing 92 capsomeres), RNA content, and structure are known that cause disease in a large number of species and produce tumors in some — the so-called wound tumor viruses. They multiply in plants but are transmitted from plant to plant by an insect, the leaf hopper.

Among the DNA viruses are those causing herpes, chickenpox, mumps, measles, smallpox (vaccinia), psittacosis, rabies, and polyoma — an exceedingly malignant tumor in rodents. The viruses of the vaccinia-psittacosis group are very large, 1,500 to 2,000 A in diameter, and at least one of them, that of vaccinia, appears to contain a single-stranded DNA. The DNA of polyoma has a molecular weight of 3.0×10^6 and was the first double-helical DNA shown to be definitely circular by chemical and physical techniques.

The smallest viral RNA isolated so far belongs to the tobacco necrosis satellite virus. The virus was given this name because it invariably occurs together with various strains of ordinary tobacco necrosis virus and is incapable of multiplying in plants in their absence. It constitutes, however, a separate and immunologically distinct entity. Its RNA (A = 28.9 per cent, C = 22.1 per cent, G = 25.0 per cent, U = 24.9 per cent) has a $M = 4.0 \times 10^5$ ($s_{20,w} = 13.5$ S; 1,200 nucleotide residues). The molecular weight of its capsid protein subunit equals 39,000 (372 residues). Thus the RNA can code, at the most, for that one protein (see page 469).

REFERENCES   Allen, F.: "Ribonucleoproteins and Ribonucleic Acids," Elsevier, Amsterdam, 1962.
Chargaff, E.: "Essays on Nucleic Acids," Elsevier, New York, 1963.
Davidson, J. N.: "Biochemistry of the Nucleic Acids," 4th ed., Wiley, New York, 1960.
"Informational Macromolecules," H. J. Vogel, V. Bryson, and J. O. Lampen (eds.), Academic, New York, 1963.
Jordan, D. O.: "The Chemistry of Nucleic Acids," Butterworth, Washington, 1960.
Martin, R. B.: "Introduction to Biophysical Chemistry," chaps. 6, 8, 10, 11, 13, and 17–20, McGraw-Hill, New York, 1964.
Michelson, A. M.: "The Chemistry of Nucleosides and Nucleotides," Academic, New York, 1963.

Nucleic Acids, in "Comprehensive Biochemistry," vol. 8, part B, M. Florkin and E. H. Stotz (eds.), Elsevier, New York, 1963.

Perutz, M. F.: "Proteins and Nucleic Acids," Elsevier, New York, 1962.

Potter, V. R.: "Nucleic Acid Outlines," vol. 1, Burgess, Minneapolis, 1960.

"Procedures in Nucleic Acid Research," G. L. Cantoni and D. R. Davies (eds.), Harper & Row, New York, 1966.

Spirin, A. S.: "Macromolecular Structure of Ribonucleic Acids," Reinhold, New York, 1964.

Steiner, R. F., and R. F. Beers, Jr.: "Polynucleotides," Elsevier, New York, 1961.

Structure and Biosynthesis of Macromolecules, *Biochem. Soc. Symp.*, **21** (1962).

Synthesis and Structure of Macromolecules, *Cold Spring Harbor Symp. Quant. Biol.*, **28** (1963).

Tanford, C.: "Physical Chemistry of Macromolecules," chaps. 5 and 6, Wiley, New York, 1961.

"The Nucleic Acids," vols. 1–3, E. Chargaff and J. N. Davidson (eds.), Academic, New York, 1955 and 1960.

"The Nucleohistones," J. Bonner and P. Ts'o (eds.), Holden-Day, San Francisco, 1964.

A very useful series is provided by "Progress in Nucleic Acid Research and Molecular Biology," *J. N. Davidson and W. E. Cohn (eds.), Academic, New York.*

Baldwin, R. L.: Molecular Aspects of the Gene: Replication Mechanisms, in "The Bacteria," vol. 5, p. 327, I. C. Gunsalus and R. Stanier (eds.), Academic, New York, 1963.

Felsenfeld, G., and H. T. Miles: The Physical and Chemical Properties of Nucleic Acids, *Ann. Rev. Biochem.*, **36**: 407 (1967).

Freese, E.: Molecular Mechanisms of Mutations, in "Molecular Genetics," p. 207, J. H. Taylor (ed.), Academic, New York, 1963.

Josse, J., and J. Eigner: Physical Properties of Deoxyribonucleic Acid, *Ann. Rev. Biochem.*, **35**: 789 (1966).

McQuillen, K.: Ribosomes, *Progr. Biophys.*, **12**: 67 (1962).

Raj, Bhandary, and A. Stuart: Nucleic Acids—Sequence Analysis, *Ann. Rev. Biochem.*, **35**: 759 (1966).

Sueoka, N.: Compositional Variation and Heterogeneity of Nucleic Acids, and Proteins, in "The Bacteria," vol. 5, p. 419, I. C. Gunsalus and R. Stanier (eds.), Academic, New York, 1963.

Thomas, C. A., Jr.: The Organization of DNA in Bacteriophage and Bacteria, in "Molecular Genetics," p. 113, J. H. Taylor (ed.), Academic, New York, 1963.

6 Enzyme Kinetics

One of the manifestations of life is the remarkable efficiency of organisms in exerting kinetic control of thermodynamic potentiality. In order to understand how this control is brought about, we must develop some understanding of the principles of kinetics that such reactions obey and study the kinetics of enzyme-catalyzed reactions.

CHEMICAL KINETICS

Kinetics of Uncatalyzed Reactions

Let us first consider some simple chemical reactions. In the simplest case

$$A \xrightarrow{k} P \tag{6-1}$$

one in which A is converted spontaneously and essentially irreversibly to P in, say, an isomerization reaction, its rate or velocity v at any time t equals $-da/dt$, the rate of disappearance of substrate, or dp/dt, the rate of appearance of product. Now, ideally, if this is a true monomolecular process, by the law of mass action this rate must be proportional to a, the concentration of A at any time t:

$$v = -\frac{da}{dt} = ka \tag{6-2}$$

This statement and its algebraic formulation constitute the *velocity*, *rate*, or *kinetic law* (or better *equation*) characteristic of the reaction in question. We observe that on the right side we have a function containing a to the first power, and the reaction is, therefore, said to be *first-order in A*. The proportionality constant k is called the *rate constant* (or *coefficient*) or *specific reaction rate*; clearly it has the dimensions of time^{-1}. Now let us consider the slightly more complex and much more general case of a bimolecular metathetical reaction in which one molecule of A must interact in the rate-determining step with a molecule of B to yield products:

$$A + B \xrightarrow{k} P + (Q) + \cdots \tag{6-3}$$

The rate equation in this instance is given by

$$v = -\frac{da}{dt} = -\frac{db}{dt} = \frac{dp}{dt} = kab \tag{6-4}$$

This reaction is *second-order overall*, for its rate is proportional to the product of two concentration terms (those of a and b, respectively) and, therefore, is first-order in a as well as in b. The rate constant k in this instance has the dimensions of concentration^{-1} time^{-1}. For the special case of two molecules of A interacting to yield products, the rate equation is

$$v = -\frac{da}{dt} = ka^2 \tag{6-5}$$

This form of the equation is also obeyed if we start with identical concentrations of A and B.

If, throughout the course of a rate-determining reaction, the concentration of any one reactant is much larger than that of all the others, its concentration remains virtually constant. This means that, as long as this condition holds, we can recast the rate equations so as to combine this concentration term with the rate constant and in effect reduce the kinetic order of the reaction by one; e.g., for Eq. (6-3) with $b_0 \gg a_0$

$$v \simeq k \, ab_0 = k'a \tag{6-6}$$

Thus the reaction, although still bimolecular, has become kinetically *apparently* or *pseudo* first-order overall. This is an important consideration, not only in chemical kinetics, but especially in enzyme kinetics, where we frequently deal only with initial velocities such that essentially $a = a_0$.

Kinetics of Catalyzed Reactions Most ordinary homogeneous chemical reactions can be accelerated in the presence of an additional reaction component, a *catalyst*, that remains unaltered in concentration during the progress of the reaction. The rate law for a typical reaction involving reactant A and catalyst C at instantaneous concentration a and c, respectively, is given by

$$v = kac = k'a \tag{6-7}$$

where $k' = kc$. The reaction is bimolecular but exhibits pseudo first-order kinetics with the observed first-order rate constant k' equal to the true second-order constant multiplied by the catalyst concentration c.

A somewhat different situation obtains if the catalyst actually combines with a reactant at one stage and is regenerated at a subsequent stage of the reaction:

$$A + C \underset{k_2}{\overset{k_1}{\rightleftharpoons}} X \xrightarrow{k_3} P + C \tag{6-8}$$

The kinetic equations for the formation of A, X, C, and P are[1]

$$-\frac{da}{dt} = k_1 ac - k_2 x \qquad (6\text{-}9a)$$

$$\frac{dx}{dt} = k_1 ac - (k_2 + k_3)x \qquad (6\text{-}9b)$$

$$\frac{dc}{dt} = (k_2 + k_3)x - k_1 ac \qquad (6\text{-}9c)$$

$$\frac{dp}{dt} = k_3 x \qquad (6\text{-}9d)$$

plus the conservation equation

$$c_0 = c + x \qquad (6\text{-}9e)$$

The larger the ratio a_0/c_0, the smaller the initial period during which a steady-state approximation does not hold. Thus we have the equation

$$\frac{dx}{dt} \simeq 0 \simeq k_1 ac - (k_2 + k_3)x \qquad \text{or} \qquad k_1 ac \simeq (k_2 + k_3)x \qquad (6\text{-}10)$$

Substituting in Eq. (6-9e), we obtain

$$x = \frac{k_1 a c_0}{k_1 a + k_2 + k_3} \qquad (6\text{-}11)$$

and substituting this in Eq. (6-9d),

$$v = -\frac{da}{dt} = \frac{dp}{dt} = k_3 x = \frac{k_1 k_3 a c_0}{k_1 a + k_2 + k_3} = \frac{k_3 c_0 a}{(k_2 + k_3)/k_1 + a} \qquad (6\text{-}12)$$

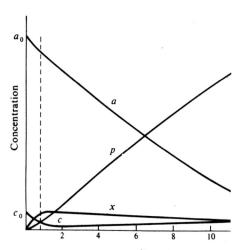

FIGURE 6-1.   Progress Curve for $A + C \underset{k_2}{\overset{k_1}{\rightleftharpoons}} X \overset{k_3}{\rightarrow} P + C$ with $k_1 \simeq k_2 \simeq k_3$; $a_0 \simeq b_0$. — *Adapted from W. W. Cleland.*

---

[1] In this book we use, for convenience's sake, the convention that k_1, k_3, k_5, ..., k_{2n-1} designate the rate constants for the individual steps in the forward direction; k_2, k_4, k_6, ..., k_{2n} those for the corresponding ones in the reverse direction, where $n =$ the step in question. The Enzyme Commission of the International Union of Biochemistry has recommended that k_{+1}, k_{+2}, k_{+3}, ..., k_{+n}, etc., and k_{-1}, k_{-2}, k_{-3}, ..., k_{-n} be used for this purpose. We shall have occasional recourse to this system for didactic purposes.

This reduces to the fundamental equation

$$v = \frac{Va}{K_a + a} \tag{6-13}$$

where $V = k_3 c_0$ and $K_a = (k_2 + k_3)/k_1$. In the integrated form this becomes

$$Vt = K_a \ln \frac{a_0}{a} + (a_0 - a) \tag{6-14}$$

which is the equation for curve a of Fig. 6-1. This rate law for the reaction of one reactant with a recycling catalyst is of mixed first and zero order. Two limiting cases may be distinguished.

$a \gg K_a$. The reaction is zero order with

$$v = V \tag{6-15a}$$

where V is a limiting, *maximal velocity*. If $a = 100K_a$, the deviation from zero order is <1 per cent; even for $a = 10K_a$, the deviation is only 9 per cent.

$a \ll K_a$. The reaction is first order with

$$v = k'a \tag{6-15b}$$

where $k' = V/K_a$. Again if $a = K_a/100$, the deviation from first order is <1 per cent; for $a = K_a/10$, the deviation is <10 per cent.

For all other values of a, and quite in general, the rate law is uniquely determined and the shape of the plot of v versus a, a rectangular hyperbola (see Fig. 6-2), completely defined by the two kinetic constants, or parameters, V and K_a.

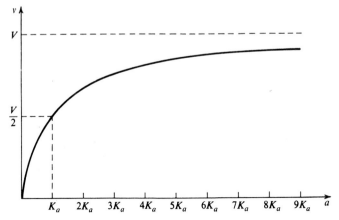

FIGURE 6-2. Graph for the Determination of the Order with Respect to Concentration for $v = \dfrac{Va}{K_a + a}$

The former, as we have already seen, is the limiting velocity as $a \to \infty$ and thus has the dimensions of conc/time; the latter equals that concentration of A, (a_K) for which $v = V/2$. Substituting in Eq. (6-13): $V/2 = Va_K/(K_a + a_K)$ or $K_a + a_K = 2a_K$; it has the dimensions of concentration or M.

KINETICS OF ENZYME-CATALYZED REACTIONS
General Observations

Provided the reaction is performed under carefully controlled conditions, the variation of rate with substrate concentration for a large number of enzyme-catalyzed reactions is that of Eq. (6-13), the so-called *Michaelis-Menten equation*, and can be graphically represented by Fig. 6-2. The two kinetic parameters V and K_a are thus both necessary and sufficient to define the rate law for these reactions explicitly, provided that:

1. They involve only a single substrate, or, in the case of multisubstrate reactions, the concentrations of all other substrates are held constant.

2. True initial velocities v_0 are measured, using different starting concentrations of A. v_0 is defined as the extrapolated rate $(-da/dt)_{t=0} = (+dp/dt)_{t=0}$.

3. $a_0 \gg e_0$, the concentration of enzyme added initially, for all values of a_0, the substrate added, and the same constant concentration e_0 is used in all measurements.[1]

For the cases in which Eq. (6-13) is obeyed, and provided these restrictions are observed, it can always be rewritten for $c_0 \equiv e_0$ and any initial substrate concentration a_0:

$$(v_0)_{a=a_0} = \frac{k_3 e_0 a_0}{K_a + a_0} = e_0 k \tag{6-16}$$

where $k = k_3 a_0/(K_a + a_0)$ and thus $(dv_0/de)_{a=\text{const}} = k$. Therefore v_0 is proportional to enzyme concentration, and this forms the basis of all enzyme assays and permits variation of enzyme concentration during initial rate measurements at the convenience of the investigator, provided the validity of Eq. (6-16) has been established.

4. All other possible variables, i.e., the temperature and the buffer used (with respect to pH, composition, and ionic strength), are defined and maintained constant in all measurements.

It thus becomes of the greatest importance to determine V and K_a as accurately as possible. The hyperbolic plot (Fig. 6-2) is not particularly useful for this pur-

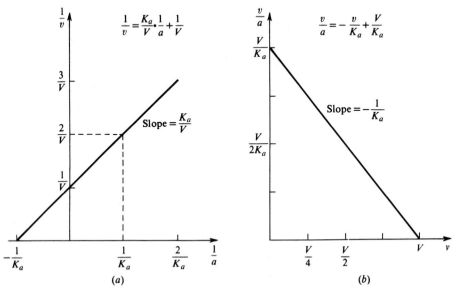

FIGURE 6-3.   Reciprocal Forms of the Rate Equation for an Enzyme-catalyzed Reaction. *(a) Lineweaver and Burk; (b) Eadie, Hofstee.*

[1] In much of the literature S, for substrate, is used rather than A. Our expressions are easily converted by appropriate substitutions of s for a, s_0 for a_0, etc.

pose, because it involves the determination of an asymptote as $a \rightarrow \infty$, a notoriously difficult task. Methods for recasting Eq. (6-13) in linear forms, which transform this equation of a hyperbola into one of a straight line, are possible, however. They are due to Lineweaver and Burk, and Eadie and Hofstee, and are given below as Eqs. (6-17) and (6-18) and Fig. 6-3, respectively; they are frequently referred to by the names of these investigators.

Double reciprocal form of Lineweaver and Burk — plot $1/v$ versus $1/a$:

$$\frac{1}{v} = \frac{K_a}{V}\frac{1}{a} + \frac{1}{V} \qquad (6\text{-}17)$$

Single reciprocal forms of Eadie and Hofstee — plot v/a versus v:

$$\frac{v}{a} = -\frac{v}{K_a} + \frac{V}{K_a} \qquad (6\text{-}18a)$$

also

$$\frac{a}{v} = \frac{K_a}{V} + \frac{a}{V} \qquad (6\text{-}18b)$$

Their use for the determination of V and K_a is indicated in the figure. Plotting of data by Eq. (6-18) appears to have some advantages, but determination of actual values for V and K_a requires statistical treatment, preferably by means of a computer program.

Although V has a well-defined meaning, both operationally and physically, as the extrapolated maximum velocity under the specified conditions, the same cannot be said for K_a. Operationally it is defined in terms of V as stated above:

$$K_a = (a)_{v=V/2} \qquad (6\text{-}19)$$

but its physical significance depends on the mechanism, which first has to be established for each reaction by other means. Experimentally values of K_a vary generally between 10^{-2} and 10^{-5} M for most single-substrate reactions. In bisubstrate cases, values as low as 10^{-8} or 10^{-9} M are occasionally observed.

Equation (6-16) allows us to define a number of terms frequently found in the literature.

An *enzyme unit* is now usually defined as the amount of substrate converted to product per unit time under certain specified conditions of pH, substrate concentration, etc., because, as stated above, the concentration of enzyme is proportional to its catalytic activity; e.g.,

Enzyme unit = mole product formed/min
Specific enzymatic activity = units/mg enzyme protein
$\qquad\qquad$ = moles product/min/mg protein
Total enzymatic activity = specific activity × total amount of enzymatic protein
$\qquad\qquad$ = total number of enzyme units

$$\text{Purification (enrichment)} = \frac{\text{specific activity (step } n)}{\text{specific activity (reference)}}$$

$$\text{Yield (recovery)} = \frac{\text{total activity (step } n)}{\text{total activity (reference)}}$$

Catalytic constant = moles product formed/min/mole pure enzyme

This follows directly from Eq. (6-16), but it requires (1) a pure enzyme and (2) a knowledge of its molecular weight. If (2) is unavailable, the catalytic constant is frequently expressed per 100,000 g of enzyme.

Turnover number = catalytic constant/number of active centers = V/c_0

It is equal to the catalytic constant provided the enzyme is monomeric and each enzyme molecule can interact with only one substrate molecule at any one time; many enzymes are, however, polymeric and contain more than one independent, catalytically active site. Turnover numbers for enzymes can vary all the way from 10^2 to 10^6.

One-substrate Reactions

In discussing mechanisms of this type, we are concerned with those in which either a single substrate participates exclusively or the much more common case where the second participating reactant is present in such a large and constant concentration as to be kinetically without significance. The latter includes the large class of reactions catalyzed by hydrolases, of many transferases in the presence of a large amount of acceptor, of many isomerases and lyases (i.e., the enzymes of classes 2, 3, 4, and 5 of the classification scheme on page 175), a very large number of instances indeed.

The Michaelis-Menten Mechanism. The simplest mechanism that can be written is the one already described — Eq. (6-8) with $C \equiv E$ for enzyme — i.e., the reversible formation of a complex or compound between A and E, followed by the virtually irreversible breakdown of this complex to yield product and regenerate the free enzyme. In the special[1] (and infrequent) case that $k_3 \ll k_2$, Eq. (6-12) reduces to

$$v_0 \simeq \frac{k_3 e_0 a_0}{k_2/k_1 + a_0} = \frac{V a_0}{\bar{K}_a + a_0} \tag{6-12a}$$

where $\bar{K}_a = k_2/k_1$, the dissociation constant for the reaction

$$A + E \underset{k_2}{\overset{k_1}{\rightleftharpoons}} X$$

In this instance, originally discussed by Michaelis and Menten in 1913, K_a, the kinetically defined *Michaelis constant*, equals $\bar{K}_a$ the dissociation constant of the enzyme-substrate complex.[2]

Reversible Formation of the Enzyme Substrate Complex. Let us now remove the restriction that the complex X breaks down irreversibly and instead admit

---

[1] In the case of bisubstrate enzymes with the second substrate in large excess, Eq. (6-12) is still obeyed. But in those instances where the reaction proceeds with an ordered release of products, i.e.

$$E + A - B \underset{k_2}{\overset{k_1}{\rightleftharpoons}} E \cdot AB \underset{k_4}{\overset{k_3}{\rightleftharpoons}} EA + B \qquad EA \xrightarrow{k_5(H_2O),etc,} E + P$$

$K_a = [(k_2 + k_3) k_5]/[(k_3 + k_5) k_1]$. This equals $\bar{K}_a$ only if $k_2 = k_5$ regardless of k_3, or if $k_3 \ll k_2$ and $k_3 \ll k_5$.

[2] The Enzyme Commission has recommended that K_M be used for the kinetically determined Michaelis constant and that K_s be used for the enzyme-substrate dissociation constant. This leads to cumbersome and ambiguous expressions in cases where more than one substrate participates in an enzymatic reaction.

the possibility that it can also be formed from the product side. Thus we have

$$A + E \underset{k_2}{\overset{k_1}{\rightleftharpoons}} X \underset{k_4}{\overset{k_3}{\rightleftharpoons}} E + P \tag{6-20a}$$

$$-\frac{da}{dt} = k_1 ae - k_2 x \tag{6-20b}$$

$$\frac{dx}{dt} = (k_1 a + k_4 p)e - (k_2 + k_3)x \tag{6-20c}$$

$$\frac{de}{dt} = (k_2 + k_3)x - (k_1 a + k_4 p)e \tag{6-20d}$$

$$\frac{dp}{dt} = k_3 x - k_4 pe \tag{6-20e}$$

$$e_0 = e + x \tag{6-20f}$$

In the steady state, which obtains when $e_0 \ll a$ and/or p, $dx/dt \simeq de/dt \simeq 0$ and

$$(k_1 a + k_4 p)e = (k_2 + k_3)x \tag{6-20c'}$$

which with Eq. (6-20f) gives us two equations in e and x:

$$x = \frac{(k_1 a + k_4 p)e_0}{D} \qquad e = \frac{(k_2 + k_3)e_0}{D} \tag{6-21}$$

where $D = k_1 a + k_4 p + k_2 + k_3$. Substituting these values into either Eq. (6-20b) or (6-20e), we obtain

$$v = \frac{-da}{dt} = \frac{dp}{dt} = \frac{(k_1 k_3 a - k_2 k_4 p)e_0}{(k_2 + k_3) + k_1 a + k_4 p} \tag{6-22}$$

Equation (6-22) reduces to the Michaelis-Menten equation in terms of the initial velocity v_1 for the forward reaction, i.e., Eq. (6-23), if we set $p = 0$, and to that for the reverse reaction with initial velocity v_2 if we set $a = 0$:

$$(v_1)_{p=0} = \frac{k_1 k_3 ae_0}{(k_2 + k_3) + k_1 a} = \frac{V_1 a}{K_a + a} = \frac{V_1}{(K_a/a) + 1} \tag{6-23a}$$

$$(v_2)_{a=0} = \frac{k_2 k_4 pe_0}{(k_2 + k_3) + k_4 p} = \frac{k_2 e_0 p}{(k_2 + k_3)/k_4 + p} = \frac{V_2 p}{K_p + p} = \frac{V_2}{(K_p/p) + 1} \tag{6-23b}$$

We can also, in this instance, calculate the values of the individual rate constants from the experimentally determined parameters K_a, K_p, V_1, V_2, provided e_0 is known. It must be expressed as "catalytic sites per liter":

$$k_1 = \frac{V_1 + V_2}{K_a e_0} \qquad k_2 = \frac{V_2}{e_0} \qquad k_3 = \frac{V_1}{e_0} \qquad k_4 = \frac{V_1 + V_2}{K_p e_0} \tag{6-24}$$

By definition $p_{eq}/a_{eq} \equiv K_{eq}$, the equilibrium constant for the overall reaction $A \rightleftharpoons B$, and at equilibrium $v = 0$; thus

$$K_{eq} = \frac{k_1 k_3}{k_2 k_4} \tag{6-25}$$

the equilibrium constant for step 1 divided by that for step 2.

We can cast the rate equations for this mechanism — Eq. (6-22) — into another useful form. In general we can write

$$v = \frac{(N_1 a - N_2 p)e_0}{C_0 + C_1 a + C_2 p} \tag{6-26}$$

where in this instance $V_1 = N_1/C_1$; $V_2 = N_2/C_2$; $K_a = C_0/C_1$; $K_p = C_0/C_2$; $K_{eq} = N_1/N_2$. Now multiply by $N_2/C_1 C_2$ and obtain

$$v = \frac{V_1 V_2 a - V_1 V_2 p/K_{eq}}{K_a V_2 + a V_2 + V_1 p/K_{eq}} \tag{6-27}$$

This is the general form of the rate equation, and equations similar to it are obtained, not only for more complicated one-substrate or pseudo one-substrate mechanisms, but for mechanisms involving two or three reactants as well. It describes the effect of reactant concentration on rate, not only at the start of the reaction in the complete absence of P (in the forward direction) or of A (in the reverse direction), but at any time during the approach to equilibrium.

It must, of course, reduce to Eq. (6-23a) and (6-23b) under appropriate restrictions. The first case, $p = 0$, is self-evident. All we have to do is set $p = 0$ (provided that $V_2 \neq 0$) and then cancel out V_2. On the other hand, for the case $a = 0$ we obtain, after multiplying both numerator and denominator by K_{eq}/V_1,

$$v = \frac{V_2 p}{K_{eq} K_a V_2/V_1 + p} \tag{6-28}$$

which at first glance is not equal to Eq. (6-23b). But from the definitions given above — Eq. (6-26) — we see that

$$\frac{K_{eq} K_a V_2}{V_1} = \frac{C_0}{C_2} = K_p \tag{6-29}$$

or

$$K_{eq} = \frac{V_1 K_p}{V_2 K_a} \tag{6-30}$$

the so-called *Haldane relationship*. Now substituting K_p for the constant numerator term in Eq. (6-28), we obtain Eq. (6-23b).

The Haldane relationship is an exceedingly interesting one, because it states that the kinetic parameters of a reversible enzyme-catalyzed reaction are not independent of one another and are limited by the thermodynamic equilibrium constant for the overall reaction; this is, of course, equivalent to saying that the rate constants for specific steps must also exhibit a definite relationship with the overall equilibrium constant — Eq. (6-25).

As the concentration of product increases, most enzymatic reactions slow down; this is due to the phenomenon of product inhibition. To see this most clearly, let us rewrite the rate equation once again in a slightly different form:

$$v = \frac{K_p V_1 a - K_a V_2 p}{K_a K_p + K_p a + K_a p} = v_1 - v_2 \tag{6-31a}$$

where v_1 is the velocity in the forward direction, v_2 the velocity in the reverse direction:

$$v_1 = \frac{V_1 a}{K_a + a + pK_a/K_p} \qquad (6\text{-}31b)$$

$$\frac{1}{v_1} = \frac{K_a}{V_1} \frac{1}{a}\left(1 + \frac{p}{K_p}\right) + \frac{1}{V_1}$$

$$v_2 = \frac{-V_2 p}{K_p + p + aK_p/K_a} \quad \text{(the minus sign indicates direction only)} \qquad (6\text{-}31c)$$

$$\frac{1}{v_2} = \frac{K_p}{V_2} \frac{1}{p}\left(1 + \frac{a}{K_a}\right) + \frac{1}{V_2}$$

Once again we find a completely symmetrical set of equations, which now state that an enzymatic reaction slows down as equilibrium is approached, not only by virtue of the thermodynamic back reaction — the negative numerator term in Eq. (6-31) — but also because, as p increases, an increasing proportion of the enzyme is immobilized as an EP complex. This kinetic effect of product inhibition is thus an intrinsic property of any realistic, i.e., reversible, mechanism of enzymatic catalysis. Its effect on a double reciprocal plot is shown in Fig. 6-4. We observe that, compared with Fig. 6-3a and Eq. (6-17), the intercept, i.e., $1/V$ is unaffected but the slope is increased by the constant factor $(1 + p/K_p)$. Behavior of this type is called *competitive inhibition*. It results whenever the inhibitor combines only with the same form of the enzyme as does the substrate under investigation, and the enzyme can exist in just two complex forms, ES and EI. In the present instance both P and A combine with E, but neither does with X.

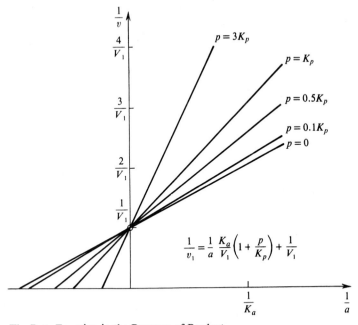

FIGURE 6-4. The Rate Equation in the Presence of Product.

Reversible Formation of Two Complexes. It is not very realistic to expect that an enzyme capable of forming a complex or compound with A and capable of converting it reversibly to P is unable to form a reversible complex with P as well. A mechanism that takes this objection into account is given by

$$A + E \underset{k_2}{\overset{k_1}{\rightleftharpoons}} X \underset{k_4}{\overset{k_3}{\rightleftharpoons}} Y \underset{k_6}{\overset{k_5}{\rightleftharpoons}} E + P \tag{6-32}$$

The pertinent steady-state and conservation equations are

$$v = \frac{dp}{dt} = k_5 y - k_6 pe \tag{6-33a}$$

$$\frac{dx}{dt} = k_1 ae - (k_2 + k_3)x + k_4 y \tag{6-33b}$$

$$\frac{dy}{dt} = k_6 pe + k_3 x - (k_4 + k_5)y \tag{6-33c}$$

$$e_0 = e + x + y \tag{6-33d}$$

In the steady state $dx/dt = dy/dt = de/dt = 0$. This yields three linear equations to be solved for three unknowns and substituted into the velocity equation (6-33a). This can be done by solving a third-order determinant (a determinant of order n for n forms of the enzyme in more general mechanisms) or more simply by a direct graphic method, due to King and Altman.

First, we write a simple geometric figure describing the mechanism; in this instance

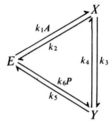

observing that the arrow heads for consecutive steps, $1 \to 3 \to 5$ (forward) and $6 \to 4 \to 2$ (reverse), are always made to point in the same direction.

Second, we write down all possible patterns (consisting of a number of lines one fewer than the number of enzyme forms; two in our case) that interconvert the possible enzyme forms; any closed loops are forbidden and must be eliminated. In our case we have

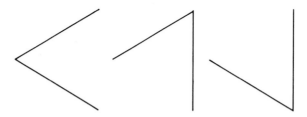

Third, we write down, for each enzyme form, an expression of the following type: form/e_0 = [sum, for all patterns, of the product of the rate constant (multiplied by concentration terms, if any) on the path along the pattern leading to that form]/Σ, where Σ represents the sum of all numerator terms. In our case we have

$$\frac{e}{e_0} = \frac{k_2 k_5 + k_2 k_4 + k_3 k_5}{\Sigma} \tag{6-34a}$$

$$\frac{x}{e_0} = \frac{k_1 k_5 a + k_1 k_4 a + k_4 k_6 p}{\Sigma} \tag{6-34b}$$

$$\frac{y}{e_0} = \frac{k_2 k_6 p + k_1 k_3 a + k_3 k_6 p}{\Sigma} \tag{6-34c}$$

Σ = sum of all numerator terms

This, then, provides us with a set of partition equations that define the proportion of enzyme in any one form in terms of the individual rate constants. This is useful, not only for the present purpose, but for determinations of inhibition patterns, of isotope exchange equilibria and rates, etc.

We now substitute these partition equations into the rate equation (6-33a) and obtain

$$v = \frac{(k_1 k_3 k_5 a - k_2 k_4 k_6 p) e_0}{k_2 k_5 + k_2 k_4 + k_3 k_5 + k_1 (k_3 + k_4 + k_5) a + k_6 (k_2 + k_3 + k_4) p} \tag{6-35}$$

In coefficient form this can be rewritten as

$$v = \frac{(N_1 a - N_2 p) e_0}{C_0 + C_1 a + C_2 p}$$

which is identical to Eq. (6-26), derived for a simpler mechanism. Thus no distinction between the two mechanisms can be made on the basis of steady-state rate measurements; indeed it can be demonstrated quite rigorously that the introduction of any number of unimolecular steps between different enzyme forms, all containing the same number of substrate (or product) molecules, does not alter the form of the rate equation, whether expressed in the form of kinetic parameters (V_i's and K_i's) or coefficients. What does change is the composition of these parameters or coefficients in terms of individual rate constants.

Formation of a Covalent Intermediate. As discussed in Chap. 7, there is now compelling evidence for the formation of acyl-enzyme compounds, i.e., covalent enzyme-reactant derivatives, in the case of several hydrolytic enzymes of different specificities, e.g., chymotrypsin, trypsin, cholinesterase, and several phosphatases.

$$E + A - B \underset{k_2}{\overset{k_1}{\rightleftharpoons}} (E \cdot A - B) \underset{k_4}{\overset{k_3}{\rightleftharpoons}} EQ' + P$$

$$EQ' \underset{k_6}{\overset{k_5}{\rightleftharpoons}} EQ \underset{k_8}{\overset{k_7}{\rightleftharpoons}} E + Q \tag{6-36}$$

As long as K_{eq} is large, the complete rate equation becomes

$$v = \frac{Va}{K_a + a + (\bar{K}_a/\bar{K}_p) p + (K_a/\bar{K}_q) q + (1/\bar{K}_p) ap + (K_a/\bar{K}_p \bar{K}_q) pq} \tag{6-37}$$

If Q is present, but P is not, this equation reduces to

$$v = \frac{Va}{K_a(1 + q/\bar{K}_q) + a} \tag{6-38a}$$

while if P is present, but not Q, it becomes

$$v = \frac{Va}{K_a[1 + (\bar{K}_a/K_a \bar{K}_p) p] + a(1 + p/\bar{K}_p)} \tag{6-38b}$$

Therefore addition of the second product gives rise to competitive inhibition, since it affects the slope of the reciprocal plot only (see Fig. 6-4), but addition of the first product affects both slope and intercept. We call this behavior *noncompetitive inhibition*. Rate measurements with product present thus allow determination of the order of release of reactants as well as of the constants V, K_a, $\overline{K}_a$, $\overline{K}_p$, and $\overline{K}_q$. Whereas $\overline{K}_a = k_2/k_1$,

$$K_a = \frac{(k_2 + k_3)\,k_5 k_7}{[k_1 k_3(k_5 + k_6 + k_7) + k_5 k_7]}$$

and thus can be larger or smaller than $\overline{K}_a$, depending on the actual values of the rate constants. $\overline{K}_q$ will equal k_7/k_8 provided that k_5 greatly exceeds k_6, which appears to hold for all known cases; $\overline{K}_p$ equals k_3/k_4.

Bisubstrate Reactions   *General Considerations.* Most enzymic reactions involve more than one substrate, and any accurate description must take account of this fact. Consider the general equation for a reversible reaction of this type:

$$A + B \rightleftharpoons P + Q \tag{6-39}$$

If we measure the initial velocity as a function of the concentration of either of the two substrates (e.g., a), then called the *variable* substrate, it obeys the Michaelis-Menten equation — (6-13), (6-17), and (6-18) — provided that (1) the same restrictions are observed as discussed on pages 153 to 154 and (2) that the second substrate (here b, the *fixed* substrate) is held constant at a concentration $b_1 \gg e_0$. If a similar set of measurements is then carried out at a different concentration $b_2 \gg e_0$, again the variation of the initial velocity as a function of a follows the Michaelis-Menten equation, but now it usually yields a different value for the two kinetic parameters, V and K_a; they are, therefore, functions of the concentration of b as well. In general the pattern of the reciprocal plots is that of two families of straight lines — Eqs. (6-39) and (6-40) and Fig. 6-5 — since, of course, the symmetry of Eq. (6-39) demands that the same consideration hold for an inversion of fixed and variable substrate and for the reverse reaction as well. In general we use A, B; a, b; K_a, $\overline{K}_a$; k_{2n-1}; V_1, K_1 for substrates; their concentrations; their Michaelis (K_a) and dissociation constants

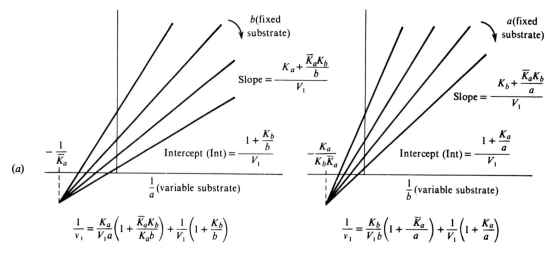

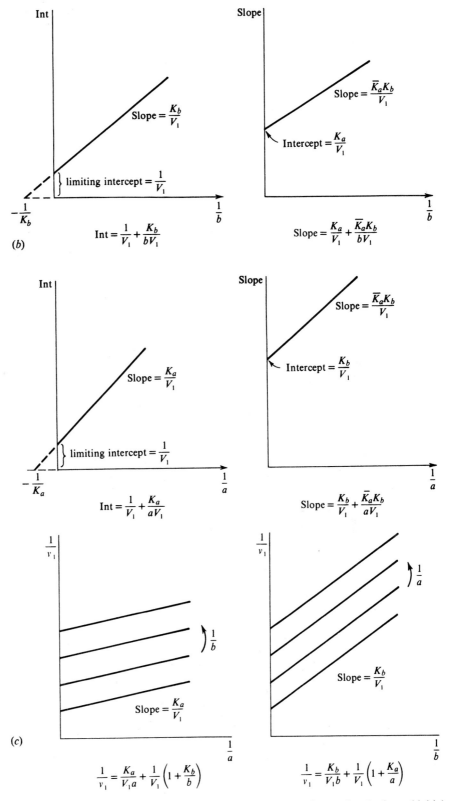

FIGURE 6-5. Reciprocal Plots for Bisubstrate Reactions [Eq. (6-40)]. *(a)* Primary plots (reciprocal initial velocity) versus 1/(variable substrate); *(b)* secondary plots (intercepts and slopes of primary plots) versus 1/(fixed substrate); *(c)* primary plots for $K_a K_b = 0$ (ping-pong mechanism), i.e., $V_1/v_1 = 1 + K_a/a + K_b/b$. [Eq. (6-43).]

$(\overline{K}_a)$; individual rate constants; the maximal velocity and the equilibrium constant for the overall reaction all in the forward direction, and P, Q; p, q; K_p, $\overline{K}_p$; k_{2n}; V_2, K_2 for the corresponding parameters in the reverse direction:[1]

$$v_1 = \frac{V_1\, ab}{\overline{K}_a K_b + K_b a + K_a b + ab}$$ (6-40a)

$$\frac{V_1}{v_1} = 1 + \frac{K_a}{a} + \frac{K_b}{b} + \frac{\overline{K}_a K_b}{ab}$$ (6-40b)

TABLE 6-1. Comparison of Different Symbolisms of Bisubstrate Kinetics

Our designation	Meaning	Dalziel	Alberty	Bloomfield et al.	Cleland	Enzyme Commission
K_a	Limiting Michaelis constant for A	$\dfrac{\phi_1}{\phi_0}$	K_A	$\dfrac{K_{AB}}{K_B}$	K_a	K_m^A
K_b	Limiting Michaelis constant for B	$\dfrac{\phi_2}{\phi_0}$	K_B	$\dfrac{K_{AB}}{K_A}$	K_b	K_m^B
$\overline{K}_a$	Dissociation constant for A	$\dfrac{\phi_{12}}{\phi_2}$	$\dfrac{K_{AB}}{K_B}$	K_A	K_{ia}	K_s^A
V_1	Limiting maximum velocity	$\dfrac{e}{\phi_0}$	V_f	V_{AB}	V_1	V
$\dfrac{V_1}{e_0}$	Turnover number	$\dfrac{1}{\phi_0}$	$\dfrac{V_1}{E_0}$	$\dfrac{V_{AB}}{E_0}$	$\dfrac{V_1}{E_t}$	None

We see that for the two-substrate case the kinetic equation requires a total of four kinetic parameters: V_1, K_a, K_b, and $\overline{K}_a$ or K_{ia}; this set is both necessary and sufficient for a unique description of the kinetics. Compare this with the one-substrate case, where just two parameters are required.

Ordinarily one determines $n \times m$ values of the initial velocity v_1, corresponding to n different concentrations of a, and m of b (with $n \simeq m$), and then plots them in the manner indicated in Fig. 6-5a(1) and (2) as functions of $1/a$ and $1/b$ (see Dalziel equation, Table 6-1). The slopes and intercepts of these *primary* plots are then replotted as shown in Fig. 6-5b to give four *secondary* plots: two — 6-5b(1) and (2) — the *intercept* replots, with identical intercepts $= 1/V_1$; and the other two — 6-5b(3) and (4) — the two *slope* replots, with identical slopes $= \overline{K}_a K_b/V_1$. *In toto* the four replots provide the investigator with 2×4 equations in the four unknowns, the kinetic parameters; he therefore has available a check on the internal consistency of his experimental measurements.

The majority of the enzymatic reactions that have been studied in detail appear to fall into just a few categories:[2]

---

[1] Other conventions have also been used. Their relationship in terms of Eqs. (6-39) and (6-40) are shown in Table 6-1.

[2] We show three methods of representing the reaction mechanism, including the graphic shorthand notation due to Cleland.

1. *Ping-pong* mechanisms of the type

$$
\begin{array}{ccccc}
A & & P \quad B & & Q \\
\downarrow & & \uparrow \quad \downarrow & & \uparrow \\
\hline
E & (AE \ PE') & E' & (E'B \ EQ) & E
\end{array}
$$

or

$$A + E \underset{k_2}{\overset{k_1}{\rightleftharpoons}} (AE \rightleftharpoons PE') \underset{k_4}{\overset{k_3}{\rightleftharpoons}} P + E'$$

$$B + E' \underset{k_6}{\overset{k_5}{\rightleftharpoons}} (BE' \rightleftharpoons QE) \underset{k_8}{\overset{k_7}{\rightleftharpoons}} Q + E$$

or

$$
\begin{array}{c}
(EA \rightleftharpoons PE') \\
{}_{k_1 A}\nearrow \quad \searrow {}^{k_3} \\
{}_{k_2}\swarrow \quad \nwarrow {}^{k_4 P} \\
E \quad\quad\quad\quad E' \\
{}_{k_8 Q}\searrow \quad \nearrow {}^{k_6} \\
{}_{k_7}\nwarrow \quad \swarrow {}^{k_5 B} \\
(EQ \rightleftharpoons BE')
\end{array}
$$

(6-41)

Here products are formed prior to reaction with the second substrate at the expense of conversion of the enzyme (or more usually of a coenzyme or prosthetic group tightly linked to the enzyme) from a form E to a form E'. Note that P is the designation of the product form of A, and Q of that of B.

Some important reactions appear to obey this mechanism; among them are those catalyzed by various pyridoxal phosphate (pyr-CHO) requiring transaminases (amino-transferases) (see page 203) and the dehydrogenation reactions catalyzed by some flavoproteins (see page 215). In the first case,

$$
\begin{array}{ccccc}
R_1CHCO_2^- + Enz\text{-pyrCHO} & \rightleftharpoons EA \rightleftharpoons E'P \rightleftharpoons & Enz\text{-pyrCH}_2NH_3^+ + R_1\overset{O}{\overset{\|}{C}}CO_2^- \\
{}^{|}_{+NH_3} & & \\
A & E & E' & P
\end{array}
$$

$$
\begin{array}{ccccc}
R_2\overset{\|}{\underset{O}{C}}CO_2^- + Enz\text{-pyrCH}_2NH_3^+ & \rightleftharpoons E'B \rightleftharpoons EQ \rightleftharpoons & Enz\text{-pyrCHO} + R_2CHCO_2^- \\
& & & {}^{|}_{N^+H_3} \\
B & E' & E & Q
\end{array}
$$

(6-42a)

in the second,

$$
\begin{array}{ccccc}
RH_2 + fp & \rightleftharpoons EA \rightleftharpoons E'P \rightleftharpoons & fpH_2 + R \\
A & E & E' & P
\end{array}
$$

$$
\begin{array}{ccccc}
Ox + fpH_2 & \rightleftharpoons E'B \rightleftharpoons EQ \rightleftharpoons & fp + OxH_2 \\
B & E' & E & Q
\end{array}
$$

(6-42b)

where RH_2 is an oxidizable substrate and Ox an electron acceptor or oxidant.

Kinetic analysis shows that for a mechanism of this kind the last term (i.e., the one in $a \cdot b$) is missing and rate equations are of the type:

$$\frac{V_1}{v_1} = 1 + \frac{K_a}{a} + \frac{K_b}{b}$$

This means that the double reciprocal plot exhibits an unusual feature: all plots of $1/v$ versus either $1/a$ or $1/b$ as variable substrates are parallel lines of identical slope, regardless of the concentration of the fixed substrate — Fig. 6-5c(1) and (2). Consideration of the complete rate equation for the reversible overall reaction shows another characteristic of this mechanism: Q (and not the product P) is a competitive inhibitor (affects slope of double reciprocal plot only, leaving identical intercept) for A, and P (not Q) for B.

2. *Ordered* mechanism of the type

$$
\begin{array}{cccccc}
A & B & & P & Q \\
\downarrow & \downarrow & & \uparrow & \uparrow \\
\hline
E & AE & (AEB \ QEP) & QE & E
\end{array}
$$

or

$$A + E \underset{k_2}{\overset{k_1}{\rightleftharpoons}} AE$$

$$AE + B \underset{k_4}{\overset{k_3}{\rightleftharpoons}} (AEB \rightleftharpoons QEP) \underset{k_6}{\overset{k_5}{\rightleftharpoons}} QE + P \qquad \text{or}$$

$$QE \underset{k_8}{\overset{k_7}{\rightleftharpoons}} E + Q$$

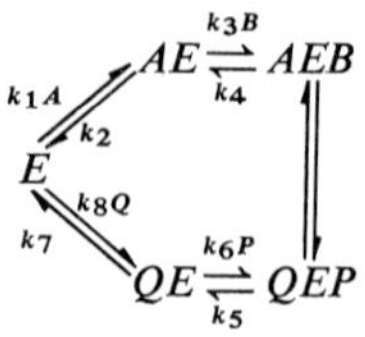

$$(6\text{-}43)$$

Here A and its product Q are called the *leading* or *obligatory* reactants and are usually the coenzymes in the reaction. Ordered mechanisms give rise to the rate laws of Eqs. (6-39) or (6-40), but because of their symmetry it is not immediately obvious which substrate is to be identified as A, the leading substrate. This identification can, however, usually be accomplished by means of binding studies; coenzymes, if they participate in a reaction, are usually bound much more tightly than their respective substrates. Furthermore only A, and not B, is competitively inhibited by its own product (Q).

Among the most important reactions obeying this mechanism are those catalyzed by a variety of NAD- and NADP-requiring dehydrogenases (see page 212). The reaction becomes

$$\text{NAD}^+ + E \rightleftharpoons \text{NAD}^+ \cdot E$$
$$A \qquad\qquad EA$$
$$\text{NAD}^+ \cdot E + \text{R}_1\text{R}_2\,\text{CHOH} \rightleftharpoons (\text{NAD}^+ \cdot E \cdot \text{CHOHR}_1\text{R}_2 \rightleftharpoons$$
$$B$$

$$\text{NADH} \cdot E \cdot \text{COR}_1\text{R}_2) \rightleftharpoons \text{NADH} \cdot E + \text{R}_1\text{R}_2\,\text{CO}$$
$$P$$

$$\text{NADH} \cdot E \rightleftharpoons E + \text{NADH}$$
$$QE \qquad\qquad Q$$

$$(6\text{-}44)$$

3. *Random Mechanisms.* For a mechanism in which all possible binary enzyme substrate complexes are formed rapidly and reversibly, the only slow step is the interconversion of the two ternary complexes:

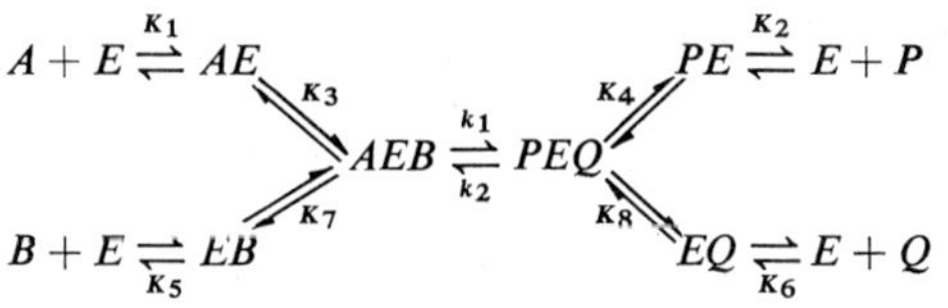

$$(6\text{-}45)$$

The rate law is given by Eq. (6-40) with

$$V_1 = k_1 e_0 \qquad\qquad V_2 = k_2 e_0$$

$$\bar{K}_a = K_1 \quad \bar{K}_b = K_5 \qquad \bar{K}_p = K_2 \quad \bar{K}_q = K_6$$

$$K_a = K_7 \quad K_b = K_3 \qquad K_p = K_8 \quad K_q = K_4$$

$$(6\text{-}46)$$

Many kinases (phosphotransferases), enzymes that catalyze the reaction $A\!-\!H + RO\!-\!PO_3^= \rightarrow APO_3^= + ROH$, appear to obey this mechanism. A good example is creatine kinase.

Enzyme
Activation

By an *activator* we mean a small molecule, frequently an inorganic ion, which is required for, or which at least stimulates, the activity of an enzyme but which, unlike a coenzyme, is not itself an explicit participant in the reaction. Although many kinetic schemes involving the interactions of such activators with various components of the system may be written, only a limited number appear to be of practical importance. We shall restrict our attention to the two most common ones: obligatory (or exclusive) interaction with the free enzyme and obligatory (or exclusive) interaction with the free substrate.

Interaction with the Free Enzyme. Many enzymes contain metal ions as part of their active sites. Among them we may mention the Zn^{+2} (or Co^{+2}) in carboxypeptidase and carbonic anhydrase, Mg^{+2} (or Mn^{+2}) in enolase and phosphoglucomutase, Mn^{+2} in isocitric dehydrogenase, malic enzyme, etc. Other enzymes appear to require the presence of a monovalent one, such as Na^{+}, K^{+}, or NH_4^{+}, for the stabilization of the particular conformation responsible for maximal catalytic activity.

One possible reaction path for activation by a dissociable metal is

$$E + M \underset{k_2}{\overset{k_1}{\rightleftharpoons}} EM$$

$$S + EM \underset{k_4}{\overset{k_3}{\rightleftharpoons}} SEM \underset{k_6}{\overset{k_5}{\rightleftharpoons}} PEM \underset{k_8}{\overset{k_7}{\rightleftharpoons}} EM + P \qquad (6\text{-}47)$$

The analogy between this mechanism and that of Eq. (6-43) is only apparent; they become kinetically equivalent only if the EM complexes with which E and P combine are not identical. The rate law for this mechanism is given by

$$v_1 = \frac{V_1 sm}{\bar{K}_m K_s + K_s m + sm} \qquad v_2 = \frac{V_2 pm}{\bar{K}_m K_p + K_p m + pm} \qquad (6\text{-}48)$$

The absence of denominator terms in s and p alone distinguishes this mechanism from those described earlier.

Interaction with the Substrate. Most, if not all, of the important reactions involving nucleoside di- and triphosphates require the simultaneous participation of a divalent metal ion (usually Mg^{+2}) in stoichiometric amounts. Investigation has shown that the probable mechanism for this activation is the obligate combination of the cation with the substrate prior to its interaction with the enzyme. Thus this substrate-metal complex rather than the free substrate itself is the true reactant. The reaction scheme is

$$S + M \underset{k_2}{\overset{k_1}{\rightleftharpoons}} SM$$

$$SM + E \underset{k_4}{\overset{k_3}{\rightleftharpoons}} (ESM \rightleftharpoons EPM) \underset{k_6}{\overset{k_5}{\rightleftharpoons}} E + PM \qquad (6\text{-}49)$$

$$PM \underset{k_8}{\overset{k_7}{\rightleftharpoons}} P + M$$

This type of mechanism is handled by using the concentration of SM instead of the concentration of free or total S in all appropriate rate equations.

Enzyme
Inhibition

General Principles. A substance that decreases the rate of a biochemical reaction is called an *inhibitor*. Classically the study of inhibitory effects on isolated enzymatic reactions and on metabolic sequences in general has been of the greatest importance in establishing the nature of the free reactants, the nature of their binding site on the enzyme, and the specificity and mechanism of the reaction. In the cell, inhibition of key reactions by substances that may be products of the reaction itself or of the same (or even of a different) metabolic sequence provide a ready and delicately poised control mechanism for the maintenance of a relatively constant intracellular environment and for its response to alterations in the extended milieu. Finally such selective inhibitions by natural or synthetic compounds (antimetabolites) must form the base of at least one broad approach toward a rational pharmacology and chemotherapy, especially if we take into account the following facts: (1) advantage can be taken of the differences in specificities of different enzymes such that the " unnatural " products of a proximal may become the inhibitors of a distal reaction, a process that has been called "lethal synthesis" by Peters; (2) enzymes are themselves also products of metabolism, and their synthesis may be similarly manipulated.

The kinetics of most enzymic reactions in the presence of varying concentrations of inhibitors are as follows. The most characteristic features are linear double reciprocal plots of $1/v$ versus $1/s$, but the slope, the intercept, or both are altered by factors $(1 + i/K_{ij})$, where i is the concentration of inhibitor and K_{ij} is a characteristic constant. The first case is called *competitive*, the second *uncompetitive*, and the third *noncompetitive*. Replots of slopes or intercepts are usually linear, but occasionally they may be parabolic, hyperbolic, or of even greater complexity. *Dead-end inhibitors* are compounds that cannot be converted to products. They usually produce linear inhibition, unless the inhibitor combines twice with the same enzyme form or unless it is a product that combines "downstream" and backs up the reactant(s) to its point of combination with the enzyme. For a single substrate all three inhibition types may be explained in terms of the following mechanism:

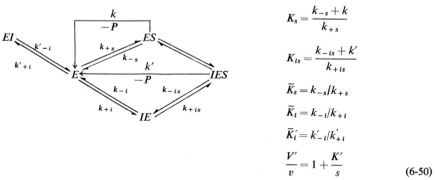

$$K_s = \frac{k_{-s}+k}{k_{+s}}$$

$$K_{is} = \frac{k_{-is}+k'}{k_{+is}}$$

$$\bar{K}_s = k_{-s}/k_{+s}$$

$$\bar{K}_i = k_{-i}/k_{+i}$$

$$\bar{K}_i' = k'_{-i}/k'_{+i}$$

$$\frac{V'}{v} = 1 + \frac{K'}{s} \qquad (6\text{-}50)$$

Inhibition type	Conditions	Effects on k's and K's	Intercept $= 1/V'$	Slope $= K'/V'$	K'
Competitive	*IES, IE* not formed	$K_{is}=\bar{K}_i=\infty$ $k'\simeq0$	$\dfrac{1}{V}=\dfrac{1}{k_0^e}$	$\dfrac{K_s}{V}(1+i/\bar{K}_i')$	$K_s(1+i/\bar{K}_i')$
Uncompetitive	*EI* not formed *IES* does not break down	$\bar{K}_i'=\infty$ $i/\bar{K}_i\ll1; k\simeq0$	$\dfrac{(1+iK_s/K_{is}\bar{K}_i)}{V}$	$\dfrac{K_s}{V}$	$\dfrac{K_s}{(1+iK_s/K_{is}\bar{K}_i)}$
Non-competitive	*EI* not formed	$K_s\neq K_{is}$ $k'\neq k\neq0$ $\bar{K}_{i'}=\infty$	$\dfrac{(1+iK_s/K_{is}\bar{K}_i)}{V(1+ik'K_s/kK_{is}\bar{K}_i)}$	$\dfrac{K_s(1+i/\bar{K}_i)}{V(1+ik'K_s/kK_{is}\bar{K}_i)}$	$\dfrac{K_s(1+i/\bar{K}_i)}{(1+iK_s/K_{is}\bar{K}_i)}$

$$\frac{1}{v} \text{ vs. } \frac{1}{s}$$

a. Competitive

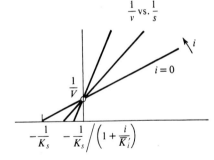

$$-\frac{1}{K_s} \quad -\frac{1}{K_s}\Big/\Big(1+\frac{i}{K_i'}\Big)$$

c. Noncompetitive

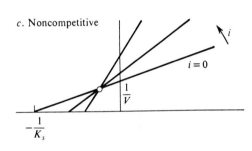

$$-\frac{1}{K_s}$$

b. Uncompetitive

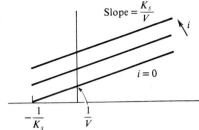

$$\text{Slope} = \frac{K_s}{V}$$

$$-\frac{1}{K_s} \qquad \frac{1}{V}$$

d. Substrate inhibition

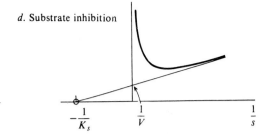

$$-\frac{1}{K_s} \qquad \frac{1}{V} \qquad \frac{1}{s}$$

FIGURE 6-6.   Kinetic Patterns for Various Inhibition Types

Multisubstrate Cases. When more than one substrate or product participates in an enzymatic reaction, the kinetic effects exerted by inhibitors can become quite complex.

If all that is required is a qualitative picture of the inhibition type to be expected (i.e., competitive, uncompetitive, or noncompetitive), this can be accomplished by inspection of the proposed mechanism with the use of the following simple rules due to Cleland:

1. An inhibitor affects the slope of a reciprocal plot ($1/v$ versus $1/s$) when it and the variable substrate S either compete directly for the same form of the enzyme or react with forms that are separated from each other in the reaction path only by reversible steps, so that either component can affect the concentration of enzyme available to the other by simple displacement of the various equilibria intervening. Thus an effect of I may be overcome by raising S.

2. An inhibitor affects the intercept of such a reciprocal plot when it combines with a form of the enzyme that differs from that responsible for combination with free S and thus lowers the amount of total enzyme available for distribution among the usual enzyme forms in a manner that cannot be overcome by saturation with S.

3. These effects can occur separately, in which case they produce competitive (case 1) or uncompetitive (case 2) patterns or, jointly, the noncompetitive pattern. If a substrate or inhibitor combines with more than one form of an enzyme, the resulting pattern is due to the sum of the different inhibitions produced singly. Any pattern can be linear or of higher order (e.g., parabolic or hyperbolic, etc.).

As a useful example we shall discuss briefly the case of adding an inhibitor (including the product Q) competing for the free enzyme with A, the first substrate bound in the case of the ordered bireactant mechanism — Eqs. (6-39), (6-40), and (6-43). The rate equation now becomes

$$\frac{V_1}{v_1} = 1 + \left(1 + \frac{i}{K_i}\right)\frac{K_a}{a} + \frac{K_b}{b}\left[1 + \left(1 + \frac{i}{K_i}\right)\frac{\bar{K}_a}{a}\right] \tag{6-51}$$

We see that, if A is the variable substrate, the inhibition is always competitive, but if a is held constant and B, the second substrate, is varied, the apparent inhibition pattern becomes noncompetitive.

If we look at the mechanism as a whole, i.e.,

$$
\begin{array}{ccccccc}
& A & & B & & P & & Q \\
& \downarrow & & \downarrow & & \uparrow & & \uparrow \\
E & & EA & & EAB \rightleftharpoons EPQ & & EQ & & E
\end{array}
$$

and consider three different types of inhibitors — a dead-end inhibitor combining with either EA or EQ, the product P, and a dead-end inhibitor combining with free enzyme — application of Cleland's rules predicts the following patterns:

Inhibition	A as variable substrate	B as variable substrate
$EA + I \rightleftharpoons EAI$	Uncompetitive	Competitive
$EQ + I \rightleftharpoons EQI$	Uncompetitive	Uncompetitive
$EQ + P \rightleftharpoons EQP$	Noncompetitive	Noncompetitive
$E + I \rightleftharpoons EI$	Competitive	Noncompetitive

Observe that the mechanisms involving EAI, EQI, or EI complexes can easily be distinguished. Product inhibition patterns are also exceedingly useful as criteria for the selection of permissible mechanisms; as already mentioned, Q added to the forward reaction, gives inhibition competitive to A, noncompetitive to B; P added is noncompetitive to both A and B for the ordered mechanism, but for the random equilibrium mechanisms both P and Q give competitive patterns with either A or B.

Effects
of pH

General Considerations. Almost all enzymes are extremely sensitive to pH; their activity is diminished at either side of a relatively narrow range. These effects are due to a combination of three factors: (1) irreversible effects of extremes of pH on protein structure, including alterations of the strength and mode of binding of prosthetic groups; (2) effects on the ionization of the substrate; and (3) effects on its binding to the enzyme and on reactivity in catalysis. It is only with the third class that we shall be concerned here; the first two can usually be determined independently of the reaction under kinetic study and corrections made for their effects.

The initial velocity of the enzymic reaction proper frequently exhibits three distinct phases as a function of pH (see Fig. 6-7a): a region of pH (at low values) where there is an increase, a region (at high values) where there is a decrease, and an intermediate range (usually around neutrality) where the activity is maximal and approximately constant — the pH *optimum* — leading to a characteristic bell-shaped curve *in toto*.[1] In a number of instances these curves have been inter-

---

[1] In other instances one or the other branch of the curve may be missing; in these cases the curve consists of only two segments: the branch (either ascending or descending) in question is joined to a horizontal portion.

preted in terms of certain proton ionization constants either on the free enzyme ($\bar{K}_{e1}$, etc.) or on the enzyme-substrate complex ($\bar{K}_{ea_1}$, etc.). In general these interpretations are not really correct; the dependence of the rate of pH can be so interpreted only in its pure first-order (i.e., $a \ll K_a$; $v = aV/K_a$) — Eq. (6-15b) — and zero-order regions (i.e., $a \gg K_a$; $v \simeq V$) — Eq. (6-15a). These two cases are indicated by the appropriate curves in Fig. 6-7a. At these extremes the inflection points, if calculated properly, may indeed correspond to such ionizations — on the enzyme in the former instance, on the enzyme-substrate complex

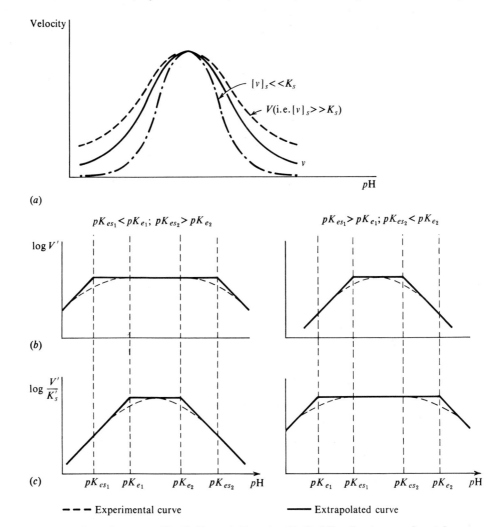

(a)

(b)

(c)

- - - Experimental curve   —— Extrapolated curve

FIGURE 6-7.   The Effect of pH on a Simple Enzymic Reaction. Dashed line denotes experimental curves; solid line denotes theoretical curves.

in the latter. But the initial velocity, as ordinarily determined, lies between these two extremes, and its pH dependence, similarly, is intermediate and cannot be explained in such simple terms.

The evaluation of these constants can best be accomplished by the use of double logarithmic plots of $\log_{10} V'$ versus pH, $\log_{10}(K')^{-1} \equiv pK'$ versus pH, and $\log_{10}[V'/K']$ (or $v_a \ll K_a$) versus pH. Idealized plots are shown in Fig. 6-7b and c. Most of them follow either the left or the right pattern with, occasionally, a combination of the left branch of the left pattern with the right branch of the right one, and vice versa. Some simple rules for the interpretation of such pK versus pH curves, due to Dixon, follow:[1]

1. The graph consists of straight-line sections joined by short curved parts.

2. The straight-line portions have integral slopes, i.e., zero or one-unit or two-unit, positive or negative.

3. Each bend indicates the pK of an ionizing group in one of the components, and the straight portions intersect at a pH corresponding to the pK.

4. Each pK produces a change of one unit in the slope.

5. Each pK of a group situated in the EA complex produces an increase in (positive) slope; each pK in the free enzyme produces a decrease in slope.

6. The curvature at the bends is such that the [actual] graph misses the [theoretical] intersection point of the neighboring straight parts by a vertical distance of 0.3 units ($=\log 2$); if two pK values occur together, the distance is equal to log 3.

7. The slope of any straight section is numerically equal to the change of charge occurring in that pH range when the complex dissociates into free enzyme and substrate.

REFERENCES   Alberty, R. A.: The Rate Equation for an Enzymic Reaction, in "The Enzymes," 2nd ed., vol. 1, p. 157, P. D. Boyer, H. Lardy, and K. Myrbäck (eds.), Academic, New York, 1959.
—— Enzyme Kinetics, *Advan. Enzymol.*, **17**: 1 (1956); The Interpretation of Steady State Kinetic Data on Enzymatic Reactions, *Brookhaven Symp. Biol.*, **15**: 18 (1962).

Bloomfield, V., L. Peller, and R. A. Alberty: Multiple Intermediates in Steady State Enzyme Kinetics: II. Systems Involving Two Substrates and Two Products, *J. Am. Chem. Soc.*, **84**: 4367 (1962); and III. Analysis of the Kinetics of Some Reactions Catalyzed by Dehydrogenases, *J. Am. Chem. Soc.*, **84**: 4375 (1962).

Cleland, W. W.: The Kinetics of Enzyme-catalyzed Reactions with Two or More Substrates or Products: I. Nomenclature and Rate Equations, *Biochim. Biophys. Acta*, **67**: 104 (1963); and II. Inhibition: Nomenclature and Theory, *Biochim. Biophys. Acta*, **67**: 173 (1963); and III. Prediction of Initial Velocity and Inhibition Patterns, *Biochim. Biophys. Acta*, **67**: 188 (1963); Enzyme Kinetics, *Ann. Rev. Biochem.*, **36**: 77 (1967).

Dalziel, K.: Initial Steady State Velocities in the Evaluation of Enzyme-Coenzyme-Substrate Reaction Mechanisms, *Acta Chem. Scand.*, **11**: 1706 (1957).

Dawes, E. A.: Enzyme Kinetics, chap. 4 in "Comprehensive Biochemistry," vol. 12, p. 89, M. Florkin and E. G. Stotz (eds.), Elsevier, New York, 1964.

Dixon, M., and E. C. Webb: "Enzymes," 2nd ed., esp. chaps. 2, 4, 8, and 9, Academic, New York, 1964.

King, E. L., and C. Altman: A Schematic Method of Deriving the Rate Laws for Enzyme-catalyzed Reactions, *J. Phys. Chem.*, **60**: 1375 (1956); King, E. L.: Unusual Kinetic Consequences of Certain Enzyme Catalysis Mechanisms, *J. Phys. Chem.*, **60**: 1378 (1956).

Laidler, K. J.: "The Chemical Kinetics of Enzyme Action," Oxford, Fair Lawn, N. J., 1958.

Peller, L., and R. A. Alberty: Multiple Intermediates in Steady State Enzyme Kinetics: I. The Mechanism Involving a Single Substrate and Product, *J. Am. Chem. Soc.*, **81**: 5907 (1959).

Reiner, J. M.: Quantitative Aspects of Enzymes and Enzyme Systems, chap. 5 in "Comprehensive Biochemistry," vol. 12, p. 126, M. Florkin and E. G. Stotz (eds.), Elsevier, New York, 1964.

---

[1] In more general cases $\log (V/K)$ versus pH depends on true dissociation constants of the variable substrate or of the enzyme forms with which it reacts. If we are interested in the latter, we must make certain that the former does not interfere.

Segal, H. L.: The Development of Enzyme Kinetics, in "The Enzymes," 2nd ed., vol. 1, p. 1, P. D. Boyer, H. Lardy, and K. Myrbäck (eds.), Academic, New York, 1959.

Walter, C.: "Steady-State Applications in Enzyme Kinetics," Ronald, New York, 1965.

Wong, J. T. F., and C. S. Hanes: Kinetic Formulations for Enzymic Reactions Involving Two Substrates, *Can. J. Biochem. Physiol.*, **40**: 763 (1962).

7| Enzymes

Protein molecules serve several independent functions in living systems. Perhaps their most striking biochemical role is the ability to affect, in a specific and efficient manner, the rates of the wide spectrum of reactions that constitute the dynamic aspect of the life process and to be themselves susceptible to a variety of controls. Proteins having such catalytic activity (see Chap. 6) are called *enzymes*.

That enzymes are, in fact, protein in nature was initially established in 1926 by Sumner. Since then, more than 100 enzymes have been obtained in crystalline form. All are proteins. The protein nature of enzymes is so well established that, as indicated above, the identification as protein is inherent in the definition of the word "enzyme."

Enzymes are exceptional catalysts in four respects. First, they are exceedingly efficient. An appreciation of the catalytic efficiency of enzymes may be gained by realizing that, under optimal conditions, most enzymatic reactions proceed 10^8 to 10^{11} times more rapidly than the corresponding nonenzymatic reactions. The turnover number (number of substrate molecules metabolized per enzyme molecule per minute) for most enzymes is approximately 1,000 and, in extreme cases, may be greater than 1 million. The rates of certain steps in enzymatic reactions are diffusion-controlled, or nearly so. Thus, many reactions that ordinarily occur only under extreme conditions of temperature or acid or base concentration proceed rapidly and quantitatively at pH values near neutrality and at room temperature in the presence of the appropriate enzymes. Second, most enzymatic reactions are specific in terms of the nature of the reaction catalyzed and the structure of the substrate utilized. Third, the spectrum of reactions catalyzed by enzymes is broad. Enzymes are responsible for catalyzing hydrolytic reactions, polymerizations, oxidation-reductions, dehydrations, aldol condensations, acyl transfer reactions, and free radical reactions, for example. Proteins, consequently, are exceptionally versatile catalysts. Finally, the enzymes themselves are subject to a variety of cellular controls. Their rate of synthesis, as well as their final concentration, is under genetic control and influenced by small molecules, such as the very substrates and products of the reaction in which they themselves participate. Furthermore, they may be present in both inactive and active forms, and the rate and extent of that interconversion is influenced by the composition of the environment at any particular instant. It is worth noting at this point that nearly all biological reactions are enzyme-catalyzed and, hence, subject to the controls indicated above. The biosynthesis of the enzymes themselves is enzyme-catalyzed.

CLASSIFICATION AND NOMENCLATURE FOR ENZYME-CATALYZED REACTIONS

A systematic classification and nomenclature for enzyme-catalyzed reactions has been established by the Commission on Enzymes of the International Union of Biochemistry. According to this classification, enzymes are divided into six general groups:

1. Oxidoreductases — catalyzing oxidation-reduction reactions
2. Transferases — catalyzing group transfer reactions
3. Hydrolases — catalyzing hydrolytic reactions
4. Lyases — catalyzing the addition of groups to double bonds or vice versa
5. Isomerases — catalyzing isomerizations
6. Ligases (synthetases) — catalyzing the condensation of two molecules coupled with the cleavage of a pyrophosphate bond of ATP or similar triphosphate.

Each broad class of enzymes is further divided into subclasses and sub-subclasses on the basis of the nature of the individual transformations involved. Such subclassifications describe the nature of the coenzyme involved, if any, the type of isomerization, the type of bond hydrolyzed, etc. This classification scheme provides a method of identifying individual enzymes by a series of four numbers. The first number indicates the main class into which the enzyme falls, the second and third indicate the subclass and sub-subclass, respectively, and the fourth is the serial number of the enzyme in its particular sub-subclass. This numbering and classification scheme is illustrated in Table 7-1, which is an abbreviated version of the comprehensive compilation.

The naming of individual enzymes is a formidable task; first, since it is difficult to establish a systematic nomenclature that accurately describes the nature of the reaction involved and, second, since an extensive and very widely used trivial nomenclature has already evolved. A systematic nomenclature has been developed (together with the systematic classification), and one must be familiar with both the systematic and trivial systems.

An examination of the systematic nomenclature presented in Table 7-1 provides familiarity with the rules for arriving at a systematic name for a given enzyme. Most trivial names attempt to give some information concerning the nature of the substrates involved and the nature of the catalyzed reaction, and most such names end with the suffix "ase." A few of the commonly employed enzyme categories are:

1. Dehydrogenases — enzymes that catalyze dehydrogenation of their substrates with a molecule other than molecular oxygen as hydrogen acceptor. If hydrogen transfer from the donor molecule is not readily demonstrated, the term *reductase* may be employed to describe such enzymes.

2. Oxidases — enzymes that catalyze oxidation of their substrates, with molecular oxygen as electron acceptor.

3. Hydroxylases — enzymes that catalyze the introduction of hydroxyl functions into their substrates, with molecular oxygen as oxygen donor.

4. Oxygenases — enzymes that catalyze the incorporation of an entire oxygen molecule into their substrates in the course of the oxidative cleavage of a carbon-carbon bond.

5. Kinases — enzymes that catalyze the transfer of phosphate from ATP or, much more infrequently, from another nucleoside triphosphate to their substrates.

6. Thiokinases — enzymes that catalyze the formation of thiol esters (of coenzyme A; see page 200) from carboxylic acid substrates in reactions involving the cleavage of ATP.

7. Phosphatases — enzymes that catalyze the hydrolytic cleavage of phosphate esters.

8. Phosphorylases — enzymes that catalyze the addition of the elements of phosphoric acid across glycosyl or related linkages.

9. Transferases — enzymes that catalyze the transfer of a particular group between two substrates. Subcategories include the transacetylases (acetyl group transfer), transcarbamylases (carbamyl group transfer), and transcarboxylases (carboxyl group transfer).

10. Mutases — enzymes that catalyze the apparent migration of some group from one site to another within the same molecule.

11. Synthetases — enzymes that catalyze the condensation of two molecules coupled with the cleavage of ATP or other nucleoside triphosphate.

In several cases, enzymes are named by simply adding the suffix "-ase" to the name of the substrate, i.e., ATPase, ribonuclease, aconitase. In addition, many trivial names bear no relationship to either the substrates or type of reaction catalyzed. Examples include many proteolytic enzymes, such as chymotrypsin, trypsin, pepsin, papain, rennin, and ficin. Finally, one must recognize that several names may be employed for the same enzyme. The enzyme that catalyzes the formation of citrate from oxaloacetate and acetyl CoA (see page 325) has been called condensing enzyme, citrate condensing enzyme, citrogenase, and citrate synthetase, in addition to the systematic names. Most other names in the trivial nomenclature are reasonably self-explanatory. Some, but by no means all, of them have been approved by the Enzyme Commission as acceptable alternatives (see Table 7-1).

TABLE 7-1. Classification and Nomenclature for Enzyme-catalyzed Reactions

Number	Systematic name	Trivial name	Reaction
1. Oxidoreductases			
1.1. Acting on CH—OH *group of donors*			
1.1.1. With NAD or NADP as acceptor			
1.1.1.1	Alcohol: NAD oxidoreductase	Alcohol dehydrogenase	Alcohol + NAD^+ = aldehyde or ketone + NADH
1.1.1.27	L-Lactate: NAD oxidoreductase	Lactate dehydrogenase	L-Lactate + NAD^+ = pyruvate + NADH
1.1.1.37	L-Malate: NAD oxidoreductase	Malate dehydrogenase	L-Malate + $NADH^+$ = oxaloacetate + NADH
1.1.3. With O_2 as acceptor			
1.1.3.4	β-D-Glucose: oxygen oxidoreductase	Glucose oxidase	β-D-Glucose + O_2 = D-glucono-δ-lactone + H_2O_2
1.2. Acting on aldehyde- or keto- group of donors			
1.2.1. With NAD or NADP as acceptor			
1.2.1.12	D-Glyceraldehyde-3-phosphate: NAD oxidoreductase (phosphorylating)	Glyceraldehydephosphate dehydrogenase, triosephosphate dehydrogenase	D-Glyceraldehyde-3-phosphate + orthophosphate + NAD^+ = 1,3-diphospho-D-glyceric acid + NADH
1.2.3. With O_2 as acceptor			
1.2.3.2	Xanthine: oxygen oxidoreductase	Xanthine oxidase	Xanthine + H_2O + O_2 = urate + H_2O_2
1.3. Acting on CH—CH *group of donors*			
1.3.1. With NAD or NADP as acceptor			
1.3.1.1	4,5-Dihydro-uracil: NAD oxidoreductase	Dihydro-uracil dehydrogenase	4,5-Dihydro-uracil + NAD^+ = uracil + NADH
1.4. Acting on CH—NH_2 *group of donors*			
1.4.1. With NAD or NADP as acceptor			
1.4.1.2	L-Glutamate: NAD oxidoreductase (deaminating)	Glutamate dehydrogenase	L-Glutamate + H_2O + NAD^+ = 2-oxoglutarate + NH_3 + NADH
1.4.3. With O_2 as acceptor			
1.4.3.2	L-Aminoacid: oxygen oxidoreductase (deaminating)	L-Aminoacid oxidase	An L-amino acid + H_2O + O_2 = a 2-oxo-acid + NH_3 + H_2O_2
1.5. Acting on C—NH *group of donors*			
1.6. Acting on NADH *or* NADPH *as donor*			
1.9. Acting on heme groups of donors			
2. Transferases			
2.1. Transferring one-carbon groups			
2.1.2. Hydroxymethyl-, formyl-, and related transferases			
2.1.2.1	L-Serine: tetrahydrofolate 5,10-hydroxymethyltransferase	Serine hydroxymethyltransferase	L-Serine + tetrahydrofolate = glycine + 5,10-methylenetetra-hydrofolate
2.1.3. Carboxyl- and carbamoyltransferases (For the trivial name, "carboxyltransferase" and "carbamoyltransferase" may be replaced by "transcarboxylase" and "transcarbamoylase," respectively)			
2.1.3.2	Carbamoylphosphate: L-aspartate carbamoyltransferase	Aspartate carbamoyltransferase	Carbamoyl phosphate + L-aspartate = orthophosphate + N-carbamoyl-L-aspartate
2.2. Transferring aldehydic or ketonic residues			
2.2.1.1	D-Sedoheptulose-7-phosphate: D-glyceraldehyde-3-phosphate glycolaldehydetransferase	Transketolase, glycolaldehyde-transferase	D-Sedoheptulose-7-phosphate + D-glyceraldehyde-3-phosphate = D-ribose-5-phosphate + D-xylulose-5-phosphate

Number	Systematic name	Trivial name	Reaction
2.3. Acyltransferases			
2.3.1. Acyltransferases			
2.3.1.8	Acetyl-CoA: orthophosphate acetyltransferase	Phosphate acetyltransferase	Acetyl-CoA + orthophosphate = CoA + acetylphosphate
2.4. Glycosyltransferases			
2.4.1. Hexosyltransferases			
2.4.1.8	Maltose: orthophosphate glucosyltransferase	Maltose phosphorylase	Maltose + orthophosphate = β-D-glucose-1-phosphate + D-glucose
2.6. Transferring nitrogenous groups			
2.6.1. Aminotransferases			
2.6.1.1	L-Aspartate: 2-oxoglutarate aminotransferase	Aspartate aminotransferase	L-Aspartate + 2-oxoglutarate = oxaloacetate + L-glutamate
2.7. Transferring phosphorus-containing groups			
2.7.1. Phosphotransferases with an alcohol group as acceptor			
2.7.1.2	ATP: glucose-6-phosphotransferase	Glucokinase	ATP + D-glucose = ADP + D-glucose-6-phosphate
2.7.1.40	ATP: pyruvate phosphotransferase	Pyruvate kinase	ATP + pyruvate = ADP + phosphoenolpyruvate
2.7.2. Phosphotransferases with a carboxyl group as acceptor			
2.7.2.1	ATP: acetate phosphotransferase	Acetate kinase	ATP + acetate = ADP + acetyl phosphate
3. Hydrolases			
3.1. Acting on ester bonds			
3.1.1. Carboxylic ester hydrolases			
3.1.1.7	Acetylcholine acetyl-hydrolase	Acetylcholinesterase	Acetylcholine + H_2O = choline + acetic acid
3.1.3. Phosphoric monoester hydrolases			
3.1.3.9	D-Glucose-6-phosphate phosphohydrolase	Glucose-6-phosphatase	D-Glucose-6-phosphate + H_2O = D-glucose + H_3PO_4
3.1.4. Phosphoric diester hydrolases			
3.1.4.1	Orthophosphoric diester phosphohydrolase	Phosphodiesterase	A phosphoric diester + H_2O = a phosphoric monoester + an alcohol
3.4. Acting on peptide bonds (peptide hydrolases)			
3.4.4. Peptide peptidohydrolases			
3.4.4.1	...	Pepsin	Hydrolyses peptides, including those with bonds adjacent to aromatic or dicarboxylic L-amino acid residues
3.4.4.4	...	Trypsin	Hydrolyses peptides, amides, esters, etc., at bonds involving the carboxyl groups of L-arginine or L-lysine
3.4.4.5	...	Chymotrypsin	Hydrolyses peptides, amides, esters, etc., especially at bonds involving the carboxyl groups of aromatic L-amino acids
3.5. Acting on C—N bonds other than peptide bonds			
3.5.1. In linear amides			
3.5.1.5	Urea amidohydrolase	Urease	Urea + H_2O = CO_2 + $2NH_3$
3.6. Acting on acid anhydride bonds			
3.6.1. In phosphoryl-containing anhydrides			
3.6.1.1	Pyrophosphate phosphohydrolase	Inorganic pyrophosphatase	Pyrophosphate + H_2O = 2 orthophosphate

TABLE 7-1. Classification and Nomenclature for Enzyme-catalyzed Reactions (*Continued*)

Number	Systematic name	Trivial name	Reaction
4. Lyases			
4.1. Carbon-carbon lyases			
4.1.1. Carboxy-lyases			
4.1.1.1	2-Oxo-acid carboxy-lyase	Pyruvate decarboxylase	A 2-oxo-acid = an aldehyde + CO_2
4.1.2. Aldehyde-lyases			
4.1.2.7	Ketose-1-phosphate aldehyde-lyase	Aldolase	A ketose-1-phosphate = dihydroxyacetone phosphate + an aldehyde
4.3. Carbon-nitrogen lyases			
4.3.1. Ammonia-lyases			
4.3.1.1	L-Aspartate ammonia-lyase	Aspartate ammonia-lyase	L-Aspartate = fumarate + NH_3
5. Isomerases			
5.1. Racemases and epimerases			
5.1.1. *Acting on amino acids and derivatives*			
5.1.1.1	Alanine racemase	Alanine racemase	L-Alanine = D-alanine
5.1.2. Acting on hydroxyacids and derivatives			
5.1.2.1	Lactate racemase	Lactate racemase	L-Lactate = D-lactate
5.1.3. Acting on carbohydrates and derivatives			
5.1.3.2	UDPglucose 4-epimerase	UDPglucose epimerase	UDPglucose = UDPgalactose
6. Ligases			
6.1. Forming C—O bonds			
6.1.1. Amino acid-RNA ligases			
6.1.1.1	L-Tyrosine: sRNA ligase (AMP)	Tyrosyl-sRNA synthetase	ATP + L-tyrosine + sRNA = AMP + pyrophosphate + L-tyrosyl-sRNA
6.2. Forming C—S bonds			
6.2.1. Acid-thiol ligases			
6.2.1.1	Acetate: CoA ligase (AMP)	Acetyl-CoA synthetase	ATP + acetate + CoA = AMP + pyrophosphate + acetyl-CoA
6.3. Forming C—N bonds			
6.3.4. Other C—N ligases			
6.3.4.2	UTP : ammonia ligase (ADP)	CTP synthetase	ATP + UTP + NH_3 = ADP + orthophosphate + CTP
6.4. Forming C—C bonds			
6.4.1.2	Acetyl-CoA: carbon-dioxide ligase (ADP)	Acetyl-CoA carboxylase	ATP + acetyl-CoA + CO_2 + H_2O = ADP + orthophosphate + malonyl-CoA

THE ACTIVE SITE OF ENZYMES The central questions in the study of reaction mechanisms are the structure of the transition state and the nature of the intermediates for the reaction under consideration. In the case of enzyme-catalyzed reactions, a knowledge of the structure of the transition state involves an understanding, not only of the geometry of the substrate molecule, but also of the three-dimensional conformation of the enzyme. The high catalytic efficiency and marked specificity exhibited by enzymatic reactions imply the participation of several distinct functional groups of the enzyme in the catalytic process. This fact, together with the structural complexities inherent in the chemistry of molecules of the size of proteins, suffices to indicate that a precise definition of the transition-state structure for enzymatic reactions is a formidable task. For the present, at least, one must be content to work toward less sophisticated goals: (1)

elucidation of the pathway; (2) identification of amino acids involved in substrate binding and in bond-making and bond-breaking reactions; (3) determination of their approximate arrangement in space; and (4) development of a rationale, through assigning specific catalytic roles to the groups involved, that explains the velocity of enzyme-catalyzed reactions to within an order of magnitude. These goals have yet to be fully realized in even a single instance.

Most enzymatic reactions involve substrates that are small compared with the size of the catalyst molecule. Consequently, only a small portion of the amino acid side chains and peptide bonds are near or in direct contact with the substrate molecule in the enzyme-substrate complex. This realization gives rise to the concept of an *active site* for enzymatic reactions. The active site of an enzyme is taken to include those side chains and peptide bonds which are in direct physical contact with the substrate (perhaps through intervening water molecules) and other side chains or peptide bonds that, although not in direct contact with the substrate, perform a direct function in the catalytic process. A schematic representation of an active site is pictured in Fig. 7-1. Part or all of the remainder of the protein serves the less direct function of providing a structural backbone suitable for maintaining the components of the active site in the three-dimensional conformation required for efficient, specific catalysis. The requirement for such a structural backbone is emphasized by the dramatic alterations in enzymatic activity that frequently result when the conformation of the protein is altered through one of the denaturing processes (heat, urea, organic solvents, etc.). Part of the enzyme molecule may, of course, play no role in the catalytic process.

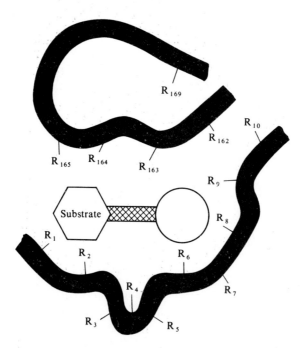

FIGURE 7-1.   A Schematic Active Site. The cross-hatched area indicates a bond to be broken in the enzyme action. The R's represent some side chains and the heavy lines the backbone of two segments of the protein chain. — *D. E. Koshland, Advan. Enzymol., 22: 45 (1960).*

The identification of amino acids present at the active site of enzymes is clearly of major importance for the understanding of the basic facets of the mechanism of enzyme-catalyzed reactions. Several methods, of varying utility, have been employed in attempts to identify at least some of the residues that constitute these active sites. The most direct method is to attach a covalent label, which itself is stable to procedures required to degrade polypeptide chains, to some residue present in the active site. For this purpose, it is convenient to distinguish two classes of enzymes: those that involve covalent enzyme-substrate intermediates in the course of the catalytic process and those that do not. In the case of the former class, the problem of specifically labeling the active site, rather than introducing a label into the protein in a nonspecific fashion, may frequently be solved by employing labeling reagents that are either the normal enzymatic substrates or structurally related compounds. As a result of the specific binding of these materials to the active site, the probability of introducing the label at alternative sites is greatly reduced. The problem of active-site labeling of enzymes of the latter class is more difficult.

The existence of covalent enzyme-substrate intermediates has been demonstrated for reactions catalyzed by an increasingly large number of enzymes. This list now includes chymotrypsin, trypsin, triose phosphate dehydrogenase, phosphoglucomutase, phosphoglyceric acid mutase, several phosphatases, several aldolases, and acetoacetic decarboxylase, among others. In a few cases, the enzyme-substrate intermediate is sufficiently stable thermodynamically to exist in amounts sufficient for isolation and study. Phosphorylated phosphoglucomutase, an intermediate in the interconversion of glucose-1-phosphate and glucose-6-phosphate, may be prepared through incubation of the dephosphoenzyme with its phosphorylated glucose substrates:

Phosphoenzyme + glucose-1-phosphate $\rightleftharpoons$

$$\text{dephosphoenzyme} + \text{glucose-1,6-diphosphate} \qquad (7\text{-}1)$$

Dephosphoenzyme + glucose-1,6-diphosphate $\rightleftharpoons$

$$\text{phosphoenzyme} + \text{glucose-6-phosphate} \qquad (7\text{-}2)$$

Chemical and enzymatic degradation of the phosphorylated enzyme yields serine phosphate, which is flanked on its C-terminal side by a histidine residue. With the exception of this histidine residue, the amino acid composition in the neighborhood of the reactive serine residue resembles that for proteases and esterases (see below). Phosphorylated phosphoglyceric acid mutase, which is quite similar to phosphoglucomutase in its overall reaction pattern, may be similarly prepared and studied.

In the majority of cases, enzyme-substrate intermediates are not sufficiently stable with respect to starting materials or products to permit their isolation in appreciable quantities. In some cases, this difficulty may be overcome by stabilizing the intermediate by chemical modification as it is being formed. For example, incubation of aldolase with radioactive dihydroxyacetone phosphate, or transaldolase with radioactive fructose-6-phosphate in the presence of sodium borohydride, a reducing agent, results in the irreversible incorporation of radioactivity into the protein. In both cases, complete acid hydrolysis of the protein has led to the identfication of *N*-ε-glyceryllysine among the hydrolysis products. Thus, these reactions must involve the formation of a Schiff base between the keto function of the substrate molecule and the ε-amino group of a lysine residue, which is then reduced by sodium borohydride, yielding a stable secondary amine:

$$\text{Enzyme—NH}_2 + \text{O}{=}\!\!\big\langle\ \rightleftharpoons \text{enzyme—N}{=}\!\!\big\langle \tag{7-3}$$

$$\text{Enzyme—N}{=}\!\!\big\langle\ + \text{NaBH}_4 \rightarrow \text{enzyme—N}\underset{H}{\overset{H}{\big|}}\!\!\big\langle \xrightarrow{\text{acid}} \text{lysine—N}\underset{H}{\overset{H}{\big|}}\!\!\big\langle \tag{7-4}$$

Similar results have been obtained in the case of acetoacetic decarboxylase. This enzyme also appears to catalyze the formation of a Schiff base between the keto function of the substrate and the ε-amino group of lysine, which can be stabilized either by reduction with sodium borohydride or by the addition of cyanide to the imine double bond.

   Of more general utility, although less elegant, are methods that involve labeling of the active site of enzymes by quasi-substrates. A quasi-substrate is a substance that is sufficiently similar to the normal substrate molecule to form the covalent enzyme-substrate complex but sufficiently different so that this intermediate decomposes slowly if at all. This method has been of particular

TABLE 7-2.   Amino Acid Sequence Around the Reactive Serine Residue of Some Esterases and Proteases

Sequence	Enzyme
Gly-Val-Ser-Ser-Cys-Met-Gly-Asp-*Ser*-Gly-Gly-Pro-Leu-Val-Cys-Lys	Chymotrypsin
$\overset{\text{NH}_2}{\underset{\|}{}}$	
Asp-Ser-Cys-Glu-Gly-Gly-Asp-*Ser*-Gly-Pro-Val-Cys-Ser-Gly-Lys	Trypsin
Asp-*Ser*-Gly	Thrombin
Asp-*Ser*-Gly	Elastase
Phe-Gly-Glu-*Ser*-Ala-Gly(Ala,Ala,Ser)	Butyryl cholin-esterase
Glu-*Ser*-Ala	(Eel)acetylcho-linesterase
Gly-Glu-*Ser*-Ala-Gly-Gly	Liver aliester-ase (horse)
$\overset{\text{NH}_2}{\underset{\|}{}}$	
Asp-Gly-Thr-*Ser*-Met-Ala-Ser-Pro-His	Subtilisin (*B. subtilis*)
Thr-*Ser*-Met-Ala	Mold protease (*Aspergillus oryzae*)
Thr-Ala-*Ser*-His-Asp	Phosphogluco-mutase
$\overset{\text{NH}_2}{\underset{\|}{}}$	
Lys-Glu-Ile-*Ser*-Val-Arg	Phosphorylase
Thr-Gly-Lys-Pro-Asp-Tyr-Val-Thr-Asp-*Ser*-Ala-Ala-Ser-Ala	Alkaline phosphatase (*E. coli*)

SOURCE: R. A. Oosterbaan and J. A. Cohen, in Goodwin, Hartley, and Harris (eds.), "Structure and Activity of Enzymes," Academic Press Inc., New York, 1964.

importance in the labeling of the active site of esterases and proteases with diisopropylfluorophosphate (see Table 7-2). With this reagent, which is not closely related structurally to the normal substrates for these enzymes, the danger of introducing a label at some position other than the active site is considerably greater than in the cases described above. Yet the rapidity, stoichiometry, and specificity of this reaction strongly suggest that the active site is in fact being labeled. For example, DFP phosphorylates one of the two serine residues of chymotrypsin specifically. Chymotrypsin may also be labeled by many additional reagents, including p-nitrophenyl acetate; in each case the same serine hydroxyl function, and no other group, is acylated. In the case of many, but not all, of the esterases and proteases studied, the group phosphorylated by DFP is a serine hydroxyl group flanked on the N-terminal side by either alanine or glycine. These results are summarized in Table 7-2. This same recurring sequence of amino acids around the reactive serine hydroxyl group for enzymes of widely varying specificity suggests that there may be a division between residues responsible for specificity and for catalyzing bond-breaking and bond-making reactions, and that those centered on serine are involved in the latter processes.

Attaching a covalent label specifically to the active site of those enzymes which do not catalyze the intermediate formation of a covalent enzyme-substrate complex is, as mentioned above, a difficult task. The basic difficulty may be illustrated by the following example. Many enzymes are known to react with p-hydroxymercuribenzoate or p-chloromercuribenzenesulfonate through mercuration of the exposed sulfhydryl groups, yielding a catalytically inactive product. However, in most such cases it is unclear whether an essential sulfhydryl group in the active site has been blocked or whether mercuration of a sulfhydryl group present in the structural backbone has caused conformation changes, which may be quite small, that have led to an inactive enzyme.

Indirect methods, which do not involve covalent labeling of the active site, may be employed for the tentative identification of amino acids involved in the catalytic process. Such methods can never locate the residue in the peptide chain, and it is difficult to know if it is at the active site or in the structural backbone.

The most widely used indirect method is the variation of some parameter of the reaction, such as the maximum velocity or the Michaelis constant, with pH. These parameters frequently vary with pH in a manner suggesting the titration of a single ionizable group (see page 171) and the pK_a for the group involved may be calculated, and its identification attempted, by comparing this value with the known pK_a values for the amino acid side chains. This process involves several difficulties. First, as a result of interactions with neighboring groups in the protein or with substrate or buffer, the pK_a for an ionizable group in a protein may differ significantly from the corresponding value for the group free in solution. Furthermore, the pK_a values for several titratable groups present in proteins overlap considerably. For instance, a group with a pK_a of 10 might be assigned to an amino group, to a phenolic hydroxyl group, or possibly to a sulfhydryl group. The assignment of a pK_a to a particular group is sometimes aided by determination of ΔH for the ionization. However, a unique assignment of pK_a to a functional group is frequently not possible. Second, the pH behavior may reflect the titration of several residues rather than of an individual group. Finally, breaks in pH-rate profiles may result from other factors, such as a change in the rate-determining step, in addition to titrations. Fortunately, all these difficulties need not always occur. Frequently an assignment made on the basis of pH effects may be corroborated by other techniques. For example, all the enzymes listed in Table 7-2 appear to involve a histidine residue in the catalytic process on the basis of the effect of pH on the maximum velocities. In the case of chymotrypsin, this conclusion is supported by the finding that a chloroketone analogue of a chymotrypsin substrate reacts specifically with one histidine residue with resultant inactivation. pH-rate behavior suggests the presence of a sulf-hydryl group at the active site of papain; this suggestion is strengthened by the inhibition of papain by reagents that bind sulfhydryl groups.

An additional method that has been widely employed in attempts to identify residues required for enzymatic activity is the loss of catalytic power with amino acid modification. The reaction of p-hydroxymercuribenzoate with sulfhydryl groups is an example of such a modification. This method is hampered a great deal by the lack of specificity of most amino acid reagents for a single type of residue and by the variability of reactivities of functional groups in proteins.

Conformation of the Active Site

The three-dimensional constellation of amino acids that constitute the active site of an enzyme is not known for any case. Indeed, it is not even certain that, in the absence of substrate, the three-dimensional conformation of the amino acids at the active site is unique and, if it is, that it corresponds to the catalyt-ically active conformation. In this regard, two theories have been proposed regarding active-site conformation. Late in the nineteenth century, Emil Fischer, in order to explain the specificity of enzyme-catalyzed reactions, proposed that the enzyme was disposed in a reasonably rigid template to which the substrate could be bound. This *lock-key hypothesis* accounts for enzyme specificity, since template rigidity would cause steric repulsions to molecules differing structurally from the normal substrate. In contrast, Koshland has advocated an *induced-fit theory* to account for the specificity of enzymic reactions. This theory involves three postulates: "(1) that a considerable alteration in the geometry of the protein is caused by the substrate as it fits into the active site; (2) that a delicate orientation of catalytic groups is required for enzyme action; (3) that the sub-strate induces this proper orientation by the change it causes in geometry."

The induced-fit theory was designed in an attempt to account for several findings not easily explained by the lock-key hypothesis. For example, in certain enzyme-catalyzed reactions, a portion of a substrate is transferred to an alcohol but not to water. A lock-key hypothesis would suggest that, in the absence of the alcohol, an appreciable reaction with water should occur, since water is almost certainly present at the active site, owing to its high concentration in aqueous solution. Since the water reaction is not observed, one may suggest that the alcohol, by binding to the active site, causes an alteration in active-site geometry to the catalytically active conformation. It also receives support from chemical findings suggesting a modification of enzyme conformation upon substrate binding.

THE PATHWAY OF ENZYME-CATALYZED REACTIONS

An obvious prerequisite for a basic understanding of a chemical reaction, enzymatic or not, is a knowledge of the bonds broken and formed and the nature of the intermediates, if any, produced in the course of the reaction. Such information constitutes a knowledge of the *pathway* for the reaction. One of the most important methods of obtaining information relevant to reaction pathways is from analysis of initial velocity and inhibition patterns from steady-state kinetic data. This topic was explored in Chap. 6. In addition, valuable information pertinent to these points can frequently be obtained by means of isotopic labeling studies. Many isotopes, such as C^{14}, H^3, P^{32}, and S^{35}, are radioactive and may be distinguished from the normal isotopes on this basis. Others, such as H^2, N^{15}, and O^{18}, differ from the ordinary isotopes only in mass and may, therefore, be assayed by recording mass spectra.

Two types of experiments with isotopes are frequently performed. *Isotope incorporation studies*, which primarily yield information concerning the position of bond breakage and formation but which may be used in attempts to identify intermediates as well, and *exchange studies*, which involve replacement of a resident group with a similar labeled group and which primarily yield information concerning the existence of reaction intermediates. As an example of the former type of study, consider the cleavage of glucose-1-phosphate as catalyzed by alkaline phosphatase. This reaction could conceivably occur with cleavage of either the C—O bond or the P—O bond. If this reaction is carried out in the presence of H_2O^{18}-enriched water, the former reaction path yields glucose containing one atom of O^{18}:

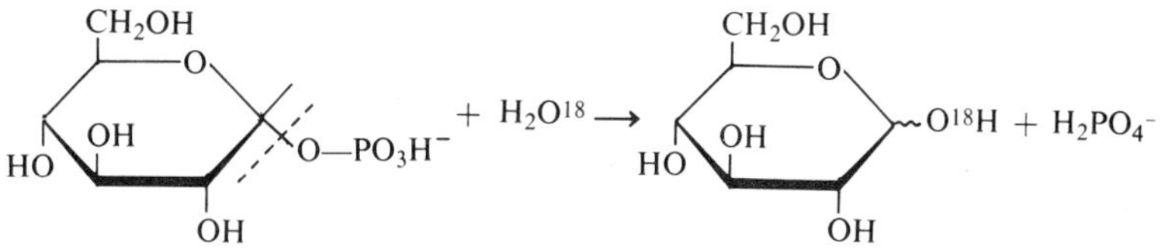

$$\text{(glucose-1-phosphate structure)} + H_2O^{18} \longrightarrow \text{(glucose-}O^{18}H\text{ structure)} + H_2PO_4^- \qquad (7\text{-}5)$$

and the latter is characterized by phosphate containing one atom of O^{18}:

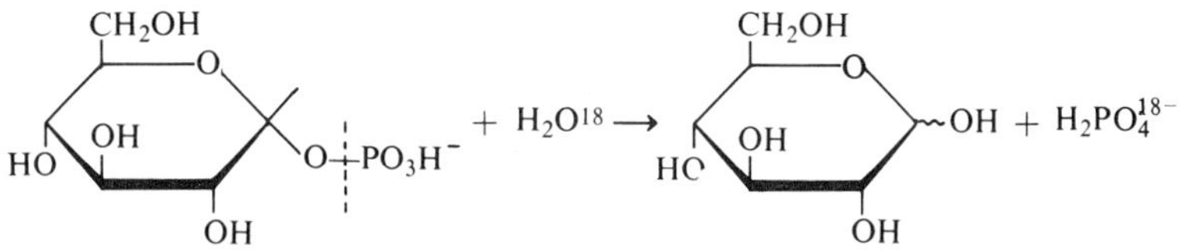

$$\text{(glucose-1-phosphate structure)} + H_2O^{18} \longrightarrow \text{(glucose-OH structure)} + H_2PO_4^{18-} \qquad (7\text{-}6)$$

The appearance of one atom of O^{18} in inorganic phosphate identifies the P—O bond as the site of cleavage of this substrate. Nearly all phosphatase reactions proceed in this fashion. On the other hand, the reaction of fructose with glucose-1-phosphate in O^{18}-enriched water yields sucrose and inorganic phosphate, which does not contain excess O^{18}. Hence this reaction must occur with C—O bond cleavage, a general characteristic of phosphorylase reactions. In summary, these experiments indicate that phosphatases are phosphoryl group transfer enzymes and phosphorylases are glycosyl group transfer enzymes.

Sucrose phosphorylase also provides an example of the use of isotope-exchange reactions. This enzyme catalyzes the following exchanges, each carried out in the absence of the second substrate:

$$\text{Glucose-1-}P + P_i{}^{32} \rightleftharpoons \text{glucose-1-}P^{32} + P_i \qquad (7\text{-}7)$$

$$\text{Glucose-fructose} + \text{fructose-}C^{14} \rightleftharpoons \text{glucose-fructose-}C^{14} + \text{fructose} \tag{7-8}$$

These findings are consistent with the possibility of a covalently linked glucosyl-enzyme intermediate; that is, the reaction may proceed via a two-step reaction path:

$$\text{Glucose-1-}P + \text{enzyme} \rightleftharpoons \text{glucosyl-enzyme} + P_i \tag{7-9}$$

$$\text{Glucosyl-enzyme} + \text{fructose} \rightleftharpoons \text{glucosyl-fructose} + \text{enzyme} \tag{7-10}$$

It is important to realize that such results are suggestive but certainly not conclusive evidence for the existence of such an intermediate, since these exchange reactions may be equally well accounted for on the basis of direct displacement reactions. Furthermore, the absence of exchange reactions does not rule out the existence of a covalent enzyme-substrate intermediate, since both substrates may have to be present for catalytic activity. For example, the reaction catalyzed by the citrate-condensing enzyme (see page 325) almost certainly proceeds with attack of the enol or carbanion of acetyl-SCoA on the carbonyl function of oxaloacetate. Yet incubation of acetyl-SCoA alone with this enzyme does not result in the exchange of the methyl hydrogens of acetyl-SCoA with the hydrogens of solvent. Thus formation of the enol or carbanion of this species requires the presence of the second substrate, oxaloacetate. Thus, although suggestive findings may be obtained in exchange experiments, they must be interpreted with caution.

An example of an isotope-exchange reaction that permits more definite conclusions to be drawn is provided by the aldolase reaction:

$$
\begin{array}{c}
CH_2-OPO_3H^- \\
| \\
C=O \\
| \\
HO-C-H \\
| \\
H-C-OH \\
| \\
H-C-OH \\
| \\
CH_2-OPO_3H^-
\end{array}
\rightleftharpoons
\begin{array}{c}
CH_2OPO_3H^- \\
| \\
C=O \\
| \\
CH_2OH
\end{array}
+
\begin{array}{c}
CHO \\
| \\
H-C-OH \\
| \\
CH_2OPO_3H^-
\end{array}
\tag{7-11}
$$

Several chemists have observed that the incubation of dihydroxyacetone phosphate with aldolase in either deuterium oxide or in water containing tritium oxide results in the incorporation of one atom of deuterium or tritium into this molecule. Similar incorporation is not observed if glyceraldehyde-3-phosphate is employed as substrate. These findings indicate that the dihydroxyacetone phosphate, and not the glyceraldehyde-3-phosphate, is activated by aldolase and strongly suggest that the carbanion, enol, or enolate of the former substrate is a (enzyme-bound) reaction intermediate. The pathway of the aldolase reaction may then be considered as the sum of two reactions (see page 268):

$$
HO-CH_2-\overset{O}{\overset{\|}{C}}-CH_2-OPO_3H^- \rightleftharpoons
$$
$$
\left[HO-{}^-CH-\overset{O}{\overset{\|}{C}}-CH_2-OPO_3H^- \leftrightarrow HO-\overset{H}{C}=\overset{O^-}{\overset{|}{C}}-CH_2-OPO_3H^- \right] \tag{7-12}
$$

$$\text{HO}\!-\!{}^-\!\underset{\underset{\text{H}}{|}}{\text{C}}\!-\!\overset{\overset{\text{O}}{\|}}{\text{C}}\!-\!\text{R} \quad + \quad \underset{\underset{\text{H}}{|}}{\overset{\overset{\text{O}}{\|}}{\text{C}}}\!-\!\overset{\overset{\text{OH}}{|}}{\text{CH}}\!-\!\text{CH}_2\text{OPO}_3\text{H}^- \;\rightleftharpoons \text{fructose-1,6-diphosphate} \qquad (7\text{-}13)$$

MECHANISM OF
ACTION OF
CHYMOTRYPSIN

The most thoroughly understood enzyme, from the standpoint of the mechanism of the catalytic process, is chymotrypsin. This enzyme provides a suitable example of the employment of the various techniques discussed above in an effort to unravel enzymatic reaction mechanisms.

Chymotrypsin is an acyl group transfer enzyme. It transfers the acyl group from a number of donors, including esters, amides, acids, hydroxamates, etc., to a number of acceptors such as water, alcohols, and amines. As indicated below, chymotrypsin-catalyzed reactions appear to proceed with the intermediate formation of an acyl enzyme. Thus this reaction is of the *double-displacement* type. Our present state of knowledge regarding the intimacies of this process derives principally from the following observations:

1. The active site of chymotrypsin has been covalently labeled with quasi-substrates, including *p*-nitrophenyl acetate, diisopropylfluorophosphate, and the nonactivated ester methyl cinnamate. These observations suggest the intermediate formation of an acyl enzyme.

2. The maximal rates of chymotryptic hydrolysis of several derivatives of *N*-acetyl-L-tryptophan are identical. Since the inherent reactivities of these derivatives are quite different, this observation suggests that an acyl enzyme is indeed formed from these, more or less, specific substrates and that deacylation is the rate-determining step in this catalytic process. Since the acyl enzyme *N*-acetyl-L-tryptophanyl chymotrypsin is identical for all the substrates, this hypothesis accounts for the identity in rates.

3. The active site of chymotrypsin may also be covalently labeled by the specific substrate *N*-acetyl tryptophan. Since chymotrypsin has, as its normal substrate, the peptide bonds adjacent to tryptophan and tyrosine residues, this experiment provides strong support for the acyl-enzyme hypothesis.

4. Chemical and enzymatic degradation of several acyl chymotrypsins reveals that the acyl group is attached to the hydroxyl function of a serine residue (see Table 7-2).

5. The conversion of this crucial serine residue to a dehydroalanyl residue renders chymotrypsin completely inactive, consistent with an obligatory acyl-enzyme intermediate involving this serine hydroxyl.

6. Studies concerning the effect of *p*H on the rate of chymotrypsin-catalyzed reactions have implicated the free base of a histidine residue, or its kinetic equivalent, as necessary for the catalysis. This conclusion is substantiated by the loss of enzymatic activity with histidine alkylation by the chloromethylketone of a chymotyrpsin substrate analogue (affinity labeling).

7. The rate of chymotrypsin-catalyzed reactions is decreased from two- to threefold in deuterium oxide compared with water. This observation is consistent with, and offers support for, proton transfer in the rate-determining step, i.e., general acid-base catalysis.

These and related observations are consistent with a mechanism of action of chymotrypsin shown in Fig. 7-2. This mechanism, which is not the only one

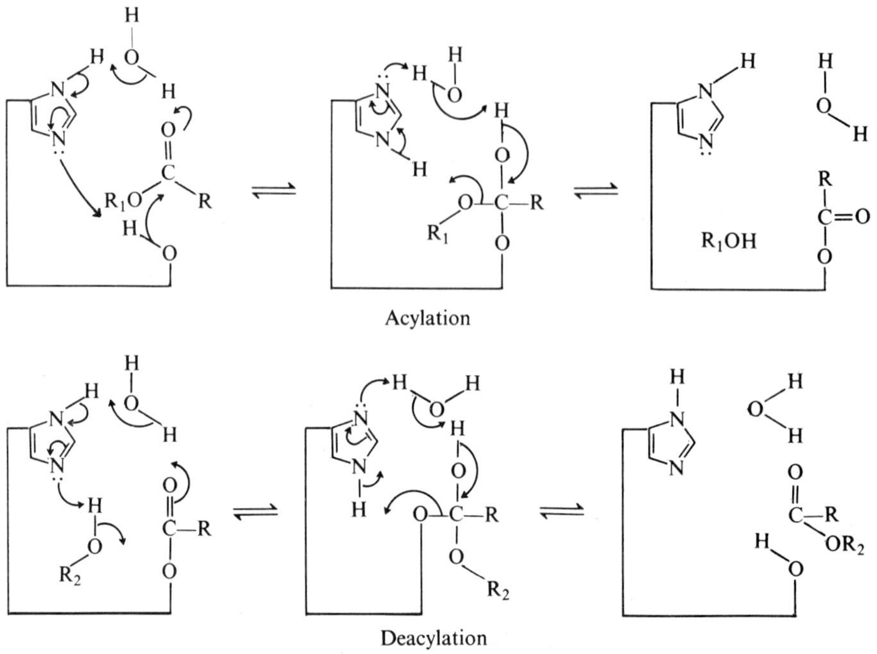

Acylation

Deacylation

FIGURE 7-2.   A Possible Mechanism for Chymotrypsin-catalyzed Acyl Transfer Reactions. The attack of the serine hydroxyl group on the carbonyl carbon atom of the substrate is pictured as being aided by both general acid and general base catalysis by an imidazole moiety of a histidine residue. A molecule of water serves as proton transfer agent for the general acid-catalyzed portion of the reaction. In a symmetrical fashion, the decomposition of the tetrahedral intermediate is also considered to proceed via a general acid-base catalyzed route, a molecule of water serving as proton transfer agent for the general base catalysis. The deacylation part of the overall reaction is considered to be essentially the microscopic reverse of the acylation part.

consistent with the data, takes explicit account of the formation of tetrahedral intermediates that are normal intermediates for esterolytic reactions.

ASPECTS OF
ENZYME
SPECIFICITY

One of the chemically most striking, and biochemically most important, aspects of enzyme-catalyzed reactions is their marked specificity. It is clear that, in the absence of a strict limitation on the range of substrates acted upon by individual enzymes, an orderly metabolic pattern is impossible to achieve.

A large number of studies of enzyme specificity have been performed. Ideally, such studies are carried out by making a series of limited structural alterations at each of several sites on the normal substrate for the reaction under consideration. An examination of the pertinent kinetic parameters for the reaction of the altered substrate serves as a measure of the degree to which the alteration has affected binding and susceptibility to reaction. The investigation of the specificity of an enzyme requires the use of pure enzyme, or at least an enzyme preparation not contaminated with enzymes catalyzing the same type of reaction as that of interest, in order to ensure that small amounts of reaction are not the result of the action of a second enzyme. In addition, such a study requires the use of carefully purified substrates to avoid the possible detection of the reaction of an impurity.

The basic goal of specificity studies is to elucidate the structural requirements for catalysis, and on this basis to obtain a picture of the catalytically active conformation of the active site, whether a rigid template or substrate-induced. Considerable progress has been made in only a few isolated cases. Frequently, such studies cannot be performed at all, since many enzymes appear to be absolutely specific for a single substrate or single pair of substrates. Only in cases in which the enzyme tolerates at least modest alterations in substrate structure is a detailed investigation of the number and spatial arrangement of groups within binding sites on the enzyme surface possible.

As many examples of the specificity of individual enzymes are presented later in this book, these will not be considered at this point. Dixon and Webb have published an extensive compilation of information of this type. One aspect of enzyme specificity does, however, merit special consideration. This is the ability of enzymes to distinguish, in some cases, between chemically identical groups. Three examples of such specificity are considered below.

The first example concerns the glycerokinase reaction:

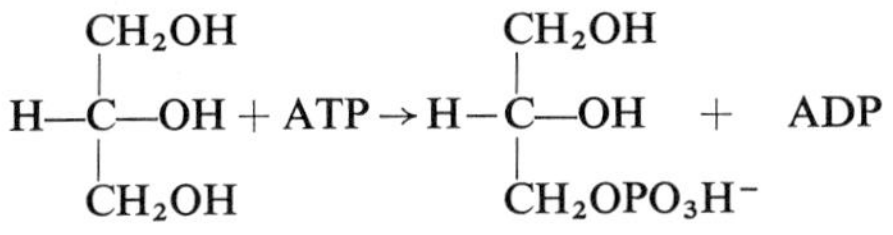

$$
\begin{array}{ccc}
CH_2OH & & CH_2OH \\
| & & | \\
H-C-OH + ATP \rightarrow & H-C-OH & + \quad ADP \\
| & & | \\
CH_2OH & & CH_2OPO_3H^-
\end{array}
\tag{7-14}
$$

L-α-Glycerophosphate

The product of this reaction is exclusively L-α-glycerophosphate. This observation suffices to indicate that this enzyme treats the chemically identical hydroxymethyl groups of glycerol in an asymmetric fashion, since if this were not so, a mixture of L-α- and D-α-glycerophosphate would have been formed. In corroboration of this conclusion, glycerol-1-C^{14}, formed enzymatically from glucose-3,4-C^{14}, is converted enzymatically to fructose-1,6-diphosphate-3,4-C^{14}

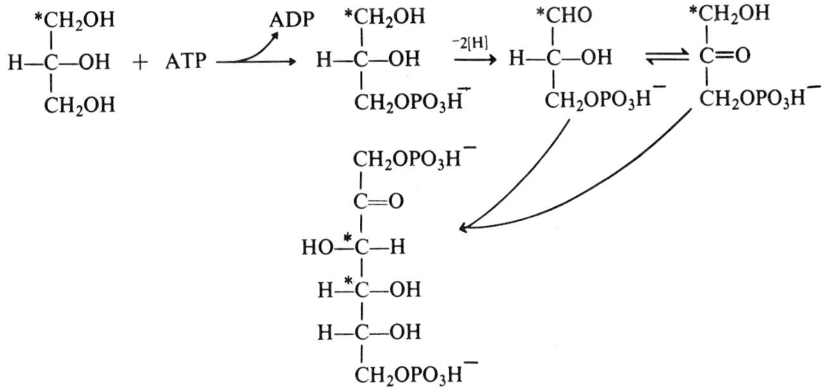

FIGURE 7-3.   Labeling Pattern of Fructose-1,6-diphosphate Derived Enzymatically from Glycerol-1-C^{14}.

by the pathway shown in Fig. 7-3. This finding indicates that the phosphorylation of glycerol occurs on the hydroxymethyl group not derived from the 3 and 4 positions of glucose, since if this molecule were handled symmetrically, the fructose-1,6-diphosphate would have been labeled at the 1 and 6 positions as well as the 3 and 4.

Related behavior is exhibited by the enzyme aconitase, which metabolizes citric acid (see page 327). Citric acid, labeled in a primary carboxyl group, prepared from labeled oxaloacetate and unlabeled acetate, as shown in Fig. 7-4, is converted enzymatically to α-ketoglutarate. The α-ketoglutarate is labeled

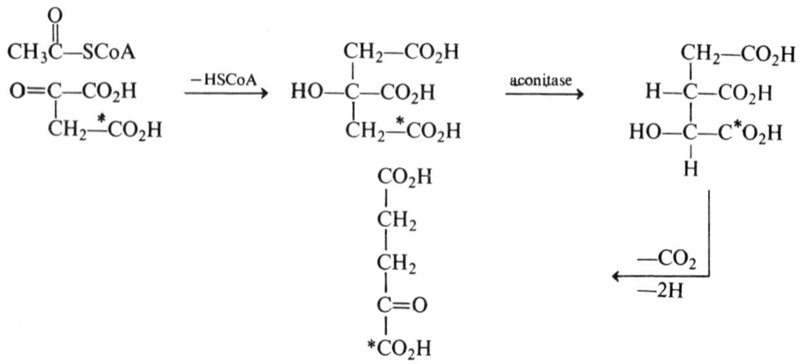

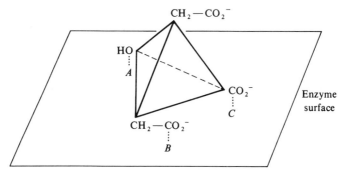

FIGURE 7-4. Labeling Pattern of α-Ketoglutarate Derived Enzymatically from Citrate-1-C^{14}.

only in the carboxyl group adjacent to the carbonyl function, indicating that aconitase distinguishes between the chemically identical carboxymethyl groups of citrate as shown.

Finally, aldolase, as noted above, catalyzes the exchange of only one hydrogen of dihydroxyacetone phosphate with solvent deuterium or tritium. If aldolase were unable to discriminate between the two hydrogens on the pertinent carbon atom, reversal of this reaction would lead to exchange of both hydrogen atoms.

Ogston has pointed out that the enzymatic differentiation of chemically identical groups can be rationalized on the basis of a three-point attachment of substrate to the enzyme surface. Such a situation is depicted schematically for the aconitase reaction in Fig. 7-5. It has been argued that the three-point-

FIGURE 7-5. A Schematic Representation of the Attachment of Citrate to Aconitase.

attachment hypothesis is unnecessary, since the two a groups on a C_{aabc} atom inherently appear distinct to an unsymmetrical reagent. The point is, in any event, that a three-dimensional match of a substrate having a C_{aabc} atom with an asymmetric enzyme surface places each of the a groups in a unique position.

REFERENCES   Bender, M. L., and R. Breslow: Mechanisms of Organic Reactions, in M. Florkin and E. H. Stotz (eds.), "Comprehensive Biochemistry," vol. 2, p. 1, Elsevier, New York, 1962.

———— and F. J. Kezdy: The Current Status of the Chymotrypsin Mechanism, *J. Am. Chem. Soc.*, **86**: 3704 (1964).

Boyer, P. D., H. Lardy, and K. Myrbäck (eds.): "The Enzymes," 2nd ed., vol. 1, Academic, New York, 1959.

Dixon, M., and E. C. Webb: "Enzymes," 2nd ed., Academic, New York, 1964.

Eigen, M., and G. G. Hammes: Elementary Steps in Enzyme Reactions, *Adv. Enzymol.*, **25**: 1 (1963).

Florkin, M., and E. H. Stotz (eds.): "Comprehensive Biochemistry," vol. 13, Elsevier, New York, 1964.

Goodwin, T. W., J. I. Harris, and B. S. Hartley (eds.): "Structure and Activity of Enzymes," Academic, New York, 1964.

Jencks, W. P.: Mechanism of Enzyme Action, *Ann. Rev. Biochem.*, **32**: 639 (1963).

Koshland, D. E., Jr.: The Active Site and Enzyme Action, *Adv. Enzymol.*, **22**: 45 (1960).

Kosower, E. M.: "Molecular Biochemistry," McGraw-Hill, New York, 1962.

Northrup, J. H., M. Kunitz, and R. M. Herriot: "Crystalline Enzymes," 2nd ed., Columbia University Press, New York, 1948.

Rose, I. A.: Mechanism of Enzyme Action, *Ann. Rev. Biochem.*, **35**: 25 (1966).

Waley, S. G.: "Mechanisms of Organic and Enzymic Reactions," Oxford, Fair Lawn, N.J., 1962.

Wolstenholme, G. E. W., and C. M. O'Connor: "Steric Course of Microbiological Reactions," Ciba Foundation Study Group no. 2, Little, Brown, Boston, 1959.

8| Coenzymes

Numerous enzymes, catalyzing a broad spectrum of biochemical reactions, require the presence of a small nonprotein *prosthetic group*, more or less tightly linked to the protein, for efficient performance of catalytic function. If this non-protein group can shuttle between two or more enzymes and thus permit group transfer between them, it is commonly referred to as a *coenzyme*. The distinction between a substrate and a coenzyme for an enzymatic reaction is often rendered unclear, since the coenzyme, as well as the substrate, may be structurally altered in the course of the reaction. However, in subsequent reactions, the original structure of the coenzyme is usually regenerated, and the substrate usually undergoes further chemical modification. In those cases in which the coenzyme emerges from a reaction step in a structurally altered form, the distinction between coenzyme and substrate may be made on this basis of eventual re-generation. Also, in coenzyme-dependent reactions the binding of coenzyme to enzyme frequently precedes substrate-enzyme interaction in an obligatory manner (see page 166).

In this chapter, the most prominent coenzymes are discussed individually. Emphasis is directed toward understanding the type or types of enzymatic reactions for which each coenzyme is required in terms of the basic reaction mechanisms involved. Extended and detailed discussions of the coenzymes treated below, and several others in addition, are presented in *The Enzymes*, vols. 2 and 3. The discussion below complements the previous comments on the mechanism of enzyme action (see Chap. 7) and is an introduction to intermediary metabolism as well. Most coenzymes perform the role of intermediate carrier for group transfer reactions.

Biological oxidations are the principal source of energy necessary to drive a multitude of endergonic biological processes. The free energy derived from the transfer of a pair of electrons from a substrate to molecular oxygen or other terminal electron acceptor is largely converted, by reactions not completely understood (see Chap. 15), into chemical energy in the form of the "energy-rich" intermediate adenosine triphosphate (ATP):

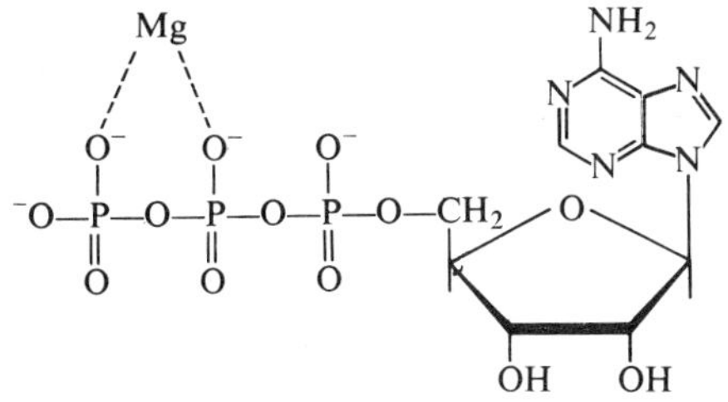

Adenosine triphosphate (ATP) · Mg chelate

The free energy derived from the ultimate hydrolysis of the pyrophosphate linkages of ATP is then available, in a coupled enzymatic reaction (see Chap. 2) to drive an otherwise unfavorable reaction more nearly toward completion. The fundamental role of the hydrolysis of ATP as the driving force for biochemical processes was first clearly recognized by Lipmann. These include muscle contraction, photosynthesis, bioluminescence, discharge of electric organs, and the biosynthesis of proteins, nucleic acids, complex carbohydrates, and lipids, among many others.

The number of individual enzymes known to require ATP as substrate or energy source is very large, and many reactions are described in the chapters of this volume dealing with intermediary metabolism. Some of the most important are summarized in Table 8-1. ATP-dependent reactions may be placed into two broad categories: the first involves the transfer of some portion of the ATP molecule to a suitable acceptor molecule, and, in the second class, the cleavage of ATP provides the driving force for otherwise unfavorable reactions. Reactions in the former category may be further classified as to the nature of the group donated from the ATP molecule: the phosphoryl, pyrophosphoryl, adenyl, and adenosinyl moieties. Those reactions in which ATP functions as an energy source are catalyzed by the ligases (or synthetases) and deserve further discussion at this point.

All ATP-dependent biosynthetic processes involve the formation of a covalent bond between two substrate molecules coupled with the cleavage of one of the pyrophosphate linkages of ATP. Most reactions of this type appear to be in one of three classes. The first involves the consecutive action of two enzymes, a phosphotransferase or pyrophosphotransferase in the first step and a phosphorylase or pyrophosphorylase in the second. For example, one route for the biosynthesis of inosine from ribose and hypoxanthine is via the initial formation of ribose-1-phosphate followed by formation of the N-glycosidic linkage:

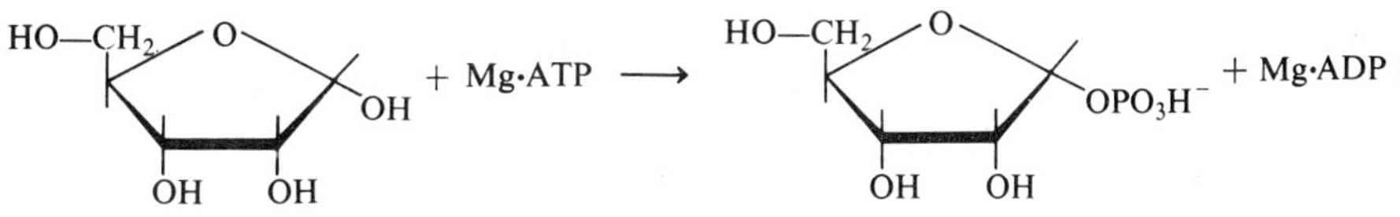

TABLE 8-1. Important Reactions Involving ATP

Reaction or reaction type	Example of stoichiometry	Name of R group	Group transferred
Oxidative phosphorylation	$A_{red} + B_{ox} + P_i + ADP \rightarrow A_{ox} + B_{red} + ATP$	Unknown	probably P_i
Photosynthetic phosphorylation	$A'_{red} + B_{ox} + ADP + P_i \xrightarrow{hv} A'_{ox} + B'_{red} + ATP$	Unknown	probably P_i
Triose phosphate dehydrogenase plus glycerate kinase	$\begin{cases} \text{D-Glyceraldehyde-3-phosphate} + P_i + NAD^+ \rightleftharpoons \\ \text{1,3-diphospho-D-glycerate} + NADH \\ \text{1,3-Diphospho-D-glycerate} + ADP \rightleftharpoons \\ \text{3-phospho-D-glycerate} + ATP \end{cases}$	$\begin{array}{c} O \\ \parallel \\ -C-O- \end{array}$	P_i
Enolase (phosphoenolpyruvate hydratase)	$\begin{cases} \text{2-Phospho-D-glycerate} \rightleftharpoons \text{phosphoenolpyruvate} + H_2O \\ \text{Phosphoenolpyruvate} + ADP \rightleftharpoons \text{pyruvate} + ATP \end{cases}$	$\begin{array}{c} H \\ \parallel \\ =C-O- \end{array}$	P_i
α-Oxoglutarate dehydrogenase (oxidoreductase)	$\alpha\text{-Oxoglutarate} + NAD^+ + CoASH \rightarrow$ succinyl-SCoA + NADH	Unknown	P_i
Plus succinate: CoA ligase (GDP) Plus nucleoside diphosphate kinase (cf. below)	$\begin{cases} \text{Succinyl-SCoA} + GDP + P_i \rightleftharpoons \text{succinate} + GTP \\ GTP + ADP \rightleftharpoons GDP + ATP \end{cases}$		
or plus succinate: CoA ligase (ADP)	$\text{Succinyl-SCoA} + ADP + P_i \rightleftharpoons \text{succinate} + ATP$		
Various kinases (ATP: donor phosphotransferases)	$ATP + \text{acetate} \rightleftharpoons \text{acetyl phosphate} + ADP \ (+H_2O)$	$\begin{array}{c} O \\ \parallel \\ -C-O- \end{array}$	P_i
	$ATP + \text{creatine} \rightleftharpoons \text{creatine phosphate} + ADP \ (+H_2O)$	$\begin{array}{c} {}^+NH_2 \\ \parallel \ \ H \\ -C-N- \end{array}$	P_i
	$ATP + ROH \rightarrow RO\text{-phosphate} + ADP \ (+H_2O)$	$R_1R_2R_3C-O-$	P_i

Enzyme	Reaction	Structure	Product
Nucleoside diphosphate kinases (ATP: nucleoside diphosphate phosphotransferases)	$ATP + NDP \rightleftharpoons ADP + NTP$	$X-\overset{\overset{\displaystyle O}{\|}}{\underset{\underset{\displaystyle O^-}{\|}}{P}}-O-$	P_i
Various nucleotidyl transferases	$ATP + FMN \rightleftharpoons FAD + PP_i$	$X-\overset{\overset{\displaystyle O}{\|}}{\underset{\underset{\displaystyle O^-}{\|}}{P}}-O-$	AMP
ATP: D-ribose-5-phosphate pyrophosphotransferase	$ATP + $ D-ribose-5-phosphate $\rightleftharpoons AMP +$ 5-phospho-α-D-ribosylpyrophosphate (PRPP)	$\overset{\displaystyle O-}{\underset{\displaystyle O-}{CH-O-}}$	PP_i
Various NMP pyrophosphorylases, pentosyltransferases	$PRPP + $ orotate $\rightleftharpoons$ orotidine-5′-phosphate $+ PP_i$	$\overset{\displaystyle O-}{\underset{\displaystyle O-}{CH-O-}}$	PP_i
Various ligases (synthetases of groups 6.1 and 6.2, first step)	$ATP + enz + RCO_2^- \rightleftharpoons \left[enz \cdot R-\overset{\overset{\displaystyle O}{\|}}{C}-O-AMP\right] + PP_i$	$\left[enz \cdot R-\overset{\overset{\displaystyle O}{\|}}{C}-O-\right]$	AMP
Various ligases (second step)	$\left[enz \cdot R-\overset{\overset{\displaystyle O}{\|}}{C}-O-AMP\right] + HX \rightleftharpoons AMP + R-\overset{\overset{\displaystyle O}{\|}}{C}-O-X$	$\left[enz \cdot R-\overset{\overset{\displaystyle O}{\|}}{C}-O-\right]$	AMP
Various ligases (group 6.3)	$ATP + $ L-pantoate $+ \beta$-alanine $\rightleftharpoons$ L-pantothenate $+ AMP + PP_i$	$\overset{\overset{\displaystyle O}{\|}}{O=C-O-}$	?
Various synthetases ($X:R$ ligases)	$ATP + $ xanthosine-5′-phosphate $+ NH_3 \rightleftharpoons GMP + AMP + PP_i$ $ATP + $ L-glutamate $+ $ L-cysteine $\rightleftharpoons \gamma$-L-glutamyl-L-cysteine $+ ADP + P_i$	$\overset{\overset{\displaystyle O}{\|}}{O=C-O-}$	probably none
ATP: L-methionine S-adenosyltransferase	$ATP + $ L-methionine $\rightarrow$ S-adenosyl-L-methionine $+$ trimetaphosphate	$X-S-CH_3$	adenosine

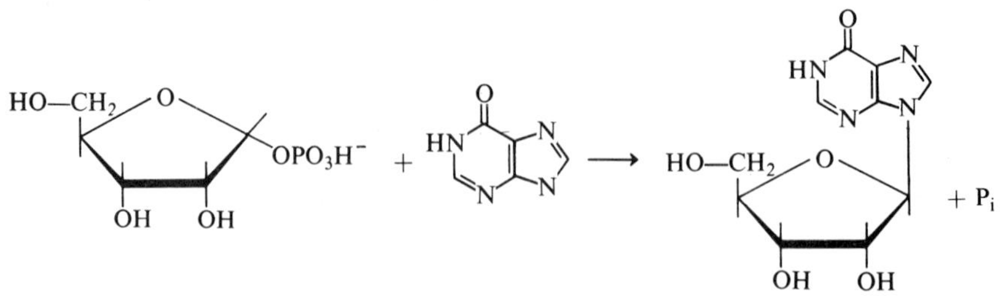

(8-2)

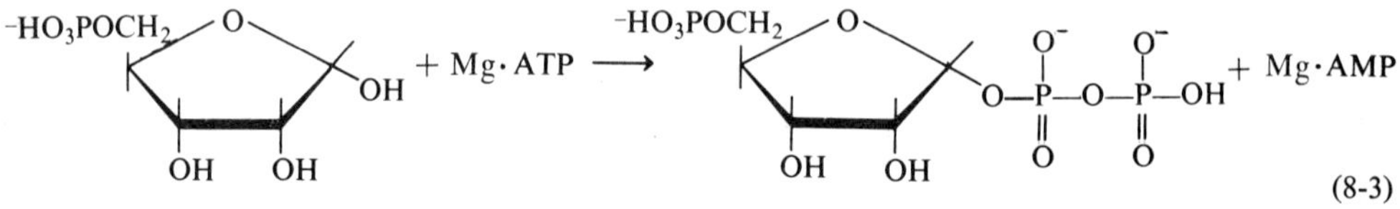

(8-3)

On the other hand, the biosynthesis of adenosine-5'-phosphate from adenine and ribose-5-phosphate involves an initial pyrophosphorylation, forming 5-phospho-α-D-ribosylpyrophosphate, followed by formation of the N-glycosidic bond:

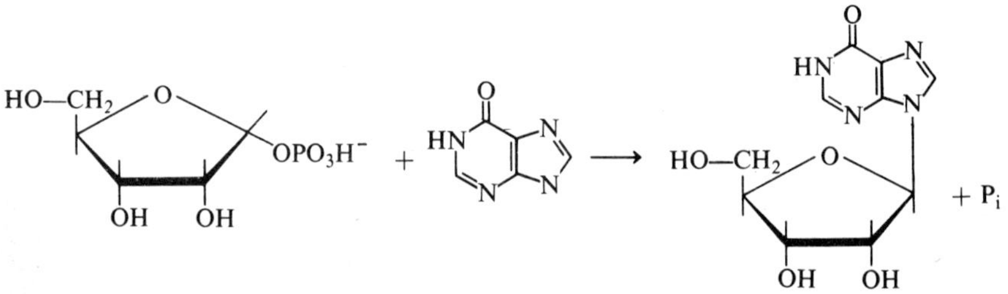

(8-4)

The second and third classes of ATP-dependent synthetase reactions involve only one enzyme, rather than two, and are usually concerned with reactions involving carboxyl group activation. They differ in the nature of the products derived from the hydrolytic cleavage of ATP. For example, the enzyme converting acetate to acetyl CoA, a thiol ester (see below), cleaves ATP into AMP and pyrophosphate, and that converting glutamate into glutamine cleaves ATP into ADP and phosphate.

Enzymes in the former class appear to catalyze a two-step reaction sequence involving the intermediate formation of enzyme-bound acyl adenylates:

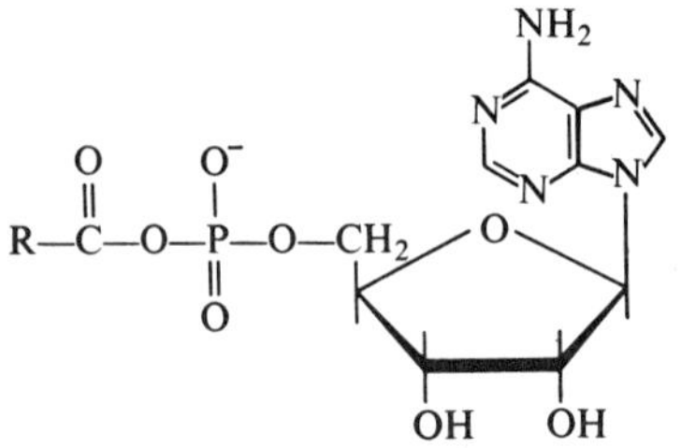

Acyl adenylate

In this regard, the acetyl-SCoA synthetase reaction mentioned above has been particularly well studied and appears to proceed as follows:

$$\text{Enz} + \text{CH}_3\text{—CO}_2{}^{18}\text{H} + \text{ATP} \underset{}{\overset{\text{Mg}^{+2}}{\rightleftharpoons}} \left[\text{CH}_3\text{—}\overset{\displaystyle O}{\overset{\displaystyle \|}{\text{C}}}\text{—O}^{18}\text{—AMP} \right] \cdot \text{enz} + \text{PP}_i \qquad (8\text{-}5)$$

$$\left[\text{CH}_3\text{—}\overset{\displaystyle O}{\overset{\displaystyle \|}{\text{C}}}\text{—O}^{18}\text{—AMP} \right] \cdot \text{enz} + \text{HSCoA} \rightleftharpoons \text{CH}_3\text{—}\overset{\displaystyle O}{\overset{\displaystyle \|}{\text{C}}}\text{—SCoA} + \text{enz}$$

$$+ \text{Ade—R—5}'\text{—O—}\overset{\displaystyle O^-}{\underset{\displaystyle O}{\overset{\displaystyle |}{\underset{\displaystyle \|}{\text{P}}}}}\text{—O}^{18}\text{H} \qquad (8\text{-}6)$$

The third class of synthetase reactions, yielding ADP and phosphate as products in reactions catalyzed by single enzymes, is less well understood. Some reactions catalyzed by enzymes in this class are known to occur with the incorporation of one oxygen of the substrate carboxyl group into the liberated phosphate, suggesting the intermediate formation of acyl phosphates:

$$\text{R—CO}_2{}^- + \text{ATP} \rightleftharpoons \text{R—}\overset{\displaystyle O}{\overset{\displaystyle \|}{\text{C}}}\text{—O—}\overset{\displaystyle O}{\underset{\displaystyle \text{OH}}{\overset{\displaystyle \|}{\underset{\displaystyle |}{\text{P}}}}}\text{—O}^- + \text{ADP} \qquad (8\text{-}7)$$

$$\text{R—}\overset{\displaystyle O}{\overset{\displaystyle \|}{\text{C}}}\text{—O—}\overset{\displaystyle O}{\underset{\displaystyle \text{OH}}{\overset{\displaystyle \|}{\underset{\displaystyle |}{\text{P}}}}}\text{—O}^- + \text{acceptor} \rightleftharpoons \text{R—}\overset{\displaystyle O}{\overset{\displaystyle \|}{\text{C}}}\text{— acceptor} + \text{P}_i \qquad (8\text{-}8)$$

URIDINE NUCLEOTIDES   One of the most important recent advances in the understanding of metabolic processes has come from the recognition of the role of *uridine nucleotide coenzymes* in carbohydrate metabolism. Numerous *uridine diphosphate sugars* have been isolated from a variety of sources and are probably of universal occurrence in nature. The structure of these compounds is basically the same, differing only in the nature of the sugar moiety, and involves a bond between the terminal phosphate of uridine diphosphate and the aldehydic carbon of the sugar:

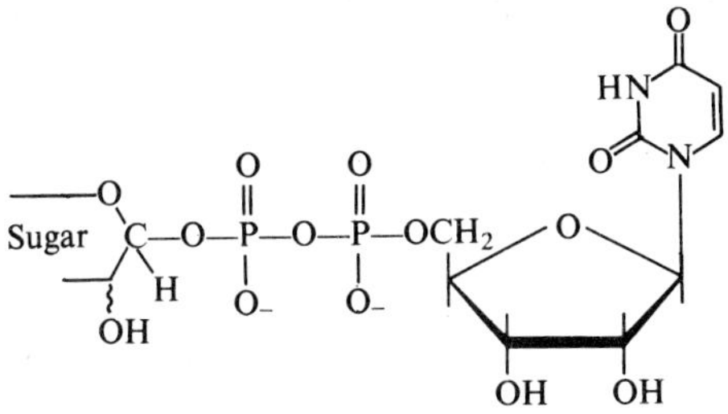

General structure for UDP-sugars

Biosynthetically, UDP-sugars are formed in enzymatic reactions between UTP and the sugar-1-phosphate:

$$\text{Sugar-1-phosphate} + \text{UTP} \rightleftharpoons \text{UDP-sugar} + \text{pyrophosphate} \qquad (8\text{-}9)$$

Enzymes catalyzing such reactions are called UDP-*sugar pyrophosphorylases* or *uridyltransferases*.

The role of UDP-sugar coenzymes in enzymatic catalysis is twofold. First, such coenzymes are involved in a variety of glycosyl transfer reactions. For example, UDP-glucose (UDPG) is involved in glucosyl group transfer reactions with fructose as acceptor, yielding sucrose; with anthranilic acid as acceptor, yielding o-aminobenzoyl glucoside; with a terminal glucose of a glycogen molecule as acceptor, lengthening the glucose chain:

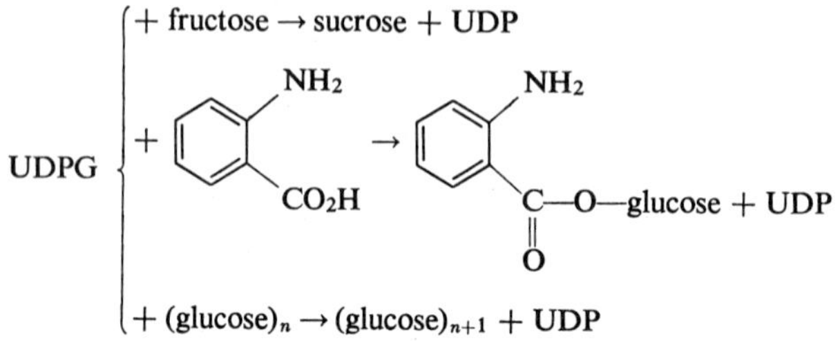

$$\text{UDPG} \begin{cases} + \text{ fructose} \rightarrow \text{sucrose} + \text{UDP} \\ \\ \\ + (\text{glucose})_n \rightarrow (\text{glucose})_{n+1} + \text{UDP} \end{cases} \tag{8-10}$$

Similarly, UDP-acetylglucosamine and UDP-glucuronic acid are intermediates in the synthesis of the complex polysaccharide, hyaluronic acid. In glycosyl group transfer reactions UDP-sugars are analogous to acyl adenylates, which, as noted above, are involved in acyl group transfer reactions also involving a variety of acceptors.

The second general type of reaction involving UDP-sugars is characterized by chemical transformation of the sugar itself. For example, UDPG-4-epimerase (UDP-glucose-4-epimerase) catalyzes the interconversion of UDPG and UDP-galactose:

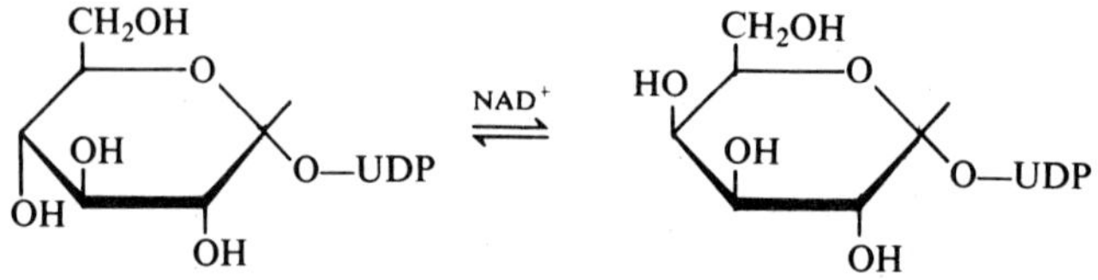

$$\tag{8-11}$$

Other examples include the nicotinamide adenine dinucleotide-dependent (see below) oxidation of UDPG to UDP-glucuronic acid:

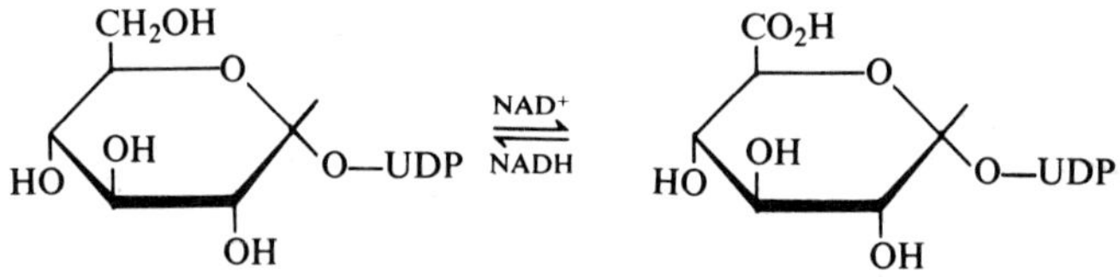

$$\tag{8-12}$$

and the decarboxylation of UDP-glucuronic acid, yielding UDP-xylose:

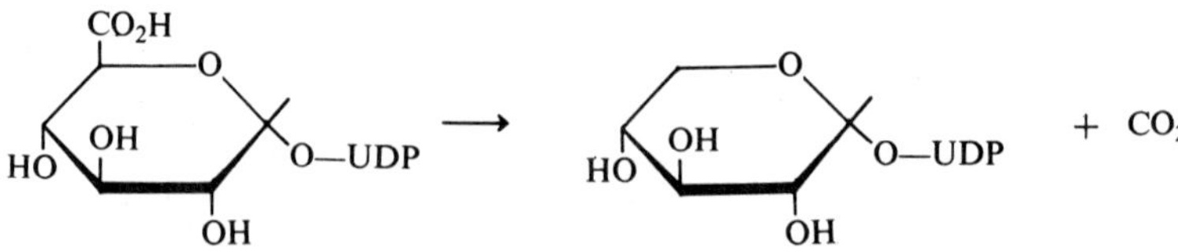

$$+ CO_2 \tag{8-13}$$

CYTIDINE NUCLEOTIDES   It was noted above that adenosine nucleotides and uridine nucleotides are involved as group transfer agents in reactions with substrates at the acyl and aldehyde level of oxidation, respectively. At the alcohol level of oxidation, group transfer reactions frequently involve *cytidine nucleotides*. Kennedy and Weiss discovered that CDP-choline and CDP-ethanolamine are essential intermediates in the biosynthesis of lecithins, an important class of lipids:

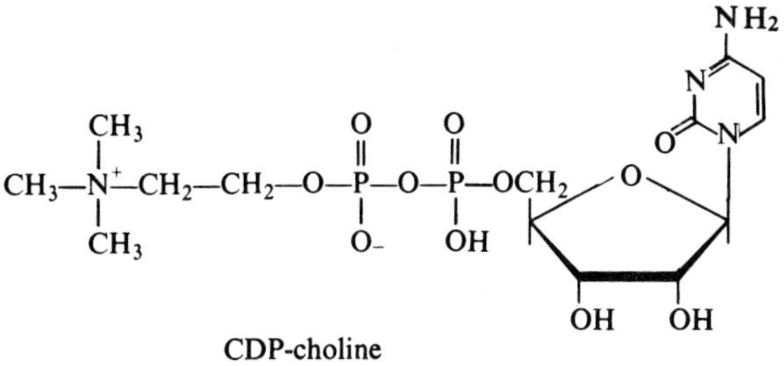

CDP-choline

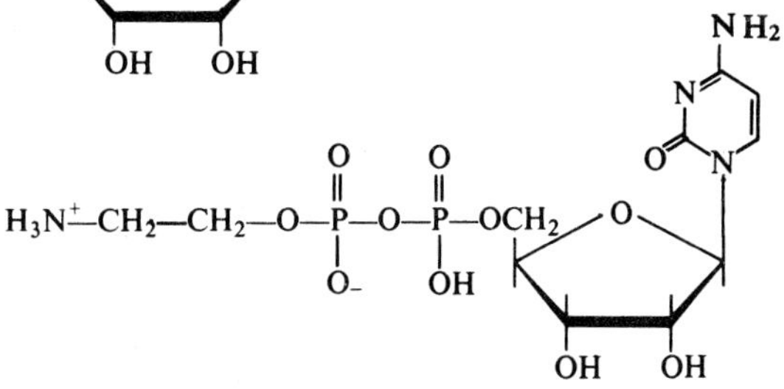

CDP-ethanolamine

CDP-alcohols are formed biosynthetically from CTP and alcohol-1-phosphate:

$$\text{CTP} + \text{alcohol-phosphate} \rightleftharpoons \text{CDP-alcohol} + \text{pyrophosphate} \tag{8-14}$$

These coenzymes transfer an alkyl phosphate group to a variety of acceptors. For example, CDP-choline reacts with α,β-diglycerides to yield lecithin and CMP:

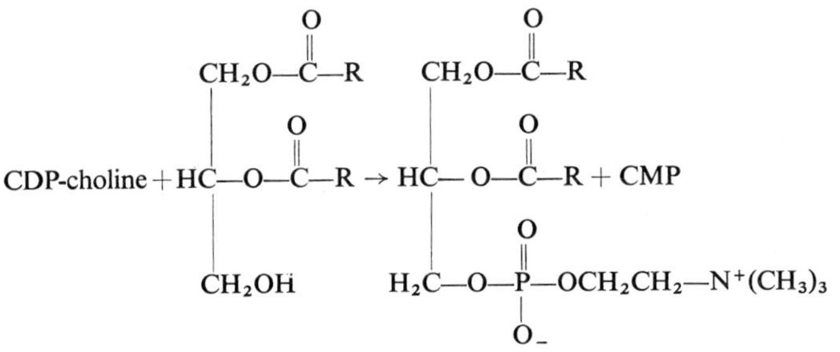

$$\tag{8-15}$$

Note that the transfer reactions involving adenosine and uridine nucleotides occur with cleavage of acylphosphate and glucosylphosphate bonds, respectively, and those involving cytidine nucleotides occur with cleavage of a pyrophosphate linkage.

GUANOSINE AND INOSINE NUCLEOTIDES

Relatively few coenzymatic functions for guanosine or inosine nucleotides have been discovered. The following are the most important: (1) GTP reacts with mannose-1-phosphate, in a manner completely reminiscent of the reaction between UTP and glucose-1-phosphate, to yield GDP-mannose as an intermediate for the transfer of mannosyl residues; (2) GTP (or ITP) is formed in the substrate-level phosphorylation accompanying the oxidation of α-oxo-glutarate by the following sequence of reactions:

$$\alpha\text{-Oxoglutarate} + NAD^+ + CoASH \rightarrow succinyl\text{-SCoA} + NADH + CO_2 \qquad (8\text{-}16)$$

$$Succinyl\text{-SCoA} + GDP\,(IDP) + P_i \rightleftharpoons succinate + CoASH + GTP(ITP) \qquad (8\text{-}17)$$

and finally (3) GTP (or ITP) is consumed in the oxaloacetic carboxykinase reaction that is responsible for the interconversion of oxaloacetate and phosphoenolpyruvate:

$$Oxaloacetate + GTP \rightleftharpoons phosphoenolpyruvate + CO_2 + GDP \qquad (8\text{-}18)$$

In addition, GTP acts as an energy donor in the formation of adenylosuccinate from IMP and L-aspartate, a key step in the biosynthesis of AMP (see page 438). The role of GTP in the biosynthesis of proteins is discussed in Chap. 21.

COENZYME A   Coenzyme A is the most prominent acyl group transfer coenzyme in living systems. This molecule is quite complex structurally and contains a multiplicity of possible functional groups:

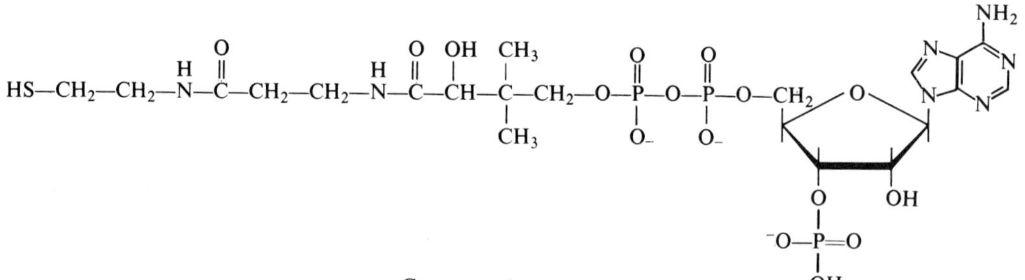

Coenzyme A

The isolation of acetyl coenzyme A from yeast by Lynen and his associates and the identification of this substance as a thiol ester demonstrate that the terminal sulfhydryl group of coenzyme A is the reactive site of this molecule in biochemical reactions. All subsequently identified acyl derivatives of coenzyme A have proved to be thiol esters as well. Hereafter we shall abbreviate coenzyme A as CoASH.

Acyl derivatives of CoASH, generally formed in ATP-dependent synthetase reactions, undergo a variety of metabolic reactions that may be classified into four groups: (1) reactions involving the attack of nucleophilic reagents on the acyl carbon atom, with transfer of the acyl function to the attacking reagent and release of CoASH; (2) reactions involving transformations (dehydrogenations, dehydrations, etc.) of the acyl moiety; (3) reactions involving condensation at the α carbon of the acyl-SCoA (such reactions almost certainly proceed through the formation of the carbanion at this position); and (4) reactions involving acyl group interchange. Reactions in each of these classes are summarized schematically in Fig. 8-1.

The choice of thiol esters rather than oxygen esters as substrates for nucleophilic reactions at the carbonyl carbon atom, for addition reactions at the β-carbon atom of α,β-unsaturated substrates, and for condensation reactions at a carbon α to a carbonyl group, is a natural one. In each case thiol esters are more reactive than oxygen esters. Simply stated, oxygen esters are less reactive than thiol esters, since (1) they are stabilized to a greater extent by resonance and

(2) such resonance is largely lost in the transition state. These arguments apply with equal force to addition reactions at the β-carbon atom of these substrates, since such reactions are just vinylogous additions to the carbonyl group.

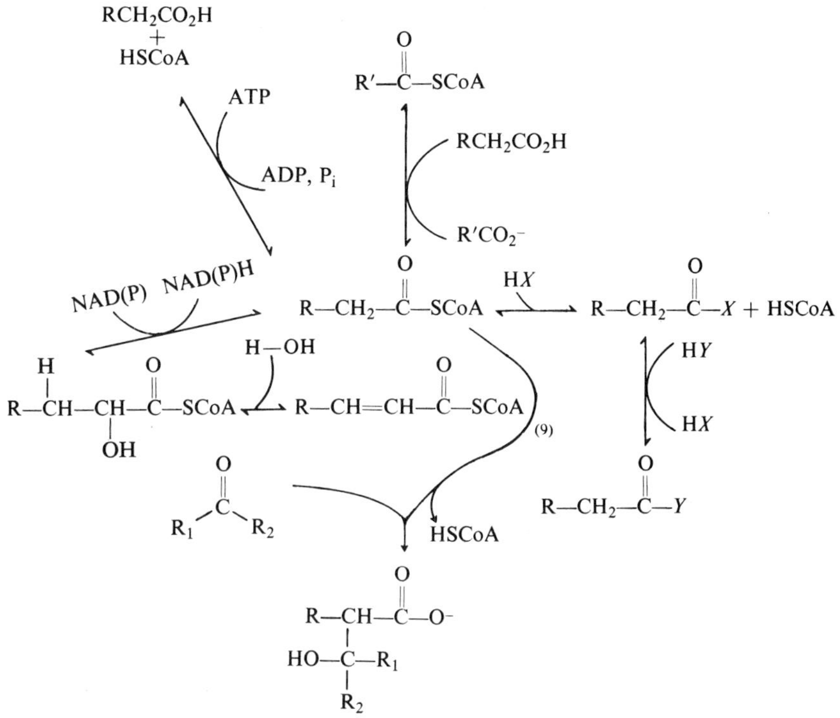

FIGURE 8-1.   A Schematic Representation of Acyl-SCoA Reaction Pathways.

LIPOIC ACID

Lipoic acid was initially isolated in crystalline form from a water-insoluble extract of beef liver. This isolation is one of the more spectacular achievements in the purification of natural products, since only 30 mg of crystalline lipoic acid was obtained from 10 tons of the liver residue. The structure of lipoic acid was subsequently demonstrated to be 1,2-dithiolane-3-valeric acid:

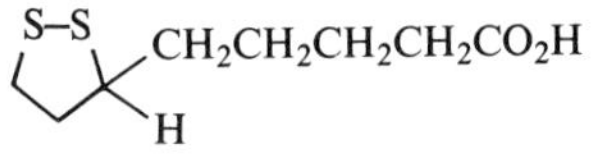

Lipoic acid

The basic coenzymatic function of lipoic acid appears to be involved with the oxidative decarboxylation of α-keto acids, such as the conversion of pyruvate to acetate and carbon dioxide. Reactions of this type are catalyzed by multi-enzyme units and involve many steps and several coenzymes (see Chaps. 11 and 14). The role of lipoic acid in the overall process is one of oxidation and acyl group transfer. The initial decarboxylation reaction yields a thiamine pyrophosphate–aldehyde intermediate (see below). In the subsequent step the acetaldehyde is transferred to lipoic acid, with the formation of 6-*S*-acetyl dihydrolipoic acid:

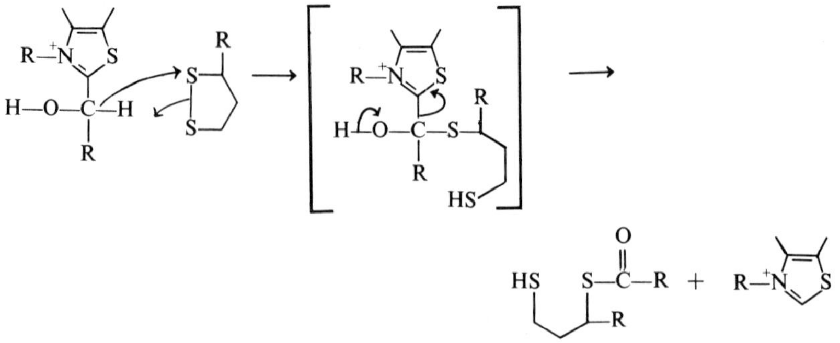

$$\text{(8-19)}$$

and the acetyl group is then transferred to HSCoA, yielding acetyl-SCoA and dihydrolipoic acid. The oxidized form of lipoic acid is regenerated by a specific dihydrolipoic dehydrogenase. Lipoic acid is covalently bound to the dehydrogenation complex involved in the overall reaction through an amide linkage between the carboxyl function of the coenzyme and an ε-amino group of a lysine residue. The formation and hydrolysis of this amide linkage are catalyzed by a specific ATP-dependent synthetase and a hydrolase, respectively.

GLUTATHIONE   The structure of glutathione, a tripeptide of universal occurrence in living material, was established in 1929 by Hopkins as γ-L-glutamyl-L-cysteinylglycine:

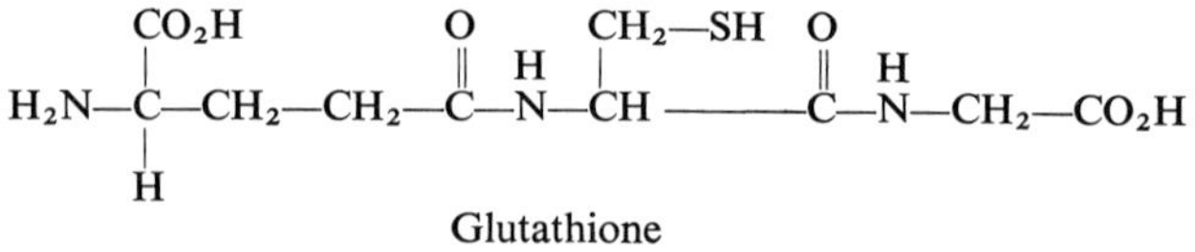

Glutathione

Although a large number of biological and biochemical functions have been suggested for glutathione since its discovery, the number of instances in which glutathione is known to function as a coenzyme are rather few. Of these, the most widely studied is the glyoxylase reaction:

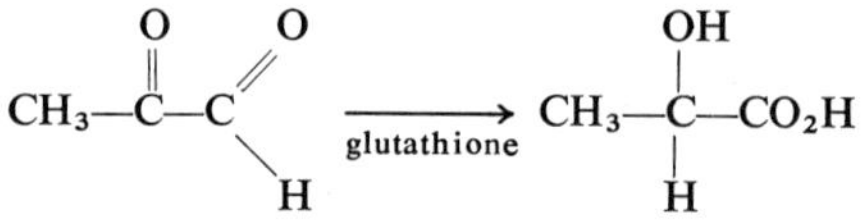

$$\text{(8-20)}$$

The conversion of methyl glyoxal into lactate occurs via a two-step reaction pathway. The first step, catalyzed by glyoxylase I, yields the thiol ester of lactate and glutathione; and the second step, catalyzed by glyoxylase II, results in the hydrolysis of this thiol ester, yielding lactate and regenerating glutathione. Studies establishing that the thiohemiacetal of methyl glyoxal and glutathione is a substrate for the glyoxylase I reaction and that the α-hydrogen of lactate is derived from the carbonyl hydrogen of methyl glyoxal rather than from solvent strongly suggest that the glyoxylase reaction involves an internal hydride shift in the thiohemiacetal intermediate

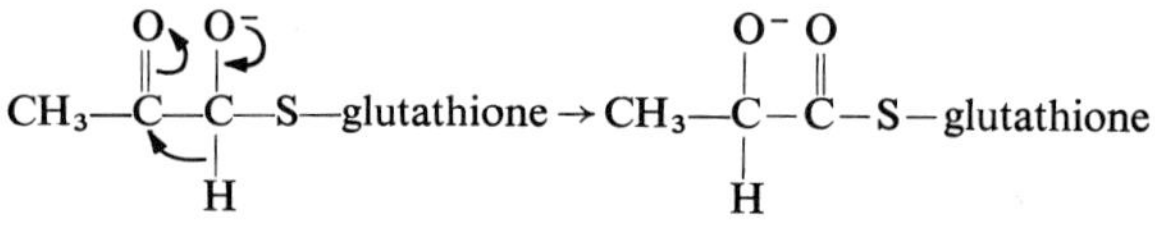

$$\text{(8-21)}$$

The most important metabolic function of glutathione (GSH) is to keep cysteine-thiols on proteins reduced by virtue of the following reactions:

$RSSR' + GSH \rightarrow RSSG + R'SH$ nonenzymatic

$RSSG + GSH \rightarrow RSH + GSSG$ nonenzymatic

$H^+ + GSSG + NADPH \rightarrow 2GSH + NADP^+$ enzymatic

PYRIDOXAL PHOSPHATE

Pyridoxal phosphate is most striking in terms of the multiplicity of different enzymatic reactions that are dependent on its presence. Nearly all these reactions are concerned with transformations of amino acids. It is not surprising, then, to learn that numerous nutritional studies in animals and microorganisms have established that a deficiency of pyridoxal (pyridoxine), a biochemical precursor of pyridoxal phosphate, results in many lesions in protein metabolism. The development of our understanding of pyridoxal phosphate-dependent reactions began in 1934 with the identification of a nutritional factor required for the cure of a specific dermatitis in young rats that developed on a deficient diet. Gyorgy called this nutritional factor vitamin B_6, a term presently used to refer to the family of substances of biochemical interest that are structurally related to pyridoxal phosphate. Its structure was established as 3-hydroxy-4,5-dihydroxymethyl-2-methyl pyridine, pyridoxol.

Following the discovery that the urine of animals that had ingested pyridoxol contained metabolites of this substance that were a great deal more effective than pyridoxol as a growth factor for the lactic acid bacteria, the metabolites were characterized by Snell in 1944 as pyridoxal and pyridoxamine. It has been subsequently demonstrated that the biocatalytically active form of pyridoxal (and in one case pyridoxamine) is the phosphorylated derivative:

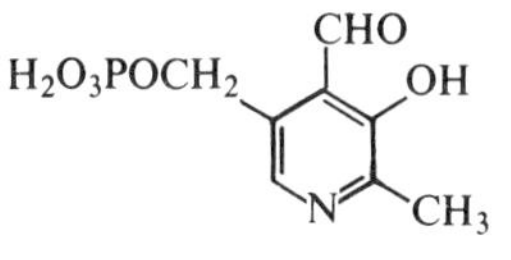

Pyridoxal phosphate 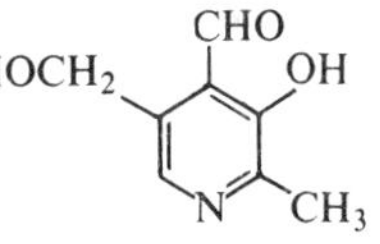   Pyridoxal

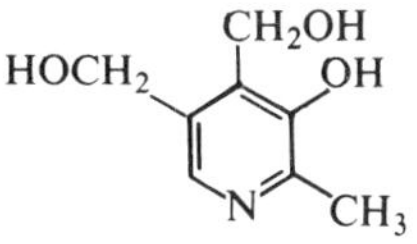

Pyridoxol 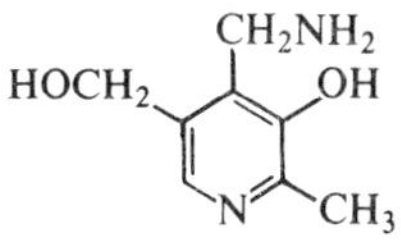   Pyridoxamine

As noted above, pyridoxal phosphate-dependent enzymes catalyze a striking variety of distinct reactions. Representative reactions include the racemization of optically active amino acids such as alanine,

$$H_2N-\overset{CH_3}{\underset{H}{C}}-CO_2H \rightleftharpoons CH_3-\overset{NH_2}{\underset{H}{C}}-CO_2H \qquad (8\text{-}22)$$

transaminations such as the interconversion of glutamate and oxaloacetate with aspartate and α-keto (α-oxo) glutarate,

$$
\begin{array}{c}
\text{CO}_2\text{H} \\
| \\
\text{CH}_2 \\
| \\
\text{CH}_2 \\
| \\
\text{H}\!-\!\text{C}\!-\!\text{NH}_2 \\
| \\
\text{CO}_2\text{H}
\end{array}
\;+\;
\begin{array}{c}
\text{CO}_2\text{H} \\
| \\
\text{CH}_2 \\
| \\
\text{C}\!=\!\text{O} \\
| \\
\text{CO}_2\text{H}
\end{array}
\;\rightleftharpoons\;
\begin{array}{c}
\text{CO}_2\text{H} \\
| \\
\text{CH}_2 \\
| \\
\text{CH}_2 \\
| \\
\text{C}\!=\!\text{O} \\
| \\
\text{CO}_2\text{H}
\end{array}
\;+\;
\begin{array}{c}
\text{CO}_2\text{H} \\
| \\
\text{CH}_2 \\
| \\
\text{H}\!-\!\text{C}\!-\!\text{NH}_2 \\
| \\
\text{CO}_2\text{H}
\end{array}
\qquad (8\text{-}23)
$$

the decarboxylation of amino acids, including histidine,

$$
\begin{array}{c}
\text{NH}_2 \\
| \\
\raisebox{0pt}{imidazole}\!-\!\text{CH}_2\!-\!\text{C}\!-\!\text{CO}_2\text{H} \\
| \\
\text{H}
\end{array}
\longrightarrow
\ \raisebox{0pt}{imidazole}\!-\!\text{CH}_2\!-\!\text{CH}_2\!-\!\text{NH}_2
\;+\; \text{CO}_2 \qquad (8\text{-}24)
$$

α,β-elimination reactions such as the dehydration of serine,

$$
\begin{array}{c}
\text{NH}_2 \\
| \\
\text{HO}\!-\!\text{CH}_2\!-\!\text{C}\!-\!\text{CO}_2\text{H} \\
| \\
\text{H}
\end{array}
\;\xrightarrow{-\text{H}_2\text{O}}\;
\begin{array}{c}
\text{NH}_2 \\
| \\
\text{CH}_2\!=\!\text{C}\!-\!\text{CO}_2\text{H}
\end{array}
\;\xrightarrow[\ -\text{NH}_3]{+\text{H}_2\text{O}}\;
\begin{array}{c}
\text{O} \\
\| \\
\text{CH}_3\!-\!\text{C}\!-\!\text{CO}_2\text{H}
\end{array}
\qquad (8\text{-}25)
$$

β,γ-elimination reactions such as the desulfuration of homocysteine,

$$
\begin{array}{c}
\text{NH}_2 \\
| \\
\text{HS}\!-\!\text{CH}_2\!-\!\text{CH}_2\!-\!\text{C}\!-\!\text{CO}_2\text{H} \\
| \\
\text{H}
\end{array}
\;\xrightarrow{-\text{H}_2\text{S}}\;
\begin{array}{c}
\text{NH}_2 \\
| \\
\text{CH}_3\!-\!\text{CH}\!=\!\text{C}\!-\!\text{CO}_2\text{H}
\end{array}
\;\xrightarrow[\ -\text{NH}_3]{+\text{H}_2\text{O}}\;
$$

$$
\begin{array}{c}
\text{O} \\
\| \\
\text{CH}_3\!-\!\text{CH}_2\!-\!\text{C}\!-\!\text{CO}_2\text{H}
\end{array} \qquad (8\text{-}26)
$$

the synthesis of tryptophan from serine and indole,

$$
\text{indole}
\;+\;
\begin{array}{c}
\text{NH}_2 \\
| \\
\text{HO}\!-\!\text{CH}_2\!-\!\text{C}\!-\!\text{CO}_2\text{H} \\
| \\
\text{H}
\end{array}
\longrightarrow
\ \text{indole}\!-\!\text{CH}_2\!-\!\overset{\text{NH}_2}{\underset{\text{H}}{\text{C}}}\!-\!\text{CO}_2\text{H} + \text{H}_2\text{O} \qquad (8\text{-}27)
$$

and the dealdolization of serine, yielding glycine and formaldehyde,

$$
\text{HOCH}_2\!-\!\overset{\text{NH}_2}{\underset{\text{H}}{\text{C}}}\!-\!\text{CO}_2\text{H} + \text{FH}_4 \rightleftharpoons \text{NH}_2\!-\!\text{CH}_2\!-\!\text{CO}_2\text{H} + (\text{HCHO})\!-\!\text{FH}_4 \qquad (8\text{-}28)
$$

The last reaction also requires the participation of an additional coenzyme, tetrahydrofolic acid (FH_4), which acts as an acceptor for the formaldehyde moiety (see below).

Studies on model systems culminated in the formulation by Snell and his associates and by Braunstein and Shemyakin of a series of similar reaction mechanisms accounting for the role of pyridoxal phosphate in these reactions. These mechanisms involve the initial formation of a metal chelate of a Schiff base between catalyst and substrate, followed by two or more bond-changing reactions within the Schiff base chelate, and terminated by hydrolysis of the chelate, regenerating catalyst and yielding products. The chelated Schiff base (I)

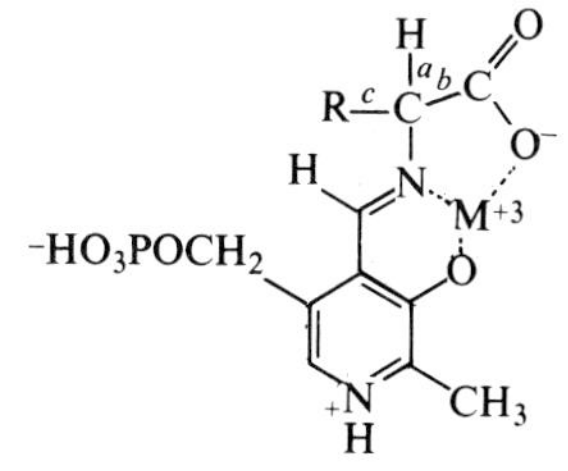

I

provides a conjugated system of double bonds extending from the reaction site to the strongly electrophilic pyridinium nitrogen atom and aiding the displacement of a pair of electrons adjacent to the α carbon of the amino acid. The labilization of these bonds, *a*, *b*, and *c* in (I), provides the basis for an understanding of pyridoxal-catalyzed reactions.

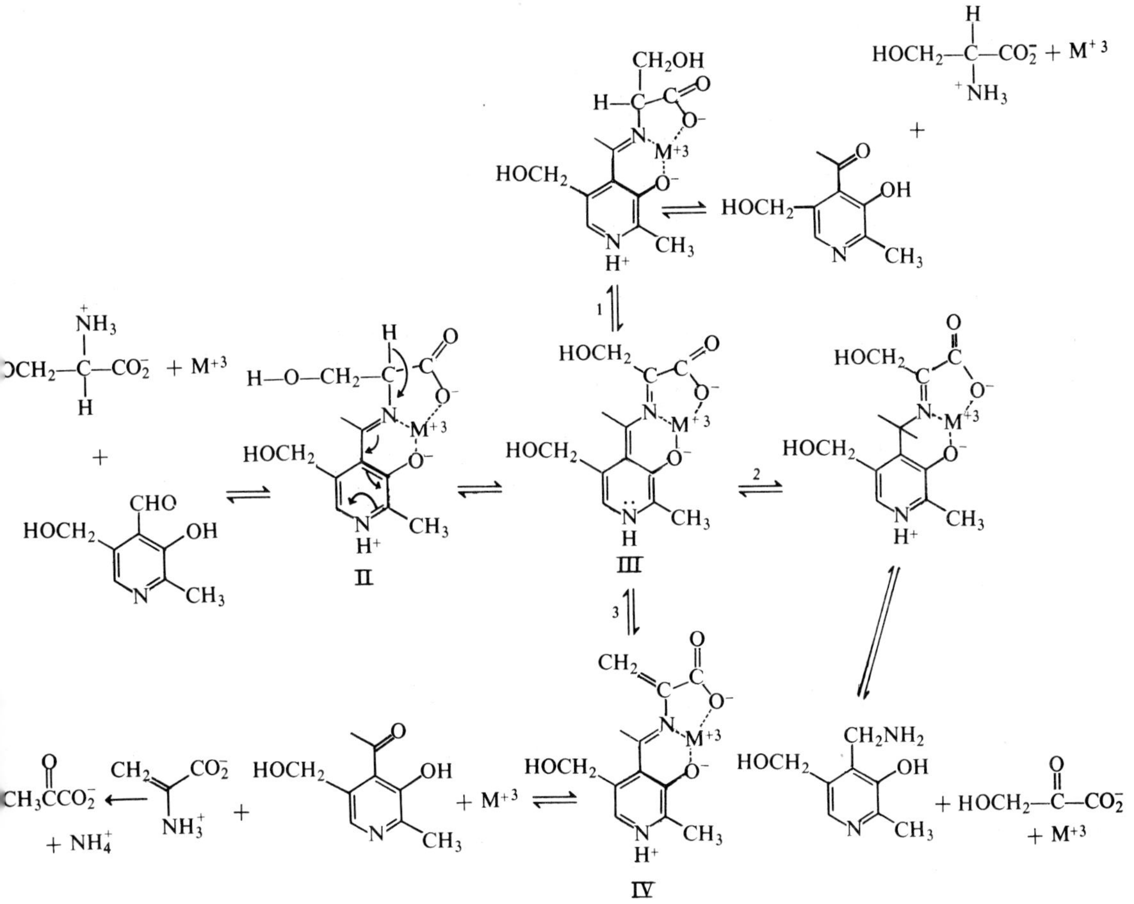

FIGURE 8-2. Pathways for Pyridoxal-catalyzed Racemization, Transamination, and Dehydration of Serine.

Some of the mechanisms that account for the observed reactions of pyridoxal-dependent enzymes are illustrated in Fig. 8-2. Pathways are illustrated with serine. *Racemization, transamination,* and *dehydration* of serine are suggested to involve the ionization of the proton attached to the α carbon of the amino acid moiety in the Schiff base chelate (II) to yield the rearranged chelate (III) — Fig. 8-2. Readdition of the proton to the same site in this optically inactive intermediate, followed by hydrolysis, completes the racemization reaction (pathway 1, Fig. 8-2). Readdition of this proton to the original carbonyl carbon atom, followed by hydrolysis, yields the transamination products, pyridoxamine and the keto acid (pathway 2, Fig. 8-2). The overall transamination reaction, as indicated in Eq. (8-23), may be completed by the reversal of this process, pyridoxamine combining with the second keto acid in the initial step. This reaction regenerates pyridoxal and converts the keto acid into the amino acid product. Finally, the unshared pair of electrons may be employed to expel hydroxide ion from (III), yielding (IV) (pathway 3, Fig. 8-2). Hydrolysis of this Schiff base chelate yields α-amino acrylic acid, which spontaneously hydrolyzes to pyruvate. Related mechanisms account for the remainder of pyridoxal phosphate-dependent reactions.

Pyridoxal-dependent enzymatic and nonenzymatic reactions differ in four important respects. First, most of the enzymatic reactions do not require metal ions for activity, but the nonenzymatic reactions are strongly dependent thereon. Plausible roles for the metal ion in the nonenzymatic reactions are stabilization of the Schiff base, inductive electron withdrawal from the reaction site, and maintenance of the planar structure required for electron withdrawal by resonance. Perhaps the protein provides all these in the enzymatic reactions. Second, the enzymatic reactions are specific in terms of both substrate structure and type of reaction catalyzed, but, as noted above, the nonenzymatic reactions are rather nonspecific. Third, the enzymatic reactions occur more rapidly by many orders of magnitude than their nonenzymatic counterparts. This reaction specificity and rate enhancement for the enzymatic reactions must be attributed to the protein moiety of the enzyme. Finally, the enzymatic reactions appear to involve a transimination reaction, rather than Schiff base formation, as the initial reaction step. Spectral studies that suggested that enzyme-bound pyridoxal phosphate existed as the Schiff base rather than as the free aldehyde have been confirmed by reduction of pyridoxal phosphate enzymes with sodium borohydride. This reagent converts Schiff bases into stable secondary amines:

$$\text{>=N— + NaBH}_4 \rightarrow \text{>}\underset{\overset{|}{\text{H}}}{\overset{\text{H}}{\text{—N—}}} \tag{8-29}$$

Sodium borohydride reduction of phosphorylase b (an enzyme for which the role of pyridoxal phosphate is not known), glutamic-aspartic transaminase, and cystathionase, followed by chemical degradation, has resulted in the isolation of reduced pyridoxal phosphate bound to the ε-amino group of a lysine residue. Assuming that enzymatic reactions, like their nonenzymatic analogues, occur with the intermediate formation of a Schiff base between pyridoxal phosphate and substrate, an early step in the enzyme-catalyzed reactions may be considered to involve the conversion of a pyridoxal phosphate–enzyme Schiff base into a pyridoxal phosphate–substrate Schiff base, a transimination reaction:

$$R' \text{—} \underset{\underset{H}{\overset{E}{\overset{\|}{N}}}}{C}\text{—}\underset{\underset{\overset{+}{N}}{}}{\underset{H}{}}\;O^- + NH_2\text{—}CHR\text{—}CO_2H \;\rightleftharpoons\; R'\text{—}\underset{\overset{R\text{—}\overset{H}{\underset{|}{C}}\text{—}CO_2H}{N}}{C}\;O^- + E\text{—}NH_2 \qquad (8\text{-}30)$$

THIAMINE PYROPHOSPHATE   Thiamine pyrophosphate, a coenzyme of universal occurrence in living systems, was originally detected as a nutritional factor required for the prevention of polyneuritis in birds and beriberi in man. The crystalline vitamin (thiamine) was obtained in 1925 by Jansen and Donath, and its structure was elucidated a decade later by Williams and Cline. Thiamine consists of a substituted pyrimidine linked by a methylene group to a substituted thiazole:

$$\underset{CH_3}{\underset{N}{}}\;\overset{NH_2}{\underset{N}{}}\;CH_2\text{—}\overset{+}{N}\underset{S}{\overset{CH_3}{}}\text{—}CH_2\text{—}CH_2\text{—}O\text{—}\underset{\overset{\|}{O}}{\overset{OH}{\underset{|}{P}}}\text{—}O\text{—}\underset{\overset{\|}{O}}{\overset{OH}{\underset{|}{P}}}\text{—}O^-$$

Thiamine pyrophosphate

Thiamine pyrophosphate serves as coenzyme for three types of enzymatic reactions: nonoxidative decarboxylations of α-keto acids, oxidative decarboxylations of α-keto acids, and formation of α-ketols (acyloins). The first implication of thiamine pyrophosphate in an enzymatic process was derived from the finding that the decarboxylation of pyruvate by yeast cells required a thermostable organic cofactor, called *cocarboxylase* by the discoverer:

$$CH_3\text{—}\overset{\overset{O}{\|}}{C}\text{—}CO_2H \xrightarrow{Mg^{+2}} CH_3\text{—}\overset{\overset{O}{\|}}{C}\text{—}H + CO_2 \qquad (8\text{-}31)$$

This cofactor was isolated and crystallized from yeast cells by Lohmann and Schuster and demonstrated to be thiamine pyrophosphate. Thiamine-dependent carboxylases of varying specificity have been detected in a wide range of living matter and are probably of universal occurrence.

The oxidative decarboxylation by α-keto acid dehydrogenases is also thiamine pyrophosphate–dependent. These reactions, with oxygen as final acceptor, can be formulated thus:

$$R\text{—}\overset{\overset{O}{\|}}{C}\text{—}CO_2H + \tfrac{1}{2}O_2 \xrightarrow{Mg^{+2}} R\text{—}\overset{\overset{O}{\|}}{C}\text{—}OH + CO_2 \qquad (8\text{-}32)$$

The role of thiamine pyrophosphate in the oxidative decarboxylations is similar to that described for the nonoxidative process. The former reactions are generally quite complicated, involving several coenzymes, lipoic acid usually serving as the actual immediate oxidizing reagent. Such reactions are quite common and occur with a variety of α-keto acids (p. 277).

The enzymatic formation of α-ketols is a common reaction apparently catalyzed by many carboxylases and α-keto acid dehydrogenases. Typical examples include the reaction of pyruvate with acetaldehyde to yield acetoin:

$$CH_3\overset{O}{\overset{\|}{C}}-CO_2H + CH_3-\overset{O}{\overset{\|}{C}}-H \rightarrow CH_3-\overset{O}{\overset{\|}{C}}-\underset{\underset{H}{|}}{\overset{\overset{OH}{|}}{C}}-CH_3 + CO_2 \tag{8-33}$$

or the reaction of 2 moles of pyruvate to yield acetoin:

$$2CH_3\overset{O}{\overset{\|}{C}}-CO_2H \rightarrow CH_3-\overset{O}{\overset{\|}{C}}-\underset{\underset{H}{|}}{\overset{\overset{OH}{|}}{C}}-CH_3 + 2CO_2 \tag{8-34}$$

Another analogous reaction involving a ketol and thiamine pyrophosphate is that catalyzed by the enzyme transketolase (see page 284).

All thiamine pyrophosphate–dependent reactions are basically similar. In each case a carbon-carbon bond adjacent to a keto group is cleaved, yielding a stable product such as a carboxylate group or an aldehyde plus an active aldehyde anion bound to thiamine pyrophosphate. Reaction of this anion with a proton generates an aldehyde; an example is the nonoxidative decarboxylation of pyruvate — Eq. (8-31). Reaction with an oxidizing agent, such as oxidized lipoic acid, generates acetate; the oxidative decarboxylation of pyruvate — Eq. (8-32) — is an example. A reaction with a carbonyl group generates an acyloin, as in acetoin formation — Eqs. (8-33) and (8-34).

An understanding of the coenzymatic function of thiamine pyrophosphate–dependent enzymatic reactions is the result of the study of analogous reactions in nonenzymatic systems. Since the initial studies of Ugai and others in 1943, several thiamine-dependent nonenzymatic reactions have been discovered that closely resemble the enzymatic processes. The mechanism of the nonenzymatic reactions was established with the striking discovery by Breslow that the aromatic hydrogen at position 2 of the thiazolium ring in thiamine exchanges readily with solvent deuterium. This exchange occurs with a half time of approximately 2 min in aqueous solution at room temperature and pH 5. At pH 7 the reaction is too fast to follow by ordinary techniques. This finding indicates that the ylid (V) is particularly stable:

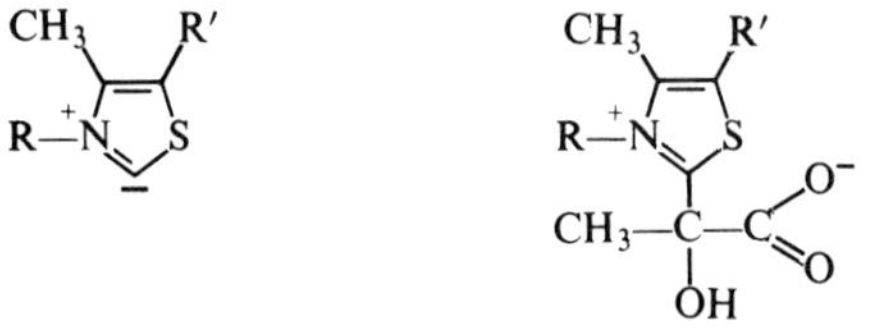

$$\underline{V} \hspace{5cm} \underline{VI}$$

On this basis, the following reasonable mechanisms may be constructed to account for thiamine-dependent reactions. Suggested mechanisms for these reactions are shown in Fig. 8-3. In all cases the initial reaction involves the addition of the carbanion to the carbonyl carbon atom of the α-keto acid, forming, e.g., compound (VI). The strongly electrophilic nitrogen atom in (VI) aids the decarboxylation of this species, yielding (VII). Subsequent addition of one of a variety of electrophilic reagents to the former carbonyl carbon atom followed by expulsion of the original carbanion yields the required reaction products. The 2-hydroxyethyl thiazolium salt of thiamine pyrophosphate has been isolated from yeast mitochondria, indicating that the suggested reaction intermediate occurs in living matter. Furthermore, hydroxyethyl thiamine pyrophosphate is enzymatically active in the formation of acetaldehyde, acetoin, and acetate, and the corresponding intermediate, dihydroxyethyl thiamine pyrophosphate, is active in the transketolase reaction.

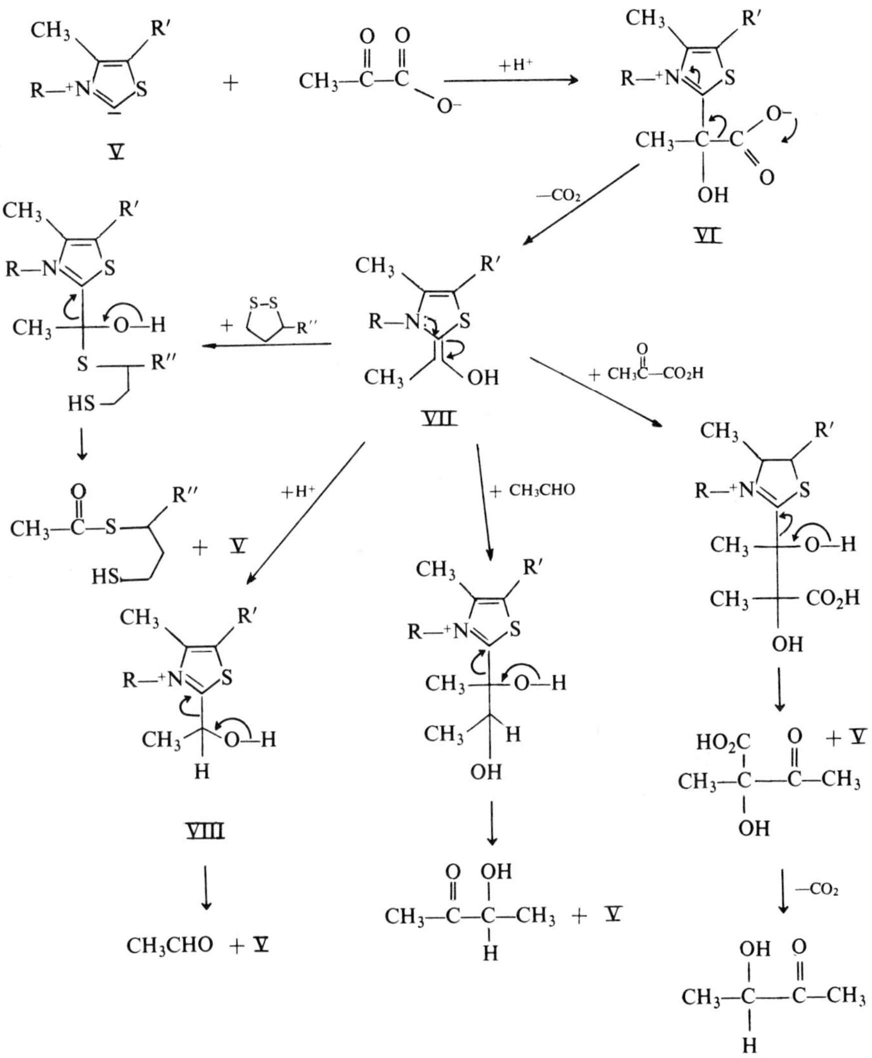

FIGURE 8-3. Mechanisms for Thiamine-dependent Reactions of Pyruvate.

TETRAHYDROFOLIC ACID

The transfer of one-carbon fragments constitutes an important class of metabolic reactions. Such transformations generally occur via coenzymes derived from tetrahydrofolic acid (FH_4):

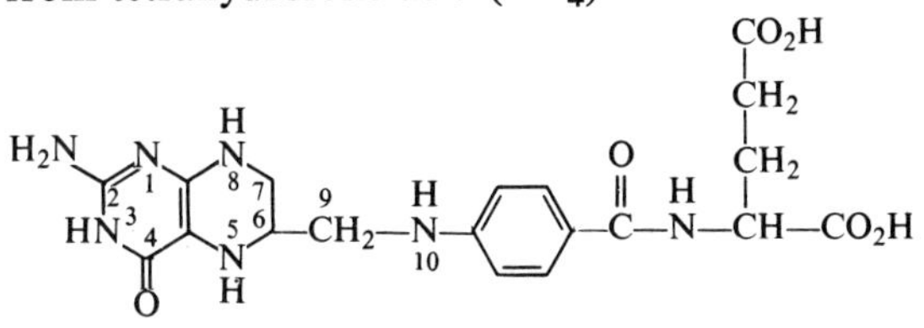

Tetrahydrofolic acid

FH_4 is composed of a reduced pteridine, p-aminobenzoic acid, and L-glutamic acid. Polyglutamic derivatives of FH_4, containing up to seven glutamate residues linked via γ-glutamyl peptide bonds, also occur in living systems and perform biochemical functions similar to those of FH_4 itself. The development of the understanding of the biochemical role of FH_4 coenzymes began with the recognition of folic acid, containing a completely aromatized pteridine ring system, as a nutritional factor for the lactic acid bacteria. The dependence of these organisms on folic acid for growth was employed as an assay system for the purification and isolation of this substance, subsequently characterized structurally. The ready oxidation of FH_4 to folic acid accounts for the isolation of the latter substance in the early studies. Folic acid may be enzymatically reduced to FH_4. There are three possible structural isomers (7,8-, 5,6-, and 5,8-) for dihydrofolate, but only the 7,8- isomer has been identified unequivocally in chemical or enzymatic reactions.

FH_4 coenzymes are concerned with the transfer of one-carbon fragments at the oxidation level of formate, formaldehyde, and methanol. At the formate level of oxidation, FH_4-formate adducts exist in four structural forms: N^{10}-formyl FH_4, N^5-formyl FH_4, N^5-formimino FH_4, and N^5,N^{10}-methenyl FH_4. Numerous examples of metabolic reactions involving these coenzymes are presented later in this volume. For the present we are concerned principally with the synthesis and interconversions of these coenzymes.

The synthesis of N^{10}-formyl FH_4 is catalyzed by formyltetrahydrofolate synthetase — formate : tetrahydrofolate ligase (ADP) — in an ATP-dependent reaction:

$$HCO_2H + FH_4 + ATP.Mg \rightleftharpoons N^{10}\text{-formyl } FH_4 + P_i + ADP.Mg \tag{8-35}$$

The hydrolysis of N^{10}-formyl FH_4 is catalyzed by a specific deacylase.

Formylglutamate formyl transferase catalyzes the formation of N^5-formyl FH_4:

$$\text{Formimino-}\gamma\text{-L-glutamate} + FH_4 \rightarrow N^5\text{-formyl } FH_4 + \text{glutamate} \tag{8-36}$$

The closely related coenzyme, N^5-formimino FH_4, may be synthesized from FH_4 and either formiminoglycine or formiminoglutamate:

$$\overset{\displaystyle H}{\underset{\displaystyle |}{}}\ \overset{\displaystyle H}{\underset{\displaystyle |}{}}$$
$$HN{=}C{-}N{-}R + FH_4 \rightarrow N^5\text{-formimino } FH_4 + RNH_2 \tag{8-37}$$

The latter reaction is catalyzed by the same enzyme that promotes the reaction in Eq. (8-36).

N^5-formyl FH_4 is converted to the N^{10}-isomer in the ATP-dependent N^5-formyltetrahydrofolate isomerase reaction:

$$N^5\text{-formyl } FH_4 + ATP \rightarrow N^{10}\text{-formyl } FH_4 + P_i + ADP \tag{8-38}$$

N^5,N^{10}-methenyl FH_4 may arise in several fashions: from N^{10}-formyl FH_4, N^5-formimino FH_4, and, perhaps, N^5-formyl FH_4. The metabolic routes for the synthesis and interconversion of the formyl derivatives of FH_4 and the other coenzymes described below are summarized in Fig. 8-4.

In contrast to transfer reactions of one-carbon fragments at the formate level of oxidation, in which several FH_4 coenzymes are involved, such reactions at the formaldehyde level of oxidation apparently involve only one coenzyme, N^5,N^{10}-methylene FH_4:

$$\underset{\substack{\\ \\ N^5,N^{10}\text{-methylene } FH_4}}{-\underset{5}{N}\underset{\substack{| \\ CH_2}}{\diagup}\underset{10}{N}-R}$$

The principal sources of this coenzyme are the reduction of N^5,N^{10}-methenyl FH_4 by a specific dehydrogenase and the L-serine hydroxymethyltransferase reaction (see Fig. 8-4). The latter enzyme requires pyridoxal phosphate, as noted in the discussion of this coenzyme above.

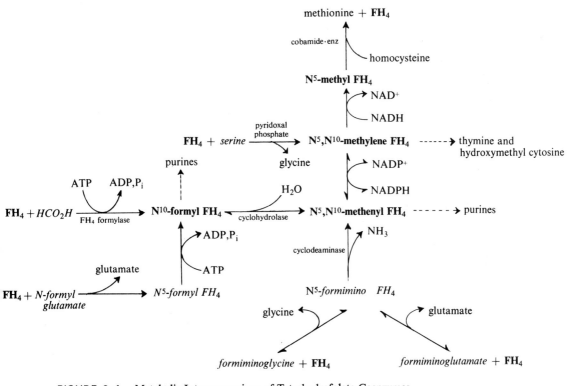

FIGURE 8-4.   Metabolic Interconversions of Tetrahydrofolate Coenzymes.

The reduction of N^5,N^{10}-methylene FH_4 by NADPH or NADH through the intermediacy of a flavoprotein (see below) yields N^5-methyl FH_4 (see Fig. 8-4), a coenzyme for the transfer of one-carbon fragments at the oxidation level of methanol:

$$\underset{\substack{\\ \\ N^5\text{-methyl } FH_4}}{\underset{5}{N}\underset{\substack{| \\ CH_3}}{\diagup}\underset{\substack{10 \\ N-R \\ | \\ H}}{}}$$

N^5-methyl FH_4 serves as the methyl group donor for the biosynthesis of methionine from homocysteine (see page 409).

PYRIDINE NUCLEOTIDES

The pyridine nucleotides were the first coenzymes to be recognized. Harden and Young, in 1904, found the conversion of glucose to ethanol by cell-free extracts of yeast required the participation of a dialyzable cofactor, called *cozymase*. The further elucidation of the structure of cozymase was greatly aided by the isolation of a dialyzable cofactor from mammalian erythrocytes, required for the aerobic oxidation of glucose-6-phosphate, by Warburg and Christian in 1934, who demonstrated that this coenzyme was composed of 1 mole of adenine, 1 mole of nicotinamide, 2 moles of pentose (D-ribose), and 3 moles of inorganic phosphate. The erythrocyte coenzyme was able to replace cozymase in a cell-free extract similar to that employed by Harden and Young, thus establishing a close relationship between the two coenzymes. Cozymase was subsequently demonstrated to be composed of a nicotinamide mono-nucleotide and adenylic acid:

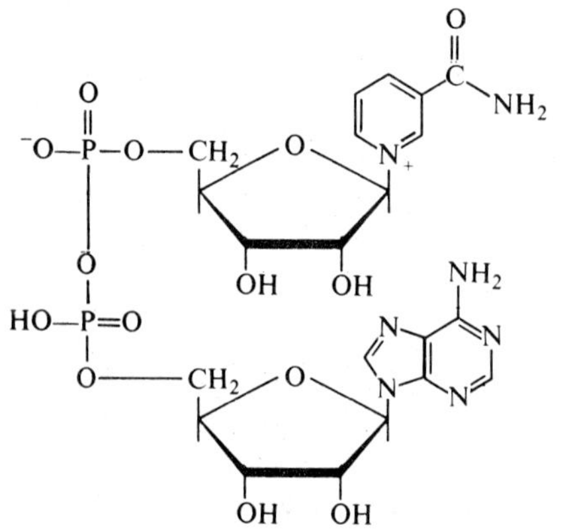

Nicotinamide adenine dinucleotide (NAD$^+$)

This coenzyme is now called *nicotinamide adenine dinucleotide* (NAD$^+$), although the older terminology of *diphosphopyridine nucleotide* (DPN) and coenzyme I (CoI) is still employed. The coenzyme isolated by Warburg and Christian differs from NAD$^+$ only in having an additional phosphate esterified at the C-2 hydroxyl group of the ribose moiety of the adenine portion of the molecule. This coenzyme is called *nicotinamide adenine dinucleotide phosphate* (NADP$^+$) or, less frequently, *triphosphopyridine nucleotide* (TPN) or coenzyme II (CoII).

NAD$^+$ and NADP$^+$ are derived biosynthetically, in the mammal, from nicotinamide (niacin) or nicotinic acid (see page 422). A nutritional deficiency of these precursors results in pellagra (in the human), a disease characterized by dermatitis, diarrhea, and dementia.

Coenzymatically, NAD$^+$ and NADP$^+$ are involved in a large number of oxidation-reduction reactions catalyzed by dehydrogenases. A typical reaction is that catalyzed by alcohol dehydrogenase:

$$CH_3CH_2OH + NAD^+ \rightleftharpoons CH_3CHO + NADH + H^+ \qquad \text{(8-39)}$$

Most pyridine nucleotide–dependent enzymes are highly specific for either NAD^+ or $NADP^+$, although some lack this degree of specificity for coenzyme.

The conversion of NAD^+ to the reduced form (NADH) is accompanied by a marked alteration in the spectrophotometric properties of the coenzyme. NAD^+ absorbs maximally near 260 mμ, the absorption being slightly less than the summation of that due to adenine and that due to nicotinamide. On reduction, the absorbance at 260 mμ decreases considerably, and a new band having a maximum at 340 mμ, characteristic of a dihydronicotinamide, appears. The alteration in spectrophotometric properties is frequently employed in assays of pyridine nucleotide–dependent enzymes. Thus the nicotinamide moiety of these coenzymes is the site of the oxidation-reduction reactions. Electronically, reduction might take place at either the 2, 4, or 6 position of the nicotinamide ring, yielding the corresponding dihydro derivatives (IX, X, and XI):

IX   X   XI

Pullman, San Pietro, and Colowick established that position 4 (X) is the actual site of reduction.

Conversion of NAD^+ to NADH results in the production of a new asymmetric center. Dithionite reduction of NAD^+ in deuterium oxide yields the two stereoisomers shown in Fig. 8-5, which differ in terms of the position occupied

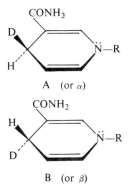

A   (or α)

B   (or β)

FIGURE 8-5.   Stereoisomers of Monodeuterio-reduced Nicotinamide Adenine Dinucleotide.

by the deuterium atom with respect to the plane of the reduced nicotinamide ring. NAD^+ and NADP-linked dehydrogenases exhibit stereospecificity for the A or B form of the reduced coenzyme (see Table 8-2). This was convincingly demonstrated by Vennesland and Westheimer for alcohol dehydrogenase (ADH) and lactic dehydrogenase (LDH). Deuterium-labeled reduced NAD^+ was prepared enzymatically with ADH and 1,1-dideuterioethanol:

$$CH_3CD_2OH + NAD^+ \xrightarrow{\text{ADH}} CH_3CDO + NADD \qquad (8\text{-}40)$$

When the reduced coenzyme was reoxidized with either acetaldehyde and ADH or pyruvic acid and LDH, the deuterium was quantitatively removed from the coenzyme and transferred to the reduced substrate. These experiments establish the following points. First, the transfer of hydrogen between substrate and coenzyme is direct. Second, ADH and LDH are stereospecific with respect to

TABLE 8-2.   Steric Specificity for NAD of Various Pyridine Nucleotide–linked Enzymes

Dehydrogenase	Source	Steric specificity
Alcohol (with ethanol)	Yeast, *Pseudomonas*, liver, wheat germ	A
Alcohol (with isopropyl alcohol)	Yeast	A
Acetaldehyde	Liver	A
L-Lactate	Heart muscle, *Lactobacillus*	A
L-Malate	Pig heart, wheat germ	A
D-Glycerate	Spinach	A
Dihydroorotate	*Zymobacterium oroticum*	A
α-Glycerophosphate	Muscle	B
3-Phosphoglyceraldehyde	Yeast, muscle	B
L-Glutamate	Liver	B
D-Glucose	Liver	B
β-Hydroxysteroid	*Pseudomonas*	B
NADH cytochrome *c* reductase	Rat liver mitochondria, pig heart	B
NADPH (transhydrogenase)	*Pseudomonas*	B
NADH diaphorase	Pig heart	B
L-β-hydroxybutyryl CoA (dehydrogenase)	Heart muscle	B

SOURCE: N. O. Kaplan, in Boyer, Lardy, and Myrbäck (eds.), "The Enzymes," vol. 3, p. 115, Academic Press Inc., New York, 1960.

coenzyme. Finally, both ADH and LDH transfer hydrogen to and from the same side of the NAD^+ molecule (form A). The stereospecificity of many dehydrogenases has subsequently been established. Some enzymes utilize form A, some form B (see Table 8-2).

In addition to stereospecificity with respect to coenzyme, Vennesland and Westheimer have elegantly demonstrated that the reduction of acetaldehyde to ethanol by ADH is also stereospecific with respect to substrate. Carbonyl carbon-labeled deuterioacetaldehyde was reduced enzymatically with unlabeled NADH, yielding the 1-monodeuterioethanol, which was isolated in aqueous solution by distillation. Enzymatic reoxidation of this substance yielded acetaldehyde containing 1 mole of deuterium per mole of acetaldehyde. Thus the same hydrogen that was transferred to acetaldehyde in the reduction step was quantitatively removed in the reoxidation. Thus, ADH is able to distinguish, in a quantitative fashion, between the two hydrogens at the 1 position of ethanol. This finding was substantiated by conversion of the monodeuterioethanol to the tosylate, followed by an SN2 hydrolysis. Since the latter reaction proceeds with stereochemical inversion, the product monodeuterioethanol must be the opposite enantiomorph of the starting material. Enzymatic reoxidation of this product yielded unlabeled acetaldehyde and NADD containing 1 mole of deuterium per mole of reduced coenzyme.

The discovery of riboflavin and the development of an understanding of its function in living systems constitutes an important chapter in the history of biochemistry. The initial detection of riboflavin or a riboflavin derivative was the isolation of an impure resinous pigment, called lactochrome, by Blyth in 1879. Following a dormant period of nearly half a century, several chemists isolated impure yellowish pigments from a variety of natural sources. Wagner-Jauregg and his associates succeeded in isolating a few milligrams of pure crystalline *ovoflavin* from egg white, an accomplishment that led to the discovery that this substance, later called vitamin B_2, was a nutritional factor for mammals. Subsequently, they prepared relatively large amounts of pure crystalline lactoflavin from whey, setting the stage for the structure determination of this substance. The structure of lactoflavin, now known as *riboflavin*, was established by synthesis in 1935 by Kuhn, Karrer, and their associates. Riboflavin is composed of a substituted isoalloxazine ring linked to D-ribitol:

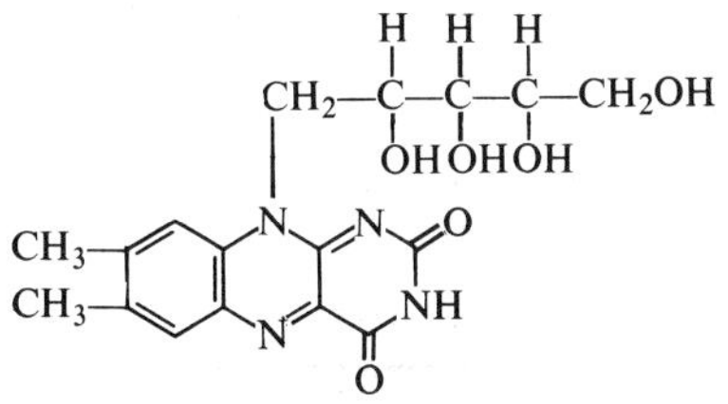

Riboflavin

A discovery of exceptional importance, both for the structure determination and for the understanding of the biochemical role of riboflavin, was the observation that the reoxidation of NADPH was catalyzed by "old yellow enzyme." Methanol treatment of the yellow enzyme resolved it into a colorless protein and a protein-free pigment, structurally related to riboflavin. Theorell demonstrated that the prosthetic group of the yellow enzyme was not riboflavin itself, but riboflavin-5'-phosphate. This substance is usually referred to as *riboflavin mononucleotide* (FMN), although this designation is not entirely correct, since the linkage between the base and sugar components is not a glycosidic one.

In 1938, Warburg and Christian discovered that an enzyme catalyzing the air oxidation of D-amino acids, called D-amino acid oxidase, was a flavoprotein containing a prosthetic group distinct from FMN. The structure of this new coenzyme, *flavin adenine dinucleotide* (FAD), was established by degradation studies and confirmed by synthesis by Todd in 1954:

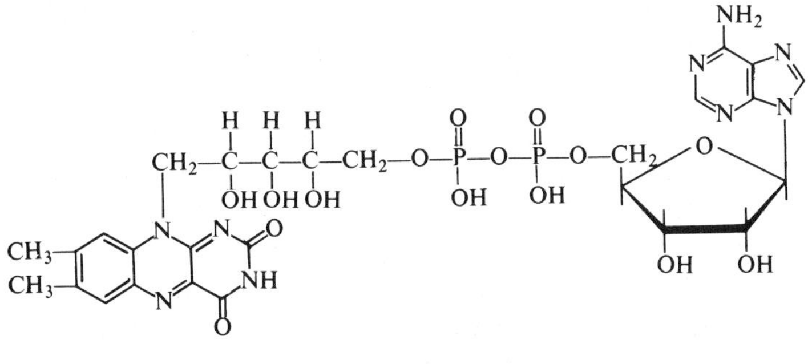

Flavin adenine dinucleotide (FAD)

The number of known flavoproteins, utilizing either FMN or FAD as coenzyme, is large, and such enzymes are universally distributed in nature. Flavoproteins are dehydrogenation catalysts. Typical substrates dehydrogenated by flavoproteins include pyridine nucleotides, α-amino acids, α-hydroxy acids, aldehydes, and substances containing saturated carbon-carbon bonds that are converted to olefins. In the course of such oxidations, the isoalloxazine ring system of the appropriate coenzyme, FMN or FAD, becomes reduced:

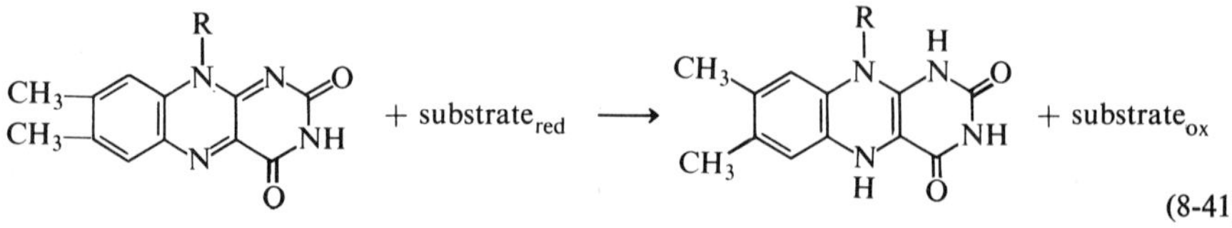

$$+ \text{substrate}_{red} \longrightarrow \qquad\qquad + \text{substrate}_{ox}$$

$$(8\text{-}41)$$

The reduced flavoproteins, in turn, become substrates for reactions involving other electron acceptors, regenerating the oxidized form of the coenzyme. Since the natural electron acceptors for these reactions are frequently unavailable, flavoproteins are often assayed with the use of artificial electron acceptors (see page 348), such as methylene blue, indophenol, phenazine or tetrazolium dyes, or molecular oxygen.

HEME COENZYMES   Coenzymes derived from a metal ion and the porphyrin nucleus occupy a central position in the life process. For example, chlorophyll, a magnesium chelate of a substituted porphyrin, is intimately involved in the photosynthetic process, the primary mode of radiant-energy utilization for living systems (see Chap. 12). In this chapter we shall concentrate on biochemical functions of coenzymes derived from porphyrins containing iron as the chelated metal.

Porphyrins are derived from the parent tetrapyrrole porphin (XII) by the replacement of hydrogens at positions 1 to 8 with a variety of side chains, particularly methyl, ethyl, vinyl, and propionic acid functions:

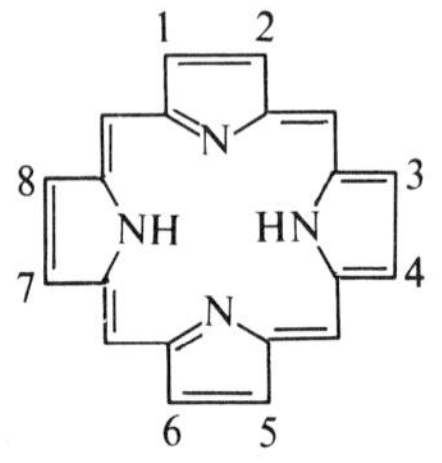

XII

Porphyrins are classified on the basis of the nature of these side chains. Particularly important classes include the *etioporphyrins*, which have four methyl and four ethyl groups as ring substituents; the *mesoporphyrins*, which have four methyl, two ethyl, and two propionic acid functions; the *protoporphyrins*, characterized by four methyl, two vinyl, and two propionic acid functions; and the *coproporphyrins*, which contain four methyl and four propionic acid groups as side chains.

Porphyrins that contain equal numbers of two types of side chains, such as the etioporphyrins or coproporphyrins, may exist in four isomeric forms, depending on the manner in which the side chains are disposed about the porphin nucleus. Porphyrins such as the protoporphyrins, which contain three types of side chains, may exist in fifteen isomeric forms.

Porphyrins form metal chelates with a variety of metal ions, including those of magnesium, iron, zinc, nickel, cobalt, copper, and silver. In such chelates, the metal ion lies in the center of the porphin nucleus, four of its ligand sites being occupied by the pyrrole nitrogen atoms. Of these complexes, that consisting of iron and protoporphyrin IX, generally referred to as *heme* if the iron is in the ferrous state and *hematin* if the iron is in the ferric state, are the most important biochemically:

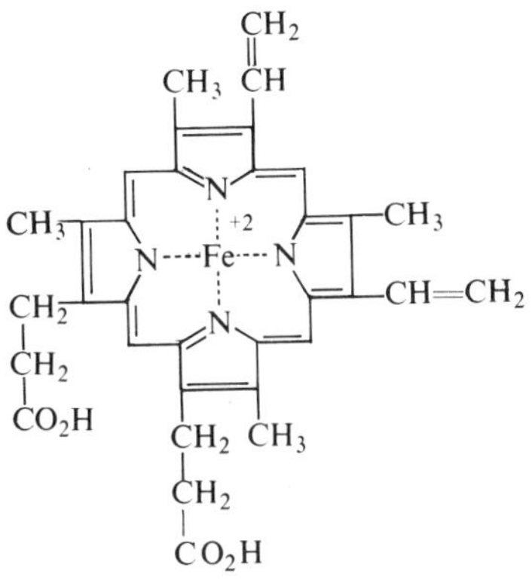

CH₂ diagram

Protoporphyrin IX

Heme serves as coenzyme for proteins involved in the transfer of oxygen from one site in the organism to another, for enzymes catalyzing a variety of oxidation reactions, and for enzymes catalyzing the cleavage of peroxides (see Chap. 15).

Human hemoglobins, a class of proteins of distinct molecular structure that perform the important function of transporting oxygen from the lungs to various tissues in the body in which oxidative metabolism occurs, are composed of four polypeptide chains of known primary structure, which usually occur in pairs, together with four heme groups bound to the globin moiety through weak forces (see Chap. 4). The fifth and sixth ligand sites of the heme iron atom are occupied by two imidazole groups of histidine residues of the globin moiety. Hemoglobin has the remarkable property of combining in reversible fashion with molecular oxygen, yielding oxyhemoglobin, in which oxygen replaces one of the imidazoles as the sixth ligand of the iron atom, without the simultaneous oxidation of the iron atom. Indeed, *methemoglobin*, in which the iron has been oxidized to the ferric state, is incapable of combining with oxygen. In addition to oxygen, hemoglobin also combines with several other small molecules or ions, including a very tight complex with carbon monoxide, accounting for the known toxicity of this substance. Heme also serves as coenzyme for other proteins performing essentially the same biochemical function, such as myoglobin, the oxygen-carrying protein of muscle, which has a molecular weight approximately one-fourth of that of hemoglobin and consists of a single polypeptide chain (see page 97).

The *cytochromes*, a class of oxidation-reduction enzymes that are principally concerned with the transfer of electrons from flavoproteins to oxygen or other electron acceptor, also employ heme as coenzyme. These enzymes are discussed in some detail in Chap. 15. In contrast to the case of hemoglobin, in which the iron remains in the ferrous state throughout the biochemical process, the iron atom in the heme moiety of cytochromes undergoes cyclic oxidation and reduction in the course of the reactions catalyzed by these enzymes.

Finally, heme also serves as cofactor for the *hydroperoxidases*. These enzymes occur in two categories: the catalases, which liberate molecular oxygen from hydrogen peroxide:

$$H_2O_2 \rightarrow H_2O + \tfrac{1}{2}O_2 \tag{8-42}$$

and the peroxidases, which transfer electrons to hydroperoxides from appropriate electron donors:

$$AH_2 + H_2O_2 \rightarrow A + 2H_2O \tag{8-43}$$

In contrast to the behavior of the heme iron atom in both hemoglobins and cytochromes, the catalytic process of the hydroperoxidases appears to result in the transient oxidation of ferric iron to higher valence (ferryl) states.

Since for all these reactions, involving oxygen transport, oxidation-reduction, and the cleavage of peroxides, the same heme coenzyme is employed, the specificity of these enzymes for reaction type, as well as substrate, must reside in the protein portion of the holoenzyme. This is certainly one of the most striking examples of the specificity attribute of enzyme-catalyzed reactions.

BIOTIN   Biotin, a growth factor of both yeast and humans (vitamin H), was first isolated by Kögl in 1935, 500 lb of dried egg yolk yielding 1 mg of this substance. The structure of biotin was established by du Vigneaud in 1942:

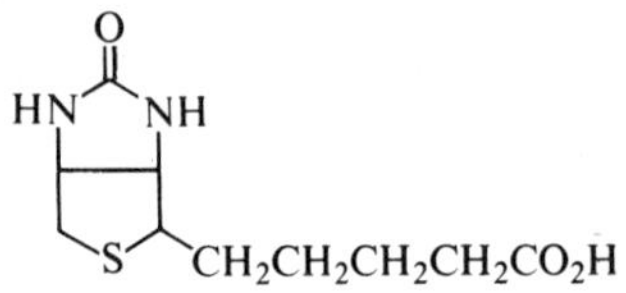

Biotin

Biotin serves as coenzyme for two types of enzymatic reactions. The first class includes ATP-dependent carboxylations, with the cleavage of the ATP to ADP and inorganic phosphate. Typical examples include the acetyl-SCoA carboxylase reaction:

$$\overset{O}{\overset{\|}{CH_3-C}}-SCoA + CO_2 + ATP \rightarrow HO_2C-CH_2-\overset{O}{\overset{\|}{C}}-SCoA + ADP + P_i \tag{8-44}$$

the propionyl-SCoA carboxylase reaction:

$$CH_3-CH_2-\overset{O}{\overset{\|}{C}}-SCoA + CO_2 + ATP \rightarrow CH_3-\underset{H}{\overset{HO_2C}{\overset{|}{C}}}-\overset{O}{\overset{\|}{C}}-SCoA + ADP + P_i \tag{8-45}$$

and the β-methylcrotonyl-SCoA carboxylase reaction:

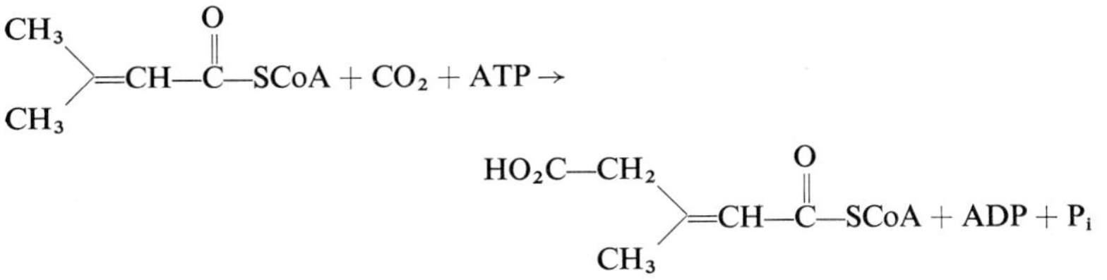

$$CH_3 \atop CH_3 \Big\rangle =CH-\overset{O}{\overset{\|}{C}}-SCoA + CO_2 + ATP \rightarrow$$

$$HO_2C-CH_2 \atop CH_3 \Big\rangle =CH-\overset{O}{\overset{\|}{C}}-SCoA + ADP + P_i \quad (8\text{-}46)$$

The second type of biotin-dependent enzymatic reaction is exemplified by the methyl malonyl-oxaloacetic transcarboxylase reaction:

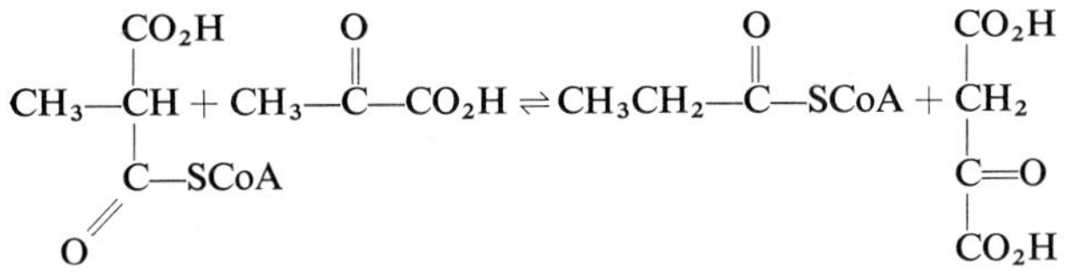

$$\overset{CO_2H}{\underset{\overset{|}{\underset{O}{\overset{\|}{C}}}-SCoA}{CH_3-CH}} + CH_3-\overset{O}{\overset{\|}{C}}-CO_2H \rightleftharpoons CH_3CH_2-\overset{O}{\overset{\|}{C}}-SCoA + \overset{CO_2H}{\underset{\underset{CO_2H}{\overset{|}{C}=O}}{CH_2}} \quad (8\text{-}47)$$

in which a carboxyl group is exchanged between substrates.

Studies indicating that biotin is very tightly bound to biotin-dependent enzymes and the existence of ε-N-biotinyllsine (biocytin)

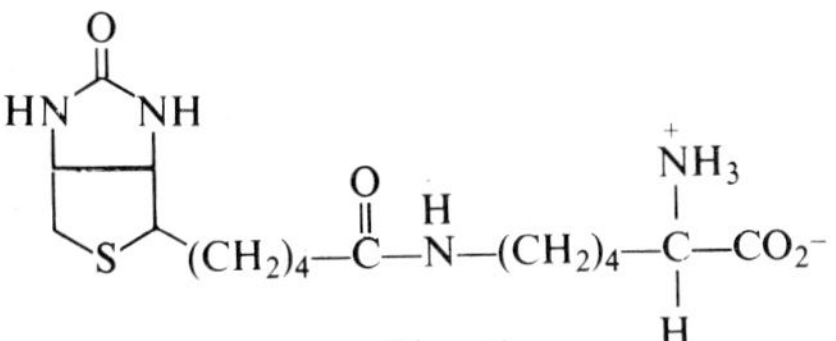

Biocytin

in natural sources suggested that biotin may be covalently bound to its enzymes through an amide linkage between the ε-amino group of a lysine residue of the enzymes and the carboxyl group of the valeric acid side chain of biotin. Lane and Lynen have definitely established that this is the case for propionyl carboxylase, and it appears very likely for other biotin enzymes, particularly acetyl carboxylase.

The key to the understanding of the mechanism of action of biotin-dependent enzymatic reactions was provided by Lynen and his coworkers, who found that incubation of free (+)-biotin with β-methyl crotonyl carboxylase, in the absence of substrates other than CO_2, resulted in the production of a *carboxy-(+)-biotin*. Carboxybiotin is a labile molecule, particularly in the presence of acids, but may be stabilized by conversion to its dimethyl ester with diazomethane. The dimethyl ester of carboxy-(+)-biotin, synthesized by β-methyl crotonyl carboxylase, is identical to the product formed from the reaction of (+)-biotin methyl ester and methyl chloroformate, suggesting structure (XIII) for carboxy-(+)-biotin:

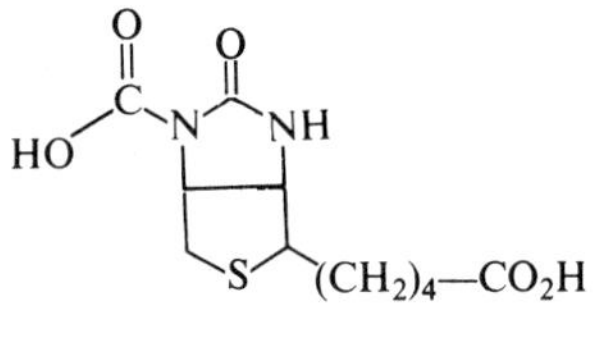

XIII

As a result of these and related studies, biotin-dependent carboxylations may be considered to proceed by a two-step reaction path involving the intermediate formation of enzyme-bound carboxybiotin:

$$CO_2 + MgATP + \text{biotinyl-enzyme} \rightarrow MgADP + P_i + \text{carboxy-biotinyl-enzyme} \qquad (8\text{-}48)$$

$$\text{Carboxy-biotinyl-enzyme} + \text{substrate} \rightarrow \text{biotinyl-enzyme} + \text{carboxy substrate} \qquad (8\text{-}49)$$

Transcarboxylations probably occur via a two-step sequence as well, enzyme-bound biotin serving as the intermediate carrier for the carboxyl group being transferred.

VITAMIN B_{12}
(COBAMIDE)
COENZYMES

Following the observation by Murphy in 1926 that liver contains a nutritional element required for the cure of pernicious anemia, more than twenty years elapsed prior to the isolation of the substance, vitamin B_{12}, in pure crystalline form. In the meantime, numerous biological manifestations of the nutritional lack of vitamin B_{12} were discovered, and, consequently, this material has received an abundance of names, including *anti-pernicious anaemia factor, Factor X, L.L.D. Factor*, and so forth. Early attempts to purify vitamin B_{12} were severely hampered by the minute quantities of vitamin B_{12} present in the liver and by the necessity of employing pernicious anemia patients as a method of assay for this vitamin. In 1948, a group headed by Folkers in the United States and one headed by E. L. Smith in England announced, almost simultaneously, the isolation and crystallization of pure vitamin B_{12} from liver.

The determination of the structure of the vitamin was nearly as difficult as its isolation. Chemical studies, particularly in the laboratories of Folkers, Smith, and Todd, together with the brilliant X-ray diffraction studies by Hodgkin and her associates, eventually led to the formulation of B_{12} as:

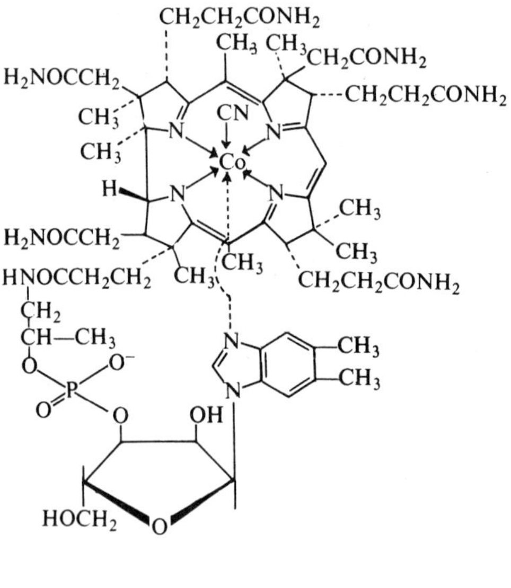

Vitamin B_{12}

Vitamin B_{12} is composed of two principal parts: the highly substituted, reduced, *corrin* nucleus and the nucleotide, which, unlike those obtained from nucleic acids, contains an α-glycosidic linkage. The macroring contains tervalent cobalt chelated to the four nitrogen atoms of this ring, a nitrogen atom of the 5,6-dimethylbenzimidazole ring, and a cyanide ion, which is an artifact of the isolation procedure. The entire structure, except for the cyanide, is termed cobalamin; hence vitamin B_{12} is frequently referred to as *cyanocobalamin*. A number of additional cobalamins have been prepared, including hydroxocobalamin, aquocobalamin, and nitritocobalamin, in which the cyanide is replaced, respectively, by hydroxide ion, water, and nitrous acid.

In addition to these vitamin B_{12} analogues, another analogue series exists in which the nitrogen base of the nucleotide moiety is varied. In addition to 5,6-dimethylbenzimidazole, adenine, 2-methyladenine, and guanine, among others, are found in naturally occurring vitamin B_{12} analogues. Many other biosynthetic analogues of this vitamin have been isolated from microorganisms grown on the desired base and factor B, a B_{12} analogue containing no nucleotide.

Vitamin B_{12} is not active as a coenzyme for any known enzymatic reaction. Rather a related family of substances, the B_{12} (or cobamide) *coenzymes*, function in this capacity. They were initially isolated by Barker and his associates in 1958. Chemical and X-ray diffraction studies indicated that 5,6-dimethylbenzimidazole B_{12} coenzyme has the structure XIV, in which the cyanide has been replaced as a cobalt ligand by the 5-deoxyadenosyl group:

XIV

Cobalt occurs in the coenzymes as Co^{+3}.

The enzymatic conversion of vitamin B_{12} derivatives to the deoxyadenosyl B_{12} coenzymes requires FAD, NADH, ATP, and glutathione as cofactors and proceeds by a multistep process. In the first step, vitamin B_{12} (Co^{+3}) is reduced to vitamin B_{12} (Co^+) in a reaction requiring FAD and NADH (reduced lipoic acid replaces the requirement for these coenzymes). The reduced form of the B_{12} then undergoes a reaction with ATP that yields the B_{12} coenzyme. Inorganic trimetaphosphate is liberated from the ATP in the course of this transformation.

Although B_{12} derivatives are known to be involved in many metabolic processes, B_{12} coenzymes have been established as required for only five enzymatic reactions. The associated enzymes are methylmalonyl-CoA mutase (see page 322), glutamate mutase, dioldehydrase, the enzyme responsible for the biosynthesis of methionine from homocysteine (see page 409), and the enzyme catalyzing the transformation CDP → dCDP (see page 442).

REFERENCES   Baddiley, J.: The Structure of Coenzyme A, *Adv. Enzymology*, **16**: 1 (1955).

Bock, R. M.: Adenine Nucleotides and Properties of Pyrophosphate Compounds, "The Enzymes," 2nd ed., vol. 2, p. 1, P. D. Boyer, H. Lardy, and K. Myrbäck (eds.), Academic, New York, 1960.

Boyer, P. D., H. Lardy, and K. Myrbäck (eds.): "The Enzymes," Academic, New York, 1958.

Braunstein, A. E.: Pyridoxal Phosphate, "The Enzymes," 2nd ed., vol. 2, p. 113, P. D. Boyer, H. Lardy, and K. Myrbäck (eds.), Academic, New York, 1960.

Brown, G. M.: Biosynthesis of Water-soluble Vitamins and Derived Coenzymes, *Physiol. Rev.*, **40**: 331 (1960).

Dixon, M., and E. C. Webb: "Enzymes," 2nd ed., Academic, New York, 1964.

Friedkin, M.: Enzymatic Aspects of Folic Acid, *Ann. Rev. Biochem.*, **32**: 185 (1963).

George, P.: The Specific Reactions of Iron in Some Hemoproteins, *Adv. Catalysis*, **4**: 367 (1952).

Huennekens, F. M.: The Role of Nucleotides and Coenzymes in Enzymatic Processes, in "Currents in Biochemical Research," D. E. Green (ed.), p. 493, Interscience, New York, 1956.

———— and M. J. Osborn: Folic Acid Coenzymes and One Carbon Metabolism, *Adv. Enzymology*, **21**: 369 (1959).

Hutchinson, D. W.: "Nucleotides and Coenzymes," Wiley, New York, 1964.

Jaenicke, L., and F. Lynen: Coenzyme A, "The Enzymes," 2nd ed., vol. 3, p. 1, P. D. Boyer, H. Lardy, and K. Myrbäck (eds.), Academic, New York, 1960.

Kaplan, N. O.: The Pyridine Coenzymes, "The Enzymes," 2nd ed., vol. 3, p. 105, P. D. Boyer, H. Lardy, and K. Myrbäck (eds.), Academic, New York, 1960.

Knox, W. E.: Glutathione, "The Enzymes," 2nd ed., vol. 2, p. 253, P. D. Boyer, H. Lardy, K. Myrbäck (eds.), Academic, New York, 1960.

Lemberg, R., and J. W. Legge: "Hematin Compounds and Bile Pigments," Interscience, New York, 1949.

Lipmann, F.: Metabolic Generation and Utilization of Phosphate Bond Energy, *Adv. Enzymology*, **1**: 99 (1941).

Metzler, D. E.: Thiamine Coenzymes, "The Enzymes," 2nd ed., vol. 2, p. 295, P. D. Boyer, H. Lardy, and K. Myrbäck (eds.), Academic, New York, 1960.

Rabinowitz, J. C.: Folic Acid, "The Enzymes," 2nd ed., vol. 2, p. 185, P. D. Boyer, H. Lardy, and K. Myrbäck (eds.), Academic, New York, 1960.

Reed, L. J.: Lipoic Acid, "The Enzymes," 2nd ed., vol. 3, p. 195, P. D. Boyer, H. Lardy, and K. Myrbäck (eds.), Academic, New York, 1960.

Sherman, H. et al.: Pyridoxine and Related Compounds, in "The Vitamins," W. H. Sebrell, Jr., and R. S. Harris (eds.), vol. III, chap. 14, Academic, New York, 1954.

Smith, E. L.: "Vitamin B_{12}," Methuen, London, 1960.

Snell, E. E.: Chemical Structure in Relation to Biological Activities of Vitamin B_6, *Vitamins and Hormones*, **16**: 77 (1958).

Strominger, J. L.: Nucleotide Intermediates in the Biosynthesis of Polysaccharides, *Angew. Chemie. (Intern. Eng. Ed.)*, **1**: 134 (1962).

Utter, M. F.: Guanosine and Inosine Nucleotides, "The Enzymes," 2nd ed., vol. 2, p. 75, P. D. Boyer, H. Lardy, and K. Myrbäck (eds.), Academic, New York, 1960.

Vallee, B. L.: Metal and Enzyme Interactions, "The Enzymes," 2nd ed., vol. 3, p. 225, P. D. Boyer, H. Lardy, and K. Myrbäck (eds.), Academic, New York, 1960.

Vennesland, B., and F. H. Westheimer: Hydrogen Transport and Steric Specificity in Reactions Catalyzed by Pyridine Nucleotide Dehydrogenases, "The Mechanism of Enzyme Action," W. D. McElroy and B. Glass (eds.), Johns Hopkins, Baltimore, 1954.

Westheimer, F. H.: Enzyme Models, "The Enzymes," 2nd ed., vol. 1, p. 259, P. D. Boyer, H. Lardy, and K. Myrbäck (eds.), Academic, New York, 1959.

Wyman, J.: Heme Proteins, *Adv. Prot. Chem.*, **4**: 407 (1948).

9 | Intracellular Organization and Particles

Studies on cellular organization and attempts to correlate structure and function at the various hierarchical levels involved — from simple molecules to macromolecules, to aggregates such as membranes or particles, to subcellular units, to cells — comprise some of the most exciting, challenging, and rewarding fields of inquiry in contemporary biology. For the biochemist and cellular physiologist an understanding in chemical terms of the various complex structural elements that have been identified inside cells is not only of fundamental importance in its own right but must of necessity form the first step in his attempts at studying their modes of synthesis, breakdown, and interaction. These complex structures, we are beginning to suspect, hold much of the secret of how cellular processes are controlled in both space and time: the secret may consist, at least in part, of isolating and maintaining the different cellular constituents — mainly enzymes, together with their substrates, products, and modifiers (activators, inhibitors) — in different compartments; sometimes allowing, sometimes denying mutual accessibility. Implicit in this statement are two premises — amply verified experimentally in the recent past — (1) that there is a distinct and discernible *localization* of some key cellular constituents, especially of enzymes, in (or on) certain cellular structures (or "organelles," which are small intracellular organs) and (2) that it should be possible to separate the latter and, *mutatis mutandis*, the former as well, by suitably mild techniques of *cell disruption* and *fractionation*.[1]

---

[1]This is the term commonly employed (see the references); grammatically it would probably be more correct to speak of a fractionation of *subcellular components*.

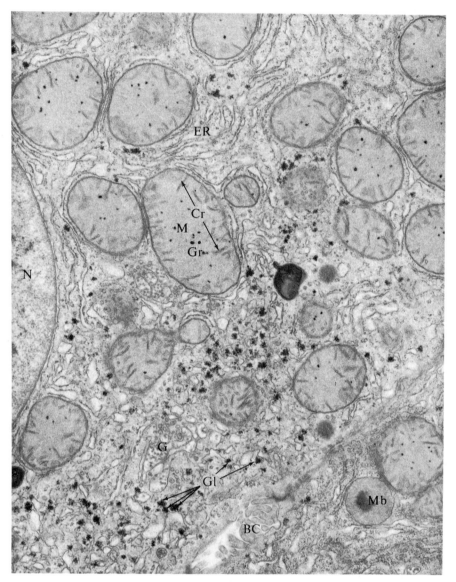

FIGURE 9-1. Cell Organelles. This electron micrograph, which shows part of a rat liver parenchymal cell, is reproduced at a magnification sufficiently high (27,000 times) to show the structural details of several common cell components. The mitochondria (M), for example, are seen to be limited by two lines, which represent the two membranes constituting the wall of these tiny organelles. The inner of the two is folded into shelflike structures, the cristae (Cr), which project into the homogeneous matrix filling the cavity of the mitochondrion. It is probable that such membrane foldings provide expanded surfaces for the organized distribution of the many enzymes resident in these organelles. Where the energy requirements of the cell are greater, as in heart muscle, the number of cristae is greater, presumably to provide a large surface area. Dense granules (Gr), 20 to 30 mμ in diameter, also evident in the matrix, are now thought to represent accumulations of bound, divalent, metallic ions required for mitochondrial enzyme systems.

A small part of the cell nucleus (N) is included at the left in the micrograph. It is limited by a membranous envelope consisting of two membranes and an intervening space of low density. The outer of the two membranes has repeatedly been shown to be continuous with the membranes limiting the vesicular elements of the endoplasmic reticulum (ER). It is therefore reasonable to regard the cytoplasmic reticulum as an extension of the nuclear envelope and to consider both as parts of a single membranous system.

Such procedures then eliminate the elegant but complex, and frequently laborious, techniques of *histo-* and *cytochemistry* and substitute for them the methodology of the ordinary biochemical laboratory. Yet ideally they lead to a complete chemical and functional characterization of the fractions. It must be emphasized, however, that any real understanding of cellular processes must always be based on two independent lines of exploration, both converging toward the central problem: structure as well as function must be explored, and phenomena observed with isolated components must constantly be referred to and checked against their counterparts in the intact cell.

In what is to follow we examine, very briefly, the results obtained on examining the anatomy of the cell by means of the electron microscope, and describe the structures observed in these investigations; second, we discuss the methodology of cell fractionation and some of the properties of the fractions obtained by this technique; and third, we try to correlate some of these findings in terms of biochemistry and enzymology.

THE STRUCTURE OF
CELLS

It may surprise the reader to learn that an unambiguous identification of the cell as the fundamental unit of higher (eukaryotic, chromosomal) organisms goes back only to the year 1839, the year that the botanist Schleiden and the zoologist Schwann independently produced their *cell theory*. The next important finding in this context came in 1859, when Virchow demonstrated that all cells derived from other preexisting cells. Since then the structure of cells of a large number of animals and plants has been subject to the scrutiny of microscopic examination of ever increasing sophistication and resolving power — first with the light microscope and more recently with the electron microscope. From these studies, there has emerged a composite picture of cells as highly complicated entities, consisting

---

In the cytoplasm of the hepatic cell, two forms of this membranous system are regularly observed. In one (ER), the cisternae have ribosomes, small, dense granules (about 150 A in diameter), on their surfaces. This is the configuration found in cells in which protein is synthesized for secretion. In the other form, the long, flat profiles of thin cisternae give way to shorter, more nearly circular profiles and are particle free, or smooth. This part of the ER is in some places continuous with the particle-covered, or rough-surfaced, units. In the hepatic cell, this smooth form is found associated with deposits of stored glycogen (Gl), and it is thought that enzyme systems important for storage and release of glycogen are associated with the limiting membranes. Ribosomes are seen throughout the field, some associated with the ER, others free on the cytoplasmic matrix.

The Golgi complex (G) also consists of vesicles limited by smooth-surfaced membranes, but in this instance they are flattened sacs or vesicles closely packed into piles or stacks. Within the Golgi vesicles, proteins and possibly other substances synthesized elsewhere in the cell are assembled into secretion granules. Rather small granules can be identified in a few sacs (near letter G), and these may represent plasma proteins known to be produced by hepatic cells. After cell homogenization, fragments of the Golgi complex, plus fragments derived from the reticulum, make up the "microsomal" fraction.

Other granular components of the liver cell, called microbodies (Mb), possess a homogeneous matrix and a dense nucleoid rich in the enzyme uricase.

In this micrograph, the structure of the bile canaliculi (BC) is clearly seen. This channel, formed by portions of the surfaces of adjacent hepatic cells, is studded with microvilli, which project from the cell surfaces into this extracellular space. Tight junctions and desmosomes seal off the canaliculus from adjoining intercellular spaces. — *Original micrograph courtesy Dr. Keith R. Porter. Legend adapted from that of Keith R. Porter and Mary A. Bonneville: "An Introduction to the Fine Structure of Cells and Tissues," Lea and Febiger, Philadelphia, 1964.*

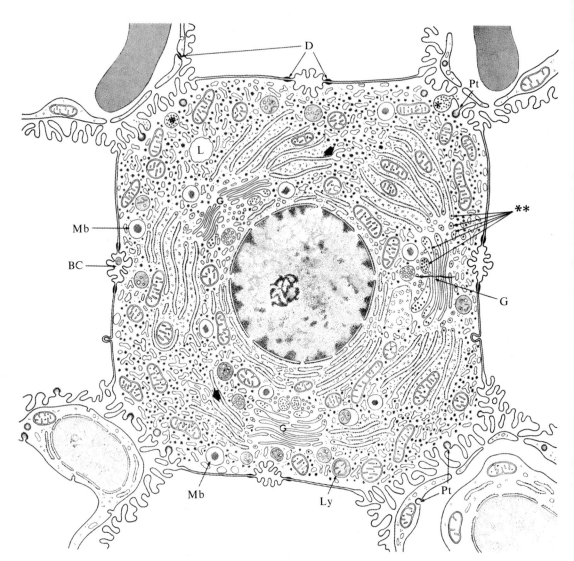

FIGURE 9-2. Diagrammatic Representation of a Liver Cell. Arrangement of the organelles shown in Fig. 9-1 within a parenchymal cell of rat liver. We observe the nucleus, mitochondria, and the long, slender profiles of cisternae belonging to the endoplasmic reticulum, or ER. Small particles or ribosomes are abundant on the surfaces of the latter and in the ground substance between them. The cisternae are ordinarily arranged in stacks of 6 to 12 units. One margin of such an assemblage frequently lies adjacent to the Golgi complex, and it will be noted that small granules of a particular type occupy the ends of these cisternae and the vesicles intervening between ER and Golgi, as well as the expanded ends of cisternae and spherical vesicles belonging to the Golgi proper (G). These images (**) are designed to show the mechanism of protein transport from ER to Golgi, where packaging for export takes place. The other margin of the stacks of ER cisternae borders on masses of glycogen and associated vesicles belonging to the so-called smooth endoplasmic reticulum, or SER. These two forms are often continuous, as though the smooth form may develop from the rough. Such continuities are indicated by thick arrows. It is thought by some, on incomplete evidence, that the smooth ER is involved in the transport of glucose from the liver cells during glycogenolysis. Other prominent components of the hepatic cell cytoplasm include lysosomes (Ly), containing remnants of organelles and ground substance apparently set aside for hydrolysis, and microbodies (Mb), of uncertain significance though probably rich in enzymes. A single lipid granule is indicated at L. — *From Keith R. Porter and Mary A. Bonneville: "An Introduction to the Fine Structure of Cells and Tissues," Lea and Febiger, Philadelphia, 1964.*

of, not just a limiting membrane enclosing a blob of cytoplasm in which the chromatin-containing nucleus is suspended, but instead a number of variegated, highly organized, structured, convoluted, and interconnected elements, which vary from organism to organism, tissue to tissue, and cell type to cell type. Yet within all the complexity, some order can be discerned: although there is no such thing as a typical cell, almost all cells appear to have certain common features. Some common subcellular structures can be identified that appear to bear a morphological and topological, and perhaps a functional, homology from cell to cell, regardless of origin. Let us then examine such a generalized animal cell on the basis of the electron micrograph of Fig. 9-1 and the drawing of Fig. 9-2, due to Porter and Bonneville. Such a cell is an exceedingly small object, with an average diameter of the order of $20\,\mu\,(2 \times 10^5 A)$ and a volume of $\sim 5,000\,\mu^3$, while the maximum resolution attainable with the electron microscope is 5 to 10 A.

The Nucleus   The largest structure visible in most cells, the one first and most easily identified with the light microscope (especially after suitable staining, or in phase contrast), and the first intracellular organelle to be isolated in bulk (by Miescher in 1871) is the nucleus: a roughly spherical body, usually one per cell, approximately $5\,\mu$ in diameter and therefore with a volume of $45\,\mu^3$. It is surrounded by and isolated from the cytoplasm by a triple-layered[1] nuclear membrane or envelope approximately 75 A thick. This separation, however, is not absolute, since the membrane may have numerous pores or apertures and is itself connected in many cells to another cytoplasmic structure, the endoplasmic reticulum (see below). It is through these pores perhaps that certain macromolecules, synthesized within the nucleus but operational in the cytoplasm (RNA and perhaps even ribonucleoprotein particles), make their way from the one compartment to the other.

The interior of the nucleus (the nucleoplasm) appears itself organized, and usually one or more distinct, denser, spherical structures, called *nucleoli*, can be distinguished against it. These bodies are particularly rich in RNA, and the bulk of the nuclear RNA, which itself accounts for 10 to 20 per cent of the total cellular RNA, appears to be localized within them. Almost all cellular DNA (≥ 95 per cent) is found in the nucleus, distributed throughout the nucleoplasm as *chromatin*, while the cell is in the " resting state," i.e., engaged in maintenance and growth between divisions. In anticipation of division and during its course, the chromatin becomes highly organized into distinct linear structures called *chromosomes*. The number of chromosomes per somatic cell is constant, and this constant complement is passed on to a daughter cell as a result of mitotic division.

Mitochondria   The next set of structures to be identified chronologically (around 1900) and, in most cells, the next largest in size are the so-called large granules, or *mitochondria*. When stained with such dyes as Janus green, they are close to the limit of resolution of light microscopy but are easily seen under phase contrast. The real advance of our understanding of their structure had to wait for the advent of the electron microscope and has only taken place during the past 15 years. Although the particles may vary considerably in number, size, and shape

---

[1] A dense double membrane with a less dense intramembranal space or separation in between. This appears to be the fundamental feature of almost all membrane systems in nature.

in different cells, their ultrastructure is sufficiently similar and distinct from that of other organelles so as to make their unambiguous identification easy in most cases and to point out their fundamental similarity, whether they are derived from man, fungus, or protozoan. Their number varies from a dozen or so in yeast to several hundred per animal cell, while their dimensions are roughly those of an ellipsoid of revolution, with long and short axes of 1.5 and 0.5 μ, respectively, and with an average volume of some 0.8 μ^3. The most salient feature of their structure is the membrane system. It consists of a relatively smooth outer membrane, an intermembranous space, and a particularly highly structured inner membrane. The last forms numerous folds or invaginations called *cristae*, which penetrate deeply into the intramitochondrial matrix or inner compartment. Linked to the inner membrane and the cristae are numerous (several thousand) distinct small knoblike attachments.

Mitochondria are probably the particles that have been studied most extensively and intensively with regard to fractionation and function. From all these studies (see also below, page 236) there has emerged a point of view that pictures mitochondria as the sites of intracellular energy production and transduction. Most of the enzymes of the citric acid cycle (see page 326) and certain accessory oxidative enzymes, such as the pyruvic dehydrogenase complex (see page 277) and the β-oxidation system for fatty acids (see page 317), appear to be localized either on the outer membrane, which also controls mitochondrial permeability, or in the matrix. The inner membrane appears to be the site of the enzymes of the electron-transport chains from NADH and succinate to molecular oxygen and of oxidative phosphorylation.

Endoplasmic Reticulum Extending from the nuclear membrane outward all the way to the cell membrane and permeating large regions of the cytoplasm there exists in many cell types a complex system of membranes, the *endoplasmic reticulum*. It consists of lipoprotein membranes in the form of flattened sacs, tubules, and vesicles. Together they enclose and define a compartment called the *intracisternal space*. Two types of endoplasmic reticulum may be distinguished, depending on the number of attached, small, electron-dense, spherical particles: the *smooth-surfaced reticulum*, with few or no particles, and the *rough-surfaced reticulum*, lined with these particles (Fig. 9-3). The functions of the endoplasmic reticulum appear to be at least fourfold: first, to carry out a large number of important complex biosynthetic processes concerned with the elaboration of proteins and perhaps of complex lipids and polysaccharides as well; second, to transport such products to their sites of utilization or storage; third, to effect and control the utilization of newly synthesized and perhaps also of ingested complex molecules; and fourth (perhaps not unrelated to the first two), to function as a precursor for other membrane systems, such as the Golgi apparatus and possibly even the nuclear and outer mitochondrial membrane.

Of all these processes the one that has received the most attention during the recent past is protein synthesis. This activity is the special province of the rough-surfaced reticulum, and more precisely of the attached ribonucleoprotein granules, called *ribosomes*. When isolated from higher organisms, they show a particle weight of $\sim 4 \times 10^6$ daltons and a sedimentation constant of 75 to 80 S. Values for bacterial ribosomes are closer to 2.7×10^6 and 70 S respectively.

Ribosomes from plants and animals contain approximately 50 per cent protein and 50 per cent RNA; those from bacteria, closer to 60 per cent RNA. In cells designed for heavy protein synthesis and for the export of the product to other parts of the organism, such as the exocrine cells of the pancreas, many of the ribosomes are attached to the reticulum in linear array, and these structures are so common as to form the predominant feature of cellular architecture (see Fig. 9-3). In other cell types, where protein synthesis is largely for internal consumption (e.g., in red blood cells, embryonic and cancer cells), we find considerable smooth reticulum, some rough-surfaced reticulum, and numerous ribosomes unattached in the cytoplasm, where they are arranged in groups or clusters (the so-called *polysomes* or *ergosomes*). Regardless of their origin or structural history (i.e., free or attached originally), ribosomes appear to be of remarkable uniformity throughout living nature. They consist of two unequal subunits, those of animal or plant origin with particle weights of roughly 1.5 and 2.5×10^6 daltons and with sedimentation coefficients of 35 to 40 S and 55 to 60 S, respectively. In bacteria, the two subunits, like the ribosome itself, appear to be somewhat lighter, with sedimentation coefficients of 30 and 50 S, respectively (mol. wt = 1×10^6 and 2×10^6 daltons). These various association-dissociation equilibria are controlled by the concentration of Mg^{+2}, high concentration of the metal favoring associations.

Another smooth membranous organelle, functionally and perhaps structurally related to the endoplasmic reticulum, is the *Golgi apparatus* or complex. It is usually localized quite close to the nucleus in the region of the so-called *centrosomes* or *centrospheres* and consists of a stacked array of smooth sacs and of variable numbers of smooth-surfaced cisternae, vesicles, or vacuoles. Golgi complexes are most prevalent and well developed in secretory cells, such as the exocrine cells of the pancreas. There is good evidence of connections between the cisternae of the rough-surfaced reticulum and the vesicles of the Golgi complex, which, in turn, are linked to larger vacuoles in the complex. Golgi vacuoles develop into secretory granules, such as *zymogen granules*, which contain and store the proteins produced by the ribosomes of the rough-surfaced reticulum (see Fig. 9-4).

Other quite large cytoplasmic bodies surrounded by a single membrane, the *lysosomes*, are found in a large number of cell types but are especially abundant in mammalian liver and kidney. They contain a sizable portion of the hydrolytic enzymes of the cell and may be the site of *intracellular digestion*, both of material ingested from the outside by the processes known as *pinocytosis* and *phagocytosis*, and — in cells undergoing rapid turnover and replacement or those subject to pathological degeneration — of cell organelles themselves. In the latter instance, they are then known as *autophagic vacuoles*. Lysosomes and bodies derived from them are also, in conjunction with the Golgi complex, concerned with the transport and secretion of newly synthesized macromolecular materials.

Numerous other small vesicular bodies occur in highly specialized cells, such as the *microbodies* of liver and the *synaptic vesicles* of nerve tissue.

The Cytoplasmic Fluid or Matrix   A considerable portion of the total cellular constituents, including numerous enzymes, nutrients, and macromolecular products, occur apparently free in the cytoplasm or cell sap. This apparent absence of structure may be an illusion,

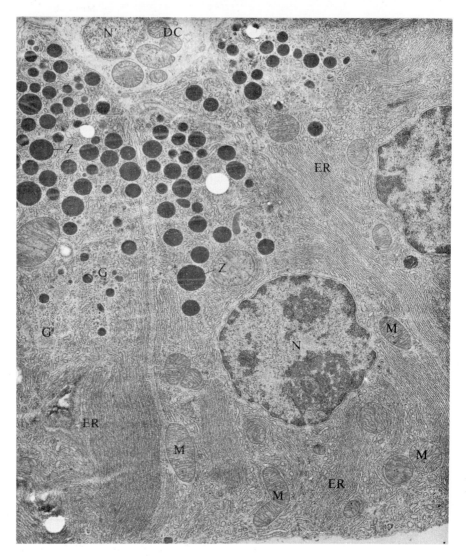

FIGURE 9-3.   Pancreatic Exocrine Cell. Pancreas of the bat, magnification 11,500 times. The intracellular architecture of a cell designed for the manufacture and export of digestive enzymes. We see concentrated layers of endoplasmic reticulum (ER), studded with ribosomes (R in insert). G = Golgi complex; Z = zymogen granule; M = mitochondria; N = nucleus. The cells lining the ducts of the exocrine pancreas seem relatively inactive when compared to their secretory relatives. In this micrograph the cytoplasm and a small part of the nucleus (N') of one such centroacinar duct cell (DC) lie near the apices of the glandular cells, and it is evident that this cell type contains only a few organelles and no complex membranous system. — *Original micrograph courtesy of Dr. Keith R. Porter.*

FIGURE 9-4.   Structures and Interrelationships in a Pancreatic Cell. *(a)* Diagram of the dispositions of organelles in a pancreatic acinar cell (see Fig. 9-3). *(b)* Schematic representation of the current views concerning the secretory pathway in the pancreatic acinar cell and the functional inter-relations of its organelles. New protein synthesized at the ribosomes is segregated in the lumen of the endoplasmic reticulum and transported to the Golgi region. There it is concentrated and formed into zymogen granules that are stored in the apical cytoplasm and ultimately released at the free surface of the cell. — *Don W. Fawcett: Structural and Functional Variations in the Membranes of the Cytoplasm, in S. Seno and E. V. Cowdry (eds.),"Intracellular Membrane Structures," Japan Society for Cell Biology, p. 15, Okayama, Japan, 1963.*

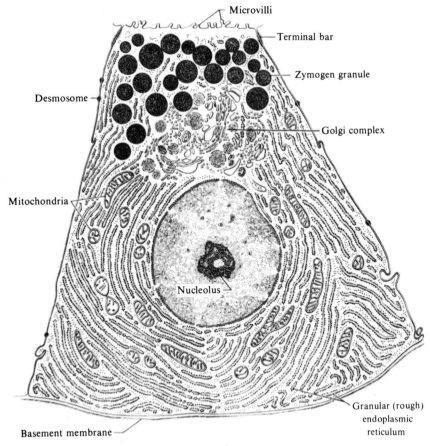

Microvilli

Terminal bar

Zymogen granule

Desmosome

Golgi complex

Mitochondria

Nucleolus

Granular (rough)
endoplasmic
reticulum

Basement membrane

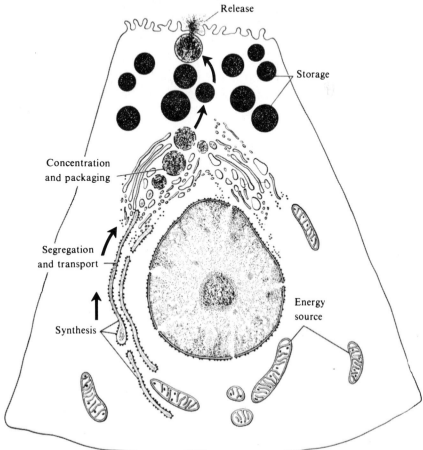

Release

Storage

Concentration
and packaging

Segregation
and transport

Energy
source

Synthesis

referable solely to our inability to visualize and investigate their organization either in situ or subsequent to cell breakage and fractionation.

The Cell or Plasma Membrane

The exterior boundary of the cell is provided by the cell (or plasma) membrane (or envelope), a typical double (but called a "unit") membrane some 80 A thick, which appears to be a relatively rigid and organized structure consisting of a bimolecular layer of polar lipids coated on both sides by protein films. However, the membrane is by no means to be regarded as homogeneous throughout its exterior. On the contrary, it is a mosaic of different functional units, differing slightly in structure, highly selective and specialized in various cells, and controlling such widely divergent but highly important cellular parameters as selective permeability to and active transport of nutrients and ions (i.e., the passage of these factors into the cell), contractile properties, and cell-to-cell associations and recognitions (i.e., in organ formation). Plasma membranes may also be the site of certain integrated enzymatic processes, such as glycolysis, or even protein synthesis in microorganisms.

Other Cell Types

The rough exposition above of the various characteristic cellular elements is applicable, not only to most animal cells, whether highly differentiated or not, but also to those of primitive unicellular plants such as molds and fungi (e.g., *Neurospora crassa*, the common bread mold, and yeast). Those of unicellular green plants (i.e., algae) or of green plants in general contain, in addition, another highly specialized and organized structure, the *chloroplast* (see page 292).

The cells of bacteria and blue-green algae, the protokaryotic or chromonemal organisms, appear grossly different. In the first place they are much smaller — their dimensions being roughly those of a cylinder 0.2 to 1 μ in diameter and 0.3 to 5 μ long. That is to say, they are in the same size class as animal mitochondria and have a volume some 500- to 1,000-fold smaller than that of animal cells. Gone are most structural features; there is no distinct membrane-bound nucleus, no endoplasmic reticulum, and no mitochondria. The only readily discernible features inside the wall of these primitive cells are numerous ribosomes scattered throughout the cytoplasm and a cell (or protoplast) membrane with numerous attachments. It is this set of structures which appears of utmost importance in providing what structural and functional organization there is in a bacterial cell, and thus it acts as an analogue and perhaps even a precursor of the more complex and highly specialized membranous elements of the more complex type of cells. In line with this hypothesis are the observations (1) that the oxidative and phosphorylative machinery of the bacterial cell is integrated into or associated with its membrane; (2) that membrane-bound ribosomes appear to be the site of the most active and effective protein synthesis; (3) that the bacterial germinal material (i.e., its DNA) appears organized with and attached to a particular region on the membrane; (4) that the membrane in certain rapidly growing plant cells appears to be capable of pinching off mitochondria-like structures; and finally (5) that the composition, structure, and some of the properties of all membranous elements appear to exhibit certain uncontestable regularities.

METHODS OF CELL FRACTIONATION

Just as there are no typical cells, so are there no standard methods of cell fractionation that are equally applicable to all cell types. Nevertheless, the methodology that was originally developed for just one tissue of one animal, the liver of the rat, has proved remarkably versatile and adaptable to numerous other tissues and organisms as well.

Principles of Centrifugation

Particles that differ in density or in size (or shape) sediment at different rates in an applied field of centrifugal force. Sedimentation rate is directly proportional to this field G, in turn given by

$$G = \omega^2 r = \frac{4\pi^2 (\text{rpm})^2}{3,600} r \qquad (9\text{-}1)$$

expressed, as relative centrifugal force in multiples of g, the gravitational constant (980 cm/sec^2). Here ω equals the angular velocity (in radians per second), r the radial distance from the axis of rotation, and rpm the revolutions per minute of the centrifuge rotor.

At a given rotor speed, the time required to centrifuge out a population of homogeneous particles is inversely proportional to the square of their radii and to the first power of the difference between their density and that of the medium, and is directly proportional to the viscosity of the medium. Thus relatively homogeneous, roughly spherical particles, of approximately equal densities, can be put into different classes solely on the basis of the time required for their sedimentation, a fact that forms the basis of the classical scheme of cell fractionation. First there are removed whole cells and large debris, then the fraction containing the large and dense nuclei (the density of DNA at 4° equals ~1.75, although that of most proteins is only 1.188), followed by one containing large particles or granules (usually largely mitochondria, but containing other structures in specialized tissues, e.g., the nerve-end particles or synaptosomes in brain, lysosomes of a variety of tissues, etc.), followed by the so-called "microsomal fraction," which contains fragments of both the smooth and the rough endoplasmic reticulum, as well as other vesicular elements of similar sedimentation characteristics originating in the Golgi, the plasma and nuclear membranes, etc., followed by free ribosomes.

One of the most significant advances in cell fractionation has been the introduction of density gradient techniques. Two types of gradients can be distinguished: *continuous*, constructed by means of gradient-building devices of varying degrees of sophistication, and *discontinuous*, produced by carefully layering zones of different density by hand, one on top of the other, usually with the heaviest at the bottom of the tube. Density gradients are used for two distinct purposes.

Zone or Band Centrifugation

In this version, the preparation is placed in a thin layer on top of the tube and centrifuged into the gradient of a medium usually less dense than the particles to be isolated. As a result of the application of the field, the particles migrate as a distinct band through the gradient, which merely serves the purpose of preventing the spreading of the zone or band through convection. This is an exceedingly useful technique of very wide applicability for both analytical and preparative purposes and has been used for the isolation and characterization of particles varying all the way from large viruses, nuclei, and mitochondria, through ribosomes, to pure proteins and nucleic acids.

Equilibrium Density or Isopycnic Centrifugation

If particles are allowed to sediment in a density gradient so designed as to include the value of the particle density, then, after equilibrium has been established, the particles will come to rest in a band centered around their own

TABLE 9-1. Distribution of Certain Key Enzymes and Other Components Suitable as Indicator or Monitors

Nuclei	Mitochondria	Smaller particles, including lysosomes	Ribosomes	Reticulum, Golgi, etc.	Soluble
			Microsomal fraction		
DNA	*Succinic dehydrogenase* (for CAC and ET)	Urate oxidase† Catalase D-amino acid oxidase 2-hydroxy acid oxidase ⎫ ^aM	RNA	*Glucose-6-P-ase^f* Nucleoside *diphosphatase*†^{f} NADPH-O_2-linked mixed-function oxidases	NADP-linked isocitric dehydrogenase
DNA-dependent RNA polymerase	*Cytochrome oxidase*† (for ET) NAD-linked isocitric deh† (for CAC) Cardiolipin (for ET) Copper EPR signal at $g = 1.94$ (for ET)	"Acid" ribonuclease† "Acid" phosphatase† "Acid" deoxyribonu-clease† β-Galactosidase† β-Glucuronidase† β-Mannosidase† Cathepsins† ⎬ ^bL		*NADPH-linked lipid peroxidase^f* Squalene cyclohy-droxylase (for steroid biosynthesis) NADPH-linked acyl- and alkoxy aryl hydroxylases	Amino-acyl-tRNA synthetase Acetyl CoA car-boxylase (for fatty acid biosynthesis) Fatty acyl CoA synthetase (n malonyl CoA + acetyl CoA $\xrightarrow{\text{NADPH}}$ fatty acid $+ nCO_2$)
	Glutamate dehydrogenase† Mg^{+2} and dinitrophenol stimulated ATPase† (for oxidative phosphorylation)	Acetyl choline ^cS Trypsinogen Chymotrypsinogen Lipase Amylase Ribonuclease ⎬ ^dZ		Cytochrome b_5 Cytochrome b_5 linked-cytochrome c reductase^f (one specific for NADH, one for NADPH)	*Glucose-6-P dehydrogenase* plus *6-P-gluconate dehydrogenase* (ox. pathway of carbo-hydrate metabolism)
	Acetyl CoA hydrolase;† fatty acyl CoA synthe-tases (for fatty acid oxidation) α-Ketoglutaric dehydro-genase complex^e Pyruvate dehydrogenase complex^e β-Hydroxybutyrate de-hydrogenase† Aspartate amino transferase† (transaminase)				*Transketolase Transaldolase* (pentose cycle) *Phospho-fructokinase* (glycolysis) *Lactic dehydrogenase*

Most frequently used indicator enzymes are italicized. These are enzymes where more than 60 per cent of the total homogenate activity is localized in the fraction indicated.

Metabolic pathways are in parentheses.

†Latent enzyme: particles must be disrupted for full activity.
ET = electron transport.
CAC = citric acid cycle.
^aM = "Microbodies" of various organs.
^bL = "Lysosomes" of vertebrate organs.
^cS = Synaptic vesicles of brain tissues.
^dZ = Zymogen granules of glandular tissue (pancreas).
^{e} = Can be readily detached from outer membranes of mitochondria as a single, homogeneous species.
^{f} = Found in "rough" reticulum.

buoyant density. Since under carefully controlled conditions the bands can be made quite narrow, particles of similar size and shape but differing only slightly in density can be separated with good efficiency.

The preferred medium for all these techniques for particle fractionation are buffered sucrose solutions. Frequently the resolution can be improved by carrying out the separations in D_2O rather than H_2O. Sorbitol, mannitol, and the polysaccharides Ficoll and glycogen have been substituted for sucrose in special instances.

INTRACELLULAR
LOCALIZATION OF
ENZYMES AND
BIOCHEMICAL
ACTIVITIES

De Duve has pointed out that any experiment of this type consists of three steps: (1) a *destructive* one, which converts a tissue or cell suspension into a homogenate; (2) a *reordering* of the components of the homogenate into "fractions" on the basis of physical properties (i.e., sedimentation coefficient, density, etc.); and (3) an *analysis* of these fractions. Interpretation of the results then requires three stages of reconstruction in return: (1) *assignment of* morphological and biochemical *properties* to the fractions: (2) *reinterpretation of the data in* (1) in terms of the components of the original homogenate and the fractionation techniques employed originally; and finally (3) an attempt to equate these *components* of a homogenate with certain *intracellular entities*.

What is done in general is to use some fractionation scheme and then select certain so-called *marker* or *indicator enzymes, activities,* or *substances* that, experience suggests, may be useful for the identification of certain intracellular particles or components. The results obtained are then used to draw up a *distribution pattern* or curve and thus *define particles in terms of characteristic biochemical activities*, and conversely to assign different characteristic biochemical properties to different particle types. Extension of the method then to a whole spectrum of enzymes, etc., allows the assignment of definite functions in the cellular economy to known ultracellular components, and conversely to define and later identify new or at least hitherto unrecognized morphological components on the basis of biochemical evidence — the identification of the "acid phosphatase particles" with *lysosomes* and the "urate oxidase particles" with *microbodies* (also called peroxidosomes), both in mammalian liver, are examples of the success of this approach. Two fundamental implicit assumptions, as also pointed out by de Duve, are (1) that enzymes are localized in but one intracellular site and (2) that populations of subcellular particles are enzymatically homogeneous.

Indicator Enzymes and
Enzyme Distributions

In Table 9-1 we have collected data concerning a number of enzymes and other components that have usually been employed (1) as indicators or monitors for certain intracellular particles and (2) for certain important biochemical processes, sequences, etc. Truly integrated metabolic activities frequently require the collaboration of two or even more fractions. It is this phenomenon, perhaps, that governs many of the parameters of metabolic control. A classic example is provided by protein synthesis (see Chap. 21). The activation of amino acids and their attachment to transfer RNA takes place within the cytoplasmic fluid; their assembly to polypeptides on ribosomal clusters, some of them forming part of the rough endoplasmic reticulum, is programmed by a series of RNAs (messenger RNA), which was originally synthesized in the nucleus under direct control of its

DNA. The energy for this process is provided by ATP formed largely in the mitochondria, and after the process is completed, the finished proteins in secretory cells at least are detached and "concentrated" by the Golgi apparatus and finally separated into storage granules.

Nuclei. Highly purified nuclear fractions contain 90 to 95 per cent of the total cellular DNA, 10 per cent of the total cellular protein, and exhibit ratios of protein to DNA of 5, and of RNA to DNA of 0.15 to 0.22.

Mitochondria. Mitochondria, from liver, are ellipsoids of revolution, which average 3.3 μ in their major and slightly less than 1 μ in their minor axes, with a dry weight of the order of 1.1×10^{-13} g per particle. There are some 800 mitochondria per rat liver cell, and they account for approximately 20 per cent of the total cell nitrogen or protein. Their density in 0.25 M sucrose equals 1.099, and their sedimentation constant is 1×10^4 S. Approximately 40 per cent of the total dry weight of the mitochondrion is phospholipid, of which cardiolipin is the most characteristic in its almost purely mitochondrial localization. Heart muscle mitochondria contain 1.46 μg atoms of nonheme Cu, between 3.3 and 6.4 μg atoms of nonheme Fe, as well as about 2.5 μg atoms of heme Fe (cytochrome) per gram of protein. They also contain about 0.5 to 0.6 μ moles of flavin and 4 μ moles of coenzyme Q (ubiquinone) per gram of protein. There is now good reason to believe that the small amounts of RNA ($\sim$1 per cent of protein) and DNA ($<$1 per cent of protein) associated even with the most highly purified preparations are not due to impurities but fulfill a functional role, probably in the biosynthesis of certain mitochondrial proteins.

Endoplasmic Reticulum and Ribosomes. The total "microsomal" fraction, consisting of bits and pieces of the endoplasmic reticulum and associated ribosomes plus other membrane fragments of similar sedimentation characteristics, accounts for approximately 20 per cent of the total cellular protein and usually better than 60 per cent (sometimes as high as 80 per cent) of the cellular RNA. This fraction from liver contains about 20 to 30 mg of protein, about 5 mg of RNA, and 5 to 8 mg of phospholipid per gram of tissue. The ratios of RNA to protein and phospholipid to protein are of the order of 0.20 and 0.30, respectively.

The reticular and free ribosomes that can be obtained by further fractionation of the "microsomal" component and prolonged centrifugation of the cytoplasm, respectively, appear to be identical. Two types of RNA can be extracted from these ribosomes, derived from and specific for one of the two ribosomal subunits. The particle weights of these two RNA species are $\sim 5 \times 10^5$ and 1.3×10^6, respectively, with sedimentation coefficients of 16 to 18 S and 23 to 28 S, depending on species. There appears to be a great multiplicity of proteins associated with or forming part of the ribosomes. Some, but by no means all of them, are probably nascent proteins, the synthesis of which has just been completed on the surface of the particle.

A large number of highly important biosynthetic reactions appear to be catalyzed by enzymes localized on the membranous part of the endoplasmic reticulum. Among them are key reactions in the biosynthesis of steroids, phospholipids, and complex polysaccharides. One of the most characteristic sets of reactions localized in this cell fraction is the hydroxylation of a large variety of organic molecules (various aliphatic and aromatic amines, steroids, etc.) requiring the simultaneous participation of O_2 and NADPH, catalyzed by the hydroxylases or mixed-function oxidases discussed on page 344.

REFERENCES

Allfrey, V.: The Isolation of Subcellular Components, in J. Brachet and A. E. Mirsky (eds.), "The Cell," vol. I, p. 193, Academic Press, New York, 1959.

Anderson, N. G.: Techniques for the Mass Isolation of Cellular Components, in G. Oster and A. W. Pollister (eds.), "Physical Techniques in Biological Research," p. 299, Academic Press, New York, 1956.

Bloom, W., and D. W. Fawcett: "A Textbook of Histology," W. B. Saunders, Philadelphia, 1962.

Claude, A.: Studies in Cells: Morphology, Chemical Constitution and Distribution of Biochemical Functions, *Harvey Lectures*; **48:** 121 (1948).

Cohn, N. S.: "Elements of Cytology," Harcourt, Brace & World, New York, 1964.

Dalton, A.: Golgi Apparatus and Secretion Granules, in J. Brachet and A. E. Mirsky (eds.), "The Cell," vol. II, p. 603, Academic Press, New York, 1961.

De Duve, C.: Principles of Tissue Fractionation, *J. Theoret. Biol.*, **6:** 33 (1964).

————: The Separation and Characterization of Subcellular Particles, *Harvey Lectures*, **59:** 49 (1965).

————, J. Berthet, and H. Beaufay: Gradient Centrifugation of Cell Particles; Theory and Applications, *Progr. Biophys.*, *Biophys. Chem.*, **9:** 325 (1959).

————, R. Wattiaux, and P. Baudhuin: Distribution of Enzymes between Subcellular Fractions of Animal Tissues, *Advan. Enzymol.*, **24:** 291 (1962).

Descriptions of Various Fractionation Schemes in S. P. Colowick and N. O. Kaplan (eds.), "Methods in Enzymology," vols. I, 1955, and V, 1962, Academic Press, New York.

Granick, S.: The Chloroplasts: Inheritance, Structure and Function, in J. Brachet and A. E. Mirsky (eds.), "The Cell," vol. II, p. 489, Academic Press, New York, 1961.

Lehninger, A.: "The Mitochondrion," Benjamin, New York, 1964.

Mirsky, A. E., and S. Osauda: The Interphase Nucleus, in J. Brachet and A. E. Mirsky (eds.), "The Cell," vol. II, p. 677, Academic Press, New York, 1961.

Novikoff, A. B.: Mitochondria (Chondriosomes), in J. Brachet and A. E. Mirsky (eds.), "The Cell," vol. II, p. 299, Academic Press, New York, 1961.

————: Lysosomes and Related Particles, in J. Brachet and A. E. Mirsky (eds.), "The Cell," vol. II, p. 423, Academic Press, New York, 1961.

Palade, G. E.: The Organization of Living Matter, *Proc. Natl. Acad. Sci. U.S.*, **52:** 613 (1964).

Petermann, M. L.: "The Physical and Chemical Properties of Ribosomes," Elsevier, New York, 1965.

Porter, K. R.: The Endoplasmic Reticulum, in T. W. Goodwin and D. Lindberg (eds.), "Biological Structure and Functions," vol. I, p. 127, Academic Press, New York, 1961.

Roodyn, D. B. (ed.): "Enzyme Cytology," Academic Press, New York, 1967.

Seno, S., and E. V. Cowdry: "Intracellular Membraneous Structure," Japan Society of Cell Biology, Okayama, 1965.

Whittaker, V. P.: The Application of Subcellular Fractionation Techniques to the Study of Brain Function, *Progr. Biophys. Mol. Biol.*, **15:** 39 (1965).

10 | The Chemistry of Carbohydrates

Carbohydrates are an important class of naturally occurring substances and are found universally distributed among plants, animals, and microorganisms. The designation "carbohydrate" derives from the fact that these organic compounds have empirical formulas $(C \cdot H_2O)_n$, in which n is three or greater, or are closely related to compounds that do. The metabolism of carbohydrates is of central importance to organisms, individually and collectively. Basically all organic foodstuffs are ultimately derived from the synthesis of carbohydrates through photosynthesis (see Chap. 12). Conversely, catabolism of carbohydrates provides the major share of the energy requirement for maintenance of life and performance of work. In addition, carbohydrates act as energy reservoirs and serve architectural functions. Prior to a consideration of the biosynthesis and metabolism of the carbohydrates, it is necessary to develop the structural chemistry of these substances in modest detail. Many excellent reference works are available and all standard textbooks of organic chemistry contain chapters devoted to it. In addition "Advances in Carbohydrate Chemistry," a yearly publication of collected review articles, provides up-to-date and detailed accounts of particular aspects of the subject. Additional references are to be found at the end of this chapter. The student is referred to these for more detailed accounts of the structural chemistry of carbohydrates and for information regarding all but the most basic reactions: only these are included here.

Carbohydrates are divided into three basic categories: monosaccharides, oligosaccharides, and polysaccharides. The *monosaccharides* usually have only four to seven or eight carbon atoms and contain only one aldehyde or ketone function or are derivatives of molecules that do. The *oligosaccharides* are oligo-mers of monosaccharides linked by formation of glycosidic bonds. These gener-ally contain two to eight or ten monomeric units. For carbohydrates character-ized by higher degrees of polymerization, the designation *polysaccharide* is reserved. Polysaccharides are frequently molecules of great size and may have molecular weights of many million. Included among them are such important substances as glycogen, cellulose, and starch. We begin our discussion with an account of the structural chemistry of the monosaccharides and, with this foundation, proceed subsequently with the chemistry of the more complex sub-stances.

MONOSACCHARIDES   The most common monosaccharide in living material is the simple six-carbon sugar *(hexose)* known as glucose. Several of the features of the structure and chemistry of this and related molecules may be appreciated from a consideration of the various means of representation of D-glucose. These are collected in Fig. 10-1. In structure I, D-glucose is indicated in a straight-chain form with an

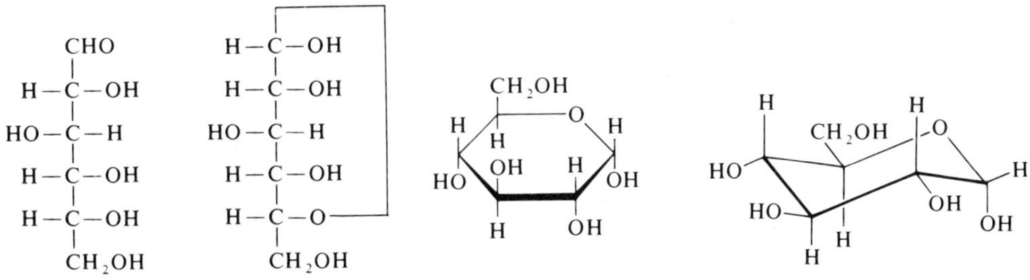

FIGURE 10-1.   Representations of the α-D-Glucose Molecule.

aldehydic function at C-1 and alcoholic functions at carbons 2 through 6. Sugars that terminate in a aldehydic function are called *aldoses*. Examination of structure I for D-glucose indicates the presence of four asymmetric carbon atoms. Thus, there exist $2^4 = 16$ optical isomers of aldohexoses, such as glucose. Assign-ment of the structure of each of the optical isomers of glucose was completed by the brilliant carbohydrate chemist Emil Fischer in 1896. In a similar fashion, we find $2^3 = 8$ optical isomers for the aldopentoses and $2^2 = 4$ for the aldotetroses. For each class of sugar, these isomers are subgrouped into D- and L- classes, depending on the relationship of the configuration at the penultimate carbon atom to that in D-glyceraldehyde. In Fig. 10-2, the steric relationships of the D-sugars are indicated. Similarly, the structures of the L-aldoses may be derived from L-glyceraldehyde and are, in each case, the mirror image of the correspond-ing D-compounds.

In structure II, D-glucose is written in a cyclic hemiacetal form. This is formed by the addition of the hydroxyl function at C-5 to the aldehyde at C-1, a general property of aldoses. This raises three additional considerations. First, formation of the hemiacetal introduces a new asymmetric center at C-1 of D-glucose. There are thus two forms of this molecule and a total of 32 optical isomers for the

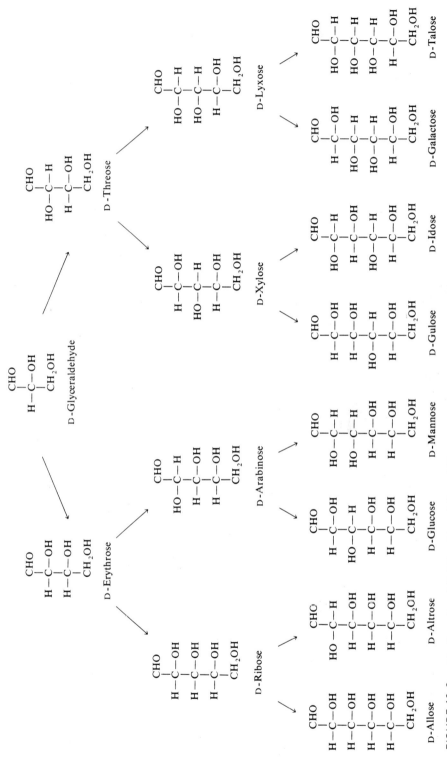

FIGURE 10-2. Configurational Relationships of the D-Aldoses.

cyclic forms of the hexoses. The former are designated α- and β- forms. In formulations such as (II), the hydroxyl at C-1 is written to the right in α- forms and to the left in β- forms. Thus, for the sake of comparison, β-D-glucose is written as

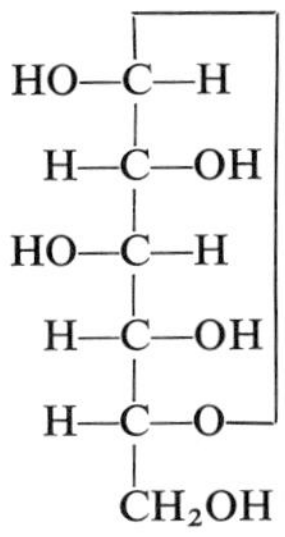

```
     ┌
HO—C—H │
  H—C—OH│
HO—C—H │
  H—C—OH│
  H—C—O—┘
     │
   CH₂OH
```

β-D-glucose

In the second place, we have the problem of ring size. In addition to six-membered rings of the type indicated in structures II and III of Fig. 10-1, several sugars form the related five-membered structures. These are designated *pyranose* and *furanose* forms, respectively, since they bear a formal resemblance to the six- and five-membered cyclic ethers pyran and furan. Thus the complete name

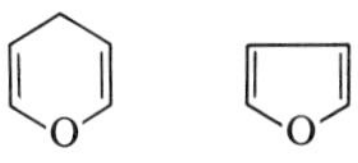

Pyran   Furan

for structure II or III in Fig. 10-1 is α-D-glucopyranose. We encounter some examples of furanoses below. Finally, to what extent do sugars exist as cyclic hemiacetals as opposed to open-chain compounds in solution? Although the extent of hemiacetal formation is certainly a function of the nature of the sugar, for most aldohexoses and aldopentoses the cyclic form is the predominant species in solution.

Although structure II indicates the basic features of α-D-glucose, it provides little insight as to the actual shape of the molecule and the spatial relationships of the various functional groups to one another. A great improvement in representation of structural formulas in carbohydrates was introduced by Haworth many years ago. An example of a Haworth projection formula is provided by structure III in Fig. 10-1. In this view, the backbone carbon atoms together with the ethereal oxygen are considered to be planar, and the configuration of each of the ring substituents is indicated as being either above or below the plane of the ring. The translation from formulas of type II to Haworth projection formulas (III) is accomplished according to the following rules: (1) substituents written to the right side of the backbone in the linear representation are written below the plane of the ring in the cyclic representation; similarly, substituents written to the left occupy positions above the ring; (2) for that single carbon atom whose hydroxyl function is involved in formation of the cyclic hemiacetal, the opposite rule applies. Thus, for D-sugars, the CH₂OH function is written in an above position, and the H atom on the same carbon is written below, despite the fact that it is to the left in the linear representation. This puzzling situation obtains because the linear representations of type II are actually misleading. The structural identity of the linear and cyclic representations is much easier to appreciate if we write the former as (this does not involve a change of configuration at carbon 5):

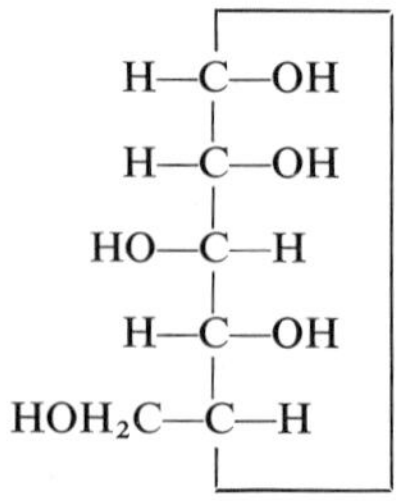

$$
\begin{array}{c}
H-C-OH \\
H-C-OH \\
HO-C-H \\
H-C-OH \\
HOH_2C-C-H
\end{array}
$$

In this formulation, the disposition of the substituents at carbon 5 follows the rule stated above for all other carbon atoms. Note that in the cyclic form, the hydroxyl function at carbon 1 will be below the ring in the α- form and above it in the β- form.

The most accurate representation of the D-glucose molecule is provided in structure IV of Fig. 10-1. In this case, the conformation of the sugar is defined as a chair form, and the substituents appear in either axial or equatorial positions. This is certainly the correct structure for the crystalline species and probably obtains in solution as well. However, since the correct conformation for many of the sugars has not been clearly established, we shall employ the Haworth projection formulas in preference to conformational structures.

Sugars that have a ketone function, usually at position C-2, rather than an aldehyde function, are known as *ketoses*. The most prominent examples are provided by the ubiquitous hexose fructose and by the pentoses ribulose and xylulose:

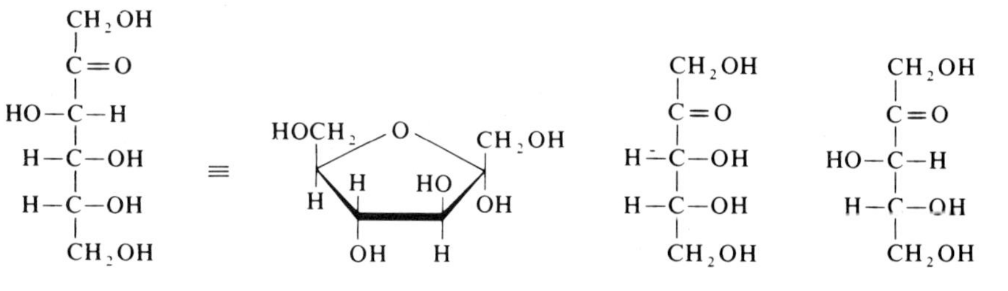

D-Fructose   D-Ribulose   D-Xylulose

Fructose exists in solution predominantly in the furanose form, as do most of the aldopentoses. Ketopentoses, such as ribulose, may exist either in the noncyclic form or in the furanose form involving the hydroxyl at C-5 in hemiacetal formation. The former configuration is preferred by these sugars.

The chemistry of the monosaccharides is, of course, dominated by the transformations of the carbonyl and alcohol moieties. Certain of these lead us to related classes of carbohydrates of biochemical interest.

Although, as noted above, most sugars exist predominantly in cyclic hemiacetal forms, the equilibrium between these and the aldehydic form is very mobile, and, in addition, sufficiently significant fractions of the sugars do exist in the aldehydic form at equilibrium, so that these substances undergo typical reactions with carbonyl reagents. Thus, aldoses reduce silver ion in ammonia solution (Tollens' reagent) and cupric ion complexed with citrate (Benedict's solution). Both of these reactions are of significant value in the detection and estimation of reducing sugars. In addition, sugars react with amines. A particularly important example is provided by the reaction with excess phenylhydrazine. Although the mechanism of this reaction is not quite clear, it seems to proceed in at least three stages: first, the formation of the phenylhydrazone of, for example, glucose; second, oxidation of the carbon atom at position 2 to the level of a carbonyl group; and, third, this function reacts with a second molecule of phenylhydrazine to yield glucose phenylosazone. The overall reaction is indicated in Eq. 10-1:

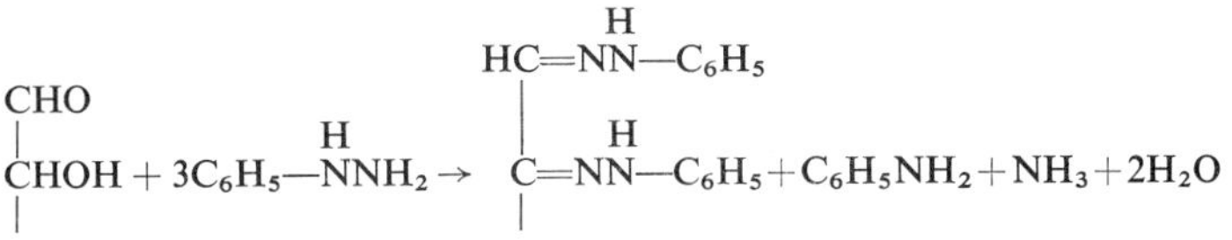

$$
\begin{array}{c}
\text{CHO} \\
| \\
\text{CHOH} \\
|
\end{array}
+ 3C_6H_5{-}\overset{H}{N}NH_2 \rightarrow
\begin{array}{c}
\overset{H}{HC}{=}NN{-}C_6H_5 \\
| \\
C{=}NN{-}C_6H_5 \\
|
\end{array}
+ C_6H_5NH_2 + NH_3 + 2H_2O
$$

$$(10\text{-}1)$$

Osazones are ordinarily crystalline compounds. This reaction was utilized with great success by Fischer in the work that established the configurations of the sugars. For example, the observation that glucose, mannose, and fructose all yield the same osazone indicates that the configuration of each of these sugars about carbons 3, 4, and 5 must be identical.

Reduction under mild conditions, with sodium amalgam for instance, converts sugars to polyhydric alcohols. That is, the aldehyde or ketone function is reduced to the alcohol level of oxidation. These alcohols are termed *pentitols*, *hexitols*, etc. Certain of them are found naturally. The most important are mannitol, sorbitol (from glucose), and ribitol. Closely related to these substances are the

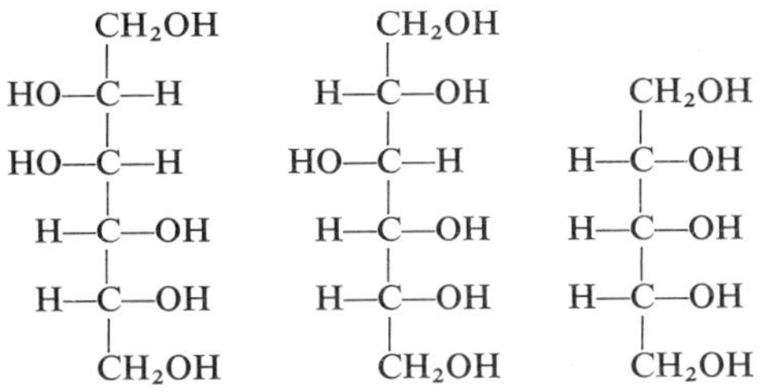

D-Mannitol   D-Sorbitol   D-Ribitol

cyclic hexitols, such as the inositols. Two of these are indicated below:

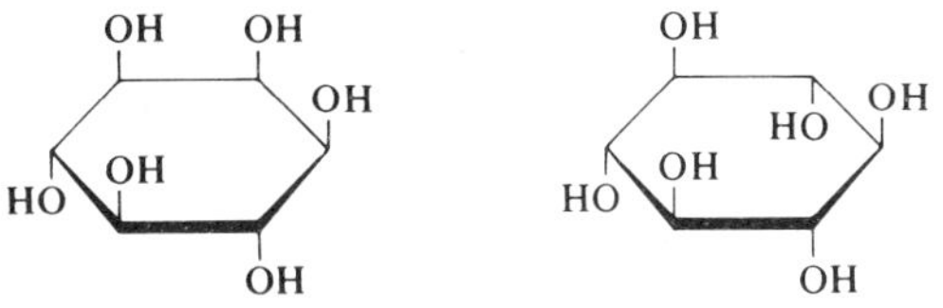

myo-Inositol   Scyllitol

Myo-inositol is found widely distributed in living material.

Monosaccharides undergo a variety of oxidation reactions: among the products of these are three classes of acids. Treatment of aldoses with an oxidizing agent, such as bromine, converts the aldehydic function at C-1 to a carboxylic acid function and gives rise to the *aldonic* acids. Use of stronger oxidizing agents, such as nitric acid, induces oxidation at both C-1 and C-6 and yields the *aldaric* acids. Finally, oxidation specifically at C-6 yields the *alduronic* acids. These three types of acids as derived from glucose are indicated below:

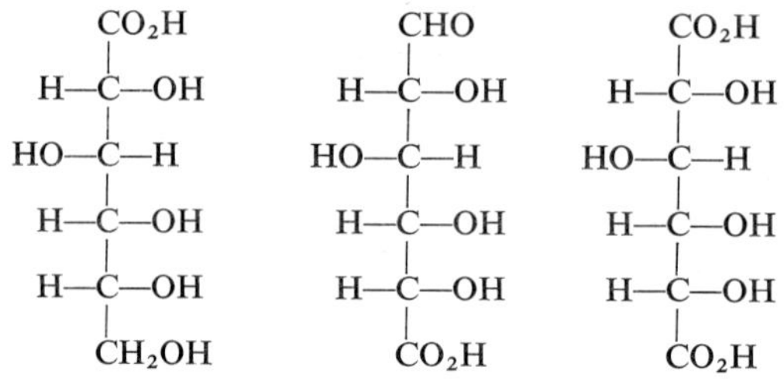

$$
\begin{array}{ccc}
\text{CO}_2\text{H} & \text{CHO} & \text{CO}_2\text{H} \\
\text{H--C--OH} & \text{H--C--OH} & \text{H--C--OH} \\
\text{HO--C--H} & \text{HO--C--H} & \text{HO--C--H} \\
\text{H--C--OH} & \text{H--C--OH} & \text{H--C--OH} \\
\text{H--C--OH} & \text{H--C--OH} & \text{H--C--OH} \\
\text{CH}_2\text{OH} & \text{CO}_2\text{H} & \text{CO}_2\text{H}
\end{array}
$$

D-Gluconic acid   D-Glucuronic acid   D-Glucaric acid

Both aldonic and alduronic acids occur frequently in nature both as constituents of polysaccharides and as intermediates in carbohydrate metabolism.

In addition to the polyols derived from monosaccharides by reduction and the various acids derived by oxidation, there are two additional classes of sugar derivatives that are of exceptional importance in biochemistry. These include the amino sugars and the methylpentoses. The two most important amino sugars are 2-D-glucosamine and 2-D-galactosamine:

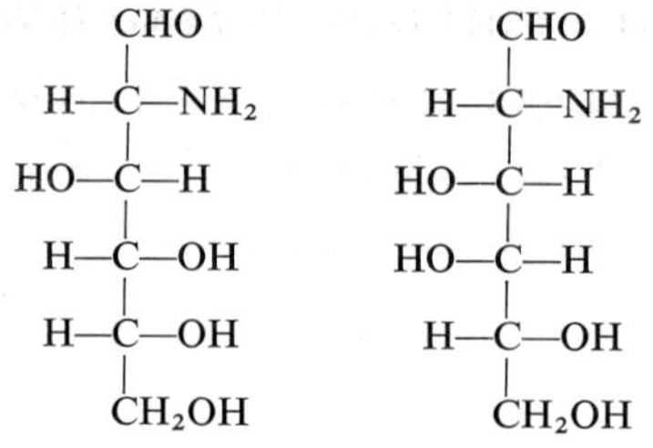

$$
\begin{array}{cc}
\text{CHO} & \text{CHO} \\
\text{H--C--NH}_2 & \text{H--C--NH}_2 \\
\text{HO--C--H} & \text{HO--C--H} \\
\text{H--C--OH} & \text{HO--C--H} \\
\text{H--C--OH} & \text{H--C--OH} \\
\text{CH}_2\text{OH} & \text{CH}_2\text{OH}
\end{array}
$$

2-D-Glucosamine   2-D-Galactosamine

Both of these occur as important constituents of many polysaccharides (usually as their *N*-acetyl derivatives; see below). The most prominent methylpentoses (or 6-deoxyhexoses) include rhamnose, fucose, and 6-deoxy-D-glucose:

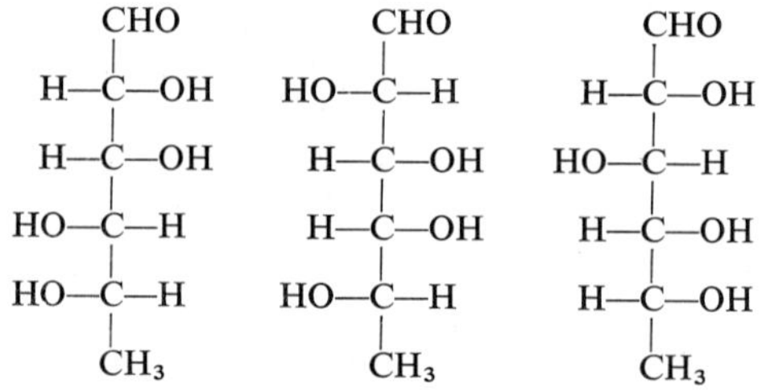

$$
\begin{array}{ccc}
\text{CHO} & \text{CHO} & \text{CHO} \\
\text{H--C--OH} & \text{HO--C--H} & \text{H--C--OH} \\
\text{H--C--OH} & \text{H--C--OH} & \text{HO--C--H} \\
\text{HO--C--H} & \text{H--C--OH} & \text{H--C--OH} \\
\text{HO--C--H} & \text{HO--C--H} & \text{H--C--OH} \\
\text{CH}_3 & \text{CH}_3 & \text{CH}_3
\end{array}
$$

L-Rhamnose   L-Fucose   6-Deoxy-D-glucose

These are widely distributed in plant materials, frequently as constituents of polysaccharides.

The interconversion of α- and β- forms of sugars, *mutarotation*, occurs readily in aqueous solution and is subject to catalysis by both acids and bases. These reactions are most easily followed by observing changes in optical rotation as a function of time. For example, α-D-glucose has a specific rotation of 112°; the β- anomer has a rotation of 18.7°. At equilibrium, the observed rotation is about 52.5°, corresponding to 64 per cent of the β- anomer and 36 per cent of the α-. The mutarotation of certain sugars is subject to enzymatic catalysis.

An exceptionally important reaction of the monosaccharides is *glycoside formation*. For example, if D-glucose is treated with methanol in the presence of HCl, two products are formed:

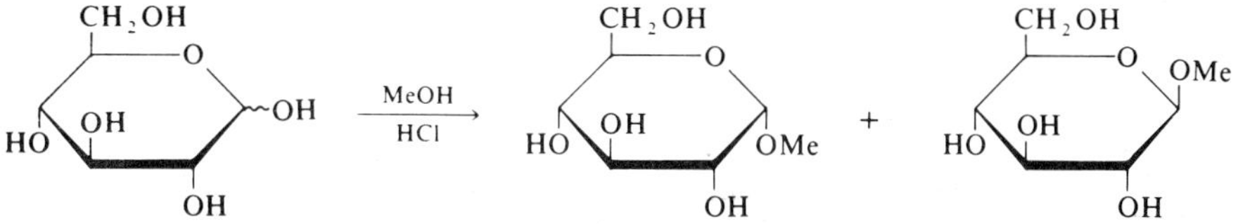

$$(10\text{-}2)$$

In each case the hydroxyl function at position 1 has been methylated. By analogy with the terminology developed above, these products are termed α-methyl-D-glucoside and β-methyl-D-glucoside. More complete designations would be α- and β-methyl-D-glucopyranosides. The nonsugar moiety of these compounds, that is the group substituted for the proton of the hydroxyl group at position C-1, is termed the *aglycone*. Compounds having one or more glycosidic linkages are of great importance biochemically. This is the basic linkage through which all polysaccharides and most oligosaccharides are formed. Thus the glycosidic bond is to carbohydrate chemistry what the peptide bond is to protein chemistry and the phosphodiester linkage is to that of nucleic acids. Glycosidic bonds are also involved in the linkages of sugars to steroids, pigments, and other substances. Some examples of such conjugates are collected in Fig. 10-3. Finally, we have already encountered an exceptionally important class of glycosides, the *N*-glycosides, in which the linkage to the aglycone is through nitrogen rather than oxygen. This is the type of linkage through which D-ribose and 2-deoxy-D-ribose are bound to the nitrogen bases in such molecules as RNA, DNA, ATP, and NAD$^+$ (see Chaps. 5 and 8).

OLIGOSACCHARIDES   The oligosaccharides are subdivided into classes termed disaccharides, trisaccharides, and so forth, depending on whether they have two, three, or more carbohydrate units. Perhaps the most abundant disaccharide is sucrose, common table sugar. Sucrose is composed of one D-glucose unit and one D-fructose unit; its structure is indicated below:

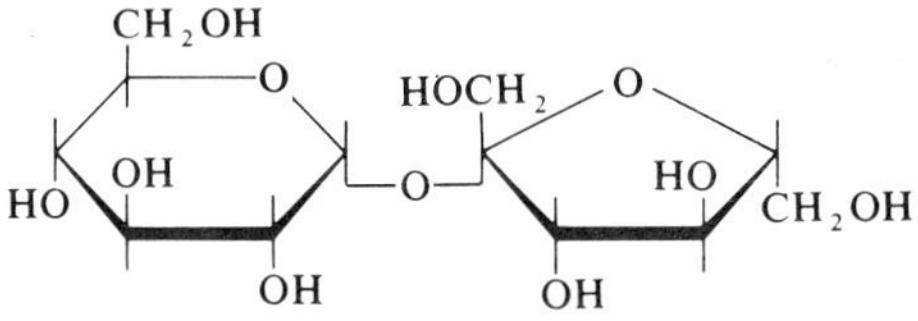

Sucrose

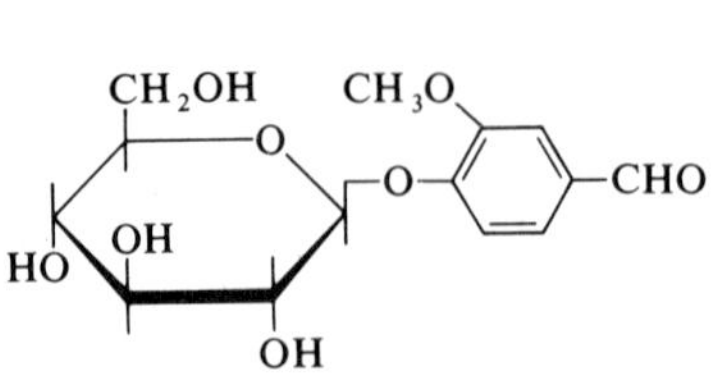

Vanillin-β-D-glucoside
(natural source of vanilla flavor)

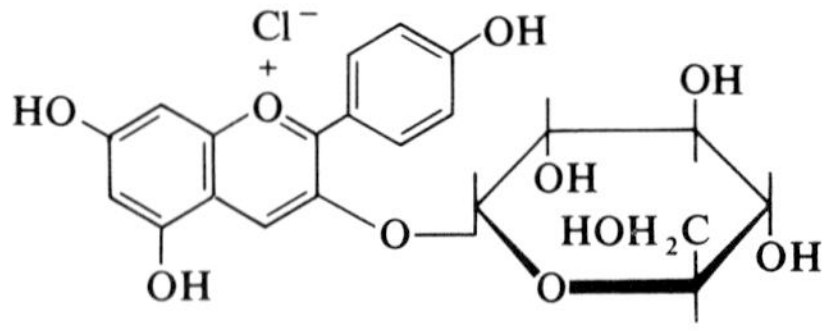

Pelargonidin-β-D-glucoside chloride
(a plant pigment)

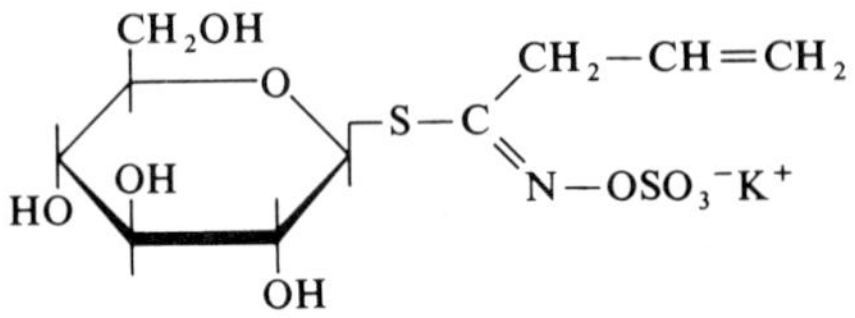

Sinigrin
(a constituent of horseradish)

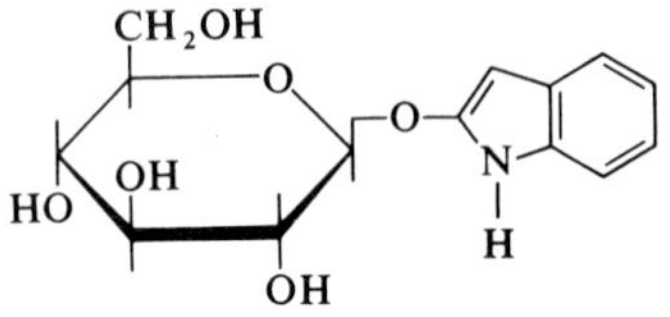

Indican
(a source of indigo dye)

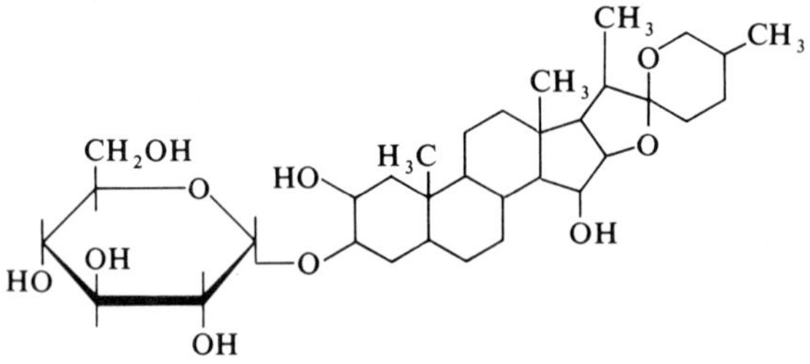

Digitogenin-α-D-glucoside
(a cardiac glycoside having the power to
stimulate cardiac muscle contraction)

FIGURE 10-3.   Some Naturally Occurring Glycosides.

The complete specification of this disaccharide or of any disaccharide requires four pieces of information. First, we must specify the nature of the monosaccharides from which the disaccharide is constituted; second, for each monosaccharide we must know the type of ring junction, furanose or pyranose, as it exists in the disaccharide; third, those carbon atoms through which the linkage is effected must be specified; and, finally, the anomeric nature of this linkage is required. Thus, a complete description of the sucrose molecule is α-D-glucopyranosyl-(1 → 2)-β-D-fructofuranoside. Notice that sucrose is not a reducing sugar, since both carbon atoms at the oxidation level of the carbonyl group are involved in the glycosidic linkage. In Fig. 10-4, several other examples of prominent disaccharides are collected together with trivial and systematic names.

Few trisaccharides are of importance as naturally occurring organic compounds. Among the more prominent are raffinose [α-D-galactopyranosyl-(1 → 6)-α-D-glucopyranosyl-(1 → 2)-β-D-fructofuranoside] and gentianose [β-D-glucopyranosyl-(1 → 6)-α-D-glucopyranosyl-(1 → 2)-β-D-fructofuranoside]:

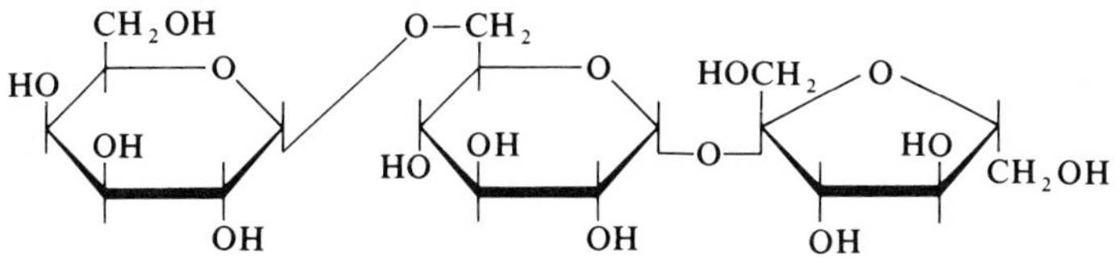

Raffinose

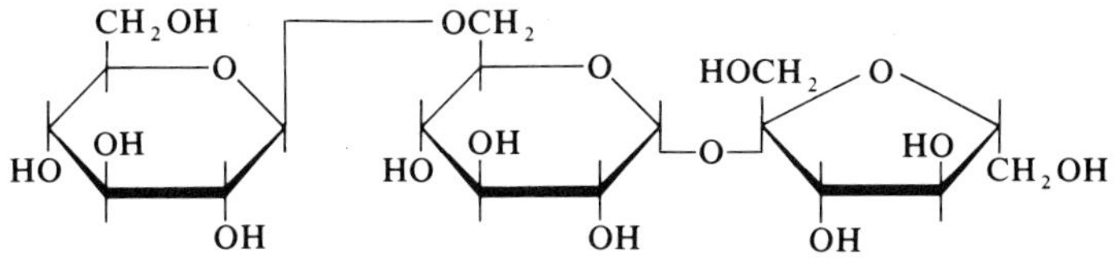

Gentianose

These sugars are constituents of plant tissues which, quite generally, have a greater variety of oligosaccharides than are found in animal tissues.

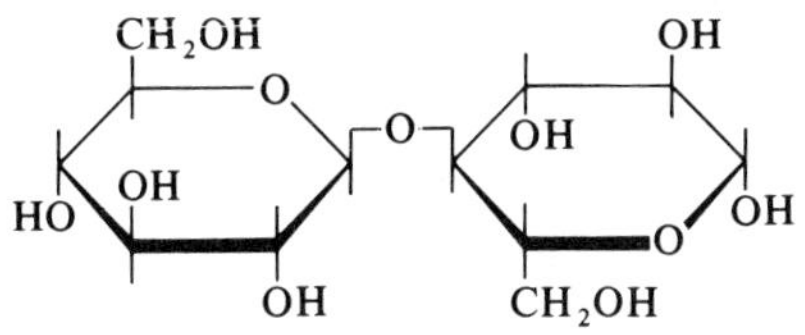

Cellobiose (β-form)
β-D-glucopyranosyl-(1→4)-β-
D-glucopyranose

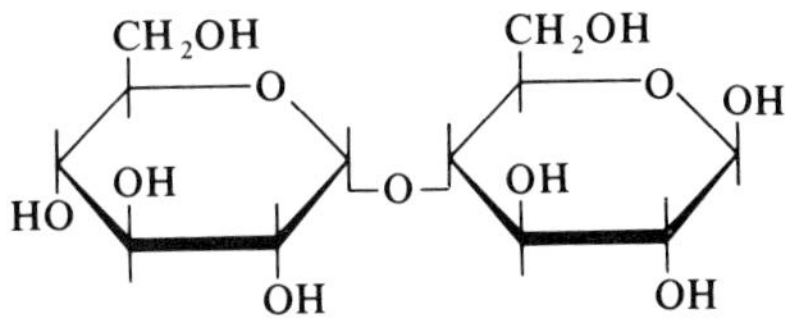

Maltose (β-form)
α-D-glucopyranosyl-(1→4)-β-
D-glucopyranose

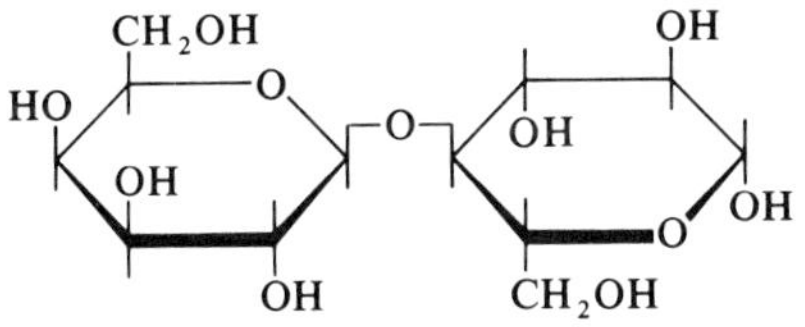

Lactose (β-form)
β-D-galactopyranosyl-(1→4)-β-
D-glucopyranose

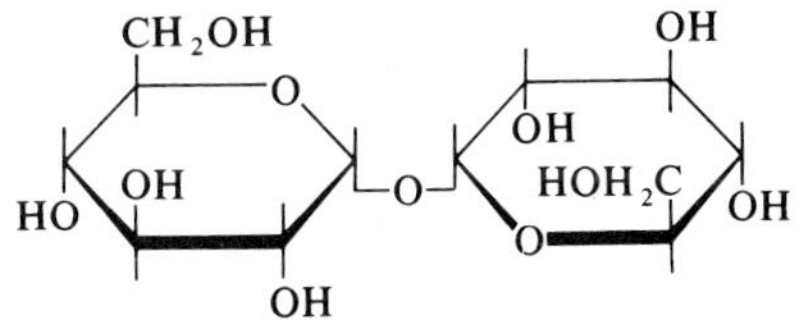

Trehalose
α-D-glucopyranosyl-(1→1)-α-
D-glucopyranoside

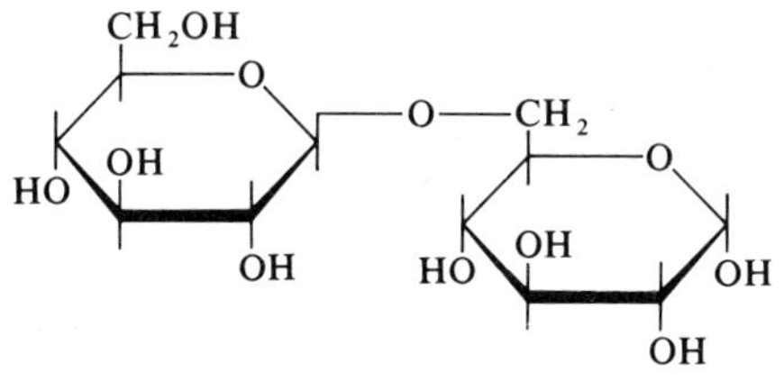

Gentiobiose (α-form)
β-D-glucopyranosyl-(1→6)-α-
D-glucopyranose

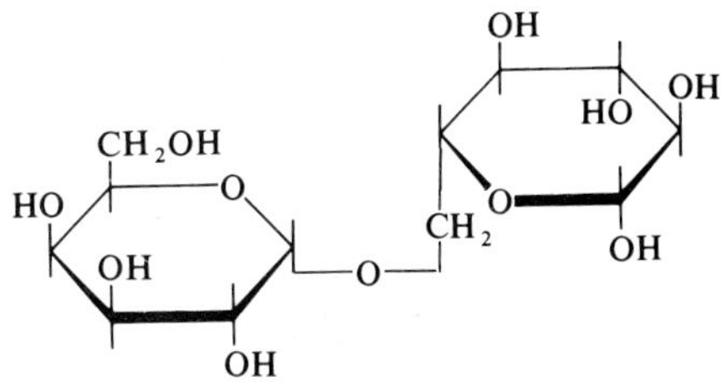

Melibiose (β-form)
α-D-galactopyranosyl-(1→6)-β-
D-glucopyranose

FIGURE 10-4. Structures and Nomenclature for Several Disaccharides.

POLYSACCHARIDES

The bulk of all carbohydrate in nature exists in the form of polysaccharides. In terms of function, polysaccharides may be divided into two principal groups. The first, which includes cellulose, for example, serves principally architectural purposes; the second, which includes substances such as glycogen, functions as nutrients. That is, molecules in this group are primarily storage centers and may be readily mobilized by conversion to monosaccharides, which may then be metabolized (see Chap. 11). In terms of gross structural features, polysaccharides may also be divided into two groups: homopolysaccharides and heteropolysaccharides. The former is characterized by the occurrence of only one sort of monosaccharide within the molecule (although different sorts of intersugar linkages may be present) and the latter by the occurrence of two or more types of monomeric units. The chemistry of the former is somewhat simpler than that of the latter, in the same sense that the chemistry of polyamino acids is simpler than that of proteins, and we turn to some examples of polysaccharides in this class first.

Before actually discussing occurrence, structure, and function for particular polysaccharides, a few words about the general state of structural studies on these molecules is in order. Considerable effort is being devoted to such studies, and great progress has been made in recent years. Perhaps 10 to 20 new polysaccharides are isolated each year. The determination of the order of occurrence of monosaccharides in polysaccharides is in some ways simpler and in some ways more difficult than the sequencing of polypeptides or nucleic acids. The basic simplifying feature in polysaccharide chemistry, compared with that of proteins or nucleic acids, is that the former substances are usually composed of reasonably small repeating units. That is, each monomeric unit occurs in a regular repeating fashion throughout the molecule. Individual amino acids or nucleotides, in contrast, appear to be distributed randomly or nearly so within the corresponding polymeric products. If a polysaccharide is, in fact, perfectly regular, then determination of the structure of the repeating unit together with a knowledge of the molecular weight suffices to establish the complete primary structure. In most cases, however, a certain number of singularities occur, such as branch points, which complicate matters considerably. A basic complicating factor in polysaccharide chemistry is the existence of a number of types of intersugar linkages. Although all amino acid residues of proteins are connected by peptide linkages and the nucleotides of nucleic acids are always joined by 3'-5' phosphodiester bonds, intersugar linkages may be α-$(1 \rightarrow 2)$, β-$(1 \rightarrow 3)$, $\alpha(1 \rightarrow 4)$, etc. In terms of the number of types of monomeric units within a particular polysaccharide, the situation is more like that of nucleic acids than of proteins. Seldom do more than four monomer types occur within a single polysaccharide molecule. It is worth noting that, quite in general, it is more difficult to establish the sequence of a polymer that contains few types of monomeric units than of one having many types.

We now direct our attention to the properties of individual polysaccharides.

Cellulose

The most abundant structural polysaccharide of plants, and indeed the most abundant organic substance on earth, is *cellulose*. About 10^{11} tons of cellulose are synthesized per year. It occurs almost exclusively in plants, in which it accounts for about 50 per cent of the total content of carbon. The following facts suffice to establish its structure. First, total hydrolysis yields only D-glucose. Second, partial hydrolysis yields cellobiose (see p. 248). Third, hydrolysis of fully methylated cellulose yields only 2,3,6-tri-O-methylglucose. It follows that cellulose is a linear array of D-glucopyranose units linked by β-$(1 \rightarrow 4)$-glycosidic bonds, as indicated below:

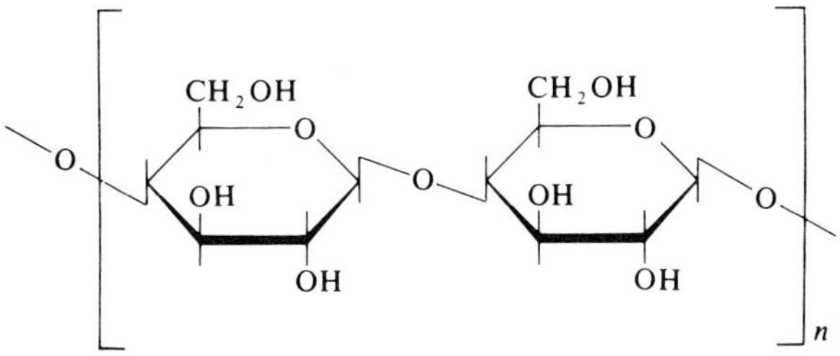

The molecular weight of isolated cellulose preparations varies from about 50,000 to more than a million. It is worth noting that these molecules, like the nucleic acids, may be subject to ready degradation in isolation procedures, and, hence, these molecular weights may be much too small. In any event, cellulose molecules exist in the cell walls of plants, not as individual molecules, but in the form of microfibrils that are several hundred angstroms long. These are formed from numerous cellulose chains arranged parallel to one another.

Chitin   *Chitin*, a polysaccharide closely related structurally to cellulose, performs similar functions in the lower forms of plant life, particularly the fungi, and in invertebrates, particularly the arthropods. It has wide distribution within these groups and is probably the second most abundant organic substance on earth. The copepods alone are considered to synthesize about 10^9 tons of chitin per year.

Chitin is composed of a linear array of β-linked 2-acetamido-2-deoxy-D-glucose units, as indicated below:

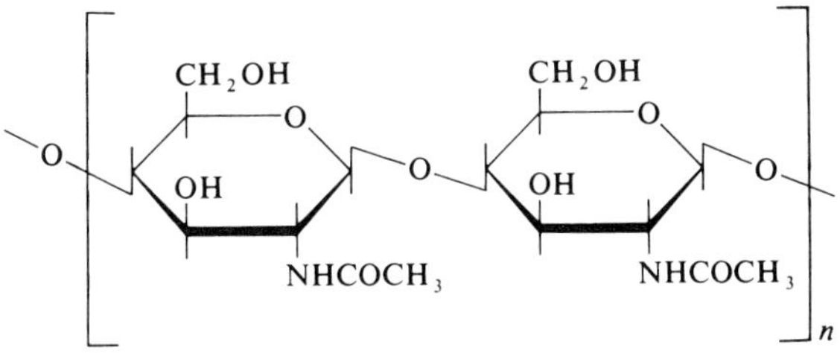

The repeating unit is identical to that for cellulose except that the hydroxyl function at C-2 has been replaced by the acetamido function. Those polysaccharides which contain amino sugars or their derivatives, such as chitin, are collectively known as *mucopolysaccharides*. It is difficult to estimate the molecular weight of chitins as they exist in nature, since they are invariably tightly linked to nonpolysaccharide material, particularly proteins and inorganic salts. Drastic methods are required to free chitin from these materials, and substantial degradation very likely occurs in these processes.

Other Structural Homopolysaccharides   In many species, neither cellulose nor chitin is employed for purposes of cell-wall construction and for related architectural functions. Their place is taken by a variety of alternative polysaccharides, including *glucans*, *mannans*, *xylans*, and so forth. For example, the glucan isolated from certain species of *Agrobacter* and *Rhizobium* has a structure that is largely, but not completely, formed by β-$(1 \rightarrow 2)$-glycosidic linkages between adjacent D-glucose units, as indicated below:

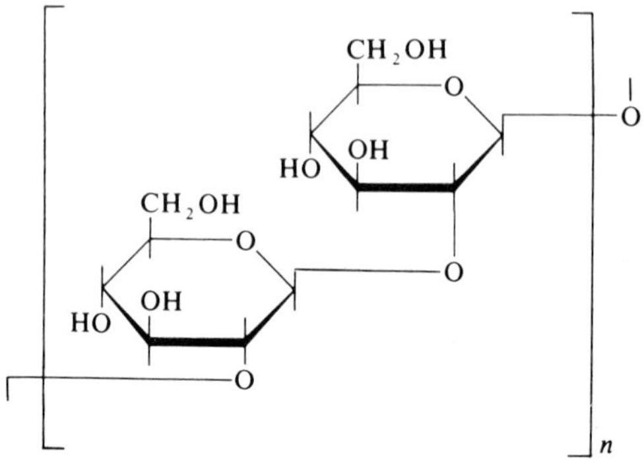

The polysaccharide is thus closely related to cellulose, differing only in the nature of the intersugar linkages. A more complicated example of a structural homopolysaccharide is provided by the mannan from baker's yeast, *Saccharomyces cerevisiae*. This polysaccharide is probably formed from the repeating units indicated below:

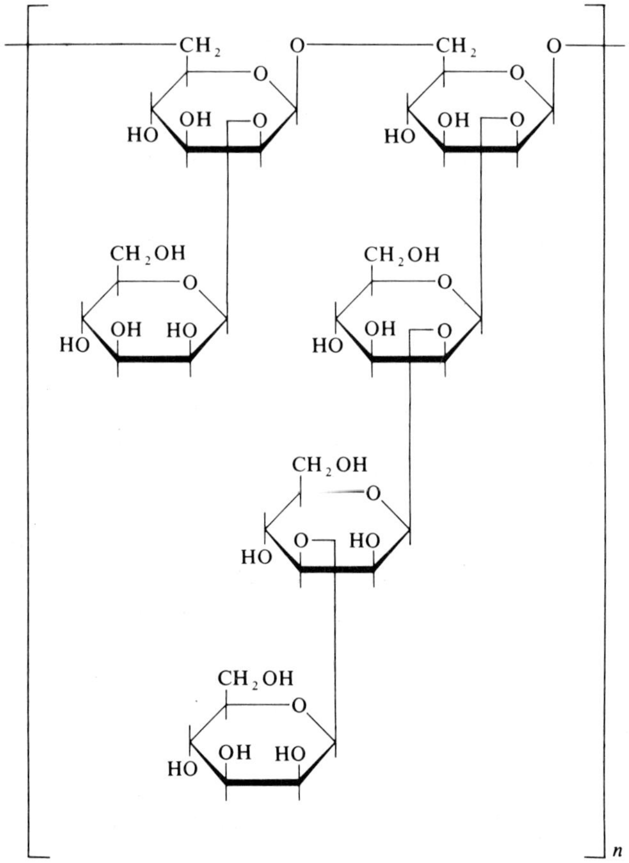

Starches Starches provide one example of the function of polysaccharides as nutritional reservoirs. They serve such a function in plants. The basic repeating unit from which the starches are synthesized involves the linkage of successive D-glucose molecules by α-$(1 \rightarrow 4)$-glycosidic bonds (contrast with cellulose):

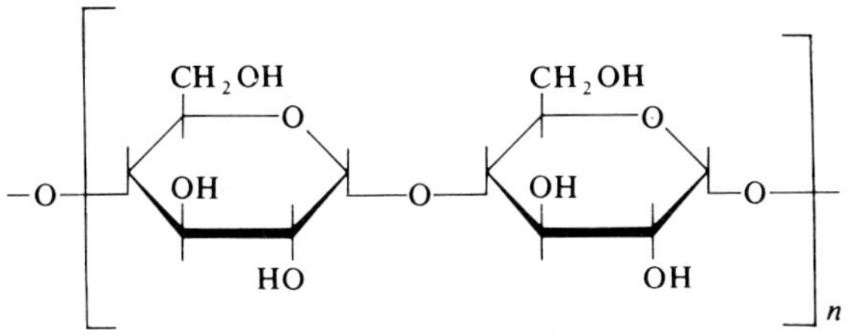

Starches fall into two distinct structural classes. The first, the *amyloses*, is constituted of long unbranched chains. In contrast, the *amylopectins* are branched-chain polysaccharides. The branch points are formed from α-$(1 \rightarrow 6)$-glycosidic linkages. A typical branch point for the amylopectins may be formulated as:

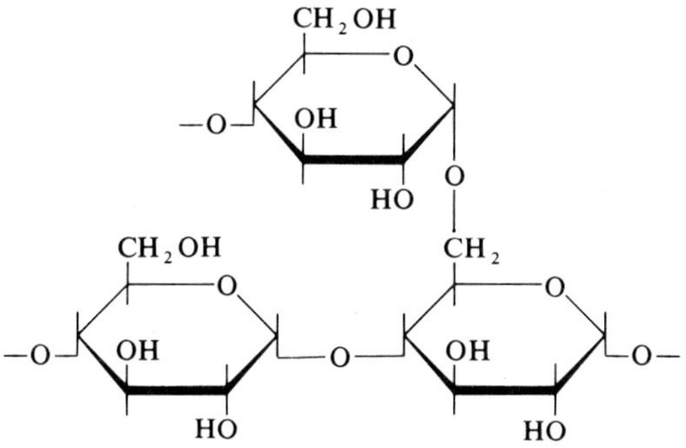

The starches vary widely in their molecular weights. This may be, in part, a result of degradation during the processes of isolation and purification. Molecular weights of a few million are not uncommon for these molecules.

Glycogen *Glycogen* is also a polyglucose that serves as a nutritional reservoir but, unlike the starches, is found in animal tissues. Its structure is similar to that of amylopectin, being a branched and highly elaborated molecule. Molecular weights of preparations range from a few hundred thousand to about 100 million. Considerable polydispersity within a single preparation is common.

Hyaluronic Acid Our first example of a heteropolysaccharide is *hyaluronic acid*. This material is composed of equimolar quantities of D-glucuronic acid and 2-acetamido-2-deoxy-D-glucose and is, therefore, a mucopolysaccharide as well. The D-glucuronic acid and 2-acetamido-2-deoxy-D-glucose occupy alternating positions in the polysaccharide. The linkages from the amino sugar to the acid are β-$(1 \rightarrow 4)$; those from the acid to the amino sugar are β-$(1 \rightarrow 3)$. Thus hyaluronic acid has the structure:

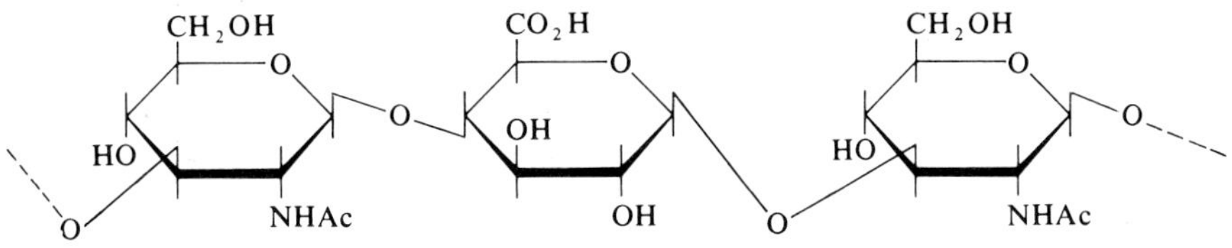

Hyaluronic acid is a widely distributed polysaccharide. It is universally present in connective tissues of animals and in their vitreous and synovial fluids as well. It is also synthesized by various strains of bacteria. Hyaluronic acid is usually found in association with protein, and hyaluronic acid-protein complexes have been isolated from natural sources. It has been suggested that the function of hyaluronic acid is to bind water in interstitial spaces and to hold cells together in a jellylike matrix. In addition, the material may provide the fluids present in joints with lubricating and shock-absorbing properties.

The molecular weight of hyaluronic acids varies considerably as a function of their source. Values ranging from a few hundred thousand to a few million have been reported.

Chondroitin Sulfates   Chondroitin, a polysaccharide identical with hyaluronic acid, except that D-galactosamine replaces D-glucosamine, is the parent substance for three polysaccharides found widely distributed in connective tissue. These are termed the *chondroitin sulfates* A, B, and C. Chondroitin sulfate B is frequently referred to as *dermatan sulfate*. The structures for these molecules are indicated below:

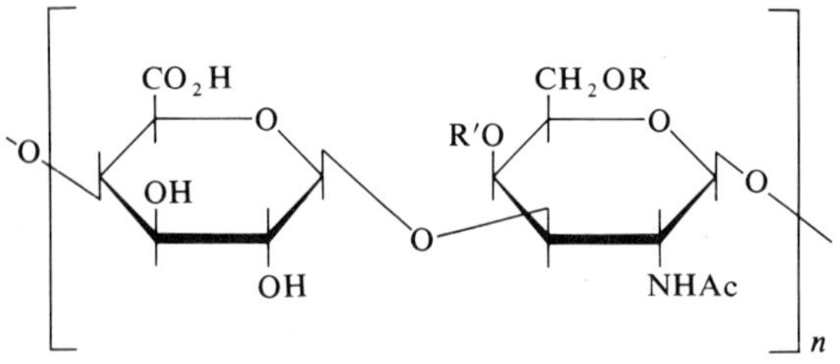

Chondroitin sulfate A: R = H, R' = SO₃H
Chondroitin sulfate C: R = SO₃H, R' = H

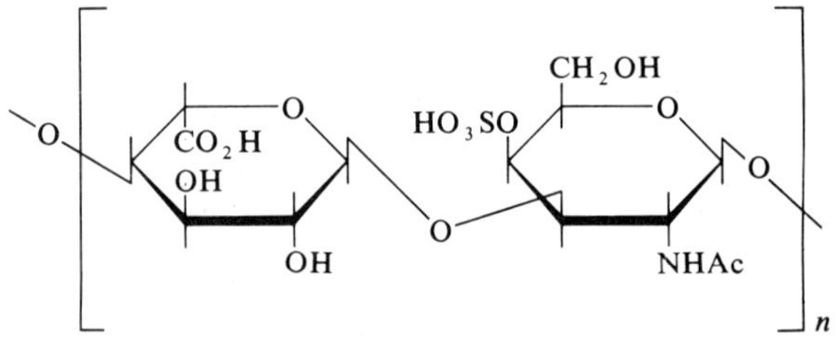

Chondroitin sulfate B
(Dermatan sulfate)

Both chondroitin sulfate A and C are composed of equimolar quantities of D-glucuronic acid, 2-acetamido-2-deoxy-D-galactose, and sulfate. The structures differ only in the position of the sulfate function. In chondroitin sulfate B, L-iduronic acid replaces the D-glucuronic acid of the A and C polysaccharides. The glycosidic bonds are, in each case, of alternating β-(1 → 3) and β-(1 → 4) types. The chondroitin sulfates are among the smaller mucopolysaccharides, ordinarily having molecular weights in the 50,000 to 100,000 range.

Keratosulfate   *Keratosulfate* is related to the chondroitin sulfates both structurally and in terms of distribution. It is the final principal polysaccharide component of connective tissue and occurs elsewhere as well. Keratosulfate consists of alternating D-galactose and 2-acetamido-2-deoxy-D-glucose-6-sulfate connected by alternating β-(1 → 4) and β-(1 → 3) linkages:

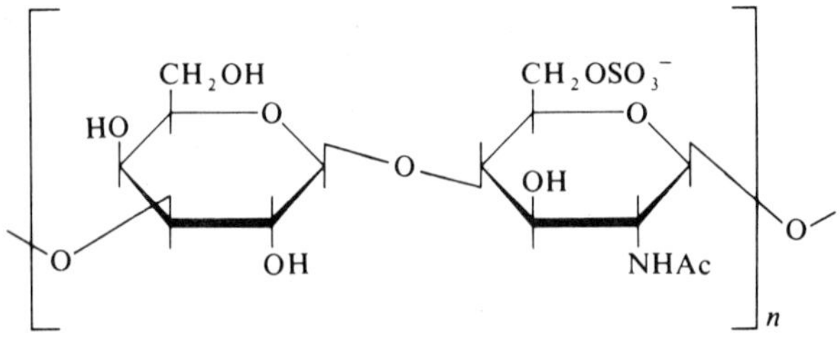

Heparin   *Heparin* is an interesting but not well understood mucopolysaccharide. It has a long history, having been discovered half a century ago, and has important biological properties, including that of an anticoagulant. Nevertheless, neither the structure nor biological function of this substance is completely clear. Heparin occurs principally in mammalian circulatory tissue and in numerous organs where mast cells occur. These are the apparent site of synthesis and storage of heparin. It occurs firmly bound to protein. Rather drastic methods are usually required to isolate it from natural sources.

The basic repeating unit of heparin is probably the tetrasaccharide illustrated below, although linkages of other sorts are present as well:

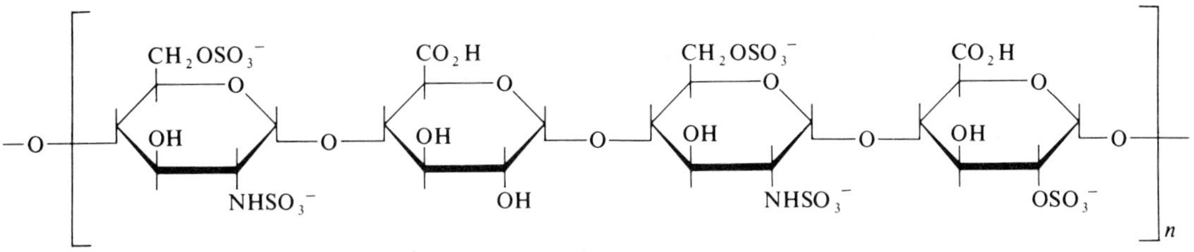

The molecular weights of heparin preparations are usually in the range of 10,000 to 20,000.

In addition to the polysaccharides specifically discussed above, these substances occur in the blood group substances, in the antigenic coats of the encapsulated bacteria, as components of bacterial cell wall materials (mureins), and in numerous glycoproteins and lipopolysaccharides.

REFERENCES   Bell, D. J.: Natural Monosaccharides and Oligosaccharides: Their Structure and Occurrence, in M. Florkin and H. S. Mason (eds.), "Comparative Biochemistry," vol. III, part A, pp. 288–354, Academic Press, Inc., New York, 1962.

Brimacombe, J. S., and J. M. Webber: "Mucopolysaccharides," Elsevier Publishing Co., New York, 1964.

Clark, F., and J. K. Grant (eds.): "Biochemistry of Mucopolysaccharides of Connective Tissue," Cambridge University Press, New York, 1961.

Florkin, M., and E. Stotz: "Comprehensive Biochemistry," Carbohydrates, sec. II, vol. 5, Elsevier Publishing Company, New York, 1963.

Gottschalk, A.: "The Chemistry and Biology of Sialic Acids," Cambridge University Press, New York, 1960.

Hirst, E. L.: The Structure of Polysaccharides, in D. J. Bell and J. K. Grant (eds.), "The Structure and Biosynthesis of Macromolecules," pp. 45–62, Cambridge University Press, New York, 1962.

Jeanloz, R. W.: Recent Developments in the Biochemistry of the Amino Sugars, *Advances in Enzymol,* **25**: 433–456 (1963).

Martin, H. N.: Biochemistry of Bacterial Cell Walls, *Ann. Rev. Biochem.,* **35**: 457 (1966).

Pigman, W. W. (ed.): "The Carbohydrates: Chemistry, Biochemistry and Physiology," Academic Press, Inc., New York, 1957.

Roseman, S.: Metabolism of Connective Tissue, *Ann. Rev. Biochem.,* **28**: 545–578 (1959).

Salton, M. R. J.: "Microbial Cell Walls," John Wiley & Sons, Inc., New York, 1960.

Sharon, N.: Polysaccharides, *Ann. Rev. Biochem.,* **35**: 485 (1966).

Stacey, M., and S. A. Barker: "Polysaccharides of Microorganisms," Clarendon Press, Oxford, 1960.

Stacey, M., and S. A. Barker: Carbohydrates of Living Tissues," D. Van Nostrand Company, Inc., Princeton, 1962.

Symposium, Synthesis of Complex Polysaccharides, *Federation Proc.*, **21**: 1064–1092 (1962).

Whistler, R. L., and C. L. Smart: " Polysaccharide Chemistry," Academic Press, Inc., New York, 1953.

———, and M. L. Wolfrom (eds.): " Methods in Carbohydrate Chemistry," Academic Press, Inc., New York, 1962.

11 The Metabolism of Carbohydrates

SOME COMMENTS CONCERNING METABOLISM

General Features

A cell's or an organism's *metabolism* may be defined as the totality of the chemical processes that it is capable of performing. Therefore the metabolism of even a simple, unicellular organism is not time-invariant; i.e., all its aspects are not actually expressed at any given instant. This immediately raises the question of what factors control this expression, and the subject of *metabolic control* or regulation occupies much current biochemical experimentation, thought, and speculation. Regulation is performed by a delicate set of interrelated checks and balances, which have both *intrinsic* (i.e., hereditary, genetic) and *extrinsic* (environmental, physiological) components. Since all metabolism forms an interconnected whole in both time and space, these effects necessarily pervade metabolism as a whole, even though it may be convenient to focus on a particular reaction and its participants as a first approximation. It is axiomatic that all metabolism and its control must be the consequence of, and be explicable either directly or indirectly in terms of, the enzymatic make-up of the organism.

In this chapter we are concerned for the first time with *metabolic pathways* (sequences, or routes), i.e., arrays of enzyme-catalyzed chemical reactions that bring about transformations of certain organic compounds vital to the organism. The compounds involved are referred to as *metabolites.* Classically, metabolic pathways have been divided into two types — *catabolic* and *anabolic.*

Metabolic Routes

Catabolic routes define essentially degradative processes in which large organic molecules, frequently supplied as food for the organism, are broken down (usually with the participation of *oxidative* reactions) to simple cellular constituents, with the attendant release of chemical free energy. This energy is

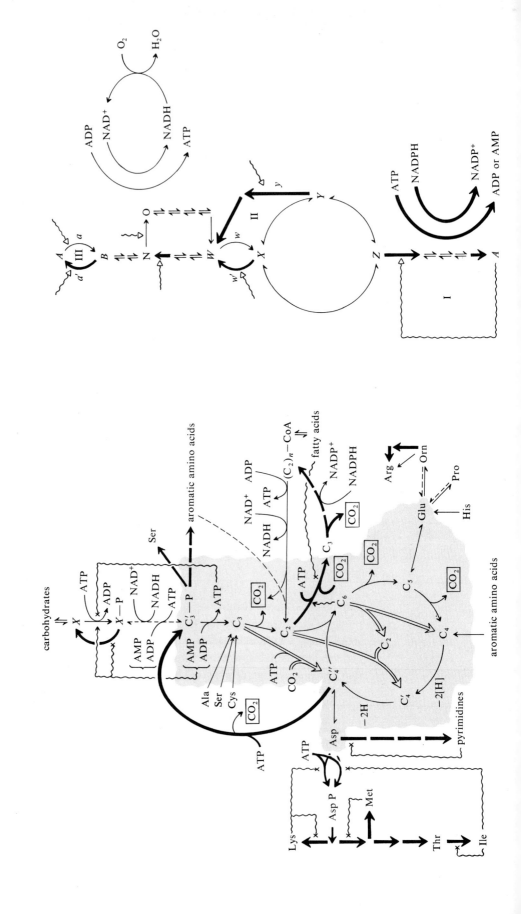

then utilized by the organism for its maintenance, growth, and replication, and for transduction into other forms of energy — mechanical or osmotic work, the generation of electrical impulses, or heat. *Anabolic routes* on the other hand define *synthetic* processes; they produce complex organic cellular constituents from simpler precursors, frequently involving the participation of *reductive* steps, and require the expenditure of chemical free energy. Inquiries into the metabolism of a wide variety of organisms have shown that there is a remarkable order and simplicity in metabolic patterns in spite of an equally remarkable diversity and individuality of metabolites consumed and produced. Of these general patterns, none is more significant than the discovery of a *central area of metabolism* joint to, and providing a direct link between, catabolic and anabolic routes.

Central Pathways During the initial stages of catabolism, each one characteristic of a particular foodstuff, large molecules are broken down to yield — apart from CO_2 and H_2O — a quite *restricted group* of small organic molecules, liberating about one-third of the available free energy in the process. These product molecules are as follows: *for carbohydrates*, triose phosphates and/or pyruvate; *for fats*, acetyl CoA (see page 317), propionyl CoA, and glycerol; *for proteins*, acetyl CoA, oxalacetate, α-ketoglutarate, fumarate, and succinate. The same compounds are also produced even when the organism, as is the case with certain bacteria, uses much more exotic carbon sources, such as certain aromatic (e.g., benzoic or mandelic acids), aliphatic (e.g., γ-aminobutyric, or itaconic acids), or heterocyclic (e.g., purines or uric acid) compounds (see Fig. 11-1*a*).

One of the major unifying and simplifying discoveries of modern, *dynamic* biochemistry was the finding that one and the same set of reactions was involved

---

FIGURE 11-1. Metabolic Principles.

Left:

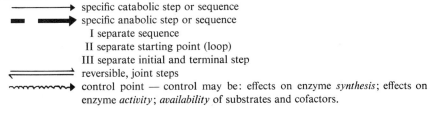

⟶ Catabolic reactions and sequences
⟹ Anabolic reactions and sequences
⟹ Anaplerotic reactions and sequences
∿∿∿ Activation by end products
∿∿∿ Inhibition by end products
Central area of metabolism is indicated by shading.

Right: Note that (1) a thermodynamically or kinetically irreversible step frequently intervenes as the first reaction of a sequence or branch; not uncommonly the last reaction in a sequence is also distinguished by the same feature. (2) These irreversible reactions provide the most sensitive loci for exertion of metabolic control *(a)* of synthesis of enzyme (induction/repression and hormonal control); *(b)* of activity of enzyme [inhibition, notably feedback (end product, retro) inhibition]; *(c)* of availability of reactants and cofactors. (3) For a reversal of the sequence, one or more separate and irreversible steps must participate, giving rise to partially or completely distinct pathways for degradation (catabolic) or synthesis (anabolic). (4) Linkage between anabolism and catabolism is provided by *(a)* common sequences; *(b)* compounds (ribonucleoside triphosphates, largely ATP) and reduced pyridine nucleotides, which are generated during catabolism and utilized during anabolism. (5) One and the same set of reactions and enzymes may participate in more than one metabolic route.

⟶ specific catabolic step or sequence
⟹ specific anabolic step or sequence
    I separate sequence
    II separate starting point (loop)
    III separate initial and terminal step
⇌ reversible, joint steps
∿∿∿⟶ control point — control may be: effects on enzyme *synthesis*; effects on enzyme *activity*; *availability* of substrates and cofactors.

in three crucial phases of metabolism: (1) the *interconversion* of the various products of catabolism just mentioned, rendering them equivalent, metabolically speaking; (2) their *complete combustion* to CO_2 and H_2O, which furnishes the organism with the remaining two-thirds of its energy supply; (3) the supply of *crucial intermediates* for biosynthetic, anabolic processes.

These central pathways are composed of relatively few reactions. In essence, they consist of the steps; triose phosphate $\rightleftharpoons$ pyruvate; pyruvate $\rightarrow$ acetyl CoA; oxalacetate $\rightleftharpoons$ aspartate; α-keto(oxo)-glutarate $\rightleftharpoons$ glutamate; and the cyclic set of reactions designed to catalyze the complete combustion of acetyl CoA (C_2 in the figure) to CO_2 plus H_2O. This device, known as the *citric acid cycle*, fulfills such a crucial role that a whole chapter (Chap. 14) is devoted to a description of its operation.

As put rather neatly by H. Kornberg:

Anabolism vs. Catabolism

" Whereas catabolic routes effect the transformations of nutrient carbon sources into the (interconvertible) intermediates of the central pathways, anabolic routes are sequences of enzymatic steps which enable the component building blocks of macromolecules to be constructed from these intermediates. Thus, while catabolic routes have clearly defined beginnings but no unambiguously identifiable end products, anabolic routes lead to clearly distinguishable end products from diffuse beginnings."

Another important distinction is that anabolic and catabolic routes rarely, if ever, follow the same pathways in detail. This is readily apparent when the product of catabolism is not identical with the carbon source in anabolism, as is the case with many amino acids. Thus, while aromatic amino acids are catabolized to acetyl CoA plus fumarate (or succinate), their synthesis utilizes phosphoenolpyruvate and an aldotetrose phosphate. Similarly serine and cysteine are easily transformed catabolically to pyruvate, but their synthesis originates with glycerophosphate and aspartate, respectively.

Another example is provided by the fatty acids. Here catabolism leads to acetyl CoA as the end product, and biosynthesis commences with the same intermediate and proceeds by what appeared at first glance a simple reversal of the catabolic sequence. But closer attention to detail disclosed that this was far from being the case. Not only did acetyl CoA first have to be converted to the more reactive malonyl CoA, which is not an intermediate in catabolism, but the sequence of enzymes responsible for the conversion of the latter to long-chain acyl CoAs (the precursors of the corresponding fatty acids—see page 375) was also not identical with that devoted to catabolism and was not even located in the same cellular compartment.

Even in the case of the biosynthesis of glucose, which proceeds, in large part, by a reversal of a number of easily reversible enzymatic reactions, biosynthesis and degradation differ, as we shall see, at the two most critical points in the whole sequence, that is, at either end. Thus, for instance, glucose is converted to glucose-6-phosphate during catabolism by a transphosphorylase reaction utilizing ATP; yet it is formed in anabolism from the phosphate ester by simple hydrolysis. Pyruvate is produced catabolically from its enol phosphate by a transphosphorylation to ADP; it is utilized anabolically in most organisms by virtue of two linked reactions, which first carboxylate it to oxalacetate and only then allow its transformation to the enolphosphate. In *Escherichia coli*, where the conversion is direct, the reactions still differ: in the forward direction, it is phosphoenolpyruvate + ADP → pyruvate + ATP; in the reverse, pyruvate + ATP → phosphoenolpyruvate + AMP + P_i.

These last few examples also serve to bring home another point. The initial and final reactions in most metabolic sequences, anabolic or catabolic, are frequently rigged in such a fashion as to render them virtually irreversible thermodynamically; i.e., they have $\Delta G^{0\prime}$ values (which we recall as the symbol for the standard free energy change at pH 7) equal to ≤ -4 kcal/mole. Teleologically the reason for this is not hard to understand. It provides for easy flux through the pathway and minimizes the possibility of a logjam of intermediates somewhere along the line. The enzymes responsible for these essentially irreversible and unique steps have often been referred to as *pacemaker enzymes*.

Is there then no *link* between anabolism and catabolism? Quite the contrary; the connection is very close indeed and is manifest on three levels:

1. *On that of the carbon sources.* As already mentioned, the products of catabolism, through the intervention of the central routes, become the substrates of anabolism.

2. *On that of energy supply.* Catabolism produces metabolic energy in the form of ATP or of compounds easily convertible to ATP; anabolism requires energy and consumes ATP.

3. *On that of reducing power.* Catabolism is essentially oxidative; it therefore consumes oxidizing and produces reducing power; the reverse is true for anabolism. Much of the reducing power generated during catabolism and consumed during anabolism is provided by the pyridine (nicotinamide) nucleotides $NAD^+/NADH$ and $NADP^+/NADPH$ (see page 212). But an important difference prevails — catabolism produces both NADH and NADPH; anabolism requires and consumes the latter almost exclusively.

Anaplerotic Routes

H. Kornberg has also directed attention to, and provided a designation for, yet a fourth type of metabolic pathway: the final stages of catabolism usually lead to complete removal of most metabolites from the common pathways, usually as CO_2 plus H_2O, plus NH_4^+ (or urea) and some other nitrogenous bases; anabolism also provides a constant drain on the pools of the intermediates of the common pathways. Thus provision must be made for their replenishment. These ancillary sequences are called *anaplerotic*. Usually they involve the insertion of either a 1-carbon (as CO_2) or a 2-carbon fragment (as acetyl CoA) into the common pool.

Metabolic Control: Regulation of the Flow of Metabolites

The flux of materials through the various pathways of metabolism does not proceed in a haphazard or random fashion but rather is attuned in a most precise manner to the needs of the organism (see Fig. 11-1*b*). These are largely determined by the composition of the medium in which it finds itself and are, in higher organisms, also responsive to the signals received by any one cell population or tissue from all other cell populations or tissues either directly or indirectly by the circulatory system, the nervous system, etc. Regulation can be exerted at many levels, but two of the most important ones are the following: One, a relatively slow and coarse control device, is to allow the composition of the environment to affect the rate and extent of synthesis of various enzymes. This control by *induction* and *repression* is described in the last chapters of this book. The other, much more rapid and finely poised, is to exert *control* on the *rates* and *extent* of one or more susceptible *enzyme-catalyzed reactions*, i.e. on metabolism proper. Frequently the most sensitive points for controls of this general nature are those which stand at the beginning or the end of specific metabolic sequences, i.e., the *pacemaker enzymes* mentioned above. Frequently also this control, which may be either positive (and thus constitutes *activation*) or negative (and thus reflects itself in *inhibition*), is exerted by one of the end products of the sequence in question. For this reason the inhibitory type, which was the first to be discovered in studies on the inhibition of one of the initial steps in a biosynthetic sequence by its end product, was called *feedback* or *retroinhibition*. Since these inhibitions, and their counterpart, the activation of early steps in catabolic sequences, involve compounds far removed metabolically and structurally from the substrates of the reactions affected, they would be expected to involve *second-site* or *allosteric* effects, that is, conformational changes of the respective enzyme proteins.

Application to Carbohydrate Metabolism

Some of the principles just enumerated may be applied to the specific problem of carbohydrate metabolism: In *phase I* of catabolism, the sugars are mobilized for their subsequent transformations by conversion to phosphorylated hexoses. This entails either simple (but virtually irreversible) phosphorylation of free hexoses at the expense of ATP or the phosphorolysis of oligo- or polysaccharides to the same type of product. No useful energy is provided by the reactions of phase I; on the contrary, energy at the expense of ATP frequently has to be provided. Both the phosphorylations and the reverse dephosphorylations are virtually irreversible thermodynamically and proceed at a significant rate only in one direction.

In *phase II* the intermediates produced in phase I are incompletely degraded, with the attendant liberation of about one-third of the free energy potentially available by their complete combustion. This degradation generates 3-carbon and 2-carbon compounds (trioses, pyruvate, acetyl CoA), which are all participants also in the central pathways comprised by the citric acid cycle and certain ancillary steps. The complete combustion of the intermediates produced in phase II (or alternatively the formation of other defined end products, such as alcohol or other compounds produced during the anaerobic fermentations with microorganisms) by means of these central pathways then constitute *phase III*.

THE GLYCOLYTIC PATHWAY
Significance

The major route of glucose catabolism in most cells is encompassed by the series of reactions that convert it to pyruvate, $CH_3COCO_2{}^-$. Such diverse processes as the generation of the ATP, which furnishes the energy for the contraction of skeletal muscle in an anaerobic environment; the generation of ATP for the continuous and stringent energy demand of heart muscle, operating in a highly aerobic environment and leading to the complete combustion of glucose; and many of the microbial fermentations of glucose to ethanol, lactate, glycerol, glycols, and a wide variety of other products, which must provide all the intermediates and most of the energy required for the growth of these organisms, all make use of this pathway. It is therefore understandable that this was the first such sequence to be completely described on the level of the interaction of the individual pure enzymes, their substrates, and cofactors.

The Overall Pathway of Glycolysis [Embden-Meyerhof-Parnas (EMP) Scheme]

For the moment we restrict our attention to the set of reactions for which this scheme was first devised. They encompass the conversion of glucose to ethanol plus CO_2 in the alcoholic fermentation by yeasts and the conversion of glucose or of a glucose unit (provided by glycogen) to lactic acid (or better, to its salt lactate) in the muscles of animals. Neither of these processes requires oxygen, and both can take place and provide the requisite cellular energy supply under completely anaerobic conditions. The sequence of intermediates and reactions is shown in Fig. 11-2, and some of their characteristics, thermodynamic and enzymatic, are summarized in Tables 11-1 and 11-2. Before considering the

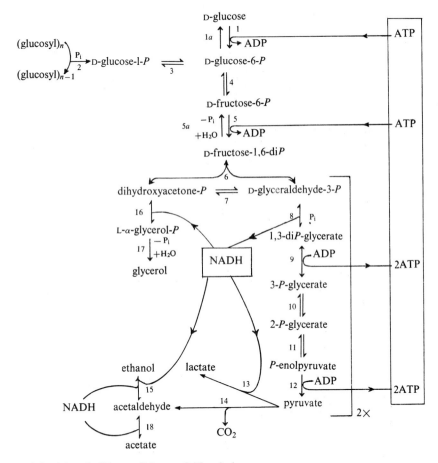

TABLE 11-2. Embden-Meyerhof-Parnas Scheme of Glycolysis.

Glycolysis: glucose + 2P$_i$ + 2ADP → 2 lactate + 2ATP (classical mammalian muscle or brain)

glucose + P$_i$ → α-glycerol-P + pyruvate (insect flight muscle, striated muscle)

Fermentations: glucose + 2P$_i$ + 2ADP → 2 ethanol + 2CO$_2$ + 2ATP + 2H$_2$O (first form)

glucose + HSO$_3^-$ → glycerol + acetaldehyde · HSO$_3$ + CO$_2$ (second form, no net ATP)

2 glucose → 2 glycerol + ethanol + acetate + 2CO$_2$ (third form, no net ATP)

glucose + (P$_i$) → α-glycerol-P + acetaldehyde + CO$_2$
↓
glycerol + P$_i$ (third form, no net ATP)

Reaction number	Equation (Cosubstrates or coenzymes shown above, activators below arrow)	Name of enzyme	Characteristic inhibitor	$\Delta G^{0\prime}$, kcal/mole
1	Glucose + ATP $\xrightarrow{\text{Mg}^{+2}}$ glucose-6-P + ADP	Hexokinase Glucokinase		−3.42
1a	Glucose-6-P + H_2O $\xrightarrow{\text{Mg}^{+2}}$ glucose + P_i	Glucose-6-phosphatase Nonspecific phosphatases	Glucose, orinase	−4.02
2	Glycogen + $nP_i \rightleftharpoons n$ glucose-1-P	(α-1,4-Glucan) phosphorylase		+0.73
3	Glucose-1-P $\underset{\xrightarrow{\text{glucose-1,6-di}P}}{\rightleftharpoons}$ glucose-6-P	Phosphoglucomutase	F^-, organophosphorus inhibitors	−1.74
4	Glucose-6-$P \rightleftharpoons$ fructose-6-P	Phosphoglucose (glucose phosphate) isomerase	2-Deoxyglucose-6-P	+0.50
5	Fructose-6-P + ATP $\xrightarrow[\text{(ADP, AMP),K}^+]{\text{Mg}^{+2}}$ fructose-1,6-di$P$ + ADP + H^+	Phosphofructokinase	ATP, citrate	−3.4
5a	Fructose-1,6-di$P$ + H_2O $\xrightarrow{\text{Mg}^{+2}}$ fructose-6-P + P_i	Fructose diphosphatase Nonspecific phosphatases	AMP, fructose-1,6-di$P$ Zn^{+2}, Fe^{+2}	−4.0
6	Fructose-1,6-di$P \rightleftharpoons$ dihydroxyacetone-P + glyceraldehyde-3-P	(Fructose-P) aldolase	Chelating agents (microbial enzymes only)	+5.73
7	Dihydroxyacetone-$P \rightleftharpoons$ glyceraldehyde-3-P	Triose phosphate isomerase		+1.83
8	$2 \times$ (Glyceraldehyde-3-P + P_i + $NAD^+ \rightleftharpoons$ 1,3-diphosphoglycerate + NADH + H^+)	Glyceraldehyde-P-dehydrogenase; triose-P-dehydrogenase	ICH_2COR D-threose-2,4-di$P$	$2 \times (+1.50)$
9	$2 \times$ (1,3-Diphosphoglycerate + ADP + $H^+ \xrightarrow{\text{Mg}^{+2}}$ 3-P-glycerate + ATP)	Phosphoglycerate kinase		$2 \times (-6.78)$
10	$2 \times$ (3-P-Glycerate $\underset{\xrightarrow{\text{glycerate-2,3-di}P}}{\rightleftharpoons}$ 2-P-glycerate)	Phosphoglyceromutase		$2 \times (+1.06)$
11	$2 \times$ (2-P-Glycerate $\xrightarrow{\text{Mg}^{+2} \text{ or Mn}^{+2}}$ phosphoenolpyruvate)	Enolase (phosphopyruvate hydratase)	Ca^{+2} F^- plus P_i	$2 \times (+0.44)$
12	$2 \times$ (phosphoenolpyruvate + ADP + $H^+ \xrightarrow[\text{K}^+(\text{Rb}^+,\text{Cs}^+)]{\text{Mg}^{+2}}$ pyruvate + ATP)	Pyruvate kinase	Ca^{+2} vs Mg^{+2} Na^+ vs K^+	$2 \times (-5.72)$
13	$2 \times$ (Pyruvate + NADH + $H^+ \rightleftharpoons$ lactate + NAD^+)	Lactate dehydrogenase	Oxamate	$2 \times (-6.00)$
14	$2 \times$ (Pyruvate + $H^+ \rightarrow$ acetaldehyde + CO_2)	Pyruvate (de)carboxylase		$2 \times (-4.72)$
15	$2 \times$ (acetaldehyde + NADH + $H^+ \rightleftharpoons$ ethanol + NAD^+)	Alcohol dehydrogenase	(HSO_3^-)	$2 \times (-5.15)$

Sums:
(Glucose)$_n$ + $H_2O \rightarrow$ 2 lactate + $2H^+$ + (glucose)$_{n-1}$ −52.43*

    (Glucose)$_n$ + $3P_i$ + 3ADP $\rightarrow$ 2 lactate + 3ATP + (glucose)$_{n-1}$ glycolysis (muscle)   −27.32†

Glucose $\rightarrow$ 2 lactate + $2H^+$ −47.4*

    Glucose + $2P_i$ + 2ADP $\rightarrow$ 2 lactate + 2ATP   glycolysis or lactate fermentation   −29.74†

Glucose $\rightarrow$ 2 ethanol + CO_2 −56.1*

    Glucose + $2P_i$ + 2ADP $\rightarrow$ 2 ethanol + $2CO_2$ + 2ATP   alcoholic fermentation   −37.48†

$\Delta G^{0\prime}$ values refer to pH 7.0 with all other reactants including H_2O at unit activity; most data from Johnson.
The free energy of formation of glucose in aqueous solution equals 217.56 kcal/mole, its ΔG^0 of combustion to $CO_2 + H_2O$ is 686 kcal/mole, and $\Delta G^{0\prime}$ for (glucose)$_n$ + $H_2O \rightarrow$ (glucose)$_{n-1}$ equals −5.03 kcal/mole.
*From $\Delta \tilde{G}^0$.
†From this table.

TABLE 11-2. Molecular Properties of Glycolytic Enzymes

Reaction number	Enzyme	Source	M	Remarks
1	Hexokinase	Yeast	96,600	
2	Phosphorylase *a*	Muscle	500,000	Tetramer
	Phosphorylase *b*	Muscle	250,000	Dimer
	Phosphorylase	Liver	200,000	Dimer (active)
3	Phosphoglucomutase	Yeast	112,000	
		Muscle	62,000	
		E. coli	60,000	
4	Phosphoglucose isomerase	Yeast	145,000	
5	Phosphofructokinase	Muscle	380,000	Dimer
6	Aldolase	Muscle	150,000	Tetramer
		Liver	150,000	Differs from muscle enzyme
		Microorganisms	~60,000	Metal-activated
7	Triosephosphate isomerase	Muscle	43,000	
8	Triosephosphate dehydrogenase	Muscle	140,000	Tetramer
9	...			
10	Phosphoglyceromutase (phosphotransferase type)	Muscle	57,000	
		Yeast	112,000	(Dimer?)
	Phosphoglyceromutase (mutase type)	Wheat germ	30,000	
11	Enolase	Muscle	85,000	Dimer
		Yeast	64,000	Monomer(?)
12	Pyruvate kinase	Muscle	250,000	Polymer
13	Lactate dehydrogenase	Vertebrate tissues	140,000	Tetramers of varying structure

individual steps, let us take a closer look at the most important features of the overall scheme.

1. The two pathways make use of the identical reactions from glucose-6-*P* to pyruvate and differ only in the eventual fate of the latter and hence in the means employed for the *regeneration of NAD^+ from $NADH$* (see item 3 below). These same two considerations also obtain for all those other metabolic sequences in which a hexose unit is initially converted to two molecules of pyruvate. In muscle glycolysis, pyruvate and NADH interact directly in the presence of *lactate dehydrogenase* to yield lactate and regenerate the NAD^+ (Table 11-1, reaction 13). In alcoholic fermentation the pyruvate is first *decarboxylated* to acetaldehyde (reaction 14) and the latter *reduced* by NADH to give alcohol.

2. The unique C—C *bond scission* reaction, which characterizes the scheme, is reaction 6, catalyzed by phosphofructose (or fructose-di-*P*) aldolase, which converts a ketohexose-diphosphate into two molecules of triosephosphate.

3. The unique *oxidation-reduction reaction* of the scheme is reaction 8, catalyzed by D-glyceraldehyde-3-*P* dehydrogenase; it requires NAD^+ and P_i and produces 1,3-diphosphoglycerate (a compound with a high $-\Delta G^{0'}$ of hydrolysis) and NADH. Note that by virtue of reaction 7, which interconverts the two triose phosphates, both the products of reaction 6 can be channeled through reaction 8.

4. For each molecule of free glucose traversing the pathway, two molecules of ATP are consumed (in reactions 1 and 5) and four molecules are produced (one each per triose in reactions 8 plus 9, and 11 plus 12, respectively). If we start with glycogen, one molecule of ATP is required per hexose unit (no ATP requirement

in reaction 2). Thus the former process generates two molecules of ATP/hexose, the latter three molecules of ATP/hexose.

5. As a corollary to item 4, catabolism of free glucose requires the consumption of two molecules of inorganic phosphate, that of a hexose unit three molecules of inorganic phosphate.

6. The overall stoichiometries, therefore, are those indicated. Since the presently accepted value of $\Delta G^{0'}$ for $ATP \rightarrow ADP + H_2O \simeq -7.5$ kcal/mole, we see three facts. (a) Only a very small proportion of the total free energy potentially derivable from the catabolism of a hexose molecule is actually rendered available by the two anaerobic processes described. (b) This is in part because both lactate and ethanol are compounds in which carbon is still at a relatively reduced level and only in part because of inherent inefficiencies. (c) The values of $\Delta G^{0'}$ assumed for the individual steps are probably nearly correct, since their sum added to the appropriate multiple of $\Delta G^{0'}$ for ATP hydrolysis pretty nearly equals the values calculated from $\Delta G^{0'}$ (formation) plus $\Delta G^{0'}$ (ATP hydrolysis).

7. The two sets of end products (lactate or ethanol plus CO_2) accumulate under anaerobic conditions. The most efficient means for the removal of the two organic compounds is their complete combustion to CO_2 plus H_2O. These processes require aerobic conditions, which can obtain either when one and the same cell is able to function in, and interact with, different physiological environments (e.g., yeast and certain mammalian cells) or, in higher organisms, when different environments interact with different specialized cells (e.g., when the lactate produced in skeletal muscle is removed by the circulation and transported to the liver for combustion).

Reaction 11-1   *Conversion of* D-*Glucose to* D-*Glucose*-6-*P.* Since glucose-6-*P* is the "mobilized" form of glucose, i.e., that in which this sugar enters, not only the glycolytic pathway, but all other pathways of carbohydrate metabolism, enzymes catalyzing reaction 1 are found extremely widely distributed throughout living nature:

Hexose + Mg·ATP → hexose-6-*P* + Mg·ADP   (11-1)

These enzymes vary greatly in their specificity: some, which may be properly referred to as *hexokinases*, are relatively nonspecific and catalyze the phosphorylation of a wide variety of hexoses of appropriate configuration, including D-fructose, D-mannose, 2-deoxy-D-glucose, and D-glucosamine. For instance, the crystalline enzyme from yeast reacts with all sugars that have the general structure shown below:

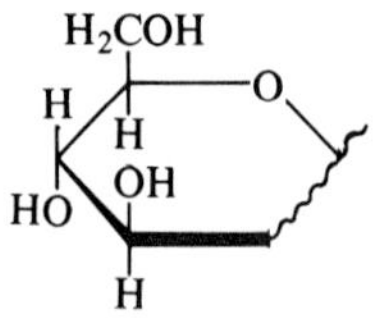

The α-pyranose form of the aldoses is acted on slightly more effectively than the β-anomer.

The enzymes from other cells and tissues appear to be highly specific for glucose and are therefore more appropriately referred to as *glucokinases*. Liver contains both enzymes.

All kinases (phosphotransferases) of this type, i.e., those forming an ordinary-

O-phosphate ester, utilize a nucleoside triphosphate (usually ATP) as a phosphate donor and require a divalent cation (usually Mg^{+2}) as an obligatory coreactant. Evidence based on kinetic studies and magnetic resonance spectroscopy indicates that the metal cofactor interacts first with ATP to yield the binary complex, which then functions as the true substrate and becomes attached to the enzyme. Experiments with O^{18}-labeled substrate have shown that the P-transfer step proper proceeds as shown below:

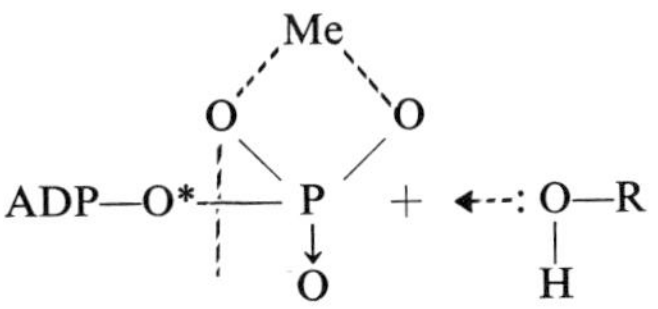

Reaction 11-1*a*   *Hydrolysis of* D-*Glucose-6-P*. The hydrolysis of glucose-6-P (reaction 1a of Table 11-1) is a key reaction, not only in *gluconeogenesis* (i.e., the re-synthesis of glucose), but also in the conversion of liver glycogen to blood glucose in mammals. It is catalyzed by the enzyme D-glucose-6-phosphatase. It is relatively specific with respect to the carbohydrate moiety; the only other substrate susceptible to rapid hydrolysis is D-glucosamine-6-P.

Reaction 11-2   *Conversion of Glycogen and Starch to* D-*Glucose-1-P*. The conversion of starch and other starchlike glucose-containing polysaccharides, such as glycogen, is catalyzed by *phosphorylases*, more correctly referred to as *α-1,4-glucan phosphorylases* widely distributed in a variety of organisms. The reaction catalyzed by the enzyme may be represented as shown below:

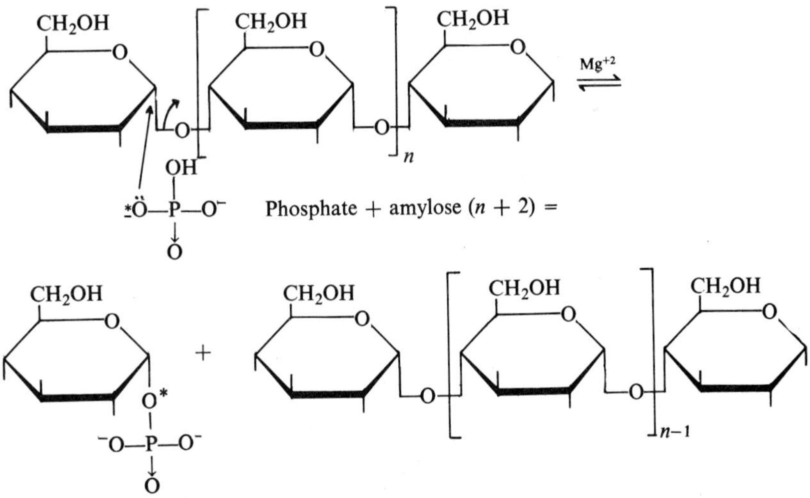

α-D-glucopyranosyl-1-P +   amylose $(n + 1)$ etc.   (11-2)
(glucose-1-P)

As written, this is a phosphorolysis commencing at the free, nonreducing, end of an *amylose chain* (see page 251), removing one glucose unit at a time, and yielding a total of $(n + 1)$ glucose-1-P molecules until the reducing end is reached (which results in the formation of free glucose). If the substrate is amylopectin (see page 252), phosphorolysis continues only until the branch points are reached and the product is a *limit dextrin*. The $1 \rightarrow 6$ bond at the branch may be cleaved by an *amylo-1,6-glucosidase*, yielding free glucose, whereupon phosphorylase is able to act again until the next branch is reached, etc. Phosphorylases are key enzymes in the mobilization of carbohydrates, converting them from their storage into their metabolically active forms. As the first step in a catabolic sequence, they would therefore be expected to be subject to a variety of control mechanisms.

The enzymes from mammalian liver and skeletal muscle have been studied extensively. Muscle phosphorylase is a tetramer composed of four identical subunits, each containing one serine residue esterified to orthophosphate as well as one molecule of pyridoxal phosphate, both essential for enzymatic activity. This active form of phosphorylase is called *phosphorylase a*. When the phosphate of the phosphoserines is hydrolyzed under the influence of a specific enzyme, called *phosphorylase phosphatase*, the enzyme disaggregates into dimeric molecules called *phosphorylase b*. In this form the enzyme is inactive under the conditions ordinarily employed with phosphorylase *a*, but activity is partially recovered in the presence of 5'-AMP.

The physiological mechanism for activation of phosphorylase *b* to *a* is different, however. It involves its phosphorylation by four molecules of ATP in the presence of a specific enzyme, *phosphorylase kinase*. This enzyme, in turn, exists in both an active and an inactive form: the interconversion of the latter and the former requires an enzyme, Mg^{+2}, and adenosine-3',5'-phosphate (also called *cyclic adenylic acid* (see page 116). The formation of this compound from ATP is catalyzed, in turn, by the specific enzyme *adenyl cyclase*, which is stimulated by the catecholamine hormone *epinephrine*. The latter is known to stimulate glycogen catabolism strongly in vivo by enhancing the conversion of glycogen to blood glucose, a condition known as *hyperglycemia*. These various interconversions are schematically represented below:

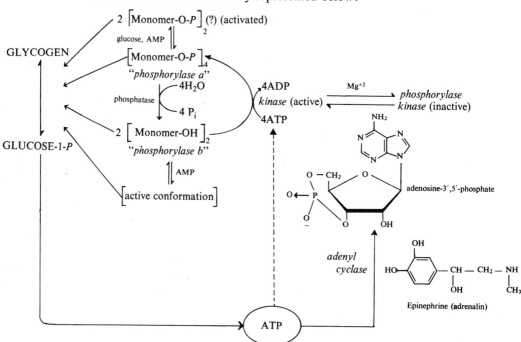

Even though the reaction catalyzed by phosphorylase is readily reversible ($K_{eq} = [C_6H_{10}O_5]_{n+1}[P_i]/[C_6H_{10}O_5]_n[\text{glucose-1-}P] \simeq 3$ at pH 7 and 25°), it is concerned with glycogen breakdown and is not responsible for *glycogenesis*, the process of glycogen resynthesis. The latter still takes place even when the ratio $P_i/\text{glucose-1-}P$ is as high as 300, and in certain hereditary disorders in which phosphorylase is completely lacking. Furthermore in the presence of epinephrine, which, as just described, stimulates phosphorylase activity, glycogen is broken down rather than synthesized. Finally and conclusively, the pathway of glycogen synthesis, thanks to the investigation of Leloir and others, is now known to involve the polymerization, not of glucose-1-*P* itself, but instead the mixed anhydride of this compound with UMP, called UDPG (see page 197), and a specific enzyme *glycogen synthetase* is involved.

Reaction 11-3 *Interconversion of D-Glucose-1-P and D-Glucose-6-P.* This reaction is important, not only in the context of glycolysis, but also in that of the metabolism of oligo- and polysaccharides in general (see page 288). It is catalyzed by the enzyme *phosphoglucomutase*, which contains one serine-OH group essential for enzymatic activity. Glucose-1,6-di*P* is an essential coenzyme; in addition the reaction requires Mg^{+2} and is inhibited by fluoride. The serine-OH becomes phosphorylated and dephosphorylated in a cyclical manner:

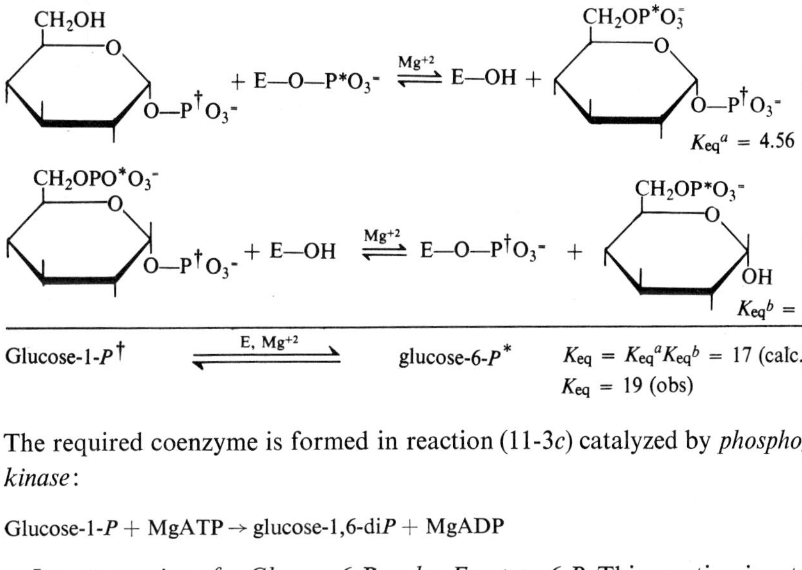

$$\text{(11-3a)} \qquad K_{eq}^a = 4.56$$

$$\text{(11-3b)} \qquad K_{eq}^b = 3.76$$

$$\text{Glucose-1-}P^\dagger \xrightleftharpoons{\text{E, Mg}^{+2}} \text{glucose-6-}P^* \qquad K_{eq} = K_{eq}^a K_{eq}^b = 17 \text{ (calc.)}$$
$$K_{eq} = 19 \text{ (obs)} \qquad \text{(11-3)}$$

The required coenzyme is formed in reaction (11-3c) catalyzed by *phosphoglucokinase*:

$$\text{Glucose-1-}P + \text{MgATP} \rightarrow \text{glucose-1,6-di}P + \text{MgADP} \qquad \text{(11-3c)}$$

Reaction 11-4 *Interconversion of D-Glucose-6-P and D-Fructose-6-P.* This reaction is catalyzed by *phosphoglucoisomerase*. This enzyme is quite specific, since the analogous anomerization mannose-6-$P \rightleftharpoons$ fructose-6-P so readily brought about by dilute alkali (the Lobry de Bruyn–Alberta van Eckenstein equilibrium) requires a separate enzyme, *phosphomannoisomerase*, also found in muscle. The two hydrogens attached to the 1-carbon of the fructose-*P* must be activated selectively by the two enzymes, since glucose-6-*P*-1-*d* does not exchange its deuterium with H_2O in the presence of the glucoisomerase but does so when both enzymes are present.

Reaction 11-5 *Formation of D-Fructose-1,6-diP from Fructose-6-P; Control of Glycolysis.* The reaction is catalyzed by a highly specific enzyme called *phosphofructokinase* and shares the other properties of kinase reactions, i.e., requirements for ATP (which in this instance can be replaced by UTP or ITP) and Mg^{+2}, and a negative $\Delta G^{0'}$:

D-Fructose-6-P + MgATP → D-fructose-1,6-di$P$ + MgADP　　　　　(11-5)

Since alternate pathways of hexose metabolism diverge from all the other hexose phosphates so far discussed, reaction 5 may be regarded as the first one characteristic of the glycolytic sequence proper and therefore constitutes an important branch and control point, subject to strong metabolic regulation: the mammalian enzyme responsible is difficult to purify — this appears to be true of most, if not all, enzymes susceptible to second-site (allosteric) control — is susceptible to strong inhibition by high concentrations of ATP, and is activated by ADP or AMP. Furthermore the enzyme is also inhibited by citrate. These various controls ensure that whenever the ratio (ATP)/(ADP + P_i) is high, e.g., when lactate and pyruvate are combusted aerobically to CO_2 by means of the citric acid cycle (see Chap. 14), glycolysis is essentially blocked and glucose synthesis favored. The obverse is also true: when glycolysis is absolutely required for energy generation, i.e., when the ratio (ATP)/ (ADP + P_i) drops, glycolysis is favored and carbohydrate synthesis turned off. To add further insurance to this control and to exert a similar one on the reverse biosynthetic sequence, most *fructose-1,6-diphosphatases*, the specific enzymes required to reconvert the diphosphate to the 6-monophosphate hydrolytically (reaction 11-5a) are inhibited by high concentration of their substrate and also, at a second (allosteric) site, specifically by AMP.

Reactions 11-6 and 11-7 　*Conversion of Fructose-1,6-diP into Two Molecules of Triose-phosphate and Interconversion of Aldo- and Ketotriose Phosphates.* The reactions catalyzed by *aldolase* and by *triose-P isomerase* are

(11-6)

D-Fructose-1,6-diP^{-4}　　　　　D-Glyceraldehyde-3-P^-　Dihydroxyacetone-P^-

$K_{eq} = 10^{-5}$,
(pH = 7.8, at 25°)

Dihydroxyacetone-P ⇌ D-glyceraldehyde-3-P　K_{eq} = 4 × 10^{-3} (same conditions)　(11-7)

Several different types of aldolases have been isolated and purified from different cells, and their properties studied. The one most thoroughly investigated is the enzyme from rabbit skeletal muscle. The active form is a trimer consisting of three polypeptide chain subunits. The enzyme is known to catalyze a hydrogen exchange in the H_2C—OH of dihydroxyacetone-P, in the absence of the aldotriose, with a stereospecificity opposite to that of triose-P isomerase, which itself exhibits a stereospecificity and mechanism identical to that of glucose-P isomerase (reaction 4). The specificity of the enzyme with regard to possible substrates indicates that dihydroxyacetone-*P* (and the corresponding portion of the hexose molecule) must interact with the enzyme in a highly selective manner,[1] although a number of different aldehydes can participate as indicated below. In all cases the product ketose has a trans configuration of hydroxyls

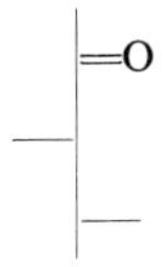
=O

around the α- and β-carbons:

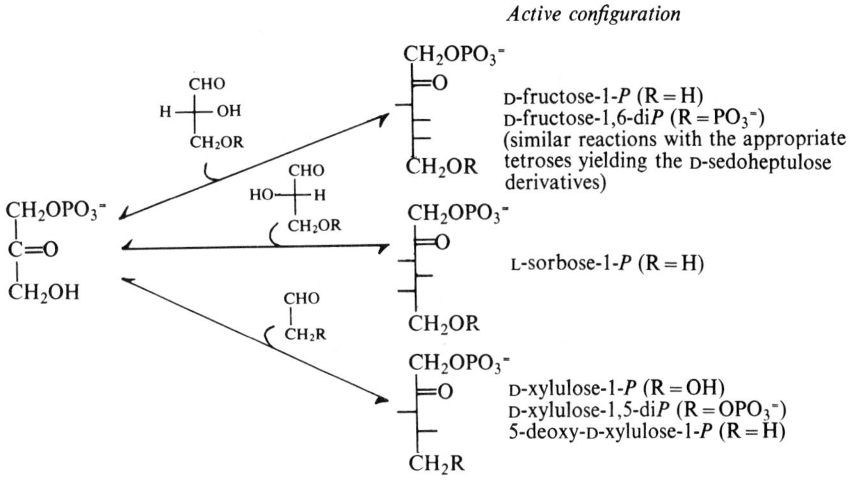
Active configuration
CHO
H—OH
CH2OR
CHO
HO—H
CH2OR
CHO
CH2R
CH2OPO3-
C=O
CH2OH
CH2OPO3-
=O
CH2OR
D-fructose-1-P (R = H)
D-fructose-1,6-diP (R = PO3-)
(similar reactions with the appropriate tetroses yielding the D-sedoheptulose derivatives)
CH2OPO3-
=O
CH2OR
L-sorbose-1-P (R = H)
CH2OPO3-
=O
CH2R
D-xylulose-1-P (R = OH)
D-xylulose-1,5-diP (R = OPO3-)
5-deoxy-D-xylulose-1-P (R = H)

A quite different type of enzyme (class II aldolase) can be isolated from microorganisms. Enzymes of this type exhibit a substrate specificity reminiscent of that of muscle aldolase, but although the muscle enzyme is devoid of a cofactor requirement and is not inhibited by metal-binding agents, the microbial enzymes require divalent metals for full activity. Perhaps a metal chelate between the carbonyl or imino group and the free α-OH is formed, as shown:

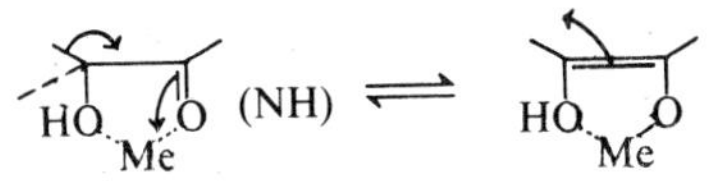
HO
O
(NH)
Me
HO
O
Me

These type II enzymes require K^+ ions as well for full activity.

Reactions 11-8 and 11-9 *Phosphorylation of ADP at the Expense of Dehydrogenation of Glyceraldehyde-P.*

$$\text{D-Glyceraldehyde-3-}P + NAD^+ + P_i \rightleftharpoons \text{D-1,3-diphosphoglycerate} + NADH \quad (11\text{-}8)$$

[1] The formation of such a complex can be demonstrated spectrophotometrically, and its structure has been shown to involve Schiff base formation between the carbonyl C of the substrate and an ε-amino group of lysine on the enzyme (see page 182): reduction and hydrolysis yield one mole per mole of enzyme of a derivative that has been identified as

$$\begin{array}{lll} H_2COH & & \\ | & & \\ HC—NH(CH_2)_4— & CH—CO_2H & \\ | & | & \\ H_2COH & NH_2 & \end{array}$$

1,3-Diphosphoglycerate + ADP + H$^+$ ⇌ D-3-phosphoglycerate + ATP   (11-9)

D-Glyceraldehyde-3-P + NAD$^+$ + ADP + P$_i$ ⇌ D-3-phosphoglycerate +

ATP + NADH   (11-8) plus (11-9)

In most cells the major fate of the triose-P formed in the preceding steps is its conversion to 1,3-diphosphoglycerate — reaction (11-8). The reaction requires the stoichiometric participation of NAD$^+$ and P$_i$ and leads to a product that, as a mixed anhydride of a carboxylic and orthophosphoric acid, shows a very high negative free energy of hydrolysis ($\Delta G^{0'} \simeq -14$ kcal). It is this fact which accounts for the driving force, not only for reactions (11-8) plus (11-9) — $\Delta G^{0'} = -5.3$ kcal/mole triose-P — but of the whole conversion of hexose-di$P$ to phosphoglycerate — reactions (11-6) to (11-9) — $\Delta G^{0'} \simeq -3$ kcal/mole hexose-di$P$.

The enzyme-catalyzing reaction (11-8), *glyceraldehyde-P dehydrogenase* (GDH), shows exceptionally wide distribution. Free —SH groups are required for activity (14 per molecule are titratable in the enzyme). Muscle GDH binds its coenzyme NAD$^+$ firmly enough so that the latter remains associated with the enzyme even on repeated recrystallization or dialysis. Adsorption of the coenzyme on a charcoal column is required for its complete removal; four molecules of NAD$^+$ can be detached in this manner and the holoenzyme reconstituted by the addition of four molecules of the pyridine nucleotide to the apoenzyme. An equal number of cysteine residues on the protein appear to be implicated in the formation of this complex, which has an absorption spectrum distinct from that of the free coenzyme. The reactions in either direction have been shown to require the formation of an acyl enzyme as an obligatory intermediate; this intermediate has the partial structure

—Cys—S—C—R
             ‖
             O

The dehydrogenase is specific for D-glyceraldehyde-3-P, the free dephosphorylated aldehyde, or acetaldehyde, and is powerfully inhibited by D-threose-2,4-diphosphate.

Reaction 11-9 is catalyzed by *phosphoglycerate kinase*. As with other enzymes of this type there is an absolute requirement for a divalent metal cofactor (Mg^{+2}, Mn^{+2}, or Ca^{+2}), and the metal interacts with the adenosine di- or triphosphate to form the reactive complex.

Reaction 11-10   *Isomerization of Phosphoglycerates.* The reversible interconversion of the primary phosphate ester 3-phospho-D-glycerate into the corresponding secondary ester 2-phospho-D-glycerate is catalyzed by *phosphoglyceromutase*:

$$\text{D-3-phosphoglycerate} \underset{\substack{\text{Mg}^{+2} \\ \text{2,3-diphosphoglycerate}}}{\rightleftharpoons} \text{D-2-phosphoglycerate} \qquad (11\text{-}10)$$

The reaction requires two obligatory cofactors: Mg^{+2} and the diester 2,3-diphosphoglycerate. The reaction mechanism is probably very similar to that established for the more thoroughly studied phosphoglucomutase reaction — reaction (11-3). In plant germ and in animal tissues a second enzyme has been identified that does not appear to require any cofactors.

Reactions 11-11 and *Conversion of 2-Phosphoglycerate to Pyruvate: The Generation of a Second*
11-12 *Molecule of ATP.*

$$H-\underset{\underset{H_2COH}{|}}{\overset{\overset{CO_2^-}{|}}{C}}-O-\underset{\underset{O^-}{|}}{\overset{\overset{O}{\uparrow}}{P}}-O^- \overset{Me^{+2}}{\rightleftharpoons} \underset{\underset{HCH}{\|}}{\overset{\overset{CO_2^-}{|}}{C}}-O-\underset{\underset{O^-}{|}}{\overset{\overset{O}{\uparrow}}{P}}-O^- + H_2O \qquad (11\text{-}11)$$

$$\underset{\underset{HCH}{\|}}{\overset{\overset{CO_2^-}{|}}{C}}-O-\underset{\underset{O^-}{|}}{\overset{\overset{O}{\uparrow}}{P}}-O^- + MgADP \rightleftharpoons CH_3COCO_2^- + MgATP \qquad (11\text{-}12)$$

Reaction (11-11) constitutes a dehydration of the phosphate ester of a dihydroxy acid (which can also be regarded as an intramolecular oxidation of C-2 and reduction of C-3), a process that is essentially isoenergetic; thus K_{eq} for the reaction as written equals 3 under physiological conditions. On the other hand, the product ester is more properly classified as a mixed anhydride, since the dephosphorylated product (enolpyruvic acid) is an α-carboxyenol. $\Delta G^{0\prime}$ for the hydrolysis of the phosphoenolpyruvate is ~ -12.8 kcal/mole, part of the driving force being provided by the position of the enol-keto tautomeric equilibrium of the product, which, in the case of pyruvate at a pH around 7, is strongly in favor of the keto form (see page 30).

Enolase, the enzyme catalyzing reaction (11-11), is very widely distributed and shows an absolute requirement for divalent cations (Mn^{+2}, Mg^{+2}, Zn^{+2}, or Cd^{+2}) that can be antagonized by other cations (Ca^{+2} or Sr^{+2}). F^- ion is an effective inhibitor at low concentration (10^{-2} M), especially in the presence of P_i, presumably by formation of a metafluorophosphate linked to the active site of the enzyme.

Pyruvate kinase, the enzyme catalyzing reaction (11-12), also requires Mg^{+2} or Mn^{+2} (with Ca^{+2} as a competitive antagonist). In addition the enzyme also requires the simultaneous presence of monovalent cations (K^+, Rb^+, or Cs^+; antagonized by Na^+ or Li^+) for optimal activity, probably for conformational stabilization. Thus this enzyme behaves like a typically easily deformable protein capable of allosteric interactions. The very unfavorable equilibrium of reaction (11-12) for the reverse reaction (pyruvate as substrate), plus the fact that the turnover number in this direction equals 12 (compared with 6×10^3 for pyruvate formation) ensures a formidable thermodynamic and kinetic block against the use of this reaction in carbohydrate synthesis.

Reaction 11-13 *The Terminal Step in Muscle Glycolysis and Homolactic Fermentation.* The reversible reduction of pyruvate to lactate, with NADH as a reducing agent, is the terminal step that characterizes glycolysis by vertebrate muscle from many other anaerobic, fermentative modes of carbohydrate catabolism:

$$CH_3COCO_2^- + NADH + H^+ \rightleftharpoons CH_3CHOHCO_2^- + NAD^+ \qquad (11\text{-}13)$$

It is shared, however, by the so-called *homolactic* fermentation (i.e., a fermentation that yields lactate as the sole product) carried out by a large number of microorganisms, the "lactic acid bacteria"; among these are various species of the genera *Lactobacilli, Bacilli, Streptococci, Clostridia*, etc. Although the product with enzymes from animal sources (L-lactate dehydrogenases, see page 108) is invariably in the L(+)- configuration, certain of the bacterial cells, and enzymes isolated from them, appear to exhibit the opposite stereospecificity; but in other instances both activities appear to be present in the same cell (e.g., *L. plantarum* ≡ *L. arabinosus*).

Reactions 11-14 and 11-15

The Terminal Steps in Alcoholic Fermentation. In certain microorganisms, among which brewer's yeast operating anaerobically is the most important, the further catabolism of pyruvate differs from that just described. The first step now is reaction 14, catalyzed by *pyruvate decarboxylase* (2-oxo-acid carboxylase, formerly called pyruvate carboxylase), the virtually irreversible decarboxylation of pyruvate to yield acetaldehyde, which requires thiamine pyrophosphate (TPP, cocarboxylase) and Mg^{+2} as indispensable cofactors. It is now known that the reaction takes place via the formation of 2-α-lactyl and -hydroxyethyl thiazolium derivatives of the coenzyme, [A] and [B]:

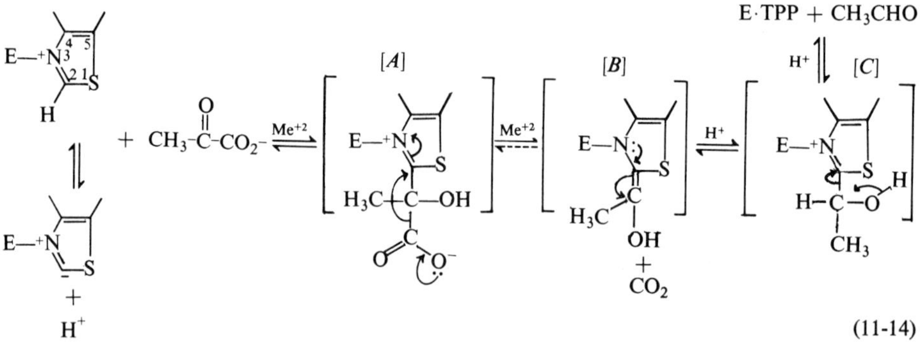

(11-14)

The general mechanism of TPP-catalyzed reactions was discussed on page 209. Enzymes capable of catalyzing reaction 14 and of releasing free acetaldehyde from complex [C] have been obtained in highly purified form from yeast, wheat germ, and other plant tissues. The metal requirement in this instance can be satisfied, not only by the usual divalent ions, but certain trivalent ones as well (Al^{+3}, Fe^{+3}).

In the final step of alcoholic fermentation, the acetaldehyde formed in reaction (11-14) is reduced to ethanol in reaction (11-15):

$$CH_3CHO + NADH^* + H^+ \rightleftharpoons CH_3-\overset{\overset{\displaystyle H^*}{|}}{\underset{\underset{\displaystyle H}{|}}{C}}OH + NAD^+ \qquad (11\text{-}15)$$

The enzyme responsible is called *alcohol dehydrogenase*. When isolated from yeast, it has a molecular weight of 151,000 and four independent catalytic sites, while an analogous enzyme with approximately half the molecular weight and two binding sites has been obtained from mammalian liver. Zn^{+2} is also present in amounts stoichiometric to the number of catalytic sites in these enzymes, which are stereospecific with regard to hydrogen transfer, both for the alcohol and for the *A*- (or α-) position of the 4-hydrogen in the nicotinamide ring (see page 214), but are relatively nonspecific with regard to structural features of the substrate alcohols and carbonyl compounds.

Alternate Glycolytic and Fermentative Pathways

The EMP pathway certainly provides the major route of glucose catabolism in most cells, with the exception of a few bacterial species. Several variants can be obtained with yeast cells, depending on the conditions employed.

The *first form* is the one already described and is the one obtained with yeast growing and multiplying under anaerobic conditions.

The *second form* leads to the formation of glycerol: it requires the trapping of the acetaldehyde formed by a carbonyl reagent, such as bisulfite, substituted hydrazines, etc. Under these conditions, reduction to ethanol does not take place, and 1 mole of triose-phosphate is diverted to glycerol production by virtue of the following reactions:

$$\text{Dihydroxyacetone-}P + \text{NADH} \rightleftharpoons \begin{array}{c} \text{CH}_2\text{OH} \\ | \\ \text{HOC—H} \\ | \\ \text{CH}_2\text{OPO}_3^= \end{array} + \text{NAD}^+ \qquad (11\text{-}16)$$

(11-17)

$$\text{L-}\alpha\text{-Glycerol-}P \text{ (L-glycerol-3-}P)$$

$$\begin{array}{c} \text{H}_2\text{O} \downarrow \\ \text{P}_i + \text{glycerol} \end{array} \quad \begin{array}{c} \nearrow \text{ADP·Mg} \\ \searrow \text{ATP·Mg} \end{array} \qquad (11\text{-}17a)$$

Reaction (11-16) is catalyzed by a soluble (cytoplasmic) enzyme called L-glycerol-3-*P*-dehydrogenase and reaction (11-17) by a specific phosphatase. Its reversal requires, as always, an ATP-dependent kinase (phosphotransferase) reaction — reaction (11-17a). It will be seen that in this sequence the NADH produced in reaction (11-8) is consumed in reaction (11-16); one triose molecule each traverses both branches — (11-16) plus (11-17) versus (11-8) through (11-14) — in a coordinated fashion, and there is no net accumulation or consumption of any of the coreactants, including ATP. Thus the net stoichiometric equation for this form of fermentation is given by the equation shown at the bottom of Fig. 11-2.

Reactions (11-16) and (11-17), in conjunction with those described as responsible for generating the triose-*P*, are also the ones concerned with the production of important intermediates of lipid metabolism (see Chap. 16) from carbohydrate precursors. Insect flight muscle is a tissue that does not produce lactate from glucose. Here the enzyme catalyzing reaction (11-16) works in conjunction with a different L-α-glycerol phosphate dehydrogenase, a flavoprotein localized in the mitochondria of this tissue, which catalyzes reaction (11-16b).

(*Extramitochondrial*) $\text{Dihydroxyacetone-}P + \text{H}^+ + \text{NADH} \rightleftharpoons \text{NAD}^+ + \alpha\text{-glycerol-}P$

(11-16a)

(*Mitochondrial*) $\alpha\text{-glycerol-}P + \text{E-FAD} \rightleftharpoons \text{dihydroxyacetone-}P + \text{E-FADH}_2$ (11-16b)

$$\underline{\text{E-FADH}_2 + \text{O}_2 + 2\text{ADP} + 2\text{P}_i \rightarrow \text{E-FAD} + \tfrac{1}{2}\text{H}_2\text{O} + 2\text{ATP}} \quad (11\text{-}16c)$$

Net (*cell*) $\text{NADH} + \text{O}_2 + 2\text{ADP} + 2\text{P}_i + \text{H}^+ \rightarrow \text{NAD}^+ + \tfrac{1}{2}\text{H}_2\text{O} + 2\text{ATP}$ (11-16d)

This sequence of reactions is of importance as a shuttle for NADH oxidation also in a number of other tissues, such as brain, smooth muscle, etc.

The *third form* of yeast fermentation takes place in an alkaline medium. Under these conditions the two branches of the EMP scheme again become closely coordinated. This leaves no net NADH for the production of ethanol from acetaldehyde. Instead another reaction must participate in the removal of this

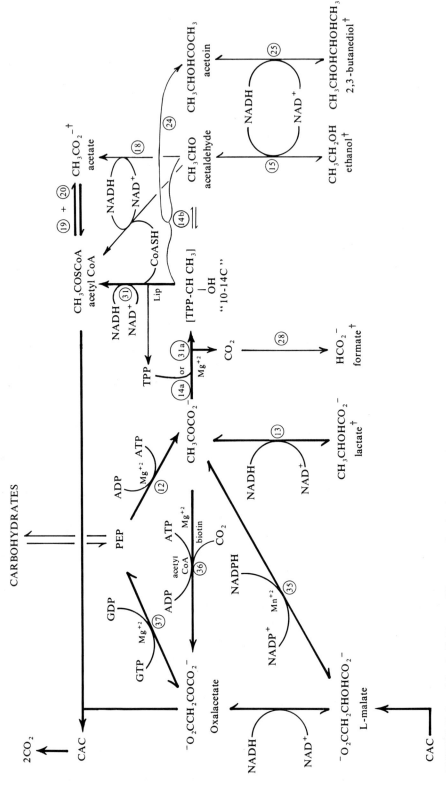

FIGURE 11-3. Metabolic Fates of Pyruvate. Predominant metabolic routes in mammals shown by heavy arrows.

† Compounds produced in microbial fermentations.

extremely toxic metabolite. This is reaction (11-18a):

$$CH_3CHO + NAD^+ + OH^- \rightleftharpoons CH_3CO_2^- + NADH + H^+ \qquad (11\text{-}18a)$$

catalyzed by an NAD-dependent *aldehyde dehydrogenase*. A similar enzyme is also found in mammalian liver. The set of reactions yields the overall balance given in Fig. 11-2.

In bacteria, a variant of reaction (11-18a) involving CoASH can take place — reaction (11-18b). Since acetyl-*S*-CoA as an acyl thioester has a high $-\Delta G^{0\prime}$ of hydrolysis (-7.7 kcal/mole), it can be equilibrated with the ATP system by reactions (11-19) and (11-20), catalyzed by *phosphotransacetylase* and *acetate kinase*:

$$CH_3CHO + NAD^+ + CoASH \rightleftharpoons CH_3COSCoA + NADH + H^+ \qquad (11\text{-}18b)$$

$$CH_3COSCoA + P_i^{=} \rightleftharpoons CH_3COP^{=} + CoASH \qquad (11\text{-}19)$$

$$CH_3COP^{=} + ADP \rightleftharpoons CH_3CO_2^- + ATP \qquad (11\text{-}20)$$

Net $CH_3CHO + NAD^+ + ADP + P_i^{=} \rightleftharpoons CH_3CO_2^- + ATP + NADH + H^+$
$$\Delta G^{0\prime} = -5.5 \text{ kcal/mole} \quad (11\text{-}21)$$

The net balance for this type of "hetero-" fermentation is

$$2 \text{ Glucose} + ADP + P_i \rightarrow 2 \text{ glycerol} + \text{ethanol} + \text{acetate} + 2CO_2 + ATP$$

ALTERNATIVE FATES OF PYRUVATE

The production of pyruvate from hexoses or hexose units is the common characteristic reaction of all cells utilizing the EMP scheme for carbohydrate catabolism and ATP production. To recapitulate, the stoichiometry observed is either

$$C_6H_{12}O_6 + 2NAD^+ + 2ADP + 2P_i \rightarrow 2CH_3COCO_2^- + 2NADH + 2ATP$$
$$\Delta G^{0\prime} = -18 \text{ kcal/mole} \quad (11\text{-}22a)$$

or

$$[C_6H_{11}O_6] + 2NAD^+ + 3ADP + 3P_i \rightarrow 2CH_3COCO_2^- + 2NADH + 3ATP$$
$$\Delta G^{0\prime} = -15 \text{ kcal/mole} \quad (11\text{-}22b)$$

where $[C_6H_{11}O_6]$ is a hexose in glycosidic linkage capable of yielding glucose-1-*P* on phosphorolysis. Different pathways diverge from, and are distinguished only by, the disposition that they assign to the NADH and pyruvate produced.

Other Fermentative Pathways in Microorganisms

Reactions Involving "Active Acetaldehyde." The 2-hydroxyethyl derivative of TPP — structure (11-14 [C]) — is exceedingly reactive and can be regarded as the metabolically "active" form of acetaldehyde. One typical reaction of this type is an acyloin condensation, the so-called *carboligase reaction* — reaction (11-23) — catalyzed by enzymes from higher plants and yeast, which appear to be either exceedingly closely associated or identical with the (de)carboxylase itself:

$$CH_3COCO_2^- + H^+ + E\cdot TPP \xrightarrow{Mg^{+2}} CO_2 + E\cdot TPP{-}CHOHCH_3 \qquad (11\text{-}14a)$$

$$E\cdot TPP{-}CHOHCH_3 \rightleftharpoons E\cdot TPP + CH_3CHO \qquad (11\text{-}14b)$$

$$E\cdot TPP{-}CHOHCH_3 + CH_3CHO \rightleftharpoons E\cdot TPP + CH_3CHOHCOCH_3 \qquad (11\text{-}23)$$

$$CH_3COCO_2^- + CH_3CHO + H^+ \xrightarrow[Mg^{+2}]{ETPP} CH_3CHOHCOCH_3 + CO_2$$
$$\text{[Eqs. (11-14a) plus (11-23)]} \quad (11\text{-}24)$$

Although with the plant enzymes, reaction (11-14b) is readily reversible, with those from certain bacteria or with the isolated pyruvic dehydrogenase complex (see page 277) free acetaldehyde is not produced, and this compound can act only as a carbonyl acceptor and not as a donor. Acetoin, in the presence of an appropriate dehydrogenase, can act as an alternative electron acceptor and provides a means for the reoxidation of NADH by virtue of reaction (11-25):

$$CH_3—CO—CHOH—CH_3 + NADH + H^+ \rightleftharpoons CH_3—CHOH—CHOH—CH_3 + NAD^+$$
$$(11-25)$$

A typical fermentation by certain bacilli and involving the reactions described would show the following stoichiometry:

$$3 \text{ Glucose} + 4ADP + 4P_i \rightarrow 2 \text{ 2,3-butanediol} + 2 \text{ glycerol} + 4CO_2 + 4ATP \qquad (11-26)$$

Reactions Involving Direct Formation of Acetyl-CoA and Acetyl-P (The "Clastic" Reaction). The high electron density on the carbon attached to the thiazolium ring in hydroxyalkyl TPP derivatives (structures 11-14 [B] and [C]) makes them highly reactive intermediates, not only in substitution, but in oxidation reactions as well:

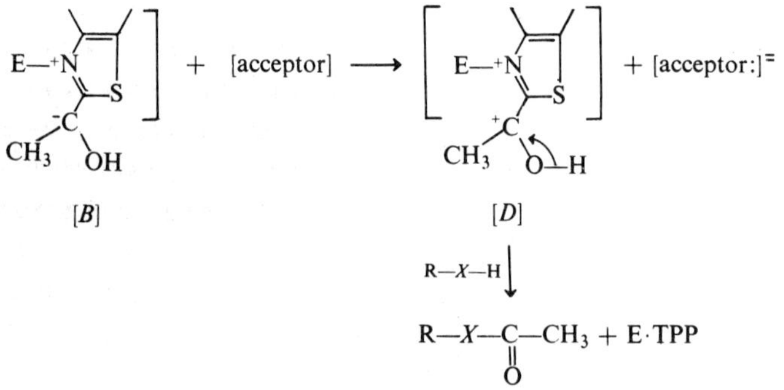

$$(11-27)$$

Most bacterial cells use CoASH (R—XH = CoA—SH) as the acetyl acceptor. The product obtained is acetyl CoA, which can be either converted to acetyl-P, in the so-called "phosphoroclastic" reaction, and then to acetate + ATP — reactions (11-19) + (11-20) — or, as the metabolically "active" form of acetate itself, participate in a large number of additional reactions. This is the route followed in a large number of microorganisms growing under anaerobic conditions. The second product ([acceptor:]$^=$ of eq. 11-27) is either H_2 (from H^+) or formate (from CO_2).

Each molecule of pyruvate undergoing the clastic reaction to formate, or CO_2 plus H_2, is capable of yielding one additional molecule of ATP. Thus we may observe the following typical fermentation balances:

$$\text{Glucose} + \begin{cases} 3ADP + 3P_i \rightarrow \text{lactate} + \text{formate} + \text{acetate} + 3ATP & (11\text{-}28a) \\ 2ADP + 2P_i \rightarrow \text{lactate} + \text{formate} + (\text{acetyl}) + 2ATP & (11\text{-}28b) \end{cases}$$

$$\text{Glucose} + <2ADP + <2P_i \rightarrow \text{2,3-butanediol} + CO_2 + \begin{cases} \text{formate} & (11\text{-}29a) \\ CO_2 + H_2 \end{cases} + <2ATP \quad (11\text{-}29b)$$

NAD-lipoate-linked Pyruvate Dehydrogenase Systems. The predominant fate of pyruvate in most animal cells and in aerobic microorganisms is its oxidation to acetyl CoA mediated by the multienzyme pyruvate dehydrogenase complexes (PDC) associated with particular cellular elements — the mitochondria of animal and plant cells, the cell membranes of bacteria (see Chap. 9). These complexes have been isolated in pure form and characterized as multicomponent aggregates of definite composition, with $M = 10 \times 10^6$ (PDC from pig heart) and 4.8×10^6 (PDC from *E. coli*). The latter has been separated into subunits, each exhibiting a separate set of enzymatic activities (eq. 11-30): (1) 16 molecules of pyruvate decarboxylase (E_a) ($M = 183,000$, containing stoichiometric amounts of enzyme-bound TPP); (2) one aggregate of lipoic reductase-transacetylase (E_b) ($M = 1.6 \times 10^6$, consisting of 64 subunits each of $M = 25,000$ and containing stoichiometric amounts of lipoyl residues — see page 201 — linked in amide linkage to ε-amino groups of lysine residues on the protein); and (3) eight molecules of dihydrolipoate dehydrogenase (E_c) ($M = 112,000$, containing stoichiometric quantities of enzyme-bound FAD, 2 per molecule). On electron micrographs, the complex exhibits a distinct polyhedral appearance with a diameter of 350 ± 50 A and a height of 225 ± 25 A (see page 108).

The reactions catalyzed are the following — note that (11-30a) is identical to (11-14a), and is catalyzed by the purified decarboxylase.

$$CH_3COCO_2^- + E_a \cdot TPP \overset{Mg^{+2}}{\rightleftharpoons} E_a \cdot TPP—CHOH—CH_3 + CO_2 \qquad (11\text{-}30a)$$

$$E_a \cdot TPP—\overset{OH}{\underset{H}{\overset{|}{\underset{|}{C}}}}—CH_3 + E_b \cdot NH—CO—(CH_2)_5— \overset{\frown}{\underset{S—S}{|}} \rightarrow$$

$$E_a \cdot TPP + E_b \cdot NHCO(CH_2)_5— \overset{\frown}{\underset{CH_3COS \quad SH}{|}} \qquad (11\text{-}30b\text{-}1)$$

$$E_b \cdot NHCO(CH_2)_5— \overset{\frown}{\underset{CH_3COS \quad SH}{|}} + CoASH \rightleftharpoons E_b \cdot NHCO(CH_2)_5— \overset{\frown}{\underset{SH \quad SH}{|}} + CH_3COSCoA \qquad (11\text{-}30b\text{-}2)$$

$$E_b \cdot NH—CO(CH_2)_5— \overset{\frown}{\underset{SH \quad SH}{|}} + E_c \cdot FAD \rightleftharpoons E_b \cdot NH—CO(CH_2)_5— \overset{\frown}{\underset{S—S}{|}} + E_c \cdot FADH_2 \qquad (11\text{-}30c\text{-}1)$$

$$E_c \cdot FADH_2 + NAD^+ \rightleftharpoons E_c \cdot FAD + NADH + H^+ \qquad (11\text{-}30c\text{-}2)$$

$$\text{Net} \quad CH_3COCO_2^- + NAD^+ + CoASH \xrightarrow[\underset{TPP, lip \langle \overset{S}{\underset{S}{|}}, Mg^{+2}}{}]{PDC(E_{a,b,c})} CoASCOCH_3 + NADH + CO_2$$

$$\Delta G^{0'} = -9.38 \text{ kcal/mole} \quad (11\text{-}31)$$

Or with O_2,

$$CH_3COCO_2^- + \tfrac{1}{2}O_2 + CoASH + H^+ \xrightarrow{\text{as above, plus electron transport}}$$
$$CoASCOCH_3 + H_2O + CO_2 \quad \Delta G^{0'} = -61.8 \text{ kcal/mole} \quad (11\text{-}32)$$

$$CH_3COCO_2^- + \tfrac{1}{2}O_2 + CoASH + 3ADP + 3P_i \xrightarrow{\text{as above, plus oxidative phosph.}}$$
$$CoASCOCH_3 + 2H_2O + CO_2 + 3ATP \quad \Delta G^{0'} = -39.3 \text{ kcal/mole} \quad (11\text{-}33)$$

The major pathway for the disposition of the acetyl CoA produced in the oxidation of pyruvate is its complete combustion to CO_2, an event which likewise takes place in the mitochondria and which, as we shall see in Chaps. 14 and 15, generates 12 molecules of ATP per molecule of $CH_3COSCoA$ or twice that number per molecule of glucose. If we assume that the 4 molecules of NADH generated during catabolism of glucose — two in reaction (11-8) and two in reaction (11-31) — are oxidized with concomitant phosphorylation — see reaction (11-16d) for a means of shuttling electrons from extramitochondrial NADH into the mitochondria — this will provide for a maximum of 12 additional molecules of ATP per molecule of glucose. Thus, for the complete conversion, we see

$$C_6H_{12}O_6 + 6O_2 + \leq 38ADP + \leq 38P_i \rightarrow 6CO_2 + 6H_2O + \leq 38ATP \qquad (11\text{-}34)$$

CARBOXYLATION REACTIONS

The continued oxidation of acetyl CoA by means of the CAC requires the simultaneous presence of oxalacetate. This is ordinarily provided for by the cyclical nature of the process, but it also means that, if there were any drain on the cycle or its members for synthetic processes — and there are many, exemplified by the biosynthesis of amino acids, purines, pyrimidines, and pentose precursors for nucleic acids and coenzymes, porphyrins, etc. — a means must be found for its replenishment. In animals these anaplerotic sequences are provided for by carboxylation reactions, which interconvert pyruvate and the dicarboxylic acids of the cycle. The circumvention of the block put on the path of carbohydrate synthesis by the pyruvate kinase reaction is another process that utilizes a preliminary carboxylation, as is the conversion of pyruvate to propionate in fermentations by propionic acid bacteria. Finally oxaloacetate is readily decarboxylated enzymatically and nonenzymatically. The following reactions constitute the major contributors to these $C_3 + C_1 = C_4$ conversions:

$$CH_3COCO_2^- + NAD(P)H + HCO_3^- \overset{Mn^{+2}}{\rightleftharpoons} {}^-O_2CCH_2CHCO_2^- + NAD(P)^+$$

$$\underset{OH \; (\text{L-malate})}{\qquad\qquad\qquad\qquad\qquad\qquad\qquad\qquad\qquad\qquad}$$

$$\Delta G^{0\prime} = 0.36 \text{ kcal/mole} \qquad (11\text{-}35)$$

$$\text{Biotinyl} \cdot E + ATP + CO_2(HCO_3^-) \overset{Mg^{+2}, \; acetyl \; CoA}{\rightleftharpoons} E \cdot \text{biotinyl} \cdot N\text{-}CO_2^- + ADP + P_i \qquad (11\text{-}36a)$$

$$E \cdot \text{Biotinyl-}N\text{-}CO_2^- + CH_3COCO_2^- \rightleftharpoons \text{biotinyl} \cdot E + {}^-O_2CCH_2COCO_2^- \qquad (11\text{-}36b)$$

$$CH_3COCO_2^- + ATP + HCO_3^- + H_2O \overset{Mg^{+2}, \; acetyl \; CoA}{\rightleftharpoons} {}^-O_2CCH_2COCO_2^- + ADP + P_i + H^+$$
$$\Delta G^{0\prime} \simeq -0.5 \text{ kcal/mole} \qquad (11\text{-}36)$$

$$CH_2{=}C{-}CO_2^- + GDP(IDP) + HCO_3^- \overset{Mg^{+2}}{\rightleftharpoons} {}^-O_2CCH_2COCO_2^- + GTP(ITP)$$
$$\underset{OPO_3^=}{\qquad\qquad} \qquad\qquad\qquad\qquad \Delta G^{0\prime} = -1 \text{ kcal/mole} \qquad (11\text{-}37)$$

$$CH_2{=}C{-}CO_2^- + P_i + HCO_3^- + H^+ \overset{Mg^{+2}}{\rightleftharpoons} {}^-O_2CCH_2COCO_2^- + PP_i + H_2O$$
$$\underset{OPO_3^=}{\qquad\qquad} \qquad\qquad\qquad\qquad \Delta G^{0\prime} \simeq -2 \text{ kcal/mole} \qquad (11\text{-}38)$$

$$CH_2{=}C{-}CO_2^- + HCO_3^- \overset{Me^{+2}}{\longrightarrow} {}^-O_2CCH_2COCO_2^- + P_i \qquad \Delta G^{0\prime} = -6.8 \text{ kcal/mole} \qquad (11\text{-}39)$$
$$\underset{OPO_3^=}{\qquad}$$

Reaction (11-35) is catalyzed by *malic enzyme*, which is usually specific for $NADP^+$, especially in higher organisms. In view of its very low affinity for HCO_3^- and the relative unavailability of NADPH in mitochondria, it is thought to function mainly to provide for the oxidation of malate for conversion to pyruvate, acetyl CoA, and other metabolites related to them, and to supply NADPH.

Reaction (11-36) is catalyzed by the *ATP-dependent pyruvate carboxylase*, an enzyme localized in the mitochondria. It has a high affinity for HCO_3^-, the carboxylation of enzyme-bound biotin is activated allosterically by acetyl CoA, and the equilibrium favors oxaloacetate formation. All these facts make it a very likely candidate as the preponderant catalyst for dicarboxylic acid (and carbohydrate) synthesis. It is most active when conditions require highest oxidative activity and energy generation.

The enzyme catalyzing reaction (11-37), *phosphoenolpyruvate carboxykinase*, interacts preferentially with the GDP/GTP or IDP/ITP systems.[1] The various nucleoside triphosphates are interconvertible by virtue of the *nucleoside diphosphate kinase* (transphosphorylase) reaction:

GDP (or IDP) + ATP = GTP (or ITP) + ADP

Reaction (11-37), reaction (11-38), catalyzed by *carboxy transphosphorylase*, and the essentially irreversible reaction (11-39), catalyzed by *phosphoenol pyruvic carboxylase* (an enzyme present in green plants and *Enterobactericeae*) all may involve oxalacetyl phosphate

$$^-O_2C-CH_2-CO-\overset{\overset{\textstyle |}{\textstyle |}}{\underset{O}{C}}-OPO_3^=$$

as an unstable intermediate; this intermediate may then be hydrolyzed — in reaction (11-39) — or transfer its phosphate to GDP — in reaction (11-37) or P_i (in reaction 11-38). Although reaction (11-39), in those cells where it occurs, may play an important role in CO_2 fixation, the function of reaction (11-37) is probably to be found in the opposite sense: reactions (11-36) and (11-37), from right to left, both catalyzed by mitochondrial enzymes and acting in concert, provide the phosphoenol pyruvate required for carbohydrate synthesis:

$$\text{Pyruvate} + \underbrace{\text{ATP} + \text{GTP}}_{\text{2 ATP}} \overset{CO_2}{=} \text{phosphoenolpyruvate} + \underbrace{\text{GDP} + \text{ADP}}_{\text{2 ADP}} \qquad (11\text{-}40)$$

THE SYNTHESIS OF GLUCOSE FROM PYRUVATE [GLUCO (NEO) GENESIS]

If a metabolic energy supply is available, mammalian liver and kidney can synthesize glucose, and hence pentoses, glycogen, and other polysaccharides from short-chain precursors. Among the latter are (1) pyruvate or lactate; (2) the so-called glycogenic amino acids (see Table 17-2); and (3) any other component that can be catabolized to pyruvate or to any member of the CAC. In resting skeletal muscle (but not in heart or smooth muscle) phosphorylated 3-carbon compounds, most notably α-glycerophosphate, are similarly converted back to glycogen at the expense of creatine-phosphate, the storage form of metabolic energy in that tissue. This resynthesis of glucose from other sources is essential for the maintenance and supplies the energy demands of certain types of cells, especially those in the nerve tissue and the blood of animals. In an analogous fashion, hexoses, pentoses, and structural polysaccharides can be synthesized by microorganisms from carbon sources containing 4- and 3-carbon atoms. The pertinent problem, then, is the mode of biosynthesis of glucose or hexosephosphates from pyruvate, summarized by the reaction:

---

[1] It is precisely GTP or ITP that is generated by oxidative phosphorylation at the substrate level during the operation of the CAC in the oxidation of α-ketoglutarate (see page 329).

$$2CH_3COCO_2^- + 2NADH + 6ATP + 4H^+ = C_6H_{12}O_6 + 2NAD^+ + 6ADP + 6P_i$$
$$\Delta G^{0'} = -7 \text{ kcal/mole} \quad (11\text{-}41)$$

It is made up of the following sequence (reaction 11-42):

$$\text{malate} \overset{H_2O}{\rightleftharpoons} \text{fumarate}$$

$$2 \times (\text{pyruvate} \xrightarrow{ATP} \text{oxaloacetate} \xrightarrow{GTP \text{ or } ATP} PEP \rightarrow P\text{-glycerate} \xrightarrow[ATP]{NADH} \text{triose-}P) \rightarrow$$
$$\text{hexose-di}P \xrightarrow{H_2O} \text{hexose-}P \xrightarrow{H_2O} \text{hexose}$$

with the controlling and unique steps again intervening at the beginning and the end of the sequence. That this is the major pathway of hexose biosynthesis is indicated by the fact that, if pyruvate labeled in either the 2- or 3-position is administered to a starved animal, the glycogen, produced after synthesis has been allowed to proceed for a while, will contain hexose units that show equilibration of the label in the 1-, 2-, 5-, and 6-positions. This suggests that a symmetrical precursor must have intervened, a process that probably involved the interconversions of the dicarboxylic acids indicated above and discussed on page 324. As already mentioned, in *E. coli* the initial step is different, and we observe the direct conversion of pyruvate to the enol phosphate without any intervention of dicarboxylic acids.

The Control of Glucose Metabolism   It may be useful at this point to review briefly those factors in animal cells that contribute most heavily to a control of glucose (and glycogen) breakdown and resynthesis and thus affect the steady state of these compounds. In general, we can say that in all cells that are capable of degrading glucose both in the presence and the absence of oxygen, the sugar disappears (and of course lactic acid or other products of anaerobic glycolysis or fermentation are formed) more rapidly under anaerobic than under aerobic conditions. This inhibition of glycolysis by oxygen was first recognized by Pasteur and later confirmed by Meyerhof and Warburg and is known as the *Pasteur effect*. Another finding, first made by A. V. Hill with muscle, but true of other tissues and cells as well, is that the resynthesis of glycogen and carbohydrates in general proceeds more rapidly under aerobic than under anaerobic conditions.

From our considerations so far we know that aerobiosis removes P_i and ADP, generates ATP, removes NADH, and produces CO_2, acetyl CoA, and di- and tricarboxylic acids a great deal more effectively than do anaerobic conditions (for further details see Chap. 14). From the overall stoichiometries -- reactions (11-22*a* and *b*) and (11-41) — and the reaction sequences responsible, we can appreciate how this set of conditions affects the overall conversions glucose (or glycogen) → pyruvate → glucose (or glycogen).

A decrease in the availability of P_i and ADP in favor of ATP certainly leads to a diminution in the rate of glycolysis and an increase in the rate of gluconeogenesis. We now turn again to a consideration of the fate of NADH. In aerobic cells it is oxidized by the mitochondrial electron transport chain (see Chap. 15); in essentially anaerobic cells it is oxidized by linked reactions, of which in animal metabolism the conversion pyruvate + NADH → lactate + NAD^+ is by far the most important.

In addition to these stoichiometric and kinetic controls, we have also discussed the quite specific regulatory mechanisms summarized in the table below:

Process	Enzymatic reaction	Activated by	Inhibited by
Breakdown	Glycogen → glucose-1-P	AMP	
	Fructose-6-P → fructose-1,6-di$P$ (FDP)	ADP, AMP, FDP	ATP, citrate
	PEP → pyruvate		ATP
Synthesis	Pyruvate → oxaloacetate → PEP	Acetyl CoA, CO_2	
	Fructose-1,6-di$P$ → fructose-6-P		AMP, FDP
	Glucose-6-P → glucose		PP$_i$, glucose
	Glucose-1-P → UDPG → glycogen	Glucose-6-P	

In this context it should also be mentioned that hepatic gluconeogenesis is under some form of *hormonal* control and that the most characteristic increases in enzyme content are found with fructose-1,6-disphosphatase, glucose-6-phosphatase, and pyruvate carboxylase.

Biosynthesis of
Carbohydrates from
2-Carbon Compounds

Higher plants and microorganisms are sometimes confronted by the problem of converting fats or 2-carbon metabolites (and hence acetyl CoA) into

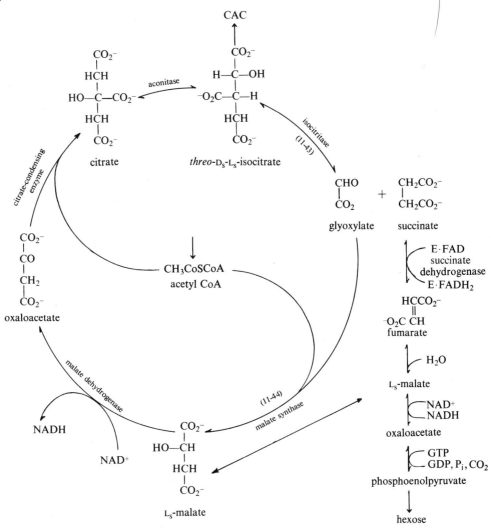

FIGURE 11-4. The Glyoxylate Cycles.

carbohydrates and other cell constituents. This takes place for instance during the germination of seeds, which contain a large amount of lipid as a metabolic store, or in microorganisms when they are required to grow on ethanol or acetate as their sole source of carbon. The task is accomplished by means of the coordinated set of reactions shown in Fig. 11-4. The two key enzymes, *isocitratase* (*isocitrate lyase*) — reaction (11-43) — and *malate synthetase* — reaction (11-44) — are absent from animal tissues, and hence the cycle cannot be operative there.

Operation of the cycle, in addition to the two novel reactions, also requires the simultaneous participation of three of the enzymes of the citric acid cycle (see Chap. 14). These are the *citrate-condensing enzyme, aconitase,* and *malate dehydrogenase.* Also required is the electron-transport chain for the oxidation of NADH by molecular oxygen — the latter plus the malate synthetase reaction providing the essential driving force. One turn of the cycle leads to the oxidation of two molecules of acetyl CoA to yield one molecule of succinate with the simultaneous removal of two reducing equivalents. The succinate so formed can then be converted to carbohydrate by the sequence of reactions shown, which includes two additional reactions catalyzed by enzymes of the citric acid cycle: *succinic dehydrogenase* and *fumarase,* with malate dehydrogenase again participating. Other cellular constituents metabolically derivable from intermediates of the CAC can be formed by a second condensation of acetyl CoA with oxaloacetate, plus follow-up reactions. Thus the glyoxylate (or Krebs-Kornberg) cycle provides an example par excellence of an anaplerotic sequence in operation. Of the various enzymes involved, isocitratase, the one at the branch point of two metabolic sequences, appears to be susceptible to second-site control: the enzyme from *E. coli* is inhibited by phosphoenol pyruvate.

HEXOSE MONOPHOSPHATE-PENTOSE PATHWAYS

The second set of major pathways for hexose catabolism has been investigated principally by Warburg, Dickens, Lipmann, S. Cohen, Horecker, Racker, and their collaborators. A number of different names have been assigned to the reaction sequence(s) involved. Since one of its pathways diverges from glycolysis at the level of glucose-6-*P*, it has been called the hexose-monophosphate "shunt"; since in the same pathway two of the first three steps are dehydrogenations and since pentoses participate catalytically, it has sometimes been designated the "oxidative pathway of hexose metabolism," or the "pentose cycle," and since phosphogluconate is a key intermediate, the designation "phosphogluconate pathway" has also been employed. We remember, however, that members of one and the same set of enzymes, operating either by themselves or in conjunction with those of other sets, can be utilized by the same or different cells to fulfill a multiplicity of functions. This appears to be especially true in the present instance, and we shall describe in this section several different ways in which this can be brought about; another very important example is provided by the CO_2 fixation cycle of photosynthesis discussed in Chap. 12 on page 305. The constituent enzymes involved are generally localized in the cytoplasm.

The Dehydrogenases — Reactions 11-45 and 11-47

The first oxidative step — reaction (11-45) — is catalyzed by *glucose-6-P dehydrogenase,* an important enzyme of very wide distribution. $NADP^+$ is the specific coenzyme for most of these enzymes. The reaction as written, i.e., with the

δ-lactone as the product or substrate, is readily reversible with a $\Delta G^{0\prime} = -100$ cal/mole. Since the enzyme from yeast can also act on free glucose, it proved possible to establish its anomeric specificity for the β-D-glucopyranose configuration.

The hydrolysis of the lactone to the 6-phosphoester of gluconate — reaction (11-46) — is strongly exergonic $(\Delta G^{0\prime} = -5000$ cal/mole) and quite rapid $(t_{1/2}$ of the order of minutes in the physiological pH range). Nevertheless, specific enzymes (*lactonases*) have been identified in plants and many species of bacteria. The second oxidative reaction (11-47) catalyzed by *6-P-gluconate dehydrogenase* requires a divalent metal cation (Mg^{+2} or Mn^{+2}) as a cofactor and constitutes a reversible oxidative decarboxylation, analogous to that catalyzed by the similarly NADP-dependent malic enzyme (see page 278) and isocitrate dehydrogenase. Presumably the 3-ketohexonic acid takes part as an intermediate.

The Isomerization of Pentose Phosphates — Reactions 11-48 and 11-49

Two isomerization reactions of pentose-5-phosphates form an integral part of all metabolic sequences that utilize this metabolic scheme. One, reaction (11-49), simply interconverts a phosphoketopentose and its aldose-phosphate counterpart. It is therefore completely analogous to reaction (11-4) in the hexose series (glucose-6-$P \rightleftharpoons$ fructose-6-P), and the mechanisms for the two reactions have been demonstrated to be identical. The other reaction (11-48) constitutes an epimerization at the 3-position, i.e. the carbon α to the carbonyl of the ketose, and may thus also involve an enediol intermediate.

The Rearrangement of the Carbon Skeleton by Transketolase and Transaldolase — Reactions 11-50a, b and 11-51

The Transketolase Reaction — *Reaction* (11-50*a* and *b*). The enzyme catalyzing this reaction requires thiamine pyrophosphate and divalent metal cations as obligatory cofactors. The reaction catalyzed can be regarded as the reversible transfer of a glycoaldehyde moiety from a donor ketose to an acceptor aldose. The specificity of the enzyme requires that the ketose have the L- configuration on the α carbon and preferably a trans configuration for the next two:

$$
\begin{array}{c}
\text{CH}_2\text{OH} \\
|\\
\text{C}{=}\text{O} \\
\text{---+---} \\
\text{HO--CH} \\
|\\
\text{HC--OH} \\
|\\
\text{R}
\end{array}
$$

In the scheme shown in Fig. 11-5, transketolase intervenes twice: first — Eq. (11-50*a*) — to form glyceraldehyde-P plus sedoheptulose-P from the two pentoses, and then again — Eq. (11-50*b*) — to form fructose-P plus triose-P from another molecule of xylulose-P reacting with tetrose-P.

The Transaldolase Reaction — *Reaction* (11-51). Transaldolase is the second enzyme characteristic of the nonoxidative portion. It catalyzes the transfer of a *dihydroxyacetone moiety* (not free dihydroxyacetone) from a donor ketose, such as, typically, D-sedoheptulose-7-P or D-fructose-6-P, to an acceptor aldose, such as D-glyceraldehyde-3-P or D-erythrose-4-P. The specificity requirements of the enzyme, the nature of the reaction catalyzed, and the apparent absence of any cofactor requirement make it appear highly likely that the mechanism of transaldolase is similar to that of aldolase — reaction (11-6). In fact the active,

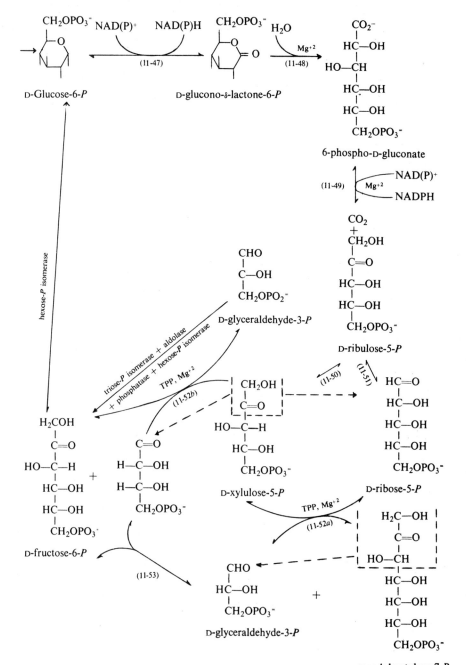

FIGURE 11-5. Enzymatic Reactions Involved in Hexose-P-Pentose-P Pathways.
Reaction (11-45) glucose-6-P-dehydrogenase
Reaction (11-46) gluconolactonase
Reaction (11-47) phosphogluconate dehydrogenase
Reaction (11-48) ribulose-P-3-epimerase
Reaction (11-49) ribose-P (phosphoribose) isomerase
Reaction (11-50a and b) transketolase
Reaction (11-51) transaldolase

enzyme-bound intermediate is again a Schiff base of the ketose, linked to the ε-amino group of a lysine residue of the enzyme.

The Pentose Oxidation Cycle   One suggestion that has been advanced is that the reactions just described plus certain ones of the glycolytic sequence may interact in the following manner to lead to the oxidative conversion of glucose either to triose-P or to CO_2:

$$3 \text{ Glucose-6-}P + 3NADP^+ \rightarrow 3 \text{ 6-}P\text{-gluconate} + 3NADPH + 3H^+ \tag{11-45}$$

$$3 \text{ 6-}P\text{-Gluconate} + 3NADP^+ \rightarrow 3 \text{ ribulose-5-}P + 3CO_2 + 3H^+ \tag{11-47}$$

$$2 \text{ Ribulose-5-}P \rightarrow 2 \text{ xylulose-5-}P \tag{11-48}$$

$$\text{Ribulose-5-}P \rightarrow \text{ribose-5-}P \tag{11-49}$$

$$\text{Xylulose-5-}P + \text{ribose-5-}P \rightarrow \text{sedoheptulose-7-}P + \text{triose-}P \tag{11-50a}$$

$$\text{Sedoheptulose-7-}P + \text{triose-}P \rightarrow \text{erythrose-4-}P + \text{fructose-6-}P \tag{11-51}$$

$$\text{Erythrose-4-}P + \text{xylulose-5-}P \rightarrow \text{fructose-6-}P + \text{triose-3-}P \tag{11-50b}$$

$$\text{Fructose-6-}P \rightarrow \text{glucose-6-}P \tag{11-4}$$

$$\textit{Net} \quad 3 \text{ Glucose-6-}P + 6NADP^+ \rightarrow 2 \text{ glucose-6-}P + \text{triose-}P + 3CO_2 + 6NADPH + 6H^+ \tag{11-52a}$$

or twice this, plus $2 \text{ triose-}P \rightarrow \text{fructose-1,6-di}P \xrightarrow{+H_2O} P_i + \text{fructose-6-}P \rightarrow \text{glucose-6-}P$:

$$\textit{Net} \quad 6 \text{ Glucose-6-}P + 12NADP^+ \rightarrow 5 \text{ glucose-6-}P + 6CO_2 + 12NADPH + 12H^+ + P_i \tag{11-52b}$$

or

$$6 \text{ Glucose-6-}P + 6O_2 \rightarrow 5 \text{ glucose-6-}P + 6CO_2 + 6H_2O + P_i \tag{11-53}$$

In theory, since the cell can oxidize (by means of O_2) the NADPH produced and thus can regenerate the $NADP^+$, the scheme provides for the complete oxidation of one molecule of glucose-P to $6CO_2 + 6H_2O$ by reaction (11-53). This entails the catalytic intervention of five additional molecules of glucose-P and the intermediates and reactions indicated. Note that the stoichiometry does not provide any clues concerning mechanism. Significantly all three — or six, in reactions (11-52b) or (11-53) — molecules of CO_2 produced have their origin in C-1 of glucose.

Nonoxidative Interconversions of Hexose and Pentose Phosphates   The oxidative route just discussed is not the only one that can lead, with the intervention of the same complement of enzymes, from hexose to pentose phosphates. Consider the following scheme of now familiar reactions:

$$2 \text{ Ribulose-5-}P \rightleftharpoons 2 \text{ ribose-5-}P$$

$$4 \text{ Ribulose-5-}P \rightleftharpoons 4 \text{ xylulose-5-}P$$

$$2 \text{ Xylulose-5-}P + 2 \text{ ribose-5-}P \rightleftharpoons 2 \text{ sedoheptulose-7-}P + 2 \text{ triose-3-}P$$

$$2 \text{ Sedoheptulose-7-}P + 2 \text{ triose-3-}P \rightleftharpoons 2 \text{ fructose-6-}P + 2 \text{ erythrose-4-}P$$

$$2 \text{ Erythrose-4-}P + 2 \text{ xylulose-5-}P \rightleftharpoons 2 \text{ fructose-6-}P + 2 \text{ triose-}P$$

$$2 \text{ Triose-}P \rightleftharpoons \text{fructose-1,6-di}P$$

$$\text{Fructose-1,6-di}P + H_2O \rightarrow \text{fructose-6-}P + P_i$$

or $$\text{Fructose-1,6-di}P + ADP \rightleftharpoons \text{fructose-6-}P + ATP$$

$$5 \text{ Fructose-6-}P \rightleftharpoons 5 \text{ glucose-6-}P$$

$$\textit{Net} \quad 6 \text{ Pentose-5-}P + H_2O \rightleftharpoons 5 \text{ glucose-6-}P + P_i \tag{11-54a}$$

$$6 \text{ Pentose-5-}P + ADP \rightleftharpoons 5 \text{ glucose-6-}P + ATP \tag{11-54b}$$

It is clear that we now have available a means of interconverting and reshuffling the carbon atoms of hexoses and pentoses. This nonoxidative pathway for the formation of ribose from glucose has been shown to occur in a variety of cells, as has the concomitant rearrangement of the hexose carbon skeleton.

Interconversions of Hexoses

The simplest interconversion or isomerization reaction is the reversible equilibrium between the α-D- and β-D- forms of the common hexoses, such as glucose (see page 245). This anomerization process is quite rapid in the physiological pH range; nevertheless specific enzymes (*mutarotases, aldose epimerases*) that further enhance the rate have been isolated from mammalian kidney and a number of molds: these enzymes catalyze mutarotation of D-glucose, D-galactose, D-xylose, L-arabinose, maltose, and lactose.

The other common hexoses besides D-glucose that have to be considered are the aldoses D-mannose and D-galactose, and the ketoses D-fructose and L-sorbose, all of which differ from one another in the configuration of only one of the six carbon atoms:

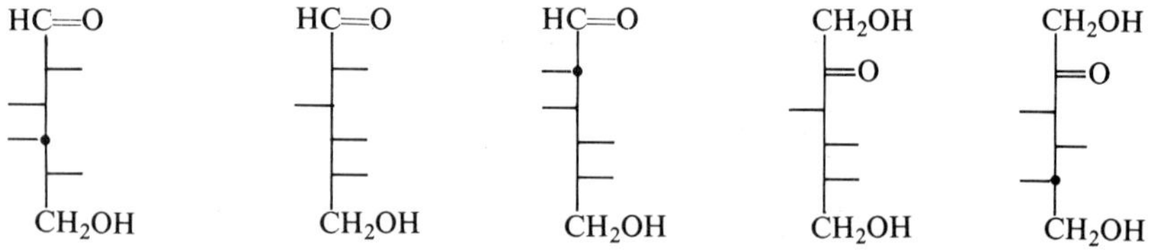

D-Galactose   D-Glucose   D-Mannose   D-Fructose   L-Sorbose

• indicates epimerized C.

Fructose and mannose are phosphorylated by the nonspecific hexokinases to yield the corresponding 6-phosphates. The mechanism of the interconversion of mannose-6-P and fructose-6-P has already been discussed. D-Galactose is phosphorylated in the presence of galactokinase in the 1-position to yield the (glycosidic) galactose-1-P. Its isomerization (Walden inversion at C-4) to glucose-1-P is discussed below.

Formation of Glucosamine

The various hexosamines found in a variety of mucopolysaccharides, glycoproteins, and bacterial cell-wall polysaccharides all have their metabolic origin in D-fructose-6-P. This compound is converted to α-D-glucosamine with the amide — NH_2 of glutamine as the nitrogen source:

$$\text{D-fructose-6-}P + \text{glutamine} \rightarrow \text{D-glucosamine-6-}P + \text{glutamate} \tag{11-55}$$

The removal of NH_3 to regenerate the ketose-P is catalyzed by separate and specific deaminases. Most of the natural products of interest contain *N*-acetyl glucosamine. This compound is formed in a reaction catalyzed by a specific *N*-acetylase with acetyl CoA as the acetyl donor:

$$\text{D-Glucosamine-6-}P + \text{acetyl CoA} \rightarrow N\text{-acetyl-D-glucosamine-6-}P + \text{CoASH} \tag{11-56}$$

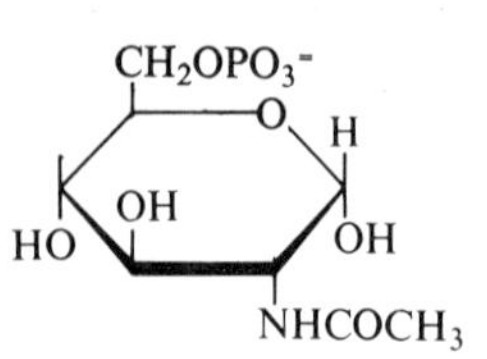

One of the most significant recent milestones in carbohydrate biochemistry

Formation and
Interconversions of
Nucleoside Diphosphate
Sugars

was the discovery by the Argentine scientist Leloir and his collaborators that a large number of interconversions and synthetic processes in this area involved as obligatory intermediates C-1 (glycosyl) esters of aldoses and nucleoside di- (occasionally mono-) phosphates. These intermediates take the place of the sugar phosphates so familiar in an earlier phase of carbohydrate biochemistry. The derivatives are formed by specific *pyrophosphorylases*. The classic case is that of the synthesis of uridine-diphosphate-glucose (UDP-glucose, UDPG) by reaction (11-57*a*) where Nu = uridine and the sugar moiety is glucose-1-*P* in (11-57):

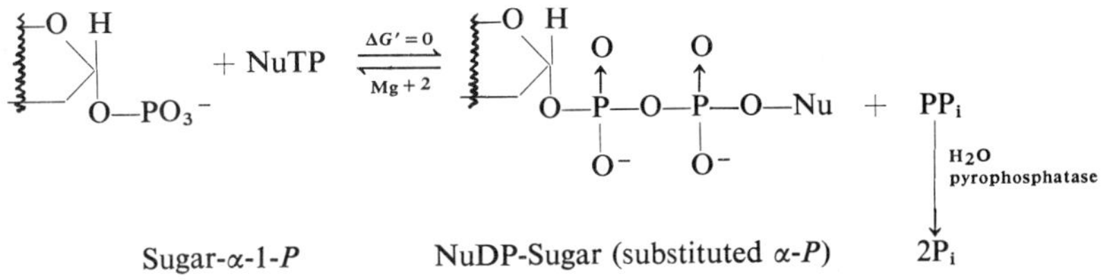

Sugar-α-1-*P*   NuDP-Sugar (substituted α-*P*) $2P_i$

$$(11\text{-}57)$$

By now a wide array of sugars and their derivatives and UTP, ATP (with glucose-1-*P* exclusively), GTP, CTP, and dTTP all have become implicated in reaction (11-57). Once formed, the NuDP sugars can undergo the following types of reactions.

The Galactose-1-P Glucose-1-P Epimerization. This sequence consists of the following steps:

Galactose-1-P + UTP $\rightleftharpoons$ UDP-galactose + PP_i
        UDP galactose pyrophosphorylase (galactose-1-P uridylyl transferase)   (11-57*b*)

UDP-Galactose $\rightleftharpoons$ UDP-glucose   *UDP glucose-epimerase*   (11-58)

UDP-Glucose + galactose-1-P $\rightleftharpoons$ UDP-galactose + glucose-1-P
                                    hexose-1-P uridylyl transferase   (11-59)

Glucose-1-P + UTP $\rightleftharpoons$ UDP-glucose + PP_i
        UDP glucose pyrophosphorylase (glucose-1-P uridylyl transferase)   (11-57*a*)

Once the UDP sugar derivative has been formed by reactions (11-57*b*) or (11-57*a*), the epimerization is brought about by reactions (11-58) and (11-59) acting in concert. The epimerase reaction proper — reaction (11-58) — takes place at the NuDP level and involves enzyme-bound NAD^+ (one molecule per protein molecule) as an obligatory cofactor.

Hereditary deficiencies in the various enzymes have been identified in micro-organisms and man: *galactosemia* in infants is caused by a lack of enzyme catalyzing reaction (11-59) and hence an inability to metabolize the galactose derived from lactose (a β-D-galactoside) in milk.

Oxidation of NuDP-Aldoses to NuDP-Uronic Acids. An oxidation of sugar nucleotides involving four reducing equivalents yields uronic acids; a typical

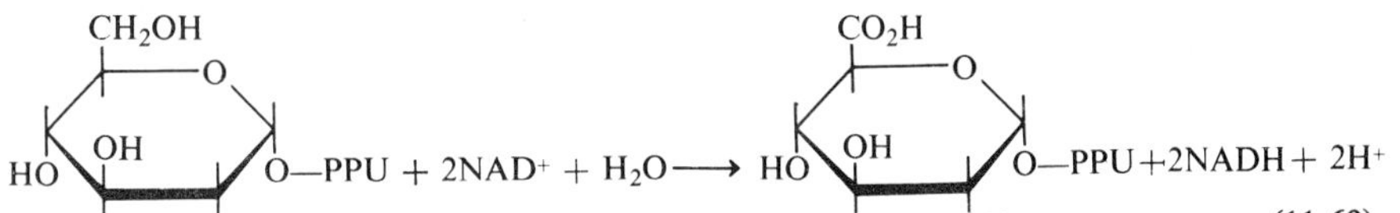

$$(11\text{-}60)$$

reaction is catalyzed by UDP-D-glucose dehydrogenase, forming UDP-D-glucuronic acid. Two molecules of NAD^+ are required, the reaction is irreversible, and there is no evidence for the participation of any half-oxidized (2-equivalent) intermediates.

Formation of Sialic Acids. Sialic acids are found in a number of mammalian glycoproteins and bacterial cell-wall structures. In mammalian liver they appear to be synthesized by the complicated pathway shown as reaction (11-61):

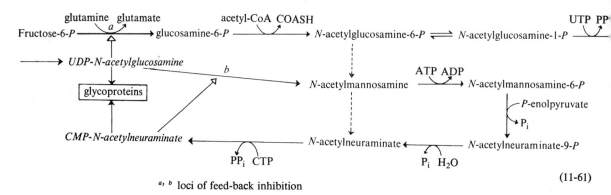

$$(11-61)$$

$^{a, b}$ loci of feed-back inhibition

BIOSYNTHESIS OF GLYCOSIDIC BONDS

By far the most important function of the nucleoside (di)phosphate sugars is to act as glycosyl donors in a wide variety of reactions, all of which involve the formation of a new glycosidic linkage. Since the $\Delta G^{0\prime}$ of hydrolysis of such bonds is of the order of -3000 cal/mole, it can readily be appreciated that their effective formation requires the expenditure of metabolic energy and hence the preferred reaction is

$$\text{NuDP-sugar} + \text{acceptor} \rightleftharpoons \text{sugar} (1\rightarrow) \text{acceptor} + \text{NuDP} \qquad (11\text{-}62)$$

Thus formation of the glycosylated product from NuTP + sugar is brought about by an exergonic pathway:

$$\text{Sugar} + 2\text{ATP} + \text{acceptor} \rightarrow \text{sugar–acceptor} + 2\text{ADP} + \text{PP}_i \qquad \Delta G^{0\prime} \simeq -3.5 \text{ kcal/mole}$$
$$\text{Sugar} + 2\text{ATP} + \text{acceptor} \rightarrow \text{sugar–acceptor} + 2\text{ADP} + 2\text{P}_i \qquad \Delta G^{0\prime} \simeq -12 \text{ kcal/mole}$$

Synthesis of Simple Glycosides and Disaccharides

The simplest reaction of the general type under consideration here is the formation of a glycoside by reaction (11-62a):

$$\text{NuDP-sugar} + \text{R—OH} \rightarrow \text{R—O—C-1-sugar} + \text{NuDP} \qquad (11\text{-}62a)$$

The enzymes responsible are referred to as NuDP-sugar–acceptor glycosyl transferases. For the formation of simple glucosides, i.e., those in which glucose (or a glucose residue in a disaccharide) is linked to an alcohol, a phenol, or an amine, reactions that can be shown to occur readily with enzyme preparations from plants and invertebrates, the $\Delta G^{0\prime}$ is approximately -3500 cal/mole and Nu = uridine.

Very similar reactions have been shown to take place with preparations from animals and plant sources in which the donor is UDP-D-glucuronic acid. In other variants, UDP-D-galactose is used to galactosylate lipids to form galactolipids, such as the cerebrosides of animal nerves; dTDP-rhamnose forms rhamnolipids in bacteria, and UDP-glucose is the glucose donor for the glucosylation of hydroxymethylcytosine in bacteriophage DNA.

If the bond formed is an *O*-glycoside of a sugar, then reaction (11-62*b*) leads to the formation of a disaccharide. The most interesting example is provided by sucrose synthesis in green plants, which proceeds largely by the path

$$\rightarrow \text{fructose-6-}P \xrightarrow{\text{UDP-glucose}} \text{sucrose-6-}P \rightarrow \text{sucrose} \tag{11-62b}$$

The $\Delta G^{0\prime}$ for the condensation step is only ~ -1000 cal/mole in this instance, since sucrose has the unusual feature of having a link between the two anomeric carbons for which $\Delta G^{0\prime}$ (hydrolysis) $\simeq -6600$ cal/mole. The overall equilibrium is still favorable for sucrose formation, however, because of the additional increment provided by the hydrolysis in the second step.

Biosynthesis of Polysaccharides   In polysaccharide synthesis (see Table 11-3) the basic reaction is modified as follows:

$$\text{Polysaccharide primer} + \text{NuDP-sugar} \rightleftharpoons \text{polysaccharide primer-sugar} + \text{NuDP} \tag{11-62c}$$

$$\text{Polysaccharide primer-sugar} + \text{NuDP-sugar} \rightleftharpoons \text{primer-sugar-sugar} + \text{NuDP} \quad \text{etc.}$$

TABLE 11-3.   Biosynthesis of Di-, Oligo-, and Polysaccharides

Oligo- or polysaccharide formed	Source of enzyme system	Acceptor or repeating unit	Linkages	Monomeric nucleotide glycosyl donor
Sucrose (-*P*)	Plants	D-Fructose (-6-*P*)	$\alpha, 1 \rightarrow 2$	UDP-D-Glucose
Lactose (-*P*)	Mammals	D-Glucose (-1-*P*)	$\beta, 1 \rightarrow 4$	UDP-D-Galactose
α-1,4-Glucan (starch amylose)	Plants	D-Glucose	$\alpha, 1 \rightarrow 4$	ADP-D-Glucose
α-1,4-Glucan (glycogen amylose)	Mammalian liver	D-Glucose	$\alpha, 1 \rightarrow 4$	UDP-D-Glucose
β-1,4-Glucan (cellulose)	Mung beans, bacteria	D-Glucose	$\beta, 1 \rightarrow 4$	UDP-D-Glucose
β-1,4-Xylan	Plants	D-Xylose	$\beta, 1 \rightarrow 4$	UDP-D-Xylose
Chitin	*Neurospora crassa*	N-Acetyl-D-glucosamine	$\alpha, 1 \rightarrow 4$	UDP-N-Acetyl-D-glucosamine
Hyaluronic acid	Bacteria, animals (umbilicus, vitreous humor, etc.)	D-Glucuronic acid; N-acetylglucosamine	$\beta, 1 \rightarrow 3$ $\beta, 1 \rightarrow 4$	UDP-D-Glucuronic acid UDP-N-Acetyl-D-glucosamine
Chondroitin	Mammalian cornea	D-Glucuronic acid; N-acetyl-D-galactosamine	$\beta, 1 \rightarrow 3$ $\beta, 1 \rightarrow 4$	UDP-D-Glucuronic acid UDP-N-Acetyl-D-galactosamine
Chondroitin sulfates	Mammalian connective tissue	D-Glucuronic acid; N-acetyl-D-galactosamine-4-, or -6-sulfate	$\beta, 1 \rightarrow 3$ $\beta, 1 \rightarrow 4$	UDP derivatives
Heparin	Mammalian liver, lung, arterial walls	D-Glucuronic acid 2-sulfate; D-galactos-amine-N, C-6-disulfate	$\alpha, 1 \rightarrow 4$ $\alpha, 1 \rightarrow 4$	UDP derivatives

$\Delta G^{0\prime}$ of reaction (11-62*c*) is of the order of -3000 cal per residue added. The classic example of polysaccharide synthesis is the biosynthesis of glycogen amylose by UDP-glucose-glycogen glucosyl transferase (*glycogen synthetase*) discovered by Leloir only in 1957. As written, it is evident that the reaction provides only for chain lengthening; i.e., it requires a primer polyglucose (glycogen itself, amylose, amylopectin, or a glucose oligosaccharide larger than maltotetraose) as glucose acceptor, and it leads to a linear polymer, an α-1 $\rightarrow$ 4-glucan.

In plants, ADP-D-glucose, rather than the UDP derivative, appears to be the glucosyl donor for starch synthesis.

The branches in naturally occurring glycogen (α, $1 \rightarrow 6$ bonds, which occur about every 8 to 12 residues in the α, $1 \rightarrow 4$ chain) arise by action of a second enzyme, a *glycogen branching enzyme* or amylo $(1,4 \rightarrow 1,6)$ transglycosylase, which cleaves off small (di- or trimeric) fragments from $1 \rightarrow 4$ linkages and transfers them to the same (or a different) polyglucose chain, but now at $1 \rightarrow 6$ linkages:

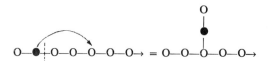

Numerous other examples of analogous polysaccharide syntheses are given in Table 11-3. If more than one type of monomeric unit participates (i.e., if the product is a hetero- rather than a homopolysaccharide), two potential pathways for its biosynthesis exist: one may envisage either a controlled alternation of incoming monomeric residues or a preliminary formation of di- or oligosaccharides still linked in the C-1 position to the nucleoside diphosphate, followed by polymerization of these more complex units.

REFERENCES

Ashwell, G.: Carbohydrate Metabolism, *Ann. Rev. Biochem.*, **33**: 101 (1964).

Atkinson, D. E.: Regulation of Enzyme Activity, *Ann. Rev. Biochem.*, **35**: 85 (1966).

Axelrod, B.: Glycolysis, in D. M. Greenberg (ed.), "Metabolic Pathways," vol. 1, p. 97, Academic Press, New York, 1960.

———: Other Pathways of Carbohydrate Metabolism, in D. M. Greenberg (ed.), "Metabolic Pathways," vol. 1, p. 205, Academic Press, New York, 1960.

Ginsburg, V.: Sugar Nucleotides and the Synthesis of Carbohydrates, *Advan. Enzymol.*, **26**: 35 (1964).

Gunsalus, I. C., and C. W. Shuster: Energy-yielding Metabolism in Bacteria, in I. C. Gunsalus and R. Y. Stanier (eds.), "The Bacteria," Academic Press, New York, vol. 2, p. 13, 1961.

Johnson, M. J.: Enzymic Equilibria and Thermodynamics, in P. D. Boyer, H. Lardy and K. Myrbäck, (eds.), "The Enzymes," 2d ed., vol. 3, p. 407, Academic Press, New York, 1960.

Kornberg, H. L.: The Coordination of Metabolic Routes, *Symp. Soc. Gen. Microbiol.*, **15**: 8 (1965).

———: Anaplerotic Sequences and Their Role in Metabolism, in P. N. Campbell, and G. D. Greville (eds.), "Essays in Biochemistry," vol. 2, Academic Press, New York, 1966.

Krebs, E. G., and E. H. Fischer: Molecular Properties and Transformations of Glycogen Phosphorylase in Animal Tissue, *Advan. Enzymol.*, **24**: 263 (1962).

Krebs, H. A., and H. L. Kornberg: "Energy Transformations in Living Matter," Springer, Berlin, 1957.

Leloir, L. F.: Nucleoside Diphosphate Sugars and Saccharide Synthesis, *Biochem. J.*, **91**: 1 (1964).

McGilvery, R. W., and B. M. Pogell: "Fructose-1,6-diphosphatase and Its Role in Gluconeogenesis," American Institute of Biological Sciences, Washington, 1964.

Northcote, D. H.: Polysaccharides, *Ann. Rev. Biochem.*, **33**: 51 (1964).

Sharon, N.: Polysaccharides, *Ann. Rev. Biochem.*, **35**: 485 (1966).

Wood, H. G., and R. L. Stjernholm: Assimilation of Carbon Dioxide by Heterotrophic Organisms, in I. C. Gunsalus and R. Y. Stanier (eds.), "The Bacteria," vol. 3, p. 41, Academic Press, New York, 1962.

——— and M. F. Utter: The Role of CO_2 Fixation in Metabolism, *Essays in Biochem.*, **1**: 1 (1965).

Wood, W. A.: Carbohydrate Metabolism, *Ann. Rev. Biochem.*, **35**: 521 (1966).

12 | Photosynthesis

Ultimately, all life on earth (the *biosphere*) depends directly on the assimilation of carbon dioxide into organic compounds, the energy for this highly endergonic process being provided by light generated in the sun. The reactions responsible for this complex conversion of photonic into chemical energy are collectively known as *photosynthesis* and the organisms responsible as *photosynthetic organisms*. Among them are, of course, plants — whether higher plants, ferns, mosses, diatoms, or algae (green, blue-green, red, or brown) — and certain microorganisms: protozoa, such as *Euglena*; and a number of different bacteria such as the purple sulfur bacteria (*Thiorhodaceae*), the purple nonsulfur bacteria (*Athiorhodaceae*), and the green sulfur bacteria (*Chlorobacteriaceae*). Photosynthesis provides them all with the organic materials required for their growth and maintenance, and their cells, in turn, or else their products in life or death, yield the foodstuffs required for all other members of the biosphere.

But the significance of photosynthesis transcends even the limits just described.

1. Organisms, in order to live, have to consume energy by means of essentially oxidative, degradative, "catabolic" processes. These demand an oxidizing environment and lead ultimately to the conversion of all carbon compounds to their most oxidized form, i.e., carbon dioxide. Photosynthesis restores the balance, both by reducing CO_2 to organic compounds, and by generating oxygen.

2. Even though all cells use some of the "catabolic" energy, in coupled reactions, to drive endergonic, synthetic, "anabolic" reactions and store it in the complex products formed, some energy is still continuously dissipated as heat — by inefficient coupling between biochemical reactions, during transduction to other forms, such as mechanical or electrical energy, etc. — and thus the

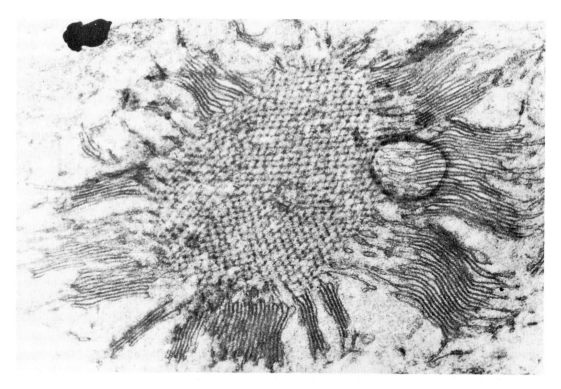

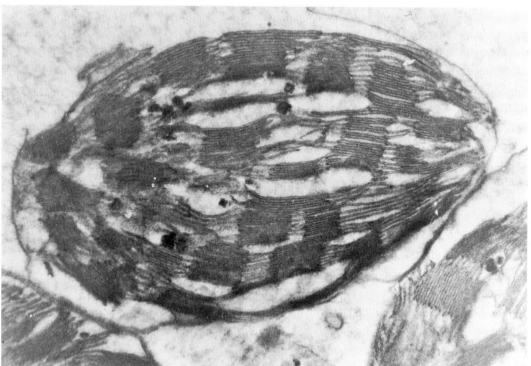

FIGURE 12-1.   The Structure of the Chloroplast. Electron micrographs: (*top*) prolamellar, paracrystalline body in a proplastid (chloroplast precursor) of *Chlorophytum*, exposed to light, showing the origin of the lamellae (magnification 50,000 : 1); (*bottom*) fully developed chloroplast in leaf of *Elodea canadenis* (magnification 24,000 : 1).—*Courtesy Professor K. Mühlethaler, Zurich.*

entropy of the biosphere increases. This is required by the second law of thermo-dynamics of any closed system, and thus, inexorably, life on earth would have to run out were it not for the continuous supply of radiant energy from outside and its utilization by photosynthesis.

3. It is not impossible that the first precursors of living things on earth, the so-called protobionts, found themselves on a planet devoid of O_2 in its atmosphere. Only the evolution of organisms capable of generating oxygen may have created the proper environment for all subsequent forms of life to develop. The early photosynthetic organisms were almost certainly procaryotic cells performing some rudimentary form of present-day bacterial photosynthesis as long as some 3 billion years ago. Later some of them evolved into ancestral forms of our blue-green algae (1 to 2 billion years ago) and started the gradual build up of oxygen in the atmosphere, eventually permitting the evolution of eucaryotic organisms at the beginning of the Cambrian era, some 600 million years ago.

THE LOCALE FOR PHOTOSYNTHESIS

In plants, photosynthesis takes place within highly specialized organelles called *plastids*. If the cells are broken and fractions of purified plastids isolated, the latter, suitably supplemented by soluble substrates and cofactors, carry out all the reactions of photosynthesis. In green plants, including green unicellular organisms, such as algae (e.g., *Chlorella, Scenedesmus*) and *Euglena*, the plastids contain chlorophyll and are referred to as *chloroplasts*. The number, shape, and size of these chloroplasts vary widely among organisms. *Chlorella* contains but one cup-shaped plastid; most other algae and the cells of green tissues of higher plants contain many chloroplasts.

When plastids are examined in thin section under the electron microscope, a wealth of fine structure is revealed (see Fig. 12-1). The most characteristic features perhaps are the many small, dark, membranous bodies (called *grana*) pervaded by a distinct lamellar structure. In *Euglena*, this dark lamellar structure fills the whole chloroplast, which can thus be regarded as a single granum; in most other cells each chloroplast contains 10 to 100 grana. The photosynthetic pigments of the cell are localized preponderantly in and around the lamellae. When the latter are isolated and purified from ruptured plastids, they are found to be also exceedingly rich in phospholipids and lipoproteins and to be able to catalyze some of the most characteristic reactions of photosynthesis: the *photolysis of water* in the presence of an added oxidant (the *Hill reaction* — see below) and the reactions responsible for electron transport.

If supplemented with a minimal complement of soluble enzymes (obtained from the lumen of the plastid) and cofactors, they also catalyze the reduction of pyridine nucleotides concomitant with the generation of ATP (photophosphorylation); when a more complete collection of soluble chloroplast enzymes is provided in addition, restoration of photosynthesis can be demonstrated.

In purified preparations of lamellar membranes from spinach chloroplasts, Park and his collaborators have identified repeating subunits, which may be arranged in a variety of arrays (see Fig. 12-2). The individual subunit, which they believe to be the morphological entity corresponding to the physiological unit of photosynthesis is estimated to be an oblate sphere 155 to 185 A in diameter and 100 A thick; its molecular weight is 2×10^6, and it contains: 230 *chlorophyll molecules* (160 *a*: 70 *b*); 48 *carotenoids*; 46 *quinones*; 116 *phospholipids*; 500 *galactosylglycerides*; 48 *sulfolipids*; sterols; and other lipids. Thus the molecular weight of total lipids is about 10^6 and that of proteins about 10^6 also; they also contain 1 *cytochrome* b_6, 1 *cytochrome f*, 10 *nonheme iron*, 2 *manganese*, and 2 *copper* ions.

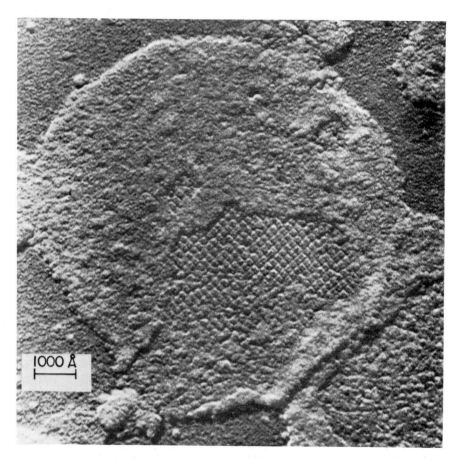

FIGURE 12-2.   Lamellae of Spinach Chloroplasts Showing Arrays of Quantasomes. The picture is that of a chromium-shadowed chloroplast lamella at a magnification of 71,000 : 1. Note the crystalline array of structural units (quantasomes) with dimensions $185 \times 155 \times 100A$. Note differences and similarities to the array shown in Fig. 12-1.—*Roderick B. Park and John Biggins, Science,* **144***: 1009–1011 (1964).*

In bacteria and blue-green algae the structures responsible for photosynthesis appear to be somewhat simpler. One can obtain roughly spherical, highly colored particles (called *chromatophores*) with a diameter of ~ 300 A (particle weight of $\sim 10^7$) containing bacteriochlorophyll, other pigments (carotenoids), phospholipid, and all the enzymes responsible for bacterial photosynthesis.

THE OVERALL
STOICHIOMETRY OF
PHOTOSYNTHESIS

Classically, photosynthesis by green plants has been formulated as

$$CO_2 + H_2O + n\ hv \xrightarrow[\text{enzymes, etc.}]{\text{chlorophyll}} \{CH_2O\} + O_2 \qquad (12\text{-}1a)$$

or

$$6CO_2 + 6H_2O + 6n\ h\nu \xrightarrow[\text{enzymes, etc.}]{\text{chlorophyll}} C_6H_{12}O_6 + 6O_2 \qquad (12\text{-}1b)$$

where $\{CH_2O\}$ signifies an organic compound at the oxidation level of carbohydrate and $C_6H_{12}O_6$ a hexose. Bacterial photosynthesis, which does not produce O_2, has been shown by Kluyver and van Niel to conform in general to the equation

$$CO_2 + 2H_2D + n\ h\nu \xrightarrow[\text{enzymes, etc.}]{\text{bacteriochlorophyll}} \{CH_2O\} + H_2O + 2D \qquad (12\text{-}2)$$

where H_2D is an oxidizable hydrogen donor, such as H_2S, thiosulfate, or selenium compounds (sulfur bacteria), hydrogen gas, or simple organic compounds, such as isopropanol, lactic acid or malic acid, fatty acids, etc. (various other genera of bacteria). Van Niel made the brilliant suggestion that fundamentally there was no difference between reaction (12-2) and reaction (12-1a), provided the latter was written as

$$CO_2 + 2H_2O* + n\ h\nu \xrightarrow[\text{enzymes, etc.}]{\text{chlorophyll}} \{CH_2O\} + H_2O + O_2* \qquad (12\text{-}3)$$

i.e., that water (on the left side) functions as the oxidizable hydrogen donor; being in this case oxidized to molecular O_2 — the $2D$ of Eq. (12-2) — while the water on the right side of both equations constitutes one of the products of CO_2 reduction.[1] This postulate was later proved correct by the use of reactants labeled with O^{18}: as indicated in the equation, all the molecular oxygen evolved has its origin in the oxygen atoms of the H_2O, and the two oxygen atoms in CO_2 become equipartitioned between the product carbohydrate and the water of the medium.

Van Niel also proposed that the primary reaction of photosynthesis in all organisms was the same: a photolysis of water giving rise to the simultaneous generation of *oxidizing* power YOH, and *reducing* power XH:

$$4H_2O + 4X + 4Y + n\ h\nu \xrightarrow[\text{accessory systems}]{\text{chlorophyll}} 4XH + 4YOH \qquad (12\text{-}4)$$

In green plants, four molecules of YOH react to generate O_2 and the product H_2O — Eq. 12-5 — and in bacteria we have the analogous reaction with H_2D — Eq. (12-6):

$$4YOH + 2H_2O \xrightarrow{\text{enzymes}} 4H_2O + 4Y + O_2 \qquad (12\text{-}5)$$

$$4YOH + 2H_2D \xrightarrow{\text{enzymes}} 4H_2O + 4Y + 2D \qquad (12\text{-}6)$$

In all cells the photosynthetic reductant, on the other hand, is used for the conversion of CO_2 to carbohydrate:

$$4XH + CO_2 \xrightarrow{\text{enzymes, etc.}} \{CH_2O\} + 2H_2O + 4X \qquad (12\text{-}7)$$

Summing over reactions (12-4), (12-5), and (12-7) yields Eq. (12-3), the overall

---

[1] An interesting physiological correlate of this postulate of van Niel's and a link between bacterial and green-plant photosynthesis is provided by certain green algae, which can be adapted to fix CO_2 anaerobically with hydrogen as the reductant, according to the reaction

$$CO_2 + 2H_2 + n\ h\nu \rightarrow \{CH_2O\} + H_2O \qquad (12\text{-}1c)$$

yet are still capable of aerobic CO_2 fixation by classic photosynthesis — reaction (12-1a).

stoichiometric equation for green-plant photosynthesis, and Eqs. (12-4), (12-6), and (12-7) generate Eq. (12-2), the corresponding one for bacterial photosynthesis.

This formulation has several important consequences: it suggests immediately that it should be possible to dissociate (1) the steps directly linked to the photochemistry of the photosynthetic pigments from a number of dark reactions and (2) those concerned with the enzyme-catalyzed reduction of CO_2 (plants and bacteria) from those of oxygen evolution (plants) — or substrate oxidation (bacteria). Indeed, washed chloroplast preparations have long been known to catalyze a light-dependent oxygen evolution in the presence of a large variety of different electron acceptors (cytochromes, quinones, indophenol dyes, ferricyanide, NAD^+, etc.):

$$4A + 2H_2O + n\, h\nu \xrightarrow{\text{chloroplasts}} 4AH + O_2 \tag{12-8}$$

This can be visualized as being the sum of Eqs. (12-4), (12-5), and Eq. (12-9):

$$XH + A \rightarrow X + AH \tag{12-9}$$

In green plants, where photooxidation and photoreduction are catalyzed by two different systems the reactions just written can be modified to accommodate the altered situation: We write Eqs. (12-10) plus (12-11) instead of reaction (12-4); Eq. (12-12) instead of reaction (12-5); Eq. (12-13) instead of reaction (12-6); and Eq. (12-14) instead of reaction (12-7):

$$4X + 4Y + n\, h\nu \xrightarrow{\text{system I}} 4X_{\text{red}}^- + 4Y_{\text{ox}}^+ \qquad \begin{array}{l}\text{generates reducing power}\\ \text{plus a weak oxidant } (Y_{\text{ox}}^+)\end{array} \tag{12-10}$$

$$4X' + 4Y' + n\, h\nu \xrightarrow{\text{system II}} 4X_{\text{red}}'^- + 4Y_{\text{ox}}'^+ \qquad \begin{array}{l}\text{generates oxidizing power}\\ \text{plus a weak reductant } (X_{\text{red}}'^-)\end{array} \tag{12-11}$$

$$4Y_{\text{ox}}'^+ + 2H_2O \rightarrow O_2 + 4Y' + 4H^+ \qquad \left\{\begin{array}{l}\text{plants} \\ \\ \text{oxidation of donor} \\ \\ \text{bacteria}\end{array}\right. \tag{12-12}$$

$$4Y_{\text{ox}}^+ + 2H_2D \rightarrow 2D + 4Y + 4H^+ \tag{12-13}$$

$$4X_{\text{red}}^- + CO_2 + 4H^+ \xrightarrow{\text{ATP}}$$

$$\{HCHO\} + 2H_2O + 4X \qquad \text{carbon assimilation} \tag{12-14}$$

$$4Y_{\text{ox}}^+ + 4X_{\text{red}}'^- \xrightarrow[\text{electron transfer system}]{\text{ADP P}_i \text{ ATP}} 4Y + 4X' \qquad \begin{array}{l}\text{combination of weak species}\\ \text{generates metabolic energy}\end{array} \tag{12-15}$$

The only new reaction is Eq. (12-15), which regenerates the two components not participating in either the reduction of CO_2 or the oxidation of H_2O (or H_2D). It is this reaction which generates the third prerequisite (besides reducing and oxidizing power) for successful photosynthetic assimilation: available biochemical energy in the form of ATP (*photosynthetic phosphorylation*—see below). Green plant photosynthesis exhibits the correct stoichiometry if we add reactions (12-10), (12-11), (12-12), and (12-14)—for photosynthetic bacteria, system II drops out and we are left with the sums of reactions (12-10), (12-13), and (12-14). One important difference between schemes of this type and van Niel's is that the splitting of water is now no longer a prerequisite, but rather a consequence, of the photochemical generation of oxidizing and reducing power.

THE PRINCIPAL
PHOTOSYNTHETIC
PIGMENTS

The most important photosynthetic pigment in all plants is chlorophyll *a* (Chl *a*); in bacteria it is bacteriochlorophyll (B Chl). The photosynthetic machinery of all these cells contains, in addition, certain pigments that used to be called "auxiliary" or "accessory"; it is now evident that these components fulfill a function as vital as that of ordinary chlorophyll *a*. Among them is a special form of Chl *a* absorbing at a shorter wavelength, in addition to chlorophyll *b*, in all green plants including algae; and also the other pigments shown in Table 12-1, especially the *carotenoids* and the *phycobilins* (phycocyanin and phycoerythrin). The structures of some of these are indicated in Fig. 12-3.

The function of the photosynthetic pigments is to harvest radiant energy and

A. The chlorophylls

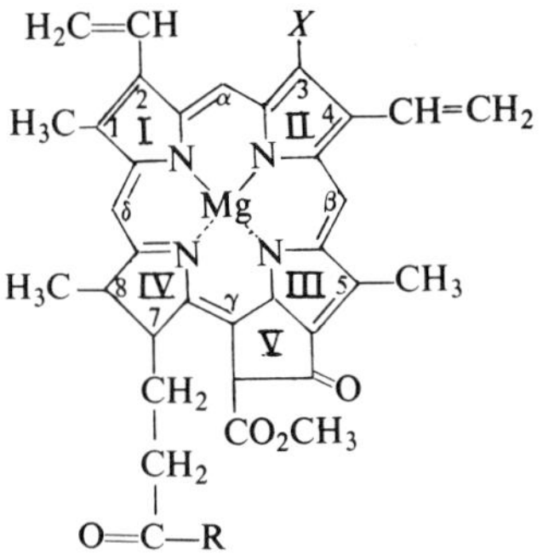

When $X =$ —CH_3 : chlorophyll *a* (Chl *a*)
$X =$ —CHO : chlorophyll *b* (Chl *b*)

R=phytyl ($C_{20}H_{39}O$—)

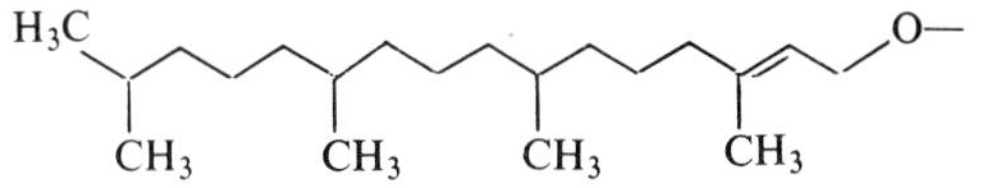

Note the chlorin (reduced porphin in ring IV) tetrapyrrole ring system IV, plus the fused cyclopentanone ring V. The complete parent ring system I-V is called phaeoporphyrin. In bacteriochlorophyll, ring II is reduced as well, i.e., positions 3 and 4 are —CH.

B. Examples of accessory pigments

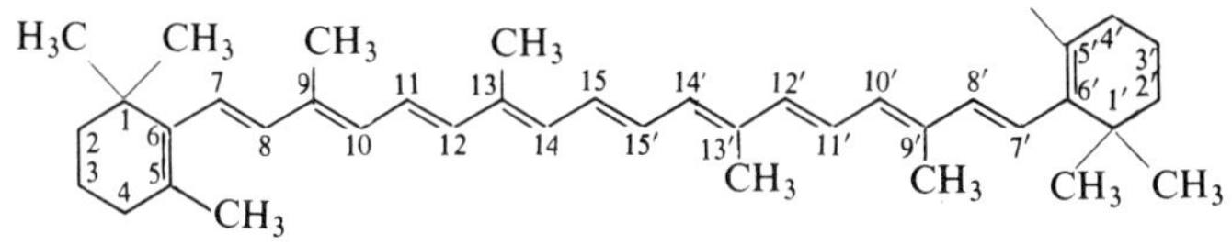

β-Carotene (all *trans*)
a *carotenoid*

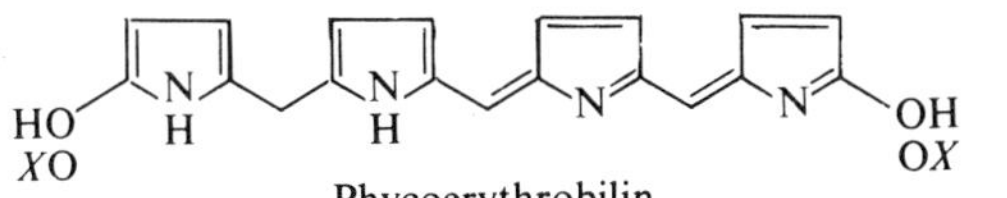

Phycoerythrobilin
a *phycobilin*

This open-chain tetrapyrrole is covalently linked, probably through the —OH group(s) to a protein (*X*). The resulting complex is called *phycoerythrin*.

FIGURE 12-3.   The Structure of Photosynthetic Pigments.

to transfer it to the photochemical reaction center proper, in a highly efficient manner. For this purpose they occur, not singly in dilute solution, but in the form of multimolecular (several hundred) organized packets, or arrays. In such arrays, absorption of a quantum of light by all members is equally effective.

TABLE 12-1.   Important Photosynthetic Pigments

Name of pigments (major absorption bands, photochemically active in vivo are shown; wavelength given in millimicrons)

Organism(s)	Principal chlorophyll	Accessory chlorophyll	Other accessory pigments
Multicellular green plants	Chl a: 683 (680–685) Chl a: 695 (695–700, 660*)	Chl b: 560, 480 Chl a: 670 (670–673)	Carotenoids (481) Mainly β-carotene
Green algae	Similar to above	Similar to above	Similar to above
Brown algae	Chl a	Chl c	β-Carotene
Diatoms, flagellates	Chl a	Chl c: 620, 470	β-Carotene
Red algae	Chl a	Chl d: (680*)	β-Carotene; phycoerythrin (570, 550, 495) plus some phycocyanin (625)
Purple bacteria (both sulfur and nonsulfur)	B Chl (800, 850, 870–890†, 773*)		Different carotenoids (among them rhodopsin, lycopene, spirilloxanthin, etc.)
Green sulfur bacteria	Chlorobium Chl 660 (725, 650*) Plus chlorobium Chl 650 (747, 660*) Plus traces of B Chl (810, 770*)		Similar to above

*In ether; amorphous monolayers of Chl a absorb at 675 mμ, crystalline ones at 735 mμ.
†Depending on species (890 mμ in *Rhodospirillum rubrum* and *Chromatium*; 870 mμ in *Rhodopseudomonas spheroides*).

The energy so absorbed is then very rapidly delocalized ($\tau \leq 10^{-10}$ sec) and is capable of migrating to any component of the aggregate, including one of its minor constituents. It is probably one of the latter that forms part of the reaction center.

EVIDENCE FOR TWO LIGHT REACTIONS   There is now abundant evidence that photosynthesis in plants requires the collaboration of two distinct systems. Some of it runs briefly as follows:

1. A qualitative comparison of action and absorption spectra in vivo had indicated that light absorbed, not only by the principal, but also by the accessory pigments was effective in photosynthesis as measured by O_2 evolution or CO_2 absorption. But when Emerson and Lewis compared the efficiency of light of different wavelengths in supporting photosynthesis quantitatively (i.e., determined the relative *quantum efficiency*), they observed that, although the efficiency was as great at the absorption maximum of the accessory pigments as that of chlorophyll a at 675 mμ, there was a remarkable decrease at somewhat longer wavelengths ($\sim$700 mμ) (the "red drop"), where there is still strong light absorption by chlorophyll.

2. Haxo and Blinks extended studies of quantum efficiency by improved techniques to a large number of algae. Oxygen evolution in red algae was found to be driven only relatively ineffectively at all wavelengths greater than 600 to 675 mμ; thus there was a red drop already at the very absorption peak of chlorophyll a. Conversely, in the same process light absorbed by accessory

pigments was two to three times as effective as that absorbed by chlorophyll *a*.

3. The low quantum yield of far-red light (e.g., $\lambda > 680$ mμ) is greatly increased by exposure of the system to other wavelengths. This "enhancement effect" is observed whether the two types of light are absorbed concurrently or even sequentially with flashes separated by several seconds of darkness.

4. The Hill reaction — Eq. (12-8) — also exhibits an enhancement phenomenon.

5. The appearance or disappearance of certain short-lived, spectrophoto-metrically identifiable intermediates (optical transients) has been observed on first turning the light on (or off). Among such transients is one photobleached (probably oxidized) at 700 mμ (*P700*) and a cytochrome (cytochrome *f*) that becomes oxidized simultaneously or shortly thereafter. This sequence is brought about by absorption in the far-red region (> 680 mμ). The reduction of oxidized P700 can be accelerated and the cytochrome can then be reduced in turn by superposition of light absorbed in the blue (~ 652 mμ).

6. Photophosphorylation (see below) can occur with far-red light alone (700 to 710 mμ). Only O_2 evolution, and not photophosphorylation or $NADP^+$ reduction, requires Mn^{+2} and is inhibited by the herbicide DCMU.

7. Mutants lacking either system I or system II have been isolated from micro-organisms in which the wild type is capable of carrying out ordinary photo-synthesis by reaction (12-1). Mutants with a defunct system II are incapable of O_2 evolution but are able to assimilate CO_2 in the presence of an oxidizable substrate DH_2, thus showing a bacterial pattern.

THE TWO REACTIONS OF PHOTOSYNTHESIS

The scheme outlined in Fig. 12-4 envisages the cooperative interaction of two distinct photochemically active systems acting in series.

One unit of *system I* consists of some 300 to 400 molecules of nonfluorescent Chl *a* with its main absorption in the far red (see Table 12-1). Associated with it is one molecule of a specialized photooxidizable pigment *P700* ($\lambda_{max} = 700$ to 705 mμ; $E_0' \simeq 0.430$ volt; probably a chlorophyll molecule in an unusual environment, perhaps associated with cytochrome *f*) directly concerned with the primary photochemical reaction. The system in green plants also contains approximately 1 molecule of *cytochrome f* per center — a cytochrome *c*-like cytochrome (see page 360) with a $\lambda_{max} = 556.3$ mμ; $E_0' = 0.365$ volt; other photosynthetic plants and bacteria contain analogous high potential cyto-chromes. In addition, and perhaps less tightly coupled, the unit also contains *ferredoxin* (see page 302) and *cytochrome b_6* — an autooxidizable cytochrome (see page 360) found in green plants, with a $\lambda_{max} = 563$ mμ and a $E_0' = -0.06$ volt — both also in concentrations approximately equal to those of cytochrome *f*; approximately 10 molecules of *plastocyanin* — a copper-protein (2 Cu per molecule of M = 20,000) — as well as equally large (or larger) quantities of naphtho- and benzoquinones — vitamin K and various plastoquinones (see page 352), respectively — NADP (see page 212), and flavins (see page 215). Carotenoids also form part of system I, and light energy absorbed by them is transferred efficiently to its chlorophyll. The principal function of system I is the simultaneous generation of reducing power and of a weak oxidant, i.e., reaction (12-10). System I, operating by itself, in the presence of an oxidizable donor DH_2, is responsible for photoreductions, such as that carried out by H_2-adapted algae (see Eq. [12-1c]).

System II is the "accessory pigment system". It contains approximately 100 molecules of *Chl a 670*, a fluorescent form of chlorophyll *a*, absorbing at shorter wavelength than the Chl *a* of system I; it also contains chlorophyll *b*, and the other accessory pigments (chlorophylls *c* and *d* as well as the phycobilin pigments phycoerythrin and phycocyanin, depending on the organism). Its function is the generation of oxidizing power as a prerequisite for the photoevolution of

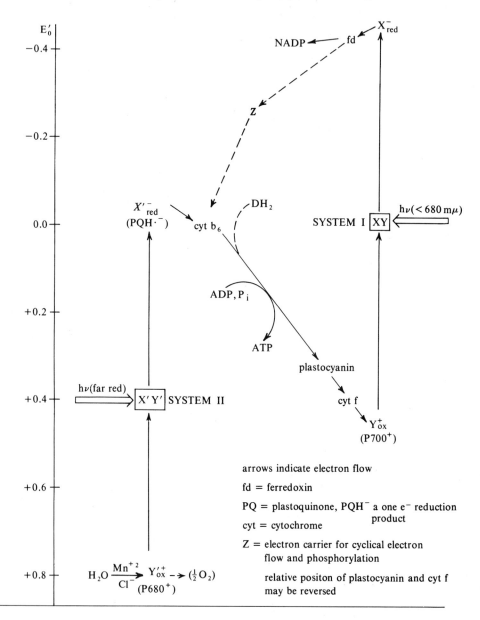

FIGURE 12-4.   The Series Formulation of Photosynthesis. Scheme shown for green plants. In bacteria System II is absent and an oxidizable substrate takes the place of X'_{red}. The detailed electron carriers are different also, ubiquinones take the place of plastoquinones, plastocyanin is absent, and other cytochromes of the *b* and *c* type take the place of b_6 and *f* respectively.

oxygen — reactions (12-11) and (12-12). The reaction(s) involved requires Mn^{+2} and Cl^- and is specifically inhibited by the herbicide 3-(3,4-dichlorophenyl)-1, 1-dimethyl urea (DCMU) at exceedingly low concentration ($\sim 10^{-7}$ M). A correlated function of system II is the formation of a weak reductant (X'^-_{red}), probably reduced plasto- or some other quinone (see page 352), capable of regenerating Y from (Y^+_{ox}) produced by system I. System II operating by itself is responsible for the Hill reaction, reaction (12-8).

The photoevolution of oxygen is a peculiarity of photosynthesis in green plants: presently available evidence suggests the presence of only one kind of photosynthetic unit (system I) in bacteria. It contains one molecule of a specialized photooxidizable pigment, *P890* (or *P870*, depending on species) — in all likelihood a form of B Chl in a special environment, in complete analogy to the situation in plants, per 30 to 50 molecules of ordinary B Chl. One molecule of *cytochrome* c_2 — a specialized cytochrome of the *c* type akin to cytochrome *f* of plants; $\lambda_{max} = 551$ to 553 mμ; $E'_0 = 0.29$ to 0.33 volt — per molecule of P890 may also form part of the reaction center. In addition the system contains other electron carriers. Functional roles have so far been assigned to ferredoxin, NAD, the benzoquinone ubiquinone, and to cytochromes of the *b* type.

1. The reaction(s) catalyzed by system I utilizes Chl *a* as a photosensitizer. As a consequence of the absorption of a quantum of far-red light by this pigment, there ensues the formation of a (hypothetical) reducing entity X^-_{red} and of an oxidizing one Y^+_{ox}. The electron, generated in this photochemical event and first localized in the short-lived intermediate X^-_{red} (with a potential $E'_0 \leq -450$ mv), is transferred first to the carrier ferredoxin (Fd) and thence (in pairs) to a pyridine nucleotide, giving rise to NADH in bacteria and NADPH in plants (see below). These compounds provide the source of stable metabolic reducing power required for CO_2 fixation. It can also be shunted from the reduced carriers Fd_{red} or NAD(P)H to ETS, the electron transfer chain (heavy diagonal arrows in Fig. 12-4), ultimately ending up by reducing Y^+_{ox} back to Y in a cyclical process.

2. The oxidizing equivalent or hole can be visualized as temporarily residing in the species Y^+_{ox} with a potential $E'_0 \simeq 400$ to 500 mv (probably oxidized P700, or P870 in bacteria).

a. In bacterial photosynthesis, it becomes reduced (thereby regenerating Y) by means of an externally added, obligatory photoreductant DH_2, which is thereby oxidized to D — Eq. (12-13). This oxidation, using a series of intermediary physiological redox carriers (diagonal line) probably generates the bulk of the ATP produced.

b. In green plants, its reduction is brought about ultimately by X'^-_{red}, the short-lived intermediate reductant generated by system II (see below). This process requires the ETS — a number of enzymes, and intermediary electron carriers. The bulk of the ATP required for carbon assimilation by green plants is probably generated in this reaction — Eq. (12-15). An essential part or parts of the requisite electron transport sequence (at the low potential side) may be absent in photosynthetic bacteria.

3. The reactions catalyzed by system II utilize the accessory pigment(s) as photosensitizer(s). The absorption of a quantum of light by these entities leads to the generation of a reductant X'^-_{red} coupled to that of an oxidant Y'^+_{ox}.

This is in complete analogy to the situation in system I, but with the important difference that their potential level is considerably higher than that of the entities comprising system I: $Y_{ox}^{'+}$ at $E_0' \geq 840$ mv and $X_{red}^{'-} \simeq 0.0$ mv.

a. The exclusive function of $Y_{ox}^{'+}$ is the oxidation of water (or hydroxyl ions) to molecular oxygen; it thus drives the O_2-generating portion of photosynthesis.

b. The function of $X_{red}^{'-}$ is the provision of reducing equivalents for the regeneration of the Y of system I by means of the electron transport chain, i.e., item 2*b* above.

THE GENERATION
OF REDUCING
POWER

One of the fundamental requirements of photosynthetic carbon assimilation is the provision of a stable biochemical reducing agent. In more formal terms, it has been demonstrated that carbon dioxide fixation probably proceeds by the following stoichiometry:

$$6 \text{ Ribulose-1,5-di}P + 6CO_2 + 18ATP + 12NADPH \rightarrow$$

$$6 \text{ ribulose-1,5-di}P + \text{hexose-}P + 18ADP + 17P_i + 12NADP^+ \qquad (12\text{-}16)$$

Thus the carbon cycle (see page 305), a series of dark reactions, requires for its operation NADPH or NADH (in bacteria) plus ATP, both generated by reaction(s) driven by light. NADPH had been shown previously to be formed in a Hill reaction with chloroplasts:

$$NADP^+ + n'h\nu + H_2O \rightarrow NADPH + \tfrac{1}{2}O_2 + H^+ \qquad (12\text{-}17a)$$

In 1958, Arnon and his collaborators were able to demonstrate that this reaction could lead to attendant phosphorylation of ADP:

$$NADP^+ + n'h\nu + H_2O + ADP + P_i \rightarrow NADPH + \tfrac{1}{2}O_2 + ATP \qquad (12\text{-}17b)$$

Since then, the evidence has become ever more compelling that reduced pyridine nucleotides are generated in a reaction linked to the photochemically active system I and that they constitute the requisite source of stable reducing power generated in stoichiometric amounts in all cells capable of photosynthesis.

More recently, an additional carrier has been identified as intervening between X_{red}^- and pyridine nucleotide. This is a relatively small, iron-containing protein called ferredoxin (Fd). It originally became implicated in another important biosynthetic reaction sequence, the conversion of atmospheric nitrogen to NH_3 by nitrogen-fixing bacteria (p. 394); similar pigments have been shown to be present in a variety of anaerobic and photosynthetic bacteria, of blue-green and green algae and of plant cells. Bacterial Fd is a small protein with a molecular weight of approximately 5.5×10^3, with a very low redox potential ($E_0' \simeq -0.425$ volt). It has a characteristic absorption spectrum [$\lambda_{max} = 390$ mμ]; this peak is bleached on chemical or photochemical reduction. Fd is reported to contain between 3 and 8 iron atoms per molecule depending on species (8 in *Clostridia*, 3 in *Chromatium*), probably linked to an equal number of cysteine residues in the protein. It also contains an equal number of acid-labile sulfur atoms (either inorganic sulfide or very labile organic residues giving rise to H_2S on acidification). Its amino acid composition is unusual, since it lacks histidine, methionine, and tryptophan. Although the iron can assume both a ferrous and a ferric oxidation state, it is not certain whether the redox properties of the protein (it is known to be a one-electron redox carrier) are to be ascribed to this valency change. Fd became implicated in the reactions of system I in plants when a soluble factor required for the photoreduction of NADP by chloroplasts and bacterial Fd were shown to be interchangeable and the bleaching and reduction of the latter could be brought about by chloroplasts in a light-induced reaction. Spinach Fd differs in several respects from its bacterial counterparts; its molecular weight is twice as great ($\sim 13,000$), it contains only two Fe- and two acid-labile sulfur residues per molecule, and its absorption spectrum is quite different. It does have an equally low E_0', however.

The ferredoxin-linked reduction of NAD(P) can be formulated as follows:

$$2X_{red}^- + 2Fd_{ox} \rightleftharpoons 2X + 2Fd_{red} \tag{12-18a}$$

where Fd_{red} contains one more electron than does $Fd_{ox,}$ and

$$H^+ + 2Fd_{red} + NAD(P)^+ \xrightarrow[\text{[Fd-NAD(P) reductase]}]{\text{transhydrogenase}} 2Fd_{ox} + NAD(P)H \tag{12-18b}$$

In bacteria and hydrogen-adapted algae, H^+ itself, in the presence of the enzyme hydrogenase, can function as an electron acceptor, leading to the formation of molecular hydrogen — reaction (12-18c).

$$2H^+ + 2Fd_{red} \xrightarrow[\text{hydrogenase}]{\text{transhydrogenase plus}} H_2 + 2Fd_{ox} \tag{12-18c}$$

PHOTOSYNTHETIC PHOSPHORYLATION (PHOTOPHOSPHORYLATION)

That light energy absorbed by a photosynthetic system could lead to the esterification of inorganic phosphate into ATP was first demonstrated by Frenkel with bacterial chromatophore fragments. Arnon and his collaborators were able to carry out the same reaction with chloroplasts, and since then the occurrence of phosphorylation during electron transport in photosynthesis (or *photophosphorylation*) has been documented at least as extensively as that of its older analogue: phosphorylation during electron transport in biological oxidation (or *oxidative phosphorylation*; see Chap. 15). The most important process that is linked to the trapping of biochemical energy in ATP is the one that — with the intervention of the ETS (quinones, cytochromes, etc.) — links the reduction of the photochemically generated oxidant of system I (Y_{ox}^+ in our formulation) to the oxidation of a reductant: X'^-_{red} generated by system II in green plants, or the external reductant DH_2 in bacteria — i.e., reaction (12-15). The overall reaction for phosphorylative NADPH formation is

$$NADP^+ + n'ADP + n'P_i + n\ hv \xrightarrow[\text{+ETS +phosph.}]{\text{complete system}}$$
$$NADPH + n'ATP + O_2 + (n'-2)H_2O \tag{12-19}$$

Under anaerobic conditions, or with system II knocked out (mutants) or inhibited (by DCMU), the addition of a redox carrier X, such as Fd, a quinone, etc. (see Fig. 12-4) can link the reductant species generated in the light reaction — X_{red}^-, Fd_{red}, or NAD(P)H — to the electron transport system. Now we observe reaction (12-20a):

$$X_{red}^- + Y_{ox}^+ + n'ADP + n'P_i \xrightarrow{\text{electron transport carriers}} X + Y + n'ATP \tag{12-20a}$$

Then by linking reaction (12-20a) to reaction (12-10) — the formation of X_{red}^- + Y_{ox}^+ — we obtain Eq. (12-20b);

$$n'ADP + n'P_i + n\ hv \xrightarrow[\text{electron transport carriers, enzymes, etc.}]{\text{system I}} n'ATP \qquad (12\text{-}20b)$$

This is the expression for *cyclic photophosphorylation*, in which the absorption of radiant energy generates only ATP and neither a reductant nor an oxidant is produced.

Current indications are that the ratio $2e^-$ transferred/NADPH/ATP produced equals unity; i.e., $n' = n/2$. Since CO_2 fixation (Eq. 12-16) requires 1.5 ATP/NADPH/CO_2 fixed, stoichiometric photophosphorylation must be complemented by an increment of the cyclical type.

THE NATURE OF THE REACTION CENTERS   The reaction center, we recall, consists of some 300 Chl a molecules per molecule of P700 in the case of system I in plants and of some 50 B Chl molecules per molecule of P870 (or 890) in photosynthetic bacteria. In addition a high potential cytochrome of the c type (cytochrome f in plants) and a low potential quinone in amounts equivalent to those of the primary reactant may also be directly implicated and may correspond to the Y and X of Fig. 12-4, respectively.

The most likely sequence of events would appear to be

$$X[Chl_n \cdot Chl]\ cyt\ (Fe^{+2}) \xrightarrow{hv} \{X[Chl_n^* \cdot Chl]\ cyt\ (Fe^{+2}) \rightarrow$$
$$\{X_{red}^-[Chl_n \cdot Chl^+]\ cyt\ (Fe^{+2})\} \rightarrow X_{red}^-[Chl_n \cdot Chl]\ cyt\ (Fe^{+3}) \quad (12\text{-}21)$$

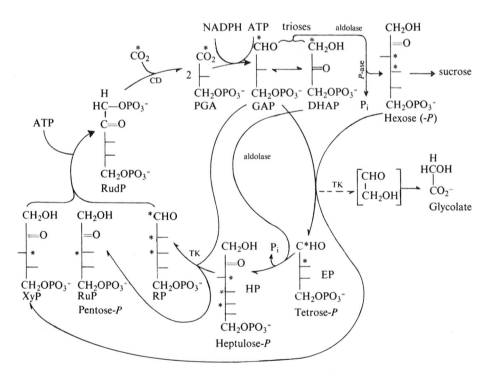

FIGURE 12-5A   Isotope Distribution on Short-term Fixation of CO_2.

The braces indicate a temperature-insensitive portion. Here Chl_n represents the chlorophyll aggregate; Chl (P700 or P870), associated with the electron donor identified with cytochrome f, or its equivalent, and X is the electron acceptor. The photochemical reaction leads to the formation of an oxidized chlorophyll and a reduced acceptor. The cytochrome later becomes reoxidized and the chlorophyll restored to its usual reduced state.

THE PATH OF CARBON IN PHOTOSYNTHESIS

The dark reactions involved in CO_2 assimilation in green plants have been intensively studied, first in vivo by means of radioactive tracers by Calvin, Benson, Bassham, and later in vitro with chloroplast and derivative preparations including purified soluble enzymes. Qualitatively, a unitary hypothesis has emerged from all these studies. The overall scheme, or "Calvin-Bassham cycle," is shown in Fig. 12-5. It is thought to be made up of the following reactions (names of enzymes are shown in italics, carbon skeleton rearrangements are indicated in brackets):

6-Ribulose-1,5-di$P$ + 6CO_2 + 6H_2O → 6[intermediate] → 12 glycerate-3-P
$[6C_5 + 6C_1 = 12C_3]$ *carboxydismutase (CD)*   (12-22)

12 Glycerate-3-P + 12ATP $\rightleftharpoons$ 12 glycerate-1,3-di$P$ + 12ADP
$[12C_3 \rightarrow 12C_3']$ *phosphoglycerate kinase*   (12-23)

12 Glycerate-1,3-di$P$ + 12NADPH $\rightleftharpoons$ 12 glyceraldehyde-3-P + 12NADP$^+$ + 12 P_i
$[12C_3' \rightarrow 12C_3'']$ D-*glyceraldehyde phosphate*
         dehydrogenase (NADP specific)   (12-24)

5 Glyceraldehyde-3-P $\rightleftharpoons$ 5 dihydroxyacetone-P
$[5C_3'' = 5C_3''']$ *triosephosphate isomerase*   (12-25)

3 Glyceraldehyde-3-P + 3 dihydroxyacetone-P $\rightleftharpoons$ 3 fructose-1,6-di$P$
$[3C_3'' + 3C_3''' = 3C_6]$ *aldolase*   (12-26)

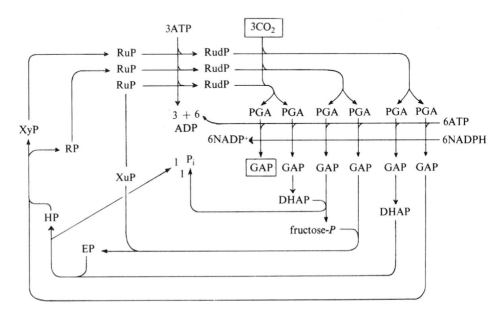

FIGURE 12-5B. Schematic Representation of the Path of Carbon in Photosynthesis.

3 Fructose-1,6-di$P$ + 3H_2O → 3 fructose-6-P + 3P_i

[3C_6 = 3C_6']   *phosphatase* (specific?)   (12-27)

2 Fructose-6-P + 2 glyceraldehyde-3-P ⇌ 2 erythrose-4-P + 2 xylulose-5-P

[2C_6' + 2C_3'' = 2C_4 + 2C_5']   *transketolase (TK)*   (12-28)

2 Erythrose-4-P + 2 dihydroxyacetone-P ⇌ 2 sedoheptulose-1,7-di$P$

[2C_4 + 2C_3''' = 2C_7]   *aldolase*   (12-29)

2 Sedoheptulose-1,7-di$P$ + 2H_2O → 2 sedoheptulose-7-P + 2P_i

[2C_7 = 2C_7']   *phosphatase* (specific?)   (12-30)

2 Sedoheptulose-7-P + 2 glyceraldehyde-3-P ⇌ 2 ribose-5-P + 2 xylulose-5-P

[2C_7' + 2C_3'' = 2C_5' + 2C_5'']   *transketolase (TK)*   (12-31)

2 Ribose-5-P ⇌ 2 ribulose-5-P

[2C_5'' = 2C_5''']   *phosphopentose isomerase*   (12-32)

4 Xylulose-5-P ⇌ 4 ribulose-5-P

[4C_5' = 4C_5''']   *phosphoketopentose epimerase* (12-33)

6 Ribulose-5-P + 6ATP → 6 ribulose-1,5-di$P$ + 6ADP

[6C_5''' = 6C_5]   *phosphopentokinase*   (12-34)

SUM

6 Ribulose-1,5di$P$ + 6CO_2 + 18ATP + 12NADPH → 6 ribulose-1,5-di$P$ + fructose-6-P
$$+ 18ADP + 17P_i + 12NADP^+$$

[6C_5 + 6C_1 = 6C_5 + C_6]   (H_2O not shown)   (12-16a)

or, after hydrolysis of the hexose phosphate, schematically,

CO_2 + 3ATP + 2NADPH + 3H_2O → ⅙ hexose + 3ADP + 3 P_i + 2NADP$^+$ (12-16b)

The net reaction — Eq. (12-16a) — leads to the formation of one molecule of a hexose-P or, (after hydrolysis, preceded if necessary by isomerization of the hexose) one hexose for each six turns of the cycle — reaction (12-16b). The cycle itself consists of one priming step — reaction (12-34), requiring ATP — one carboxylation step proper — reaction (12-22) — leading to phosphoglyceric acid as the first identifiable product, another priming step — reaction (12-23) — and a reductive step — reaction (12-24). All other subsequent reactions — Eqs. (12-25) to (12-33) — are merely rearrangements designed to (1) regenerate the starting material and (2) eliminate the product. All these steps, plus reaction (12-23), are catalyzed by enzymes that are not restricted to green plants but are distributed ubiquitously among all living organisms (see Chap. 11).

To recapitulate, the requirements for green-plant photosynthesis — Eqs. (12-35a to d) = (12-36) — are

PART I: Photoelectron transport system

Light-phase linked: $n\ hv$ + 2H^+ + 2NADP$^+$ + 4Y $\xrightarrow[Fd]{\text{system I}}$ 2NADPH + 4Y_{ox}^+ (12-35a)

$n\ hv$ + 2H_2O + 4X' $\xrightarrow{\text{system II}}$ O_2 + 4X'_{red} + 4H^+ (12-35b)

Dark-phase linked: 4X'_{red} + 4Y_{ox}^+ + n'ADP + $n'P_i$ $\xrightarrow[\text{system}]{\text{ET and P}}$ 4X' + 4Y + n'ATP + $n'H_2O$

ET and P = electron transport and phosphorylation

(12-35c)

PART II: CO_2 assimilation system

$$CO_2 + 2NADPH + 3ATP + 3H_2O \xrightarrow[\text{system}]{\text{Calvin cycle}} \tfrac{1}{6} \text{ hexose} + 2NADP^+ + 3ADP + 3P_i$$
$$(12\text{-}35d)$$

GRAND TOTAL

$$2n \ hv + CO_2 + (n' - 3)ADP + (n' - 3)P_i + 5H_2O \xrightarrow[\text{accessory systems}]{\text{chloroplast plus}} \tfrac{1}{6} \text{ hexose} + O_2$$
$$+ (n' - 3)ATP + (n' - 3)H_2O \qquad (12\text{-}36)$$

Compare this with Eq. (12-3), and remember that for our purposes here $ADP + P_i = ATP + H_2O$. This formulation again suggests that if n'/n is indeed 0.5, then there is a deficit in ATP that has to be provided by cyclic phosphorylation. See Eq. (12-20b).

QUANTUM YIELD
AND ENERGETICS

The question of the magnitude of the quantum yield, i.e., the value of n in Eq. (12-3), has been difficult and controversial. Warburg, Burk, and their collaborators believed it to be equal to 4, but Emerson and most others consistently obtained values near 8. The mechanism involving two linked light reactions — Eq. (12-35) — suggests strongly that the value of $n/4$ cannot be less than unity. This then leads to $2n = 8$ in complete agreement with higher values suggested by the work of a large number of investigators.

Eight einsteins (mole quanta) of light at, e.g., 700 mμ, utilized with 70 per cent efficiency, correspond to approximately 205 kcal; for the reaction $CO_2 + H_2O \rightarrow \{CH_2O\} + O_2$, $\Delta G^{0'} = 114$ kcal; for $ADP + P_i \rightarrow ATP + H_2O$, the $\Delta G^{0'} \simeq +7.5$ kcal. Thus we can calculate that the overall process has an efficiency of $\sim 122/205 \simeq 0.60$. Of the approximately 75 kcal thus apparently "wasted," $\geq 6 \times 3 = 18$ kcal are dissipated in the hydrolytic steps — Eqs. (12-27), (12-30), and the hydrolysis of hexose-P — and $6 \times 7 = 42$ kcal in the formation of ribulose-di$P$ — Eq. (12-34) — a total of 60 kcal. This represents energy used to ensure essentially unidirectional flow of carbon through the biosynthetic sequence. We see that the "true" efficiency of the process virtually equals 190/205, or 0.92. Thus only 8 per cent of the available energy is dissipated in ways not capable of rationalization by the biochemist.

OTHER REDUCTIVE
REACTIONS DRIVEN
BY LIGHT

In organisms containing the enzyme hydrogenase (i.e., photosynthetic bacteria and hydrogen-adapted algae), the Fd_{red} produced as the primary stable reducing species by light can give rise to the photoevolution of hydrogen (Eq. [12-18c]). Alternatively, Fd can be used by the same organisms to reverse the phosphoroclastic reaction of pyruvate (p. 276) — Eq. (12-37):

$$CH_3COCO_2^- + P_i \xrightarrow{\text{phosphoroclastic split}} \text{acetyl phosphate} + CO_2 + H_2 \qquad (12\text{-}37)$$

$$CH_3COCO_2^- + P_i + 2Fd_{ox} \rightleftharpoons \text{acetyl phosphate} + CO_2 + 2Fd_{red} \qquad (12\text{-}38)$$

Since pyruvate (with the intervention of additional carboxylation steps, see p. 278) is the precursor of the various di- and tri-carboxylic acids of the citric acid cycle and hence of all carbohydrates and all those amino acids which originate from these compounds, reaction (12-38) provides the photosynthetic cell with a key step in the reductive synthesis of important constituents.

Yet another role has been discovered for reduced ferredoxin: Nitrogen fixation, i.e., the conversions of N_2 to NH_3 by the ATP-requiring enzyme(s) nitrogenase, can utilize either molecular hydrogen or Fd_{red} as a source of reducing power (Chap. 17). These various possibilities are outlined below as reaction (12-39), which indicates alternative paths, some of them reversible, for the utilization of Fd_{red} and its reconversion to the oxidized form:

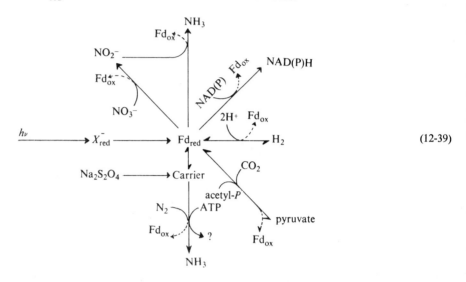

$$(12\text{-}39)$$

Finally, Fd_{red}, either with or without the intervention of reduced pyridine nucleotides, has also been implicated in the assimilation of oxidized nitrogen compounds, and in the reduction of nitrate to nitrite, as well as the complete reduction of the latter to ammonia (see Chap. 17).

REFERENCES   Bassham, J. A.: Photosynthesis: Energetics and Related Topics, *Advan. Enzymol.*, **25**: 39 (1963).
————, and M. Calvin: "The Path of Carbon in Photosynthesis," Prentice-Hall, Englewood Cliffs, N.J., 1957.
Brookhaven Symposia in Biology: "The Photochemical Apparatus: Its Structure and Function," **11** (1959).
Calvin, M., and J. A. Bassham: "The Photosynthesis of Carbon Compounds," Benjamin, New York, 1962.
Clayton, R. K.: "Molecular Physics in Photosynthesis," Blaisdell, New York, 1965.
————: Photosynthesis: Primary Physical and Chemical Processes, *Ann. Rev. Plant. Physiol*, **14**: 159 (1963).
Duysens, L. N. M.: Photosynthesis, *Progr. Biophys. Mol. Biol.*, **14**: 3 (1964).
Gest, H., A. San Pietro, and L. P. Vernon (eds.): "Bacterial Photosynthesis," Antioch Press, Yellow Springs, Ohio, 1963.
Gibbs, M.: Photosynthesis, *Ann. Rev. Biochem.*, **36**: 757 (1967).
Giese, A. C. (ed.): "Photophysiology," Academic Press, New York, 1964.
Hill, R., and C. P. Whittingham: "Photosynthesis," Wiley, New York, 1957.
Jagendorf, A.: Photosynthesis, *Surv. Biol. Progr.*, **4**: 183 (1962).
Kamen, M. D.: "Primary Processes in Photosynthesis," Academic Press, New York, 1963.
Kok, B., and A. Jagendorf (eds.): "Photosynthetic Mechanisms of Green Plants," Publication 1145, National Academy of Sciences, National Research Council, Washington, 1963.
McElroy, W. D., and B. Glass (eds.): Symposium on Light and Life, Johns Hopkins, Baltimore, 1961.
San Pietro, A. (ed.): "Non-heme Iron Proteins: Role in Energy Conversion," Antioch Press, Yellow Springs, Ohio, 1965.

Smith, J. H. C., and C. S. French: The Major and Accessory Pigments in Photosynthesis, *Ann. Rev. Plant Physiol.*, **14:** 181 (1963).

Vernon, L. P.: Bacterial Photosynthesis, *Ann. Rev. Plant Physiol.*, **15:** 73 (1963).

———, and M. Avron: Photosynthesis, *Ann. Rev. Biochem.*, **34:** 269 (1965).

Vishniac, W., B. L. Horecker, and S. Ochoa: Enzymatic Aspects of Photosynthesis, *Advan. Enzymol.*, **19:** 1 (1957).

13 | The Oxidation of Fatty Acids and Degradation of Complex Lipids

The *lipids* are a heterogeneous class of substances characterized by a variable solubility in organic solvents and insolubility, for the most part, in water. The principal classes of complex lipids are the neutral *fats* and *oils, phospholipids* (derivatives of phosphatidic acid), *sphingolipids*, and *steroids*. The basic features of the chemistry of lipids have been summarized many times, and this is not our main concern. Consequently, lipid chemistry will be discussed only to the extent necessary to facilitate an understanding of lipid metabolism.

FATTY ACIDS   The names and structures of the most common, as well as a few of the more exotic, fatty acids are collected in Table 13-1. The most common fatty acids in nature are straight-chain saturated or unsaturated compounds containing an even number of carbon atoms. Particularly prevalent are palmitic, stearic, and oleic acids. Saturated straight-chain acids containing an odd number of carbons seldom appear in large quantity but do seem to occur universally. On the other hand, branched-chain fatty acids have been identified in relatively few natural sources. Fatty acids containing a cyclopropane ring have been identified in at least three cases: *cis*-11,12-methyleneoctadecanoic acid (lactobacillic acid) is a major lipid constituent of *Lactobacilli* and *Agrobacterium tumefaciens*, and *cis*-9,10-methylenehexadecanoic acid has been isolated from *E. coli*. Fatty acids containing a cyclopropene ring — sterculic acid — and a cyclopentene ring — chaulmoogric acid — have been isolated from plant sources.

Free fatty acids occur in the diet to a minor extent only. The major fraction of the ingested fatty acids occurs incorporated into more complex lipids, principally the triglycerides and the phosphatides.

310

TABLE 13-1. Some Naturally Occurring Fatty Acids

Saturated fatty acids

Butyric acid	$CH_3(CH_2)_2CO_2H$
Caproic acid	$CH_3(CH_2)_4CO_2H$
Caprylic acid	$CH_3(CH_2)_6CO_2H$
Capric acid	$CH_3(CH_2)_8CO_2H$
Lauric acid	$CH_3(CH_2)_{10}CO_2H$
Myristic acid	$CH_3(CH_2)_{12}CO_2H$
Palmitic acid	$CH_3(CH_2)_{14}CO_2H$
Stearic acid	$CH_3(CH_2)_{16}CO_2H$
Arachidic acid	$CH_3(CH_2)_{18}CO_2H$
Lignoceric acid	$CH_3(CH_2)_{22}CO_2H$

Unsaturated fatty acids

Crotonic acid	$CH_3CH{=}CHCO_2H$
Palmitoleic acid	$CH_3(CH_2)_5CH{=}CH(CH_2)_7CO_2H$
Oleic acid	$CH_3(CH_2)_7CH{=}CH(CH_2)_7CO_2H$
Linoleic acid	$CH_3(CH_2)_3(CH_2CH{=}CH)_2(CH_2)_7CO_2H$
Linolenic acid	$CH_3(CH_2CH{=}CH)_3(CH_2)_7CO_2H$
Arachidonic acid	$CH_3(CH_2)_3(CH_2CH{=}CH)_4(CH_2)_3CO_2H$
Nervonic acid	$CH_3(CH_2)_7CH{=}CH(CH_2)_{13}CO_2H$
Ximenynic acid	$CH_3(CH_2)_5CH{=}CH{-}C{\equiv}C{-}(CH_2)_7CO_2H$
Mycomycin	$HC{\equiv}CC{\equiv}C{-}CH{=}C{=}CH{-}CH{=}CH{-}CH{=}CHCH_2CO_2H$

Others

Lactobacillic acid	$(CH_2)_5CH_3$ / $(CH_2)_9{-}CO_2H$
Sterculic acid	$(CH_2)_7{-}CH_3$ / $(CH_2)_7{-}CO_2H$
Chaulmoogric acid	$(CH_2)_{12}CO_2H$ / H

DEGRADATION OF TRIGLYCERIDES

Triesters of glycerol and fatty acids, the *triglycerides*, compose two of the several important classes of complex lipids, the fats and the oils. Their distinction is based on the physical state of the triglyceride at room temperature, the oils being liquid and the fats being solid. The melting point of triglycerides is, of course, determined by their fatty acid composition. In general, the higher the proportion of short-chain acids and unsaturated acids, the lower the melting point.

The hydrolysis of ingested triglycerides in higher animals occurs largely in the small intestine and is catalyzed by lipolytic enzymes elaborated by the pancreas. The pancreatic *lipases* (glycerol ester hydrolases) appear to be of two types: one specific for ester linkages at the α position of triglycerides and the second for ester linkages at the β position. The complete hydrolysis of triglycerides proceeds in a stepwise fashion, with rapid hydrolysis of the α and α' linkages followed by slow hydrolysis of the β-monoglyceride (see Fig. 13-1). These reactions are accelerated by the *bile salts*, sodium taurocholate and glycocholate, which serve the function of emulsification and solubilization of lipids:

Glycocholic acid

Taurocholic acid

The bile salts are contained in the bile, a secretion of the liver that passes into the intestine by way of the gall bladder. The discharge of bile into the intestine is evoked by the hormone *cholecystokinin*, which is synthesized in the small intestine and liberated into the circulation in response to the presence of lipid in the duodenum.

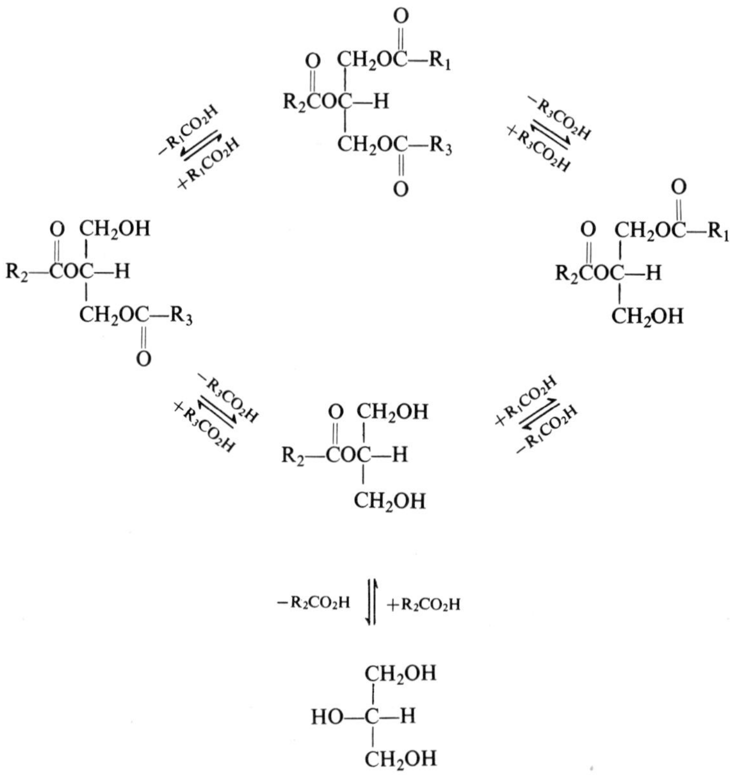

FIGURE 13-1.   Probable Reaction Sequence for the Complete Hydrolysis of Triglycerides.

It should be noted that the hydrolysis of triglycerides by lipases is, in principle, a reversible reaction, thus providing a possible pathway for the biosynthesis of these compounds.

Both free fatty acids and glycerides of varying levels of esterification are absorbed through the intestinal wall. Short-chain fatty acids and glycerol are then transported to the liver via the portal blood, while long-chain fatty acids and glycerides are reconverted to triglycerides in the intestinal mucosa, released into the lymph, and transported to the blood via the lymphatic system. Transport of triglycerides in the lymph and blood occurs in the form of *chylomicrons*, microscopic lipoproteins approximately 50 μ in diameter. Chylomicrons are composed chiefly of triglycerides and, to a lesser extent, of other forms of lipid and protein and exist as a lipid particle surrounded by a protein coat. Lipid-protein complexes, such as chylomicrons, serve as substrates for an additional lipase contained in some tissues, *lipoprotein lipase*. This enzyme catalyzes the hydrolysis of triglycerides only when they are associated with protein. In the course of this hydrolysis, there is no buildup of mono- or diglycerides, in contrast with the hydrolysis catalyzed by pancreatic lipase.

DEGRADATION OF
PHOSPHOLIPIDS

Several very important classes of complex lipids are derived from *phosphatidic acid*. These include phosphatidyl *cholines*, also termed *lecithins*, phosphatidyl *ethanolamines*, and phosphatidyl *serines*. The phosphatidyl cholines and ethanolamines are major phospholipid constituents, but phosphatidyl serines occur to a quite limited extent and are principally involved in ethanolamine synthesis (see page 381). The latter two classes are sometimes termed *cephalins*. Each of these designations describes, of course, a class of compounds whose individual members are distinguished by the nature of the esterified fatty acids. Most phosphatidyl cholines contain one saturated fatty acid, esterified at the α' position, and one unsaturated fatty acid, esterified at the β position.

Derivatives of phosphatidic acids contain a center of asymmetry at the β-carbon atom. Naturally occurring derivatives have been demonstrated to be stereochemically related to L-α-glycerophosphate (see page 273).

Free phosphatidic acid has been demonstrated to occur naturally, although it does not appear to account for an appreciable fraction of total phospholipid. The lecithins and cephalins are very widely distributed in nature and are frequently the major lipid constituent of tissues.

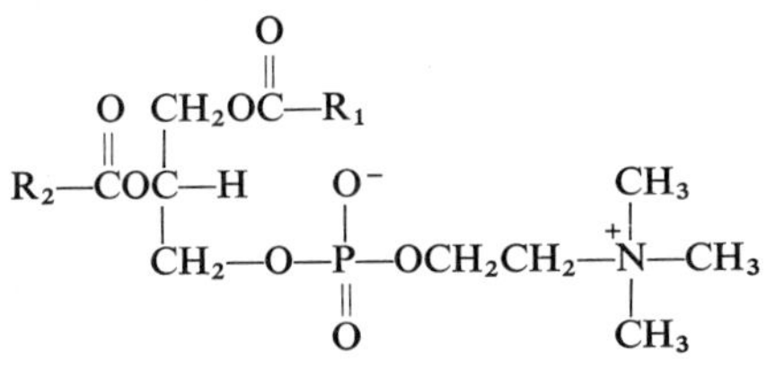

Phosphatidyl choline

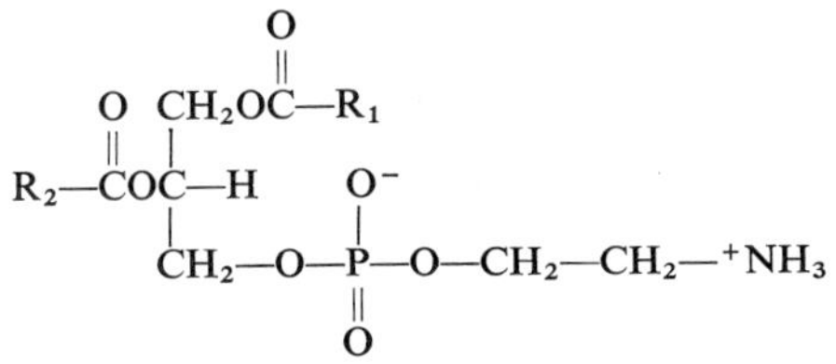

Phosphatidyl ethanolamine

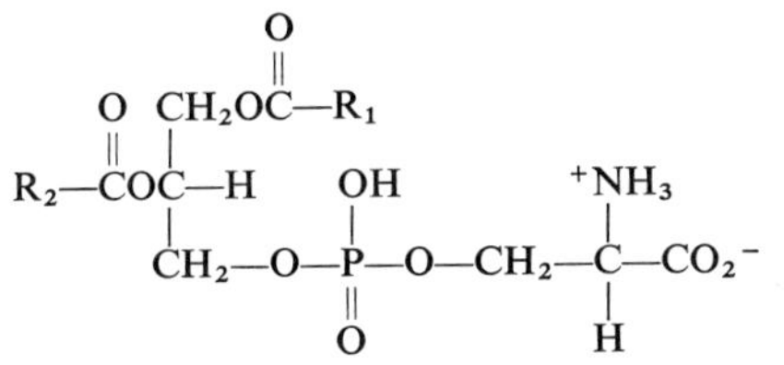

Phosphatidyl serine

The enzymatic degradation of lecithins and cephalins is incompletely understood. We distinguish the following five enzymes that cleave one or more of the ester linkages of the phosphatides: *phosphatidases A, B, C, D*, and *lysophosphatidase*.

Phosphatidase A occurs in snake venom, bee and wasp poisons, animal tissues, and perhaps in plants and bacteria, and cleaves one fatty acid from phosphatides, yielding a lysophosphatide:

Phosphatide $\xrightarrow{\text{phosphatidase A}}$ RCO$_2$H + lysophosphatide   (13-1)

Cleavage occurs specifically at the β position.

Lysophosphatidase completes the removal of fatty acids from phosphatides by catalyzing the conversion of lysophosphatides to the appropriate glycerylphosphoryl derivative:

$$
\begin{array}{c}
\overset{\displaystyle O}{\overset{\|}{\underset{}{}}} \\
\text{CH}_2\text{OC—R}_1 \\
\text{HO—CH} \quad \text{O}^- \\
\text{CH}_2\text{OP—OR} \\
\overset{\|}{\text{O}}
\end{array}
+ \text{H}_2\text{O} \rightarrow
\begin{array}{c}
\text{CH}_2\text{OH} \\
\text{HO—CH} \quad \text{O}^- \\
\text{CH}_2\text{OP—OR} \\
\overset{\|}{\text{O}}
\end{array}
+ \text{R}_1\text{CO}_2\text{H}
\qquad (13\text{-}2)
$$

Phosphatidase B combines the functions of phosphatidase A and lysophosphatidase. This enzyme catalyzes the hydrolysis of both fatty acyl esters yielding the glycerylphosphoryl base directly:

$$
\begin{array}{c}
\quad\quad \overset{\displaystyle O}{\overset{\|}{}} \\
\text{O} \;\; \text{CH}_2\text{OC—R}_1 \\
\overset{\|}{} \;\;\;\; \\
\text{R}_2\text{—COCH} \quad \text{O}^- \\
\text{CH}_2\text{—OP—OR} \\
\overset{\|}{\text{O}}
\end{array}
+ 2\text{H}_2\text{O} \rightarrow
\begin{array}{c}
\text{CH}_2\text{OH} \\
\text{HO—CH} \quad\quad \text{O}^- \\
\text{CH}_2\text{—O—P—OR} \\
\overset{\|}{\text{O}}
\end{array}
+ \text{R}_1\text{CO}_2\text{H} + \text{R}_2\text{CO}_2\text{H}
\qquad (13\text{-}3)
$$

Phosphatidases C and D catalyze the hydrolysis of the phosphodiester linkages between L-α-phosphatidic acid and nitrogenous base (13-4), and between α, β-diglyceride and phosphorylated base (13-5), respectively:

$$
\begin{array}{c}
\quad\quad \overset{\displaystyle O}{\overset{\|}{}} \\
\text{O} \;\; \text{CH}_2\text{OC—R}_1 \\
\overset{\|}{} \\
\text{R}_2\text{—COCH} \quad\quad \text{O}^- \\
\text{CH}_2\text{—O—P—O—CH}_2\text{CH}_2\text{—N}^+(\text{R}')_3 \\
\overset{\|}{\text{O}}
\end{array}
\xrightarrow{\text{H}_2\text{O}}
$$

$$
\begin{array}{c}
\quad\quad \overset{\displaystyle O}{\overset{\|}{}} \\
\text{O} \;\; \text{CH}_2\text{OC—R}_1 \\
\overset{\|}{} \\
\text{R}_2\text{—COCH} \quad\quad \text{O}^- \\
\text{CH}_2\text{—O—P—OH} \\
\overset{\|}{\text{O}}
\end{array}
+ \text{HO—CH}_2\text{CH}_2\text{—N}^+(\text{R}')_3
\qquad (13\text{-}4)
$$

$$
\begin{array}{c}
\quad\quad \overset{\displaystyle O}{\overset{\|}{}} \\
\text{O} \;\; \text{CH}_2\text{OC—R}_1 \\
\overset{\|}{} \\
\text{R}_2\text{—COCH} \quad\quad \text{O}^- \\
\text{CH}_2\text{—O—P—OCH}_2\text{CH}_2\text{—N}^+(\text{R}')_3 \\
\overset{\|}{\text{O}}
\end{array}
\xrightarrow{\text{H}_2\text{O}}
$$

$$
\begin{array}{c}
\quad\quad \overset{\displaystyle O}{\overset{\|}{}} \\
\text{O} \;\; \text{CH}_2\text{OC—R}_1 \\
\overset{\|}{} \\
\text{R}_2\text{—COCH} \\
\text{CH}_2\text{OH}
\end{array}
+ {}^-\text{HO}_3\text{P—OCH}_2\text{CH}_2\text{—N}^+(\text{R}')_3
\qquad (13\text{-}5)
$$

The stepwise fashion in which these and related enzymes degrade phosphatides to their components has not been established.

OXIDATION OF
FATTY ACIDS

The *oxidative degradation of fatty acid*s is a universal biochemical capacity among living organisms. In mammals, such oxidation occurs in a variety of tissues, including liver, kidney, and heart. Intracellularly, fatty acid oxidation occurs principally in the mitochondria.

Early Considerations

The essential features of the pathway for oxidation of fatty acids were clearly detailed by Knoop in 1904 and shortly thereafter by Embden and Dakin. Nearly fifty years were required before the brilliant conclusions of Knoop received full experimental confirmation. Knoop arrived at the theory of "β-oxidation" through feeding experiments employing fatty acids labeled in the terminal position with phenyl groups. The latter permitted the identification of the end products in the urine of the experimental animals. When ω-phenyl fatty acids containing an even number of carbons in the straight chain were fed, *phenylaceturic acid*, formed by the condensation of phenylacetic acid and glycine in vivo, accumulated in the urine:

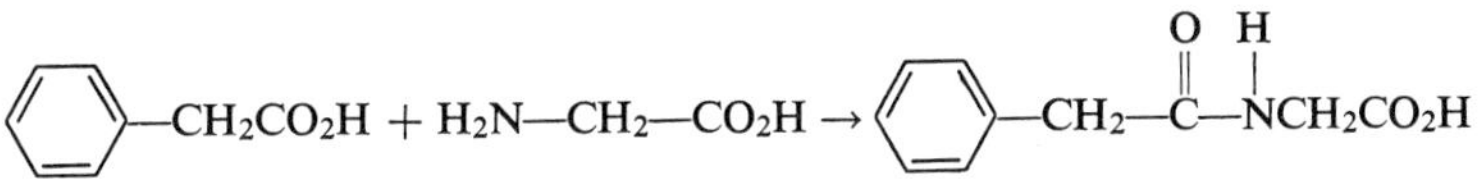

$$\text{—CH}_2\text{CO}_2\text{H} + \text{H}_2\text{N—CH}_2\text{—CO}_2\text{H} \rightarrow \text{—CH}_2\text{—}\overset{\overset{\displaystyle O}{\|}}{C}\text{—}\overset{\overset{\displaystyle H}{|}}{N}\text{CH}_2\text{CO}_2\text{H} \qquad (13\text{-}6)$$

Phenylaceturic acid

In contrast, when similarly labeled fatty acids containing an odd number of carbon atoms were fed, *hippuric acid*, formed by condensation of benzoic acid and glycine in vivo, accumulated in the urine:

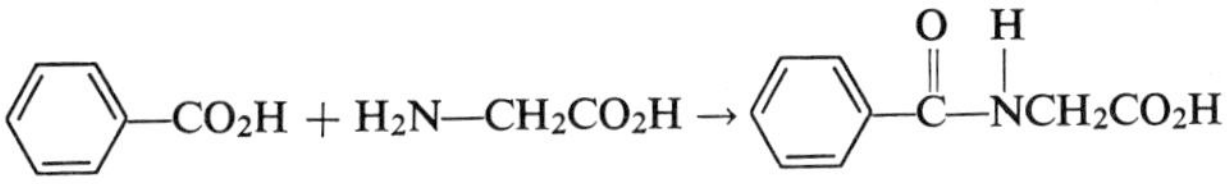

$$\text{—CO}_2\text{H} + \text{H}_2\text{N—CH}_2\text{CO}_2\text{H} \rightarrow \text{—}\overset{\overset{\displaystyle O}{\|}}{C}\text{—}\overset{\overset{\displaystyle H}{|}}{N}\text{CH}_2\text{CO}_2\text{H} \qquad (13\text{-}7)$$

Hippuric acid

These are precisely the results that one would expect, provided the fatty acids were degraded by the successive removal of two-carbon fragments from the parent molecule. The individual reactions leading to the cleavage of two-carbon units from fatty acids were visualized as indicated in Fig. 13-2.

One of the principal difficulties with the early conclusions of Knoop, Embden and Dakin lay in accounting for the production of acetoacetate and other "ketone bodies," such as hydroxybutyrate and acetone (which arise from acetoacetate), in the course of fatty acid oxidation. The latter pair of authors

$\longrightarrow \text{RCH}_2\text{CH}_2\text{CO}_2\text{H}$	
$\downarrow$	
$\text{RCHOHCH}_2\text{CO}_2\text{H} \rightleftharpoons \text{RCH}{=}\text{CHCO}_2\text{H}$	β-Oxidation to unsaturated, or β-OH acid.
$\downarrow$	
$\text{RCOCH}_2\text{CO}_2\text{H}$	Oxidation to β-keto acid.
$\downarrow$	
$\text{RCO}_2\text{H} + \text{"CH}_3\text{CO}_2\text{H"}$	Removal of 2-carbon units and formation of fatty acid with two less carbon atoms than parent acid.

FIGURE 13-2.   The Oxidative Metabolism of Fatty Acids According to the β-oxidation Theory of Knoop.

assumed that the terminal four-carbon fragment of normal fatty acids was not oxidized beyond the stage of acetoacetate. Thus acetoacetate was considered to be produced in stoichiometric amounts from the oxidation of even-numbered fatty acids. Odd-numbered fatty acids would yield stoichiometric amounts of propionic acid and no ketone bodies at all according to the same reasoning. Subsequent experiments revealed that these conclusions were untenable and necessitated modifications in the theory of fatty acid oxidation. In 1940, MacKay, Wick, and Barnum proposed a "β-oxidation-condensation" theory that incorporated most of Knoop's original suggestions, but held that acetoacetate was formed through condensation of two acetate fragments as indicated below:

$$CH_3CH_2CH_2CH_2CH_2CH_2CH_2CO_2H \rightarrow 4\text{"}CH_3CO_2H\text{"} \rightarrow 2CH_3COCH_2CO_2H$$

$$CH_3CH_2CH_2CH_2CH_2CH_2CO_2H \begin{cases} \rightarrow 2\text{"}CH_3CO_2H\text{"} \rightarrow CH_3COCH_2CO_2H \\ \rightarrow CH_3CH_2CO_2H \rightarrow CH_3COCO_2H \end{cases} \qquad (13\text{-}8)$$

This scheme clearly predicts that both the carbonyl and carboxyl carbons of acetoacetate have their origin in the carboxyl carbon of the parent fatty acid, a prediction fully substantiated by experiments subsequently performed with the aid of radioactive tracers.

The Pathway for Fatty Acid Oxidation   The key milestones in the understanding of the pathway of fatty acid oxidation, following the work of Knoop, were (1) the observation of fatty acid oxidation in cell-free preparations from the guinea pig liver by Leloir and Muñoz in 1939 and (2) the elucidation of the structure of "activated" fatty acids as the S-acyl derivatives of coenzyme A by Lynen and Reichert in 1951. The use of cell-free preparations permitted the identification of the individual enzymes involved in fatty acid oxidation and the determination of the properties of the catalytic reactions. The discovery of the acyl derivatives of CoASH, which followed the discovery of coenzyme A by Lipmann, provided a solution to the most perplexing problem of fatty acid oxidation — the failure to detect any of the postulated intermediates or any free short-chain fatty acids in the course of oxidation of longer molecules. It is now clear that all the intermediates, including the short-chain fatty acids formed in the course of oxidation, occur only as the acyl-SCoA derivatives.

The pathway for the oxidation of fatty acids is indicated in Fig. 13-3. The parent fatty acid is activated by conversion to the fatty-acyl-SCoA, oxidized to the α, β-unsaturated compound, hydrated, oxidized to the β-keto derivative, and finally subjected to a thiolytic cleavage yielding acetyl-SCoA and the fatty acyl-SCoA containing two less carbon atoms, which, in turn, undergoes the same series of reactions. We now consider each of the steps individually.

Fatty Acid Activation   Conversion of fatty acids to fatty acyl derivatives of CoASH may occur by any of a variety of routes. These include reactions catalyzed by acetate thiokinase, medium- and long-chain fatty acid thiokinases, thiophorases, and a GTP-specific acid thiokinase.

Acetate thiokinase. Acetate thiokinase, a widely distributed enzyme, catalyzes the overall reaction indicated below:

$$CH_3CO_2H + ATP + HSCoA \underset{}{\overset{Mg^{+2}}{\rightleftharpoons}} CH_3\overset{\displaystyle O}{\overset{\displaystyle \|}{C}}-SCoA + AMP + PP_i \qquad (13\text{-}9)$$

The equilibrium constant for reaction (13-9) is near unity in the presence of approximately equimolar concentrations of Mg^{+2} and ATP. This result indicates that the standard free energy of hydrolysis of ATP to AMP and PP_i is about the same as that for hydrolysis of acetyl-SCoA. Acetate thiokinase is activated by

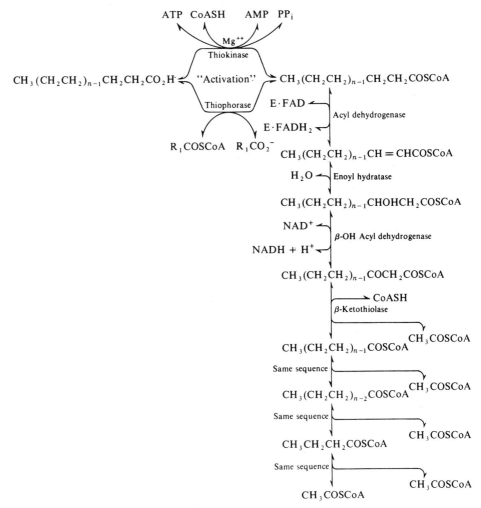

FIGURE 13-3   The Pattern of Fatty-acid Oxidation.—*H. R. Mahler, in K. S. Markley (ed.), "Fatty Acids," 2nd ed., Part 3, Interscience, New York, 1964.*

K^+, Rb^+, and ammonium ions but inhibited by Na^+ and Li^+ ions. The enzyme activates acetate, propionate, and acrylate but does not handle long-chain acids. The acetate thiokinase reaction is, in fact, the sum of two reactions involving the intermediate formation of acyladenylates, tightly bound to the surface of the enzyme:

$$E + CH_3CO_2H + ATP \overset{Mg^{+2}}{\rightleftharpoons} \left[\underset{\underset{\displaystyle CH_3—C—AMP}{\|}}{\overset{O}{}} \right] \cdot E + PP_i$$

$$\left[\underset{\underset{\displaystyle CH_3C—AMP}{\|}}{\overset{O}{}} \right] \cdot E + HSCoA \rightleftharpoons CH_3—\overset{O}{\underset{\|}{C}}—SCoA + AMP + E$$

(13-10)

Fatty Acid Thiokinase (*Medium Chain*). A widely distributed enzyme catalyzes the formation of acyl-SCoAs from saturated fatty acids containing four to twelve carbon atoms. With the exception of the nature of the substrates, this reaction seems closely related to that of acetate thiokinase — Eqs. (13-9) and (13-10). In addition to the saturated fatty acids, this enzyme also activates benzoates, unsaturated acids, hydroxyacids, picolinic acid, and several others. In contrast, this enzyme is specific for AMP and HSCoA as acceptors for the acyl function.

Fatty Acid Thiokinase (*Long Chain*). A fatty acid thiokinase capable of activating fatty acids containing up to 22 carbon atoms has been identified in mammalian liver. The reaction appears closely related to those discussed above.

Thiophorases. The thiophorases catalyze the interconversion of acyl-SCoAs and free acids:

$$R_1-\overset{\overset{\text{O}}{\|}}{C}-SCoA + R_2CO_2H \rightleftharpoons R_1CO_2H + R_2-\overset{\overset{\text{O}}{\|}}{C}-SCoA \qquad (13\text{-}11)$$

The thiophorases may be divided into two classes: (1) those that catalyze the transfer of HSCoA from acetyl-SCoA to aliphatic acids and (2) those that catalyze the transfer of HSCoA from succinyl-SCoA to acetoacetate and other β-keto acids.

GTP-specific Acid Thiokinase. An acyl thiokinase that specifically requires GTP as coenzyme has been isolated from the mitochondria of beef liver. The overall stoichiometry of this reaction is:

$$RCO_2H + HSCoA + GTP \overset{Mg^{+2}}{\rightleftharpoons} R-\overset{\overset{\text{O}}{\|}}{C}-SCoA + GDP + P_i \qquad (13\text{-}12)$$

Phosphotransacetylase. In certain microorganisms, acetyl-SCoA may be formed from acetate by a two-step reaction path not involving acetyl adenylate as an intermediate. The initial reaction, catalyzed by acetate kinase, involves the formation of acetyl phosphate from acetate and ATP. The second reaction, catalyzed by phosphotransacetylase, involves the transfer of the acyl function from phosphate to HSCoA:

$$CH_3CO_2H + ATP \rightleftharpoons CH_3\overset{\overset{\text{O}}{\|}}{C}-OPO_3H_2 + ADP$$

$$\qquad (13\text{-}13)$$

$$CH_3-\overset{\overset{\text{O}}{\|}}{C}-OPO_3H_2 + HSCoA \rightleftharpoons CH_3\overset{\overset{\text{O}}{\|}}{C}-SCoA + P_i$$

The various routes for acyl-SCoA formation are summarized in Table 13-2.

Fatty Acyl-SCoA Dehydrogenases. Four distinct fatty acyl-SCoA dehydrogenases have been isolated and purified from the mitochondria of mammalian liver. Each of these enzymes catalyzes the reaction indicated below and each requires FAD as coenzyme:

$$E \cdot FAD + R-CH_2-CH_2-\overset{\overset{\text{O}}{\|}}{C}-SCoA \rightleftharpoons E \cdot FADH_2 + R-\overset{\overset{\text{H}}{|}}{C}=\overset{}{C}-\overset{\overset{\text{O}}{\|}}{C}-SCoA \qquad (13\text{-}14)$$
$$\underset{|}{}\underset{\text{H}}{}$$

TABLE 13-2. A Summary of Routes to Acyl-SCoA Formation

Reaction	Enzymes	Chain length	Occurrence
$RCO_2H + ATP + HSCoA \rightleftharpoons$ $RC\overset{O}{\overset{\|}{—}}SCoA + AMP + PP_i$	Acetate thiokinase Fatty acid thiokinase Fatty acid thiokinase	C_2–C_3 C_4–C_{11} C_{10}–C_{18}	Yeast, higher organisms
$RCO_2H + GTP + HSCoA \rightleftharpoons$ $RCOSCoA + GDP + P_i$	Acid thiokinase	?	Liver
$R_1C\overset{O}{\overset{\|}{—}}SCoA + R_2CO_2H \rightleftharpoons$ $R_1CO_2H + R_2C\overset{O}{\overset{\|}{S}}CoA$	Acetic thiophorase Butyric-succinic thiophorase Acetoacetic-succinic thiophorase	$R_1 = CH_3$ $R_2 = C_2$–C_5 $R_1 = CH_2CH_2CO_2H$ $R_2 = C_3$–C_5 $R_1 = CH_2CH_2CO_2H$ $R_2 = RCOCH_2$	Microorganisms Heart, kidney Extrahepatic mammalian tissues
$RCO_2H + ATP \rightleftharpoons$ $RC\overset{O}{\overset{\|}{O}}PO_3H_2 + ADP$	Acyl kinases	C_2; C_4 (separate)	Microorganisms
$RC\overset{O}{\overset{\|}{O}}PO_3H_2 + HSCoA \rightleftharpoons$ $R—C\overset{O}{\overset{\|}{—}}SCoA + H_3PO_4$	Phosphotransacylases	C_2; C_4 (separate)	Microorganisms

These enzymes differ in their physical properties and in their substrate specificity, in particular in terms of the lengths of the carbon chains of the substrates.

Enoyl Hydratases. The mitochondria of mammalian liver contain an enoyl hydrase (crotonase), which catalyzes the conversion of *trans*-2-enoyl derivatives of CoASH to the corresponding L-β-hydroxyacyl compounds:

$$R—\overset{H}{\underset{H}{C}}=C—C\overset{O}{\overset{\|}{—}}SCoA + H_2O \rightleftharpoons R—\overset{OH}{\underset{H}{C}}—CH_2—C\overset{O}{\overset{\|}{—}}SCoA \qquad (13\text{-}15)$$
L-

As implied by this equation, the addition of water is stereospecific and only the L-β-hydroxyacyl-SCoA derivatives are formed. This enzyme also catalyzes the hydration of the *cis* isomer, probably with identical stereospecificity, yielding D-β-hydroxyacyl-SCoAs.

β-Hydroxyacyl-SCoA Dehydrogenases. Enzymes that specifically catalyze the dehydrogenation of L-β-hydroxyacyl-SCoA substrates have been highly purified from beef liver mitochondria and pig heart. The overall reaction is indicated below, and the enzymes appear to be nonspecific with respect to the chain length of the substrate:

$$R—\overset{OH}{\underset{H}{C}}—CH_2—C\overset{O}{\overset{\|}{—}}SCoA + NAD^+ \rightleftharpoons R—C\overset{O}{\overset{\|}{—}}CH_2—C\overset{O}{\overset{\|}{—}}SCoA + NADH + H^+ \qquad (13\text{-}16)$$

Since this reaction liberates a proton, the equilibrium is strongly pH dependent, favoring β-hydroxyacyl-SCoA formation at pH 7 and β-ketoacyl-SCoA formation in solutions more basic that pH 9.

β-*Ketothiolase.* β-Ketothiolase catalyzes the thiolytic cleavage of β-ketoacyl-SCoA substrates:

$$R\overset{\overset{O}{\|}}{C}-CH_2-\overset{\overset{O}{\|}}{C}-SCoA + HSCoA \rightleftharpoons R-\overset{\overset{O}{\|}}{C}-SCoA + CH_3-\overset{\overset{O}{\|}}{C}-SCoA \qquad (13\text{-}17)$$

The equilibrium strongly favors cleavage. A highly purified enzyme of this type from beef liver mitochondria catalyzes the cleavage of substrates containing between 4 and 12 carbon atoms. In contrast, a similar enzyme from heart is specific for the 4-carbon substrate. Hence, in certain tissues at least, several β-ketothiolases may be required in the course of oxidation of long-chain fatty acids.

Summation of all the preceding reactions yields the overall reaction for the oxidation of even-numbered fatty acids to acetyl-SCoA fragments. The balanced complete equation is indicated below:

$$CH_3(CH_2CH_2)_nCO_2H + ATP + (n+1)CoASH + nNAD^+ + nE\cdot FAD + nH_2O$$
$$= (n+1)CH_3COSCoA + \binom{ADP + P_i}{AMP + PP_i} + nNADH$$
$$+ nE\cdot FADH_2 + nH^+ \qquad (13\text{-}18)$$

The sequence of reactions indicated above for the oxidation of fatty acids provides a ready explanation for the "sparking" phenomenon. This term refers to the fact that catalytic amounts of certain di- or tricarboxylic acids must be present for fatty acid oxidation to occur. Oxidative reactions of these acids yield ATP (see Chaps. 14 and 15), which is, in turn, required for the activation of the fatty acids. The second function for the "sparking" substrate is to provide a partner for condensation of the acetyl-SCoA produced as the oxidation product. Following such condensation, degradation of these 2-carbon fragments proceeds via the citric acid cycle, as detailed in Chap. 14.

Carnitine, γ-trimethylamino-β-hydroxybutyrate, is known to stimulate the oxidation of long-chain fatty acids in a variety of tissues. For example, fatty acyl derivatives of CoASH present in the soluble portion of the cell may undergo acyl transfer reactions in which carnitine serves as acyl group acceptor. The acylated carnitines are then supposed to cross the mitochondrial membrane (impermeable to esters to coenzyme A) and, intramitochondrially, be reconverted to the corresponding HSCoA derivatives (see page 375). Overall, this sequence of events results in the exposure of fatty acyl-SCoA present extramitochondrially to the oxidation enzymes present intramitochondrially.

FORMATION OF KETONE BODIES   The ketone bodies, acetoacetate, β-hydroxybutyrate, and acetone, accumulate in the blood under certain abnormal conditions, e.g., diabetes. Each of these substances arises from the metabolism of acetoacetyl-SCoA. The principal fate of acetoacetyl-SCoA in the liver is conjugation with acetyl-SCoA, yielding β-hydroxy-β-methylglutaryl-SCoA, an important precursor of cholesterol (see page 388):

$$CH_3\overset{O}{\overset{\|}{C}}-CH_2-\overset{O}{\overset{\|}{C}}-SCoA + CH_3\overset{O}{\overset{\|}{C}}-SCoA \rightarrow$$

$$HO_2C-CH_2-\underset{OH}{\overset{CH_3}{\underset{|}{\overset{|}{C}}}}-CH_2-\overset{O}{\overset{\|}{C}}-SCoA + HSCoA \qquad (13\text{-}19)$$

Under normal conditions, virtually all this intermediate is channeled into cholesterol synthesis. In certain instances, a distinct enzyme from that involved in its synthesis catalyzes the cleavage of β-hydroxy-β-methylglutaryl-SCoA to acetyl-SCoA and acetoacetate:

$$HO_2C-CH_2-\underset{OH}{\overset{CH_3}{\underset{|}{\overset{|}{C}}}}-CH_2-\overset{O}{\overset{\|}{C}}-SCoA \rightarrow CH_3\overset{O}{\overset{\|}{C}}-SCoA + CH_3\overset{O}{\overset{\|}{C}}-CH_2-CO_2H \qquad (13\text{-}20)$$

The sum of Eqs. (13-19) and (13-20) represents the major route for the formation of free acetoacetate in the liver. Alternatively, free acetoacetate may be produced through the action of a deacylase, which appears to be localized in the liver:

$$CH_3\overset{O}{\overset{\|}{C}}-CH_2-\overset{O}{\overset{\|}{C}}-SCoA \xrightarrow{H_2O} CH_3\overset{O}{\overset{\|}{C}}-CH_2-CO_2H + HSCoA \qquad (13\text{-}21)$$

β-Hydroxybutyrate is formed by the reduction of free acetoacetate in a reaction catalyzed by an enzyme obtained in highly purified form from the soluble portion of the liver cytoplasm:

$$CH_3\overset{O}{\overset{\|}{C}}-CH_2-CO_2H + NADH + H^+ \rightleftharpoons CH_3\underset{H}{\overset{OH}{\underset{|}{\overset{|}{C}}}}-CH_2-CO_2H + NAD^+ \qquad (13\text{-}22)$$

This reduction is *stereospecific*, and only D-(−)-β-hydroxybutyrate is formed.

Acetone also arises from the metabolism of free acetoacetate. The mechanism of acetoacetic decarboxylase, the enzyme responsible for this conversion, has been the subject of a penetrating investigation by Westheimer and his collaborators;

$$CH_3\overset{O}{\overset{\|}{C}}-CH_2-CO_2H \rightarrow CH_3\overset{O}{\overset{\|}{C}}-CH_3 + CO_2 \qquad (13\text{-}23)$$

This reaction occurs with the formation of a Schiff base between enzyme and substrate, followed by its decarboxylation and hydrolysis:

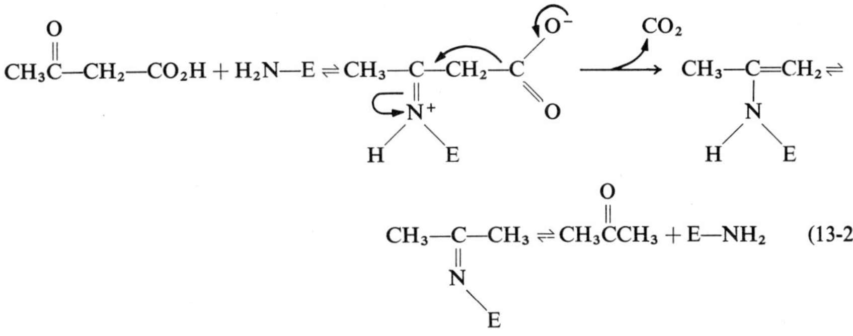

$$CH_3\overset{O}{\overset{\|}{C}}-CH_2-CO_2H + H_2N-E \rightleftharpoons CH_3-\underset{\underset{H \quad E}{N^+}}{\overset{}{C}}-CH_2-\overset{O^-}{\underset{O}{C}} \xrightarrow{CO_2} CH_3-\underset{\underset{H \quad E}{N}}{C}=CH_2 \rightleftharpoons$$

$$CH_3-\underset{\underset{E}{N}}{\overset{}{C}}-CH_3 \rightleftharpoons CH_3\overset{O}{\overset{\|}{C}}CH_3 + E-NH_2 \qquad (13\text{-}24)$$

OXIDATION OF ODD-NUMBERED FATTY ACIDS: THE FATE OF PROPIONATE

The sequence of reactions detailed above for the oxidation of even-numbered fatty acids is also applicable to the oxidation of those with an odd number of carbon atoms. The main distinction between the two pathways lies in the products. The terminal cleavage of acetoacetyl-SCoA yields two molecules of acetyl-SCoA, and that of β-ketovaleryl-SCoA yields one of acetyl SCoA and one of propionyl-SCoA. Further metabolism of propionyl-SCoA may occur via several reaction paths. The most important of these, the methyl malonyl pathway, involves the ATP-dependent carboxylation of propionyl-SCoA, which, in turn, is first converted to its enantiomer and then isomerized to succinyl-SCoA in a vitamin B_{12} coenzyme-dependent reaction catalyzed by methyl malonyl mutase:

$$CH_3CH_2\overset{\overset{\displaystyle O}{\|}}{C}-SCoA + ATP + CO_2 \underset{Mg^{+2}}{\overset{biotin \cdot E}{\rightleftharpoons}} CH_3-\overset{\overset{\displaystyle HO_2C}{|}}{\underset{\underset{\displaystyle H}{|}}{C}}-\overset{\overset{\displaystyle O}{\|}}{C}-SCoA + ADP + P_i \qquad (13\text{-}25)$$

$$CH_3-\overset{\overset{\displaystyle HO_2C}{|}}{\underset{\underset{\displaystyle H}{|}}{C}}-\overset{\overset{\displaystyle O}{\|}}{C}-SCoA \rightleftharpoons CH_3-\overset{\overset{\displaystyle H}{|}}{\underset{\underset{\displaystyle CO_2H}{|}}{C}}-\overset{\overset{\displaystyle O}{\|}}{C}-SCoA \qquad (13\text{-}26)$$

$$CH_3-\overset{\overset{\displaystyle H}{|}}{\underset{\underset{\displaystyle CO_2H}{|}}{C}}-\overset{\overset{\displaystyle O}{\|}}{C}-SCoA \xrightarrow{B_{12}\ coenzyme} HO_2C-CH_2-CH_2\overset{\overset{\displaystyle O}{\|}}{C}-SCoA \qquad (13\text{-}27)$$

Succinyl-SCoA is metabolized further by the citric acid cycle sequence of reactions, as outlined in Chap. 14. Metabolism of propionate according to Eqs. (13-26) and (13-27) occurs in a variety of mammalian tissues, in propionic acid bacteria, and in other microorganisms.

OXIDATION OF BRANCHED-CHAIN FATTY ACIDS

The oxidation of the principal branched-chain fatty acids, isobutyrate, α-methylbutyrate, and isovalerate, occurs via pathways largely identical to those for the degradation of valine, isoleucine, and leucine, respectively. These pathways are developed in Chap. 17.

REFERENCES

Davidson, F. M., C. Long, and I. F. Penny: "Biochemical Problems of Lipids," Butterworths, London, 1956.

Deuel, H. J.: "The Lipids," Interscience, New York, 1951.

Green, D. E.: Fatty Acid Oxidation in Soluble Systems of Animal Tissues, *Biol. Rev. Cambridge Phil. Soc.*, **29**: 330 (1954).

————, and S. J. Wakil: Enzymatic Mechanism of Fatty Acid Oxidation and Synthesis, in K. Bloch (ed.), "Lipide Metabolism," Wiley, New York, 1960.

Hanahan, D. J., and G. A. Thompson, Jr.: Complex Lipids, *Ann. Rev. Biochem.*, **32**: 215 (1963).

————, F. R. N. Gurd, and I. Zabin: "Lipide Chemistry," Wiley, New York, 1960.

Jaenicke, L., and F. Lynen: Coenzyme A, in P. D. Boyer, H. Lardy, and K. Myrbäck (eds.), "The Enzymes," 2d ed., vol. 3, p. 3, Academic Press, New York, 1960.

Jencks, W. P.: Acyl Activation, in P. D. Boyer, H. Lardy, and K. Myrbäck (eds.), "The Enzymes," 2d ed., vol. 6, p. 373, Academic Press, New York, 1962.

Kates, M.: Lipolytic Enzymes, in K. Bloch (ed.), "Lipide Metabolism," Wiley, New York, 1960.

Lovern, J. A.: "The Chemistry of Lipids of Biochemical Significance," Methuen, London, 1955.

Lynen, F.: Lipide Metabolism, *Ann. Rev. Biochem.*, **24**: 654 (1955).

Mahler, H. R.: Biological Oxidation of Fatty Acids, in K. S. Markley (ed.), "Fatty Acids," 2d ed., Part 3, p. 1487, Interscience, New York, 1964.

14| The Citric Acid Cycle

The *citric acid cycle* — frequently also called the *tricarboxylic acid cycle,* with both designations sometimes linked to the name of Krebs[1], its most illustrious proponent — forms the hub of metabolism of almost all cells and must therefore assume an equally central place in our discussion. Originally proposed to account for the complete combustion of pyruvate (and hence of carbohydrates), and of the 2- and 3-carbon end products of fatty acid oxidation, its importance transcends these and other purely catabolic, energy-yielding functions. As the focus of the central pathways (see page 257) many of its reactions and substrates fulfill an equally crucial role in the biosynthesis (anabolism) of a host of important metabolites, ranging from amino acids, purines, and pyrimidines to long-chain fatty acids and porphyrins.

THE CYCLICAL
OXIDATION OF
ACETYL-SCoA
Historical

The study of the oxidation of a number of organic compounds, including certain mono-, di-, and tricarboxylic acids by preparations from animal tissues (minces, extracts of all sorts, homogenates, and later separated and purified fractions — see Chap. 9) was initiated over fifty years ago by Thunberg and by Batelli and Stern. These investigators found that of many substances tested with frog muscle preparations, only succinate, fumarate, malate, and citrate were susceptible to oxidation rapid enough to be of any possible significance as intermediates in the oxidation of fats and carbohydrates. In 1936, Martius and Knoop suggested that the following set of conversions intervened between citrate and succinate (see Fig. 14-1 for the structure of the intermediates):

[1]Sir Hans A. Krebs, German-born British biochemist, who received the Nobel Prize for Physiology and Medicine in 1953 for his work in intermediary metabolism.

citrate → isocitrate → oxalosuccinate → α-ketoglutarate → succinate. In the next year, Krebs, on the basis of his demonstration of the formation of citrate from pyruvate plus oxalacetate in pigeon breast muscle, proposed that these reactions

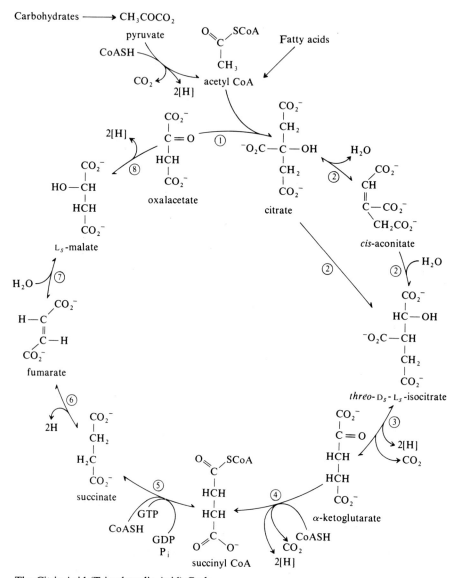

FIGURE 14-1. The Citric Acid (Tricarboxylic Acid) Cycle.

could be used in cyclical fashion to account for the complete oxidation of pyruvate to three molecules of CO_2 as follows:

$$\text{Pyruvate} + \text{oxalacetate} \xrightarrow[-CO_2]{-2H} \text{citrate} \rightarrow \textit{cis}\text{-aconitate} \rightarrow \text{isocitrate} \xrightarrow[-CO_2]{-2H}$$
$$\alpha\text{-ketoglutarate} \xrightarrow[-CO_2]{-2H} \text{succinate} \rightarrow \text{fumarate} \rightarrow \text{malate} \xrightarrow{-2H} \text{oxalacetate}$$

The following set of observations contributes strong evidence that this sequence of reactions, with the modifications discussed below, does constitute the major pathway for the catabolism of pyruvate and acetate (as acetyl-CoA) in the tissue of all animals, from man to *Paramecium* and in those of higher plants and many microorganisms:

1. The various postulated intermediates can all be demonstrated to be present in most tissues examined and to be oxidized at rates rapid enough to make them suitable for participation in such a cycle.

2. Addition of any of the various di- and tri-carboxylic acids greatly stimulates the rate of endogenous respiration and furthermore leads to an uptake of oxygen far above and beyond that accountable for by the addition of the intermediates alone. It is the latter observation that most forcefully indicates the cyclical nature of the process of oxidation: clearly, since the added substrates act catalytically rather than stoichiometrically, they are being (at least in part) regenerated in the course of the reaction. Similar effects are also observed if instead of endogenous respiration we study that resulting from the oxidation of glucose, pyruvate, lactate, or fatty acid.

3. Malonate at low concentrations (<0.01 M) is a highly specific inhibitor for one step and one step only of the postulated scheme, namely, the conversion of succinate to fumarate. Addition of malonate to a respiring system leads to an abolition of the catalytic effect and to an accumulation of succinate.

4. The distribution of C^{14} in the various intermediates during the oxidation of a typical labeled substrate, such as glucose or fatty acid, is in complete accord with the scheme.

5. The individual reactions postulated can be demonstrated to occur both in crude minces and homogenates (with other steps blocked by means of selective inhibitors), as well as with highly purified enzymes extracted therefrom.

6. In cells of animals or plants all the reactions of the cycle can be shown to be localized in just one subcellular organelle, namely, the mitochondrion. Furthermore, the various enzymes of the cycle are present in the mitochondria of different cells in different amounts but in nearly constant proportion to one another.

The Reactions of the Cycle

A contemporary version of the cycle and its component parts is shown in Fig. 14-1 and Table 14-1. We observe that the cycle proper consists of a total of eight reactions: one (reaction 1) forms a C—C bond between a dicarboxylic and a derivative of a monocarboxylic acid (oxalacetate and acetyl CoA); four reactions are dehydrogenations; of them, two are oxidative decarboxylations (reactions 3 and 4), leading to the formation of a 4-*C*-dicarboxylic from a 6-*C*-tricarboxylic acid; two (reactions 5 and 8) together oxidize a saturated 4-*C*-dicarboxylic acid to the α-keto dicarboxylic acid required to start the sequence anew; two of the remaining reactions (2 and 6) are hydration-dehydration reactions (the former used to bring about an isomerization), and one (reaction 5) leads to phosphorylation (i.e., the conversion of P_i into a nucleoside triphosphate) at the expense of the oxidation of a substrate in the reaction just preceding.

ENZYMES OF THE CYCLE AND THE INDIVIDUAL REACTIONS
Reaction 14-1

Reaction 1 is catalyzed by an enzyme that has had a large number of different designations in its short history. The simplest, but hardly descriptive, trivial name is simply *condensing enzyme*. This has been variously modified to *citrate condensing enzyme* or *citrogenase*; the two suggested systematic names are also indicated in the table.

TABLE 14-1. The Reactions of the Citric Acid Cycle

Reaction	Equation (Additional coenzyme or cosubstrate above, cofactors or activators below arrow)	Name of enzyme	Characteristic inhibitor (competitive inhibitors*)	$\Delta G^{0'}$, in kilocalories per mole[h]
1	Acetyl-SCoA + oxalacetate$^=$ + $H_2O \rightarrow$ citrate^{-3} + CoASH + H^+	Citrate condensing enzyme [citrate synthase, citrate oxalacetate lyase (CoA acetylating), citrogenase]	None	-9.08
2a	Citrate^{-3} $\xrightarrow{\text{Fe}^{+2},\text{ GSH}}$ isocitrate^{-3}	Aconitase (aconitate hydratase)	Fluorocitrate* trans-aconitate*	$+1.59$
2b	Citrate^{-3} $\xrightarrow{\text{Fe}^{+2},\text{ GSH}}$ cis-aconitate^{-3}	Aconitase (aconitate hydratase)		$(+2.04)$
2c	cis-Aconitate^{-3} $\xrightarrow{\text{Fe}^{+2},\text{ GSH}}$ isocitrate^{-3}	Aconitase (aconitate hydratase)		(-0.45)
3[b]	Isocitrate^{-3} + NAD$^+$ $\xrightarrow[\text{Mg}^{+2}\text{ or Mn}^{+2},\text{ ADP}^a]{}$ α-Keto(α-oxo)glutarate$^=$ + NADH + CO_2	Isocitrate dehydrogenase ($_D$S-isocitrate: NAD oxido-reductase)	ATP	-1.70
4	α-Ketoglutarate$^=$ + CoASH + NAD$^+$ $\xrightarrow[\text{Mg}^{+2}]{\text{TPP, lip S}_2}$ succinyl-S-CoA$^-$ + CO_2 + NADH	α-Ketoglutarate dehydrogenase (complex)	Arsenite Parapyruvate*[c]	-8.82
5	Succinyl-SCoA + GDP + P$_i$ + H_2O $\xrightarrow{\text{Mg}^{+2}}$ succinate + GTP + CoASH	Succinic thiokinase [succinyl-CoA synthase, succinate: CoA ligase (GDP)]	NH$_2$OH[d]	-2.12^e
6	Succinate$^=$ + (FAD)^f $\underset{}{\overset{\text{Fe}^{+2}}{\rightleftharpoons}}$ fumarate$^=$ + (FADH$_2$)	Succinic(-ate) dehydrogenase [$-$: (acceptor) oxidoreductase]	Malonate* Oxalacetate*	~ 0
7	Fumarate$^=$ + H_2O $\rightleftharpoons$ L-malate$^=$	Fumarase (fumarate hydratase)	meso-Tartrate*	-0.88
8	L-Malate$^=$ + NAD$^+$ $\rightleftharpoons$ oxalacetate$^=$ + NADH + H^+	Malate dehydrogenase (L-malate: NAD oxidoreductase)	β-F-Oxalacetate* Fluoromalate*	$+6.69$
Sum 1–8	Acetyl-SCoA + 3NAD$^+$ + (FAD) + GDP + P$_i$ + 2H_2O $\xrightarrow{\text{cycle}}$ 2CO$_2$ + CoASH + 3NADH + (FADH$_2$) + GTP			-14.32
9a	3 × [NADH + 0.5O$_2$ + H^+ $\rightarrow$ NAD$^+$ + H_2O]	Electron transport chain (NADH branch)	Barbiturates Rotenone Antimycin A Cyanide	-52.4
9b	3 × [NADH + 0.5O$_2$ + 3ADP + 3P$_i$ $\rightarrow$ NAD$^+$ + 3ATP + 4H_2O]	Same as above, plus oxidative phosphorylation	Dinitrophenol Oligomycin	-30
10a	(FADH$_2$) + 0.5O$_2$ $\rightarrow$ (FAD) + H_2O	Electron transport chain (succinate branch)	Thienyltrifluo-roacetone Antimycin A Cyanide	-36.2
10b	(FADH$_2$) + 0.5O$_2$ + 2ADP + 2P$_i$ $\rightarrow$ (FAD) + 2ATP + 3H_2O	Same as above, plus oxidative phosphorylation	Dinitrophenol Oligomycin	-21
Sum total	Acetyl-SCoA + 3O$_2$ $\rightarrow$ 3CO$_2$ + 2H_2O + CoASH	Cycle + electron transport		-215.2
	Acetyl-SCoA + 3O$_2$ + 11ADP + GDP + 12P$_i$ $\rightarrow$ 3CO$_2$ + 2H_2O + 11ATP + GTP + CoASH	Cycle + electron transport + oxidative phosphorylation		-125.3

In general, the reactions shown are those occurring with the mitochondrial enzymes from various animal tissues (mammalian heart, liver; avian breast muscle, insect flight muscle, etc.). Extramitochondrial enzymes from these sources and the enzymes from microorganisms frequently have different characteristics from those shown.
[a] AMP is the specific cofactor with the mitochondrial enzyme from yeast and the enzyme from *Aspergillus niger.*
[b] An important extramitochondrial enzyme catalyzes the reaction with NADP as obligatory coenzyme.

The enzyme is large and exceptionally stable; its specificity for the substrates indicated appears to be quite stringent in all respects, with monofluoroacetyl CoA as the only alternate reactant. This compound in the presence of oxalacetate (OAA) is converted to fluorocitrate at about one-tenth the rate of the natural substrate. Another enzyme, called the *citrate cleavage enzyme* (*citrate lyase, ATP requiring*), is known that catalyzes reaction (14-1a). This reaction as well as reaction 14-1 may require the formation of enzyme-bound citryl CoA as an intermediate:

$$\text{Citrate} + \text{ATP} + \text{CoASH} + \text{E} \rightleftharpoons [\text{E citryl} \sim \text{SCoA}] + \text{ADP} + P_i$$
$$\downarrow \text{H}_2\text{O}$$
$$\text{acetyl CoA} + \text{OAA} + \text{E}$$

$$(14\text{-}1a)$$

In reaction (14-1), the intermediate is spontaneously and irreversibly hydrolyzed to citrate, and in reaction (14-1a), its formation from citrate requires activation by ATP.

Reaction 14-2 The enzyme *aconitase* (aconitate hydratase) catalyzes reactions (14-2b) and (14-2c) — see Table 14-1 — the reversible hydration-dehydration equilibria between citrate and *cis*-aconitate and also between (+)-isocitrate and *cis*-aconitate. The specificity for these three substrates appears to be absolute. Evidence is very strong that both reactions are catalyzed by the same enzyme. On dialysis, activity is lost, which can be restored by Fe^{+2} ions in the presence of a reducing agent. The question whether the interconversion of citrate and isocitrate requires *cis*-aconitate as an obligatory intermediate has been vexing. It is clear that the simultaneous occurrence of the two partial reactions (14-2b) and (14-2c) could account for the isomerization; the question is, does it? The bulk of the currently available evidence would indicate that it does not.

Reaction 14-3 Most animal and plant cells contain two enzymes capable of dehydrogenating the naturally occurring (+)-isocitrate — one specific for $NADP^+$ and the other for NAD^+. For a long time it was believed that the former, which appeared to exhibit much greater activity in cell homogenates or extracts, was the one primarily involved in the citric acid cycle. There was one disturbing feature, viz., that the bulk of the isolated activity was almost invariably found to be localized in the soluble portion of the cytoplasm, although the overall cycle had quite generally been assigned to mitochondria as one of their most characteristic properties. The situation became clarified when it became evident that the NAD^+-linked mitochondrial enzymes were unstable and exhibited some rather peculiar molecular and kinetic properties. The latter, however, were precisely those to be expected from an enzyme that is to fulfill a key regulatory function in as important an area of metabolism as is the citric acid cycle. ADP not only

---

[c] A dimer of pyruvate accumulating on storage, its structure is

$$\text{OH}$$
$$|$$
$$^-\text{O}_2\text{CC}(\text{CH}_3)\text{CH}_2\text{COCO}_2^-$$

[d] Acts by virtue of forming the hydroxamic acid derivative of the substrate succinyl CoA.
[e] For the reaction succinyl—CoA^- + $\text{Mg} \cdot \text{GDP}^-$ + P_i = succinate= + $\text{Mg} \cdot \text{GTP}^=$ + CoASH; $\Delta G^{0\prime} = -0.8$ kcal/mole.
[f] (FAD) stands for tightly enzyme-bound flavin.
[g] Estimated on the basis of the ready reversibility of the reaction.
[h] Most of the $\Delta G^{0\prime}$ values are those calculated by M. J. Johnson for 25°, a pH of 7.0, an ionic strength of 0.15, and total analytical concentrations for all reactants (1 atm for gases, 1 molar for all others, including H_2O) — M. J. Johnson, in P. D. Boyer, H. Lardy, and K. Myrbäck (eds.), "The Enzymes," 2d. ed., vol. 3, p. 407, Academic Press, New York, 1960.

enhances the stability of the enzyme but is also specifically required for full activity at low substrate concentrations because of a pronounced effect on the K_s for isocitrate; i.e., ADP may be acting as an allosteric effector. There is good indication that besides ADP, (+)-isocitrate can also activate the enzyme. Part of the inhibition by ATP is accounted for by chelation of the divalent metal ion (Mg^{+2} or Mn^{+2}) required as an obligatory cofactor. Enzymes from molds and fungi exhibit somewhat different properties: e.g., the enzyme from yeast is activated by 5′-AMP (or ADP at higher concentrations).

The $NADP^+$-dependent enzymes show none of these peculiar features. They also differ from the NAD^+-requiring ones in their size, their intracellular localization, and in the nature of the reaction catalyzed. There is no evidence for oxalosuccinate either as a free or an enzyme-bound intermediate with the NAD^+-linked enzymes; with the $NADP^+$-requiring ones there is good proof for the occurrence of the following partial reactions (note that free oxalosuccinate can react with the enzyme to afford the corresponding complex and reactions but does not readily dissociate from the enzyme surface and is not an intermediate):

$$\text{Isocitrate} + E \rightleftharpoons [E \cdot \text{isocitrate}] \underset{-NADP^+}{\overset{+NADP^+}{\rightleftharpoons}} [E \cdot \text{oxalosuccinate}] + NADPH + H^+ \qquad (14\text{-}3a)$$

$$\text{Oxalosuccinate} + E \rightleftharpoons [E \cdot \text{oxalosuccinate}] \qquad (14\text{-}3b)$$

$$[E \cdot \text{oxalosuccinate}] \rightleftharpoons [E \cdot \alpha\text{-ketoglutarate}] + CO_2$$
$$\updownarrow$$
$$\alpha\text{-ketoglutarate} + E \qquad (14\text{-}3c)$$

The overall reaction — reaction 3, Table 14-1, i.e., (14-3a) + (14-3c) — requires Mn^{+2}, as does the reductive carboxylation of α-ketoglutarate — (14-3c) + (14-3a) in reverse — and the decarboxylation of oxalosuccinate — (14-3b) + (14-3c).

Reaction 14-4   One of the peculiarities of the cycle is the fact that it contains two successive decarboxylative dehydrogenation steps of quite different reaction types. Reaction 4 is catalyzed by the α-ketoglutarate dehydrogenase complex of enzymes (α-KDC), an entity that bears a striking resemblance to that responsible for the analogous reactions of pyruvate (PDC), already described on page 277. The α-KDC isolated from pig heart is somewhat smaller than the PDC from the same source ($M = 3.3 \times 10^6$ versus 10×10^6). It contains approximately six molecules of protein-bound lipoate, eight molecules of FAD, and six molecules of TPP per particle. The reactions catalyzed by the various components are

$$^-O_2CCH_2CH_2COCO_2^- + E_a \cdot TPP \underset{}{\overset{Mg^{+2}}{\rightleftharpoons}} E_a \cdot TPP{-}\overset{\overset{\displaystyle OH}{|}}{CH}(CH_2)_2CO_2^- + CO_2 \qquad (14\text{-}4a)$$
$$\text{α-hydroxy-γ-carboxypropyl TPP}$$

$$E_a \cdot TPP{-}\overset{\overset{\displaystyle OH}{|}}{CH}{-}(CH_2)_2CO_2^- + E_b \cdot NH{-}CO{-}(CH_2)_5{-}\langle\quad\rangle \longrightarrow$$
$$\qquad\qquad\qquad\qquad\qquad\qquad\qquad\qquad S{-}S$$

$$E_a \cdot TPP + E_b \cdot NH{-}CO{-}(CH_2)_5{-}\langle\quad\rangle \qquad (14\text{-}4b\text{-}1)$$
$$^-O_2C(CH_2)_2{-}COS \quad SH$$

$$E_b \cdot NHCO(CH_2)_5{-}\langle\quad\rangle + CoASH \rightleftharpoons E_b \cdot NHCO(CH_2)_5{-}\langle\quad\rangle + \text{succinyl-SCoA}$$
$$^-O_2C{-}(CH_2)_2{-}CO{-}S \quad SH \qquad\qquad\qquad\qquad HS \quad SH$$
$$\qquad\qquad\qquad\qquad\qquad\qquad\qquad\qquad\qquad\qquad\qquad\qquad (14\text{-}4b\text{-}2)$$

$$E_b \cdot NHCO(CH_2)_5 \!-\!\!\!\begin{smallmatrix} \\ HS \quad SH \end{smallmatrix} + E_c\!-\!FAD \rightleftharpoons E_b \cdot NHCO(CH_2)_5 \!-\!\!\!\begin{smallmatrix} \\ S\!-\!S \end{smallmatrix} + E_c \cdot FADH_2$$

(14-4c-1)

$$E_c \cdot FADH_2 + NAD^+ + E_c \cdot FAD + NADH + H^+$$ (14-4c-2)

$E_a = \alpha$-ketoglutarate decarboxylase; $E_b = $ lipoic reductase-transacetylase; $E_c = $ dihydrolipoic dehydrogenase

It will be noted that only enzyme (E_a) and the overall stoichiometry of the complex distinguishes α-KDC from PDC. The net reaction — sum of (14-4a) + (14-4b-1) + (14-4b-2) + (14-4c-1) + (14-4c-2) — is that shown in Table 14-1.

Reaction 14-5   While acetyl CoA can undergo a wide variety of metabolic reactions, the fate of the succinyl CoA generated in reaction (14-4) is much more limited. Its preponderant route is to continue in the cycle. Since the appropriate step (the conversion of succinyl CoA to succinate) is highly exergonic, the stage is set for the utilization of the thiolester bond generated in step 4 for conversion into, and storage as, a nucleoside triphosphate. The reaction is catalyzed by *succinic thiokinase*:

$$\text{Succinyl-SCoA} + \text{MgGDP} + P_i \rightleftharpoons \text{succinate} + \text{MgGTP} + \text{CoASH}$$ (14-5)

and both the guanosine and inosine di- and triphosphates can function as cosubstrates in the reaction. GTP can enter the metabolic pool of high energy currency in the form of ATP, by virtue of the reaction catalyzed by *nucleoside diphosphate kinase*:

$$\text{GTP (or NTP in general)} + \text{ADP} \xrightarrow{Mg^{+2}} \text{ATP} + \text{GDP (or NDP in general)}$$

Reaction 14-6   This key dehydrogenation of the cycle is catalyzed by *succinic dehydrogenase*, an enzyme that appears to be tightly integrated into the particulate matter of all aerobic cells — the mitochondria of animals and plants, or the oxidative mosaic of bacterial cell membranes — and has therefore been frequently employed as a marker enzyme for such particles. It is not surprising therefore that several of the most important features of the enzyme in its native physiological state still continue to elude us, most notably the precise nature of the true electron acceptor for ($FADH_2$), as well as the function of the nonheme iron associated with the enzyme. These points are discussed further in Chap. 15.

The homogeneous soluble enzyme has an $M \simeq 1.75 \times 10^5$, and contains tightly bound to the protein 4 g-atoms of nonheme iron and 1 mole of FAD in covalent (probably amide) linkage. One of the difficulties in the early history of the enzyme was that of its assay after its detachment from other electron-transport carriers. While in the native, particulate form it reacts readily with numerous acceptors, utilizing more or less of the whole respiratory chain, as a "succin-oxidase" or "dye reductase" — reactions (14-6a) and (14-6b) — the number of electron acceptors capable of oxidizing the flavin in the solubilized enzyme — reaction (14-6c) — is strictly limited:

$$\text{Succinate} + E_s \cdot FAD \rightleftharpoons \text{fumarate} + E_s \cdot FADH_2 \qquad (fp_s H_2)$$ (14-6)

$$E_s \cdot FADH_2 + \tfrac{1}{2}O_2 \xrightarrow[\text{transport chain}]{\text{mitochondrial electron}} E_s \cdot FAD(fp_s) + H_2O$$ (14-6a)

$$E_s \cdot FADH_2 + \begin{Bmatrix} 2 \text{ dye } (1e \text{ acceptor}) \\ \text{or} \\ \text{dye } (2e \text{ acceptor}) \end{Bmatrix} \xrightarrow[\text{electron transport chain}]{\text{components of}} E_s \cdot FAD + \begin{Bmatrix} 2 \text{ (dye)}^- + 2H^+ \\ \text{dye } H_2 \end{Bmatrix}$$

$$(14\text{-}6b)$$

$$E_s \cdot FADH_2 + \begin{Bmatrix} 2 \text{ dye } (1e \text{ acceptor}) \\ \text{dye } (2e \text{ acceptor}) \end{Bmatrix} \xrightarrow{\text{direct}} E_s \cdot FAD + \begin{Bmatrix} 2 \text{ (dye)}^- + 2H^+ \\ \text{dye } H_2 \end{Bmatrix} \qquad (14\text{-}6c)$$

(E_s is succinic dehydrogenase apoprotein; fp_s is succinate dehydrogenase flavoprotein.)

Only phenazine methosulfate (*N*-methyl phenazinium methosulfate) and K-ferricyanide are of practical importance. Reaction (14-6) is readily reversible, and the overall reduction of fumarate to succinate can easily be studied if a dye of sufficiently low potential ($FMNH_2$, viologen dyes, etc.) is used to drive reaction (14-6b) or (14-6c) from right to left.

Reaction 14-7   The reversible hydration-dehydration between fumarate and L-malate is catalyzed by the enzyme *fumarase*. The kinetics and mechanism of the crystalline enzyme from pig heart ($M = 2.2 \times 10^5$), consisting of four identical polypeptide subunits ($M = 48.5 \times 10^3$), have been thoroughly investigated. No cofactors are required, but the participation of an acidic (i.e., protonated) and a basic (deprotonated) residue has been clearly implicated. Their *pK* values at an ionic strength of 0.01 are 6.2 and 6.8, respectively, and probably refer to two histidine residues, or one histidine and one carboxylic acid residue. The reaction is stereo-specific in either direction, and the addition and removal of the elements of water is *trans*, as shown by the use of D_2O and analysis of the product L-malate by organic or physical (NMR, ORD) techniques:

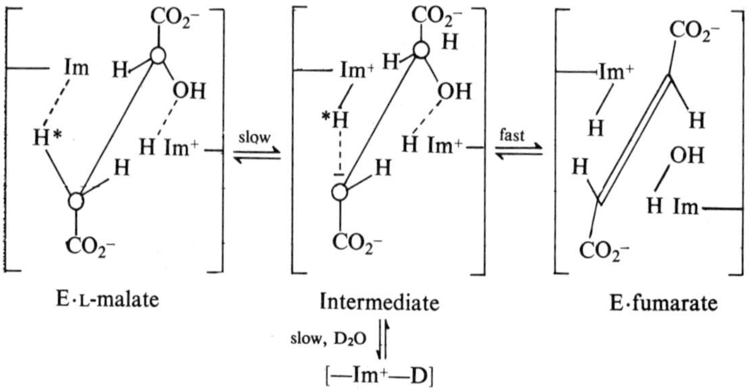

E·L-malate   Intermediate   E·fumarate

slow, D_2O $\updownarrow$

$[-Im^+-D]$

Alternative representations for the 3-monodeuterio-L-malate (*erythro*-L$_s$-malate-3-*d*), shown in brackets at the left, are as follows:

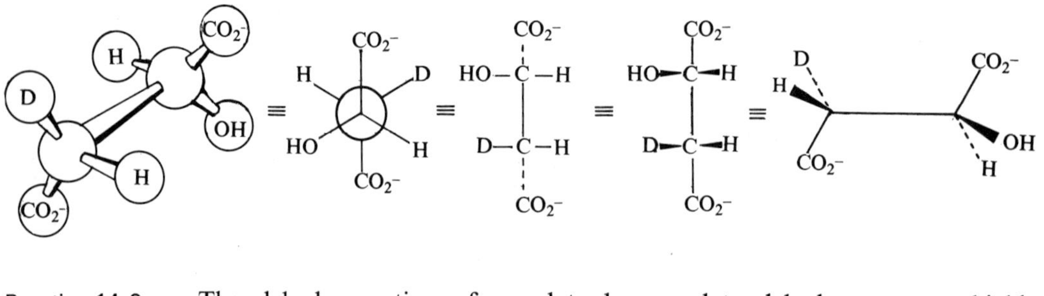

Reaction 14-8   The dehydrogenation of L-malate by L-malate dehydrogenase, a highly

stereoselectly NAD-requiring enzyme — strictly specific for malate in the L-(R)- configuration, hydrogen transfer to the α (or A) side of the pyridine ring — completes the reactions of the cycle and regenerates oxalacetate, the starting material. Mammalian cells appear to contain two isozymes of malate dehydrogenase, one species probably being mitochondrial in localization.

The Overall Reactions We have just seen how one turn of the cycle, involving eight enzyme-catalyzed reactions, leads to the conversion of one molecule of acetyl CoA — or of pyruvate, if we remember that the pyruvate dehydrogenase complex (see page 277) catalyzes the reaction $pyruvate^- + CoASH + NAD^+ \rightarrow acetyl\text{-}SCoA + NADH + CO_2$ — to CO_2 plus H_2O. The overall stoichiometry for acetyl CoA is given in Table 14-1. The analogous one for pyruvate is $pyruvate^- + 2.5O_2 + H^+ \rightarrow 3CO_2 + 2H_2O$.

Now it is clear that the cycle as a metabolic device for the complete oxidation of pyruvate or acetyl CoA requires the reoxidation of the reduced coenzymes produced during its operation. This is brought about by the sequence of carriers that in their aggregate are referred to as the electron-transport sequence or system (ETS). These entities are housed in general in the very same particles that are responsible for the substrate-level oxidations of the cycle. Thus, *particulate* citric acid cycle activity is characterized by a linkage of the various dehydrogenases to molecular oxygen, with the stoichiometry shown. Since the main purpose of the cycle is not just the disposition of the carbon and hydrogens of all those compounds that can generate acetyl CoA or any of the cycle members, but is the conversion of potential chemical energy into metabolic energy in the form of ATP, provision must also be made for the formation of the latter at the expense of the oxidations of the cycle. Only one of its reactions, namely, reaction 5, performs this task directly, at the substrate level. This is an insignificant part of the total potential energy available, which, as the table shows, amounts to some -215 kcal/mole of acetyl CoA or -275 kcal/mole of pyruvate metabolized. Practically all this energy — specifically, 11 out of 12 moles of ATP from the oxidation of one mole of acetyl CoA, or 14 out of 15 from that of 1 mole of pyruvate (and corresponding to 34 out of 38 for 1 mole of glucose; see page 278) — is generated as a consequence of oxidative phosphorylation accompanying mitochondrial electron transport. We shall address ourselves to these problems in Chap. 15.

We have just stated that the cycle is a catalytic device par excellence, employed for the complete combustion, not only of acetyl CoA and all those compounds capable of generating this intermediate, but also of any or all of its members, or of any compound capable of generating any of these members. How is this brought about? It is clear that reactions 14-2 to 7 or 8 by themselves can bring about the dehydrogenation (and when linked to electron transport, the aerobic oxidation) of any of the di- or tricarboxylic acids of the cycle to malate or oxalacetate, but no further. The problem, therefore, resolves itself into the question of how to generate acetyl CoA from malate or oxalacetate. Once we know the solution to this problem, the subsequent steps can be regarded simply as a dismutation of OAA, which continues until only catalytic amounts of this compound are left:

Malate (or oxalacetate) $\rightarrow$ acetyl CoA $+ 2CO_2$ (14-11)

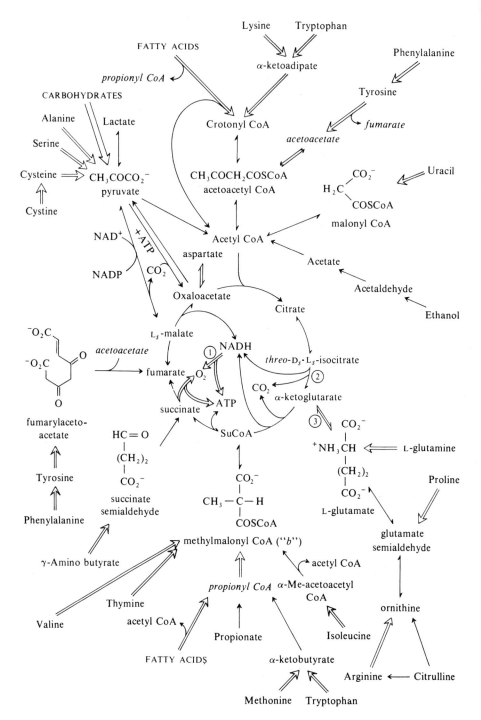

FIGURE 14-2. The Citric Acid Cycle in Catabolism. Multistep reactions indicated by ⇒. The terms in italics are joint intermediates.

$$\text{Acetyl CoA} + \text{oxalacetate} \rightarrow \text{citrate} \rightarrow 2CO_2 + H_2O + \text{oxalacetate} \qquad (14\text{-}12)$$

The steps primarily responsible for reaction 14-11 probably consist of malic enzyme and pyruvic dehydrogenase working in conjunction.[1] It will be recalled that the first-named one is an extramitochondrial NADP-requiring enzyme (see page 278), which brings about the conversion of malate to pyruvate. The same enzyme is also capable of decarboxylating OAA irreversibly:

$$\text{Malate}^= + NADP^+ \overset{Mn^{+2}}{\rightleftharpoons} \text{pyruvate}^- + CO_2 + NADPH \qquad (14\text{-}13a)$$

$$OAA^= \rightarrow \text{pyruvate}^- + HCO_3^- \qquad (14\text{-}13b)$$

Now to recapitulate briefly the fate of pyruvate. This compound is produced in the cytoplasm either from carbohydrates or lactate. It enters the mitochondria, there to be first converted to acetyl CoA, and is then combusted, provided a sufficient supply of one of the cycle acids is present to allow initiation of the first condensation step. If this requirement is not fulfilled or if there is a steady drain on one or more of the participants of the cycle, as a consequence of other metabolic demands, pyruvate must first be converted by CO_2 fixation to a C_4-dicarboxylic acid in an anaplerotic step. In animals the ATP-dependent pyruvate carboxylase (see page 278) is a likely candidate for this task. In *E. coli*, pyruvate is converted directly to PEP at the expense of ATP with the liberation of AMP and P_i. The phosphoenolpyruvate is then carboxylated to OAA in the reaction catalyzed by PEP carboxylase (see page 279).

THE CYCLE AS A CATABOLIC AND ENERGY-GENERATING DEVICE

We have already stressed the role of the cycle (supplemented by the appropriate accessory enzymes) as a most effective catalytic device for the complete combustion of carbohydrates (through pyruvate and acetyl CoA), of acetyl CoA, and of all the members of the cycle itself; linked to the simultaneous generation of some 12 molecules of ATP per turn. It is clear, therefore, that any metabolite capable of being catabolized to one of the compounds just described serves equally well to keep the furnace stoked (see Fig. 14-2).

There exist three great classes of organic compounds in a relatively reduced state that serve as common metabolic fuels: carbohydrates, lipids, and proteins. We already discussed the oxidation of carbohydrates in Chap. 11, and pointed out there how acetyl CoA is generated from these metabolites and certain other related compounds, such as lactate, acetate, acetaldehyde, and ethanol. The fatty acids that form the bulk of the energy supply available in lipids also produce acetyl CoA as a consequence of enzymatic β-oxidation reactions catalyzed by a group of mitochondrial enzymes, which were described in Chap. 13. Acetyl CoA is the sole product, if, as is usually the case, the fatty acid in question contains an even number of carbon atoms in an unbranched chain. Other fatty acids lead to propionyl CoA in addition (see Chap. 13). As is readily appreciated from Fig. 14-2, acetyl CoA and succinyl CoA account for the bulk

---

[1] In bacteria, we must also consider the alternative,

$$OAA \xrightarrow[+P_i]{-CO_2} PEP \xrightarrow{-P_i} \text{pyruvate} \xrightarrow{-CO_2} \text{acetyl CoA}$$
$$\underset{-CO_2}{\underline{\qquad\qquad\qquad\qquad}}$$

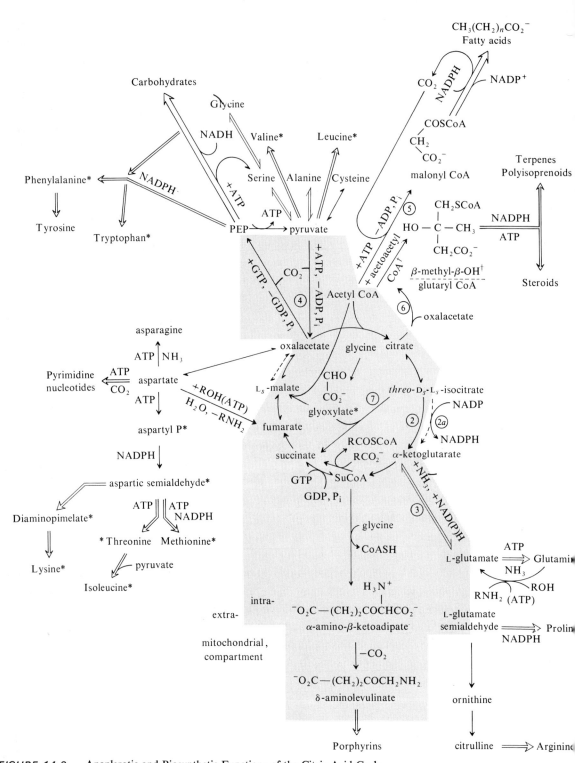

FIGURE 14-3. Anaplerotic and Biosynthetic Functions of the Citric Acid Cycle.

The amino acid intermediates marked * probably are not formed by the routes indicated in higher animals.
† The enzyme responsible may be localized in mitochondria.
↳ indicate intra- and extramitochondrial isoenzymes.

of the flux of carbon atoms entering the cycle. Enough has already been said about the former pathway; therefore some comment about the latter is now appropriate. The methylmalonyl CoA ("form a") produced as a product of the oxidation of odd carbon or branched-chain fatty acids, or of aliphatic amino acids, has a configuration around the asymmetric carbon opposite to that ("form b") required by the specificity of the methylmalonyl CoA mutase, the enzyme capable of converting this compound to succinyl CoA. For this reason a methylmalonyl CoA racemase (or epimerase) must first intervene to inter-convert the two stereoisomers.

The catabolism of the various amino acids shown will be discussed in Chap. 17. Here we want to emphasize only the following. In general, there exist two main pathways for the conversion of α-amino acids to the corresponding α-keto acids — the first step in the catabolism of the majority of compounds of this class: dehydrogenation by flavoprotein amino acid oxidases with the general reaction

$$
\underset{\overset{|}{+}NH_3}{RCHCO_2^-} + O_2 \xrightarrow{\text{flavoprotein}} \underset{\overset{||}{NH}}{R-C-CO_2^-} + H_2O_2 + H^+
$$

$$
\xrightarrow{H_2O} NH_3 + \underset{\overset{||}{O}}{R-C-CO_2^-} \qquad \xrightarrow{\text{catalase}} H_2O + \tfrac{1}{2}O_2 \tag{14-14}
$$

and transamination with α-ketoglutarate by a series of pyridoxal phosphate-dependent transaminases (aminotransferases). Here pyCHO is the pyridoxal and $pyCH_2^+-NH_3^-$ the pyridoxamine form of the coenzyme:

$$
\underset{\overset{|}{+}NH_3}{RCHCO_2^-} + E \cdot pyCHO \rightleftharpoons \underset{\overset{||}{O}}{R-C-CO_2^-} + E \cdot pyCH_2^+NH_3 \tag{14-15a}
$$

$$
{}^-O_2C(CH_2)_2COCO_2^- + E \cdot pyCH_2^+NH_3 \rightleftharpoons {}^-O_2C(CH_2)_2-\underset{\overset{|}{+}NH_3}{CH}-CO_2^- + E \cdot pyCHO \tag{14-15b}
$$

In mammals, at least, reaction (14-15) predominates for the naturally occurring L-amino acids except for L-proline. This metabolism of amino acids by trans-amination constitutes a dead end as far as the $-NH_2$ group is concerned unless provision for its conversion to a "free" form as NH_3 or NH_4^+ can be found. It is this consideration that ascribes a very special role to L-glutamate. The interconversion L-glutamate $\rightleftharpoons \alpha$-ketoglutarate is catalyzed by L-glutamate dehydrogenase:

$$
\text{L-glutamate}^- + \left.\begin{matrix} NAD^+ \\ NADP^+ \end{matrix}\right\} + H_2O \rightleftharpoons \alpha\text{-ketoglutarate}^= + \left.\begin{matrix} NADH \\ NADPH \end{matrix}\right\} + NH_4^+ + H^+
$$

$$
\Delta G^{0\prime} = 7.65 \text{ kcal/mole} \tag{14-16}
$$

Enzymes of this type are very widely distributed throughout living nature, attesting to their great importance in metabolism (see also Figs. 14-2 and 14-3). The enzyme from vertebrate tissues is a polymer of $M \simeq 10^6$, relatively easily dissociated into subunits of much lower enzymic activity and affected through second-site (allosteric) interactions by a wide variety of agents, most notably the purine nucleoside diphosphates. It exhibits almost equal activity with either of the two nicotinamide coenzymes. The enzymes from microorganisms, on the other hand, appear to be specific either for the NAD^+/NADH or the $NADP^+$/ NADPH couple and are relatively insensitive to second-site modifiers.

FUNCTION OF THE CYCLE IN BIOSYNTHESIS

A large number of biosynthetic pathways emanate from the cycle and its constituents. It therefore plays a pivotal role in this branch of metabolism as well (see Fig. 14-3). Stress must be laid on the fact that any time any intermediate is bled off from the cycle, steady-state operation demands its replenishment at the same or a different locus by an anaplerotic reaction.

Carbohydrates

In most cells (except those of bacteria capable of growth on organic compounds containing just two carbon atoms and of certain plant tissues), the synthesis of carbohydrates requires the presence of *stoichiometric* amounts of one of the di- or tricarboxylic acids of the cycle or of compounds that can give rise to one of these intermediates (see Fig. 14-2 and the previous section). Since pyruvate, in the presence of ATP and the pyruvic carboxylase, can fix carbon dioxide to yield oxalacetate (see page 278), this requirement is met by a large number of organic intermediates containing a minimum of three carbon atoms. As outlined in Fig. 14-3 and discussed in more detail on page 279, the synthesis of carbohydrates from such sources involves, at the very outset, two mitochondrial reactions that have no counterpart in carbohydrate breakdown:

$$Pyruvate + ATP + CO_2 \rightarrow OAA + ADP + P_i$$
$$OAA + GTP \rightarrow PEP + GDP + P_i + CO_2 \qquad PEP = \textit{P}\text{-enolpyruvate}$$
$$\downarrow$$
$$carbohydrates$$

Those cells containing the two enzymes peculiar to the glyoxylate cycle (or bypass), viz., *isocitrate lyase* and *malate synthetase* (page 282), are capable of generating 4-carbon dicarboxylic acids and hence carbohydrate from 2-carbon precursors. The biosynthesis of carbohydrate from fats, and more specifically from acetyl CoA, can take place only in such cells. Animals are therefore incapable of affecting this conversion.

Lipids

The biosynthesis of lipids is discussed in Chap. 16. Here we wish to emphasize only the following points. Acetyl CoA, the key intermediate in all these reactions (see Fig. 14-3), is generated by just two main processes (see Fig. 14-2), both localized in the mitochondria or equivalent particles — by the thiolytic cleavage of acetoacetyl CoA (generated by the oxidation of fatty acids and certain amino acids) and the oxidative decarboxylation of pyruvate. Yet the biosynthesis of fatty acids requires as an obligatory first step the carboxylation of acetyl CoA to malonyl CoA, and this reaction, as well as all subsequent steps of the process, are probably catalyzed by an extramitochondrial complex of enzymes. How is this brought about? Does acetyl CoA simply diffuse out of the mitochondria, or is some more complex, energy-requiring process implicated? Recent studies suggest that the latter may be the case: acetyl CoA is first metabolized to citrate inside the particle by condensation with OAA; the citrate so formed is then lost to the cytoplasm, there to be cleaved back to oxalacetate plus acetyl CoA by the ATP-requiring citrate lyase — Eq. (14-1a). The levels of this enzyme appear to be controlled strongly by genetic and environmental factors, such as nutritional state, on the one hand, and pathological conditions, such as diabetes or obesity, on the other. This reaction sequence, unlike that responsible for the synthesis of carbohydrates, requires only catalytic amounts of OAA (or of pyruvate plus CO_2), and synthesis of fatty acids, therefore, does not require the obligatory participation of 4-carbon dicarboxylic acids.

Proteins   Protein synthesis requires metabolic energy in the form of ATP — as do all the other synthetic processes already discussed — a commodity amply provided for by the operation of the cycle. In addition, this process, again like all the others, requires a supply of monomeric units or precursors, in this instance the twenty or so common L-amino acids. Of this number, most higher animals, including man and the laboratory rat, are unable to synthesize in amounts sufficient for their needs about half (Arg, His, Ile, Leu, Lys, Met, Phe, Thr, Trp, and Val). Plants and most microorganisms, on the other hand, are capable of generating most if not all of these as well. The compounds in question are marked with an asterisk in Fig. 14-3. Again the citric acid cycle provides a means for the generation of both groups, the "nonessential" amino acids in animals and the bulk of all amino acids in other cells and organisms.

The metabolic sequences responsible are discussed in more detail in Chap. 17, but several points are worth noting now: there exist three "families" of amino acids that originate from the three α-keto acids pyruvate, OAA, and α-ketoglutarate, and the corresponding α-amino acids, Ala, Asp, and Glu. The group related to α-ketoglutarate and Glu appears to be formed throughout living nature; only some of those originating from pyruvate are synthesized in higher organisms, and those for which OAA and Asp provide the carbon skeleton are simply not produced at all by mammals, and perhaps not by other animals either.

Purines and Pyrimidines   The synthesis of these important constituents of coenzymes and of nucleic acids is described in Chap. 18 and is intimately connected with a functioning cycle: aspartate provides the carbon skeleton of pyrimidines; and the ureido nitrogens of purines, as well as the amino nitrogen for both the amino purines and amino pyrimidines, are variously contributed by aspartate and glutamine.

Porphyrins   Porphyrins are vital cellular constituents as essential components of respiratory pigments and enzymes (see Chaps. 8, 12, and 15). Their biosynthesis is discussed in detail on page 429 of Chap. 17. Its initial mitochondrial phase emanates from succinyl CoA and thus constitutes yet another significant and continuous drain on the cycle.

SOME FACTORS INFLUENCING ACTIVITY OF CITRIC ACID CYCLE

Enzyme Levels   The levels of a number of mitochondrial enzymes, including the characteristic dehydrogenases of the citric acid cycle and the carriers of the respiratory chain, appear to be present in constant relative proportion in mitochondria from widely different sources, ranging from the flight muscle of the locust to various tissues of the rat. Enzymes behaving in this fashion include the various cytochromes (see page 359), succinic dehydrogenase, malate dehydrogenase, and glycerol-P dehydrogenase. These observations suggest that there exists a (probably genetic) mechanism for the control of the synthesis or perhaps the integration of key mitochondrial enzymes in the course of *mitochondriogenesis*.

Substrate Levels   One of the controlling features for any reaction sequence is the availability

TABLE 14-2. Controls on the Citric Acid Cycle

Control point	Name of enzyme(s)	Localization	Requires	Liberates	Activated by	Inhibited by	Biosynthesis and/or activity affected by	Remarks
1	Coupling of ox. phos. to electron transport and respiration	Particulate	ADP, P_i	ATP, CO_2 by virtue of respiration	...	Uncouplers, ATP	State of particles, cations, etc.	Variety of agents can disrupt coupling leading to oxidation but no ATP formation
2	NAD-linked isocitrate dehydrogenase	Particulate	NAD^+	NADH, CO_2	ADP	ATP, NADH	?	At high levels of cycle activity isocitrate probably oxidized by 2a
2a	NADP-linked isocitrate dehydrogenase	Soluble and particulate	$NADP^+$	NADPH, CO_2	OAA?	...	...	Generates NADPH for biosynthesis in appropriate compartment
3	Glutamate dehydrogenase (α-ketoglutarate $\rightleftharpoons$ Glu)	Particulate	NADPH or NADH, NH_3	$NADP^+$ or NAD^+	ADP	GDP plus NADH	?	Precise nature of control exerted not yet known
4	Pyruvate carboxylase	Particulate	ATP, CO_2	ADP	Acetyl CoA		Hormones, genetic makeup, nutritional state	Controls carbohydrate synthesis, NADH-dependent pathway
5	Acetyl CoA carboxylase	Soluble	ATP, CO_2	ADP	Citrate, etc.	Long-chain acyl CoAs	?	Controls fat synthesis, an NADPH-dependent pathway
6	Citrate lyase (ATP requiring)	Soluble	Citrate (from acetyl CoA)	Acetyl CoA, OAA†			Nutritional state, other factors (e.g., obesity)	Makes available extra-particulate acetyl CoA for lipid synthesis
7	Condensing enzyme	Particulate	Acetyl CoA, OAA	Citrate, CoA		Long-chain acyl CoAs, ATP†		Controls diversion of acetyl CoA to other pathways
8	Isocitrate lyase	Soluble	Citrate (from acetyl CoA)	C_4 acids		PEP	PEP	Bacteria (and plants) only

†Recent experiments suggest that ATP also decreases the affinity of fumarase for fumarate and hence the conversion fumarate $\rightarrow$ malate.

of various initiating substrates. It is also evident that a good indicator of metabolic activity is provided by the steady-state concentration or the half-life of the various substrates involved. In rat liver and kidney, half-lives are all of the order of seconds, except for OAA which is at least an order of magnitude lower. In *E. coli*, all these values must be divided by at least a factor of 10. These data testify to the high demand placed on the OAA molecule and its big role in controlling mitochondrial metabolism (see Figs. 14-2 and 14-3).

Coenzyme Levels   Examination of Figs. 14-2 and 14-3 discloses the important fact that, at least in higher organisms, degradative, catabolic, energy-yielding sequences generally involve NAD^+, while biosynthetic, energy-requiring ones almost invariably require NADPH. A cell operating efficiently in the steady state, engaged in carrying out two neatly balanced sets of tasks, ought to and does reflect this principle.

Respiratory Control   The rate of mitochondrial respiration observed depends, not only on the nature and concentration of the substrate to be oxidized, but also, in a most profound manner, on the coupling of respiration to phosphorylation. Intact mitochondria are usually (i.e., when substrate and P_i are not limiting) "tightly" coupled, so that their rate of respiration is actually controlled by the ratio [ADP]/[ATP]. When this ratio is high ("state 3"), most of the intramitochondrial adenine nucleotide is in the form of ADP, and respiration is fast; in contrast, when ATP accumulates at the expense of ADP, i.e., under conditions when the rate of its dephosphorylation by phosphate- and energy-requiring reactions cannot keep pace with the rate of its formation, respiration wanes ("state 4"). Added ATP can even inhibit respiration by virtue of bringing about reversed electron flow.[1] These phenomena, are now known as *respiratory control*.

Accessibility   The mitochondrial membrane itself provides a means for the admission of some substrates and the exclusion of others. For instance, intact mitochondria simply do not admit NADH and this important metabolite, when produced on the outside, is not oxidized as such by the particles but instead participates in a substrate-linked shuttle, as shown below:

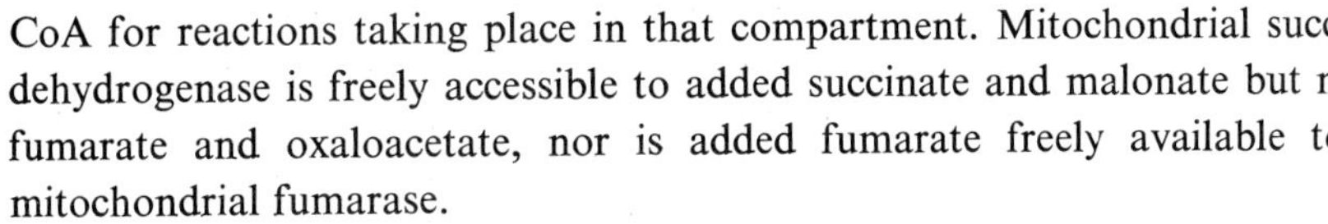

$$H^+ + NADH \rightarrow \quad ox.\ substrate \leftarrow ---- || ---- ox.\ substrate \rightarrow H_2O$$
$$NAD^+ \leftarrow \quad substrate\ H_2 ------ || --- \rightarrow substrate\ H_2 \rightarrow \tfrac{1}{2}O_2$$

cytoplasm ("outside")   mitochondria ("inside")

A number of other instances of this type of compartmentation are known. Intramitochondrial acetyl CoA does not readily diffuse out but is usually first converted to citrate, which is then cleaved in the cytoplasm to generate acetyl CoA for reactions taking place in that compartment. Mitochondrial succinate dehydrogenase is freely accessible to added succinate and malonate but not to fumarate and oxaloacetate, nor is added fumarate freely available to the mitochondrial fumarase.

Control of Enzyme Activity   In Table 14-2 we summarize some facts, many of them already described in

---

[1] This term is used, as more fully discussed on page 369, to describe certain oxidation-reduction reactions not ordinarily observed because of their unfavorable equilibrium, which, however, can be reversed by the addition of ATP; e.g., $NADH + 2\ cytochrome\ c\ (Fe^{+3}) \rightarrow NAD^+ + 2\ cytochrome\ c\ (Fe^{+2}) + H^+$, but $NADH + 2\ cytochrome\ c\ (Fe^{+3}) + 2ADP + 2P_i \rightleftharpoons NAD^+ + 2\ cytochrome\ c\ (Fe^{+2}) + 2ATP$.

these pages, concerning the control of some of the key enzymes of the cycle and some accessory enzymes by a variety of common metabolites.

REFERENCES   Alberty, R. A.: Fumarase, in P. D. Boyer, H. Lardy, and K. Myrbäck (eds.), "The Enzymes," 2d ed., vol. 5, p. 531, Academic Press, New York, 1961.

Atkinson, D. E.: Regulation of Enzyme Activity, *Ann. Rev. Biochem.*, **35**: 85 (1966).

Dickman, S. R.: Aconitase, in P. D. Boyer, H. Lardy, and K. Myrbäck (eds.), "The Enzymes," 2d ed., vol. 5, p. 495, Academic Press, New York, 1961.

Krebs, H. A., and J. M. Lowenstein: The Tricarboxylic Acid Cycle, in D. M. Greenberg (ed.), "Metabolic Pathways," vol. 1, p. 129, Academic Press, New York, 1960.

Kun, E.: Malate Dehydrogenase, in P. D. Boyer, H. Lardy, and K. Myrbäck (eds.), "The Enzymes," 2d ed.. vol. 7, p. 149, Academic Press, New York, 1963.

Lehninger, A. L.: "The Mitochondrion," Benjamin, New York, 1964.

Plaut, G. W. E.: Isocitrate Dehydrogenases, in P. D. Boyer, H. Lardy, and K. Myrbäck (eds.), "The Enzymes," 2d ed., vol. 7, p. 105, Academic Press, New York, 1963.

Sanadi, D. R.: Pyruvate and α-Ketoglutarate Oxidation Enzymes, in P. D. Boyer, H. Lardy, and K. Myrbäck (eds.), "The Enzymes," 2d ed., vol. 7, p. 307, Academic Press, New York, 1963.

Singer, T. P., and E. B. Kearney: Succinate Dehydrogenase, in P. D. Boyer, H. Lardy, and K. Myrbäck (eds.), "The Enzymes," 2d ed., vol. 7, p. 383, Academic Press, New York, 1963.

Stern, J. R.: Oxaloacetate Transacetase, in P. D. Boyer, H. Lardy, and K. Myrbäck (eds.), "The Enzymes," 2d ed., vol. 5, p. 367, Academic Press, New York, 1961.

15 | Biological Oxidations

Biological oxidation reactions provide the cell with a means for supplying its energy demand. They belong to four classes, which, in turn, can be grouped into two main categories, as follows:[1]

A. Dehydrogenations

    1. With O_2 as acceptor   Catalyzed by aerobic dehydrogenases (oxidases), substrate: O_2 oxidoreductases

    2. With some other acceptor   Catalyzed by coenzyme or cofactor-linked dehydrogenases, substrate: acceptor oxidoreductases

B. Oxygen insertion reactions

    1. Yielding dihydroxyderivatives   Catalyzed by oxygenases

    2. Yielding monohydroxyderivatives Catalyzed by hydroxylases

Of these, type *A* probably represents the primordial one; it is the only one observed in anaerobic cells and provides for the bulk of the energy supply both in anaerobic and aerobic cells. Catalysis of simple dehydrogenation reactions probably was among the first characteristics of the ancestral living entities long before the emergence of oxygen into the earth's atmosphere. The importance of

---

[1]We shall use DH_2 as an abbreviation for substrate in the reduced state, D for the molecule in the oxidized form, in order to avoid any possible confusion with sulfur compounds arising from the use of SH_2, etc. Similarly, $A \rightarrow AH_2$ or $A^n \rightarrow A^{n-1}$ will be used for $2e^-$ and $1e^-$ oxidants or acceptors.

dehydrogenations in biochemistry was first pointed out by Wieland in the twenties, based on studies in which colloidal palladium acted as dehydrogenation catalyst or hydrogen carrier for the oxidation of a variety of organic compounds by an acceptor A, such as molecular oxygen, benzoquinone, methylene blue, etc.:

$$
\begin{array}{l}
\overset{X}{\underset{H}{R-\overset{|}{\underset{|}{C}}-OH}} + (Pd) \rightleftharpoons R\,X C{=}O + (Pd)H_2 \\
\qquad\qquad\quad \text{alcohol } X = H \\
\qquad\qquad\quad \text{aldehyde hydrate } X = OH
\end{array}
\tag{15-1a}
$$

or

$$
\begin{array}{l}
DH_2 + (Pd) \rightleftharpoons D + (Pd)H_2 \\
(Pd)H_2 + A \rightarrow Pd + AH_2 \\
\hline
DH_2 + A \xrightarrow{\ Pd\ } D + AH_2
\end{array}
\tag{15-1b}\tag{15-1c}
$$

The apparent generality of these reactions compelled Wieland to the conclusion that oxygen was simply the most physiological of a number of possible acceptors and led him to postulate that all biological oxidations proceeded by means of dehydrogenations involving one or more intermediate hydrogen carriers, A', etc. (also referred to as electron or redox carriers). This may be portrayed by a convenient notation, modified from Baldwin:

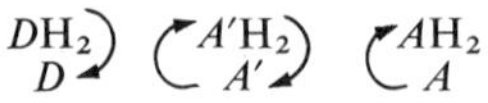

$$
\overset{DH_2}{\underset{D}{\Big)}}\ \overset{A'H_2}{\underset{A'}{\Big(}}\ \overset{AH_2}{\underset{A}{\Big(}}
\tag{15-2a}
$$

or

$$
DH_2 + A' \rightleftharpoons A'H_2 + D \qquad A'H_2 + A \rightleftharpoons AH_2 + A'
\tag{15-2b}
$$

$$
Net \quad DH_2 + A \overset{A'}{\rightleftharpoons} AH_2 + D
\tag{15-2c}
$$

Subsequent studies, especially by Thunberg and by Keilin, showed that living cells and their extracts were able to bring about the dehydrogenation of metabolically important compounds, such as glucose, lactate, succinate, various amino acids, etc., either aerobically at the expense of oxygen or anaerobically at the expense of artificial electron acceptors, such as methylene blue. As a result of these studies, biological oxidations were postulated to conform to Eq. (15-2c), i.e., dehydrogenations of the substrate catalyzed by *dehydrogenases* (now called *oxidoreductases*) capable of transferring reducing equivalents to an intermediate carrier A'.

Two corollaries also emerged: if the first acceptor A' (reduced to $A'H_2$ by the first dehydrogenase) can in turn act as the substrate for a second enzyme, several such respiratory carriers may act in series and produce an array called a *respiratory chain*, or an *electron-transfer system* or *chain*. This then intervenes between the substrate and its primary dehydrogenase on the one hand, the reduction of the terminal acceptor (shown here as oxygen) on the other:

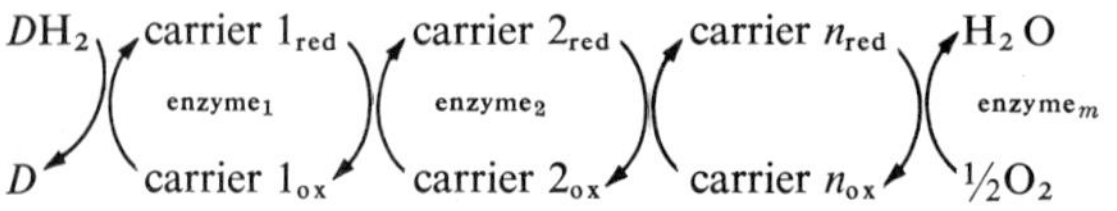

$$
\overset{DH_2}{\underset{D}{\Big)}}\!\!\overset{\text{carrier }1_{red}}{\underset{\text{carrier }1_{ox}}{\Big(\!\!\overset{\text{enzyme}_1}{}\!\!\Big)}}\!\!\overset{\text{carrier }2_{red}}{\underset{\text{carrier }2_{ox}}{\Big(\!\!\overset{\text{enzyme}_2}{}\!\!\Big)}}\!\!\overset{\text{carrier }n_{red}}{\underset{\text{carrier }n_{ox}}{\Big(\!\!\overset{}{}\!\!\Big)}}\!\!\overset{H_2O}{\underset{\frac{1}{2}O_2}{\Big(\!\!\overset{\text{enzyme}_m}{}\!\!\Big)}}
\tag{15-3}
$$

or $\quad DH_2 \xrightarrow{\ E_1\ } \text{carrier } 1 \xrightarrow{\ E_2\ } \text{carrier } 2 \rightarrow \cdots \rightarrow \text{carrier } n \xrightarrow{\ E_m\ } O_2$

Another corollary is that if one carrier can intervene between two dehydrogenases using two different substrates (DH_2 and $D'H_2$), we observe a *linked* reaction:

$$\begin{array}{c} DH_2 \\ \diagdown \\ D \end{array} \underset{\text{enzyme}_1}{\overset{\text{carrier}_{\text{red}}}{\diagup\diagdown}} \underset{\text{enzyme}_2}{\overset{D'H_2}{\diagup\diagdown}} \begin{array}{c} \\ \diagup \\ D' \end{array} \qquad (15\text{-}4)$$

Thus, there are two alternative ways of reconverting the reduced intermediary carrier back to its oxidized form: reoxidation by other carriers, and eventually by a terminal acceptor, or oxidation by a second substrate, which is reduced in the process. Two of the principal carriers, the nicotinamide (or pyridine) coenzymes and the flavin nucleotide coenzymes, were discussed in Chap. 8, and examples of linked reactions during glycolysis and fermentation were described in Chap. 11. In mitochondrial systems, coenzyme Q, cytochromes, nonheme iron, and copper intervene between flavin and the terminal acceptor oxygen. The terminal member of this sequence is cytochrome oxidase, first identified by Warburg as *Atmungsferment*.

We shall first consider briefly reactions involving oxygen, catalyzed by oxygenases or hydroxylases, and then turn our attention to the various types of dehydrogenases, the cytochromes, and other hemoproteins, and conclude with a discussion of respiratory chains and of oxidative phosphorylation.

OXYGENASES AND HYDROXYLASES
Oxygenases

Oxygenases (also called oxygen transferases) are enzymes that catalyze the introduction of both atoms of molecular oxygen into the substrate:

$$DH_2 + O_2^{18} \xrightarrow{\text{oxygenase}} D(O^{18}H)_2 \qquad (15\text{-}5)$$

The first product, which may or may not be stable, can be regarded as the dihydroxy-derivative of the substrate. Properties of some well-characterized oxygenases are tabulated in Table 15-1.

TABLE 15-1. Oxygenases

Enzyme	Source	Prosthetic group	Substrate	Product
Pyrocatechase (catechol-1,2-oxygenase)	*Pseudomonas*	$[Fe^{+2}]$*	Catechol	*cis, cis*-Muconate
Homogentisate oxygenase	Liver, kidney, bacteria	$[Fe^{+2}]$	Homogentisate	4-Maleylacetoacetate
3-Hydroxy-anthranilate oxygenase	Liver, kidney		3-Hydroxyanthranilate	Picolinate† Quinolinate
Tryptophan oxygenase	Animal tissues, bacteria	[Fe porphyrin] (heme)	L-Tryptophan	L-Formyl-kynurenine
Inositol oxygenase	Kidney	$[Fe^{+2}]$	*Myo*inositol	*D*-Glucuronate
Lipoxygenase	Plants		Unsaturated carboxylic acid	Peroxyacid

*[Fe] indicates circumstantial evidence for the involvement of Fe^{+2} at the catalytic site.
†The first product is 2-amino-3-carboxymuconate semialdehyde = 1-amino-4-formyl-1,3-butadiene-1,2-dicarboxylate.

Cleavage of Aromatic Rings. Many oxygenases are concerned with cleavage of an aromatic double bond, which may be located between two phenolic groups, adjacent to a single phenolic group, or in an indole ring. The corresponding products are a dicarboxylic acid, a semialdehyde, and a formylated amino ketone:

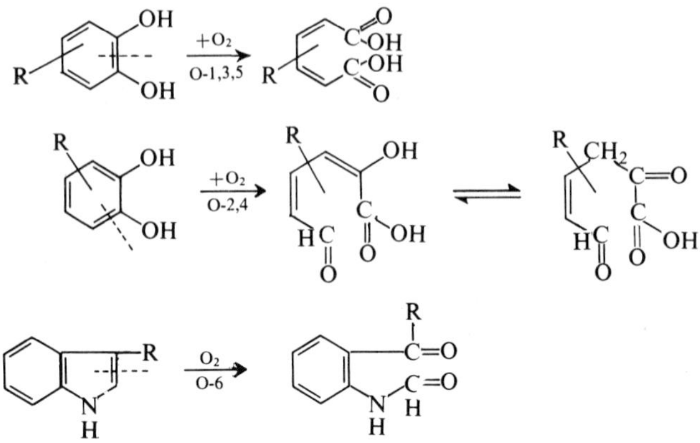

$$(15\text{-}6a)$$

$$(15\text{-}6b)$$

$$(15\text{-}6c)$$

Other reactions catalyzed by oxygenases are also summarized Table 15-1.

Hydroxylases Hydroxylases are responsible for the introduction of a single atom of molecular oxygen into the substrate, which is converted first into the monohydroxy derivative:

$$DH_2 + O_2{}^{18} + XH_2 \xrightarrow{\text{hydroxylase}} DHO^{18}H + X + H_2O^{18} \tag{15-7}$$

The appearance of labeled oxygen in H_2O and the absolute requirement for a second, oxidizable substrate (XH_2) differentiate the hydroxylase (or "mixed function oxidase") reactions from either the oxygenase or dehydrogenase reactions — compare reaction (15-7) with reactions (15-5) and (15-1a) or (15-1b).

We must be concerned, therefore, not only with the substrate, but also with the *cosubstrate* (see examples in Table 15-2). A number of different types of reaction are catalyzed by enzymes in this class. One is catalyzed by copper-containing plant enzymes capable of catalyzing both the conversion of mono-phenols to diphenols, and the dehydrogenation of the latter to *o*-quinones (Eq. 15-8). These enzymes are usually referred to as the *phenolase complex*.

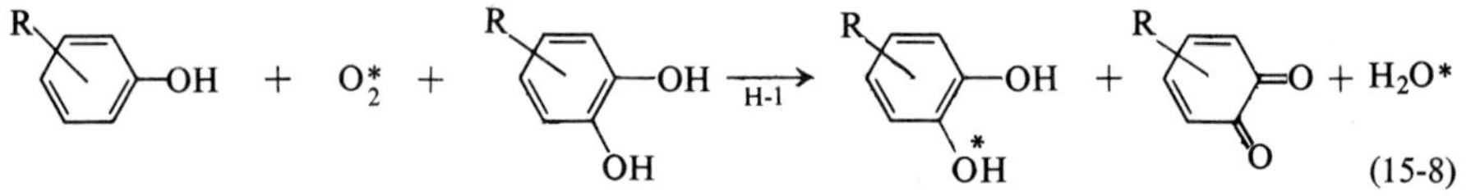

$$(15\text{-}8)$$

Here the cosubstrate is itself a product of the reaction. Thus, the net reaction catalyzed by phenolase is the conversion of one molecule of a monophenol to an *o*-quinone. The oxygen molecule is split during the reaction, one atom being reduced to H_2O, the other entering the aromatic ring. Other reducing agents such as ascorbate or hydroquinone can substitute for *o*-diphenol as the cosubstrate.

Mammalian dopamine hydroxylase is a copper protein that requires ascorbate as the obligatory cosubstrate.

An important hydroxylase obtained from rat liver catalyzes the conversion of L-phenylalanine to L-tyrosine. The natural cosubstrate in this case is a 5,6,7,8-tetrahydropteridine that is oxidized to a dihydropteridine (see page 424) and regenerated by NADPH in the presence of a second enzyme:

$$H^+ + NADPH + phenylalanine + O_2 \xrightarrow{\text{tetrahydropteridine}} NADP^+ + tyrosine + H_2O \quad (15\text{-}9)$$

"*Microsomal*" *Hydroxylases.* Reaction (15-9) is the prototype of a large number of reactions catalyzed by enzyme systems localized largely in the microsomal fraction of organs such as liver, the adrenals, and female sex glands. As shown in Table 15-2, enzymes in the liver are concerned with the metabolism and detoxification of a large number of aromatic compounds of pharmacological interest and with key steps in lipid metabolism. Of special significance are the large number of related reactions that lead to the introduction of hydroxyl or

TABLE 15-2. Some Hydroxylases

Enzyme	Source	Prosthetic group	Substrate	Product	Cosubstrate
Phenolase (monophenol oxidase)	Plants	[Cu]	Substituted phenol	Substituted catechol	Substituted catechol
Peroxidase	Horseradish	Heme	Salicylic acid	Gentisic acid	Dihydroxy-fumarate
Phenylalanine hydroxylase	Liver, plants	?	L-Phenylalanine	L-Tyrosine	5,6,7,8-Tetra-hydropteridine
Aryl-4-hydroxylase	Liver	Heme	Aniline, acetanilide	4-Hydroxyaryl cpds.	NADPH
Alkoxylaryl-hydroxylase	Liver	Heme	RCH_2O-ArR′	RCHO + HOArR′	NADPH
Arylalkylamine hydroxylase	Liver	Heme	RNH-Ar	N-oxides	NADPH
Steroid-2-hydroxylase	Liver	?	Estriol	2-Hydroxyestriol	NADPH
Steroid-11-β-hydroxylase	Adrenals (liver)	Heme (P450)	11-Deoxycorticosterone	Corticosterone	NADPH
Steroid-17-α-hydroxylase	Adrenals	Heme (P450)	Progesterone	Deoxycorticosterone	NADPH
Squalene oxidocyclase	Liver	?	Squalene	Lanosterol	NADPH
Fatty acid hydroxylase	Liver	?	Fatty acids	ω-Hydroxy fatty acids	NADPH
Fatty acid desaturase	Various	?	Saturated or unsaturated fatty acyl CoA	Unsaturated or poly-unsaturated fatty acyl CoA	?
Kynurenate hydroxylase	*Pseudomonas*	?	Kynurenate	7,8-Dihydroxy-kynurenate	NADH
Octane hydroxylase	Bacteria	?	Octane	Octanol	?

ketone groups into a steroid ring. A number of the steroid hormones are synthesized by this route. Some of these reactions are catalyzed by liver enzymes and
by those of the female sex glands, but by far the largest number are found, as
might be expected, in the cortex and the medulla of the adrenal gland. Many
positions in the steroid nucleus are capable of being hydroxylated. In some
reactions a ferredoxin-like carrier (see page 302) intervenes between NADPH
and the steroid, and a cytochrome pigment (called P450), capable of interacting
with CO, is the entity responsible for interaction with oxygen.

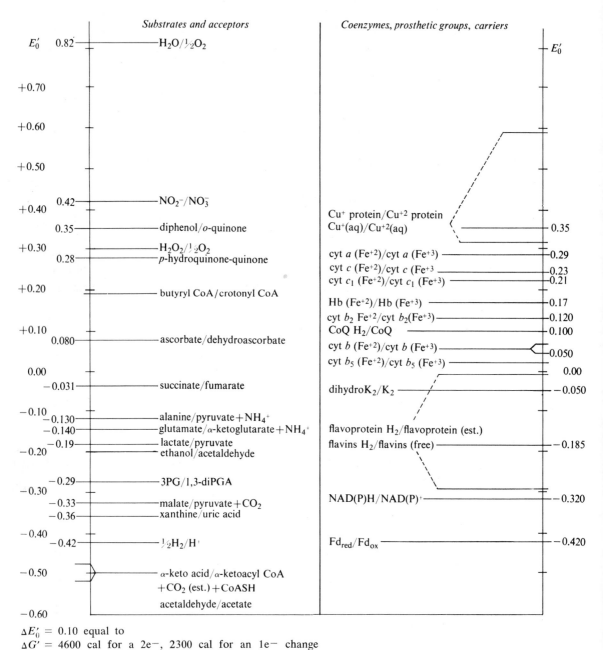

$\Delta E_0' = 0.10$ equal to
$\Delta G' = 4600$ cal for a $2e^-$, 2300 cal for an $1e^-$ change

FIGURE 15-1.   Classification of Coenzymes, Carriers, and Substrates by Their E_0' Value (25°, pH 7).

DEHYDROGENASES
Classification and
General Remarks

Three groups of dehydrogenases (called "oxidoreductases" by the International Commission on Enzymes) can readily be distinguished by the nature of the electron (hydrogen) acceptor and by the type of reaction involved: (1) nicotinamide nucleotide–dependent, (2) flavoproteins, and (3) cuproproteins. Some of the characteristic properties of these dehydrogenases are apparent from Figure 15-1. Thus, the copper enzymes, which have a relatively high oxidation potential, are concerned with the dehydrogenation, using oxygen as the acceptor, of substrates that also have a high potential. Cuproprotein enzymes are therefore ideally suited as the terminal members of respiratory chains. Even cytochrome oxidase, which fulfills this role in animals and plants, contains both an iron porphyrin and copper; the latter may be responsible for the interaction with O_2.

The nicotinamide nucleotide–dependent enzymes, on the other hand, catalyze the transfer of two reducing equivalents from the substrate to the coenzyme, which usually functions as a readily dissociable carrier. They are ideally designed, therefore, for the initial dehydrogenation of most substrates. The reduced coenzyme formed as a result of this reaction can shuttle freely to a second site where it can (1) be utilized to reduce a second substrate via a linked reaction, (2) provide reducing power for biosynthetic sequences, or (3) be reoxidized by a respiratory chain with the attendant conversion of ADP to ATP.

Flavoproteins occupy an intermediate position between the first two classes. They catalyze the oxidation of substrates of intermediate redox potential and interact either with oxygen directly or with a number of alternate acceptors.

Cuproprotein
Enzymes

Some of the cuproprotein enzymes are listed in Table 15-3. Many of these proteins contain an even number of Cu atoms per molecule and exhibit the characteristic blue color (λ max $\geq$ 580 mμ) of the tetragonal complexes of

TABLE 15-3. Properties of Some Cuproproteins

Protein	Source	Molecular weight	Copper per mole	λ_{max}, mμ
Ascorbate oxidase	Plants	150,000	6	606
Uricase	Animals (liver, kidney)	120,000	1	330?
Cytochrome oxidase*	Animals, fungi	200,000	2	820?
Cytochrome oxidase-cuproprotein	Heart muscle	25,000	1	820?
Galactose oxidase	Molds	42,500	1	?
Phenolase†	Plants	34,000	1	340?
Plastocyanin	Plant chloroplasts	21,000	2	597
Pseudomonas aeruginosa blue pigment	*Ps. aeruginosa*	16,600	1	630
Amine oxidase (spermine)	Mammalian plasma	225,000	4?	380
Dopamine β-hydroxylase	Adrenals	290,000	4–7	480

*Also contains iron-porphyrin.
†Also known as tyrosinase, monophenol oxidase, diphenol oxidase, catecholase. Systematic name, o-diphenol: O_2-oxidoreductase.

Cu^{+2} with nitrogenous ligands (amino, imino, and imidazole side chains of amino acids).

All cuproprotein enzymes except plastocyanin (see page 299) utilize only O_2 as the electron acceptor. This characteristic property may be an indication of structural specificity leading to a particularly high affinity for O_2 or else is a reflection of the fact that the high E_0' of the substrates makes it difficult to find alternate acceptors. Since o-quinones, p-quinones, and dehydroascorbate are all reduced by plant enzymes at the expense of NAD(P)H, this combination, plus phenolase, or ascorbate oxidase, provides the plant with alternative respiratory chains from reduced pyridine nucleotide to O_2 that do not involve the participation of cytochromes or cytochrome oxidase:

$$DH_2 \xrightarrow{\text{dehydrogenase}} NAD(P) \xrightarrow{\text{quinone reductase}} \text{quinone} \xrightarrow{\text{Cu enzyme}} O_2 \qquad (15\text{-}10)$$

Flavoproteins   Flavoproteins are mainly concerned with three important areas of oxidative metabolism: (1) the oxygen-linked dehydrogenation of certain substrates, such as amino acids; (2) the cytochrome-linked dehydrogenation of the initial members of the particle-bound respiratory chain (i.e., NADH and succinate in almost all cells, α-glycerophosphate, choline, sarcosine, fatty acyl CoAs in appropriate mitochondria from various sources, D- and L-lactate in aerobically grown yeast, etc.); and (3) the NAD(P)-linked dehydrogenation of certain low-potential substrates (e.g., dihydrolipoate, dihydroorotate, reduced ferredoxin). Enzymes in group 1 usually contain only a flavin prosthetic group, those in group 2 frequently contain additional components (usually metals), and those in group 3 sometimes

TABLE 15-4A.   Properties of Flavoproteins

Enzyme	Source	Molecular weight	Prosthetic groups		Physiological acceptor
			Flavin	Other	
D-Amino acid oxidase	Liver, kidney	~100,000	2(?)FAD	...	O_2
L-Amino acid oxidase	Kidney	138,000	2FMN	...	O_2
	Snake venoms	~140,000	2FAD	...	O_2
Glucose oxidase	Molds	154,000	2FAD	...	O_2
Glycolate oxidase	Plants	~100,000	FMN	...	O_2
Luciferase	Photobacterium fisheri	76,000	FMN	...	O_2
Acyl CoA dehydrogenase (three separate enzymes known)	Liver, heart mitochondria	200,000(?)	$2n$FAD	...	ETF
Electron-transferring flavoprotein (ETF)	Liver, heart mitochondria	70,000	FAD	...	Respiratory chain
NADPH-ferredoxin reductase	Plants, adrenal microsomes	35,000	FAD(?)	...	$NADP^+$
Lipoyl dehydrogenase	All respiratory particles	100,000	2FAD	—S—S—	NAD^+
NADH-cytochrome b_5 reductase	Liver microsomes and mitochondria	40,000	FAD	$2Mg^{+2}$ (not for electron transfer)	Cytochrome b_5
NADPH-cytochrome c reductase	Microsomes	68,000	FAD	...	Cytochrome c
	Yeast	78,000	FMN	...	Cytochrome c
NADPH-glutathione reductase	E. coli, plants	?	FAD	?	Oxidized glutathione

do (dihydroorotate) and sometimes do not contain a metal ion (lipoyl dehydrogenase).

Catalysis by Simple Flavoproteins. The two flavin coenzymes FMN and FAD (see page 215) are tightly bound to the various proteins, thus acting as prosthetic groups rather than as freely dissociating coenzymes (see Table 15-4A). By raising the ionic strength and lowering the pH, the protonated flavins may be detached to produce the apo-enzyme. In general, this treatment has been more successful with the simple flavoproteins than with the more complex metalloflavoproteins. Among the most characteristic features of flavins is their light absorption at 260, ~ 370, and ~ 450 mμ. Upon reduction of flavins with borohydride or dithionite, or enzymatically in the presence of various substrates, the two long wavelength peaks are bleached, and the extinction coefficient in the 450-mμ region is reduced to ≤ 10 per cent of the value of the oxidized form. Flavins also exhibit a strong, yellow-green fluorescence ($\lambda_{max} \simeq 500$ mμ). The fluorescence of FAD is only 10 per cent of that of the vitamin or FMN, because of internal quenching by the adenine ring. Upon binding to the protein, the optical

TABLE 15-4B. Properties of Purified Metalloflavoproteins

Enzyme	Source	Molecular weight	Prosthetic group		Physiological acceptor
			Flavin	Other	
Xanthine oxidase (dehydrogenase)	Milk	300,000	2FAD	8Fe* 2Mo	O_2 (cyt c)
	Mammalian liver		2FAD	8Fe* 2Mo	O_2 (cyt c), NAD^+
	Avian liver or kidney		2FAD	16Fe* 4Mo	NAD^+
Dihydroorotic dehydrogenase	*Zymobacterium oroticum*	125,000	1FAD +1FMN	2Fe*	O_2, NAD^+ for dihydro-orotate O_2, orotate for NADH
NADH dehydrogenase	Heart mitochondria	$\sim 200,000$ (particle)	1FMN	8Fe*	Respiratory chain (not cytochrome c!)
		$\sim 250,000$	1FMN	2–3Fe*	Ferricyanide, CoQ‡
		80,000	1FMN	4Fe*	Cytochrome c‡
Succinate dehydrogenase	Beef heart mitochondria	$\sim 300,000$	1FAD†	8Fe*	Respiratory chain
	Beef heart mitochondria, yeast	250,000	1FAD†	4Fe*	PMS, ferricyanide
Choline dehydrogenase	Mammalian liver mitochondria	800,000	1FAD	4Fe*	PMS
α-Glycerophosphate dehydrogenase	Pig brain mitochondria	2×10^6(!)	1FAD	1Fe*	Ferricyanide, PMS
NADP-nitrate reductase	*Neurospora crassa*		? FAD	? Mo	NO_3^-
L-Lactate dehydrogenase	Aerobic yeast respiratory particles	200,000	2FMN	1 heme	Respiratory chain through cyt c
D-Lactate dehydrogenase	Aerobic yeast respiratory particles	?	? FMN	? Zn^{+2}	Same as above

*The nonheme iron in these enzymes appears to be associated with a stoichiometric quantity of acid-labile sulfur, such as is found in ferredoxin. Many of these enzymes also exhibit a characteristic EPR signal ($g = 1.94$). In general, this EPR signal is lost on solubilization of the mitochondrial enzymes.
†FAD linked covalently to protein and can be released only by enzymatic treatment.
‡Once solubilized, these enzymes must be assayed with artificial acceptors such as ferricyanide or PMS.

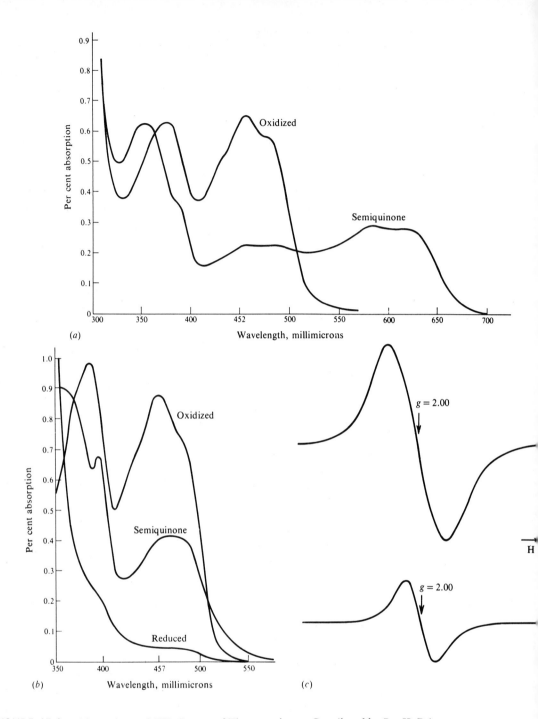

FIGURE 15-2. Absorption and ESR Spectra of Flavoproteins. — *Contributed by Dr. H. Beinert.*

(a) Absorption spectrum of blue semiquinone of flavoproteins (Type A, according to G. Palmer and V. Massey, Mech nisms of Flavoprotein Catalysis, in T. P. Singer (ed.), "Biological Oxidations," Wiley, New York, 1967). A soluti of *Azotobacter* flavoprotein (Y. I. Shethna, P. W. Wilson, and H. Beinert, *Biochem. Biophys. Acta*, in press) in 0.03 phosphate of pH 7.4, 5.7×10^{-5} M with respect to bound flavin, was reduced anaerobically with dithionite to t semiquinone state. Excess dithionite was oxidized with oxygen. The spectrum is very close to that of the pure semiquinor The amount of the oxidized form does not exceed 8 per cent of the total flavin present.

(b) Absorption spectrum of red semiquinone of flavoproteins (Type B, according to G. Palmer and V. Massey, Mech nisms of Flavoprotein Catalysis, in T. P. Singer (ed.), "Biological Oxidations," Wiley, New York, 1967). A solution oxynitrilase [W. Becker, U. Benthin, E. Eschenhof, and E. Pfeil, *Biochem. Z.*, **337**: 156 (1963)] in 0.02 M phosphate pH 7.4, 7.66×10^{-5} M with respect to bound flavin, was reduced anaerobically with dithionite and reoxidized to t semiquinone state by oxygen. In this case, a considerable amount of the reduced and oxidized forms are in equilibrium wi the semiquinone; however, the characteristic features of the absorption spectrum of the red semiquinone are appare properties of the flavins are profoundly affected — there is usually a significant shift of the absorption maxima to longer wavelengths and a quenching of the fluorescence.

Flavin coenzymes are able to undergo a reduction to both a half-reduced ($1e^-$ equivalent) and a fully reduced ($2e^-$ equivalent) state. Thus a flavoprotein containing a single flavin coenzyme might participate in the catalytic cycle by shuttling back and forth between the oxidized and the fully reduced, between the oxidized and the semiquinone, or between the semiquinone and the fully reduced states. Various semiquinone forms (II, III, VI, VII) of the flavoprotein enzymes are frequently observed by spectrophotometry and EPR measurements (see Fig. 15-2):

$$
\begin{bmatrix} E \begin{smallmatrix} \text{FlavH} \\ \\ \text{FlavH} \end{smallmatrix} D \end{bmatrix} \rightarrow \begin{bmatrix} E \begin{smallmatrix} \text{FlavH·} \\ \\ \text{Flav} \end{smallmatrix} \cdot HD \end{bmatrix} \rightleftharpoons \begin{bmatrix} E \begin{smallmatrix} \text{FlavH·} \\ \\ \text{FlavH·} \end{smallmatrix} D \end{bmatrix} \rightleftharpoons \begin{bmatrix} E \begin{smallmatrix} \text{FlavH}_2 \\ \\ \text{Flav} \end{smallmatrix} D \end{bmatrix}
$$

$$\quad\quad\quad \text{I} \quad\quad\quad\quad \text{II} \quad\quad\quad\quad \text{III} \quad\quad\quad\quad \text{IV}$$

$$\downarrow \begin{smallmatrix} DH_2 \\ \\ D \end{smallmatrix}$$

$$
\begin{bmatrix} E \begin{smallmatrix} \text{FlavH}_2 \\ \\ \text{Flav} \end{smallmatrix} H_2D \end{bmatrix} \rightleftharpoons \begin{bmatrix} E \begin{smallmatrix} \text{FlavH}_2 \\ \\ \text{FlavH·} \end{smallmatrix} \cdot HD \end{bmatrix} \rightleftharpoons \begin{bmatrix} E \begin{smallmatrix} \text{FlavH·} \\ \\ \text{FlavH·} \end{smallmatrix} H_2D \end{bmatrix} \rightarrow \begin{bmatrix} E \begin{smallmatrix} \text{FlavH}_2 \\ \\ \text{FlavH}_2 \end{smallmatrix} D \end{bmatrix}
$$

$$\quad\quad\quad \text{V} \quad\quad\quad\quad \text{VI} \quad\quad\quad\quad \text{VII} \quad\quad\quad\quad \text{VIII}$$

Metalloflavoproteins. A number of isolated, highly purified flavoproteins contain additional prosthetic groups (see Table 15-4B) usually metal ions. The precise role of the metals has proved to be elusive. The main problem is that many of these enzymes, even though highly purified and with the various prosthetic groups in definite and constant proportions, were originally part of more complex particulate structures. In order to render the enzymes soluble, these structures had to be disrupted by enzymatic, chemical, or physical means, and in the course of such treatments the enzymes may have suffered alterations in their properties.

The outlook is more promising with flavoproteins, such as xanthine and dihydroorotate dehydrogenases, which, in the cell, were probably not tightly connected to any larger structural and functional unit. Both enzymes contain NHI and an equal amount of labile sulfide. Dihydroorotate dehydrogenase is the simpler in composition and in the type of reaction catalyzed; it is unusual in containing both one molecule of FAD and one of FMN per molecule of enzyme. Perhaps each of the flavins is responsible for the initial interaction with one of the two substrate pairs, NAD/NADH and dihydroorotate/orotate.

Nonheme Iron Proteins (NHI proteins) Certain electron carrier proteins (existing either as independent entities or as part of more complex structures) contain an even number of iron atoms linked

---

(*c*) EPR spectra of flavoproteins taken at $-159°$. Top curve: Blue semiquinone from *Azotobacter* flavoprotein (cf. Fig. 15-2*a*); lower curve: red semiquinone of oxynitrilase (cf. Fig. 15-2*b*).

in an unusual fashion to cysteine residues, forming "acid-labile" sulfide. Some of the proteins so far identified, with the number of iron atoms given in brackets, include bacterial ferredoxin [6 to 8] (see page 302), plant ferredoxin or PPNR [2] (see page 303), dihydroorotic dehydrogenase [2], xanthine oxidase [8], hepatic aldehyde oxidase [8]; the NADH dehydrogenase branch of the respiratory chain [8] (complex I; see page 363), and various soluble NADH-dehydrogenating enzymes derived from this complex ([4] or [2]), the succinate dehydrogenase branch of the respiratory chain (complex II), and soluble, derived enzymes ([8], [4], and [2]); $CoQH_2$-cytochrome c portion of the respiratory chain [2] (complex III; see page 363) — and a ferredoxin-like pigment linked to the cytochrome c and the P450 reductase of microsomes (see page 364). Therefore, entities of this sort are widely distributed in nature and appear to fulfill key functions in electron transport in regions varying greatly in oxidation potential but invariably utilizing flavoproteins as either donors or acceptors.

Quinone Coenzymes   Another group of respiratory carriers that are capable of interacting with the flavoproteins of the respiratory chain (see page 362) is comprised of certain benzoquinones called *coenzymes* Q(CoQ) or *ubiquinones* (UQ) of the structure:

Ubiquinone

n in the formula varies from 6 in certain microorganisms — in which case the compound is referred to as CoQ_6 or UQ_{30} — to 10 in the mitochondria of most mammals — when its designation is CoQ_{10} or UQ_{50}.

The closely related *plastoquinones*, which fulfill analogous carrier roles in photosynthetic electron transport (see page 303), differ from ubiquinones in the alkyl substituents of the benzene ring: two —CH_3 groups instead of the two —OCH_3; H instead of —CH_3. Plastoquinones B and C carry one hydroxyl group in the side chain.

Nicotinamide Coenzyme-dependent Dehydrogenases   The structure and function of NAD and NADP, the two pyridine (nicotinamide) nucleotide coenzymes, were discussed in Chap. 8. These coenzymes are generally reversibly dissociable from their apoenzymes. Frequently the reduced coenzymes are bound more tightly to the protein than the oxidized form. Zn^{+2} ions are part of coenzyme-binding sites of several of the highly purified dehydrogenases. Thiol groups on the enzyme have also been implicated in substrate interaction in many instances.

The reactions catalyzed by these enzymes are readily followed by taking advantage of the optical properties of the coenzymes: light absorption at 340 mμ and strong fluorescence (λ max at 440 mμ) by the reduced forms. Catalysis by the enzymes involves the reversible and rapid formation of four binary (i.e., enzyme-substrate and enzyme-coenzyme) and two ternary (enzyme-coenzyme-substrate) complexes. Frequently there exists a compulsory order of binding and an ordered or constrained path for the reaction with the coenzymes as the "leading" substrate (see page 166). The oxidation-reduction step takes place within the ternary complex and probably involves the transfer of a hydride ion (or one proton plus two electrons):

$$R DH^* + NAD(P)^+ + H_2O \rightleftharpoons R DOH + NAD(P)H^* + H^+ \tag{15-11a}$$

$$DH_2 + NADP^+ \rightleftharpoons D + NAD(P)H + H^+ \tag{15-11b}$$

In Eq. (15-11a), the transfer of hydrogen is reversible, stereospecific with respect to both the substrate and the coenzyme, and direct (i.e., not involving the solvent or any component of the enzyme capable of proton exchange with the solvent more rapid than the hydrogen transfer step). If the oxidized form of the substrate ($R DOH$) contains one more oxygen atom than does the reduced substrate (RDH), both the oxygen and the proton liberated must be provided by the solvent. In both reactions (15-11a) and (15-11b), a proton is liberated and oxidation of the substrate is favored by high pH.

Several hundred dehydrogenases, differing in substrate specificity and in the molecular properties of the protein, have been isolated to date. Among this bewildering array, however, are a relatively small number of reaction types:

$$R''\!-\!\overset{\overset{\displaystyle R'}{|}}{\underset{\underset{\displaystyle H}{|}}{C}}\!-\!OH + NAD(P)^+ \rightleftharpoons R''\!-\!\overset{\overset{\displaystyle R'}{|}}{C}\!=\!O + NAD(P)H + H^+ \tag{15-12}$$

$$R\!-\!\overset{\overset{\displaystyle H}{|}}{C}\!=\!O + NAD(P)^+ + A^- \rightleftharpoons R\!-\!\overset{\overset{\displaystyle O}{\|}}{C}\!-\!A + NAD(P)H \qquad A^- = OH^-, PO_3H^-, CoAS^- \tag{15-13}$$

$$HCO_2H + NAD(P)^+ \rightarrow CO_2 + NAD(P)H + H^+ \tag{15-14}$$

$$R'\!-\!\overset{\overset{\displaystyle }{|}}{\underset{\underset{\displaystyle R''}{|}}{CH}}\!-\!NH\!-\!R''' + NAD(P)^+ \rightleftharpoons R'\!-\!\overset{\overset{\displaystyle }{|}}{\underset{\underset{\displaystyle R''}{|}}{C}}\!=\!N\!-\!R''' + NAD(P)H + H^+ \tag{15-15}$$

HEMOPROTEINS
Prosthetic Groups
and Reactions

Hemoproteins are ubiquitously distributed in nature, where they participate in the following important reactions: (1) as O_2-carrying entities, (2) in the reduction of peroxides, and (3) in electron transfer between dehydrogenases and acceptors. The prosthetic groups of all these proteins are derived from protoporphyrin IX, an Fe^{+2} chelate, which is also called *protoheme* or simply *heme* (Fig. 15-3). Other important heme prosthetic groups are also indicated.

Hemes are square-planar chelates of Fe, in which the metal can form complexes with two additional ligands, combination with the first ligand greatly facilitating interaction with the second. These hexacoordinate octahedral complexes are called *hemochromes*. In many hemoproteins, at least one of these coordination positions is occupied by histidine groups on the protein. If the sixth coordination position is occupied by a ligand with a relatively weak field (H_2O, Cl^-, $-CO_2^-$) as in myo- or hemoglobin, it is possible to replace it with one capable of interacting more strongly with the central metal atom. This is especially true if the latter ligand is capable of forming π bonds (O_2, CO, CN^-, N-heterocycles). In this manner, high-spin complexes may be transformed into low-spin complexes.

Hemes are oxidized by O_2 or other oxidizing agents to the corresponding Fe^{+3} derivatives called ferriprotoporphyrins, or *hemins*. These ferric complexes

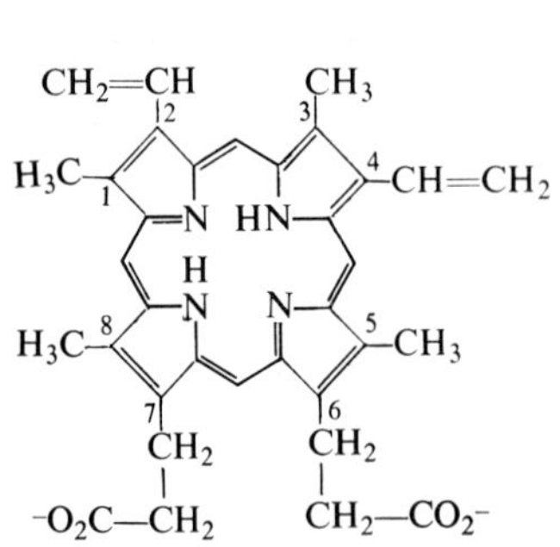

Protoporphyrin IX

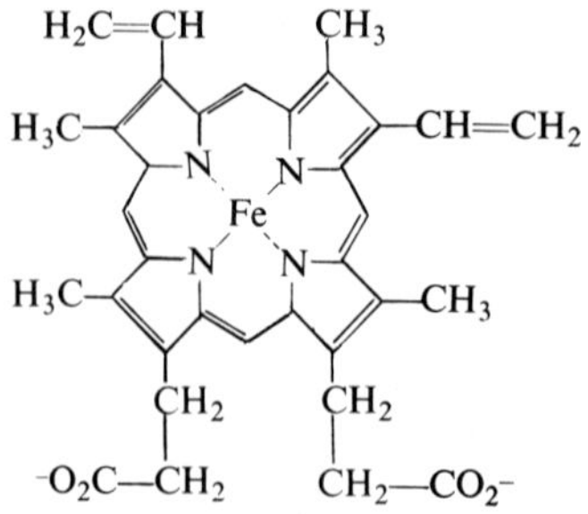

Ferroprotoporphyrin IX*
(proto)heme (IX)

Prosthetic group of

hemoglobin
myoglobin
erythrocruorin
catalase
peroxidase
cytochromes of class B

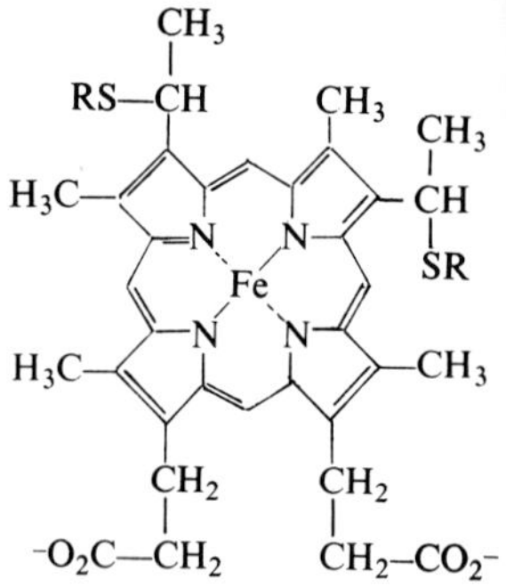

Heme C
Prosthetic group of
cytochromes of class C

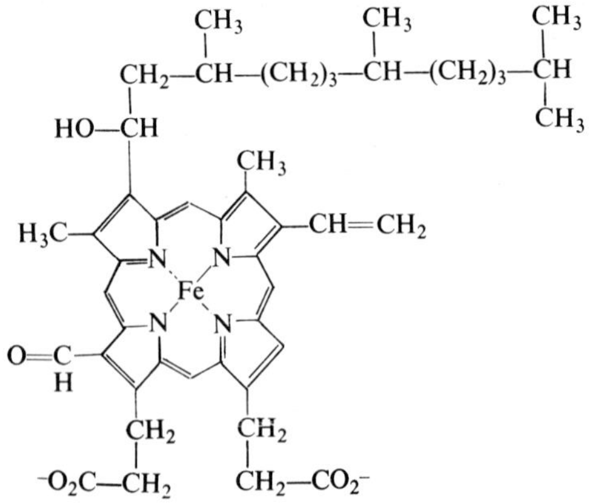

Heme A
Prosthetic group of
cytochromes of class A

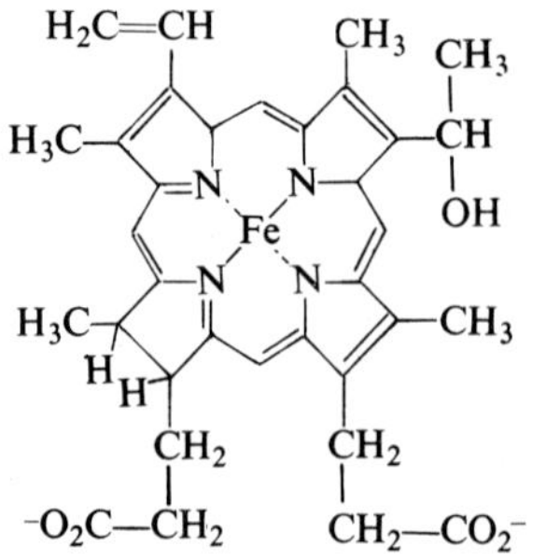

Heme a_2
Prosthetic group of
cytochromes of class a_2

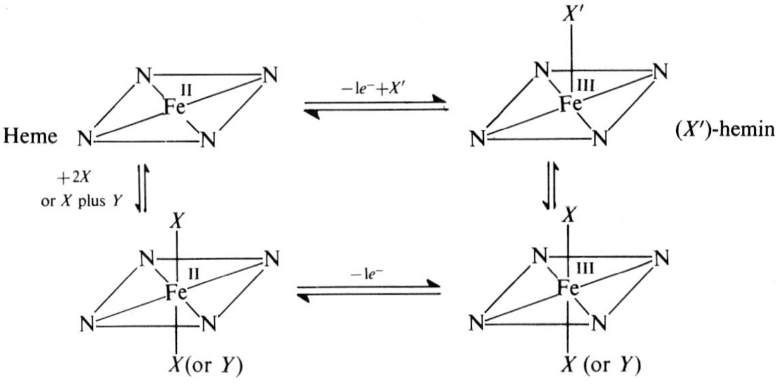

Heme

$-1e^- + X'$

(X')-hemin

$+2X$
or X plus Y

$-1e^-$

X (or Y)
Hemochrome

X (or Y)
Hemichrome

$X = OH$
$Y = OH_2$ } hematin $\underset{pK=7.5}{\overset{+H^+}{\rightleftharpoons}}$ OH_2
OH_2 } hydroxyhemin

FIGURE 15-3. Prosthetic Groups of Hemoproteins.

* Chlorocruoroheme, the prosthetic group of chlorocruorin, differs from heme only in having a formyl group in position 2.

have one residual positive charge, which, in the isolated complex, must be neutralized by an anion. The resulting pentacoordinate, square-pyramidal complex is called, in the case of chloride, *hemin chloride*, or *chlorohemin*. In alkaline solution the chloride is replaced by hydroxide, and *hematin* is formed. Hemins readily form hexacoordinate octahedral complexes with additional ligands, called *hemichromes*.

One of the most characteristic features of hemoproteins is their absorption spectrum (see Fig. 15-4). Low-spin ferrous complexes show a typical three-banded spectrum. High-spin ferrous complexes have spectra with only two bands: the Soret peak, near 420 mμ, plus a band around 550 mμ. Ferric complexes show less apparent regularity in their spectra; the porphyrin contributes two bands, the Soret band, and a second one in the range 540 to 570 mμ, which is of significant intensity only in low-spin complexes. There are also two additional bands: one in the vicinity of 600 mμ, and a weaker one around 500 mμ.

Hemoglobin and Other Respiratory Pigments

The most important respiratory pigment of higher vertebrates is hemoglobin, a tetramer having a molecular weight of 64,450. The structure of hemoglobin was considered in earlier chapters. In its reduced, oxygen-free form, it is a rare species among hemoproteins: a *high-spin* Fe^{+2} complex of exceedingly low potential; one in which the central iron of a square-planar heme group is further coordinated with one strong-field ligand (histidine) and one weak-field ligand (water). Only by virtue of the iron's being coordinated to a *protein-bound* histidine residue could such a compound exist at all. These considerations explain the great avidity of hemoglobin for π-bonding substituents, such as O_2, CO, or CN^-. The latter two groups bind many times more strongly than the first and yield photoreversible complexes. Substitution of them for H_2O in the sixth coordination position leads to a profound structural rearrangement, as a result of which the whole complex changes to one of low spin. Free hemoglobin is easily oxidized to its ferri form, *methemoglobin*, by a variety of oxidizing agents.

All four heme residues in a hemoglobin molecule are capable of binding oxygen, but the respective binding constants are dependent on one another; each successive O_2 molecule affects the binding of the next. The ratio of the four stepwise constants is approximately 1 : 4 : 24 : 9. This phenomenon of linked, cooperative interactions results in a sigmoid, rather than a hyperbolic, binding curve when the extent of O_2 binding is plotted against O_2 tension (see Fig. 15-5). Similar curves are also obtained for the formation of the CO complex, but the association constants are about 10^2 greater.

In vertebrates, hemoglobin does not exist in solution but is contained in highly concentrated form within the red blood cells, or erythrocytes. A closely related pigment, myoglobin, is found inside muscle cells. The structure of myoglobin has been studied at an even higher resolution than that of hemoglobin (see page 99). This protein ($M = 17,000$) can be regarded as closely related to the monomeric units of hemoglobin. Since it contains only one heme prosthetic group per molecule, it exhibits a hyperbolic rather than a sigmoid oxygen dissociation curve. Closely related to myoglobin are the hemoglobins found in the blood cells of certain primitive vertebrates, such as the lamprey eels: they have an $M = 17,500$ and contain only one heme per molecule A variety of respiratory pigments are found in invertebrates: *erythrocruorins* are large

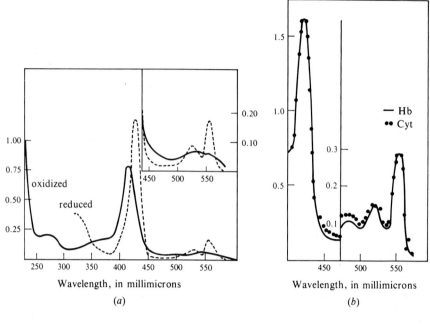

Wavelength, in millimicrons

(a)

Wavelength, in millimicrons

(b)

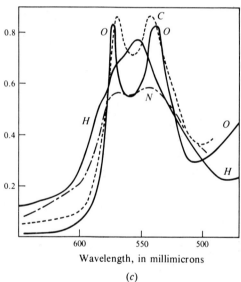

Wavelength, in millimicrons

(c)

FIGURE 15-4. Absorption Spectra of Heme Compounds.
(a) Absorption spectrum of a typical cytochrome b (cytochrome b_5 from liver respiratory particles). Reduced spectrum obtained by reduction with dithionite or, enzymatically, with NADH. (b) Spectra of pyridine hemochromes, of hemoglobin and of the cytochrome from (a). Obtained by adding alkaline pyridine to the compounds and reducing with dithionite.—(a) and (b) from I. Raw, R. Molinari, D. do Amaral, and H. R. Mahler, J. Biol. Chem., 233: 225 (1958). (c) Absorption spectra of hemoglobin (H), oxyhemoglobin (O), and nitric oxide hemoglobin (N). Abscissa: wavelength in millimicrons; ordinate: extinction of 0.1 per cent solutions in 10-mm absorption cell.—From F. Haurowitz and R. Hardin, Respiratory Proteins, in H. Neurath and K. Bailey (eds.), "The Proteins," vol. II, part A, p. 296, Academic Press, New York, 1954.

hemoglobin-like molecules existing extracellularly in the circulating blood of many polychete and oligochete annelid worms and of mollusks, with a $M = 4 \times 10^5$ to 6.7×10^6 and contain 30 to 400 heme groups per molecule. Certain other annelid worms, such as *Spirographis*, have in their blood green hemoproteins, called *chlorocruorins*, of $M = 3.5 \times 10^6$, containing 190 *chlorocruoroheme* groups (see Fig. 15-3) per molecule. Regardless of size, all these hemoproteins bind one molecule of O_2 per heme group.

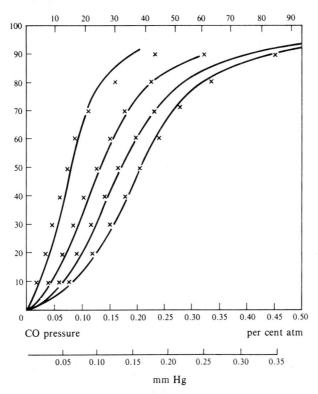

FIGURE 15-5. O_2 and CO Saturation Curves for Hemoglobin. Equilibrium curves of CO-hemoglobin (full lines) and O_2-hemoglobin (crosses) at 0-, 19-, 41-, and 79-mm CO_2 pressure (from left to right). Abscissa at bottom: CO pressure; abscissa at top: O_2 pressure in millimeters Hg; ordinate: per cent saturation.—*From J. Barcroft, "The Respiratory Function of the Blood," part II, Cambridge University Press, New York, 1928.*

Hemerythrins and *hemocyanins* are nonheme respiratory pigments found, respectively, in the blood cells of sipunculid worms and in the plasma of certain mollusks and crustaceans. The hemerythrin of *Sipunculus* contains 16 nonheme iron atoms linked to the protein in a structure that may be related to that found for other NHI proteins. Two atoms of metal are required to bind each molecule of O_2. The same holds true also for the hemocyanins, which are large copper-containing proteins that, in the lobster, contain 20 atoms of metal per protein ($M = 780,000$). Other hemocyanins are known (for instance, in snails) that are approximately ten times as large.

The Hydroperoxidases

The hydroperoxidases are a group of hemiproteins which include *catalase*, widely distributed throughout nature (vertebrate liver, blood, various microorganisms), and *peroxidase*, found in plants, leucocytes, and milk. Catalases and peroxidases catalyze the same type of reaction:

$$RO{-}OH + \left.\begin{array}{c} H_2X \\ 2X^n \end{array}\right\} \rightarrow ROH + H_2O + \left.\begin{array}{c} X \\ 2X^{n+1} \end{array}\right\} \tag{15-16a}$$

Catalases utilize H_2O_2 (R = H) as the most effective oxidant, but can react with alkyl hydroperoxides if R is of short-chain length, the order being $H \gg CH_3 > C_2H_5$. The preferred electron donor, or coreductant, is a second molecule of H_2O_2 ($X = O_2$). In this case, and with R = H, Eq. (15-16a) becomes the "catalatic" one:

$$2H_2O_2 \rightarrow 2H_2O + O_2 \tag{15-16b}$$

An alternative reaction is the "peroxidative" one — Eq. (15-16a) — in which H_2X or X^n can be (1) ascorbate or ferrocyanide; (2) phenols; (3) short-chain alcohols or formate; (4) sodium nitrate; and (5) azide or hydroxylamine. If the hydrogen peroxide is generated in situ (e.g., by a flavoprotein dehydrogenase), then the addition of catalase plus a coreductant produces the following:

$$DH_2 + XH_2 + O_2 \xrightarrow{\text{fp + catalase}} D + X + 2H_2O \tag{15-17}$$

Although peroxidases can catalyze reaction (15-16b), their preferred mode of action is that of reaction (15-16a). Among the cosubstrates are phenols, aliphatic and aromatic amines, leuco dyes, enediols, and cytochrome c. These facts, the nature of the prosthetic group (all catalases and most peroxidases appear to contain ferriprotophyrin IX in a high-spin state), and the observation that all complexes of this type have weak catalatic and peroxidative activity have led to their assignment to one common class of enzymes, the hydroperoxidases.

The Cytochromes   In hemoglobin and related pigments the function of the prosthetic group is to carry O_2 while remaining in the Fe^{+2} state; in the hydroperoxidases the prosthetic group carries and decomposes RO—OH while remaining in the Fe^{+3} state. The cytochromes, in contrast, do not combine with any substrate but, instead, shuttle back and forth between the Fe^{+2} and Fe^{+3} states. Cytochromes are, therefore, redox carriers designed to shuttle between the dehydrogenases on one side and the terminal acceptors on the other. Depending on the potential of the final acceptor (-0.20 to 0.80 volt) a multiplicity of carriers may have to intervene in the respiratory (or electron-transport) chain (this is discussed in the next section).

Table 15-5 illustrates the great diversity of properties of the known cytochromes. Even more complications are in the offing: for instance, there are at least two different isozymes of cytochrome c in yeast, and this situation probably occurs in other cells as well. Yet as far as the prosthetic group is concerned, as well as its linkage to protein, there appears to be uniformity. For if we disregard cytochromes of the a type (class A), all others are derivatives of heme itself. The basic structure is modified somewhat in cytochromes C by addition of protein cysteine residues across the vinyl side chains, leading, in this instance only, to a prosthetic group that is linked to the protein both through its metal and through these additional covalent bonds.

The cytochromes were discovered in 1886 by MacMunn, a Scottish physician who observed their characteristic absorption spectra by means of a hand spectroscope and found them to be distributed widely in tissues. He called them "histo-" and "myohaematin," since they appeared to him to be related to heme and hemin. He thus clearly recognized their chemical nature and also assigned to them a respiratory function, which he believed to be connected with oxygen transfer, no other form of respiratory activity being then known. In 1925, D. Keilin, studying the respiration, first of wax moths, bees, and other insects, observed the apparently universal occurrence of these pigments, which he called "cytochrome." He quickly established reversible redox changes as crucial to its function, obtained evidence that related it to the hemochromogens, and showed that two classes of respiratory poisons introduced by Warburg, namely, cyanide and narcotics (urethane and barbiturates), strongly affected "cytochrome" but in an opposite sense, the former inhibiting oxidation and the latter blocking reduction. By 1930, Keilin had realized that "cytochrome" consisted of three spectroscopically distinct components, which he called a, b, and c, in the order of their absorption maxima: a absorbs at the longest wavelength and c at the shortest (see Table 15-5). He also obtained some evidence that cytochrome b was closest to the substrate side and believed that there existed a CO-, KCN-, and H_2S- sensitive entity which linked the cytochromes to O_2 and which he therefore called "cytochrome oxidase." He did not believe this to be a cytochrome or even a hemoprotein but thought it might contain Cu. Meanwhile, Warburg had obtained good evidence from action spectra that his CO-sensitive *Atmungsferment* was also a hemoprotein (see Fig. 15-6). Keilin and Hartree then

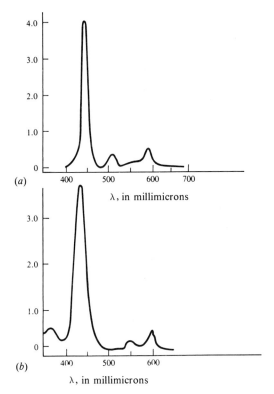

FIGURE 15-6.   The Photochemical Action Spectrum of *Atmungsferment* and Cytochrome Oxidase.
(*a*) Cytochrome oxidase (mammalian); (*b*) *Atmungsferment* (yeast). The spectrum is determined by measuring the efficiency of light at various wavelengths in overcoming the CO-inhibited O_2 uptake of whole cells (*b*) or the inhibition of an enzyme preparation (*a*). Curves in *a* and *b* redrawn from the data of Melnick and Warburg. Ordinate: relative efficiency of light of wavelength λ compared to that of $\lambda = 436$ mμ.

TABLE 15-5. Properties of the Cytochromes

Class	Name	Source	Spectra λ_{max} [ε_{mM}] Reduced α	Reduced β	Reduced γ	Oxidized γ	E_0'	Molecular weight $M \times 10^3$	Physiological Reductant	Oxidant
A	a	Mitochondria[b]	600 [23]	—[a]	439 [94]	425 [76]	+0.28	240	c	a_3
	a_3	Mitochondria[b,c]	(603.5) [19.4]	—	443 [79], 430 (CO)		(+0.30)		c + a	O_2
A_2	a_1	Bacteria	590						C	O_2
	a_2	Pseudomonas[d]	652	629	460	412	0.05[e]	90	C551	O_2, c_1
B	b	Mitochondria[b,l]	563 [21]	532	429 [114]			30	CoQ, NHI	Q_1,Q_2
	b_1	E. coli[f]	560	530	426	415	0.250		fp?	NO_3^-
		Other bacteria	559	528	426	415			fp	
	b_2	Yeast	557 [33]	528 [17]	424 [198]	413 [117]		170[g]	fp	c_1 or c
	b_3	Plant microsomes	559	529	425			40	fp	?
	b_5	Microsomes, liver mitochondria	556 [26]	526 [13]	423 [171]	413 [115]	0.02	14	fp	c, P450
	b_6	Chloroplasts	563				−0.06		fp?	f?
	b_7	Spadix of Arum plant	560	529			−0.03		b	O_2?
	B420	Microsomes[h]	—	—	420, 450 (CO)				b_5, hydroxylase	O_2
C	o	Acetobacter, E. coli	568 (CO)	521 [15.9]	415 [125]	407	0.254	13	C	O_2
	c	Mitochondria[b]	550 [27.7]	524 [11.6]	418 [116]	410	0.220	37	c_1	a
	c_1	Mitochondria[b,l]	554 [24.1]	522–25	416–18	410–12	0.25	32	b	c
	c_2	Denitrifying bacteria	550–52	522	418	410			fp?	NO_3^-?
	c_3	Desulfovibrio desulfuricans	552	522	414	414	−0.205	11.3[j]	fp?	SO_4^-
	c_4	Azotobacter[h]	551	524	418	414	0.30		B	c_5
	c_5	Azotobacter[h]	555	521	415		0.32		c_4	a_1,a_2
	C554	Halotolerant bacteria[i]	554						?	?
	C555 or f	Chloroplasts	555	525	423	413	0.365	110[k]	b_6?	Chl a
	C556 or h	Hepatopancreas of gastropods	556	527	422	408		18.5	?	?

[a]The dash indicates component or reaction absent; an empty space indicates information not available.

[b]Component has been identified in (and in some cases isolated from) the mitochondrial electron transport chain in animals, plants, yeasts, and molds (*Neurospora*).

[c]Defined as the entity in cytochrome oxidase that reacts with CO in the reduced and with HCN, HNO_2, and probably O_2 in the oxidized state. Monomeric cytochrome oxidase has an $M \simeq 240{,}000$ and contains 2 hemes per molecule $[a \cdot Cu : a_3 \cdot Cu = 1]$. The minimal functional unit is three times larger ($M \simeq 700{,}000$).

[d]*Pseudomonas* cytochrome oxidase and the terminal oxidase of certain bacteria do not possess cyt a_3. The isolated protein contains one mole of heme *c* plus one mole of a_2. The systematic name is cytochrome CD.

[e]Estimated value for particulate form. The isolated, solubilized forms show considerably lower values. Similarly, partially denatured particulate enzymes show different E_0' values and become autoxidizable.

[f]The *b*-type cytochrome of many bacteria.

[g]Part of the L-lactate dehydrogenase. *M* shown is for dimeric form containing 2 hemes and 2FMN.

[h]Perhaps the terminal oxidase for microsomal electron transport with either cyt b_5 or the microsomal hydroxylase functioning as an electron donor. Only the γ peak is evident in the spectrum; this is also referred to as P450 because of λ_{max} of CO compound of particulate form.

[i]Formerly called cyt b_4.

[j]Two hemes per molecule.

[k]Two hemes per molecule.

[l]Pure preparations of these cytochromes with enzymatic activity have not yet been obtained from mitochondrial sources.

showed in 1939 (1) that cytochrome oxidase was identical with cytochrome a_3, a special component of cytochrome a; (2) that the cytochromes probably acted as a linear chain of carriers; and (3) that the terminal portion of the chain consisted of cytochrome c in close association with the oxidase.

THE
MITOCHONDRIAL
ELECTRON-
TRANSPORT
CHAIN
Methods of
Investigation

Several types of experiment have contributed to the present state of information in this area: (1) application of sophisticated spectroscopic techniques to measure the content of various suspected carriers (NAD, flavoproteins, cytochromes) and the kinetics of their reduction and reoxidation in various respiratory particles; (2) attempts to strip mitochondria of the enzymes involved in substrate oxidation, oxidative phosphorylation, and other respiration-linked activities, in order to be able to focus on those reactions responsible and essential for electron transport per se; (3) attempts at further comminution of mitochondria and respiratory subparticles to obtain respiratory enzyme complexes free of structural proteins, and susceptible to further purification, in order to yield essentially homogeneous preparations whose properties, function, and interdependence could be investigated; (4) attempts at reconstructing mitochondrial electron transport by the use of such preparations together with soluble enzymes; and (5) the use of respiratory inhibitors.

Electron Transport in
Beef Heart
Mitochondria

For a variety of reasons, the use of mitochondria from bovine heart muscle offers particular advantages for the study of mitochondrial electron transport, i.e., oxidation by O_2 of NADH and succinate. It was the first tissue from which a modified respiratory particle had been isolated (the "Keilin-Hartree" preparation first described in 1940); the electron-transport system appears to be particularly stable in these mitochondria, perhaps because of a particularly low content of proteolytic enzymes; there is a minimal number of other respiratory-chain-linked dehydrogenases present; and there do not appear to be any alternate pathways for the oxidation of NADH, such as exist in mitochondria from mammalian liver.

Heart mitochondria have been utilized by Green and his associates for the preparation of a number of ever smaller submitochondrial electron transport particles (ETP), leading finally to four complexes, each capable of catalyzing one of the component reactions of electron transport and of recombining to yield more complicated arrays, in turn, capable of catalyzing two or more of these steps. The composition of mitochondria with respect to the components of the essential chain — Eq. (15-18) — the reactions catalyzed, and their kinetics are quite similar in many cells:

$$\text{Substrate} \rightarrow \text{NAD} \rightarrow \text{fp}_D \rightarrow \text{cyt } b \rightarrow \text{cyt } c_1 \rightarrow \text{cyt } c \rightarrow \text{cyt}(a \text{ plus } a_3) \rightarrow O_2$$
$$\text{succinate} \rightarrow \text{fp}_S \underset{\uparrow}{}$$

(15-18)

The Complexes
of the Respiratory
Chain

The four complexes carry out the following characteristic reactions (see Fig. 15-7):

$$\text{NADH} + \text{H}^+ + \text{CoQ} \xrightarrow{\text{Complex I}} \text{NAD}^+ + \text{CoQH}_2 \qquad \text{NADH : CoQ (oxido)}$$
$$\text{reductase}$$

(15-19)

$$\text{Succinate} + \text{CoQ} \xrightarrow{\text{Complex II}} \text{fumarate} + \text{CoQH}_2 \qquad \text{succinate : CoQ (oxido)}$$
$$\text{reductase}$$

(15-20)

$$\text{CoQH}_2 + 2 \text{ cyt } c(\text{Fe}^{+3}) \xrightarrow{\text{Complex III}} \text{CoQ} + 2 \text{ cyt } c(\text{Fe}^{+2})$$

hydro CoQ : cytochrome c (oxido)reductase   (15-21)

$$4 \text{ cyt } c(\text{Fe}^{+2}) + \text{O}_2 \xrightarrow{\text{Complex IV}} 4 \text{ cyt } c(\text{Fe}^{+3}) + \text{H}_2\text{O}$$

cytochrome oxidase (cytochrome c: O_2 oxidoreductase)   (15-22)

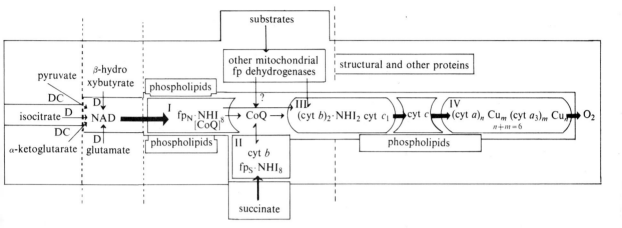

FIGURE 15-7. The Electron Transport System of Mitochondria from Beef Heart.
D = dehydrogenase (NAD-linked)
DC = dehydrogenase complex (NAD-linked)
fp = flavoprotein
fp_N = NADH dehydrogenase
fp_S = succinate dehydrogenase
NHI = nonheme iron
Black lines indicate the mitochondrial system, containing enzymes and other components localized on outer and inner membranes and in the intramitochondrial matrix. Thus, the systems linked to the outer membranes can be stripped away and the intramitochondrial content liberated; electron transport particles (ETP) are obtained and are capable of catalyzing the key reactions NADH→O_2 and succinate→O_2, and sometimes also of retaining the capacity for oxidative phosphorylation. By further comminutive procedures there can then be obtained the unit of electron transport, consisting of four complexes, I through IV. Complex I: NADH-CoQ (oxido) reductase; complex II: succinate-CoQ (oxido) reductase; complex III: CoQH_2-cytochrome c (oxido) reductase; complex IV: cytochrome oxidase.

It is evident that in the presence of the two mobile carriers, CoQ and cytochrome c (which become almost completely detached during isolation of the complexes), this accounts for all the oxidation-reduction reactions of the mitochondrial electron-transport system. Thus, complex I plus complex III reconstitute the mitochondrial NADH: cytochrome c (oxido) reductase; complex II plus III, the mitochondrial succinate: cytochrome c (oxido) reductase; complex I plus III plus IV, the mitochondrial NADH oxidase; complex II plus III plus IV, the mitochondrial succinoxidase; and finally I plus II plus III plus IV, the complete electron-transport sequence, i.e., a combined NADH- and succinoxidase Eq. (15-18). Efficient reconstitution requires the stoichiometric recombination of the various complexes when admixed at relatively high concentrations together with cytochrome c and coenzyme Q. The latter two components are mobile, lipid-soluble carriers, capable of linking the various activities both in the reconstructed system and in the intact ETP or mitochondria; CoQ, because of its long aliphatic side chain, has considerable lipid solubility, and cytochrome c, which is ordinarily a water-soluble protein, can be made lipid-soluble by complexing with mitochondrial phospholipids. One of the strongest lines of evidence that mitochondrial electron transport is adequately represented by reconstitution of the four complexes is provided by studies with inhibitors.

Respiratory Inhibitors   Inhibitors, especially cyanide, CO, and certain narcotics, played a useful role in developing our understanding of cellular respiration. Extension of these studies to include a number of additional inhibitors and the use of spectrophotometric techniques[1] has provided a valuable tool for disrupting the chain at various points, thereby elucidating the sequence of components and their mode of interaction. Specific inhibitors are summarized in Table 15-6. In general, some degree of structural integrity of the complex appears to be required for its interaction with most inhibitors, since soluble, phospholipid-free enzymes do not exhibit the characteristic inhibition pattern.

Role of Mitochondrial Lipids   Mitochondria contain a relatively large amount of lipid — more than 90 per cent of which is phospholipid — as an integral part of the membrane system, and

TABLE 15-6.   The Different Classes of Respiratory Inhibitors

Class	Examples	Specifically affected complex or reaction	Concentrations usually employed
A	HCN, HN$_3$, CO	IV Cyt c (Fe^{+2}) $\rightarrow$ O$_2$	$\leq 10^{-4}$ M (CN$^-$)
B	Antimycin A^a	III Cyt b (Fe^{+2}) $\rightarrow$ cyt c_1 (Fe^{+3}) (perhaps at NHI)	Stoichiometric with cytochromes
	2-Alkyl-4-hydroxyquinoline-N-oxide	III Same as above	$\sim 10^{-6}$ M
	3(2-Methyloctyl) naphthoquinone	III ?	$\sim 10^{-5}$ M
	BAL + O$_2$	III ?	$\sim 10^{-3}$ M
C	Rotenone^b	I FMN $\rightarrow$ Q and/or cyt b (Fe^{+3})	Stoichiometric with fp$_N$
	Barbiturates (amytal, seconal)	I Same as above	$\geq 10^{-3}$ M
D	Thenoyltrifluoroacetone^c	II Peptide-FAD $\rightarrow$ Q and/or cyt b	$\geq 10^{-4}$ M
E	Oligomycin^d Atractylate^e	Inhibit respiration (NADH $\rightarrow$ O$_2$ or succinate $\rightarrow$ O$_2$) when coupled to phosphorylation	
F	Uncoupling agents (substituted phenols, phenylhydrazones, gramicidin, arsenate, dicoumarol)	Stimulate respiration when rate is limited by phosphorylation or blocked by oligomycin	
G	Arsenite, Cd^{+2}	Inhibit respiration for α-ketoglutarate and pyruvate only by virtue of blocking dihydrolipoyl dehydrogenase. Inhibit phosphorylation, probably at or prior to site 3.	

^{a}An antibiotic elaborated by a *Streptomyces* species.
^{b}A potent fish poison isolated from plant roots and having the following structure:

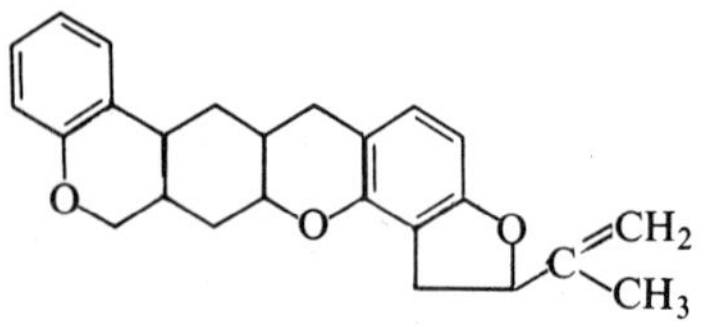

^{c}4,4,4-Trifluoro-1(2-thienyl)-1,3-butanedione.
^{d}Polypeptide antibiotics obtained from an Actinomycete.
^{e}N-glucoside from the plant *Atractylus*.

---

[1] Localization of inhibitor action is facilitated by application of the "crossover theorem" of Chance and Williams, which states that, if an inhibitor is added to an array of redox carriers in their steady state, then those on the reduced side become more reduced, those on the oxidized side more oxidized.

the isolated submitochondrial particles and purified complexes still retain this component.

The mitochondrial lipids from heart muscle consist of approximately equal proportions of phosphatidylcholine and phosphatidyl ethanolamine, each accounting for about 35 per cent of the total lipid and about 16 per cent of cardiolipin.

Mitochondrial phospholipids exhibit a particularly high degree of unsaturation: in heart muscle there are 3.2 double bonds per atom of phospholipid-P. This unsaturation appears to be of functional significance, since the catalytic activity of any of the four complexes can be reduced upon extraction with lipid solvents. Activity is restored by unsaturated phospholipids, such as those from mitochondria, by egg, beef, or soybean lecithin, or by synthetic oleyl lecithin. The greater the degree of unsaturation, the greater the activation. The function of phospholipid appears to be twofold: (1) to stabilize the active conformations of the various proteins of the respiratory chain both individually and collectively; and (2) to permit their interaction with other essential components, such as CoQ, factors required for oxidative phosphorylation, and the structural protein(s).

Other Components In addition to the components already described, most mitochondria also contain vitamin K and other related naphthoquinones, as well as vitamin E or related compounds. Although the particles and derived preparations can interact with added naphthoquinones, hydroquinones, and certain vitamin E derivatives, the functional significance of these observations remains obscure, except in certain bacteria (e.g., *Mycobacteria*):

$$H_3C - \overset{\overset{\displaystyle CH_3}{|}}{} \quad O \quad \overset{CH_3}{|}$$

Vitamin E (α-tocopherol), structure with $(CH_2)_3\overset{\overset{\displaystyle CH_3}{|}}{CH}(CH_2)_3\overset{\overset{\displaystyle CH_3}{|}}{CH}(CH_2)_3\overset{\overset{\displaystyle CH_3}{|}}{CH}CH_3$

K_1: R $= CH{=}\overset{\overset{\displaystyle CH_3}{|}}{C}(CH_2)_3\overset{\overset{\displaystyle CH_3}{|}}{CH}(CH_2)_3\overset{\overset{\displaystyle CH_3}{|}}{CH}(CH_2)_3\overset{\overset{\displaystyle CH_3}{|}}{CH}CH_3$

K_2: R $= CH{=}\overset{\overset{\displaystyle CH_3}{|}}{C}CH_2(CH_2CH{=}\overset{\overset{\displaystyle CH_3}{|}}{C})_4CH_2CH{=}C\overset{CH_3}{\underset{CH_3}{<}}$

K_3: R $= H$ (menadione)

Vitamins K

OXIDATIVE PHOSPHORYL-ATION AND RELATED PROCESSES During the period 1937 to 1941 it was recognized by Belitzer and Tsibakova and by Kalckar that the large amount of free energy liberated during the complete oxidation of metabolites via the citric acid cycle could be utilized to drive the synthesis of ATP, a process now referred to as oxidative phosphorylation. These studies were continued and extended vigorously in several laboratories, and by 1950 it was clear that the ability to catalyze oxidative phosphorylation was a property exclusively of mitochondria; that respiration (i.e., oxidation) and phosphorylation could be dissociated or "uncoupled" from each other by certain agents, such as 2,4-dinitrophenol; that phosphorylation was almost exclusively linked to the electron-transport chain rather than to substrate level oxidations;[1] and that the number of moles of ATP formed relative to the gram-atoms of oxygen consumed, i.e., the P/O ratio, approached integral values for different substrates undergoing one-step oxidation. P/O ratios → 4 were reported for α-ketoglutarate going to succinate, 3 for malate → OAA, glutamate → α-ketoglutarate, or β-hydroxybutyrate (BOB) → acetoacetate, and 2 for succinate → fumarate or malate.

For purposes of discussion, we shall now recast Eq. (15-18) and Fig. 15-7 in the following manner (Fig. 15-8, upper part), which also incorporates information concerning oxidative phosphorylation (lower part).

Phosphorylation Sites and P/O Ratios

Estimation of the number of phosphorylation sites and their localization in the electron-transport chain has been accomplished by a number of different techniques, both direct and indirect. A direct comparison of P/O ratios — measured most frequently by means of polarographic techniques for oxygen uptake and by sensitive tracer (P^{32}) or enzymatic measurements for ATP formation or ADP disappearance — disclosed that true respiratory-chain-linked phosphorylation in the oxidation of NADH, or of NAD-dehydrogenase-dependent substrates, yielded a value of 3, and that of flavoprotein-dependent substrates, such as succinate, led to a value of 2. Since all steps beyond the initial flavoproteins are similar for all substrates, one phosphorylation site (1) must be localized within complex I. The remaining two sites are thus located in the span between CoQ (cyt b) and O_2. One of these (site 2) may be localized between CoQ and cytochrome c_1 (or c), i.e., in the area of complex III. This assignment is supported by the observation that in a system in which cytochrome oxidase is blocked by HCN, the oxidation of NADH or of BOB by added cyt c takes place with a $P/2e^-$ (equals P/O) ratio of 2. Localization of the third site (3) in the area of cytochrome oxidase follows from the experiments just cited, and from the fact that ascorbate — plus tetramethyl-p-phenylenediamine (TMPD) as carrier — which can donate electrons only to cyt c, is oxidized with a P/O of unity. Neither the rate nor stoichiometry of this reaction is affected by the addition of antimycin A. Essentially identical conclusions were reached by Chance and Williams on the basis of "crossover" experiments (see page 364). When intact mitochondria are supplied with substrate and P_i, they exhibit the phenomenon of respiratory control in that their rate of respiration becomes very low in the absence of ADP (state 4). Addition of this component converts the system to state 3. Thus, state 4 can be regarded as inhibited and the transition $3 \rightarrow 4$ as analogous to that obtaining when a respiratory inhibitor is added to the chain operating in its steady state. A comparison of the state of oxidation of the various spectrophotometrically identifiable carriers occurring as a result of the transition should therefore identify those carrier pairs capable of interacting with ADP at a phosphorylation site. These experiments suggested that phosphorylation takes place coincidentally with the reactions NADH → fp_D, $b \rightarrow c_1$, and $a \rightarrow a_3$. Finally, if one postulates a model in which each phosphorylation step requires the interaction of one reduced carrier with the adjacent oxidized carrier, it is clear

---

[1]Of all the citric acid cycle (CAC) substrates only α-ketoglutarate is capable of undergoing a live *substrate-level* phosphorylation to produce one molecule of ATP per molecule of substrate oxidized (see page 328).

that efficient chemical coupling demands an absolute free energy span between these carrier couples greater than for the reaction $ATP + H_2O \rightarrow ADP + P_i$. This argument implies a $\Delta G'$ of ≤ -10 kcal or a $\Delta E_0'$ of ~ 250 mv for the complex in question: examination of Fig. 15-1 shows that only the pairs NADH/fp, fp/cyt b (CoQ), cyt b (CoQ)/cyt c_1, and cyt a/cyt a_3 (or O_2) can qualify on this basis. The overall energy available between NADH and O_2 amounts to 1.14 volts or 51.3 kcal/mole. Since, at physiological concentrations, the formation of three molecules of ATP corresponds to the expenditure of 30 kcal/mole, it is clear that a P/O ratio of 3 is equivalent to an observed efficiency of >fifty per cent.

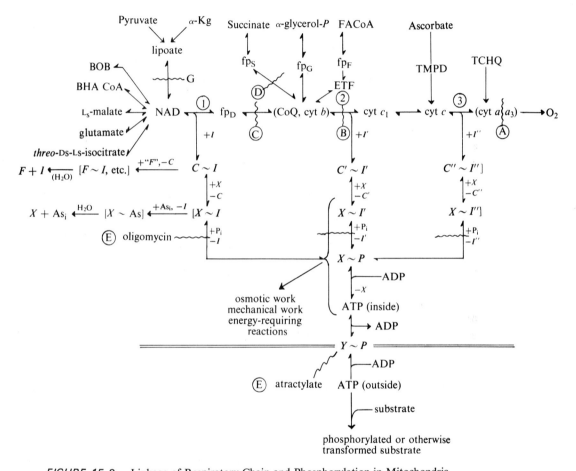

FIGURE 15-8.   Linkage of Respiratory Chain and Phosphorylation in Mitochondria.

①, ②, and ③ are phosphorylation sites. Ⓐ, Ⓑ, Ⓒ, Ⓓ, and Ⓔ are sites of action of respiratory inhibitors (see Table 15-6).

BOB = D-β-Hydroxybutyrate

BHA = L-β-Hydroxyacyl-

fp_F = fatty acyl dehydrogenase (see page 318)

ETF = electron transferring flavoprotein (see page 348)

TMPD = tetramethyl-p-phenylene diamine

TCHQ = tetrachlorohydroquinone

$C \sim I$, etc.: intermediates of oxidative phosphorylation with $\Delta G^{0\prime} \leqslant 0$ for reaction $C \sim I \xrightarrow{(H_2O)}$ $C + I$, etc.

E = uncouplers, such as dinitrophenol (see Table 15-6)

$As_i = HAsO_4^=$

Nature has had to develop a highly complex and integrated device to accomplish oxidative phosphorylation with such high efficiency. It is provided by an array of membrane-bound mitochondrial components. Bacterial systems, which make use of nonmitochondrial and less highly integrated complexes generally produce P/O ratios lower than those observed for equivalent reactions in mitochondrial systems.

The Partial Reactions of Phosphorylation

General Models. The key to the riddle of oxidative phosphorylation consists of determining how free energy liberated by oxidation-reduction reactions in the chain can be utilized to generate a chemical bond that, after a series of iso-energetic displacement reactions, is capable of generating ATP from ADP. Following a suggestion of Lipmann, such bonds are indicated by the sign $\sim$ (the "tilde"), e.g., $ADP \sim P$ or generally $A \sim B$.[1] By analogy with reactions already discussed, most investigators have postulated *direct* chemical coupling, involving joint intermediates, rather than indirect models involving the generation of gradients across the mitochondrial membrane. One such model, proposed by Mitchell, envisions a chemi-osmotic coupling for the "vectorial" oxidation of a carrier, C_{red}, localized on one side of a membrane (symbolized by the double line with the arrow pointing toward the "inside"), by means of a second one, C'_{ox}, bound on the other side:

$$H_2O + C_{red} \,\|\!\!\rightarrow\! C'_{ox} + H_2O \rightleftharpoons OH^- + HC_{ox}^+ \,\|\!\!\rightarrow\! C'_{red} - OH + H^+ \tag{15-23a}$$

or

$$C_{red} \,\|\!\!\rightarrow\! C'_{ox} \rightleftharpoons OH^- + C_{ox} \,\|\!\!\rightarrow\! C'_{red} + H^+ \tag{15-23b}$$

If the membrane is impermeable to small ions, including H^+ and OH^-, the primary consequence of the redox reaction is the generation of a pH gradient. One can then conceive of this gradient's being used for the vectorial reversal of any reaction having a high negative free energy of hydrolysis with the highly exergonic formation of H_2O from its ions providing the driving force.

In searching for appropriate chemical models, investigators have relied heavily on possible analogies to well-authenticated instances of oxidative phosphorylation at the substrate level — Eqs. (15-24) and (15-25):

$$\text{Glyceraldehyde-3-}P + NAD^+ + P_i \rightleftharpoons 1,3\text{-di}P\text{-glycerate} + NADH \tag{15-24a}$$

$$\text{1,3-Di}P\text{-glycerate} + ADP \rightleftharpoons \text{glycerate-3-}P + ATP \tag{15-24b}$$

$$\alpha\text{-Ketoglutarate} + NAD^+ + CoASH \rightleftharpoons \text{succinyl CoA} + NADH \tag{15-25a}$$

$$\text{Succinyl CoA} + GDP + P_i \rightleftharpoons \text{succinate} + GTP \tag{15-25b}$$

These sets of reactions differ: reactions (15-24) lead to the *direct* incorporation of inorganic phosphate into one of the products of the redox reaction, whereas in reactions (15-25), oxidation leads to the generation of a reactive intermediate

---

[1] In the older literature, they were called "high-energy bonds," but this term has now been largely abandoned. In general, a compound $A \sim B$ has a relatively high negative free energy of hydrolysis (≤ -7 kcal/mole) or is in equilibrium (i.e., linked through a series of isoenergetic steps) with one that does (see Chap. 2).

not containing either P_i or ADP (succinyl CoA), which subsequently produces GTP (equivalent to ATP) by a series of displacement reactions. The following two mechanisms (types 1 and 2) for respiratory-chain-linked phosphorylations have therefore been considered. Type 1 involves a nonphosphorylated intermediate and is analogous to reactions (15-25), but type 2 does not and hence is analogous to reactions (15-24):

$$\text{Type 1} \quad (C_{red}, C'_{ox}) + I \rightleftharpoons (C_{ox}, C'_{red}) \sim I \tag{15-26a}$$

$$(C_{ox}, C'_{red}) \sim I + P_i + \text{ADP} \rightleftharpoons (C_{ox}, C'_{red}) + \text{ATP} + I \tag{15-26b}$$

$$\text{Type 2} \quad (C_{red}, C'_{ox}) + P_i \rightleftharpoons (C_{ox}, C'_{red}) \sim P \tag{15-27a}$$

$$(C_{ox}, C'_{red}) \sim P + \text{ADP} \rightleftharpoons (C_{ox}, C'_{red}) + \text{ATP} \tag{15-27b}$$

In these formulations, both partial reactions (a and b) may consist of more than one step, just as an acyl enzyme and acyl lipoate are intermediates in reactions (15-24a) and (15-25a). (Reaction (15-25b) probably also involves the sequence acyl enzyme → acyl $\sim$ P.) The reactive intermediate linked to the carrier is abbreviated as ( ) $\sim I$, and we have left unspecified the precise linkage of I to C_{ox}, C'_{red}, or to the complex as a whole. Perhaps I is a protein and $\sim I$ represents a particular conformation. At present, the type 1 mechanism appears to be the more plausible. Thus, in the presence of dinitrophenol (DNP) (see below) respiration does not require the presence of P_i even at low concentrations, a result consistent with reaction (15-26a) but not (15-27a); also the kinetics for the transition for stage 4 (ADP limited) to stage 3 (normal) respiration are consistent with a type 1 system.

ATPase. Mitochondria and phosphorylating particles in general catalyze a rapid hydrolytic breakdown of ATP to ADP plus P_i. Unlike such reactions catalyzed by other membrane systems, this reaction is relatively insensitive to the presence of Na^+ and K^+ and to the specific inhibitor, ouabain (G-strophantin, a steroid rhamnoside). The mitochondrial ATPase, low in fully functional particles where the rate of respiration is controlled by phosphorylation, becomes unmasked whenever the two processes can no longer act in concert, i.e., when the particles are aged or mistreated or exposed to "uncouplers," such as DNP. These results have been interpreted in terms of a reversal of ATP formation with attendant enhancement of the hydrolytic breakdown of some labile intermediate.

Respiratory Control. The observations that led to the concept of respiratory control in fully functional, or "tightly coupled," respiratory particles were described on page 366. The overall mechanism responsible is evident from Fig. 15-8 and the reversibility of its constituent reactions.

Reversed Electron Flow. Electron transport reactions in the direction from right to left (Fig. 15-8) can be energized by the addition of ATP. The following reactions have been demonstrated: [(TMPD) → cyt c → NAD → (oxidized substrate, i.e., acetoacetate, α-ketoglutarate, etc.)] and [succinate → NAD → (substrate)].

The Use of Uncouplers and Inhibitors

Uncouplers of Oxidative Phosphorylation. Agents of this class (Table 15-6, class F) show the following properties.

(1) They stimulate respiration in the absence of either an intermediate (ADP) or a terminal phosphate acceptor (glucose plus hexokinase). (2) This stimulation

does not require the presence of P_i, and it is accompanied by abolition of respiratory-chain-linked phosphorylation. (3) Respiration in particles still susceptible to complete inhibition by "true" phosphorylation inhibitors (Table 15-6, class E) can be restored to normal levels. And (4) they stimulate ATPase in particles or soluble preparations but inhibit reversed electron flow either in mitochondria or in submitochondrial particles, whether ATP is added externally or generated in situ (e.g., by α-ketoglutarate dehydrogenase, plus succinate thiokinase).

The classical uncoupler of this class is 2,4-dinitrophenol (DNP), introduced by Loomis and Lipmann. A number of other compounds that have also been shown to react in essentially the same fashion include various other substituted phenols, especially pentachlorophenol, a circular polypeptide antibiotic (gramicidin), dicumarol[1] — a potent anticoagulant isolated from rotting sweet clover — and various substituted phenylhydrazones, such as m-chlorocarbonyl-cyanide-phenylhydrazone (CCCP), and arsenate. In Mitchell's hypothesis uncouplers are agents capable of destroying the vectorial, anisotropic structure of the membrane, leading to elimination of the pH gradient.

Inhibitors of Energy-linked Electron Transfer. Agents of this group (class E) are true inhibitors of respiration in intact, tightly coupled phosphorylating particles. The compounds are ineffective, therefore, with those respiratory particles that no longer have the requisite degree of structural integrity even though they may still be able to produce ATP. Also they, in contrast to agents of class F, inhibit, rather than stimulate, the particulate ATPase. When respiration is blocked by inhibitors (class E), it can be completely restored by uncouplers (class F); conversely, ATPase is stimulated by uncouplers (class F) and depressed by inhibitors (class E). Reversed electron flow and other energy-requiring mito-chondrial activities are inhibited only when the energy source is ATP itself or some other equivalent compound added to the system, and not when it is provided by high-energy intermediates generated continuously in situ as a consequence of respiration. Two groups comprise this class of inhibitors. The first, exemplified by oligomycin, appears to block one of the primary phosphoryl-ation steps. Atractyloside, also called atractylate, a representative of the second class of agents, blocks the system only when external ATP is used, inhibits the entry of ADP and ATP into mitochondria, and the labeling of extramitochondrial (but not intramitochondrial) ATP by P^{32} during oxidative phosphorylation. It also blocks the hydrolysis of external, but not of internal, ATP. All these effects require intact mitochondria and disappear when sub-mitochondrial, though still phosphorylating, oligomycin-sensitive particles are used. Evidently atractyloside inhibits at a step beyond that blocked by oligomycin, i.e., one specifically concerned with the entry and exit of ADP/ATP into a mitochondrial compartment.

---

[1] Also spelled dicoumarol:

Other Reactions
Energized by
Electron Transport

ATP production is not the only reaction that is directly dependent on mito-chondrial electron transport. On the contrary, most energy-requiring processes occurring in the particles can be driven by ATP supplied in the medium, by ATP generated as a result of energy-linked respiration, or by the coupling reactions themselves. This direct coupling is inhibited by respiratory inhibitors and by DNP, but it is relatively independent of (or sometimes stimulated by) oligomycin and atractylate. Among the endergonic reactions that can thus be driven directly by reactive intermediates in the energy coupling sequence are (1) reversed electron flow; (2) accumulation of ions (both cations, such as Mg^{+2} or Ca^{+2}, or anions such as phosphate) inside the particle against an osmotic gradient (active trans-port or translocation); (3) mitochondrial contraction, i.e., the performance of mechanochemical work; (4) the energy-dependent reduction of $NADP^+$ at the expense of NADH; (5) the formation of acyl CoA derivatives from fatty acids prior to their oxidation by the β-oxidation sequence; and (6) mitochondrial protein synthesis.

REFERENCES

Beinert, H.: Flavin Coenzymes, in P. Boyer, H. Lardy, and K. Myrbäck (eds.), "The Enzymes," 2d ed., vol. 2, p. 339, Academic Press, New York, 1960.

Chance, B. (ed.): "Energy-linked Functions of Mitochondria," Academic Press, New York, 1963.

————, and G. R. Williams: The Respiratory Chain and Oxidative Phosphorylation, *Advan. Enzymol.*, **17**: 65 (1956).

Ehrenberg, A.: Flavin Free Radicals, in B. Pullman (ed.), "Electronic Aspects of Bio-chemistry," p. 379, Academic Press, New York, 1964.

Ernster, L., and C. P. Lee: Biological Oxidoreductions, *Ann. Rev. Biochem.*, **33**: 729 (1964).

Falk, J. E.: "Porphyrins and Metalloporphyrins," Elsevier, New York, 1964.

Frieden, E., S. Osaki, and H. Kobayashi: Copper Proteins and Oxygen, *J. Gen. Physiol.*, **49**: 213 (1965).

George, P., and J. S. Griffith: Electron Transfer and Enzyme Catalysis, in P. Boyer, H. Lardy, and K. Myrbäck (eds.), "The Enzymes," 2d ed., vol. 1, p. 347, Academic Press, New York, 1959.

Griffiths, D. E.: Oxidative Phosphorylation, in P. N. Campbell and G. D. Greville (eds.), "Essays in Biochemistry," p. 91, Biochemical Society/Academic Press, New York, 1965.

Haurowitz, F.: "The Chemistry and Function of Proteins," pp. 256–279, Academic Press, New York, 1963.

Hayashi, O.: Direct Oxygenation by O_2, Oxygenases, in P. Boyer, H. Lardy, and K. Myrbäck, (eds.), in "The Enzymes," 2d ed., vol. 8, p. 353, Academic Press, New York, 1963.

Lehninger, A. L.: "The Mitochondrion," Benjamin, New York, 1964.

Mahler, H. R.: Nature and Function of Metalloflavoproteins, *Advan. Enzymol.*, **17**: 233 (1956).

Malkin, R., and J. C. Rabinowitz: Non-heme Iron Electron-Transfer Proteins, *Ann. Rev. Biochem.*, **36**, 113 (1967).

Mason, H. S., and M. Morrison (eds.): "Oxidases and Related Redox Systems," Wiley, New York, 1965.

Massey, V., and C. Veeger: Biological Oxidations, *Ann. Rev. Biochem.*, **32**: 579 (1963).

Mitchell, P.: The Chemiosmotic Hypothesis and Oxidative Phosphorylation, *Biol. Rev. Cambridge Phil. Soc.* (1967).

Nicholls, P.: Cytochromes: A Survey, in P. Boyer, H. Lardy, and K. Myrbäck (eds.), "The Enzymes," 2d ed., vol. 8, p. 3, Academic Press, New York, 1963.

Racker, E.: "Mechanisms in Bioenergetics," Academic Press, New York, 1965.

San Pietro, A. (ed.): "Non-heme Iron Proteins: Role in Energy Conversion," Antioch Press, Yellow Springs, Ohio, 1965.

Singer, T. P.: Flavoprotein Dehydrogenases of the Respiratory Chain: A Survey, in P. Boyer, H. Lardy, and K. Myrbäck (eds.), "The Enzymes," vol. 7, p. 345, Academic Press, New York, 1963.

Singer, T. P. (ed.): "Biological Oxidations," Wiley, New York, 1966.

Sund, H., H. Diekman, and K. Wallenfels: Die Wasserstoffübertragung mit Pyridinnucleotiden, *Advan. Enzymol.*, **26**: 115 (1964).

Williams, R. J. P.: Coordination and Catalysis, in P. Boyer, H. Lardy, and K. Myrbäck (eds.), "The Enzymes," 2d ed., vol. 1, p. 391, Academic Press, New York, 1959.

16 | Biosynthesis of Lipids

To a substantial extent, the biosynthesis of lipids reflects the variety of fashions in which the repeated condensation of two-carbon fragments, derived from acetate, is employed for the construction of natural products. It includes the *fatty acids*, many *aromatic* and *heterocyclic* compounds, *steroids*, and *terpenes*. The biosynthesis of representative members of these structural classes, together with the formation of complex lipids resulting from further metabolism of the fatty acids, is considered in this chapter.

BIOSYNTHESIS OF FATTY ACIDS

The main classes of naturally occurring fatty acids were described in Chap. 13 (see Table 13-1). At this point we discuss the biosynthesis of fatty acids of each of these structural types, beginning with the saturated straight-chain members containing an even number of carbon atoms.

Each step in the enzymatic pathway responsible for the oxidation of fatty acids is reversible (see page 317). Consequently the proposition was advanced that fatty acid biosynthesis might occur by simple reversal of the oxidative pathway. Indeed, incubation of acetyl-SCoA with purified enzymes of the oxidative pathway, together with NADH, NADPH, and an enzyme able to reduce unsaturated fatty acyl-SCoAs irreversibly to the saturated derivatives, results in synthesis of fatty acids. Furthermore, several workers were able to demonstrate the incorporation of acetyl-SCoA into fatty acids in mitochondrial systems supplemented with NADH, NADPH, and ATP. However, it now seems certain that at least two pathways for fatty acid biosynthesis exist in the mito-chondrion: one similar to that occurring in the soluble portion of the cell (discussed below), which catalyzes the *de novo* synthesis of fatty acids, and one that catalyzes the elongation of preformed fatty acids through condensation with acetyl-SCoA. It appears that only the latter pathway is similar to the reverse of fatty acid oxidation.

Although fatty acid oxidation occurs principally or entirely in the mitochondria or other particulate cellular fractions, fatty acid synthesis can be brought about by soluble extracts of pigeon liver and mammary gland. Cofactor requirements for fatty acid synthesis in soluble cell extracts, determined by Wakil and his associates, include an absolute dependence upon bicarbonate, ATP, Mn^{+2}, and NADPH. These cofactor requirements alone clearly distinguish the synthetic and oxidative pathways, since (1) bicarbonate has no effect upon fatty acid oxidation and (2) NAD, rather than NADP, is the oxidation-reduction coenzyme in the oxidative pathway.

The principal product of fatty acid synthesis by soluble, cell-free extracts is palmitic acid, although other long-chain fatty acids, C_{10} to C_{14}, are formed in lesser amounts.

The basic building block for fatty acid synthesis is acetyl-SCoA. The principal cellular source of this substance is the intramitochondrial oxidation of pyruvate. Since the mitochondrial membrane is rather impermeable to acetyl-SCoA, the question has been raised as to the origin of the extramitochondrial acetyl-SCoA for fatty acid biosynthesis. The only known reactions leading to the extramitochondrial generation of acetyl-SCoA are the ATP-dependent cleavage of citrate:

$$\text{Citrate} + \text{ATP} \cdot \text{Mg} + \text{HSCoA} \rightleftharpoons \text{acetyl-SCoA} + \text{oxaloacetate} + \text{ADP} \cdot \text{Mg} + P_i \qquad (16\text{-}1)$$

and the acetate thiokinase reaction:

$$\text{Acetate} + \text{ATP} \cdot \text{Mg} + \text{HSCoA} \rightleftharpoons \text{acetyl-SCoA} + \text{AMP} + PP_i \cdot \text{Mg} \qquad (16\text{-}2)$$

The substrates for both of these reactions can be generated from intramitochondrial acetyl-SCoA. Thus intramitochondrial acetyl-SCoA may be cleaved to acetate and, as such, diffuse into the soluble cell portion, or alternatively it may be condensed with oxaloacetate and the citrate product diffuse into the soluble portion. These processes, together with the citrate cleaving enzyme and acetate thiokinase, account for the overall transport of acetyl-SCoA across the mitochondrial membrane. In view of the fact that extramitochondrial citrate is known to stimulate and act as precursor for fatty acid synthesis, it has been suggested that this metabolite may be a major source of acetyl-SCoA for this process. In addition, citrate acts as activator for the enzyme responsible for the first step in fatty acid synthesis.

In addition, a fraction of the extramitochondrial acetyl-SCoA may be derived from the intramitochondrial pool through carnitine-mediated transport across the mitochondrial membrane. Evidence cited previously (see page 320) suggests that carnitine:

$$(CH_3)_3 N^+ — CH_2 — CH — CH_2 — COO^-$$
$$|$$
$$OH$$

Carnitine

may function as an acyl group carrier for the transport of acyl functions from the cytoplasm into the mitochondria in the course of fatty acid oxidation. This compound may well carry out the reverse role as well. Indeed, carnitine stimulates the incorporation of those compounds which are known to give rise to intramitochondrial acetyl-SCoA (pyruvate, glucose, acetate) into long-chain fatty acids in mammalian systems. The role of carnitine as acetyl group carrier for fatty acid synthesis is indicated schematically in Fig. 16-1.

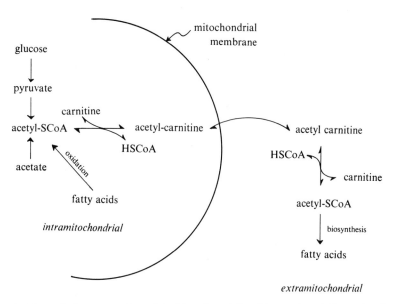

FIGURE 16-1. A Schematic Representation of the Function of Carnitine as Acetyl Group Carrier Across the Mitochondrial Membrane.

An important key to the present understanding of the route of fatty acid synthesis was provided by the discovery of Wakil, and subsequently by Formica and Brady, of acetyl-CoA carboxylase. This large, complex, biotin-dependent enzyme (see page 218) catalyzes the ATP-dependent synthesis of malonyl-SCoA from CO_2 and acetyl-SCoA:

$$CH_3 - \overset{\overset{\displaystyle O}{\|}}{C} - SCoA + CO_2 + ATP \xrightarrow{Mg^{+2}} HO_2C - CH_2 - \overset{\overset{\displaystyle O}{\|}}{C} - SCoA + ADP + P_i \qquad (16\text{-}3)$$

Malonyl-SCoA is the first specific intermediate of fatty acid biosynthesis. In the presence of soluble enzyme fractions, malonyl-SCoA is rapidly converted into fatty acids. This conversion requires, absolutely, the presence of acetyl-SCoA.

Numerous investigators have observed the marked stimulation of fatty acid synthesis in vitro by citrate, isocitrate, and related di- and tricarboxylic acids. It has been demonstrated that this stimulatory effect is not the consequence of the generation of NADPH, through metabolism of these acids by the citric acid cycle enzymes, but is involved in the synthesis of malonyl-SCoA. As mentioned above, acetyl-CoA carboxylase is activated, in a process involving displacement of a monomer-polymer equilibrium, by citrate, isocitrate, and, to a lesser extent, by other polybasic acids. The enzyme appears to be inhibited, on the other hand, by the overall products of the reaction sequence, long-chain fatty acyl-SCoAs.

Fatty acid–synthesizing systems from three sources have been investigated in some detail: that from *E. coli* by Vagelos, that from yeast by Lynen, and that from pigeon liver by Wakil. Of these systems, that from *E. coli* is perhaps best understood at the moment. In Fig. 16-2, the probable route for fatty acid synthesis is diagrammed. Repeated passages through the biosynthetic scheme of Fig. 16-2 yield the following stoichiometry for the synthesis of palmitate from acetyl-SCoA and malonyl-SCoA:

$$CH_3-\overset{O}{\underset{||}{C}}-SCoA + 7HO_2C-CH_2-\overset{O}{\underset{||}{C}}-SCoA + 14NADPH + 14H^+ \rightarrow$$
$$CH_3-(CH_2)_{14}-CO_2H + 7CO_2 + 8CoASH + 14NADP^+ + 6H_2O \quad (16\text{-}4)$$

Starting from acetyl-SCoA alone, the corresponding stoichiometry reads

$$8CH_3-\overset{O}{\underset{||}{C}}-SCoA + 7CO_2^* + 14NADPH + 7ATP + 14H^+ \rightarrow$$
$$CH_3-(CH_2)_{14}-CO_2H + 7CO_2^* + 8CoASH + 14NADP^+ + 7ADP + 7P_i + 6H_2O \quad (16\text{-}5)$$

CO_2^* is shown on both sides of the equation, since it is an indispensable stoichiometric reactant, which, however, is regenerated intact in the course of the reaction sequence (see below).

$$CH_3-\overset{O}{\underset{||}{C}}-SCoA + HS-ACP \rightleftharpoons CH_3-\overset{O}{\underset{||}{C}}-S-ACP + CoASH \quad (1)$$

$$\overset{HO_2C}{\underset{|}{C}}H_2-\overset{O}{\underset{||}{C}}-SCoA + HS-ACP \rightleftharpoons \overset{HO_2C}{\underset{|}{C}}H_2-\overset{O}{\underset{||}{C}}-S-ACP + CoASH \quad (2)$$

$$CH_3-\overset{O}{\underset{||}{C}}-S-ACP + \overset{HO_2C}{\underset{|}{C}}H_2-\overset{O}{\underset{||}{C}}-S-ACP \rightleftharpoons CH_3-\overset{O}{\underset{||}{C}}-CH_2-\overset{O}{\underset{||}{C}}-S-ACP + HS-ACP + CO_2 \quad (3)$$

$$CH_3-\overset{O}{\underset{||}{C}}-CH_2-\overset{O}{\underset{||}{C}}-S-ACP + NADPH + H^+ \rightleftharpoons CH_3-\overset{OH}{\underset{H}{\underset{|}{C}}}-CH_2-\overset{O}{\underset{||}{C}}-S-ACP + NADP^+ \quad (\text{D, isomer}) \quad (4)$$

$$CH_3-\overset{OH}{\underset{H}{\underset{|}{C}}}-CH_2-\overset{O}{\underset{||}{C}}-S-ACP \rightleftharpoons CH_3-CH=CH-\overset{O}{\underset{||}{C}}-S-ACP + H_2O \quad (5)$$

$$CH_3-CH=CH-\overset{O}{\underset{||}{C}}-S-ACP + NADPH + H^+ \rightarrow CH_3CH_2CH_2-\overset{O}{\underset{||}{C}}-S-ACP + NADP^+ \quad (6)$$

$$CH_3CH_2CH_2-\overset{O}{\underset{||}{C}}-S-ACP + HS-CoA \rightleftharpoons CH_3CH_2CH_2\overset{O}{\underset{||}{C}}-SCoA + HS-ACP \quad (7)$$

$$\overset{HO_2C}{\underset{|}{C}}H_2-\overset{O}{\underset{||}{C}}-SCoA + CH_3-\overset{O}{\underset{||}{C}}-SCoA + 2NADPH + 2H^+ \rightarrow CH_3CH_2CH_2\overset{O}{\underset{||}{C}}-SCoA + CO_2 + CoASH$$
$$+ 2NADP^+ + H_2O \quad (8)$$

FIGURE 16-2.   Pathway for Fatty Acid Biosynthesis in *E. Coli.*

The proposed pathway of Fig. 16-2 is consistent with, and supported by, the following important observations. First, the fatty acid–synthesizing system of *E. coli* is soluble and has been fractionated into several components. These include an acetyl transferase, a malonyl transferase, a condensing enzyme, a β-ketoacyl-ACP reductase, and an enoyl-ACP hydrase (Eqs. 1 through 5 in Fig. 16-2). In addition, the synthetase system contains an acyl-carrier protein (ACP), molecular weight 9,600, to which the acyl intermediates are bound throughout the course of the synthetic process. The linkage between the ACP and the intermediates is of the thiolester type. The crucial sulfhydryl group of the ACP has recently been identified as that of a 4′-phosphopantetheine prosthetic group. This prosthetic group is evidently covalently bound to a serine hydroxyl function of the ACP through a phosphodiester linkage.

Second, in the presence of excess malonyl-SCoA, acetyl-SCoA is incorporated only into carbons 15 and 16 of palmitic acid. This is exactly the result expected on the basis of an initial condensation of acetyl-SCoA and malonyl-SCoA followed by successive chain elongation through condensation of the developing fatty acid with additional molecules of malonyl-SCoA. Thus acetyl-SCoA functions as a primer for fatty acid synthesis.

Third, C^{14}-labeled CO_2 is not incorporated into fatty acids. This finding implies a catalytic role for CO_2: the same CO_2 that is utilized in the acetyl-CoA carboxylase reaction is freed in the acetyl-SCoA-malonyl-SCoA condensation.

Fourth, malonyl-SCoA is bound to the fatty acid–synthesizing complex from pigeon liver by sulfhydryl groups, and condensation of the malonyl enzyme with acetyl-SCoA is accompanied by decarboxylation.

Fifth, the product of the condensation reaction in the *E. coli* system has been identified as acetoacetyl-S-ACP. A similar observation has been made by Lynen for the system from yeast.

Sixth, an enoyl hydrase, specific for acyl-carrier protein thiolesters, has been detected in and purified from *E. coli*. This enzyme catalyzes the reversible hydration of crotonyl-S-ACP to yield D(−)-β-hydroxybutyryl-S-ACP.

Seventh, in soluble systems from rat brain or adipose tissue, acetoacetyl-SCoA, D(−)-β-hydroxybutyryl-SCoA, and crotonyl-SCoA, the acyl-SCoA derivatives of the suggested intermediates, are incorporated into palmitate. In accordance with the scheme of Fig. 16-2, these substrates appear to undergo reduction prior to incorporation.

Eighth, tritium from tritiated NADPH is incorporated into the odd-numbered carbon atoms of palmitic acid, beginning with carbon 3. Since FMN is involved coenzymatically in the reduction of the α,β-unsaturated species, the tritium incorporation presumably comes from direct hydrogen transfer from labeled NADPH to the β-ketoacyl species yielding the β-hydroxyacyl compound.

Ninth, in the yeast system, each of the postulated enzymatic activities may be individually demonstrated with the use of model substrates.

Finally, attempts at detection of free intermediates in fatty acid biosynthesis have proved fruitless. This is consistent with, and provides support for, the existence of the various intermediates in a form tightly bound to the pertinent enzyme system.

The enzymatic machinery involved in fatty acid synthesis differs significantly from species to species. Highly purified preparations of the fatty acid synthetase from yeast behave like a single particulate component, clearly of a multienzyme nature, of molecular weight 2,300,000. In contrast, the fatty acid synthetases from avian liver and *Cl. kluyveri* have been resolved into two components, and, as mentioned above, that from *E. coli* has been resolved into several components.

Since propionyl-SCoA replaces acetyl-SCoA to some extent in the initial condensation reaction with malonyl-SCoA, the biosynthesis of fatty acids containing an odd number of carbon atoms may be accounted for in terms of the enzymatic pathway indicated above.

It may be well at this point to summarize the features that distinguish fatty acid *biosynthesis* from fatty acid *oxidation*; similar considerations appear to obtain for the biosynthesis versus degradation of other compounds. (1) Although the enzymatic reactions comprising a catabolic sequence are reversible in principle and microscopically, actual reversal for biosynthesis occurs by a pathway that is distinct in one or more of the following features. (2) Some or all of the enzymes responsible are localized in different subcellular components. (3) One (or more) key steps usually located at the end of the degradative, and consequently at the beginning of the biosynthetic, sequence are virtually irreversible and hence distinct. In the present instance, these are the reactions catalyzed by β-ketothiolase and acetyl-SCoA carboxylase, which lead to the generation and utilization of acetyl-SCoA, respectively. (4) The enzyme responsible for the initiation of a biosynthetic pathway is subject to feedback inhibition and other control mechanisms. (5) Catabolic sequences are energy-providing and generate ATP and (immediately) oxidized pyridine nucleotides; anabolic ones are reductive energy-requiring, and utilize ATP and reduced pyridine nucleotides. The two pyridine nucleotides are again distinct: NAD^+ for degradation, NADPH for biosynthesis (see also page 259). (6) The stereochemistry of apparently similar reactions and intermediates is distinct (here L($+$)-β-hydroxyacyl-SCoA for degradation, the D($-$)- enantiomer for biosynthesis).

The metabolic pathways yielding unsaturated fatty acids are incompletely understood. The participation of molecular oxygen in the desaturation process in aerobic organisms was first suggested by the observation that under anaerobic conditions, but not in the presence of air, yeast requires oleic acid as a growth factor. This finding was subsequently corroborated in studies on a purified system from yeast: under anaerobic conditions only saturated acids were synthesized, but in the presence of oxygen both saturated and unsaturated products were obtained in approximately equal amounts. This system, in the presence of O_2 and NADPH, catalyzes the desaturation of preformed acids, such as palmitate or stearate. The acyl-SCoA or acyl-S-ACP derivatives are substrates for this reaction, which appears to result from the desaturation of the preformed fatty acids in a ferredoxin-dependent process. The intracellular site for aerobic fatty acid desaturation is on particles concentrated in the microsomal fraction. Again this appears to be a general feature for hydroxylation, desaturation, and other oxidation reactions that require the simultaneous participation of O_2 and a reducing agent, such as NADPH (mixed function oxidase; see page

344). The general reaction type is

$$RH + NADPH + O_2^* + 2H^+ \rightarrow R^+ + NADP^+ + 2H_2O^*$$

or $RO^*H + NADP^+ + H_2O^*$ (16-6)

Localization in microsomal membranes is characteristic, not only of these reactions, but also of most of the reactions of lipid biosynthesis except those for the initial synthesis of fatty acids. It is the membranous portion of the microsomes, derived from the endoplasmic reticulum, rather than the ribosomes, that is involved in these reactions (see Chap. 9).

Anaerobic organisms may either catalyze the desaturation of fatty acids by some pathway not involving the participation of oxygen or may follow an alternative pathway. The ability to introduce a double bond directly into a preformed fatty acid is lacking in several anaerobic bacteria, suggesting that the latter alternative is correct. Unsaturated fatty acids may arise through the condensation of unsaturated acyl-SCoA intermediates directly with additional malonyl-SCoA units. Thus, rather than reducing the double bond, as in synthesis of saturated fatty acids, the bond remains intact and is moved away from the carboxyl group as the chain is lengthened. A survey of the unsaturated fatty acids that occur in bacteria, in terms of the position of the double bond, suggests that a β-dehydration of C_{10} and C_{12} hydroxyacyl-SCoA intermediates accounts for the observed products. For example, the synthesis of palmitoleic and vaccenic acids from octanoate may be visualized as in Fig. 16-3. Support for

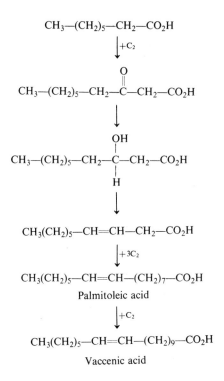

FIGURE 16-3.   Anaerobic Pathway for the Synthesis of Palmitoleic and Vaccenic Acids from Octanoate.— *K. Bloch, P. Baronowsky, H. Goldfine, W. J. Lennarz, R. Light, A. T. Norris, and G. Scheuerbrandt, Federation Proc.,* **20:** *921 (1961).*

this pathway comes from the finding that the fatty acid synthetase from *E. coli* contains a dehydrase specific for D(−)-β-hydroxydecanoate. This may well be the key enzyme for the synthesis of unsaturated fatty acids in organisms of this type.

SYNTHESIS OF TRIGLYCERIDES

The biosynthetic pathway for the formation of triglycerides in liver was first formulated by Weiss and Kennedy in 1956. Free glycerol is phosphorylated at the α-position in the presence of glycerokinase and ATP, yielding L-glycerophosphate, which, alternatively, may arise from reduction of dihydroxyacetone phosphate. One mole of this is subsequently acylated with two moles of fatty

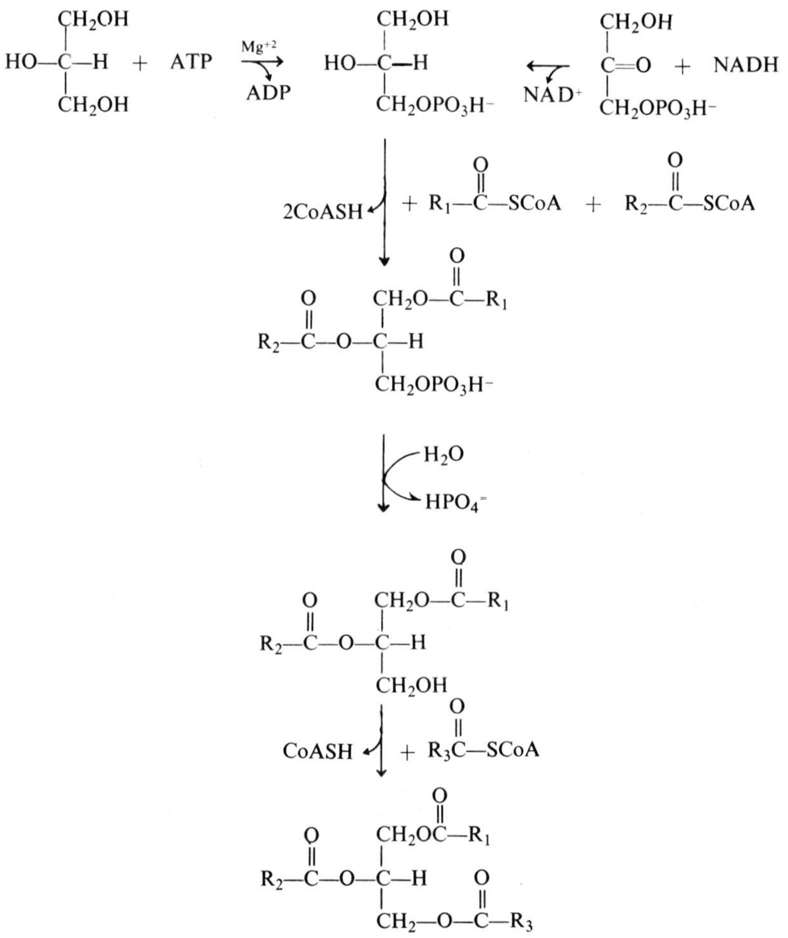

FIGURE 16-4.   Biosynthetic Pathway for Triglyceride Formation.

acyl-SCoA, yielding an α,β-diglyceride phosphate, termed a phosphatidic acid. Phosphatidic acids are, as indicated below, key intermediates in the biosynthesis of several classes of complex lipids. The synthesis of the triglycerides is completed by dephosphorylation, yielding an α,β-diglyceride, followed by esterification with a third mole of fatty acyl-SCoA. The synthesis of triglycerides is summarized in Fig. 16-4.

BIOSYNTHESIS OF
PHOSPHOLIPIDS

The biosynthetic pathways leading to the formation of phosphatidyl choline, -ethanolamine, and -serine are indicated in Fig. 16-5. Phosphatidyl choline and phosphatidylethanolamine arise from the reaction of D-α,β-diglyceride with CDP-choline and CDP-ethanolamine, respectively (see page 199). Phosphatidyl-

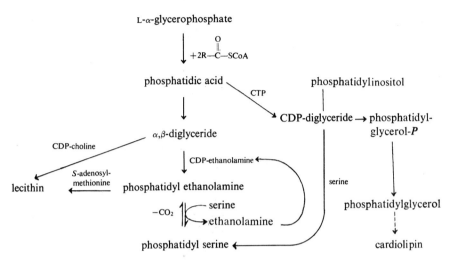

FIGURE 16-5. Biosynthetic Pathways for Formation of Lecithins and Cephalins.

ethanolamine may also arise from the decarboxylation of phosphatidylserine and may give rise to phosphatidylcholine via S-adenosylmethionine-mediated methylation reactions. Phosphatidylserine is formed in liver by an exchange reaction between phosphatidylethanolamine and free L-serine:

$$\text{Phosphatidylethanolamine} + \text{L-serine} \rightleftharpoons \text{phosphatidylserine} + \text{ethanolamine} \qquad (16\text{-}7)$$

Alternatively, phosphatidylserine may be formed in a reaction catalyzed by an enzyme that was isolated from *E. coli*, involving the condensation of free serine with CDP-diglyceride, formed from phosphatidic acid and CTP.

Although the bulk of phosphatides that occur naturally is composed of lecithins, cephalins, and phosphatidyl glycerol, several additional classes of phosphatides do occur in nature to a substantial extent. These include the *inositol phosphatides*, *plasmalogens*, and derivatives of *α-glyceryl ethers*, among others.

The simplest inositol lipid, phosphatidyl inositol, has been demonstrated to have the structure 1-phosphatidyl-L-*myo*-inositol:

1-Phosphatidyl-L-*myo*-inositol

Phosphatidylinositol is synthesized from CDP-diglyceride and free inositol in a fashion similar to that for one route to phosphatidylserine:

$$\text{CDP-diglyceride} + \text{inositol} \rightarrow \text{1-phosphatidyl-L-}myo\text{-inositol} + \text{CMP} \qquad (16\text{-}8)$$

Although the plasmalogens have been known since 1924, when Feulgen detected aldehydogenic material in phosphatide preparations, the correct structure for this class of compounds has been established only recently. It is now clear that the aldehydic behavior of plasmalogens is a consequence of an α,β-unsaturated ether structure. The unsaturated ether is linked to glycerol at the α'- position, and the β- position is occupied by a fatty acid:

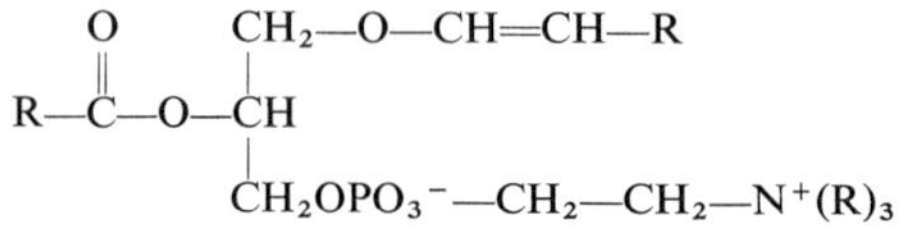

$$
\begin{array}{l}
\quad\;\text{O} \qquad \text{CH}_2\text{—O—CH=CH—R} \\
\quad\;\|\qquad\;\; | \\
\text{R—C—O—CH} \\
\qquad\qquad | \\
\qquad\quad \text{CH}_2\text{OPO}_3{}^-\text{—CH}_2\text{—CH}_2\text{—N}^+(\text{R})_3 \\
\end{array}
$$

A plasmalogen

Plasmalogens containing choline or ethanolamine have been identified and are, therefore, closely related structurally to the lecithins and cephalins.

Rather little is currently known regarding the synthesis of plasmalogens, although some indications do support the reasonable hypothesis that the pathways are similar to those for synthesis of lecithins and cephalins and that the corresponding saturated species are the direct plasmalogen precursors.

Several α-glyceryl ethers are widely distributed in nature, notably chimyl alcohol, batyl alcohol, and selachyl alcohol:

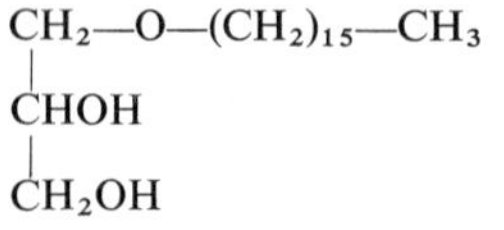

$$
\begin{array}{ll}
\text{CH}_2\text{—O—(CH}_2)_{15}\text{—CH}_3 \qquad\qquad & \text{CH}_2\text{—O—(CH}_2)_{17}\,\text{CH}_3 \\
| & | \\
\text{CHOH} & \text{CHOH} \\
| & | \\
\text{CH}_2\text{OH} & \text{CH}_2\text{OH} \\
\end{array}
$$

      Chimyl alcohol 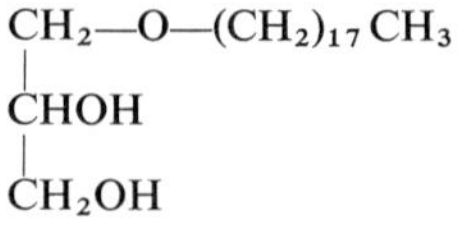   Batyl alcohol

$$
\begin{array}{l}
\text{CH}_2\text{—O—(CH}_2)_8\text{—CH=CH—(CH}_2)_7\text{—CH}_3 \\
| \\
\text{CHOH} \\
| \\
\text{CH}_2\text{OH} \\
\end{array}
$$

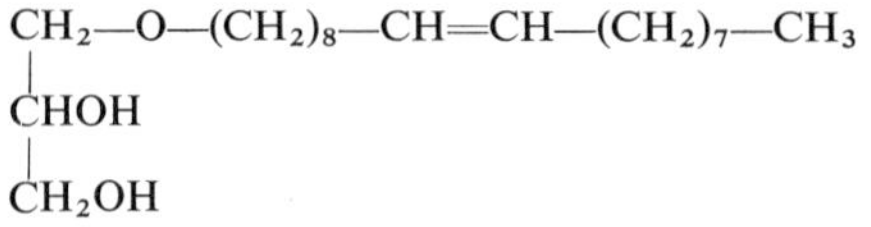

              Selachyl alcohol

Several types of lipid materials containing α-glyceryl ethers have been identified, including structural analogues of phosphatidylcholine and phosphatidylethanolamine. The biosynthetic routes leading to these complex lipids are unknown.

As noted above, phosphatides are of near universal occurrence in nature. Intracellularly, phosphatides are found concentrated in the nuclear, mitochondrial, and microsomal membranes. There they are considered to perform several functions, including those of structure maintenance, ion transport, and permeability regulation. The important role of phosphatides and other lipids in the maintenance of the integrity of the oxidative phosphorylation process in mitochondria was considered in Chap. 15.

BIOSYNTHESIS OF SPHINGOLIPIDS

Sphingolipids are a heterogeneous collection of lipids characterized by the presence of the long-chain aminoalcohol *sphingosine*, or a closely related substance:

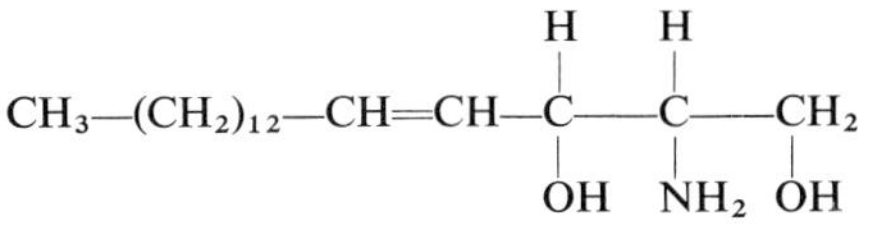

$$CH_3-(CH_2)_{12}-CH=CH-\underset{\underset{OH}{|}}{\overset{\overset{H}{|}}{C}}-\underset{\underset{NH_2}{|}}{\overset{\overset{H}{|}}{C}}-\underset{\underset{OH}{|}}{CH_2}$$

Sphingosine

Studies by several workers have established the stereochemistry of naturally occurring sphingosine: the configuration about the double bond is trans, the configuration of carbon 2 is D, and the relationship of the substituents on carbon 3 to those on carbon 2 is erythro-. Sphingosine is, therefore, *trans*-D-*erythro*-1,3-dihydroxy-2-amino-octadec-4-ene, as confirmed by total synthesis. In addition to lipids from sphingosine itself, closely related substances are derived from dihydrosphingosine, in which the double bond of sphingosine has been saturated — phytosphingosine, a 4-hydroxy derivative of dihydrosphingosine (1,3,4-trihydroxy-2-amino-octadecane) — and dehydrophytosphingosine, an unsaturated derivative of phytosphingosine. The former pair of compounds forms the basis for the sphingolipids occurring in animal tissues, the latter pair for those occurring in plant tissues.

In living materials, sphingosine and its close relatives do not occur in the free form to an appreciable extent, but instead in principal lipid types, sphingomyelins, cerebrosides and gangliosides.

Sphingomyelins yield, on complete hydrolysis, equimolar quantities of sphingosine, choline, phosphate, and fatty acid. Early studies demonstrated that the fatty acid was attached in amide linkage to the primary amino group of sphingosine. Incomplete hydrolysis products of sphingomyelin include phosphorylcholine and sphingosine phosphate, indicating that phosphorylcholine is esterified at the hydroxy group at either the 1 or 3 position of sphingosine. Subsequent studies have identified the site of attachment as the C-1 hydroxyl. Sphingomyelin, therefore, has the following structure:

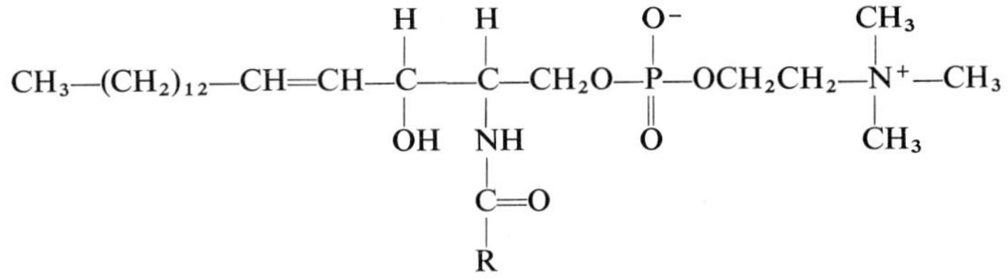

$$CH_3-(CH_2)_{12}-CH=CH-\underset{\underset{OH}{|}}{\overset{\overset{H}{|}}{C}}-\underset{\underset{NH}{|}}{\overset{\overset{H}{|}}{C}}-CH_2O-\underset{\underset{O}{||}}{\overset{\overset{O^-}{|}}{P}}-OCH_2CH_2-\underset{\underset{CH_3}{|}}{\overset{\overset{CH_3}{|}}{N^+}}-CH_3$$

$$\underset{\underset{R}{|}}{\overset{\overset{|}{C=O}}{}}$$

Sphingomyelin

Complete hydrolysis of *cerebrosides* yield sphingosine (or dihydrosphingosine), fatty acid, and a sugar, usually galactose. Structure-determination studies have revealed the structure below as the formula for cerebrosides:

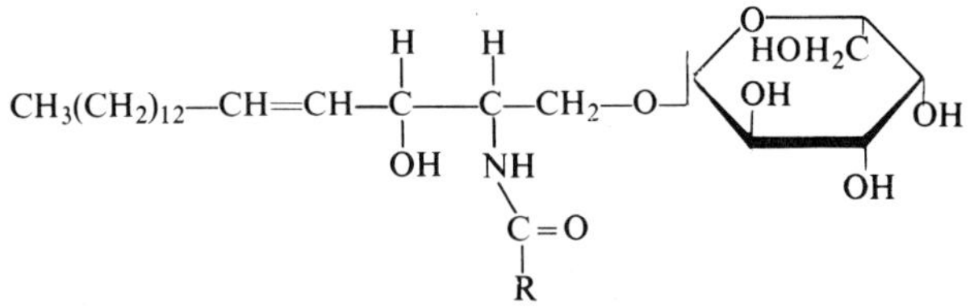

Cerebroside

The configuration of the galactosidic bond is ordinary β. Although galactose usually predominates as the sugar moiety in cerebroside preparations from human brain and spleen, glucose largely replaces it in certain pathological states, including Gaucher's disease.

Cerebrosides are characterized by the nature of the fatty acid components. For example, kerasin contains lignoceric acid $[CH_3(CH_2)_{22}CO_2H]$, phrenosin contains cerebronic acid $[CH_3(CH_2)_{21}CHOH\!-\!CO_2H]$, nervon contains nervonic acid $[CH_3(CH_2)_7CH\!=\!CH(CH_2)_{13}CO_2H]$, etc. The related substance sphingosine galactoside, in which the fatty acid moiety is missing, is termed psychosine.

The *gangliosides* are complex sphingolipids composed of sphingosine, fatty acid, one or more sugars, and, characteristically, neuraminic acid:

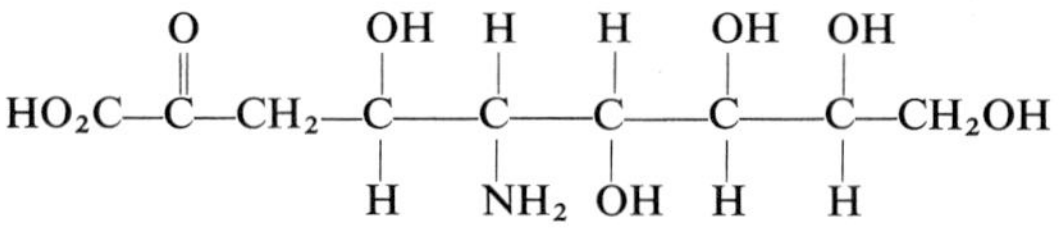

$$HO_2C\!-\!\overset{\displaystyle O}{\overset{\|}{C}}\!-\!CH_2\!-\!\underset{H}{\overset{}{C}}\!-\!\underset{NH_2}{\overset{OH}{C}}\!-\!\underset{OH}{\overset{H}{C}}\!-\!\underset{H}{\overset{H}{C}}\!-\!\underset{H}{\overset{OH}{C}}\!-\!\overset{OH}{C}\!-\!CH_2OH$$

Neuraminic acid

The structures of gangliosides have been established in only a few cases. A pure crystalline ganglioside from horse erythrocyte contains equimolar amounts of sphingosine, fatty acid, glucose, galactose, and N-acetylneuraminic acid (sialic acid; see page 288). Methylation and degradation studies are consistent with the following structure:

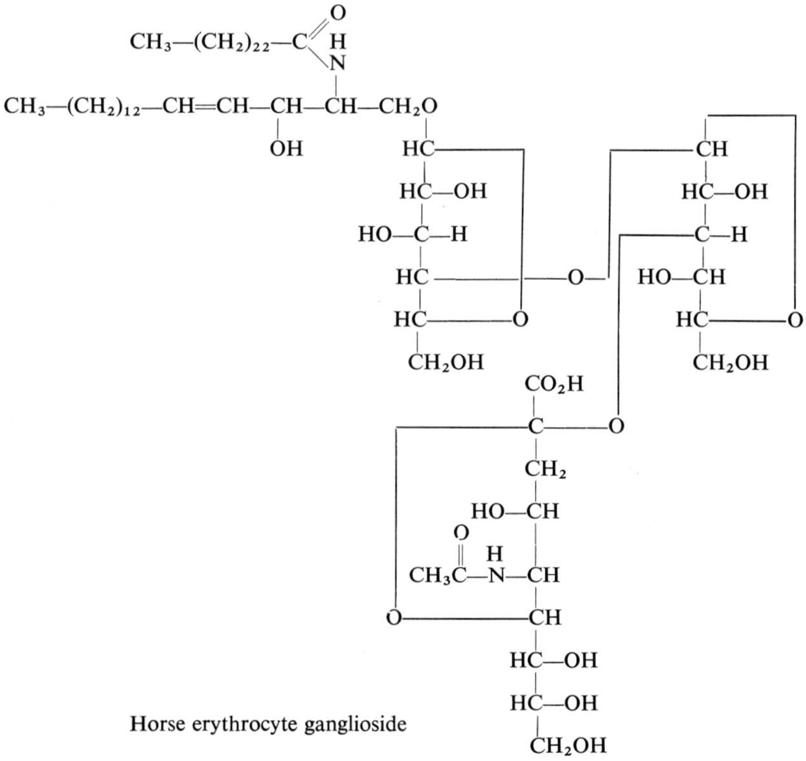

Horse erythrocyte ganglioside

In vivo studies utilizing labeled substrates have revealed that carbons 1 and 2 and the amino nitrogen of sphingosine are derived from serine. The remaining 16 atoms are derived from acetate, probably by way of a sixteen-carbon intermediate. An enzyme system has been found in rat brain that synthesizes sphingosine from palmityl-SCoA and serine in a fashion consistent with the results of the in vivo studies. The following sequence of reactions accounts for the biosynthesis of sphingosine:

$$\text{Palmityl-SCoA} + \text{NADPH} \rightarrow \text{palmitic aldehyde} + \text{NADP}^+ + \text{CoASH} \tag{16-9}$$

$$\text{Palmitic aldehyde} + \text{L-serine} \rightarrow \text{dihydrosphingosine} + \text{CO}_2 \tag{16-10}$$

$$\text{Dihydrosphingosine} \xrightarrow{\text{oxidation}} \text{sphingosine} \tag{16-11}$$

The condensation of palmitic aldehyde and L-serine may be dependent on pyridoxal phosphate and Mn^{+2} ions.

The biosynthesis of sphingomyelin from sphingosine may occur via the intermediate formation of an N-acyl sphingosine (ceramide):

$$\text{Sphingosine} + \text{R}-\overset{\overset{\text{O}}{\|}}{\text{C}}-\text{SCoA} \rightarrow N\text{-acyl sphingosine} \tag{16-12}$$

Ceramide transferase catalyzes the formation of sphingomyelin from N-acyl sphingosine and CDP-choline:

$$N\text{-acyl sphingosine} + \text{CDP-choline} \rightarrow \text{sphingomyelin} \tag{16-13}$$

Curiously, this enzyme is specific for *trans-threo-N*-acyl sphingosine and yields the threo sphingomyelin. As noted above, naturally occurring sphingomyelin is of the erythro configuration. The significance of these facts is not clear.

It remains entirely possible that sphingomyelin synthesis may also occur via acylation of sphingosine phosphorylcholine. The mammalian brain contains the enzymes, localized in the microsomal fraction, necessary for the incorporation of galactose or glucose into cerebrosides. The sugars are donated to the sphingosine moiety from the UDP-derivatives (see page 197):

$$\text{Sphingosine} + \text{UDP-galactose} \rightarrow \text{psychosine} + \text{UDP} \tag{16-14}$$

The sequence of biochemical reactions leading to the formation of the gangliosides is not known.

The sphingolipids, together with the phosphatides, account for most of the lipid content of the brain, a lipid-rich organ. In addition, the sphingolipids are the principal lipid components of the myelin sheath of nerve.

BIOSYNTHESIS OF STEROIDS The various classes of lipids previously discussed in this chapter are saponifiable; that is, alkaline hydrolysis converts them into water-soluble substances. Chevreul, in 1812, recognized that not all lipids are saponifiable. Unsaponifiable lipids include a biochemically very important class of substances, the *steroids*. The steroids are derived from the cyclopentanoperhydrophenanthrene skeleton:

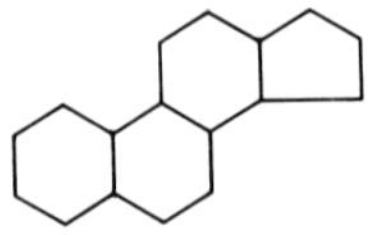

Cyclopentanoperhydrophenanthrene

A large number of steroids are synthesized by the mammal and other organisms, and these play a variety of biochemical and physiological roles. In man, the quantitatively predominant steroid is the unsaturated alcohol *cholesterol*:

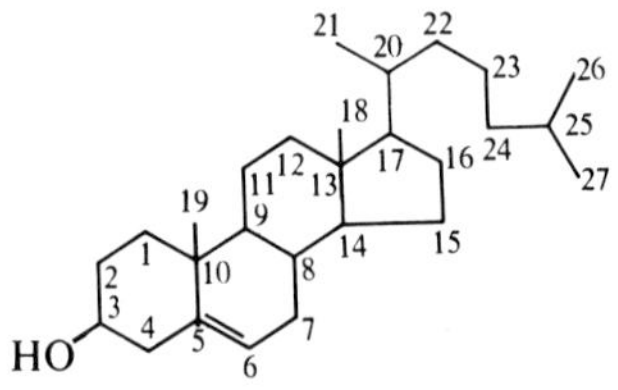

Cholesterol

Cholesterol is a key intermediate in the biosynthesis of related steroids.

Physiologically important steroids include the bile acids, the adrenocortical hormones, the androgens, and the estrogens. The bile acids that occur to the greatest extent in the human include cholic acid, deoxycholic acid, and chenocholic acid:

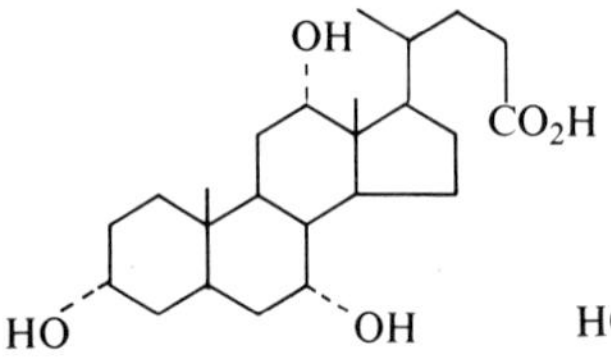

Cholic acid 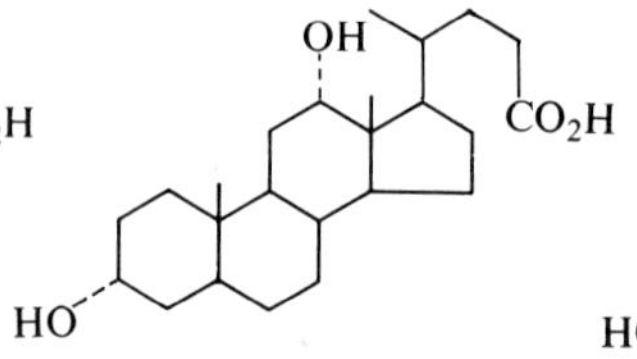   Deoxycholic acid 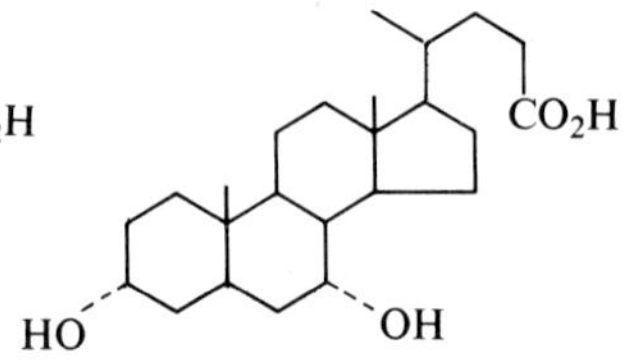   Chenocholic acid

The bile acids do not occur free in bile but are esterified at the terminal carboxyl group with either glycine, yielding glycocholic acid, or taurine, yielding taurocholic acid:

$$C_{23}H_{36}(OH)_3-\overset{\overset{\textstyle O}{\|}}{C}-\overset{\overset{\textstyle H}{}}{N}-CH_2-CO_2H \qquad C_{23}H_{36}(OH)_3-\overset{\overset{\textstyle O}{\|}}{C}-\overset{\overset{\textstyle H}{}}{N}-CH_2CH_2SO_3H$$

Glycocholic acid   Taurocholic acid

Their salts aid the intestinal hydrolysis of neutral fats by serving as emulsifying and solubilizing agents.

The cortex of the adrenal gland elaborates a large number of steroids, the adrenocortical hormones, which are important for controlling proper electrolyte balance, and for the control of rates of carbohydrate and nitrogen metabolism. The most important include aldosterone, corticosterone, deoxycorticosterone, and cortisone:

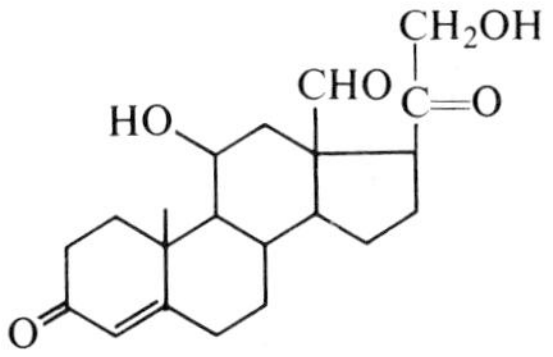

Aldosterone

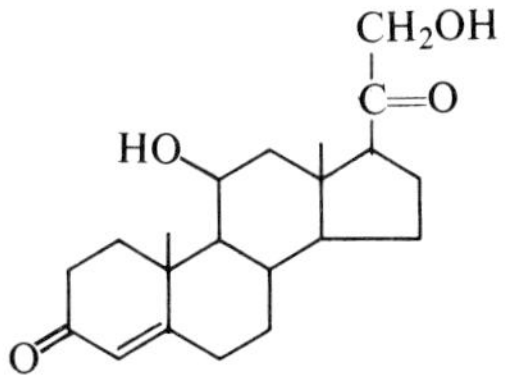

Corticosterone

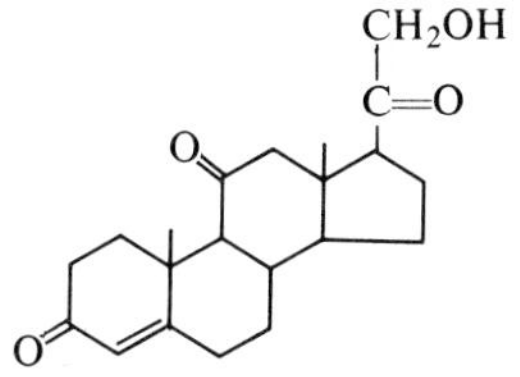

Deoxycorticosterone

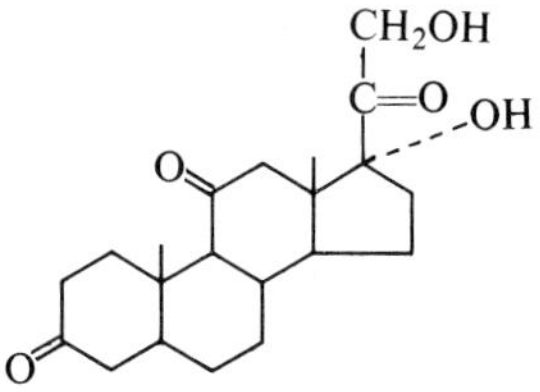

Cortisone

All are derivatives of C_{21} hydrocarbons.

The estrogens are elaborated by the ovary and are responsible for the development of the typical secondary sexual characteristics of the female. A particularly potent estrogen is estrone. Similarly, the androgens, including testosterone and androsterone, are synthesized in, and liberated from, the testis and are responsible for the secondary male characteristics:

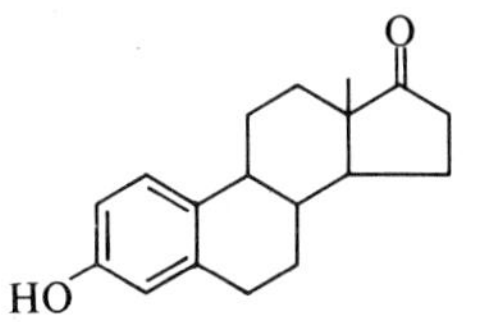

Estrone

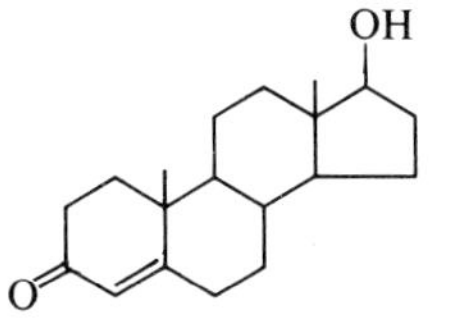

Testosterone

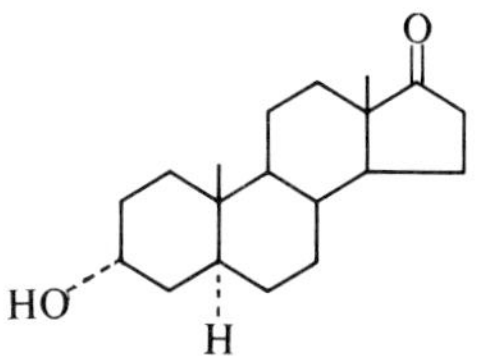

Androsterone

The development of an understanding of the biosynthesis of cholesterol is one of the most interesting and important achievements in biochemistry in the past several years. In the 1940s, Bloch and his collaborators demonstrated that isotopically labeled acetate is incorporated into cholesterol both in vivo and in liver tissue slices. Subsequently, it was determined that both carbons of acetate are incorporated, and that the entire cholesterol molecule is derived from acetate. Degradation of cholesterol synthesized from both carboxyl-labeled and methyl-labeled acetate in liver-slice preparations localized the incorporated label in the individual carbons of this molecule. The carbons of cholesterol derived from the methyl group (m) and from the carboxyl group (c) of acetate are indicated below:

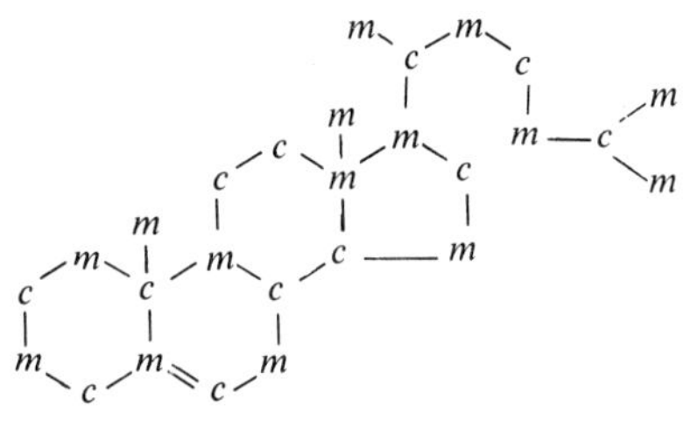

At this stage the problem was to elucidate a biosynthetic pathway leading to cholesterol that accounted for the indicated labeling pattern. Subsequent discoveries implicated *mevalonic acid* and *squalene* as key intermediates in cholesterol biosynthesis from acetate. It is convenient to discuss this pathway in three

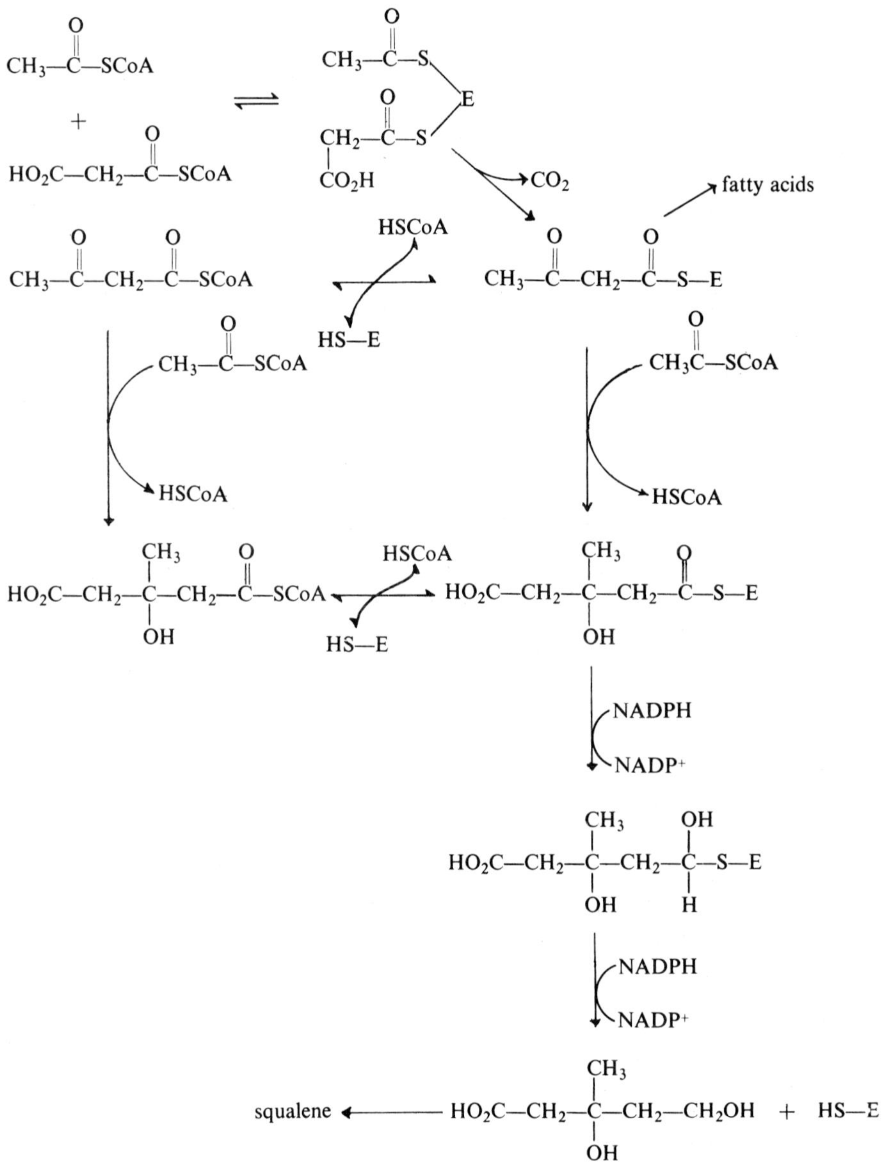

$$CH_3-\underset{\underset{\text{O}}{\|}}{C}-SCoA$$

$$+$$

$$HO_2C-CH_2-\underset{\underset{\text{O}}{\|}}{C}-SCoA$$

$$\rightleftharpoons$$

$$CH_3-\underset{\underset{\text{O}}{\|}}{C}-S\diagdown E$$

$$CH_2-\underset{\underset{\text{O}}{\|}}{C}-S\diagup$$

$$\underset{\text{CO}_2H}{}$$

$$\rightarrow CO_2 \qquad \rightarrow \text{fatty acids}$$

$$CH_3-\underset{\underset{\text{O}}{\|}}{C}-CH_2-\underset{\underset{\text{O}}{\|}}{C}-SCoA$$

HSCoA

HS—E

$$CH_3-\underset{\underset{\text{O}}{\|}}{C}-CH_2-\underset{\underset{\text{O}}{\|}}{C}-S-E$$

$$CH_3-\underset{\underset{\text{O}}{\|}}{C}-SCoA \qquad\qquad CH_3\underset{\underset{\text{O}}{\|}}{C}-SCoA$$

HSCoA \qquad\qquad HSCoA

$$HO_2C-CH_2-\underset{\underset{\text{OH}}{|}}{\overset{\overset{\text{CH}_3}{|}}{C}}-CH_2-\underset{\underset{\text{O}}{\|}}{C}-SCoA$$

HSCoA

HS—E

$$HO_2C-CH_2-\underset{\underset{\text{OH}}{|}}{\overset{\overset{\text{CH}_3}{|}}{C}}-CH_2-\underset{\underset{\text{O}}{\|}}{C}-S-E$$

NADPH

NADP+

$$HO_2C-CH_2-\underset{\underset{\text{OH}}{|}}{\overset{\overset{\text{CH}_3}{|}}{C}}-CH_2-\underset{\underset{\text{H}}{|}}{\overset{\overset{\text{OH}}{|}}{C}}-S-E$$

NADPH

NADP+

$$\text{squalene} \longleftarrow HO_2C-CH_2-\underset{\underset{\text{OH}}{|}}{\overset{\overset{\text{CH}_3}{|}}{C}}-CH_2-CH_2OH \quad + \quad HS-E$$

FIGURE 16-6.   Pathways from Acetyl-SCoA to Mevalonic Acid.

sections: the conversion of acetate to mevalonate, the conversion of mevalonate to squalene, and the conversion of squalene to cholesterol. The biosynthesis of mevalonate from acetate was initially demonstrated in a cell-free preparation from rat liver and required soluble enzymes, microsomes, CoASH, ATP, glutathione, NADPH, and Mg^{+2}:

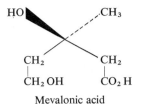

Mevalonic acid

There appear to be two related pathways for synthesis of mevalonate: (1) the earlier established pathway, involving acetoacetyl-SCoA and 3-hydroxy-3-methyl glutaryl-SCoA as intermediates, and (2) a pathway recently discovered in pigeon liver in which these intermediate acyl compounds are bound to the sulfhydryl functions of enzymes. These routes are summarized in Fig. 16-6.

FIGURE 16-7. Biosynthetic Pathway from Mevalonic Acid to Isopentenyl Pyrophosphate and Dimethallyl Pyrophosphate.

In 1932, Robinson, following even earlier proposals, suggested that squalene might well be an intermediate in cholesterol biosynthesis:

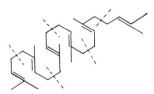

Squalene

Subsequently, Bloch and his collaborators demonstrated both the formation of squalene from acetate and the conversion of squalene to cholesterol in the liver of the intact rat, strongly suggesting that squalene is an intermediate in the pathway from acetate to cholesterol.

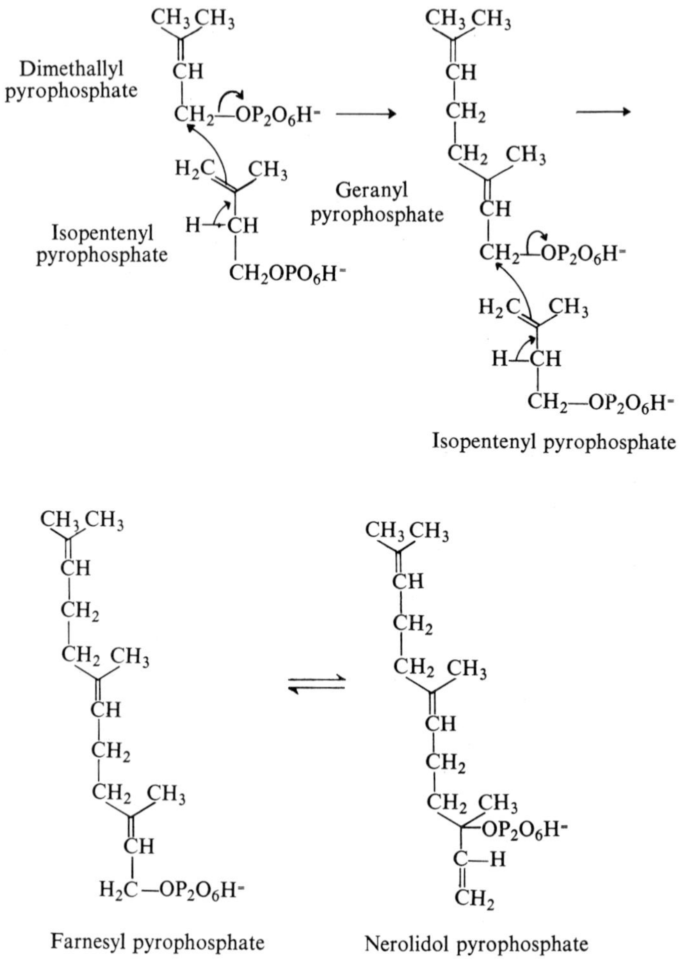

FIGURE 16-8.   Postulated Pathway for the Conversion of Isopentenyl and Dimethallyl Pyrophosphate to Farnesyl and Nerolidol Pyrophosphate.

The intermediacy of squalene, a dihydrotriterpene, is reasonable in terms of the labeling pattern of cholesterol. The isoprenoid unit

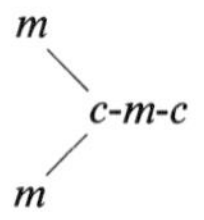

is detectable in three places in cholesterol, suggesting that it is formed from such units. Hence, mevalonic acid must first be converted into an isoprenoid structure, and, second, six of these must be condensed to yield squalene.

The metabolic route from mevalonic acid to isopentenyl pyrophosphate, a precursor of squalene, is indicated in Fig. 16-7. Mevalonic acid is first converted to mevalonic acid-5-phosphate by mevalonic kinase, an enzyme isolated and purified from several sources, and subsequently to mevalonic acid-5-pyrophosphate. The latter substrate then undergoes a concerted dehydration and

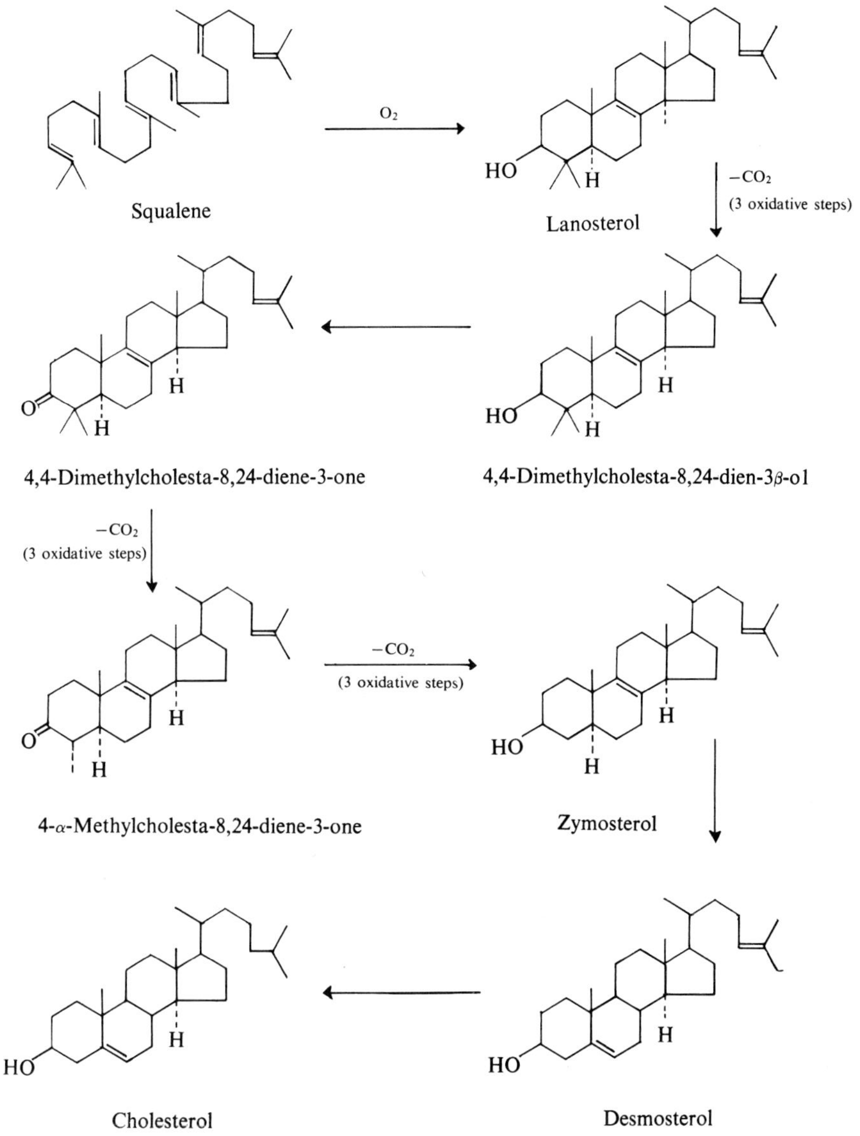

Squalene

O_2

Lanosterol

$-CO_2$
(3 oxidative steps)

4,4-Dimethylcholesta-8,24-diene-3-one

4,4-Dimethylcholesta-8,24-dien-3β-ol

$-CO_2$
(3 oxidative steps)

4-α-Methylcholesta-8,24-diene-3-one

$-CO_2$
(3 oxidative steps)

Zymosterol

Cholesterol

Desmosterol

FIGURE 16-9.   Biosynthetic Pathway from Squalene to Cholesterol in the Rat.

decarboxylation, yielding isopentenyl pyrophosphate. This reaction, possibly, involves the formation of 3-phosphomevalonic acid-5-pyrophosphate as an intermediate. Finally, isopentenyl pyrophosphate is reversibly converted to dimethallyl pyrophosphate in an enzymatic reaction, which may be formulated as follows:

$$\underset{H^+\ \ H_2C}{\overset{CH_3}{\diagdown}}C\underset{H}{\overset{H}{|}}{-}CH_2{-}OP_2O_6H^= \longrightarrow \underset{CH_3}{\overset{CH_3}{\diagdown}}{=}CH{-}CH_2{-}OP_2O_6H^= \qquad (16\text{-}15)$$

The conversion of the isoprenoid pyrophosphates to squalene occurs via several successive condensations, as shown in Fig. 16-8. The condensation of isopentenyl pyrophosphate with dimethallyl pyrophosphate yields the monoterpene, *trans*-geranyl pyrophosphate. Geranyl pyrophosphate, in turn, condenses with an additional molecule of dimethallyl pyrophosphate to yield the sesquiterpene, *trans,trans*-farnesyl pyrophosphate. Farnesyl pyrophosphate may be isomerized, in part, to the sesquiterpene, nerolidol pyrophosphate, which is, however, not an intermediate.

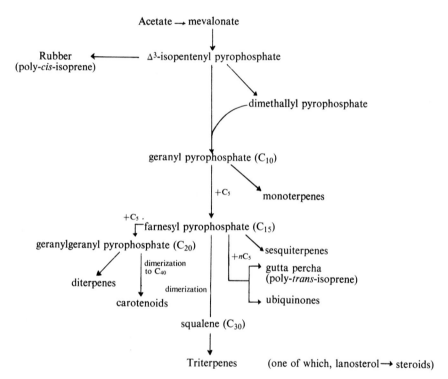

FIGURE 16-10.   A Summary of the Metabolic Fates of Isopentenyl Pyrophosphate.—*J. H. Richards and J. B. Hendrickson, Biosynthesis of Steroids, Terpenes, and Acetogenins," page 205, Benjamin, New York, 1964.*

Two moles of farnesyl pyrophosphate then condense to yield a dehydrosqualene, which is reduced to squalene by a dehydrogenase.

The conversion of squalene to cholesterol is thought to occur in the rat via the pathway indicated in Fig. 16-9. The key step in this pathway is the generation of lanosterol from squalene. It has been postulated that the cyclization of squalene is a concerted process accompanied by two 1 : 2 methyl group shifts. Elegant labeling experiments by Bloch, Cornforth, and their associates have

confirmed that the conversion of squalene to lanosterol involves successive
1 : 2 methyl group shifts rather than a single 1 : 3 shift:

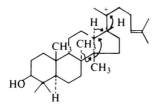

In addition to the steroids, biological isoprenoid units yield a variety of
additional important natural products. An overall view of the metabolic role
of isopentenyl pyrophosphate is given in Fig. 16-10. Repeated condensation of
isopentenyl functions yield poly-*cis*-isoprene (rubber). In contrast, repeated
condensations of *trans,trans*-farnesyl pyrophosphate with C-5 units yield poly-
trans-isoprene (gutta percha), a material without elastic properties.

REFERENCES Bloch, K.: Biological Synthesis of Cholesterol, *Harvey Lectures*, **48**: 68 (1952).

————: Biogenesis and Transformations of Squalene, *Ciba Found. Symp.*, *Biosyn. Terpenes Sterols*, p. 4, Little, Brown, Boston (1959).

Clayton, R. B.: Biosynthesis of Sterols, Steroids, and Terpenoids, *Quart. Rev.*, **19**: 168 (1965).

Cornforth, J. W., R. H. Cornforth, M. G. Horning, A. Pelter, and G. Popjak: The Mechanism of a Rearrangement Occurring During Biosynthesis of Cholesterol, *Ciba Found. Symp.*, *Biosyn. Terpenes Sterols*, p. 119, Little, Brown, Boston (1959).

Davidson, P. M., C. Long, and I. F. Penny: "Biochemical Problems of Lipids," Butterworths Scientific Publications, London, 1956.

Fieser, L. F., and M. Fieser: "Steroids," Reinhold, New York, 1959.

Folkers, K., C. H. Shunk, B. O. Linn, F. M. Robinson, P. E. Wittreich, J. W. Huff, J. L. Gilfillan, and H. R. Skeggs: Discovery and Elucidation of Mevalonic Acid, *Ciba Found. Symp.*, *Biosyn. Terpenes Sterols*, p. 119, Little, Brown, Boston (1959).

Frantz, I. D., Jr., and G. J. Shroepfer: Sterol Biosynthesis, *Ann. Rev. Biochem.*, **36**: 691 (1967).

Hanahan, D. J., and G. A. Thompson, Jr.: Complex Lipids, *Ann. Rev. Biochem.*, **32**: 215 (1963).

Kennedy, E. P.: Biosynthesis of Complex Lipids, *Federation Proc.*, **20**: 934 (1961).

Lynen, F.: Acetyl Coenzyme A and the Fatty Acid Cycle, *Harvey Lectures*, **48**: 210 (1952).

————: Biosynthesis of Saturated Fatty Acids, *Federation Proc.*, **20**: 941 (1961).

————, H. Eggerer, U. Henning, J. Knappe, I. Kessel, and E. Ringelman: New Aspects of Acetate Incorporation into Isoprenoid Precursors, *Ciba Found. Symp.*, *Biosyn. Terpenes Sterols*, p. 95, Little, Brown, Boston (1959).

Rapport, M. M., and W. T. Norton: Chemistry of the Lipids, *Ann. Rev. Biochem.*, **31**: 103 (1962).

Richards, J. H., and J. B. Hendrickson: "The Biosynthesis of Steroids, Terpenes, and Acetogenins," Benjamin, New York, 1964.

Rossiter, P. J.: in K. A. C. Elliott, I. H. Page, and J. H. Quastel (eds.), "Neurochemistry," p. 10, C. C Thomas, Springfield, Illinois, 1955.

Shapiro, B.: Lipid Metabolism, *Ann. Rev. Biochem.*, **36**: 247 (1967).

Vagelos, P. R.: Lipid Metabolism, *Ann. Rev. Biochem.*, **33**: 139 (1964).

Wakil, S. J.: Mechanism of Fatty Acid Synthesis, *J. Lipid Res.*, **2**: 1 (1961).

————: Lipid Metabolism, *Ann. Rev. Biochem.*, **31**: 369 (1962).

Wright, L. D.: Biosynthesis of Isoprenoid Compounds, *Ann. Rev. Biochem.*, **30**: 525 (1961).

17 | Metabolism of the Amino Acids

In this chapter, we consider the metabolism of the amino acids, individually and as a group. This material is organized into five categories: (1) the assimilation of inorganic nitrogen; (2) the cleavage of peptide bonds; (3) the biosynthesis of the amino acids; (4) general aspects of amino acid metabolism; and (5) specific aspects of the metabolism of the amino acids. The assembly of amino acids into proteins, a closely related subject, is considered in Chap. 21.

ASSIMILATION
OF INORGANIC
NITROGEN
Nitrogen Fixation

Inorganic nitrogen, which may be converted into ammonia and subsequently into inorganic materials, consists principally of molecular nitrogen and nitrate salts.

The ultimate source of nitrogen for the construction of nitrogenous organic compounds is atmospheric nitrogen. Throughout the plant and microbial kingdoms, there is a category of species that maintains the capacity to reduce nitrogen to ammonia. These are termed "nitrogen-fixing" organisms. Such organisms include certain species of heterotrophic bacteria, both aerobic (*Azotobacter vinelandii*) and anaerobic (*Clostridium pasteurianum*); photosynthetic bacteria (*Rhodospirillum rubrum*); several algae; and a symbiotic system, consisting of bacteria of the genus *Rhizobium* together with certain plants, principally legumes. In the last case, neither the bacteria nor the plant alone can fix nitrogen. The combined abilities of the bacteria, which live in the root nodules of the plant, and the plant create a very efficient and important nitrogen-fixing cooperative.

The reduction of nitrogen is an extraordinary biochemical capacity. Molecular nitrogen is an extremely stable molecule, as evidenced by the value of 225 kcal/ mole for the strength of the triple bond in N_2 (compare with the corresponding value of 110 kcal/mole for acetylene), and strenuous conditions are required for its reduction in the laboratory. Nevertheless, several million tons of nitrogen per year are converted, by the above organisms and their relatives, to ammonia under very mild conditions.

Much remains to be established concerning the sequence of events comprising nitrogen fixation. A major breakthrough in the understanding of nitrogen fixation was the development of nitrogen-fixing, cell-free preparations from a variety of organisms. This permits the fractionation, purification, and characterization of those cellular components actually involved in nitrogen fixation.

In view of the diverse characteristics of the organisms that fix nitrogen, it is not surprising that the properties of the cell-free, nitrogen-fixing systems from different sources exhibit considerable individuality. This individuality takes the form of varying responses to the presence of oxygen, to changes of nitrogen pressure, and to variations in pH and substrate concentration. The best-studied system is derived from *Clostridium pasteurianum*.

Reaction Product. The final product of nitrogen fixation is ammonia. Possible intermediates on the route from N_2 to NH_3, which include $NH\!\!=\!\!NH$, hydrazine, and hydroxylamine, have been searched for but not detected. Reaction intermediates may, hence, exist only transiently or be tightly bound to appropriate enzymes.

Role of Pyruvate. Pyruvate metabolism is absolutely required for nitrogen fixation (α-ketobutyrate substitutes for pyruvate in some systems). On a quantitative basis, approximately 100 moles of pyruvate are oxidized per mole of nitrogen fixed, suggesting that the two processes are only loosely coupled. Pyruvate oxidation could provide electrons and ATP for nitrogen reduction, and it seems almost certain that it does serve at least the former function. The pathway for pyruvate oxidation in *C. pasteurianum* is indicated in Fig. 17-1. The function of the electron acceptor ferredoxin is discussed below. The precise role of ATP in nitrogen fixation remains to be established. It may be a part of the "hydrogen-donating" system (see below).

Role of Ferredoxin. Investigations concerning nitrogen fixation led directly to the discovery of a novel electron-transferring enzyme — ferredoxin. Clostridial ferredoxin is discussed in detail in Chaps. 12 and 15. It is found widely distributed among hydrogen-evolving anaerobes but is not found in aerobes. As indicated in Fig. 17-1, ferredoxin can function as an electron acceptor in pyruvate oxidation. Reduced ferredoxin can then be reoxidized in systems that reduce nitrite and hydroxylamine to ammonia, and $NADP^+$ to NADPH. Ferredoxin is absolutely required for nitrogen fixation in *C. pasteurianum*. Hence ferredoxin is almost certainly an important electron-transfer agent coupling the oxidation of pyruvate to the reduction of nitrogen.

Resolution of System. The nitrogen-fixing extracts of *C. pasteurianum* have been resolved into two components (each a complex mixture); one a "nitrogen-activating" system and the other a "hydrogen-donating" system.

Metabolic Control. The "nitrogenase" of *C. pasteurianum* appears to be under metabolic control and is repressible by ammonium ion.

Reduction of nitrate by plants and microorganisms serves one of two purposes: (1) as a source of ammonia for synthetic purposes, or (2) as a terminal
electron acceptor. In the latter case, the product of the reduction may be either
N_2, N_2O, or NO, depending on the species in which the reduction occurs. These
materials are not further involved in the cellular metabolism, and hence, no
assimilation of nitrate is involved.

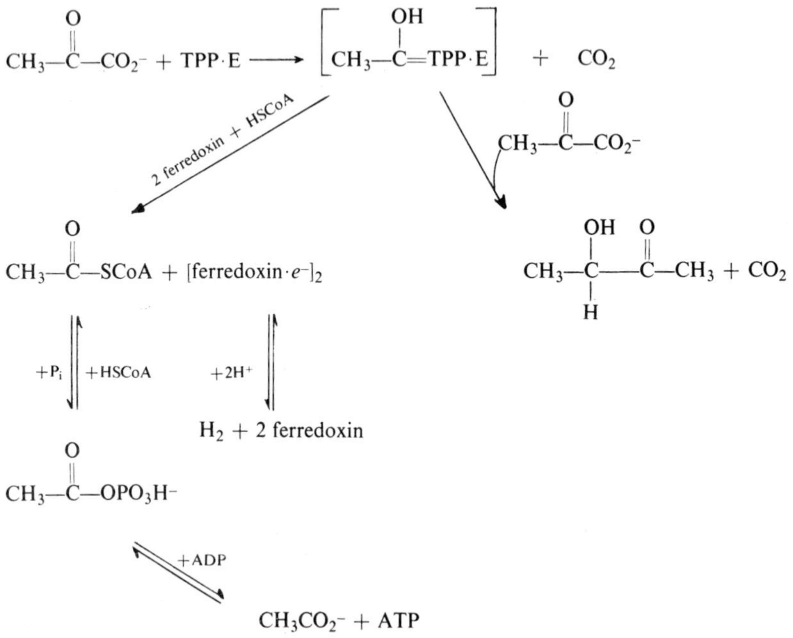

FIGURE 17-1.   Oxidation of Pyruvate in *Clostridium Pasteurianum*.

Nitrate *assimilation* proceeds in two steps. First, nitrate reductase catalyzes
the conversion of nitrate to nitrite, and, second, nitrite reductase catalyzes the
nitrite-to-ammonia reaction. In certain species, the reverse reactions occur:
Nitrosomonas converts ammonia to nitrite and *Nitrobacter* converts nitrite to
nitrate.

Nitrate reductase, which occurs in many higher plants, fungi, and microorganisms, is a pyridine nucleotide-linked molybdoflavoprotein. Either NADPH
or NADH is employed as initial electron donor, depending on the source of the
enzyme. The sequence in which each of the electron-transfer agents participates
in the overall transfer from reduced pyridine nucleotide to nitrate has been
elucidated for the nitrate reductase from *Neurospora*:

$$Fd_{red} \xrightarrow{fp} NADPH \rightarrow FAD \rightarrow Mo \rightarrow NO_3^- \tag{17-1}$$

Nitrite reductases are usually pyridine nucleotide-linked metalloflavoproteins.
However, a diversity of initial electron sources, including NADPH, H_2, and
photoreduction, are employed for the reduction of nitrite to ammonia. As in
the case of nitrogen fixation, ferredoxin appears to play a central role as electron-

transfer agent for nitrite reduction. In this context, ferredoxin appears to be reduced by the agents above and subsequently donates these electrons to nitrite directly or through another intermediate carrier.

CLEAVAGE AND FORMATION OF PEPTIDE BONDS

In mammals the predominant dietary source of nitrogen is protein. These complex molecules must be degraded, through the digestive process, to their constituent amino acids. These may be directly employed for synthesis of specific proteins or further metabolized, yielding a variety of products, as discussed later in this chapter. The digestive enzymes of man and other mammals occupy an important position in the historical development of intermediary metabolism, beginning with the researches of Schwann and Kuhne in the nineteenth century. As a consequence of this early development, the proteolytic enzymes are a relatively well-understood group.

The importance of proteolytic enzymes is by no means restricted to the digestive process in mammals. They are of universal occurrence in living material and function in a variety of capacities. We begin by discussing the digestive enzymes of man and continue with those from other sources.

Proteolytic Enzymes of the Gastrointestinal Tract

Pepsin. Pepsin was probably the entity recognized by Spallanzani in 1783 and may be regarded as the earliest known protein. It was obtained in crystalline form by Northrup in 1930.

Pepsin, the principal proteolytic enzyme in the gastric juice, apparently occurs in all vertebrates, although the properties of the individual enzymes vary somewhat. The enzyme from swine has been most thoroughly investigated. Since the pH of gastric juice is generally near 1 or 2, pepsin must have unusual stability in strongly acidic solutions. Indeed, it is characterized by an isoelectric point below 1, exhibits maximal catalytic activity in moderately acidic solutions, and is denatured at values of pH above 5. In these respects, pepsin is perhaps unique and certainly unusual among known enzymes.

Like the pancreatic proteolytic enzymes, pepsin is synthesized in the form of a precursor, termed a *zymogen*, pepsinogen. *Pepsinogen*, a crystalline protein, occurs in the gastric mucosa and is characterized by a molecular weight near 42,000 and an isoelectric point near 3.7. The conversion of pepsinogen to pepsin is catalyzed by hydrogen ions, and hence would be expected to occur on liberation of pepsinogen into the strongly acidic gastric juice, and also by pepsin itself. The activation reaction, in consequence, is autocatalytic. Since pepsin itself has a molecular weight of 35,000, the pepsinogen-pepsin conversion involves loss of a substantial portion of the polypeptide chain. In this conversion, the N-terminal portion of pepsinogen, containing all the basic amino acid residues, is split off. Included in the cleavage products is a *pepsin inhibitor* of molecular weight 3,242 and five smaller fragments having a combined molecular weight near 4,000. The sites of pepsin attack on pepsinogen are illustrated in Fig. 17-2.

As indicated in Fig. 17-2, pepsin consists of a single polypeptide chain with an N-terminal isoleucine and a C-terminal valine. The molecule contains three disulfide bridges (accounting for all the cysteines present), two of which are required for enzymatic activity. Hydrodynamic measurements indicate that pepsin is a highly compact protein, although little α helix appears to be present.

Pepsin is a discriminating enzyme in terms of the types of susceptible linkages. Requirements for susceptibility to pepsin-catalyzed hydrolysis include (1) that the substrate must have a peptide linkage; (2) that both amino acids in the peptide bond must be of the L- configuration; (3) that residues containing aromatic side chains are attacked most rapidly, although some reaction at cysteine and cystine sites is observed. Pepsin is an *endopeptidase*, attacking peptide linkages in the interior of polypeptide chains.

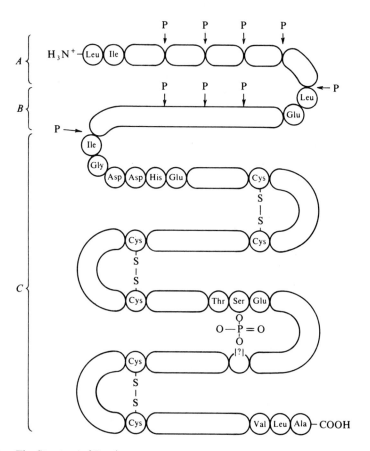

FIGURE 17-2.   The Structure of Pepsinogen.
The principal attack by pepsin is at points marked P, releasing miscellaneous peptides (*A*), pepsin inhibitor (*B*), and pepsin (*C*). The undetermined sequences are actually much larger in relation to the known sequences than is indicated. The location of the phosphoserine residue with respect to the disulfides is also uncertain.—*F. A. Bovey and S. Yanari, in Boyer, Lardy, and Myrbäck (eds.), " The Enzymes," 2d ed., vol. 4, page 69, Academic Press, New York, 1960.*

Rennin. Rennin, an enzyme from the fourth stomach of the calf, has properties similar to those of pepsin. Rennin is composed of a single polypeptide chain with a molecular weight near 40,000 and an isoelectric point of 4.5. Its specificity is nearly identical to that of pepsin. The individuality of rennin was established by its crystallization and subsequent determination of its amino acid composition and other properties.

Chymotrypsin. The process of protein digestion, initiated in the stomach by pepsin, is continued in the duodenum (upper loop of the small intestine) by enzymes present in a pancreatic secretion. The enzymes, trypsin and chymotrypsin, have distinctly similar properties.

Chymotrypsin occurs in the pancreatic juice as a mixture of two zymogens, chymotrypsinogens A and B. The former protein has been thoroughly characterized. It has a molecular weight of 25,000 and an isoelectric point near 9.1. Chymotrypsinogen A is composed of a single polypeptide chain whose amino acid sequence, together with that for trypsinogen, is indicated in Fig. 17-3.

```
                      1     2     3     4     5     6     7     8     9    10    11    12    13    14    15    16    17    18
Chymotrypsinogen     Cys - Gly - Val - Pro - Ala - Ile - Gln - Pro - Val - Leu - Ser - Gly - Leu - Ser - Arg - ILE - VAL-GLY-
Trypsinogen                                                                 Val - Asp - Asp - Asp - Asp - Lys - ILE -VAL-GLY-
                                                                             1     2     3     4     5     6     7     8     9

 19    20    21    22    23    24    25    26    27    28    29    30    31    32    33    34    35    36    37    38    39    40    41
Asp - Glu - Glu - Ala - Val - Pro - Gly - Ser - Trp -PRO- Trp -GLN-VAL-SER-LEU- Gln - Asp - Lys - Thr -GLY- Phe - HIS -PHE-
Gly - Tyr - Thr - Cys - Gly - Ala - Asn - Thr - Val -PRO- Tyr -GLN-VAL-SER-LEU- Asn -               Ser -GLY- Tyr - HIS -PHE-
 10    11    12    13    14    15    16    17    18    19    20    21    22    23    24    25                26    27    28    29    30

 42    43    44    45    46    47    48    49    50    51    52    53    54    55    56    57    58    59    60    61    62    63    64
CYS-GLY-GLY-SER-LEU- ILE -ASN- Glu - Asn -TRP-VAL-VAL- Thr -ALA-ALA- HIS -CYS- Gly - Val - Thr - Thr - Ser - Asp -
CYS-GLY-GLY-SER-LEU- ILE -ASN- Ser - Gln -TRP-VAL-VAL- Ser -ALA-ALA- HIS -CYS- Tyr - Lys - Ser - Gly - Ile - Gln -
 31    32    33    34    35    36    37    38    39    40    41    42    43    44    45    46    47    48    49    50    51    52    53

 65    66    67    68    69    70    71    72    73    74    75    76    77    78    79    80    81    82    83    84    85    86    87
VAL-Val -Val - Ala - Gly - Glu - Phe - Asp - Gln - Gly - Ser - Ser - Ser - Glu - Lys - Ile - Gln - Lys - Leu - Lys - Ile - Ala - Lys -
VAL- Arg - Leu - Gly - Glu - Asp - Asn - Ile - Asn - Val - Val - Gly - Asp - Glu - Gln - Phe - Ile - Ser - Ala - Ser - Lys - Ser -
 54    55    56    57    58    59    60    61    62    63    64    65    66    67    68    69    70    71    72    73    74    75    76

 88    89    90    91    92    93    94    95    96    97    98    99   100   101   102   103   104   105   106   107   108   109   110
Val - Phe - Lys - Asn -SER- Lys -TYR-ASN- Ser - Leu - Thr - Ile -ASN-ASN- Asn - ILE - Thr -LEU- Leu -LYS-LEU- Ser - Thr -
Ile - Val - His - Pro -SER-      -TYR-ASN( Pro , Leu , Thr , Asn )ASN-ASN- Asp - ILE - Met -LEU- Ile -LYS-LEU- Lys - Ser -
 77    78    79    80    81          82    83    84    85    86    87    88    89    90    91    92    93    94    95    96    97    98

111   112   113   114   115   116   117   118   119   120   121   122   123   124   125   126   127   128   129   130   131   132   133
ALA-ALA-SER- Phe - Ser - Gln - Thr -VAL- Ser - Ala - Val - Cys -LEU-PRO- Ser - Ala - Ser - Asp - Asp - Phe - Ala -ALA-GLY-
ALA-ALA-SER- Leu - Asn - Ser - Arg -VAL- Ala - Ser - Ile - Ser -LEU-PRO- Thr - Ser - Cys -             Ala - Ser -ALA-GLY-
 99   100   101   102   103   104   105   106   107   108   109   110   111   112   113   114   115               116   117   118   119

134   135   136   137   138   139   140   141   142   143   144   145   146   147   148   149   150   151   152   153   154   155   156
THR- Thr -CYS- Val - Thr - Thr -GLY-TRP-GLY- Leu -THR- Arg - Tyr - Thr - Asn - Ala - Asn - Thr -PRO-ASP- Arg -LEU- Gln -
THR- Gln -CYS- Leu - Ile - Ser -GLY-TRP-GLY- Asn -THR- Lys - Ser - Ser - Gly - Thr - Ser - Tyr -PRO-ASP- Val -LEU- Lys -
120   121   122   123   124   125   126   127   128   129   130   131   132   133   134   135   136   137   138   139   140   141   142

157   158   159   160   161   162   163   164   165   166   167   168   169   170   171   172   173   174   175   176   177   178   179
Gln - Ala - Ser -LEU-PRO- Leu -LEU-SER- Asn - Thr - Asn -CYS-LYS- Lys - Tyr - Trp - Gly - Thr - Lys -ILE- Lys - Asp - Ala -
Cys - Leu - Lys - A? -PRO- Ile -LEU-SER- Asp - Ser - Ser -CYS-LYS- Ser - Ala - Tyr - Pro - Gly - Gln - ILE- Thr - Ser - Asn -
143   144   145   146   147   148   149   150   151   152   153   154   155   156   157   158   159   160   161   162   163   164   165

180   181   182   183   184   185   186   187   188   189                     190   191   192   193   194   195   196   197   198   199   200
MET- Ile -CYS-ALA-GLY- Ala - Ser - Gly - Val - Ser -                       -SER-CYS- Met -GLY-ASP-SER-GLY-GLY-PRO- Leu -VAL-
MET- Phe -CYS-ALA-GLY- Tyr - Leu - Glu - Gly - Gly - Lys - Asn -SER-CYS- Gln -GLY-ASP-SER-GLY-GLY-PRO- Val -VAL-
166   167   168   169   170   171   172   173   174   175   176   177   178   179   180   181   182   183   184   185   186   187   188

201   202   203   204   205   206   207   208   209   210   211   212   213   214   215   216   217   218   219   220   221   222   223
CYS- Lys - Lys - Asn - Gly - Ala - Trp - Thr - Leu - Val -GLY- ILE -VAL- Ser -SER-TRP-GLY-SER- Ser - Thr - Cys - Ser - Thr -
CYS- Ser - Gly - Lys - Let - Gln -                    -GLY- ILE -VAL-      -SER-TRP-GLY-SER- Gly - Cys - Ala - Gln - Lys -
189   190   191   192   193   194                     195   196   197      198   199   200   201   202   203   204   205   206

224   225   226   227   228   229   230   231   232   233   234   235   236   237   238   239   240   241   242   243   244   245   246
Ser - Thr -PRO-GLY-VAL-TYR- Ala - Arg -VAL- Thr - Ala - Leu -VAL- Asn -TRP- Val - Gln -GLN-THR- Leu -ALA- Ala -ASN
Asn - Lys -PRO-GLY-VAL-TYR- Thr - Lys -VAL- Cys - Asn - Tyr -VAL- Ser - Thr -TRP- Ile - Lys -GLN-THR- Ile -ALA- Ser -ASN
207   208   209   210   211   212   213   214   215   216   217   218   219   220   221   222   223   224   225   226   227   228   229
```

FIGURE 17-3. The Structural Similarity of Trypsinogen and Chymotrypsinogen.
The sequence 84–87 in trypsinogen has not yet been established. Gaps in sequence have been arbitrarily inserted to draw attention to the resulting areas of homology. Amino acid residues that are homologous in the two proteins are shown in capital letters.—*K. A. Walsh and H. Neurath, Proc. Nat. Acad. Sci., U.S., 52: 884 (1964).*

The chymotrypsinogen A–chymotrypsin conversion is a complicated process, actually yielding a family of chymotrypsins α-, δ-, π-, etc. These reactions are catalyzed by trypsin and by chymotrypsin. Since chymotrypsin has a molecular weight near 25,000, activation of the zymogen must entail rather small losses of the polypeptide chain. A general scheme for the activation of chymotrypsinogen A is indicated in Fig. 17-4. Trypsin-catalyzed cleavage of a single peptide linkage between arginine and isoleucine yields π-chymotrypsin. Subsequent cleavage of a

second peptide bond, splitting out a seryl-arginine dipeptide, yields δ-chymotrypsin. Chymotrypsin-catalyzed elimination of a threonyl-aspartic dipeptide
from δ-chymotrypsin yields α-chymotrypsin. The same product may be arrived
at by reversing the order of dipeptide eliminations, neochymotrypsinogen being
formed as intermediate.

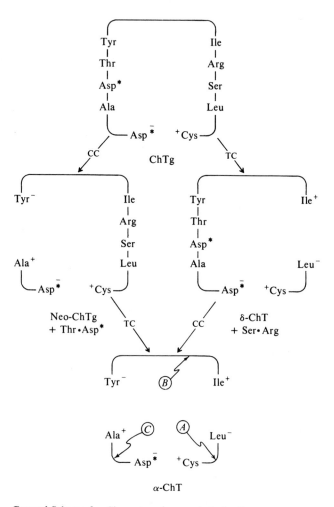

FIGURE 17-4.   General Scheme for Chymotrypsinogen A Activation.
                ChTg, chymotrypsinogen A; neo-ChTg, neochymotrypsinogen; δ- and α-ChT, δ- and α-
                chymotrypsins, respectively; TC, reactions catalyzed by trypsin; CC, reactions catalyzed by
                chymotrypsin; + and −, N- and C-terminal residues, respectively; A, B, and C, chains A, B,
                and C of α-chymotrypsin; Asp*, asparagine residue. The two chains of neochymotrypsinogen
                and δ-chymotrypsin and the three chains of α-chymotrypsin are held together by disulfide
                bridges.—P. Desnuelle, in Boyer, Lardy, and Myrbäck (eds.), "The Enzymes," 2d ed., vol. 4,
                page 107, Academic Press, New York, 1960.

     α-Chymotrypsin, like pepsin, is an endopeptidase. In addition, this enzyme
catalyzes the hydrolysis of esters, amides, hydroxamates, and other acyl derivatives. Although chymotrypsin catalyzes the hydrolysis (and aminolysis and
alcoholysis) of a broad spectrum of substrates, activity is maximal when the
carboxyl function of the peptide linkage is donated by an aromatic amino acid.

Catalysis by chymotrypsin is more thoroughly understood than that for any other enzyme and was discussed in modest detail in Chap. 7 (see page 187).

Trypsin. The structural similarities of trypsin and chymotrypsin are emphasized by the striking homologies in amino acid sequences of the zymogens (see Fig. 17-3). Specific similarities between the two enzymes include (1) site of origin, (2) rate of synthesis, (3) endopeptidase activity, (4) molecular weight, (5) isoelectric point, (6) amino acid composition, and (7) nature of the catalytic process. In regard to the last point, most of the comments concerning the mechanism of chymotryptic reactions apply with equal force to trypsin as well. The principal difference is the enzymatic specificity. Trypsin is maximally active on peptides whose carboxyl group is donated by a basic residue.

The trypsinogen-trypsin conversion is simpler than the corresponding chymotrypsinogen reaction in that only one product is formed. The activation can be catalyzed by trypsin itself, by the enzyme enterokinase, and also by certain proteinases derived from molds. Activation involves cleavage of the N-terminal hexapeptide from the polypeptide chain, as depicted schematically in Fig. 17-5.

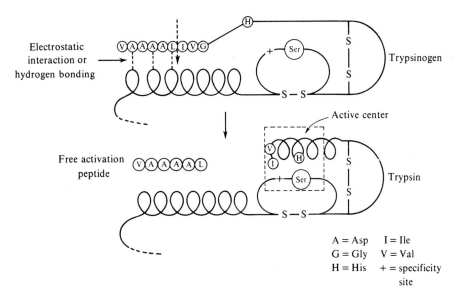

FIGURE 17-5. Proposed Model for the Activation of Bovine Trypsinogen.—*P. Desnuelle, in Boyer, Lardy, and Myrbäck (eds.), "The Enzymes," 2d ed., vol. 4, page 128, Academic Press, New York, 1960.*

Calcium ion plays an important role in the activation process, both accelerating cleavage at the pertinent peptide linkage and retarding cleavage at other sites. Cleavage at the latter sites yields enzymatically inactive products.

Enterokinase is a proteolytic enzyme elaborated by the duodenal mucosa. It is a glycoprotein and has not yet been completely characterized.

Carboxypeptidase. Accompanying trypsin and chymotrypsin in the pancreatic juice is the *exopeptidase* carboxypeptidase. This enzyme (really a family of enzymes) degrades polypeptides in a sequential fashion, beginning at the C terminus. Employment of this enzyme for amino-acid-sequence studies was discussed in Chap. 4 (see page 81).

Two carboxypeptidases, A and B, are involved in protein digestion in the duodenum. Carboxypeptidase A exhibits maximal catalytic activity with C-terminal aromatic residues, and carboxypeptidase B is specific for C-terminal basic residues.

As in the case of the other proteolytic enzymes, carboxypeptidase A occurs in the pancreatic juice in the form of a zymogen, procarboxypeptidase A.

It is a zinc protein when isolated from natural sources and contains one atom of the metal ion per molecule of protein, to which it is bound, in part, by means of a specific sulfhydryl function. Zinc carboxypeptidase A exhibits both peptidase and esterase activity, a dual specificity that is sensitive to minor structural alterations in the enzyme molecule. If the zinc ion is replaced by either cadmium or mercuric ions, the esterase activity of carboxypeptidase A is enhanced, although, in marked contrast, the peptidase activity is abolished. Similarly, acetylation of two tyrosyl residues with either acetylimidazole or acetic anhydride abolishes peptidase activity while enhancing esterase activity some sixfold. Acetylation or metal-ion exchange does not lead to detectable alterations in the tertiary structure of the carboxypeptidase A molecule. Thus the peptidase and esterase activities exhibit strikingly distinct dependencies on subtle alterations of the molecular architecture.

Carboxypeptidase B, specific for terminal peptide bonds involving lysine or arginine residues, is probably a metalloenzyme as well. This conclusion follows from its inhibition by chelating agents, such as 1,10-phenanthroline. The nature of the metal ion present remains to be established.

Leucine Aminopeptidase. Leucine aminopeptidase, an enzyme found in the intestinal mucosa and other tissues, is an exopeptidase, which degrades polypeptide chains sequentially from the N terminus (see page 81). The enzyme from swine kidney has been highly purified, though not crystallized.

Leucine aminopeptidase is activated by either magnesium or manganese ions. The enzyme exhibits both esterase and peptidase activity and hydrolyzes a broad range of substrates, which, if they have an asymmetric α-carbon atom, must be of the L- configuration. As the name of the enzyme implies, hydrolysis is most rapid in the case of N-terminal leucine. The relative rates at which substrates are cleaved is largely independent of the nature of the activating ion.

In addition to leucine aminopeptidase and the carboxypeptidases, the intestinal mucosa contains a variety of additional peptidases. Many of these exhibit specificity for chain length of the substrate, particularly the dipeptidases and tripeptidases. Such enzymes must function to complete the digestion of proteins begun by the enzymes previously discussed. A summary of the enzymes involved in the digestive process in man is presented in Table 17-1.

Proteolytic Enzymes of Animal Tissues

A group of proteolytic enzymes, the cathepsins, are localized intracellularly in kidney, spleen, liver, and lung tissue, among other sites. The cathepsins are endopeptidases that hydrolyze both proteins and small synthetic substrates. The substrate specificities of cathepsins A, B, and C are similar to those of pepsin, trypsin, and chymotrypsin, respectively. These enzymes have not been obtained in sufficiently pure states to permit investigation of their molecular and catalytic properties.

Plant Proteinases

Papain. Papain is a proteolytic enzyme from the fruit of the tropical melon tree, *Carica papaya*. This enzyme occurs in high concentration in the papaya latex, from which it may be crystallized in large amounts. Papain is composed of a single polypeptide chain, whose amino acid sequence is known. The molecular weight of this enzyme is near 21,000, and its isoelectric point is 8.75.

TABLE 17-1. Proteolytic Enzymes in the Mammalian Gastrointestinal Tract

Secretion	Enzyme	Comments
Gastric	Pepsin	A proteinase also found in the gastric juice of birds, reptiles, and fish
	Rennin	A milk-coagulating enzyme present in the juice of the fourth stomach of the calf
Pancreatic	Trypsin	A proteinase
	Chymotrypsin	A proteinase
	Carboxypeptidase	A peptidase
Intestinal	Aminopeptidases Prolidase Tripeptidase Dipeptidases }	Peptidases

SOURCE: J. Fruton and S. Simmonds, "General Biochemistry," p. 685, Wiley, New York, 1958.

Papain exhibits a broad substrate specificity. Peptides, amides, esters, and thiolesters are all susceptible to papain-catalyzed hydrolysis, and a variety of nucleophilic reagents, in addition to water, will serve as acyl-group acceptors. Peptides involving a variety of amino acids are effectively cleaved by papain, although the constituent amino acids must be of the L- configuration. A good deal of evidence has implicated a thiol group of cysteine as essential for catalytic activity of papain.

Ficin. An enzyme from plants of the fig family, ficin is an endopeptidase similar to papain. Ficin has a molecular weight near 26,000 and, like papain, is a sulfhydryl enzyme. *p*H-rate profiles implicate a carboxylate ion or the kinetic equivalent in the catalytic process of this enzyme as well. Ficin is maximally active with substrates derived from L-arginine but exhibits catalytic activity toward a broad spectrum of substrates.

Other important proteolytic enzymes of plants include *bromelin* from pineapple, *chymopapain* from papaya latex, and *asclepain* from the roots and latex of the milkweed.

Bacterial Proteinases

Many proteolytic enzymes have been isolated from bacterial sources. As a group, these enzymes exhibit both exopeptidase and endopeptidase activity and are characterized by a strikingly broad specificity (or lack of it). In extreme cases, certain bacterial proteinases may cleave as many as 80 per cent of the peptide bonds of a protein.

BIOSYNTHESIS OF THE AMINO ACIDS

Organisms differ markedly in terms of their ability to carry out the *de novo* synthesis of the protein-containing amino acids. Most microorganisms and plants are competent in all such syntheses, but most animals lack about half of these synthetic capacities. For the latter organisms, amino acids may then be classified as "essential" or "nonessential."

The distinction between essential and nonessential amino acids may be made on the basis of a variety of experimental criteria. On the basis of those most frequently employed, an amino acid is considered essential if it must be included in the diet for (1) optimal growth or (2) the maintenance of nitrogen balance. An animal is said to be in nitrogen balance if its daily intake of nitrogen is just balanced by its daily excretion of nitrogen. The classic studies of Rose have established that, for the white rat, leucine, isoleucine, valine, lysine, methionine, phenylalanine, tryptophan, threonine, histidine, and arginine are essential amino acids. The first eight of these amino acids have been found to be essential for all species of higher animals studied. In contrast to the white rat, the human organism can synthesize (or recover from protein breakdown) sufficient histidine for optimal growth and maintenance of nitrogen balance. Among the essential amino acids for the white rat, only the carbon chains of arginine and threonine can be synthesized at all (their synthesis is simply too slow to permit optimal growth). This organism has lost, therefore, through evolution, the capacity to accomplish the synthesis of the carbon chains of the remaining essential amino acids.

The dietary requirement for a particular amino acid is a function of several variables, including the presence of metabolically related substances in the diet. For example, tyrosine exerts a sparing effect on phenylalanine, as does glutamic acid on arginine. In the rat, the requirement for methionine may be satisfied by homocysteine plus an adequate supply of methyl group donors. Thus, the "essentiality" of an amino acid is not only a function of the criteria employed for its determination but also of the other components of the diet. In addition, amino acid requirements vary with the physiological state of the animal (i.e., in pregnancy, lactation, and disease), with age, and, perhaps, with the nature of the intestinal flora.

It is worth emphasizing that the "essential" feature of the essential amino acids is their carbon skeleton; most of these amino acids may be derived from the corresponding keto acids through transamination (see page 417).

Assimilation of Ammonia: The Synthesis of Glutamic Acid and Glutamine

As indicated above, the assimilation of molecular nitrogen and nitrate, the principal inorganic nitrogen sources, yields ammonia as the immediate product. How is ammonia incorporated into organic nitrogen compounds? Although a number of reactions result in such incorporation, three processes appear to be quantitatively most important in many species. These are the reactions catalyzed by glutamic dehydrogenase, glutamine synthetase, and carbamyl phosphate synthetase.

Glutamic dehydrogenase catalyzes the pyridine nucleotide-linked formation of glutamic acid from α-ketoglutarate and ammonia:

$$\left.\begin{array}{l}\text{NADH} \\ \text{(NADPH)}\end{array}\right\} + \alpha\text{-ketoglutarate} + \text{NH}_4^+ \rightleftharpoons \left.\begin{array}{l}\text{NAD}^+ \\ \text{(NADP}^+\text{)}\end{array}\right\} + \text{L-glutamate} + \text{H}_2\text{O} \qquad (17\text{-}2)$$

This enzyme is widely distributed throughout living systems. Either NADPH or NADH is employed as coenzyme—the former usually in cases in which glutamic dehydrogenase functions in a biosynthetic capacity and the latter when this enzyme serves principally a catabolic function. Some of the aspects of the structural organization of this interesting enzyme were considered in Chap. 4, and its integration with the citric acid cycle in Chap. 14.

The principal alternate route for the biosynthesis of glutamate is the pyridoxal-phosphate dependent *transamination* involving α-ketoglutarate (see Chap. 8 for discussion of mechanisms involved in transaminations):

$$\alpha\text{-Ketoglutarate} + \text{amino acid} \xrightleftharpoons{\text{pyridoxal phosphate}} \text{L-glutamate} + \text{keto acid} \qquad (17\text{-}3)$$

The interconversion of α-ketoglutarate and glutamate is an important link directly coupling the metabolism of amino acids and that of the carbohydrates. This reaction provides for the incorporation of carbon derived from glucose into glutamate and, subsequently, into other amino acids.

The second important reaction incorporating ammonia into organic compounds is the ATP-dependent *formation of glutamine*:

$$\text{L-Glutamate} + NH_3 + ATP \xrightleftharpoons{Mg^{+2}} \text{L-glutamine} + ADP + P_i \qquad (17\text{-}4)$$

Finally, the *carbamyl phosphate synthetase* reaction is an important means for the incorporation of ammonia into several biosynthetic products, notably the pyrimidines and urea. The stoichiometry of this reaction for mammalian enzymes is indicated below:

$$CO_2 + NH_3 + 2ATP + H_2O \xrightarrow[\text{glutamate}]{\text{acyl}} NH_2\overset{\overset{\text{O}}{\|}}{-C}-OPO_3H^- + 2ADP + P_i \qquad (17\text{-}5)$$

With the mammalian enzymes at least, an acyl glutamate is a required cofactor. With bacterial enzymes, only a single ATP is involved.

Amino Acids Derived from Glutamate

The route for the transformation of glutamate to *proline* is indicated in Fig. 17-6.

In animal tissues, 4-hydroxy-L-proline occurs principally in collagen. The biosynthesis of collagen hydroxyproline is incompletely understood. The following facts concerning this synthesis do, however, seem clear. First, the oxygen

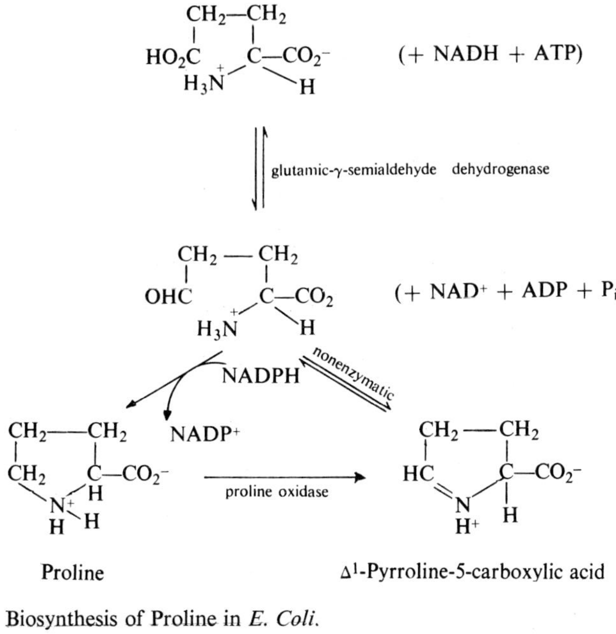

FIGURE 17-6. Biosynthesis of Proline in *E. Coli.*

atom of the hydroxyproline hydroxyl function is derived from atmospheric oxygen, as revealed by isotope incorporation experiments. Second, proline is a precursor of collagen hydroxyproline. This conclusion follows from experiments in which the administration of labeled proline to rats yielded tissue proteins containing highly labeled hydroxyproline. Third, free proline is not the substrate for the hydroxylation reaction; that is, free hydroxyproline is not an intermediate in the synthesis of collagen hydroxyproline. Experiments in a cell-free microsomal system from chick embryos that incorporates labeled proline into labeled peptide-bound hydroxyproline reveal that the appearance of this amino acid lags well behind the incorporation of proline. This result suggests that peptide-bound proline is the actual substrate for the hydroxylation reaction. Fourth, synthesis of collagen hydroxyproline is catalyzed by an enzyme system associated with the ribosomal fraction of the cell.

The conversion of glutamate to *arginine*, as it occurs in microorganisms, is outlined in Fig. 17-7. *Ornithine*, an amino acid which does not occur in proteins but which is intimately involved in the synthesis of urea (see page 431), is a key intermediate in this transformation. Ornithine may arise (1) from glutamic-γ-semialdehyde through transamination or (2) from N-acetylglutamic-γ-semialdehyde through transamination followed either by deacetylation or acetyl group transfer to glutamic acid. The latter alternative yields a cyclic pathway in which the acetyl group is preserved.

Biosynthesis of Aspartic Acid and Asparagine

Biosynthetic routes leading to *aspartic acid* closely parallel those for formation of glutamic acid. Thus aspartic acid may be derived from oxaloacetic acid by transamination:

$$\text{Oxaloacetic acid} + \text{amino acid} \xrightleftharpoons[]{\text{pyridoxal phosphate}} \text{L-aspartate} + \text{ketoacid} \quad (17\text{-}6)$$

Such reactions provide an additional important link between amino acid and carbohydrate metabolism. In addition, aspartate may be derived by direct amination of fumarate, a reaction catalyzed by aspartase, one of the earliest studied bacterial enzymes:

$$\quad (17\text{-}7)$$

The synthesis of *asparagine* in microorganisms and animals is incompletely understood. The asparagine synthetase of microorganisms catalyzes the condensation of ammonia and aspartate with the concomitant cleavage of ATP to AMP and PP_i (in contrast to the glutamine synthetase reaction, in which ADP and P_i are formed). In plants, asparagine arises from the enzymatic hydrolysis of β-cyanoalanine.

Amino Acids Derived from Aspartate

The biosynthesis of *threonine, methionine,* and *lysine* all involve the intermediate formation of aspartic-β-semialdehyde. This intermediate is derived from aspartate in a two-step reaction sequence. First, aspartyl kinase catalyzes the formation of β-aspartyl phosphate, which is subsequently reduced to the aldehyde in a pyridine nucleotide-linked reaction (see Fig. 17-8).

The synthesis of *threonine* from aspartic-β-semialdehyde proceeds via the amino acid homoserine as indicated in Fig. 17-8. *O*-homoserine phosphate is synthesized from homoserine and ATP in a reaction catalyzed by *homoserine*

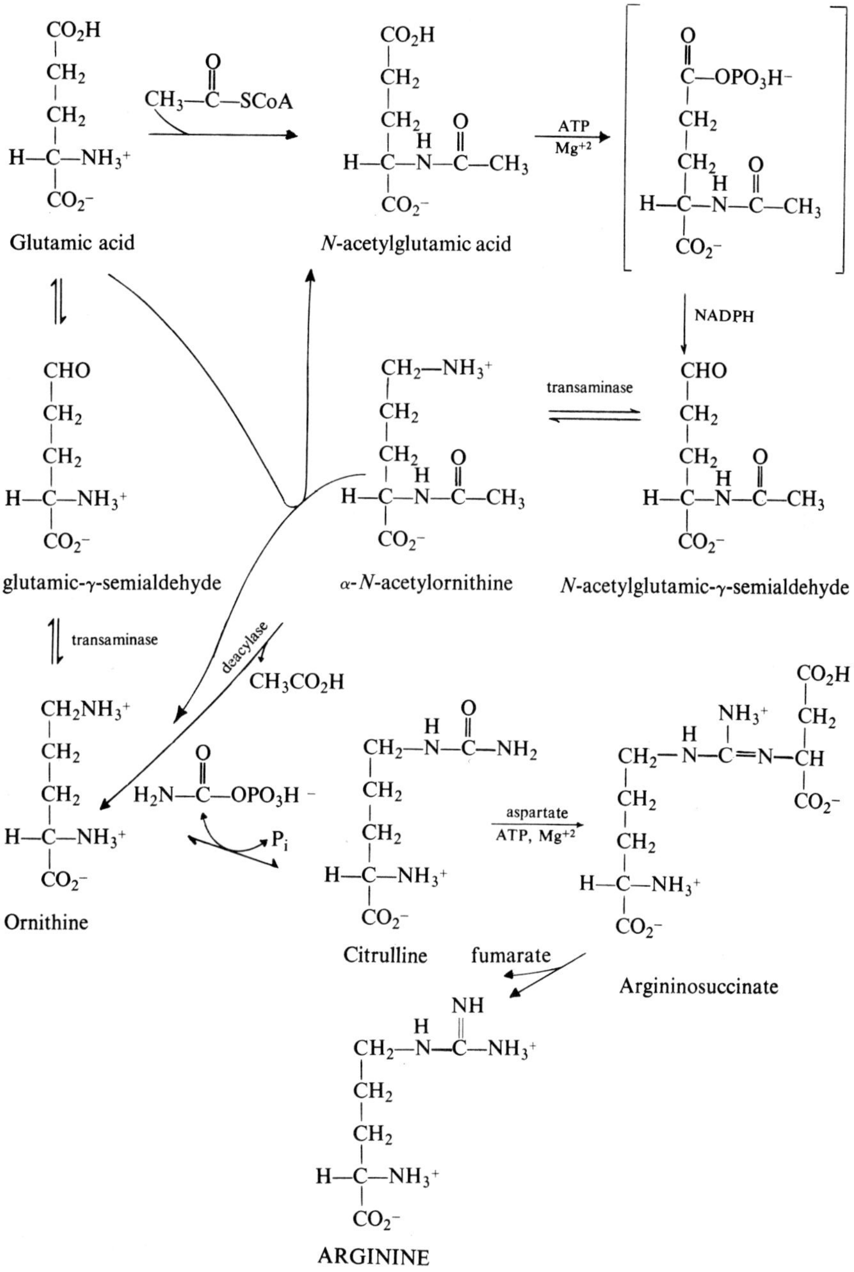

FIGURE 17-7. Biosynthesis of Arginine in Microorganisms.

kinase. The terminal step in threonine synthesis is a very interesting reaction, in which *threonine synthetase*, a pyridoxal phosphate-dependent enzyme, converts *O*-phosphohomoserine to threonine.

Alternatively, threonine may be synthesized in the threonine aldolase reaction:

$$CH_3CHO + H_3N^+\!-\!CH_2\!-\!CO_2^- \rightleftharpoons \begin{array}{c} CH_3 \\ | \\ CHOH \\ | \\ H_3N^+\!-\!CH\!-\!CO_2^- \end{array} \qquad (17\text{-}8)$$

Glycine   Threonine

This enzyme, which is pyridoxal phosphate-dependent, occurs in certain microorganisms and certain mammalian tissues. Particularly in the latter, threonine aldolase may primarily serve a catabolic, rather than a biosynthetic function.

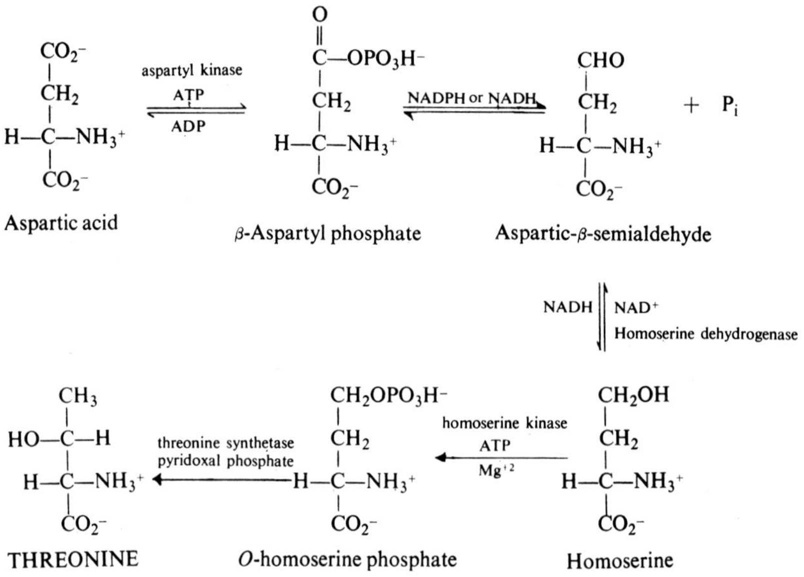

FIGURE 17-8.   Biosynthesis of Homoserine and Threonine.

In microorganisms, *methionine* is synthesized in a multistep process from cysteine and homoserine. The overall pathway may be divided into three stages: (1) synthesis of cystathionine from homoserine and cysteine, (2) conversion of cystathionine to homocysteine, and (3) conversion of the latter substrate to methionine. The overall pathway is indicated in Fig. 17-9.

The incorporation of a 1-carbon fragment into homocysteine yields methionine. Such incorporation may result from the *de novo* synthesis of the methyl function or involve the transfer of preformed methyl groups. The former type of synthesis has been studied most thoroughly in microorganisms, although it also occurs in animal tissues. In *E. coli* there are two pathways for the conversion of homocysteine to methionine. The simplest involves the direct transfer of a methyl group from N^5-methyltetrahydropteroyltriglutamate to homocysteine:

N^5-methyltetrahydropteroyltriglutamate + homocysteine →

methionine + tetrahydropteroyltriglutamate   (17-9)

N^5-methyl FH_4 is inactive in this reaction.

The second pathway is quite complicated and requires NADH, FAD, S-adenosylmethionine (see page 427), N^5-methyl FH_4, and a vitamin B_{12} enzyme:

$$N^5\text{-methyl } FH_4 + \text{homocysteine} \xrightarrow[\text{S-adenosylmethionine, } B_{12}\text{-enzyme}]{\substack{\text{NADH}\\\text{FAD}}} \text{methionine} + FH_4 \qquad (17\text{-}10)$$

The details of this reaction are far from clear. It has been established that the methyl group of S-adenosylmethionine is not transferred to homocysteine in this reaction and that this substance acts catalytically. Recent experiments suggest

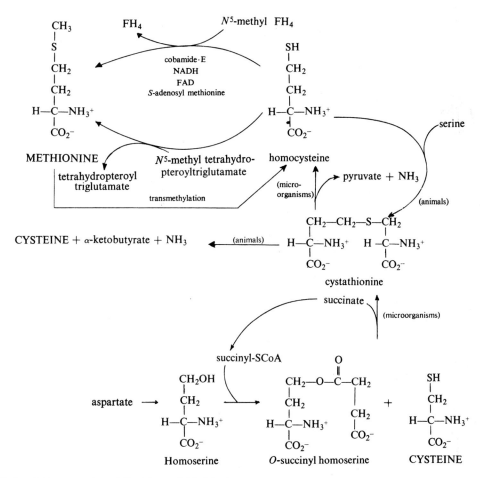

FIGURE 17-9. Interconversion of Cysteine and Methionine.

that a novel (Co^I) form of a cobalamin coenzyme may participate in methionine biosynthesis. Methylation of this fully reduced hydroxocobalamin yields the methyl analogue of the cobalamin coenzymes (the methyl function replaces the deoxyadenosyl moiety in the structure on page 221). Methyl cobalamin transfers its methyl group to homocysteine both nonenzymatically and, at an increased rate, enzymatically, in the presence of the B_{12} apoenzyme. In mammalian systems, N^5-methyl FH_4 serves as methyl group donor for methionine biosynthesis in a reaction requiring catalytic amounts of S-adenosylmethionine. No requirement for the participation of vitamin B_{12} coenzymes has been established for this system.

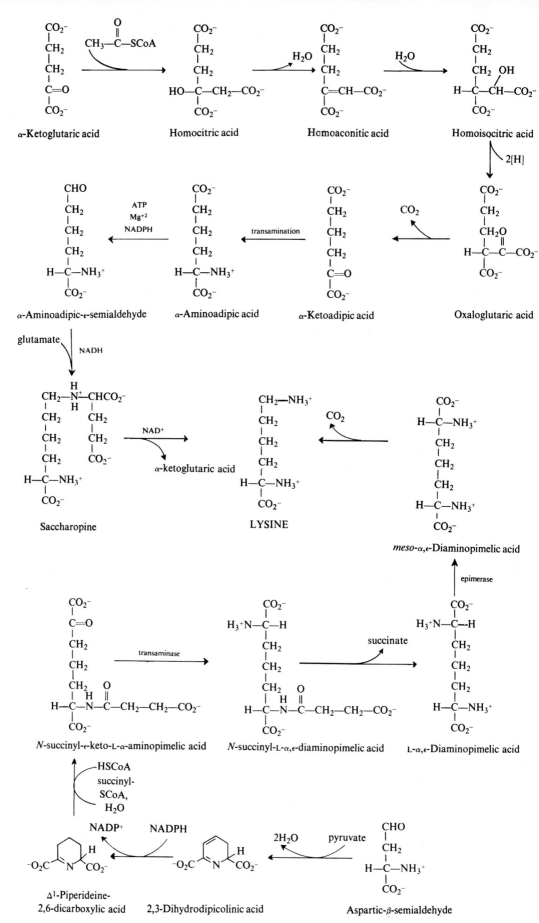

FIGURE 17-10. Biosynthesis of Lysine via the α-Aminoadipic and Diaminopimelic Acid Routes.

In addition to those reactions involving the participation of FH_4 coenzymes, methionine may arise from direct methyl group transfer from a variety of donor molecules. These reactions are considered more fully on page 428.

Inasmuch as animal tissues lack the capacity to synthesize the carbon chain of homocysteine, mammals do not accomplish the *de novo* synthesis of methionine but, as noted above, may convert homocysteine to this amino acid.

The biosynthesis of *lysine* is particularly striking in that two separate and distinct reaction pathways are employed. In bacteria, higher plants, and in certain algae and fungi, the carbon skeleton of this amino acid is derived from pyruvate and aspartate with the intermediate formation of α,ε-diaminopimelic acid. In other algae and fungi, acetate and α-keto-glutarate provide the carbon skeleton of lysine, and the reaction sequence proceeds through the intermediate α-aminoadipic acid. The overall reaction pathways are outlined in Fig. 17-10.

Biosynthesis of Serine, Glycine, and Cysteine

Serine, an important intermediate in the interconversion of cysteine and methionine (see Fig. 17-9) and in the synthesis of cysteine and glycine, is derived from the carbon chain of D-3-phosphoglyceric acid, as indicated in Fig. 17-11, or

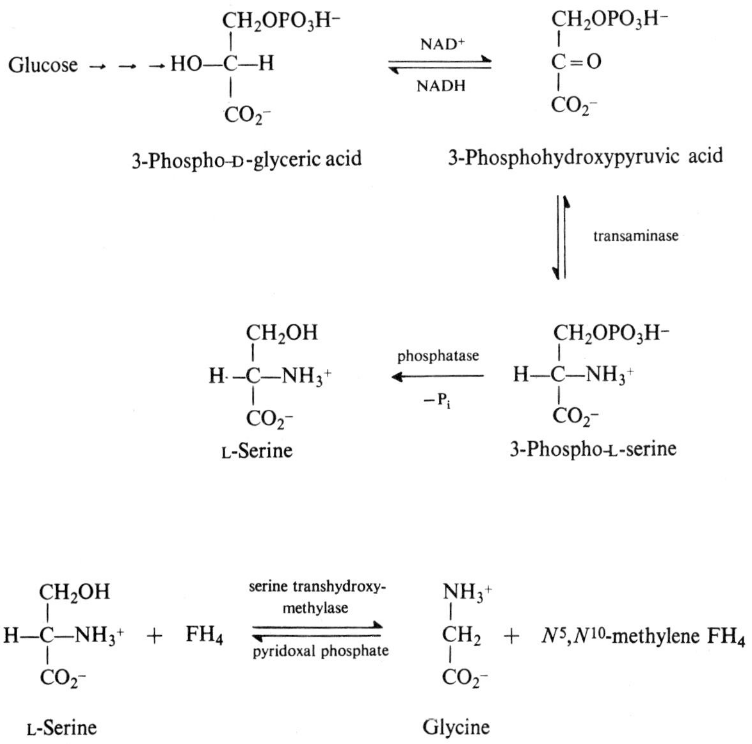

FIGURE 17-11. Biosynthesis of Serine and Glycine.

may arise from glycine in the serine transhydroxymethylase reaction (see page 204). Phosphoglyceric acid dehydrogenase catalyzes the NAD-dependent oxidation of 3-phosphoglyceric acid, yielding 3-phosphohydroxypyruvic acid. Transamination and hydrolysis of the phosphate ester complete the synthesis of serine.

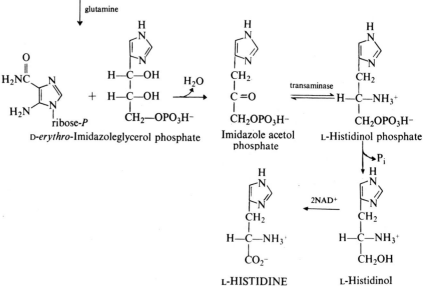

FIGURE 17-12.   Biosynthesis of Histidine in Microorganisms.

In the presence of FH_4, serine is readily converted to glycine and N^5,N^{10}-methylene FH_4 in a reaction catalyzed by serine transhydroxymethylase, a pyridoxal phosphate enzyme (see Fig. 17-11).

Cysteine may be synthesized from serine and homocysteine, as indicated in Fig. 17-9. An alternative route for cysteine synthesis is known. Serine sulfhydrase, a pyridoxal phosphate enzyme, catalyzes cysteine synthesis from serine and H_2S:

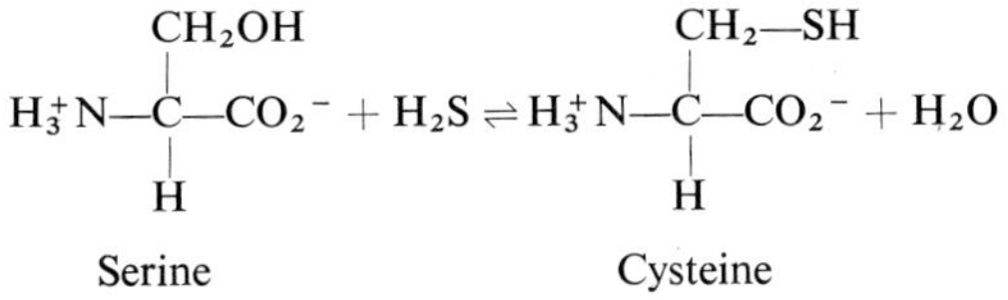

$$
\underset{\text{Serine}}{\overset{\overset{\displaystyle CH_2OH}{|}}{H_3^+N-\underset{|}{\overset{|}{C}}-CO_2^-}} + H_2S \rightleftharpoons \underset{\text{Cysteine}}{\overset{\overset{\displaystyle CH_2-SH}{|}}{H_3^+N-\underset{|}{\overset{|}{C}}-CO_2^-}} + H_2O \qquad (17\text{-}11)
$$

The disulfide bridges of proteins are formed by oxidation following the incorporation of cysteine into polypeptide chains, rather than by direct incorporation of cystine.

Synthesis of Alanine Several routes for the biosynthesis of alanine are known. For example, transaminases that convert pyruvate to alanine have been observed in several organisms:

$$
\text{Pyruvate} + \text{amino acid} \underset{\text{phosphate}}{\overset{\text{pyridoxal}}{\rightleftharpoons}} \text{L-alanine} + \text{ketoacid} \qquad (17\text{-}12)
$$

In addition, an enzyme from *Bacillus subtilis* catalyzes the direct reductive amination of pyruvate, yielding alanine. Finally, a microbial enzyme catalyzes the β-decarboxylation of aspartic acid, again yielding alanine:

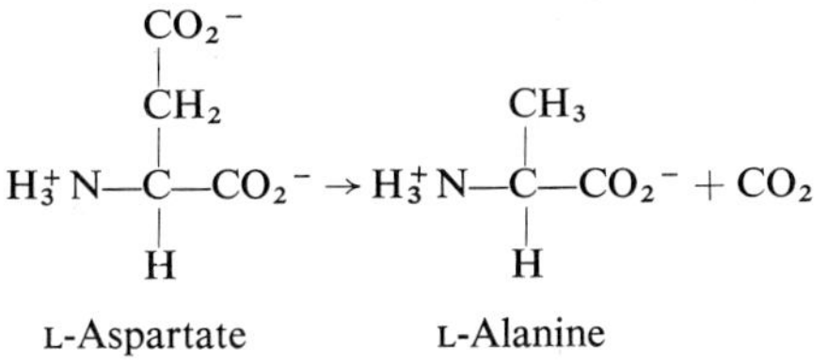

$$
\underset{\text{L-Aspartate}}{\overset{\overset{\displaystyle CO_2^-}{|}}{\overset{\displaystyle CH_2}{|}}{H_3^+N-\underset{|}{\overset{|}{C}}-CO_2^-}} \rightarrow \underset{\text{L-Alanine}}{\overset{\overset{\displaystyle CH_3}{|}}{H_3^+N-\underset{|}{\overset{|}{C}}-CO_2^-}} + CO_2 \qquad (17\text{-}13)
$$

Biosynthesis of Histidine The key to the understanding of the synthesis of histidine was the finding, based on isotope tracer studies, that N-1 and C-2 of the imidazole ring are derived from N-1 and C-2 of the purine nucleus:

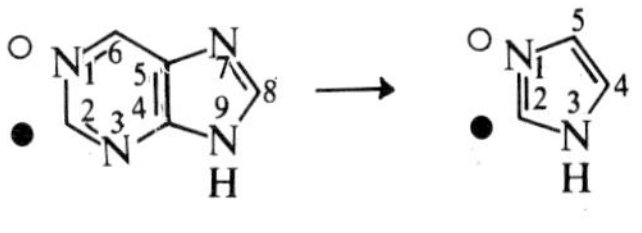

Subsequently, Moyed and Magasanik were able to demonstrate that bacterial extracts, can, with the addition of ATP and ribose-5-phosphate, catalyze the synthesis of *compound III*, an important intermediate for the synthesis of the imidazole ring. Compound III has been identified as an intermediate derived from condensation of ribose-5-phosphate with N-1 of a ring-opened AMP derivative, *N*-(5′-phospho-D-1′-ribulosylformimino)-5-(5″-phosphoribosyl)-4-imidazole-carboxamide (see Fig. 17-12). Addition of the amide nitrogen of glutamine to compound III with closure of the imidazole ring yields imidazole-glycerol phosphate and 5-aminoimidazole-4-carboxamide ribonucleotide, which is employed for the resynthesis of purines.

Synthesis of the Branched-chain Amino Acids

As might have been expected, the routes for synthesis of *valine*, *leucine*, and *isoleucine* are closely related. The biosynthesis of valine and leucine proceeds through the common intermediate, α-ketoisovaleric acid, and is outlined in Fig. 17-13. The thiamine pyrophosphate–dependent condensation of pyruvate

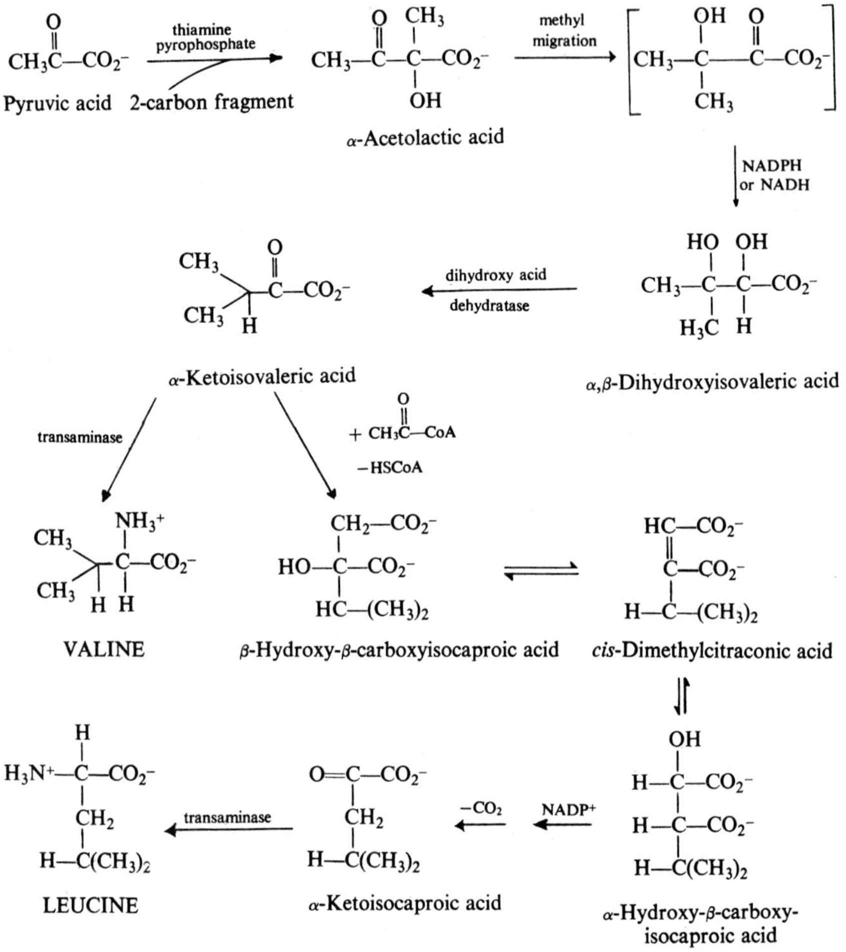

FIGURE 17-13. Biosynthesis of Valine and Leucine in Microorganisms and Plants.

with a 2-carbon fragment yields acetolactic acid (see Chap. 11), which is converted directly to α,β-dihydroxyisovaleric acid in an interesting reaction. This transformation, which is closely related to the classic pinacol rearrangement, is catalyzed by *acetohydroxy acid isomeroreductase* and requires Mg^{+2} and a reduced pyridine nucleotide. *Dihydroxyacid dehydratase* catalyzes the dehydration of α,β-dihydroxyisovaleric acid, yielding α-ketoisovaleric acid, which, by transamination, yields valine directly.

α-Ketoisovaleric acid is condensed with acetyl-SCoA, yielding β-hydroxy-β-carboxyisocaproic acid. This substance is converted to α-hydroxy-β-carboxyisocaproic acid by a dehydration-rehydration sequence closely related to that for the citrate-isocitrate conversion catalyzed by aconitase. However, the *β-hydroxy-β-carboxyisocaproate isomerase* has been purified and shown to be distinct from aconitase. Oxidative decarboxylation and transamination complete the synthesis of leucine.

Threonine dehydratase catalyzes the conversion of threonine to α-ketobutyrate. The latter substance is condensed with "active acetaldehyde," yielding α-aceto-α-hydroxybutyric acid, a key intermediate for synthesis of isoleucine. The synthesis of isoleucine from this intermediate closely parallels the synthesis of valine from acetolactate, and, indeed, the same enzymes appear to be involved in both reaction sequences for the terminal transamination step. There are two transaminases for valine but only one for isoleucine. This accounts for mutants that require isoleucine but not valine. The biosynthetic route to isoleucine is detailed in Fig. 17-14.

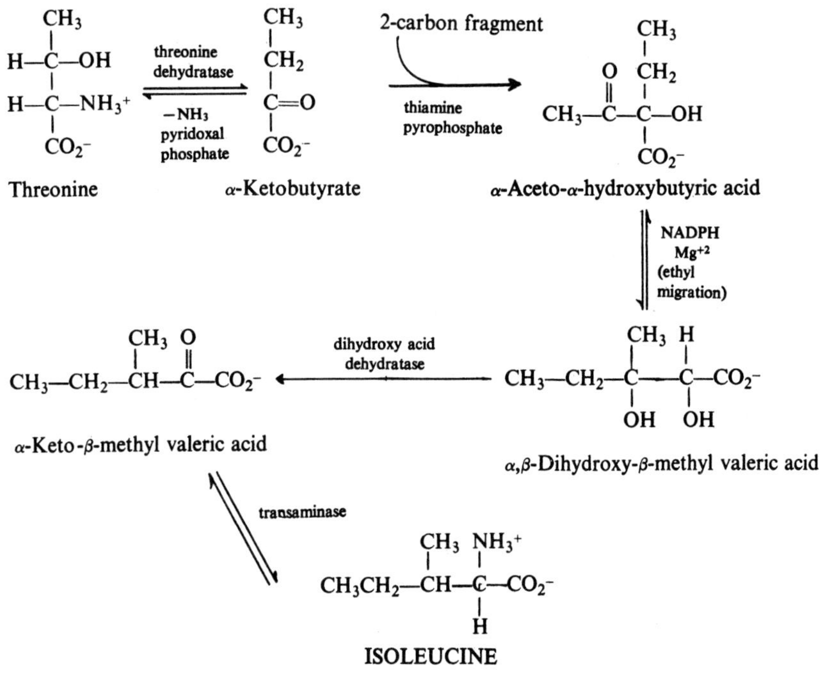

FIGURE 17-14. Biosynthesis of Isoleucine in Microorganisms and Plants.

Biosynthesis of Phenylalanine, Tyrosine, and Tryptophan

A number of reactions are common to the synthesis of *phenylalanine, tyrosine,* and *tryptophan.* These steps culminate in the synthesis of shikimic acid-5-phosphate, as indicated in Fig. 17-15. The role of shikimic acid as an intermediate in the synthesis of aromatic amino acids from D-glucose was discovered by Davis. The route from D-glucose to shikimic acid was elucidated in part by isotope tracer experiments employing glucose variously labelled with C^{14}. Subsequent experiments revealed that phosphoenolpyruvate condenses with erythrose-4-phosphate to yield the 7-carbon precursor of shikimic acid, 3-deoxy-D-arabinoheptulosonic acid-7-phosphate. Cyclization yields 5-dehydroquinic acid, which gives shikimic acid-5-phosphate following dehydration, oxidation, and phosphorylation (see Fig. 17-15). Most of the enzymes involved in this reaction sequence have not yet been purified and characterized.

3-Enolpyruvylshikimate-5-phosphate synthetase catalyzes the condensation of phosphoenolpyruvic acid and shikimic acid-5-phosphate as detailed in Fig. 17-16. The product, 3-enolpyruvylshikimate-5-phosphate, yields chorismic acid, which on rearrangement, gives anthranilic acid, a precursor of tryptophan

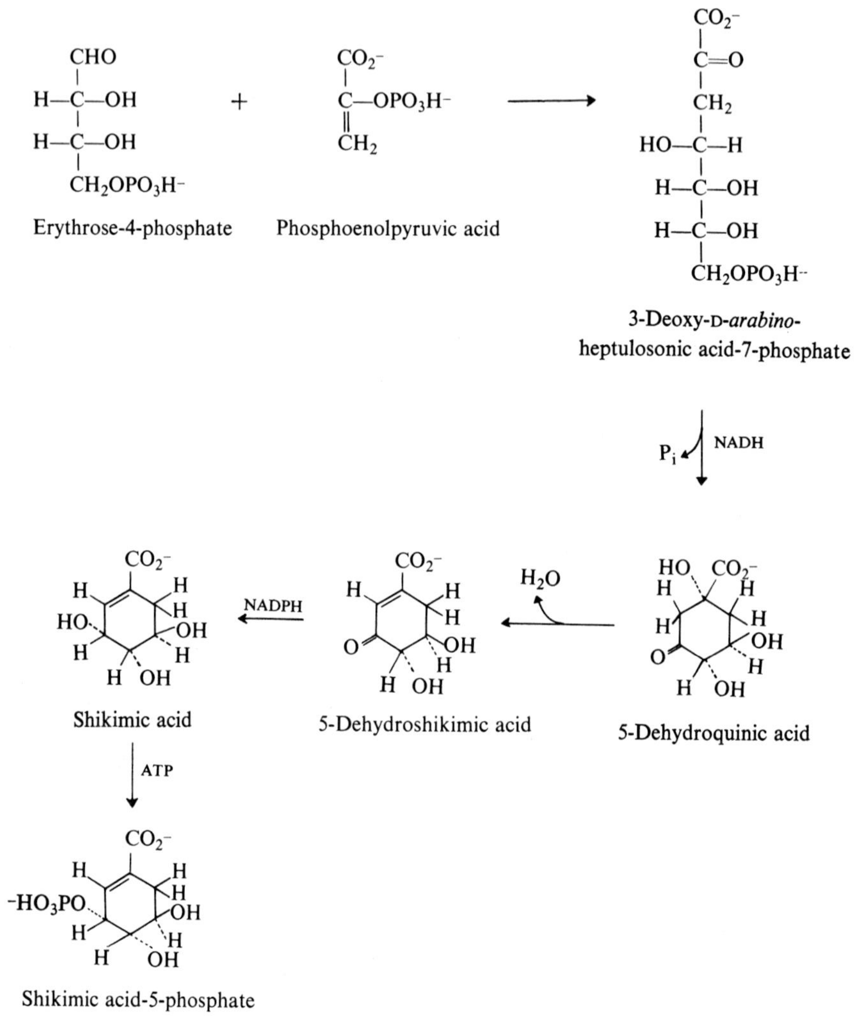

FIGURE 17-15.   Biosynthesis of Shikimic Acid-5-Phosphate.

and prephenic acid, a precursor of phenylalanine and tyrosine. Decarboxylation and reductive decarboxylation of prephenic acid yield the immediate precursors of tyrosine and phenylalanine, respectively. The latter two are finally formed by transamination (see Fig. 17-16).

Conversion of anthranilic acid to tryptophan occurs in yeast and *E. coli*, as indicated in Fig. 17-17. The terminal step is catalyzed by *tryptophan synthetase* (see page 468), a remarkable enzyme thoroughly studied by Yanofsky and Bonner.

GENERAL ASPECTS OF AMINO ACID METABOLISM

General reactions of the amino acids include transamination, decarboxylation, racemization, and deamination (oxidative and nonoxidative). The first three reaction types indicated above are generally (but not invariably) pyridoxal phosphate-dependent, and the reaction mechanisms were discussed in Chap. 8. Consequently, we consider only metabolic aspects of these reactions below.

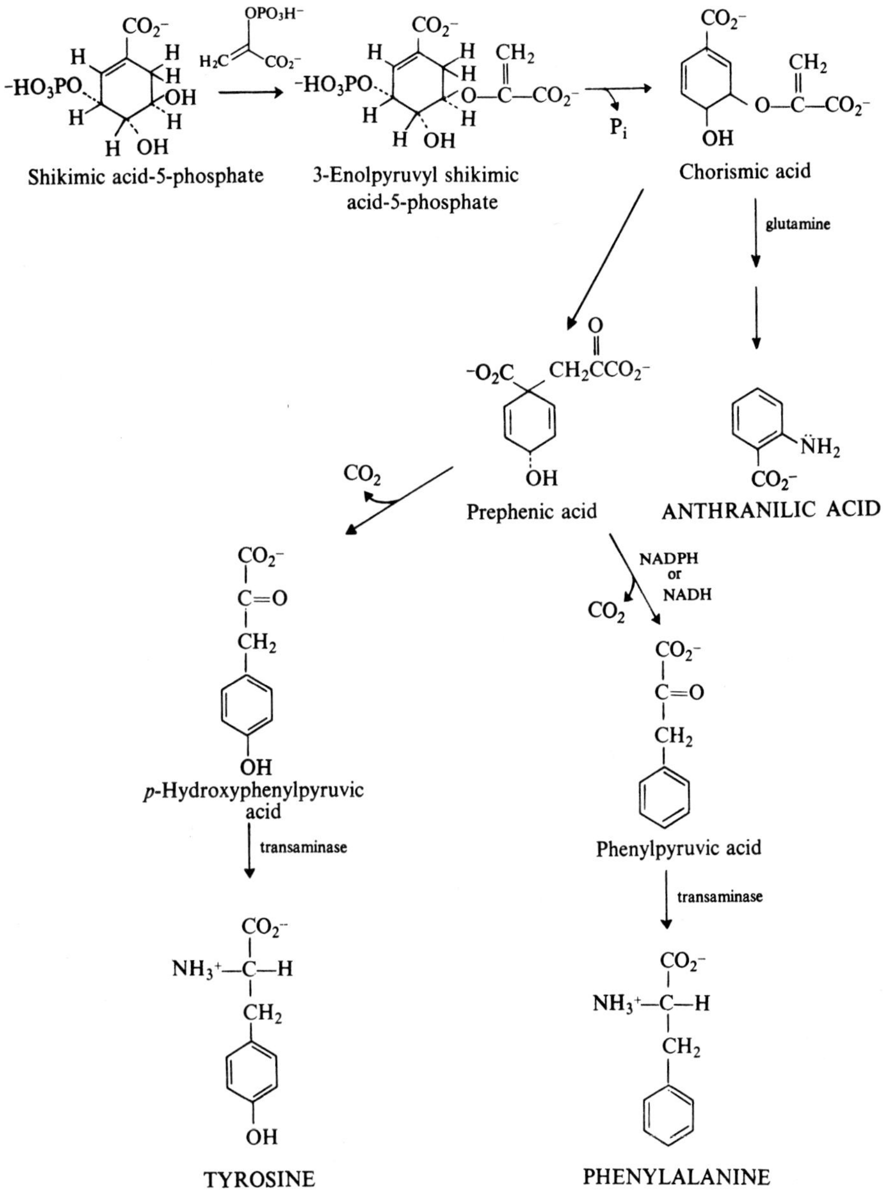

FIGURE 17-16. Conversion of Shikimic Acid-5-Phosphate to Tyrosine, Phenylalanine, and Anthranilic Acid.

Transamination

The scope of biological transaminations is broad indeed. Early studies were principally concerned with reactions involving dicarboxylic acid substrates — glutamic-oxaloacetic transaminase, for example. Subsequently, similar reactions involving other amino and keto acids were identified. At present, the known transamination reactions include nearly all the L-amino acids, and a number of such reactions involving D-amino acids, ω-amino acids, and aldehydes are recognized as well.

The metabolic roles of transaminations are several and significant. Important functions include (1) amino acid biosynthesis (transamination is directly involved in the synthesis of at least eleven of the amino acids), (2) amino acid degradation (see below), (3) liaison between carbohydrate and amino acid metabolism, and (4) synthesis of several specific compounds, including urea and γ-amino butyric acid.

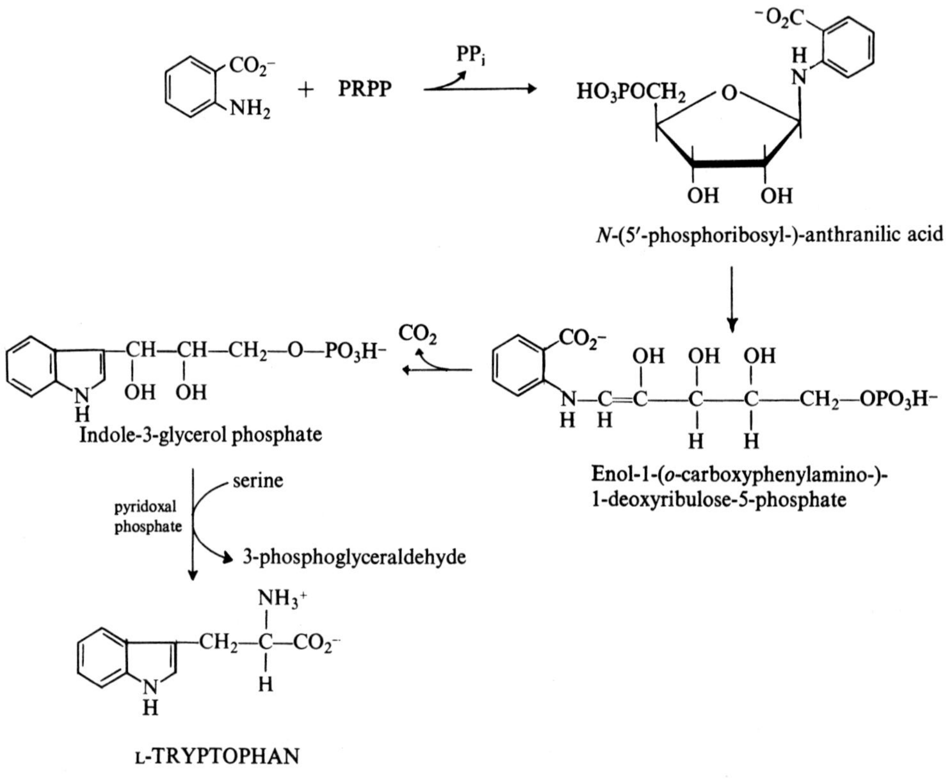

FIGURE 17-17.   Biosynthesis of Tryptophan.

Decarboxylation   Amino acid decarboxylases are distributed widely throughout living material. For the most part, they catalyze the α-decarboxylation of L-amino acids. Interesting exceptions include D-lysine decarboxylase and L-β-aspartic acid decarboxylase. These enzymes occur in certain microorganisms. Certain of the decarboxylases are quite specific enzymes, and others exhibit activity with a variety of substrates.

Racemization   Enzymes catalyzing the racemization of alanine, methionine, glutamate, proline, lysine, and serine and for the epimerization of hydroxyproline and diaminopimelate have been identified in bacteria. The last enzyme is, of course, involved in the biosynthesis of L-lysine. In addition, proline and alanine are metabolized in certain organisms via the D-amino acids rather than the L-isomers.

The metabolic functions of the other enzymes are less well defined but probably include synthesis of D-amino acids for cell-wall construction.

Deamination   Enzymes that catalyze the complete reaction indicated below are termed amino acid oxidases:

$$R{-}CH{-}CO_2^- + O_2 + H_2O \rightarrow R{-}\overset{\overset{\displaystyle O}{\|}}{C}{-}CO_2^- + NH_4^+ + H_2O_2 \qquad (17\text{-}14)$$
$$\overset{|}{{}^+NH_3}$$

In the presence of catalase, the hydrogen peroxide formed in this reaction is decomposed to oxygen and water. In its absence, the hydrogen peroxide reacts with the ketoacid product nonenzymatically in an oxidative decarboxylation reaction:

$$R{-}\overset{\overset{\displaystyle O}{\|}}{C}{-}CO_2^- + H_2O_2 \rightarrow RCO_2^- + CO_2 + H_2O \qquad (17\text{-}15)$$

Under certain conditions, reaction (17-15) occurs much more slowly than reaction (17-14), so that α-ketoacid can accumulate even in the absence of catalase.

The amino acid oxidases fall into two broad categories: those which catalyze the oxidative deamination of L-amino acids and those which perform a similar function employing the D-isomers as substrates. Enzymes of both classes are reasonably widely distributed in living material. L-*Amino acid oxidases* have been detected in the venom of most poisonous snakes, in avian liver, in molds, and in bacteria. The corresponding D-*amino acid oxidases* occur in the kidney and liver of mammals, and in birds, amphibians, insects, bacteria, and molds. Aside from the specificity requirement in terms of configuration about the α-carbon of the substrate, most amino acid oxidases exhibit a rather broad, though not unlimited, specificity. A typical amino acid oxidase utilizes perhaps ten of the amino acids as substrates. The reaction rates of course vary with the substrate.

Glycine is oxidized by the D-amino acid oxidase, which occurs in the liver and kidney of mammals. The reaction products are ammonia and glyoxylic acid:

$$H_3N^+{-}CH_2{-}CO_2^- + O_2 + H_2O \rightarrow H{-}\overset{\overset{\displaystyle O}{\|}}{C}{-}CO_2^- + NH_4^+ + H_2O_2 \qquad (17\text{-}16)$$

The L-amino acid oxidases of snake venoms exhibit molecular weights near 150,000 and contain 2 moles of FAD per mole of protein.

The role of the enzymes that catalyze the deamination of L-amino acids in metabolism seems clear. These enzymes, whether they act in an oxidative or nonoxidative fashion, permit the reshuffling of amino functions between various carbon skeletons. Thus the amino function of a dietary amino acid may be employed to complete the biosynthesis of a different amino acid in vivo. In most cases, the inability of an organism to catalyze the *de novo* synthesis of an amino acid reflects an inability to construct the carbon skeleton, not an inability to introduce the amino function into a formed carbon skeleton.

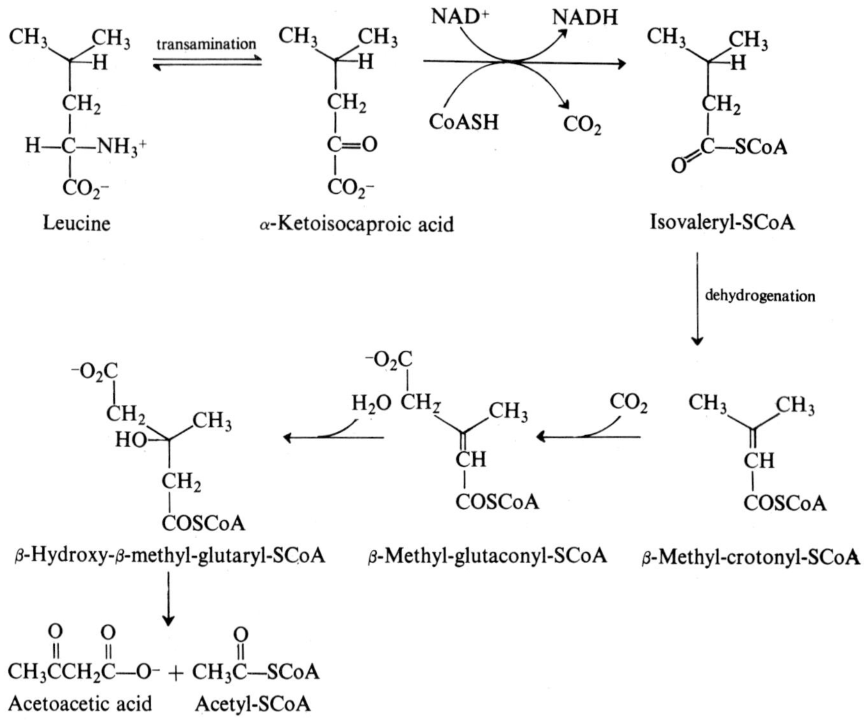

CH$_3$ CH$_3$ —transamination⇌ CH$_3$ CH$_3$ NAD$^+$ NADH CH$_3$ CH$_3$

CH$_2$ CH$_2$ CoASH   CO$_2$ CH$_2$

H—C—NH$_3^+$ C=O   O=C—SCoA

CO$_2^-$ CO$_2^-$

Leucine   α-Ketoisocaproic acid   Isovaleryl-SCoA

dehydrogenation

$^-$O$_2$C   H$_2$O CH$_2$ CH$_3$ CO$_2$ CH$_3$ CH$_3$

CH$_2$ CH$_3$ CH   CH

HO—   COSCoA   COSCoA

CH$_2$

COSCoA

β-Hydroxy-β-methyl-glutaryl-SCoA   β-Methyl-glutaconyl-SCoA   β-Methyl-crotonyl-SCoA

O O   O

CH$_3$CCH$_2$C—O$^-$ + CH$_3$C—SCoA

Acetoacetic acid   Acetyl-SCoA

FIGURE 17-19.   Pathway for Leucine Degradation.

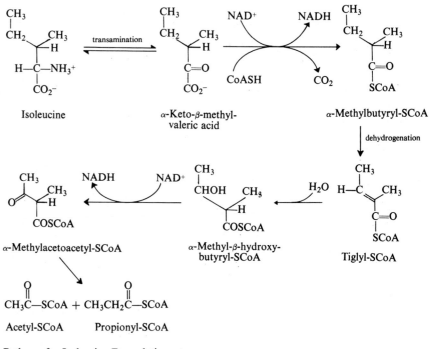

CH$_3$ CH$_3$ NAD$^+$ NADH   CH$_3$

CH$_2$ CH$_3$ —transamination→ CH$_2$ CH$_3$ CH$_2$ CH$_3$

H—C—NH$_3^+$ C=O   CoASH   CO$_2$ C=O

CO$_2^-$ CO$_2^-$ SCoA

Isoleucine   α-Keto-β-methyl-valeric acid   α-Methylbutyryl-SCoA

dehydrogenation

CH$_3$ NADH   NAD$^+$ CH$_3$ CH$_3$

CH$_3$ CHOH CH$_3$ H$_2$O H—C   CH$_3$

O=   H   H   C=O

COSCoA   COSCoA   SCoA

α-Methylacetoacetyl-SCoA   α-Methyl-β-hydroxy-butyryl-SCoA   Tiglyl-SCoA

O   O

CH$_3$C—SCoA + CH$_3$CH$_2$C—SCoA

Acetyl-SCoA   Propionyl-SCoA

FIGURE 17-20.   Pathway for Isoleucine Degradation.

SPECIFIC ASPECTS
OF AMINO ACID
METABOLISM

In addition to the transformations discussed above, which are common to most or all the amino acids, each amino acid is involved in reaction pathways that are unique to it. We now wish to direct attention to the more important of these. We begin with a discussion of the catabolism of several of the amino acids and subsequently consider particular aspects of metabolic interconversions involving amino acids.

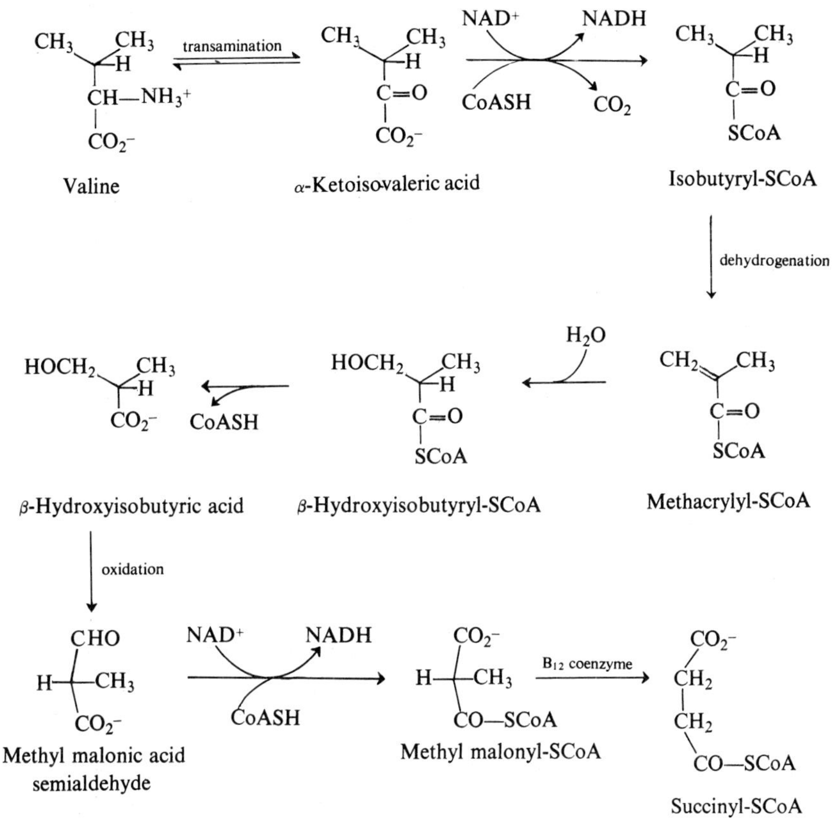

FIGURE 17-18.   Pathway for Valine Degradation.

Degradation of
the Branched-chain
Amino Acids

In Figs. 17-18, 17-19, and 17-20, the pathways for oxidative degradation of valine, leucine, and isoleucine are presented. These catabolic pathways have the first three steps in common. Then the pathways diverge, although the remaining steps in each case bear a distinct resemblance to the reactions of fatty acid oxidation. Of note is the occurrence of β-hydroxy-β-methylglutaryl-SCoA in leucine oxidation. This compound is an important intermediate for the synthesis of cholesterol and other steroids from acetyl-SCoA (see page 387).

Early studies led to the historical classification of amino acids as *ketogenic* or *glycogenic* for the mammal. The distinction between the two classes depends on whether ketone bodies (acetoacetic acid, acetone, and the like) or glucose (or glycogen) are formed as a result of administration of the particular amino acid (a distinction that is frequently a function of experimental conditions). On this basis, valine is a glycogenic amino acid, leucine is ketogenic, and isoleucine exhibits both glycogenic and ketogenic behavior. These results may be readily

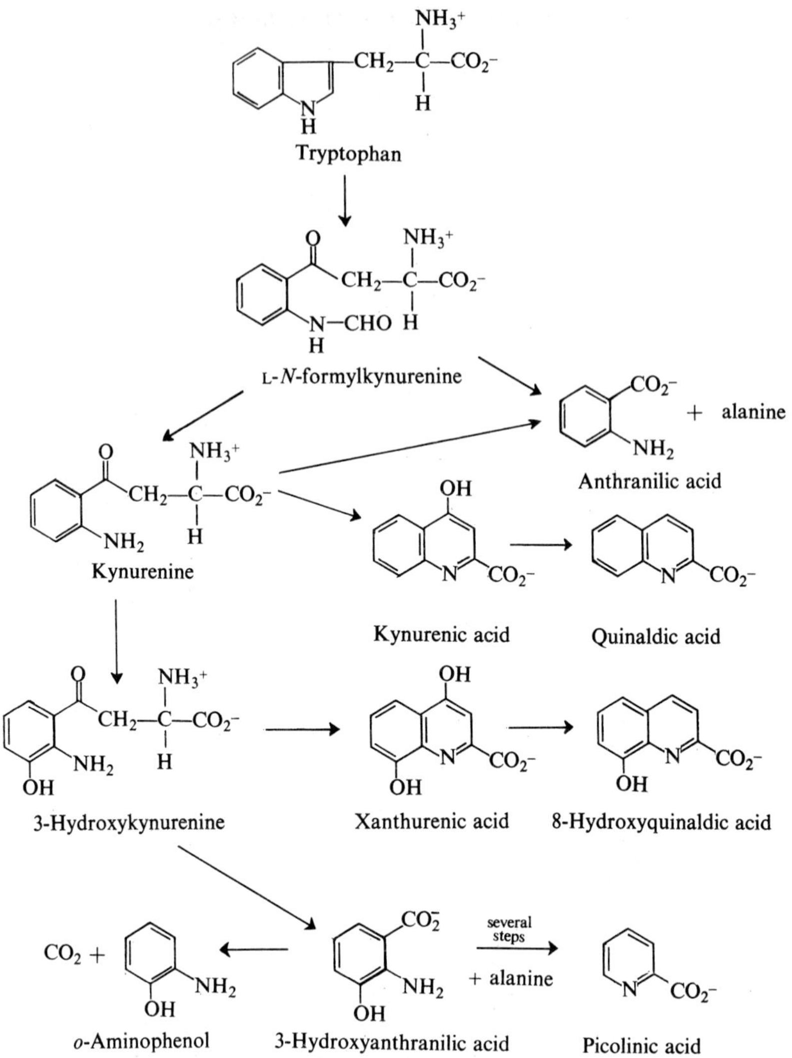

FIGURE 17-21. Some Pathways Involved in Tryptophan Oxidation.

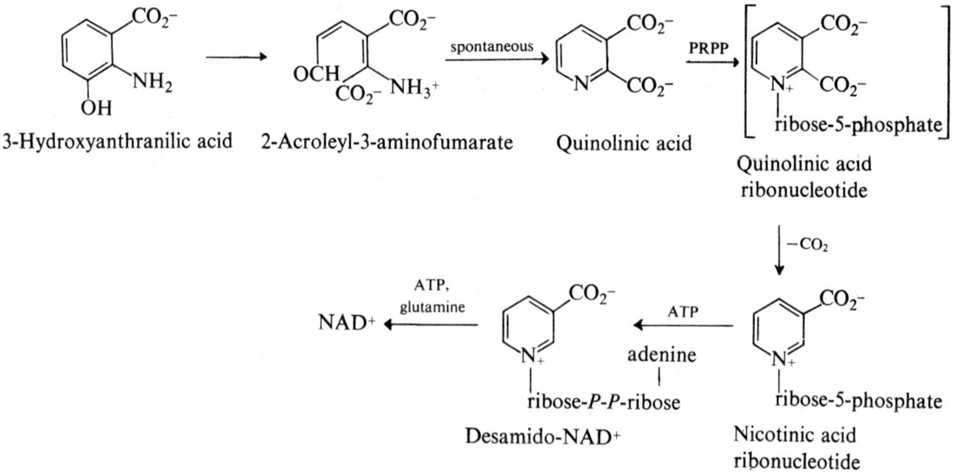

FIGURE 17-22. Synthesis of Some Nicotinic Acid Derivatives from 3-Hydroxyanthranilic Acid.

understood in terms of the nature of the final degradation products. Valine yields succinyl-SCoA, which, via the tricarboxylic acid cycle and related enzymes, may be converted to pyruvic acid and thence to glucose (see page 279). In contrast, leucine yields directly a ketone body, acetoacetic acid, and acetyl-SCoA. The latter may, of course, be converted to acetoacetic acid as well (see page 321). Isoleucine yields acetyl-SCoA and propionyl-SCoA. Propionyl-SCoA is converted to succinyl-SCoA via methylmalonyl-SCoA (see page 322) and hence is glycogenic. Since, as noted above, acetyl-SCoA is ketogenic, isoleucine should (and does) fall into both categories. A classification of all the amino acids as ketogenic or glycogenic is presented in Table 17-2.

TABLE 17-2.   Glycogenic and Ketogenic Amino Acids

Glycogenic	Ketogenic	Glycogenic and Ketogenic
Alanine	Leucine	Isoleucine
Arginine		Lysine
Aspartic acid		Phenylalanine
Cystine		Tyrosine
Glutamic acid		
Glycine		
Histidine		
Hydroxyproline		
Methionine		
Proline		
Serine		
Threonine		
Tryptophan		
Valine		

Metabolism of Tryptophan

The metabolism of tryptophan yields a variety of interesting and important substances, including serotonin, a powerful vasoconstrictor found in mammalian nervous tissue and elsewhere, indoleacetic acid, a growth-promoting substance for plants (an auxin), eye pigments in certain insects, and the vitamin niacin (nicotinic acid). The relationship between the metabolism of tryptophan and nicotinic acid has been recognized for many years, following nutritional studies in mammalian species that established that dietary requirements for nicotinic acid may be met by ingestion of excess tryptophan. The metabolic transformation of tryptophan to nicotinic acid is quite complex and has only recently been unraveled in detail. The first part of the pathway, involving the formation of 3-hydroxyanthranilic acid from tryptophan, has been well established for several years and is indicated schematically in Fig. 17-21.

The oxidation of tryptophan is initiated by the enzyme *tryptophan pyrrolase*. This enzyme, which has an iron protoporphyrin IX prosthetic group (see page 216), catalyzes the conversion of tryptophan to L-*N*-formylkynurenine, employing molecular oxygen as oxidant. Tryptophan pyrrolase is an inducible enzyme, whose levels in mammalian tissues are elevated by administration of tryptophan, α-methyl tryptophan, or glucocorticoids.

3-*Hydroxyanthranilic oxidase*, an enzyme requiring ferrous ions, catalyzes the oxidation, by molecular oxygen, of 3-hydroxyanthranilic acid to 2-acroleyl-3-aminofumarate, which undergoes a spontaneous ring closure, yielding quinolinic acid (see Fig. 17-22).

Additional important metabolic transformations of tryptophan, alluded to above, are summarized in Fig. 17-23.

Degradation of Phenylalanine and Tyrosine

The oxidative metabolism of phenylalanine and tyrosine is of particular interest in that (1) a number of diseases resulting from "inborn errors of metabolism" are associated with this pathway of metabolism and (2) the associated enzymes require coenzymes that, in some instances, are quite unusual. The

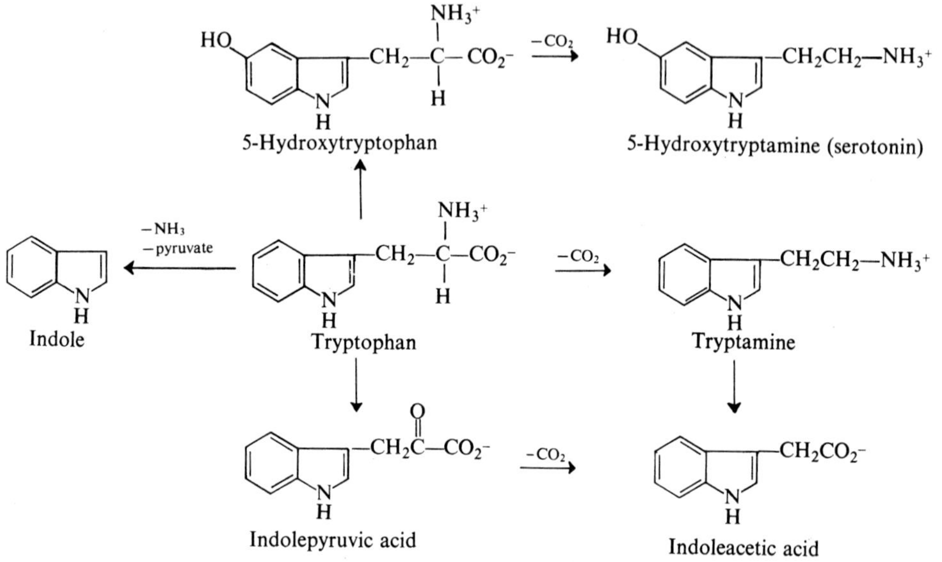

FIGURE 17-23.   Some Metabolic Transformations of Tryptophan.

principal routes for oxidative degradation of these amino acids are indicated in Fig. 17-24.

Under normal physiological conditions, the bulk of phenylalanine is metabolized through its initial conversion to tyrosine. The enzyme responsible for catalyzing this reaction, phenylalanine hydroxylase, is typical of most hydroxylases (see page 344), in that molecular oxygen and NADPH participate in the reaction. This enzyme is localized in the microsomal fraction of the cell. A striking and unusual feature of the reaction is the requirement of a pteridine, whose structure is indicated below, as coenzyme for the reaction:

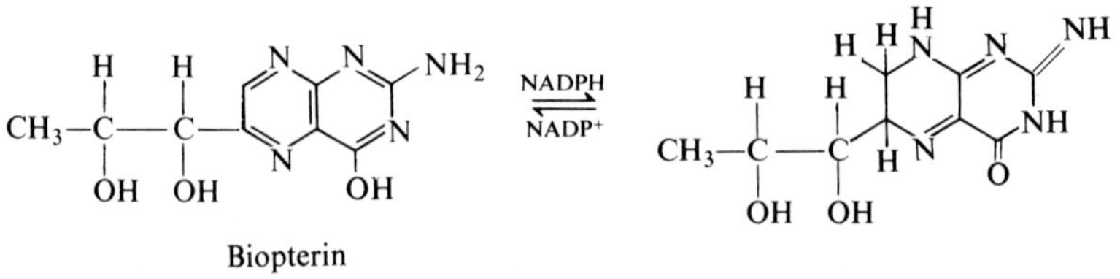

(17-17)

The apparent function of NADPH in this reaction is to maintain the pteridine in the quinoid dihydro form.

As in the case of several other amino acids, the degradation of tyrosine is initiated by a transamination yielding, in this case, *p*-hydroxyphenylpyruvic acid.

This intermediate is metabolized in an interesting (and mechanistically puzzling) fashion. Apparently a single enzyme, *p-hydroxyphenylpyruvic acid oxidase*, a copper-containing protein, catalyzes the conversion of its substrate to homogentisic acid — a reaction involving decarboxylation, oxidation, hydroxylation of the aromatic ring, and migration of a side chain. The reaction requires ascorbic acid, whose function remains obscure. *Homogentisic acid oxidase*, an enzyme requiring ferrous ions, catalyzes the formation of maleylacetoacetic acid from

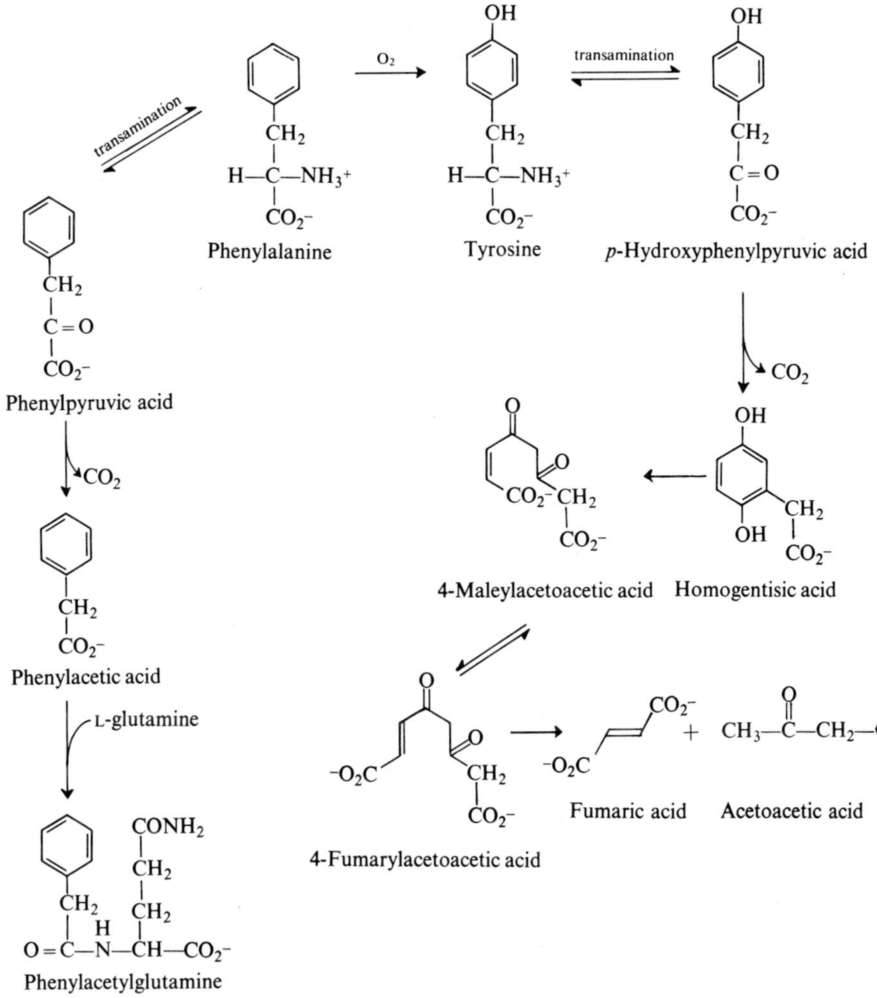

FIGURE 17-24. Principal Routes for the Metabolism of Phenylalanine and Tyrosine.

homogentisic acid. Maleylacetoacetic acid is converted to the corresponding trans compound, fumarylacetoacetic acid, in a reaction catalyzed by maleylacetoacetic isomerase and requiring glutathione — one of the few known instances in which this species is involved coenzymatically. Cleavage of fumarylacetoacetic acid yields fumaric acid, which is further metabolized by enzymes of the citric acid cycle, and acetoacetic acid, which may either enter the citric acid cycle (following conversion to acetyl-SCoA) or be converted to fatty acids.

In Chap. 4, mention was made of the fact that humans afflicted with sickle-cell anemia have a hemoglobin that is structurally distinct from that of normal individuals. Sickle-cell hemoglobin is an inherited disease; that is, the genetic information transmitted from parent to progeny does not have the correct information for synthesis of a normal hemoglobin molecule (see the discussion of genetics in Chap. 19). This disease is one of a general class that may be termed "inborn errors of metabolism." Several such diseases were recognized many years ago by Garrod, who considered cystinuria, alcaptonuria, and albinism, for example, to be the consequence of the inability of the organism to carry out a particular metabolic transformation in the normal sequence of events. This conclusion has certainly been fully corroborated by subsequent findings. In many cases, it has been possible to demonstrate that inborn errors of metabolism are associated with the lack or partial lack of a particular enzymatic activity. This may reflect failure to synthesize the pertinent enzyme at all, the synthesis of a structurally altered enzyme, or synthesis of the normal enzyme in altered amounts. Several inborn errors of metabolism are concerned with amino acid metabolism. We consider three examples from the metabolism of phenyl-alanine and tyrosine: albinism, alcaptonuria, and phenylketonuria.

Albinism is characterized by lack of pigment in skin, hair, and retina. This disease assumes several forms and may be either complete, involving total lack of pigment, or incomplete, in which case pigment loss is restricted to particular areas. Melanin, the pigment of hair, skin, and eyes, is a polymeric material of unknown structure that arises from the oxidation of tyrosine. The only enzyme concerned with the conversion of tyrosine to melanin is tyrosinase, a copper-containing protein, which catalyzes the conversion of tyrosine to dihydroxy-phenylalanine and subsequently to dihydroxyphenylalanine quinone, as indicated below and on page 344:

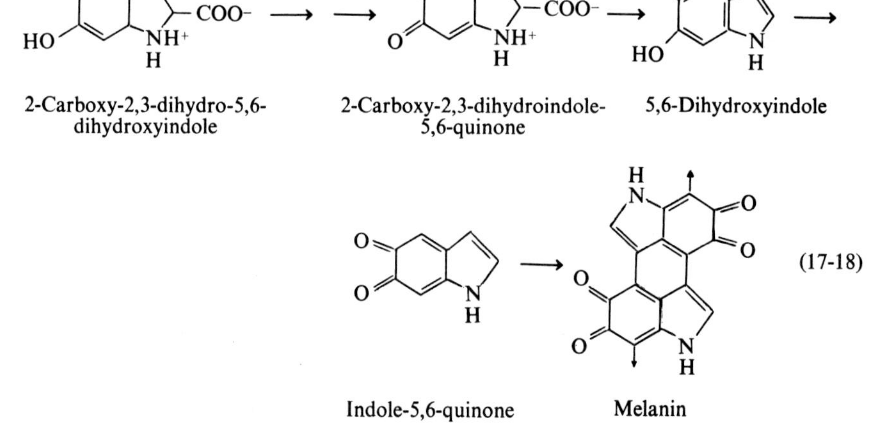

Tyrosine   3,4-Dihydroxyphenylalanine   Phenylalanine-3,4-quinone
                              (DOPA)

2-Carboxy-2,3-dihydro-5,6-   2-Carboxy-2,3-dihydroindole-   5,6-Dihydroxyindole
     dihydroxyindole   5,6-quinone

(17-18)

Indole-5,6-quinone   Melanin

The conversion of the last substrate to melanin is apparently spontaneous. Albinism results from the lack of normal tyrosinase activity.

Phenylketonuria results from the absence of normal phenylalanine hydroxylase activity. Under these conditions, phenylalanine cannot be converted to tyrosine, and its metabolism to phenylpyruvic and phenyllactic acids (see Fig. 17-24) is greatly exaggerated. These substances, as the name of the disease implies, are excreted in the urine. This is a severe disorder and results in marked mental retardation in children. The disease may be prevented if the intake of dietary phenylalanine is restricted from birth.

Alcaptonuria is characterized by the excretion of homogentisic acid in the urine, which rapidly darkens on exposure to oxygen as a result of the oxidation of this substance to the pigment alcapton. This disease is caused by the congenital absence of homogentisic acid oxidase. Other than darkening of the urine, alcaptonuriacs experience no symptoms early in life. Subsequently, pigmentation of the connective tissue occurs, which is usually associated with the development of arthritis.

Methionine and Biological Transmethylations

As noted above, the *de novo* synthesis of methyl groups involves the reduction of N^5, N^{10}-methylene FH_4 to N^5-methyl FH_4 (see pages 211 and 409). N^5-methyl FH_4 donates its methyl function in only one known reaction: the biosynthesis of methionine (see page 409). For the most part, the remaining transmethylation reactions employ methionine as methyl group donor. Methyl group transfers from methionine require ATP and Mg^{+2}. These requirements are readily understood on the basis of the intermediate formation of *S*-adenosylmethionine, which serves as the actual methyl group donor:

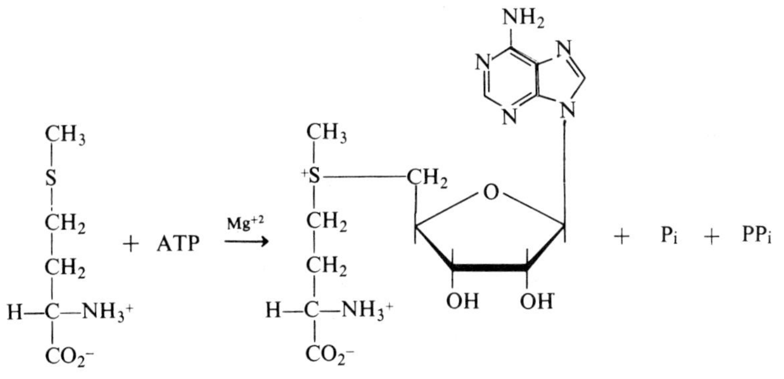

$$\text{methionine} + \text{ATP} \xrightarrow{Mg^{+2}} \text{S-adenosylmethionine} + P_i + PP_i \qquad (17\text{-}19)$$

S-adenosylmethionine

It will be recalled that this compound is classed with the "high-energy" metabolites. The synthesis of *S*-adenosylmethionine is unusual among ATP-dependent reactions in that the three phosphates of ATP are converted to enzyme-bound trimetaphosphate, which is cleaved on the enzyme to yield phosphate and pyrophosphate.

The number of known transmethylations is quite large. In several of these reactions, the participation of *S*-adenosylmethionine as methyl group donor has been established or strongly suggested. A few are collected in Table 17-3. In each instance, the transmethylation conforms to the general formulation below:

S-adenosylmethionine + substrate → adenosylhomocysteine + methyl-substrate
Adenosylhomocysteine → homocysteine + adenosine   (17-20)

TABLE 17-3.   A Partial Compilation of Transmethylation Reactions Involving
S-Adenosylmethionine

Enzyme	Reaction	Source
Norephinephrine methyl-transferase	Norepinephrine → epinephrine	Bovine adrenal medulla
Catechol methyl transferase	Catechol and derivatives → 3-methoxycatechols	Liver
Acetylserotonin O-methyltransferase	Acetylserotonin → melatonin	Nervous tissue and pineal gland
2,6-Diaminopurine methyltransferase	2,6-diaminopurine → 2-methylamino-6-aminopurine	E. coli
Polynucleotide methyltransferase	Polynucleotides → methylated polynucleotides	E. coli, liver
Guanidinoacetate methyltransferase	Guanidinoacetate → creatine	Liver
Nicotinamide methyltransferase	Nicotinamide → N-methylnicotinamide	Liver
Phosphatidyl ethanolamine methyltransferase	Phosphatidyl ethanolamine → phosphatidyl choline	Liver, Neurospora

The homocysteine product may be reconverted to methionine either through methylation with N^5-methyl FH_4 or in reactions in which alternate substances serve as methyl group donors. The latter class of methyl group donors, which serve only as donors to homocysteine, include dimethylthetins, methyl methionine, and betaine. The overall reaction is indicated below:

$$\begin{array}{ccccccc}
 & & & & & CH_3 & \\
 & & SH & & & S & \\
 & & | & & & | & \\
CH_3 \quad CH_3 & & CH_2 & & CH_3 & CH_2 & \\
\diagdown \quad \diagup & + & | & \longrightarrow & | & | & + H^+ \\
S^+ & & CH_2 & & S & CH_2 & \\
| & & | & & | & | & \\
CH_2 & & H-C-NH_3^+ & & CH_2 & H-C-NH_3^+ & \\
| & & | & & | & | & \\
CO_2^- & & CO_2^- & & CO_2^- & CO_2^- &
\end{array} \qquad (17\text{-}21)$$

Dimethylthetin

Dimethylthetin homocysteine methyltransferase, for example, is a widely distributed enzyme that has been obtained in homogeneous form. This enzyme appears to be distinct from that which catalyzes the synthesis of methionine employing betaine as methyl group donor.

Glycine and the Synthesis of Tetrapyrroles

As emphasized in Chap. 8, structures derived from the tetrapyrrole nucleus perform a variety of essential functions in living organisms. Most organisms have the capacity to synthesize these complicated molecules *de novo*. The biochemical pathways through which simple precursors give rise to tetrapyrroles were completely unknown prior to the advent of isotopic tracer methods. Employing these methods, Shemin and his colleagues, in a series of elegant experiments, elucidated the principal features of these pathways. Glycine, which is an important precursor of purines (see page 433) and serine (see page 411), proved to be one of the basic building blocks for these molecules. Tracer experiments demonstrated that both in vivo (man and rats) and in vitro (duckling erythrocytes) labeled acetate and glycine were incorporated into the protoporphyrin IX nucleus of the prosthetic group of hemoglobin. Careful degradation of the labeled material sufficed to establish the source of each atom of the protoporphyrin IX molecule. The results are indicated in Fig. 17-25. The important conclusions derived from this work include (1) that glycine donated the nitrogen atoms for each ring as well as carbon for the methylene bridges; (2) that the remaining atoms were derived from either acetate or the methylene group of acetate; (3) that all rings were identically labeled, indicating a common precursor for all rings; (4) that the labeling pattern indicated the existence of a common precursor for both sides of each pyrrole ring; and (5) that the labeling pattern of the atoms derived from acetate indicated that this substrate had been metabolized via the tricarboxylic acid cycle. All these results can be readily accommodated by the reaction pathway indicated below, for which unequivocal evidence has been garnered:

$$
\text{Acetate} \xrightarrow{\text{CAC}}
\begin{array}{c} CO_2^- \\ | \\ CH_2 \\ | \\ CH_2 \\ | \\ O=C-SCoA \end{array}
+
\begin{array}{c} NH_3^+ \\ | \\ CH_2 \\ | \\ CO_2^- \end{array}
\longrightarrow
\begin{array}{c} CO_2^- \\ | \\ CH_2 \\ | \\ CH_2 \\ | \\ C=O \\ | \\ H-C-NH_3^+ \\ | \\ CO_2^- \end{array}
\xrightarrow{CO_2}
$$

α-Amino-β-ketoadipic acid

(17-22)

$$
\begin{array}{c} CO_2^- \\ | \\ CH_2 \\ | \\ CH_2 \\ | \\ C=O \\ | \\ CH_2 \\ | \\ NH_3^+ \end{array}
\xrightarrow{2H_2O}
$$

δ-Aminolevulinic acid   Porphobilinogen

The initial reaction involves condensation of glycine with succinyl-SCoA (derived from acetate via the tricarboxylic acid cycle), yielding δ-aminolevulinic acid and carbon dioxide. This reaction is pyridoxal phosphate–dependent. Two molecules of δ-aminolevulinic acid are then condensed, with the loss of two molecules of water, to yield the crucial intermediate, *porphobilinogen*. This reaction is catalyzed by δ-aminolevulinic acid dehydrase. Porphobilinogen is apparently the immediate precursor to the tetrapyrroles.

The general pathways by which the various tetrapyrroles of biochemical interest are derived from porphobilinogen are indicated in Fig. 17-26.

Arginine and the Biosynthesis of Urea

The end product of nitrogen metabolism varies markedly from species to species. Of particular interest is the fact that in man and other terrestrial

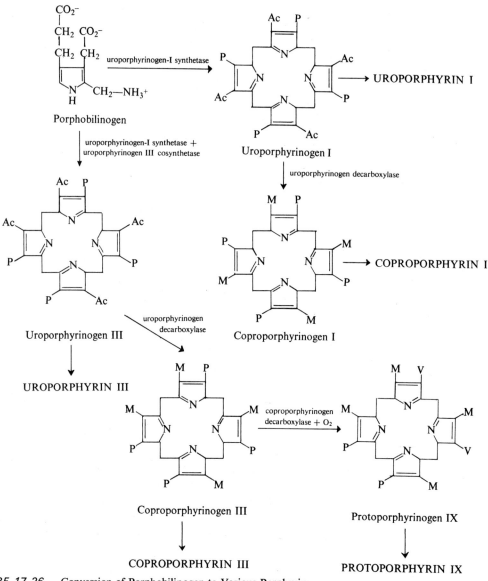

FIGURE 17-25. Metabolic Sources of Atoms of Protoporphyrin IX, as Shown by Isotope Experiments. All 4 N atoms are derived from glycine; atoms marked with asterisks are derived from the methylene carbon of glycine; atoms marked with solid circles are derived from the methyl carbon of acetate; atoms marked with open circles are derived mainly from the methyl carbon of acetate and in small part from the carboxyl carbon of acetate; the unmarked carbon atoms of the COOH groups are derived solely from the carboxyl carbon of acetate.—*J. Fruton and S. Simmonds, "General Biochemistry," page 865, Wiley, New York, 1958.*

FIGURE 17-26. Conversion of Porphobilinogen to Various Porphyrins.

vertebrates (ureotelic organisms) this end product is urea. Although nitrogen-containing substances other than urea certainly occur in the urine of man, urea is quantitatively the most important. The principal sources of ammonia for biosynthesis of urea were discussed above. These include the oxidative and non-oxidative deaminations of amino acids and the hydrolysis of the amides of glutamic and aspartic acids.

The overall pathway for synthesis of urea from carbon dioxide and ammonia is indicated in Fig. 17-27. The initial step in this reaction sequence, formation of

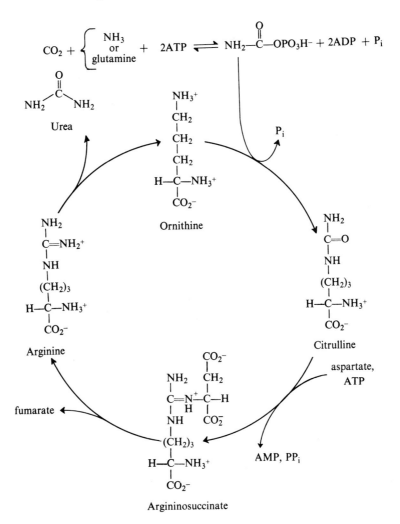

FIGURE 17-27.   The Urea Cycle.

carbamyl phosphate, is also the initial step in synthesis of the pyrimidines, and is discussed in some detail on page 439. Ornithine transcarbamylase (carbamoyl phosphate : 1-aspartate carbamoyl-transferase) catalyzes the condensation of carbamyl phosphate and ornithine, yielding citrulline. This enzyme occurs in mammalian (but not avian) liver, in higher and lower plants, and in certain microorganisms. Conversion of citrulline to arginine occurs via a two-step reaction path bearing a close resemblance to that for synthesis of adenylic acid (see page 438). *Argininosuccinate synthetase* catalyzes the ATP-dependent formation of an acyl guanidinium linkage between aspartic acid and citrulline. The product, argininosuccinate, is cleaved to fumarate and arginine in an *argininosuccinase* (L-argininosuccinate arginine-lyase) catalyzed process that bears a formal resemblance to the reaction catalyzed by aspartase (see page 406). The terminal step in urea production is the hydrolysis of arginine, catalyzed by *arginase*, yielding urea and regenerating ornithine, which, subsequently, may condense with an additional mole of carbamyl phosphate. Thus, urea formation is a cyclic process in which carbon dioxide and ammonia enter at one site and urea leaves at another.

REFERENCES
Aebi, H. E., Inborn Errors of Metabolism, *Ann. Rev. Biochem*, **36**: 271 (1967).

Bogorad, L.: Enzymatic Mechanisms in Porphyrin Syntheses, *Ann. N.Y. Acad. Sci.*, **104**: 676 (1963).

Bovey, F. A., and S. Yanari: Pepsin, in P. Boyer, H. Lardy, and K. Myrbäck (eds.), "The Enzymes," 2d ed., vol. 4, p. 63, Academic Press, New York, 1960.

Carnahan, J. E., and J. E. Castle: Nitrogen Fixation, *Ann. Rev. Plant Physiol.*, **14**: 125 (1963).

Davis, B. D.: Intermediates in Amino Acid Biosynthesis, *Advan. Enzymol.*, **16**: 247 (1955).

Desnuelle, P.: Chymotrypsin, in P. Boyer, H. Lardy, and K. Myrbäck (eds.), "The Enzymes," 2d ed., vol. 4, p. 93, Academic Press, New York, 1960.

————: Trypsin, in P. Boyer, H. Lardy, and K. Myrbäck (eds.), "The Enzymes," 2d ed., vol. 4, p. 119, Academic Press, New York, 1960.

Fruton, J. S.: Cathepsins, in P. Boyer, H. Lardy, and K. Myrbäck (eds.), "The Enzymes," 2d ed., vol. 4, p. 233, Academic Press, New York, 1960.

Greenberg, D. M.: Biological Methylation, *Advan. Enzymol.*, **25**: 395 (1963).

————: Amino Acid Metabolism, *Ann. Rev. Biochem.*, **33**: 633 (1964).

Larner, J.: Inborn Errors of Metabolism, *Ann. Rev. Biochem.*, **31**: 569 (1962).

Meister, A.: Amino Group Transfer, in P. D. Boyer, H. Lardy, and K. Myrbäck (eds.), "The Enzymes," 2d ed., vol. 6, p. 193, Academic Press, New York, 1962.

————: "Biochemistry of the Amino Acids," 2d ed., Academic Press, New York, 1965.

Mortenson, L. E.: Inorganic Nitrogen Assimilation and Ammonia Incorporation, in I. C. Gunsalus and R. Y. Stanier (eds.), "The Bacteria," vol. III, p. 119, Academic Press, New York, 1962.

————: Nitrogen Fixation: Role of Ferredoxin in Anaerobic Metabolism, *Ann. Rev. Microbiol.*, **17**: 115 (1963).

Moyed, H. S., and H. E. Umbarger: Regulation of Biosynthetic Pathways, *Physiol. Rev.*, **42**: 444 (1962).

Nason, A.: Enzymatic Pathways of Nitrate, Nitrite, and Hydroxylamine Metabolism, *Bacteriol. Rev.*, **26**: 16 (1962).

Neurath, H.: Carboxypeptidases A and B, in P. Boyer, H. Lardy, and K. Myrbäck (eds.), "The Enzymes," 2d ed., vol. 4, p. 11, Academic Press, New York, 1960.

————: Structure and Function of Proteolytic Enzymes, in M. Sela (ed.), "New Perspectives in Biology," p. 28, Elsevier, New York, 1964.

Sakami, W., and H. Harrington: Amino Acid Metabolism, *Ann. Rev. Biochem.*, **32**: 355 (1963).

Smith, E. L., and J. R. Kimmel: Papain, in P. Boyer, H. Lardy, and K. Myrbäck (eds.), "The Enzymes," 2d ed., vol. 4, p. 133, Academic Press, New York, 1960.

Sprinson, D. B.: The Biosynthesis of Aromatic Compounds from D-Glucose, *Advan. Carbohydrate Chem.*, **15**: 235 (1960).

Umbarger, E., and B. D. Davis: Pathways of Amino Acid Biosynthesis, in I. C. Gunsalus and R. Y. Stanier (eds.), "The Bacteria," vol. III, p. 167, Academic Press, New York, 1962.

Wellner, D., Flavoproteins, *Ann. Rev. Biochem.*, **36**: 669 (1967).

18 | Metabolism of the Nucleotides

Many features of nucleic acid metabolism relate directly to questions of central importance in the biological sciences. These include an understanding, on a molecular basis, of the mechanisms involved in the specification of macromolecular structures, the principal features of the transfer of biochemical specificity from parent to progeny, the basis of cellular differentiation, and the mechanism by which certain compounds are able to inhibit tumor and bacterial growth selectively.

In this chapter, we deal with the synthesis and degradation of the nucleotides, precursors of the nucleic acids. Subsequently, the role of nucleic acids as genetic material, the biosynthesis of the nucleic acids themselves, and the relationship of nucleic acids to the biosynthesis of proteins is considered.

BIOSYNTHESIS OF NUCLEOTIDE TRIPHOSPHATES
Purines

The ability to synthesize the purine ring system *de novo* is a very nearly universal biochemical capacity. Only a few known species require a nutritional source of preformed purines. The first major step toward a resolution of this metabolic pathway was the determination, through the use of labeled isotopes, of the origin of each of the atoms of the purine ring system. Studies principally from the laboratory of Buchanan demonstrated that carbons 2 and 8 are derived from formate, carbon 6 is derived from CO_2, and carbons 4 and 5 come from the carboxyl and methylene carbons of glycine respectively. In addition, nitrogen 7 is derived from glycine as well. This information is depicted schematically for the purine hypoxanthine in Fig. 18-1. Subsequent studies have revealed that nitrogen 1 is derived from aspartic acid and that nitrogens at positions 3 and 9 come from the amide nitrogen of glutamine. A major contribution to the elucidation of the pathway of purine nucleotide biosynthesis was the finding by G. R. Greenberg that the nucleotide, inosinic acid, is the first product formed with a complete purine ring structure.

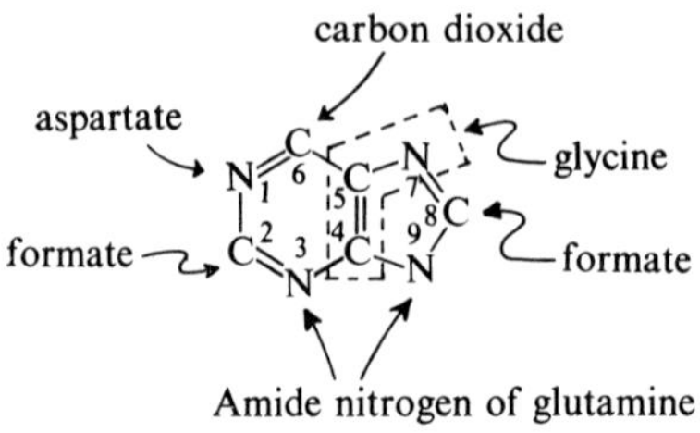

FIGURE 18-1.   The Basic Precursors of the Purine Skeleton.

The initial step in the biosynthesis of the purine ribonucleotides is the ATP-dependent pyrophosphorylation of ribose-5-phosphate, yielding 5-phosphoribosyl-l-pyrophosphate (PRPP):

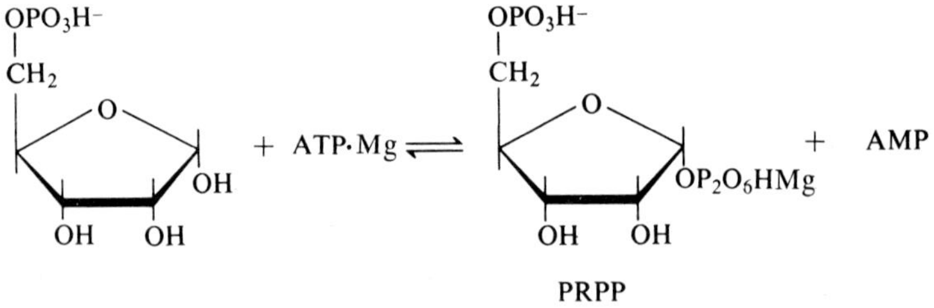

$$+ \text{ ATP·Mg} \rightleftharpoons \qquad + \quad \text{AMP} \qquad (18\text{-}1)$$

PRPP

This is an interesting reaction in that it is one of the few known cases in which a pyrophosphate group is transferred intact from ATP.

The second step of this pathway involves the glutamine-dependent amination of PRPP, yielding the acid-labile sugar 5-phosphoribosyl-l-amine:

Mg · 5-Phosphoribosyl-1-pyrophosphate + glutamine $\longrightarrow$

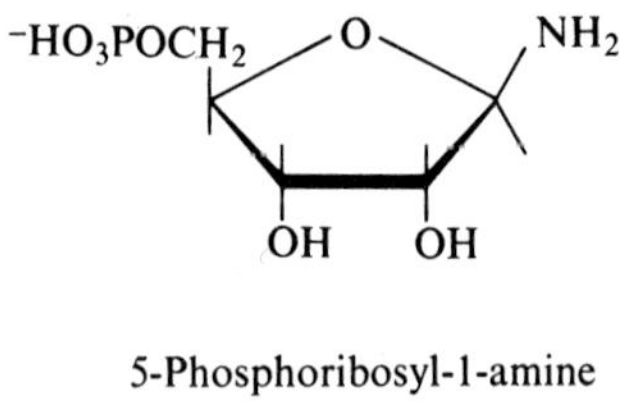

$$+ \text{ glutamate } + \text{MgPP}_i \qquad (18\text{-}2)$$

5-Phosphoribosyl-1-amine

Thus, the overall result of the first two steps is an ATP-dependent amination of ribose-5-phosphate. The amination step involves an inversion at C-1 of the ribose moiety, yielding the amino sugar with the β configuration. Hence, the N-glycosidic bond of proper stereochemistry is introduced early in the reaction sequence.

5-Phosphoribosyl-l-amine is subsequently conjugated, through formation of an amide linkage, with glycine in an ATP-dependent reaction:

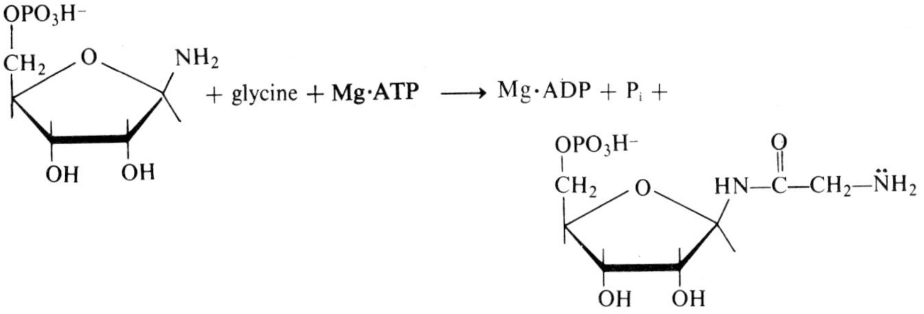

$$\text{(ribose-5-phosphate-amine)} + \text{glycine} + \text{Mg·ATP} \longrightarrow \text{Mg·ADP} + P_i +$$

Glycinamide ribonucleotide   (18-3)

Glycinamide ribonucleotide, the product of reaction (18-3), is formylated to yield N-formyl glycinamide ribonucleotide. N^5,N^{10}-methenyl tetrahydrofolate serves as coenzyme for this reaction (see Chap. 8):

$$\text{Glycinamide ribonucletoide} + N^5,N^{10}\text{-methenyl tetrahydrofolate} + H_2O \longrightarrow$$

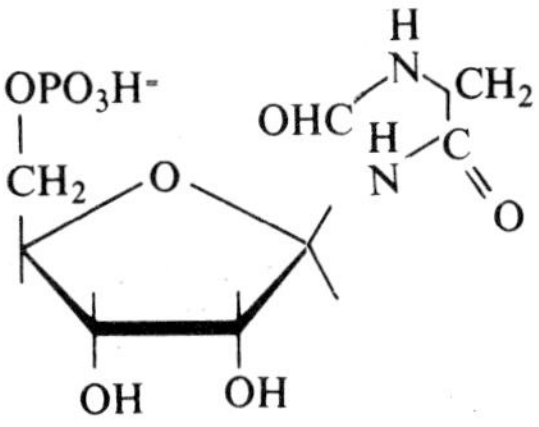

$$\text{(product)} + \text{tetrahydrofolate} + H^+ \quad (18\text{-}4)$$

α-N-formylglycinamide ribonucleotide

A second ATP-dependent amination in which glutamine serves as amine donor is encountered in the transformation of N-formyl glycinamide ribonucleotide to N-formyl glycinamidine ribonucleotide:

$$\alpha\text{-}N\text{-formylglycinamide ribonucleotide} + \text{glutamine} + H_2O + \text{Mg·ATP} \longrightarrow$$

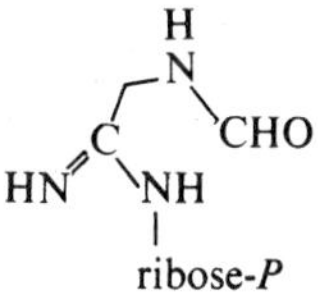

$$\text{(product)} + \text{glutamic acid} + \text{Mg·ADP} + P_i \quad (18\text{-}5)$$

N-formylglycinamidine ribonucleotide

N-formyl glycinamidine ribonucleotide has all the structural features of the imidazole ring of purines. This ring is formed by an ATP-dependent dehydration, yielding 5-aminoimidazole ribonucleotide:

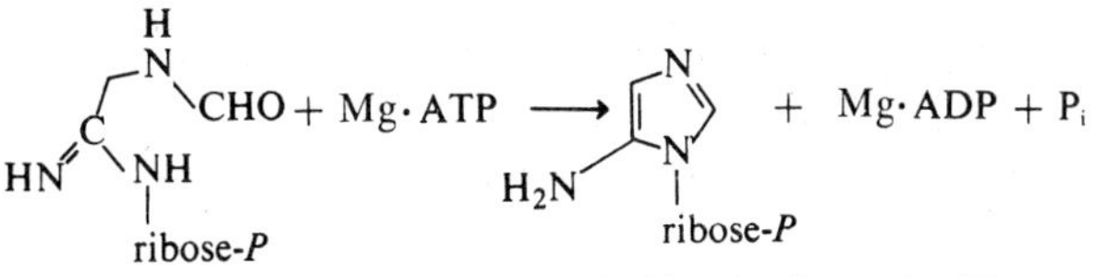

$$\text{(reactant)} + \text{Mg·ATP} \longrightarrow \text{(imidazole product)} + \text{Mg·ADP} + P_i \quad (18\text{-}6)$$

5-Aminoimidazole ribonucleotide

Aminoimidazole ribonucleotide carboxylase catalyzes the carboxylation of the immediate ring-closure product, yielding 5-amino-4-imidazolecarboxylic acid ribonucleotide:

5-Aminoimidazole ribonucleotide $+ CO_2 \rightleftharpoons$

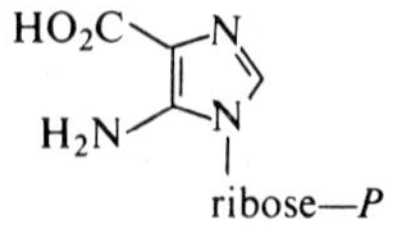

$$
\begin{array}{c}
\text{HO}_2\text{C}\diagdown\diagup\text{N} \\
\text{H}_2\text{N}\diagdown\diagup\text{N} \\
| \\
\text{ribose—}P
\end{array}
\tag{18-7}
$$

5-Aminoimidazole-4-carboxylic
acid ribonucleotide

Bicarbonate, in equilibrium with free carbon dioxide, serves as a source of the carboxylic function.

The conversion of 5-amino-4-imidazolecarboxylic acid ribonucleotide to the corresponding amide, 5-amino-4-imidazole carboxamide ribonucleotide, occurs in a two-step process. First, an amide linkage between the substrate and aspartic acid is introduced in an ATP-dependent process; this produces the intermediate 5-aminoimidazole-4-N-succinocarboxamide ribonucleotide:

5-Aminoimidazole-4-carboxylic acid ribonucleotide + aspartic acid + Mg·ATP $\rightleftharpoons$

$$
\begin{array}{c}
\text{CO}_2\text{H} \\
| \\
\text{CH}_2 \quad \text{O} \\
| \quad\ \text{H} \quad \| \\
\text{H—C—N—C}\diagdown\diagup\text{N} \\
| \qquad\ \ \text{H}_2\text{N}\diagup\text{N} \\
\text{CO}_2\text{H} \qquad\quad | \\
\text{ribose-}P
\end{array}
+ \text{Mg·ADP} + P_i
\tag{18-8}
$$

5-Aminoimidazole-4-N-succinocarboxamide ribonucleotide

This product subsequently undergoes an elimination reaction with the expulsion of fumaric acid.

5-Aminoimidazole-4-N-succinocarboxamide ribonucleotide $\rightleftharpoons$

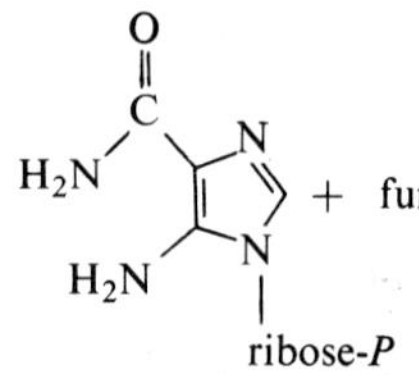

$$
\begin{array}{c}
\text{O} \\
\| \\
\text{C}\diagdown\diagup\text{N} \\
\text{H}_2\text{N} \diagup\ \diagup \diagup\text{N} \\
\text{H}_2\text{N}\diagup\ \ | \\
\text{ribose-}P
\end{array}
+ \text{fumarate}
\tag{18-9}
$$

5-Aminoimidazole-4-carboxamide
ribonucleotide

The last carbon atom required to yield all the elements of the purine ring system is now introduced as a formyl group attached to the 5-amino function of the imidazole carboxamide ribonucleotide:

5-Aminoimidazole-4-carboxamide ribonucleotide + N^{10}-formyl tetrahydrofolic acid $\xrightarrow{K^+}$

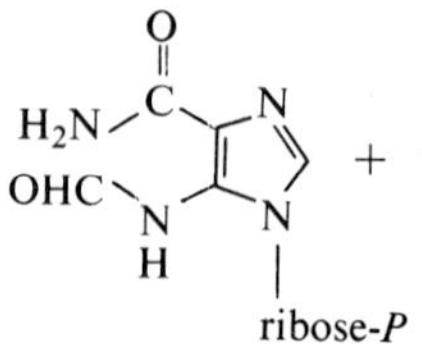

$$
\begin{array}{c}
\text{O} \\
\| \\
\text{H}_2\text{N}\diagup\text{C}\diagdown\diagup\text{N} \\
\text{OHC}\diagdown\ \diagup\diagup\text{N} \\
\quad\ \ \text{N} \ \ | \\
\quad\ \ \text{H} \quad \text{ribose-}P
\end{array}
+ \text{tetrahydrofolic acid}
\tag{18-10}
$$

5-Formamidoimidazole-4-carboxamide
ribonucleotide

This reaction, like the previous formylation in this reaction sequence, involves the participation of a FH_4 coenzyme, but, unlike the previous case, N^{10}-formyl FH_4 is the form of the coenzyme involved.

Ring closure with dehydration, yielding inosinic acid, completes the formation of the purine ring system:

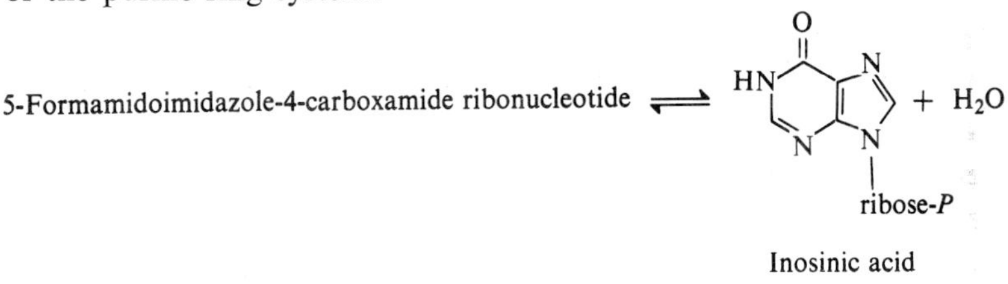

5-Formamidoimidazole-4-carboxamide ribonucleotide $\rightleftharpoons$ [structure] $+ H_2O$

(18-11)

Inosinic acid

It remains only to convert inosinic acid to adenylic and guanylic acids to complete the synthesis of the purine ribonucleotides. The metabolic pathway from ribose-5-phosphate to inosinic acid is summarized in Fig. 18-2. The sources of

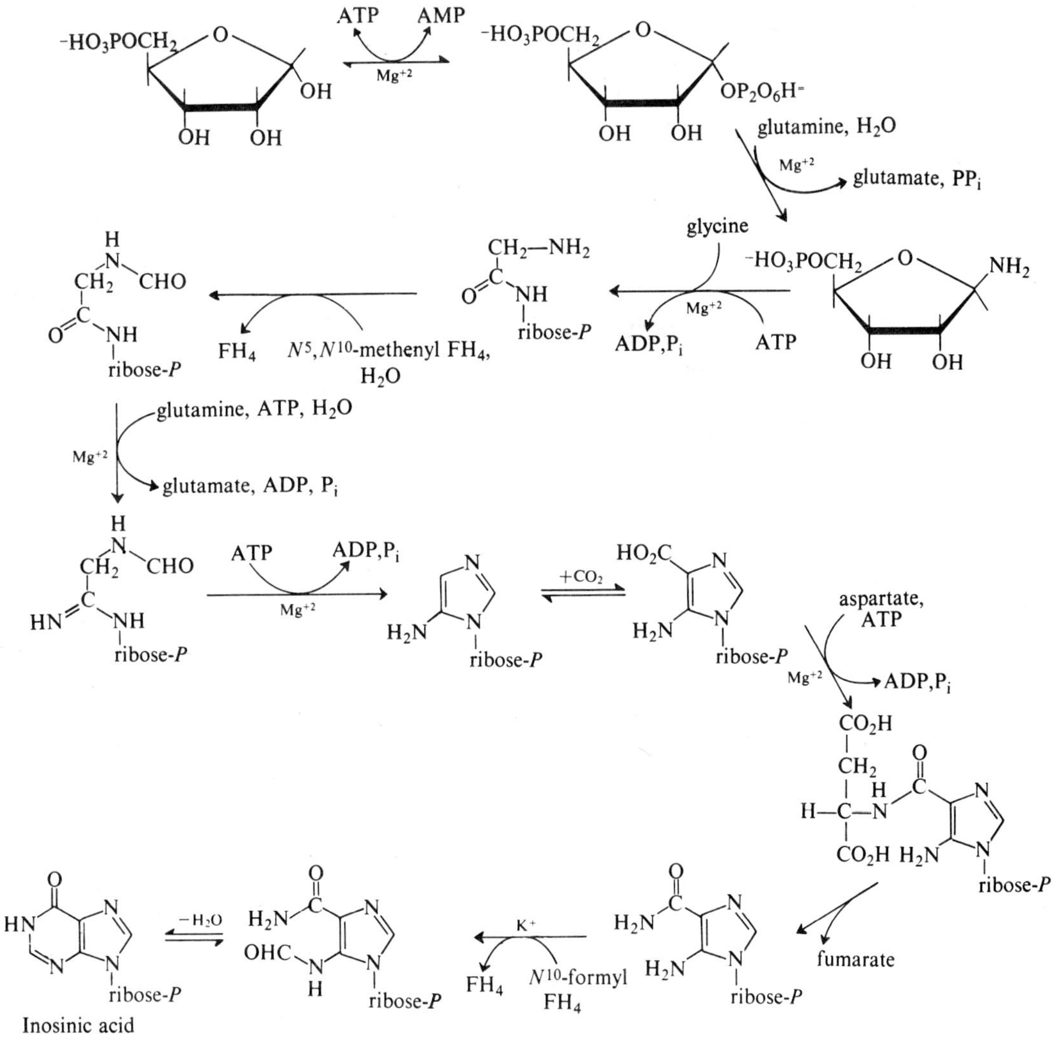

FIGURE 18-2. The Metabolic Pathway Leading to the Synthesis of Inosinic Acid.

the various atoms of the purine ring system as indicated in Fig. 18-1 are correctly accounted for by this pathway.

The biochemical transformations converting inosinic acid to adenylic and guanylic acids are indicated in Fig. 18-3. The amination of inosinic acid to yield

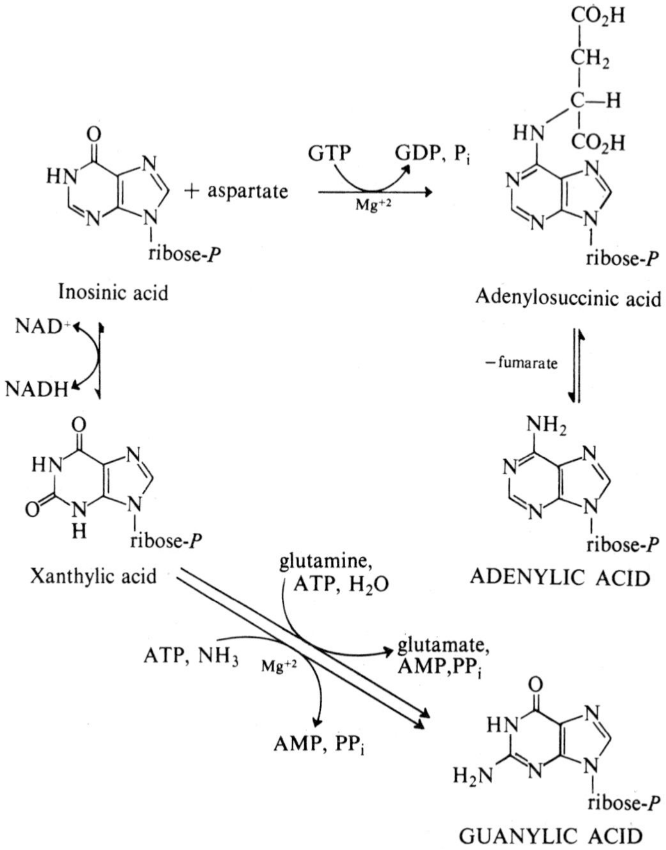

FIGURE 18-3.   The Conversion of Inosinic Acid to Adenylic and Guanylic Acids.

adenylic acid proceeds via a two-step reaction path very similar to that involved in the synthesis of 5-amino-4-imidazolecarboxamide ribonucleotide — Eqs. (18-8) and (18-9). The enzyme catalyzing the elimination of fumaric acid from adenylosuccinate, adenylosuccinase, very probably also catalyzes the analogous reaction indicated above — Eq. (18-9). It is significant that the reaction yielding adenylosuccinic acid, on the pathway to adenine nucleotides, requires GTP as coenzyme. As noted below, a similar situation exists in the synthesis of guanine nucleotides, ATP being required as a coenzyme. A regulatory role is implied in these requirements, since, clearly, an excess of GTP shunts synthesis in the direction of ATP, and conversely, an excess of ATP produces more GTP.

Conversion of inosinic acid to guanylic acid also proceeds in a two-step process. First, xanthylic acid is produced in an oxidation reaction, NAD^+ serving as coenzyme. Second, xanthylic acid is converted to guanylic acid in an ATP-dependent amination reaction. Either glutamine or ammonia serves as amine group donor, depending on the species in which the reaction occurs.

The actual purine precursors of RNA, the nucleoside triphosphates, are formed from the monophosphates by two successive kinase reactions:

$$\text{NMP} \underset{Mg^{+2}}{\overset{\text{ATP} \quad \text{ADP}}{\rightleftharpoons}} \text{NDP} \underset{Mg^{+2}}{\overset{\text{ATP} \quad \text{ADP}}{\rightleftharpoons}} \text{NTP} \qquad (18\text{-}12)$$

The kinases responsible for catalyzing these reactions are not specific for the base, and they phosphorylate adenine, guanine, uracil, or cytosine nucleotides. These reactions clearly do not account for net synthesis of ATP. This triphosphate is derived, of course, as the end product of exergonic oxidation reactions.

Pyrimidines A central distinction between the metabolic routes leading to the formation of purine and pyrimidine nucleotides is timing in the formation of the N-glycosidic bond. In purine synthesis, this link is formed in the very early steps, and the ring system is built upon this foundation. In contrast, the complete pyrimidine nucleus is synthesized prior to its attachment to ribose-5-phosphate. The key intermediate introduced into the N-glycosidic linkage is orotic acid, which contains the pyrimidine nucleus:

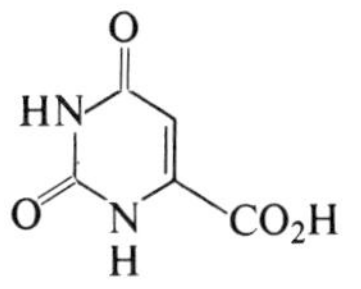

Orotic acid

The initial step for pyrimidine biosynthesis is the formation of carbamyl phosphate, an important intermediate in other respects as well. Of the known routes leading to the formation of carbamyl phosphate, the synthesis from ammonia, carbon dioxide, and ATP is certainly the most important. This synthesis assumes two forms. In *microorganisms* carbamate kinase catalyzes the reaction indicated below:

$$\text{NH}_2\text{CO}_2^- + \text{ATP} \rightleftharpoons \text{H}_2\text{N}-\overset{\overset{\text{O}}{\|}}{\text{C}}-\text{OPO}_3\text{H}_2 + \text{ADP}$$
$$\text{Carbamyl phosphate} \qquad (18\text{-}13)$$

The equilibrium position for this reaction lies well to the left, consistent with the "energy-rich" nature of carboxylic-phosphoric acid anhydrides. The rate of this reaction is unaffected by the presence of acyl glutamates.

In contrast, the synthesis of carbamyl phosphate, catalyzed by *carbamyl phosphate synthetase*, which is the only route in *mammalian* systems, occurs with the stoichiometry indicated below:

$$\text{CO}_2 + \text{NH}_3 + 2\text{ATP} \xrightarrow{\overset{\text{acetyl}}{\text{glutamate}}} \text{H}_2\text{N}-\overset{\overset{\text{O}}{\|}}{\text{C}}-\text{OPO}_3\text{H}_2 + 2\text{ADP} + \text{P}_i \qquad (18\text{-}14)$$

This reaction is largely irreversible and requires N-acetyl glutamate or a related substance as coenzyme. In microoganisms there occurs a similar reaction, but here glutamine — which is converted to glutamate in the course of the reaction — is required as an activator.

In the second step of pyrimidine biosynthesis, the carbamyl phosphate donates its carbamyl moiety to the α-amino group of aspartate in a reaction catalyzed by *aspartate-carbamyl transferase*:

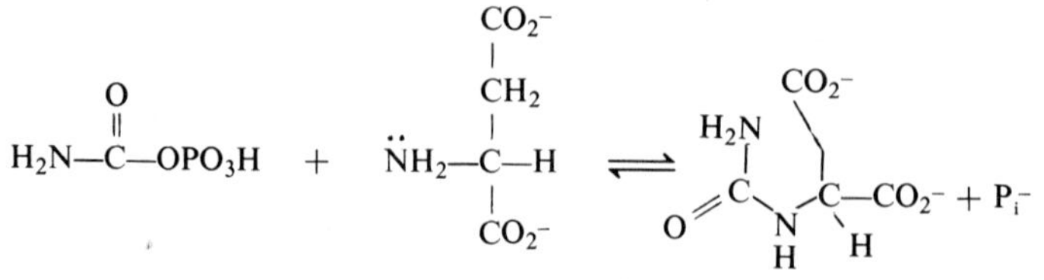

$$H_2N-\overset{\overset{O}{\|}}{C}-OPO_3H \;+\; \overset{..}{N}H_2-\overset{\overset{\displaystyle CO_2^-}{|}\overset{\displaystyle CH_2}{|}}{\underset{\underset{\displaystyle CO_2^-}{|}}{C}}-H \;\rightleftharpoons\; \text{Carbamyl aspartate} \;+\; P_i^-$$

(18-15)

Carbamyl aspartate

Carbamyl aspartate is converted to dihydroorotic acid in a reversible cyclo-dehydration catalyzed by *dihydroorotase*:

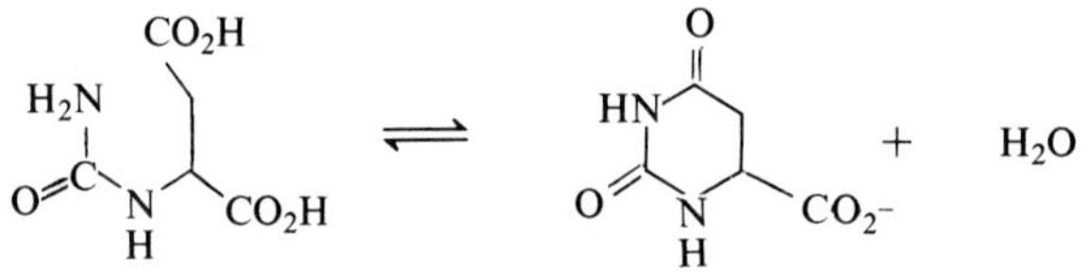

$$\rightleftharpoons \quad \text{Dihydroorotic acid} \;+\; H_2O$$

(18-16)

Dihydroorotic acid

This substrate is subsequently oxidized to orotic acid by *dihydroorotic dehydrogenase*, a flavoprotein (see page 351), in a pyridine coenzyme–linked reaction:

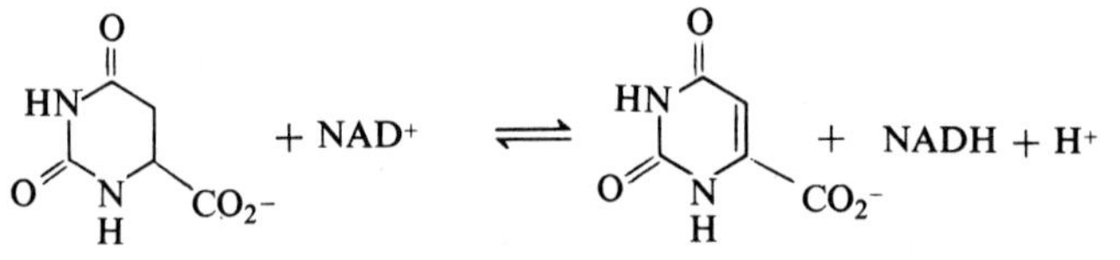

$$+\; NAD^+ \quad\rightleftharpoons\quad \text{Orotic acid} \;+\; NADH + H^+$$

(18-17)

Orotic acid

The synthesis of the pyrimidine ring is now complete, and attachment of ribose-5′-phosphate is the next concern. This is accomplished by coupling orotic acid to PRPP in a reaction catalyzed by *orotidine-5′-phosphate pyrophosphorylase*:

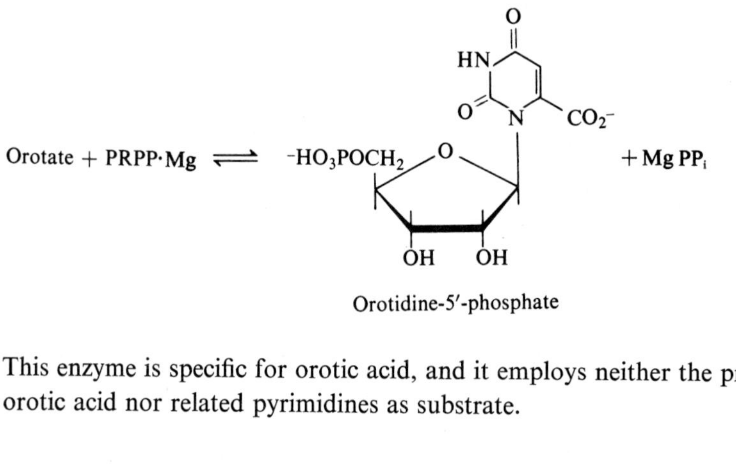

$$\text{Orotate} + \text{PRPP·Mg} \;\rightleftharpoons\; ^-HO_3POCH_2 \cdots \text{(Orotidine-5′-phosphate)} \;+\; \text{Mg PP}_i$$

(18-18)

Orotidine-5′-phosphate

This enzyme is specific for orotic acid, and it employs neither the precursors to orotic acid nor related pyrimidines as substrate.

The synthesis of uridylic acid (UMP) is completed by the irreversible decarboxylation of orotidine-5′-phosphate by an appropriate decarboxylase:

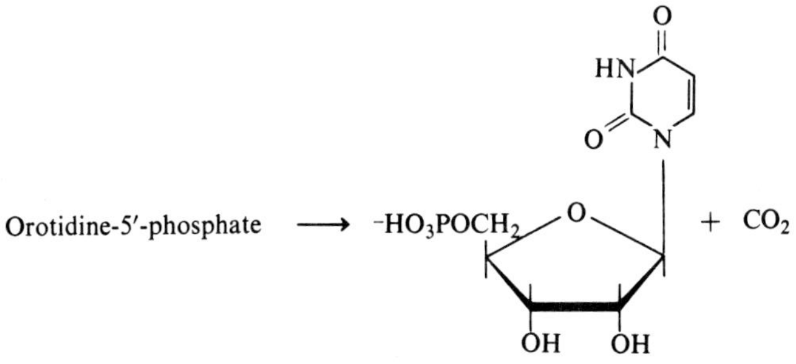

$$\text{Orotidine-5′-phosphate} \longrightarrow \text{-HO}_3\text{POCH}_2 \quad + \text{ CO}_2 \qquad (18\text{-}19)$$

Uridylic acid

Isotopically labeled orotic acid is incorporated, in vivo, much more rapidly into RNA-uracil than into RNA-cytosine. This observation suggests that uridine nucleotides are intermediates in the conversion of orotic acid into cytidine nucleotides. Indeed, the only known pathway for the formation of cytidine nucleotides involves the amination of UTP:

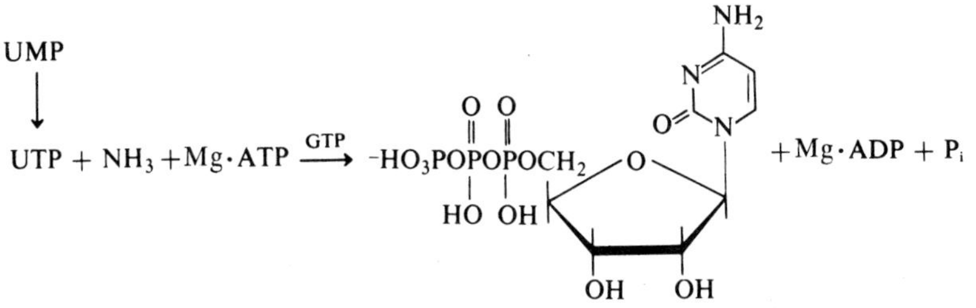

UMP

$$\text{UTP} + \text{NH}_3 + \text{Mg·ATP} \xrightarrow{\text{GTP}} \text{-HO}_3\text{POPOPOCH}_2 \quad + \text{Mg·ADP} + \text{P}_i \qquad (18\text{-}20)$$

Cytidine triphosphate

UTP is formed from UMP by successive kinase reactions as indicated in Eq. (18-12). The reactions leading to the formation of uridine and cytidine nucleotides are summarized in Fig. 18-4.

BIOSYNTHESIS OF DEOXYNUCLEOSIDE TRIPHOSPHATES

The most straightforward means by which the deoxynucleoside triphosphates might be presumed to arise are by reduction of the corresponding ribonucleoside polyphosphates or by metabolic routes parallel to those previously discussed but employing the reduced sugar moiety. That the former possibility is correct, a supposition not necessarily excluding a minor contribution from the latter pathway, was initially suggested by the following experiment. Cytidine, labeled uniformly in all carbon atoms with C^{14}, was injected into rats and, after a suitable time period, the DNA-cytidine was isolated and examined. The ratio of radioactivity, 0.80, in the base and sugar moieties of the isolated deoxycytidine was identical to that of the administered material. This experiment indicates that the cytidine was incorporated into the DNA without cleavage of the glycosidic bond. Thus the reduction of cytidine to deoxycytidine must have occurred at the nucleoside or nucleotide level of organization and not at the sugar level.

The enzymatic reduction of ribonucleotides by extracts of *E. coli* has been carefully examined by Reichard and his associates. The principal conclusions derived from this work include the following. First, the substrates for reduction are the diphosphates. Second, ATP, Mg^{+2}, NADPH, two enzymes, and a sulfhydryl protein cofactor are required for reaction. Third, the immediate hydrogen donor for the reaction is the reduced, sulfhydryl form of the protein cofactor. This cofactor has been termed *thioredoxin*. In the course of the reduction, thio-

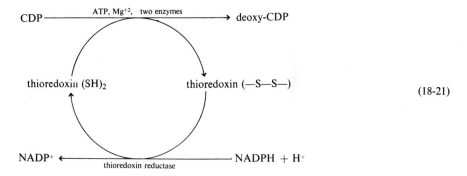

FIGURE 18-4. Metabolic Pathway Leading to the Synthesis of Uridine and Cytidine Nucleotides.

redoxin is converted to a disulfide form. Fourth, the reduced form of thioredoxin is regenerated by reduction of the disulfide form in an NADPH-dependent process catalyzed by thioredoxin reductase. These interconversions are summarized in Eq. (18-21).

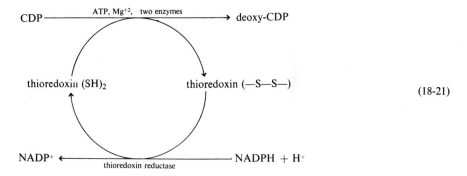

(18-21)

Biosynthesis of Thymidylate

Metabolic routes for the production of the nucleotides and deoxynucleotides of adenine, guanine, uracil, and cytosine have just been discussed. In addition to these species, *thymidylic acid*, a major constituent of nearly all DNA, and *5-hydroxymethyldeoxycytidylic acid*, which replaces thymine in the DNA of the T-even bacteriophages, must be accounted for.

A priori thymidylic acid could arise from uridylic acid by either (1) reduction followed by methylation or (2) methylation followed by reduction. The observation that deoxyuridine is a far better precursor than uridine for the synthesis of DNA-thymidylic acid suggests that the former alternative is correct. The complete *de novo* pathway for thymidylic acid synthesis is $CMP \rightarrow CDP \rightarrow dCDP \rightarrow dCMP \rightarrow dUMP \rightarrow dTMP$.

Thymidylate synthetase from *E. coli* catalyzes the synthesis of thymidylic acid according to the following stoichiometry:

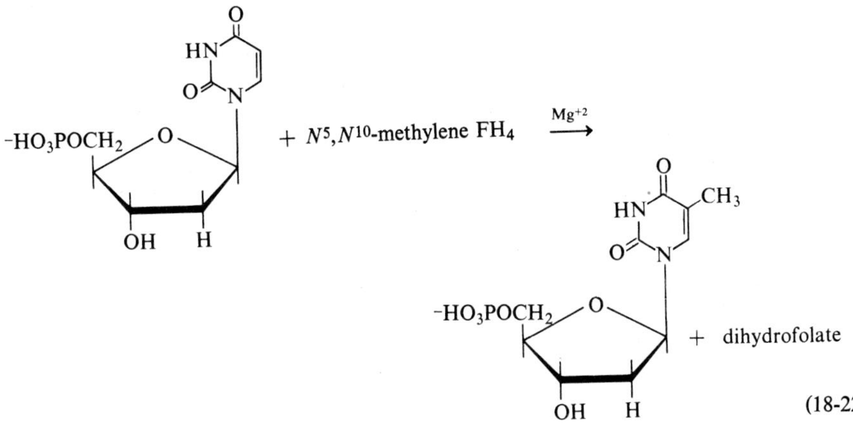

$$(18\text{-}22)$$

In this reaction, FH_4 serves a dual function in that it acts as both carrier of the one-carbon fragment and as reducing agent. The transfer of hydrogen from the pteridine ring system of FH_4 to the methyl group of thymidylate is direct, as revealed by the incorporation of one atom of tritium into the methyl group when tritiated FH_4 is employed as coenzyme:

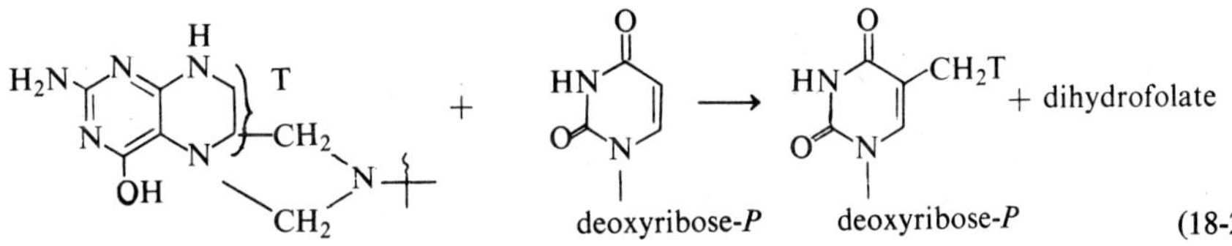

$$(18\text{-}23)$$

Hydroxymethyldeoxycytidylic acid is derived from the parent compound in a reaction that also involves the participation of N^5,N^{10}-methylene FH_4 as a donor of a one-carbon fragment:

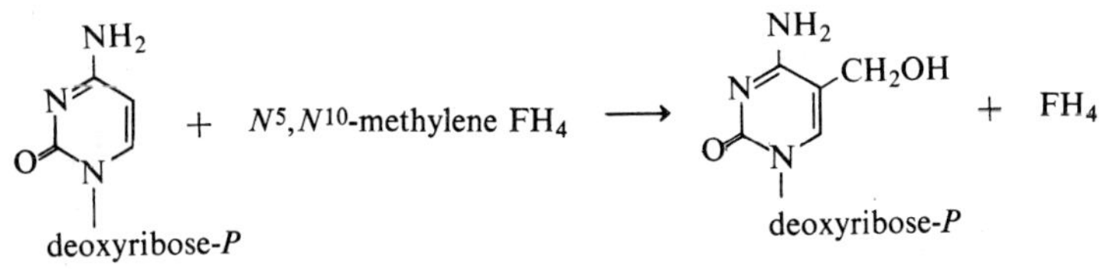

$$(18\text{-}24)$$

In this case, reduction does not accompany carbon transfer.

Ribothymidylic acid occurs as a minor constituent in tRNA. Its synthesis occurs as the organizational level of the intact tRNA molecule. *S*-adenosyl methionine (see page 427) acts as methyl group donor to tRNA-uracil groups with the resultant formation of tRNA-thymine functions. The same situation also prevails with regard to the methylation of other bases in both RNA and DNA.

Alternate Pathways
for the Biosynthesis
of Nucleotides

The pathways described above almost certainly represent the major routes by which purine and pyrimidine nucleotides are synthesized. However, additional routes for the formation of these structures are known. These appear to be "salvage" mechanisms and are employed to utilize exogenous sources of preformed bases or endogenous sources for this purpose.

In the liver, specific pyrophosphorylases catalyze the formation of purine nucleotides from the free base and PRPP:

$$\text{Purine} + \text{PRPP} \rightleftharpoons \text{purine ribonucleotide} + \text{PP}_i \tag{18-25}$$

A corresponding reaction employing uracil as substrate has been identified in microorganisms:

$$\text{Uracil} + \text{PRPP} \rightleftharpoons \text{uridylic acid} + \text{PP}_i \tag{18-26}$$

In addition, nucleoside phosphorylases catalyze the formation of nucleosides from the bases and ribose-l-phosphate:

$$\text{Base} + \begin{array}{c}\text{(ribose structure: CH}_2\text{OH, O, OPO}_3\text{H}^-, \text{OH OH)}\end{array} \rightleftharpoons \begin{array}{c}\text{(ribonucleoside structure: CH}_2\text{OH, O, base, OH OH)}\end{array} + \text{P}_i \tag{18-27}$$

The nucleosides are converted to the nucleotides through the action of an appropriate kinase:

$$\text{Ribonucleoside} + \text{ATP} \rightarrow \text{ribonucleotide} + \text{ADP} \tag{18-28}$$

REGULATION OF
PYRIMIDINE AND
PURINE BIO-
SYNTHESIS

The synthesis of both pyrimidines and purines is under metabolic control involving both feedback inhibition and feedback repression by end products.

In pyrimidine biosynthesis, the primary site of control is the enzyme aspartate transcarbamylase, responsible for catalyzing the initial reaction concerned solely with assembling the pyrimidines. The type and specificity of control exhibit an interesting variation with species. Aspartate transcarbamylases from *E. coli*, *A. aerogenes*, and *Serratia marcescens* are all subject to feedback inhibition by CTP, whereas that from *P. fluorescens* is most strongly inhibited by UTP and that from lettuce seedlings is most sensitive to UMP. Furthermore, aspartate transcarbamylase from *B. subtilis* seems not to be subject to feedback inhibition at all but is subject to feedback repression. These results certainly demonstrate the versatility and species specificity of cellular control mechanisms.

Regulation of the synthesis of the purines is both complex and elegant. The principal facts are the following. First, IMP-dehydrogenase, which is involved in the conversion of IMP to GMP (see Fig. 18-3), is subject to feedback inhibition by GMP and to repression by guanine. Hence, the IMP-to-GMP conversion is retarded or stopped under conditions in which adequate supplies of the guanine nucleotides are available. Second, the GMP reductase system, which catalyzes the reduction of GMP to IMP and permits utilization of GMP for synthesis of AMP, is inhibited by ATP. Hence, an adequate supply of adenine nucleotides inhibits synthesis of these compounds at the expense of the guanine nucleotides.

Third, as mentioned above, the formation of AMP and GMP is further regulated in that ATP is required for synthesis of GMP and GTP is required for synthesis of AMP. These controls ensure that conversion of IMP to the adenine or guanine nucleotides occurs in conformance with the requirements of the cell. If an excess of one type is present intracellularly, then there is no necessary requirement for *de novo* synthesis of the purines at all, since the adenine and guanine nucleotides are interconvertible. Another control mechanism exists for this situation, since both adenine and guanine nucleotides are inhibitors of glutamine phosphoribosylpyrophosphate amidotransferase, the enzyme catalyzing the initial step in purine synthesis. These control mechanisms are depicted schematically in Fig. 18-5.

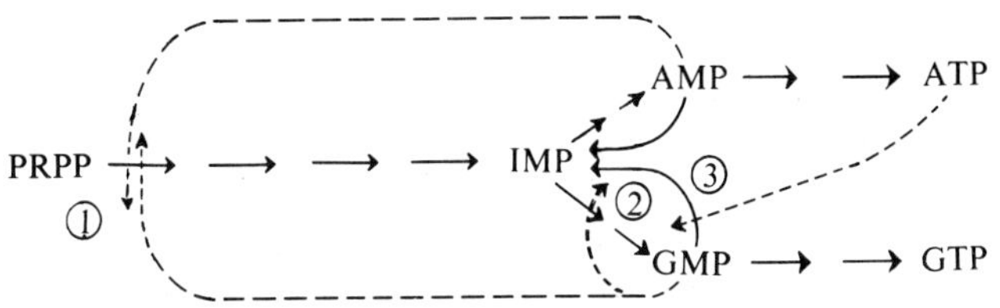

FIGURE 18-5.   A Schematic Representation of Control of Purine Biosynthesis.
The dashed lines indicate regulatory pathways. (1) is glutamine phosphoribosylpyrophosphate amidotransferase; (2) is IMP dehydrogenase; and (3) is GMP reductase system.— *B. Magasanik, in McElroy and Glass (eds.), "The Chemical Basis of Development," Johns Hopkins Press, Baltimore, 1959.*

CATABOLISM OF PURINES

The extent of degradation of the purine ring system varies greatly from species to species. In man and other primates, the principal excretory product resulting from purine catabolism is uric acid, in which the purine ring system is intact, whereas in some marine invertebrates, ammonia and carbon dioxide are the end products.

An important intermediate in purine catabolism is xanthine. Following cleavage of the *N*-glycosidic bond, guanine is converted in one step to xanthine by the hydrolytic enzyme *guanase*:

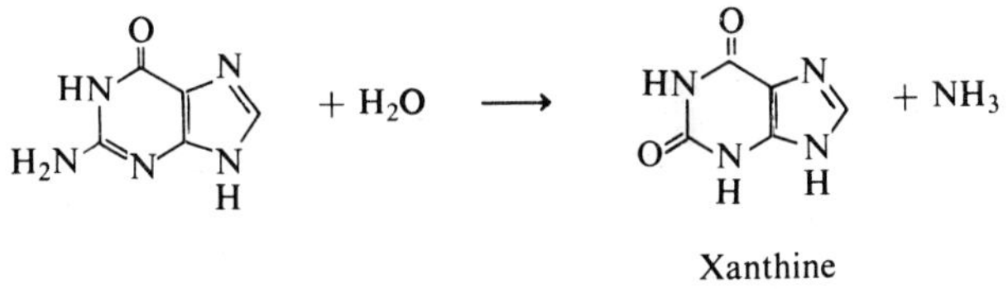

$$+ H_2O \longrightarrow \qquad + NH_3 \qquad (18\text{-}29)$$

Xanthine

The degradation of adenine derivatives in mammals and birds occurs with deamination of adenosine and adenylic acid, followed by conversion to hypoxanthine:

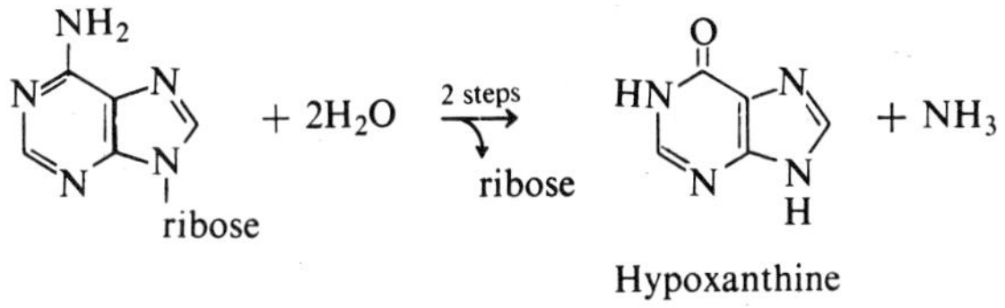

$$+ 2H_2O \xrightarrow{\text{2 steps}} \qquad + NH_3 \qquad (18\text{-}30)$$

Hypoxanthine

Hypoxanthine is converted to xanthine and subsequently to uric acid by the enzyme *xanthine oxidase*:

Hypoxanthine $+ O_2 + H_2O \longrightarrow$ xanthine $+ H_2O_2$

(18-31)

Xanthine $+ O_2 + H_2O \longrightarrow$

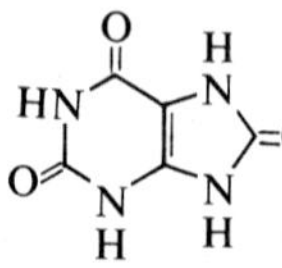

$+ H_2O_2$

(18-32)

Uric acid

The disease gout, which occurs principally in males, is the apparent result of an overproduction of uric acid. This results in the deposition of the rather insoluble salt sodium urate in the form of crystals (tophi) in the cartilage, accounting for the extreme and characteristic sensitivity of the joints.

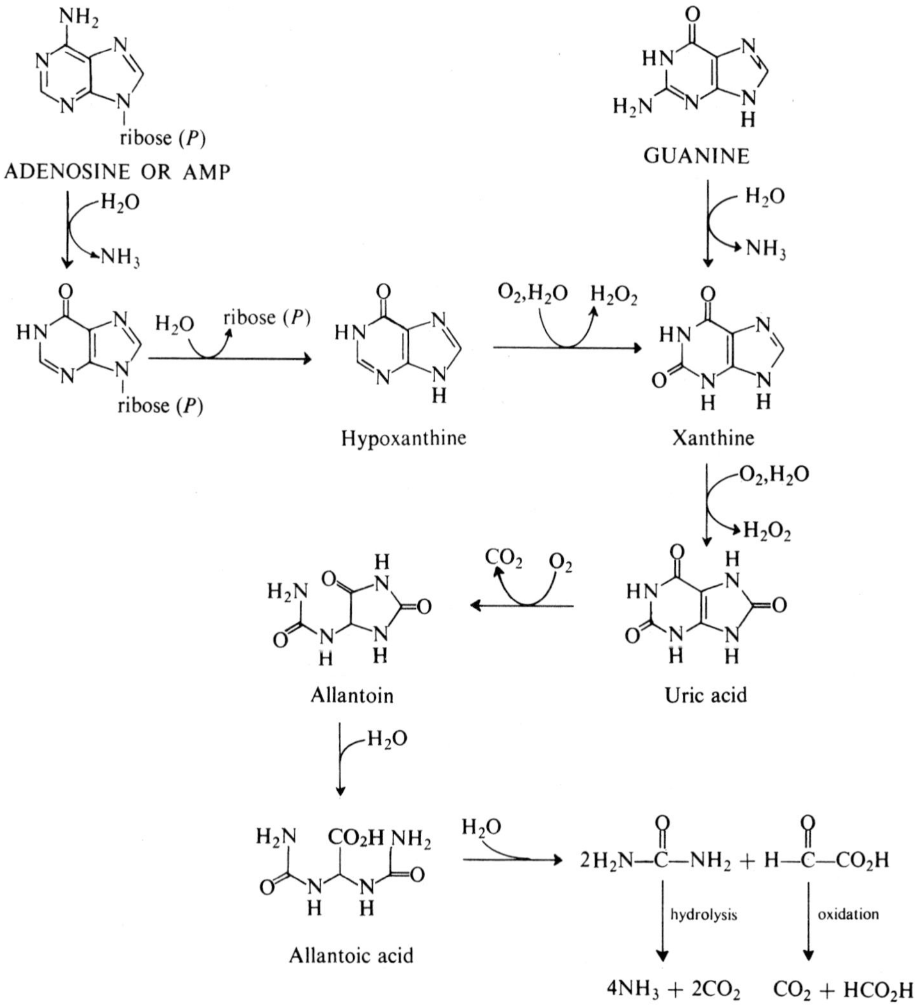

FIGURE 18-6.   The Metabolic Route for the Degradation of Purines.

In most species in which uric acid is not the final excretory product of purine metabolism, it is oxidized to allantoin, with the loss of carbon dioxide:

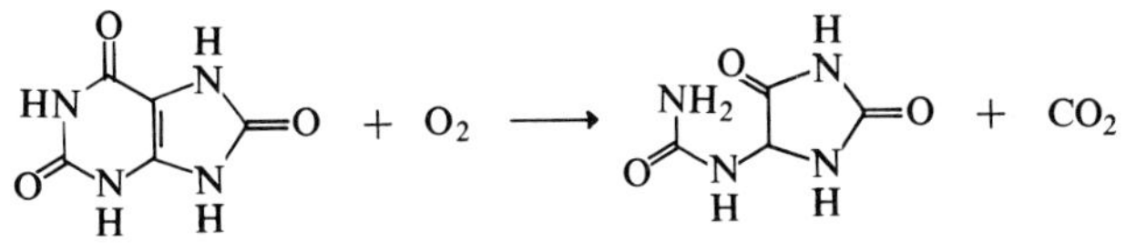

$$\text{(uric acid)} + O_2 \longrightarrow \text{(allantoin)} + CO_2 \tag{18-33}$$

Allantoin

The enzyme responsible for catalyzing this transformation, *uricase*, is a copper protein (see page 347). Allantoin, the excretory product of purine catabolism in mammals other than man and in some reptiles, undergoes an *allantoinase*-catalyzed hydrolysis, yielding allantoic acid:

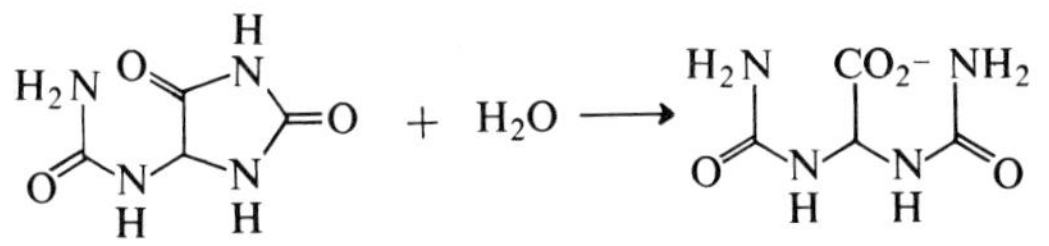

$$\text{(allantoin)} + H_2O \longrightarrow \text{(allantoic acid)} \tag{18-34}$$

Allantoic acid

This product is excreted by some teleost fishes, but in most species it is further hydrolyzed to urea and glyoxylic acid by the enzyme *allantoicase*:

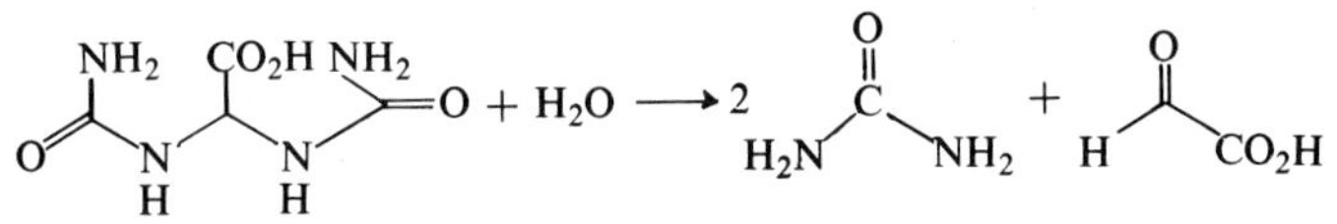

$$\text{(allantoic acid)} + H_2O \longrightarrow 2\ \underset{H_2N}{\overset{O}{\underset{\|}{C}}}_{NH_2} + \underset{H}{\overset{O}{C}}_{CO_2H} \tag{18-35}$$

In most fishes and amphibia purine degradation stops at this stage. In a few cases, as noted above, urea is further cleaved to yield carbon dioxide and ammonia. The metabolic route for the complete degradation of the purines is summarized in Fig. 18-6.

REFERENCES   Brachet, J.: "The Biological Role of Ribonucleic Acids," Elsevier, New York, 1960.

Buchanan, J. M., and S. C. Hartman: Enzymatic Reactions in the Synthesis of the Purines, *Advan. Enzymol.*, **21**: 199 (1959).

Davidson, J. N.: "The Biochemistry of the Nucleic Acids," Methuen London, 1960.

"Progress in Nucleic Acid Research," Academic Press, New York. A continued series of volumes containing review articles pertinent to the nucleic acids.

Reichard, P.: The Enzymatic Synthesis of Pyrimidines, *Advan. Enzymol.*, **21**: 263 (1959).

Schmidt, G.: Metabolism of Nucleic Acids, *Ann. Rev. Biochem.*, **33**: 667 (1964).

19 | Nature and Function of the Gene

The questions with which genetics has been traditionally concerned are the following: what is the nature, the organization, and the mode of self-duplication of the substance(s) that transmit information from parent to progeny, generation after generation, in a form so precise as to allow only a negligible amount of alteration in the final product? How can they permit equal fidelity in specification and information transfer from generation to generation for an altered product formed as a result of an initial alteration in the appropriate determinant? What is the nature of the processes by which the genetic determinants find their expression in determining all the chemical, metabolic, and morphological characteristics of any cell, of all organisms? In this chapter we shall briefly examine the evidence that proves that DNA is the genetic material of all cellular organisms and that its role as genetic determinant is expressed by virtue of its specification of the proteins in these organisms. This process is now known to be mediated by three different species of RNA. Gene duplication thus requires DNA synthesis, and gene action RNA and protein synthesis. The biosynthesis of nucleic acids is discussed in Chap. 20, and Chap. 21 is devoted to a consideration of the biosynthesis of proteins.

Before embarking on a brief discussion of molecular or biochemical genetics, we direct our attention to classical genetics, but only in so far as it allows us to define operationally a number of terms that we shall use in the remainder of the chapter. Of necessity our account will be rudimentary.

CLASSICAL
GENETICS

Mendelian Genetics. Mendel, the originator of the science, performed his experiments with 22 true-breeding strains of the garden pea (*Pisum sativum*). His conclusions were as follows. Provided that both parents came from the same strain, all descendants completely resembled these parents with respect to one of several easily distinguishable external characteristics, or *phenotypes*. Now let us perform a hypothetical experiment similar to one of Mendel's called a *genetic cross*, in which we mate two parents belonging to two different strains of different genetic constitution, or *genotype*. Let us cross one parent with a purple flower with one that produces white flowers. What is the result? The offspring called the *first filial*, or F_1, generation, consists exclusively, not of pink or of mottled, but of purple flowers. We say that the trait for purple is *dominant*; conversely, that for white, or the absence of purple, is *recessive*. Quite generally this is what was observed by Mendel for each of the seven traits examined by him: all the members of the F_1 generation always resembled either one parent or the other. There was no hybrid phenotype. What happens if we cross two members of the F_1 generation with each other and analyze the property of the resulting F_2 generation? The two traits now *segregate*, and we observe both types of plants, those with purple and those with white flowers, in the precise ratio of 3 : 1, provided that we examine a reasonably large number of progeny. How can we explain these results? Mendel reasoned — and this reasoning has been borne out by countless subsequent experiments and by the remarkable coherence and self-consistency of the whole edifice of Mendelian genetics built thereon — that we have the following sequence of events:

1. In the parental, or F_0, generation, the hereditary determinants for the genetic locus of flower color can exist in two and only two stable alternative forms, or *alleles*, the *homozygous* allele for purple, or *PP*, and the equally homozygous allele for white, or *pp*. These alleles segregate independently during formation of the gametes, the male and female germ cells, and are recombined at fertilization.

2. In the hybrid F_1 generation we have formed *heterozygotes*, i.e., hybrids of unstable alleles, *Pp* or *pP*. Since *P* is dominant over the recessive *p*, the phenotypic expression of this particular genotype is purple, and thus indistinguishable from that characteristic of the *PP* parent.

3. A distinction becomes possible, however, by the cross of the F_1 hybrids with themselves, or by backcrosses with the white parents. The two alleles again segregate independently into their unit factors *P* and *p*, and we observe, after recombination, their appropriate phenotypes expressed thus — (pu) stands for the purple, (w) for the white, phenotype:

$$\begin{array}{c} PP \\ (pu) \end{array} \times \begin{array}{c} pp \\ (w) \end{array} = \begin{array}{c} Pp \\ (pu) \end{array} + \begin{array}{c} pP \\ (pu) \end{array} \qquad \begin{array}{c} Pp \\ (pu) \end{array} \times \begin{array}{c} pP \\ (pu) \end{array} = \begin{array}{c|c|c} & P & p \\ \hline P & PP(\text{pu}) & Pp(\text{pu}) \\ \hline p & pP(\text{pu}) & pp(\text{w}) \end{array}$$

$$Pp \times pp = \begin{array}{c|c|c} & p & p \\ \hline P & Pp(\text{pu}) & Pp(\text{pu}) \\ \hline p & pp(\text{w}) & pp(\text{w}) \end{array} \qquad Pp \times PP = \begin{array}{c|c|c} & P & P \\ \hline P & PP(\text{pu}) & PP(\text{pu}) \\ \hline p & pP(\text{pu}) & pP(\text{pu}) \end{array}$$

In an analogous fashion strains were crossed that differed in two separate traits. The first, say, yellow flower (ye), was carried by the allele, *Y*, dominant over green (gr), carried by the allele *y* of the same unit factor; the second, say, appearance of seed, was carried by the allele S for smooth (sm), dominant over the allele s for wrinkled (wr). The cross of the two genotypes $PPSS \times ppss$ yielded a uniform F_1 generation with phenotype yellow and smooth, determined by the genotype $PpSs$. Members of this generation were then crossed to produce an F_2 generation. We observe progeny with various traits in the following distribution, on the average: nine yellow-smooth, three green-smooth, three yellow-wrinkled, and one green-wrinkled. Constructing the matrix governing a re-assortment of units segregating independently and randomly, we would predict that the following statistics would result in complete agreement with the experiments:

	YS	Ys	yS	ys
YS	YS YS(ye-sm)	YS Ys(ye-sm)	YSyS(ye-sm)	YSys(ye-sm)
Ys	Ys YS(ye-sm)	Ys Ys(ye-wr)	YsyS(ye-sm)	Ysys(ye-wr)
yS	yS YS(ye-sm)	yS Ys(ye-sm)	ySyS(gr-sm)	ySys(gr-sm)
ys	ysYS(ye-sm)	ys Ys(ye-wr)	ysyS(gr-sm)	ysys(gr-wr)

The model that emerged from these studies, a purely formal and statistical one, envisaged the *unit factors* involved as separate, indivisible *units of segregation*, capable of existing in two or more completely and sharply defined configurations or allelic forms and of being transmitted and recombined in complete independence of any other. Following a suggestion by Johannsen in 1911, these unit factors were called *genes*.

Linkage. Soon Mendel's conclusions were checked by studies with other organisms, especially with the fruit fly *Drosophila melanogaster* performed by Thomas Hunt Morgan. It was found that Mendel's conclusions had to be modified in one important respect. Frequently genes did not appear to be assorted and transmitted independently but acted as if they were formally linked to one another. Different genes appeared to fall within several groups. All those within any one of the *linkage groups* appeared to be transmitted together to a varying degree, yet were transmitted independently of the members of a second group, and so forth. Within any one linkage group the genes could be ordered in a linear manner so that their separation on this one-dimensional *genetic map* was directly proportional to their *recombination frequency*, i.e., the ratio formed by multiplying the number of joint appearances of any pair of genes by 100 and dividing by the total progeny. On the map short distances correspond to un-common recombinational events and long distances to frequent occurrences. Thus the map is composed of a number of *genetic loci* arranged in linear array, with each new locus fixed or ordered into the array by means of two-factor crosses with genetic markers, say, A or B, whose position on the map had been established previously. Obviously the map so constructed (see Fig. 19-1) must be internally consistent such that, with the marker X located between A and B, the distances $A \to X$ plus $X \to B$ must add up to $A \to B$. The genes, therefore, become elements of recombination that can be localized at definite loci along a linear map.

Mutation. In classical genetics a mutation, a phenomenon first observed by De Vries, is defined as an abrupt or discontinuous change from one allelic form to another, thus producing a visible alteration of phenotype (see Fig. 19-1b).

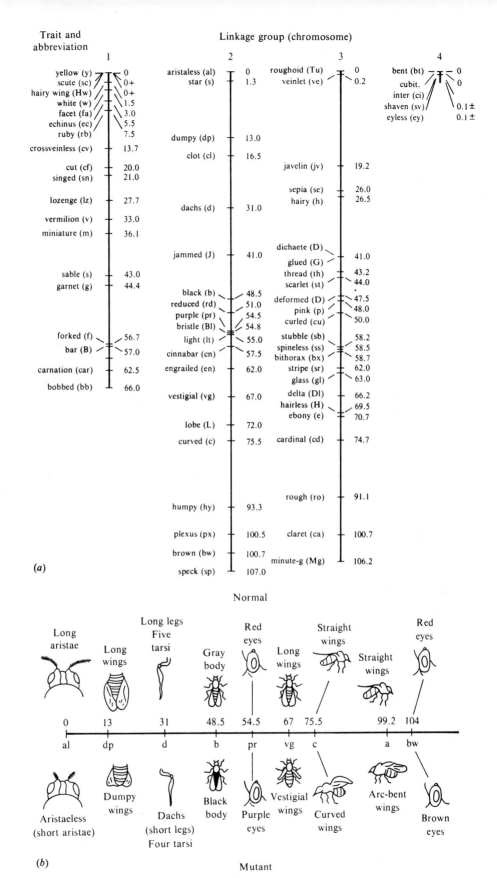

FIGURE 19-1. (a) Linkage Map for *Drosophila* Showing Four Linkage Groups (Chromosomes). (b) A portion of the genetic map of *Drosophila* (chromosome 2).—From C. B. Anfinsen, "*The Molecular Basis of Evolution*," Wiley, New York, 1959.

Mutations can arise spontaneously, i.e., be manifest by the existence of the allelic forms in the preexisting population, as was the case with Mendel's peas. Mutations can also be induced by various mutagenic agents, or *mutagens*, such as certain chemicals (see page 135) or, as discovered by Muller, by irradiation with X rays. Were it not for mutations, the observations on which genetics rests could never have been made.

The Physical Basis of Classical Genetics: Chromosomes as Linkage Groups. Morgan's investigations also led him to another important conclusion. The number of linkage groups in *Drosophila* corresponded precisely to the number of chromosomes in the nuclei of somatic cells of this organism. The chromosomes of the salivary glands are abnormally large and quite readily studied in the light microscope. Furthermore, various mutations operationally defined originally in purely genetic terms, as distinct phenotypic traits caused by configurational changes in the alleles of various hypothetical genes, now produced observable alterations in the appearance of distinct small regions of the chromosomes. Finally, the order of these morphologically distinct regions on the chromosome was the same as the order of the mutational loci on the genetic map (see Fig. 19-2).[1]

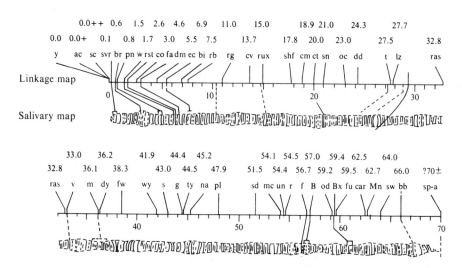

FIGURE 19-2.   Arrangement of Genetic Determinants on Salivary Chromosomes.
Microscopic appearance of a salivary chromosome of *Drosophila.—From C. B. Anfinsen, "The Molecular Basis of Evolution," Wiley, New York, 1959.*

Thus we can say that the genetic map is an analogue of the chromosome map, or that there is an approximate colinearity of the two maps. Finally Morgan also provided a physical explanation of linkage in terms of the phenomena of *chiasmata* and *crossing over* occurring during cell division, which are discussed in all texts on genetics.

Haploid Organisms. Although classical genetics was concerned chiefly with diploid, higher organisms, both animal, such as *Drosophila*, and plant, such as

---

[1] Map distance cannot be brought into precise one-to-one correspondence with chromosome distance, since multiple crossovers occur and chromosomes break during cell division.

corn, most recent revolutionary advances have come from studies on certain unicellular microorganisms. The favorite organisms have been the bread mold *Neurospora crassa*, the fungus *Aspergillus niger*, the bacteria *Salmonella typhimurium* and *Escherichia coli*, and certain bacteriophages, which utilize the last named bacterium as a host. All these organisms have the property in common that in their usual vegetative state they are haploid, i.e., contain but a single chromosome (viruses, bacteria) or set of chromosomes (fungi, molds, e.g., *Neurospora*).

How is exchange of genetic material brought about in such organisms, which largely or entirely propagate their kind by simple asexual division? In certain rare instances in bacteria — for example, the unique K12 strain of *E. coli*, originally discovered by Tatum and Lederberg — two mating types, called F^+ (males) and F^- (females), do exist. The male F^+ cell has an infectious and dominant sex factor, or *F agent*, that can be transmitted to F^- cells on direct

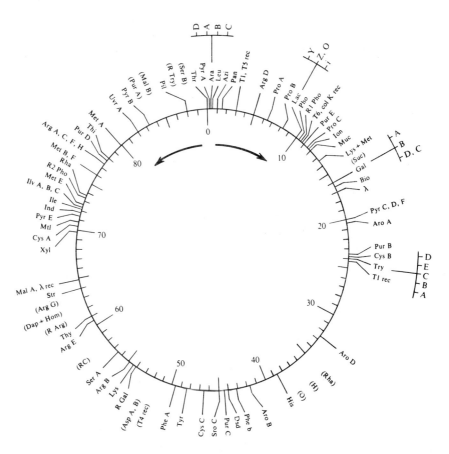

FIGURE 19-3.   Genetic Map of *E. Coli*. Drawn to Scale.
The map is graduated in 1-min intervals (89 min total) and numbered at 10-min intervals to facilitate analysis. Markers enclosed in parentheses are only approximately mapped at the positions indicated. The exact sequence of markers in crowded regions is not always known. The genetic map in terms of recombination units closely corresponds to that in time units, with the normalization factor 1 time unit (corresponding to approximately 10^5 nucleotide pairs) equals about 22 recombination units.—*From A. L. Taylor and M. S. Thomann, Genetics, 50: 659 (1964).*

contact, thereby converting them to the F^+ form. A process akin to sexual conjugation also takes place between F^+ and F^- in which a considerable portion of the chromosome of the F^+ cell, which thus acts as a donor, is transferred to the F^- cell, which acts as a recipient. Conjugation between the mating types is a relatively uncommon event, and the efficiency of transfer of genetic determinants is very low and amounts to only 10^{-4} of that of the F factor. However with certain mutant males called Hfr (high frequency of recombination), this efficiency is increased by a factor of 10^3. In these mutants the F factor is no longer infectious: unlike the F^+ males, conjugation usually no longer leads to a transfer of the F factor into the recipient, and the attendant conversion from F^- to F^+ does not take place. The conjugation process and the concomitant transfer of genes from Hfr to F^- may be interrupted at any time by separating the cells mechanically in a Waring blendor and can be monitored by testing the zygotes formed with respect to their ability to express various characters phenotypically (see page 449). In this manner we can establish the sequence of certain genes, A, B, C, etc., both qualitatively with respect to their order on the chromosomes and quantitatively by their relative time of entry into the recipient cells. We can then compare a map constructed on this basis, i.e., in terms of the ratio of time for any marker divided by time for the total chromosome, with the usual map based on recombination frequency, i.e., the ratio of number of recombinants receiving a marker divided by total Hfr cells mated. Remarkably good agreement is obtained by the two techniques (see Fig. 19-3). In the same strain of *E. coli* two additional means for the exchange of genetic information have been observed. The first is a process called *F-duction*, which consists of the transfer of a small number of genetic determinants coincident with the transfer of the F factor already mentioned. The latter acts as if it had originally been very closely associated with, and even integrated into, the chromosome of the F^+ cell but was capable of being detached with a small chunk of chromosome still adhering, which it could then transfer to a recipient bacterium. The factor thus leads both an integrated and a semiautonomous existence. A genetic unit or particle behaving in this manner was called an *episome* by Jacob, Wollman, and Monod.

An analogous but much more widely applicable example of genetic exchange and transfer by an episomal entity in bacteria is provided by the process known as *transduction*, brought about through the agency of temperate bacteriophages (see Fig. 19-4A and B). These bacteriophages may or may not be capable of replication in their own right.

A final means, for genetic exchange in bacteria is provided by *transformation*, i.e., the direct transfer of genetic material from donor to recipient. If a cell-free extract of an appropriate bacterial species (*Diplococcus pneumoniae, Haemophilus influenzae, Bacillus subtilis*) bearing a characteristic genetic marker (e.g., resistance to a particular antibiotic, nature of the cell wall, requirements for a particular growth factor) is added to a growing culture of a different strain of the same bacterium but lacking that particular trait, a fraction of the cells incorporate this trait into their genome. Thus, cells from the first strain act as donor, and those of the second as acceptors or recipients of a genetic marker and are transformed in the process from, say, streptomycin sensitivity to streptomycin resistance; this transformation is permanent and passed on from generation to generation. The active *transforming principle* has been unambiguously identified as pure DNA.

What about bacterial viruses, haploid organisms incapable even of vegetative reproduction, let alone sexual union in the absence of a host cell? A process that is operationally identical to sexual recombination is obtained by simultaneous infection of one and the same bacterial cell by two virus particles differing from each other in one or more genetic markers. The parental types segregate independently, and one obtains, out of this phage cross, progeny viruses of the two parental and various recombinant genotypes, the latter with frequencies that can be correlated once again on the basis of a one-dimensional map. Incidentally, quite compelling genetic evidence has forced investigators to postulate a circular rather than a linear map in the case of *E. coli* K12 and in those of bacteriophages T2 and T4 (see Fig. 19-3). Since phage crosses can be performed with great speed and elegance and one can examine a very large number of progeny in each experiment, some of the most significant findings in modern genetics have been based on such studies. Their significance is enhanced further by the discovery, first made by Hershey and Chase, that only the viral DNA, and not its protein, enters the host bacterium, in the manner schematically indicated in the left hand (lytic) cycle of Fig. 19-4A.

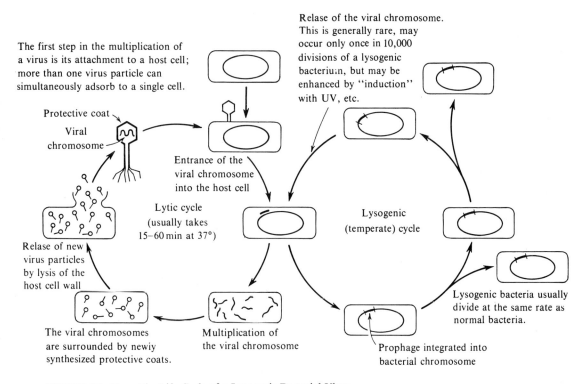

The first step in the multiplication of a virus is its attachment to a host cell; more than one virus particle can simultaneously adsorb to a single cell.

Relase of the viral chromosome. This is generally rare, may occur only once in 10,000 divisions of a lysogenic bacterium, but may be enhanced by "induction" with UV, etc.

Protective coat
Viral chromosome

Entrance of the viral chromosome into the host cell

Lytic cycle (usually takes 15–60 min at 37°)

Lysogenic (temperate) cycle

Relase of new virus particles by lysis of the host cell wall

Lysogenic bacteria usually divide at the same rate as normal bacteria.

The viral chromosomes are surrounded by newiy synthesized protective coats.

Multiplication of the viral chromosome

Prophage integrated into bacterial chromosome

FIGURE 19-4A.   The Life Cycle of a Lysogenic Bacterial Virus.
We see that, after its chromosome enters a host cell, it sometimes multiplies immediately, like a lytic virus, and at other times becomes transformed into prophage. The lytic phase of its life cycle is identical to the complete life cycle of a lytic (nonlysogenic) virus. Lytic bacterial viruses are so called because their multiplication results in the rupture (lysis) of the bacteria.—*Adapted from J. Watson, " Molecular Biology of the Gene," Benjamin, New York, 1965, with permission.*

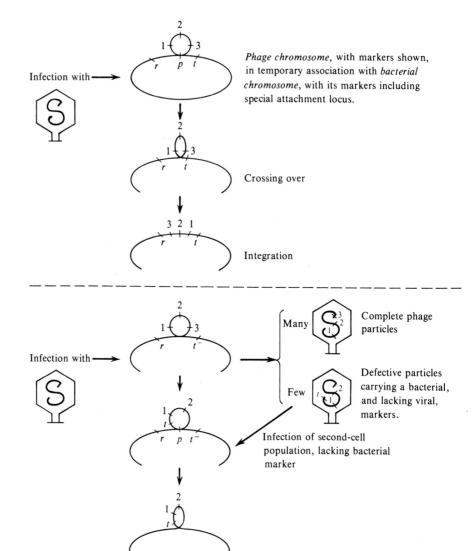

Phage chromosome, with markers shown, in temporary association with *bacterial chromosome*, with its markers including special attachment locus.

Crossing over

Integration

Complete phage particles

Defective particles carrying a bacterial, and lacking viral, markers.

Infection of second-cell population, lacking bacterial marker

FIGURE 19-4B.   Lysogeny and Transduction.
Integration of prophage into bacterial chromosome (*top*) and passive transfer of bacterial genetic material by (defective) carrier phages (*bottom*).

DNA AS GENETIC
MATERIAL

It now becomes appropriate to summarize some of the most cogent evidence upon which the identification of DNA as the genetic material of all cells rests. The most compelling set is provided by the following:

1. Naked DNA unaccompanied by any other structured macromolecular component can transmit (*a*) single genetic markers, (*b*) linked groups of markers, or (*c*) all the markers of a chromosome in the processes of genetic exchange in

microorganisms called respectively (*a*) transformation, (*b*) transduction and F-duction, and (*c*) bacterial conjugation, or infection by viral DNA. In all these processes there is good correlation between physical length, or weight, of DNA and map length.

2. For any species of higher organisms DNA is constant in amount and composition in all resting, somatic, diploid (2*N*) cells. It increases in amount during the process of mitotic division but returns to the resting value in the daughter cells. The haploid (*N*) germ cells (gametes) contain DNA of identical composition but in one-half the amount.

3. Genetic relatedness between different species of both macro- and micro-organisms has been positively correlated with DNA composition and with the extent of homologies of polynucleotide sequences in the molecules.

4. Physical and chemical agents (mutagens) are known that produce muta-tions with high efficiency; correlations can be established between this efficiency and the extent of distinct chemical alterations in DNA (see page 133).

5. The Watson-Crick-Wilkins model of DNA structure (see page 123) provides a convenient framework to accommodate all these and numerous other observa-tions in modern genetics and has been of tremendous heuristic value in the formulation of models and the design of critical experiments for the purpose of testing additional predictions in this general area.

It has therefore become customary to equate the chromosome, especially that of microorganisms, with a DNA molecule. By extension, then, the individual genes heretofore defined operationally only in terms of certain types of experi-ments now become definite segments of this molecule, i.e., long tracts or sequences of a polydeoxyribonucleotide duplex. Chromosome replication is discussed in the next chapter. Recombination, at least in haploid organisms, is believed to proceed by a process of breakage and rejoining involving the parental chromosomes.

MOLECULAR OR BIOCHEMICAL GENETICS: THE ONE-GENE-ONE-ENZYME HYPOTHESIS

The conclusion that the phenotypic expression of many mutational events in genes must be due to resultant alterations in certain enzymatically active proteins seems almost inescapable in retrospect, and certainly was foreshadowed in 1908 by Garrod's careful documentation of various inherited abnormalities in man as "inborn errors of metabolism." He observed, for instance, that the disease alcaptonuria, which is inherited as a simple recessive Mendelian trait, was invariably accompanied and therefore probably caused by an inability to oxidize homogentisic acid, a normal metabolite of phenylalanine (see page 425). Many additional examples of such hereditary diseases have since come to light. A representative sample is presented in Table 19-1.

The modern era was initiated by Beadle and Tatum. Using *Neurospora* they were able to isolate a large number of independent biochemical mutants that, in general, were unable to synthesize one (or more) amino acid, purine, pyrimidine, sugar, or B vitamin. Thus the *prototrophic* wild type cell had been converted to an *auxotrophic* mutant that required for growth the addition to a minimal medium of the requisite component as an essential growth factor. Further analysis of a large number of such mutants of various types showed that, in general, the growth requirements for individual components could be sub-divided and grouped further in the following manner. Let us assume that we find that one mutant, which we call z, requires compound Z and only compound Z as a growth factor. Frequently, then, we can also find a second mutant y that grows when either Z or Y is added to the medium. There may also occur a mutant x, which is also an auxotroph for Z but which grows on X, Y, or Z. Finally we obtain w, yet a fourth auxotroph for Z, but one which can grow on W, X, Y or Z. Now if W turns out to be a well-known product or intermediate of metabolism, we can say first of all that the pathway from W to Z includes the stages $W \xrightarrow{1} X \xrightarrow{2} Y \xrightarrow{3} Z$. For this reason auxotrophic mutants have turned out to be exceedingly useful tools for the elucidation of novel metabolic pathways.

TABLE 19-1.   Some Hereditary Disorders in Man in Which the Specific Lacking or Modified Enzyme or Protein Has Been Identified

Disorder	Affected enzyme or protein
Acanthocytosis	β-Lipoproteins
Acatalasemia	Catalase
Afibrinogenemia	Fibrinogen
Agammaglobulinemia	γ-Globulin
Albinism	Tyrosinase
Alcaptonuria	Homogentisic acid oxidase
Analbuminemia	Serum albumin
Argininosuccinic acidemia	Argininosuccinase
Galactosemia	Galactose-1-phosphate uridyl transferase
Glycogen storage diseases	
Type I (von Gierke's)	Glucose-6-phosphatase
Type III	Amylo-1,6-glucosidase
Type IV	Amylo-$(1,4 \rightarrow 1,6)$-transglycosylase
Type V (McArdle's)	Muscle phosphorylase
Type VI (Hers')	Liver phosphorylase
Goiter (familial)	Iodotyrosine dehalogenase
Hemoglobinopathies	Hemoglobins
Hemophilia A	Antihemophilic factor A
Hemophilia B	Antihemophilic factor B
Histidinemia	Histidase
Homocystinuria	Cystathionine synthetase
Hyperbilirubinemia (Gilbert's disease)	Uridine diphosphate glucuronate transferase
Hypophosphatasia	Alkaline phosphatase
Maple syrup urine disease	Enzymes that decarboxylate branched-chain α-keto acids
Mastocytosis	Histidine decarboxylase (excess)
Methemoglobinemia	Methemoglobin reductase
Orotic aciduria	Orotidine 5'-phosphate pyrophosphorylase
Parahemophilia	Accelerator globulin
Pentosuria	L-Xylulose dehydrogenase
Phenylketonuria	Phenylalanine hydroxylase
Prolinemia	Proline oxidase (some cases)
Tyrosinosis	p-Hydroxyphenylpyruvic acid oxidase
Vitamin B_{12} deficiency	Methylmalonyl-coenzyme A isomerase
Wilson's disease	Ceruloplasmin
Xanthinuria	Xanthine oxidase

We can also propose as a working hypothesis that mutant z behaves as it does because it is "blocked" between Y and Z; i.e., it is incapable of synthesizing a functional enzyme 3, the one responsible for the conversion $Y \rightarrow Z$, in anywhere near normal amounts. We phrase this statement in precisely these terms because subsequent investigations have amply demonstrated that such *genetic blocks*, i.e., alterations of the z gene from the standard to a mutant type of allele,[1] can manifest themselves phenotypically in a number of ways, including the following: (*a*) the complete absence of enzyme 3 or any protein related to it, (*b*) the synthesis of normal enzyme 3 but in subnormal amounts, or (*c*) the synthesis of an abnormal enzyme 3, related to the normal form structurally or immunologically but devoid of or much lowered in enzymatic activity. We can test the hypothesis by showing that on investigation of the intracellular content of mutant *z*, either directly or after administration of *W*, we find accumulation of *Y*, *X*, and *W* in that order and that extracts of cell *z* show normal ability to catalyze steps 1 and 2 but grossly impaired activity for step 3; analogous experiments with mutants *x* and *y* disclose similar deficiencies in enzymes 1 and 2, respectively. We are now entitled to expand our scheme as follows:

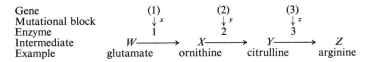

Gene   (1)   (2)   (3)
Mutational block   ↓ *x*   ↓ *y*   ↓ *z*
Enzyme   1   2   3
Intermediate   *W*———→   *X*———→   *Y*———→   *Z*
Example   glutamate   ornithine   citrulline   arginine

By the use of standard genetic techniques a very large number of mutants could be mapped, and the appropriate linear genetic maps for the seven linkage groups of *Neurospora* established. With the discovery of conjugation in *E. coli* K12 and by the use of transduction techniques as a means of affecting partial genetic exchange, similar maps could be constructed for this bacterium employing the same type of biochemical auxotrophs,[2] and the same form of reasoning could be shown to be valid with regard to the correlation of its genetic and enzymatic constitution. *E. coli* K12 has only a single linkage group, and map distances can, in this instance, be correlated on the one hand with time of penetration of the male chromosome into the recipient cell—and is so correlated in the example shown in Fig. 19-3 — and on the other with total chromosome length, which is identical, as we already know, with total DNA length. In this instance, therefore, time of penetration as measured by physical time of contact, time of appearance of markers in the recipient cell, and amount of P^{32}-labeled DNA transferred from donor to recipient all correspond rather neatly.

As far as bacterial viruses are concerned, one has several different types of mutants available. Classically their phenotypic expression had to do with host range and plaque morphology and thus was a function of the various protein components of the mature phage. More recently many others, i.e., "conditional lethals," have been discovered which can be selected either on the basis of temperature sensitivity (*ts* mutants that are capable of multiplication, say, at 30° but not at 40°) or on the basis of their ability to multiply in one type of cell (the "permissive host") coupled with an inability to multiply in closely related

---

[1] The nomenclature for the standard or wild type and the corresponding mutant is somewhat ambiguous, since both *x*, for wild type, and *x*⁻, for mutant, as well as *x*⁺ or just (+), for wild type, and *x* or (−), for mutant, have been employed in different systems. Finally the system *X* for wild type and *x* for mutant has also been used.

[2] With bacteria, selection of auxotrophs is simple, thanks to a discovery by Lederberg. Penicillin kills only growing cells. Thus in a population of wild type plus auxotrophs treated with the antibiotic on minimal medium the former grows and is eliminated. The latter are incapable of growth and remain viable and resume growth upon supplementation with the appropriate growth factor.

bacterial strains (the " restrictive host "). This latter type is known as the class of "amber" (*am*) mutants. Both *am* and *ts* mutants in T2 and T4 have been shown to map in many different regions of the phage chromosome. These segments are known to control not only the ordinary kind of phage proteins but also a variety of other protein molecules elaborated by the infected cell, vitally concerned in the biosynthesis of viral components, especially its DNA, to the exclusion of the corresponding bacterial entity. Thus elaborate and detailed maps could be constructed for some of the bacterial viruses as well.

From the foregoing it is now clear what the experimental foundations are for the famous *one-gene-one-enzyme hypothesis* originally enunciated explicitly by Norman Horowitz of the California Institute of Technology. To anticipate some points to which we shall return later in their proper context, two important sets of observations emerged as corollaries of some of these studies: (1) frequently, though by no means always, the genes controlling the various steps of a biosynthetic sequence, for example,

$$\overset{1}{\underset{}{\downarrow}} \quad \overset{2}{\underset{}{\downarrow}} \quad \overset{3}{\underset{}{\downarrow}}$$
$$W \to X \to Y \to Z$$

are closely linked and map in the same general region of the chromosome, perhaps even in the order 1, 2, 3, or its reverse; (2) often the synthesis of the cluster of enzymes, for example, 1, 2, 3, corresponding to and controlled by this cluster of genes appeared to be turned on (*induction*) or off (*repression*) in a coordinated manner in response to changes in the physiological environment.

As to actual examples, out of a large number available we mention only two. The genes concerned with galactose metabolism are clustered at gal A-D in Fig. 19-3. They control the sequence of enzymes (see page 287) catalyzing the following reactions:

$$\text{galactose} \xrightarrow[\text{galactokinase}]{} \text{galactose-1-}P \xrightarrow[\substack{\text{Gal-1-}P\text{-uridyl} \\ \text{transferase}}]{+\text{UTP}-\text{PP}_i} \text{UDP-Gal} \xrightarrow[\text{epimerase}]{} \text{UDPG}$$

$$\qquad\quad \underset{Gal\ A}{\uparrow} \qquad\qquad\qquad\qquad \underset{Gal\ B}{\uparrow} \qquad\qquad\quad \underset{Gal\ C}{\uparrow}$$

Those concerned with isoleucine and valine biosynthesis are marked *Ilv A, B, C, D* and control enzymes (see page 414) as follows:

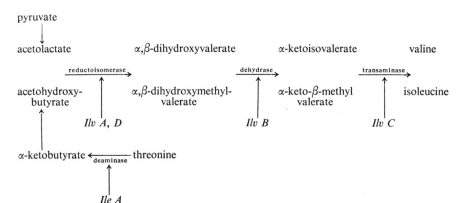

THE GENE AS
FUNCTIONAL UNIT:
ONE GENE – ONE
POLYPEPTIDE

Fine-structure Genetics: The Units of Recombination and Mutation. In all the foregoing the classic definition of a gene was still employed and appeared to suffice in the vast majority of cases: a discrete, essentially quantized, indivisible unit, defined operationally as being able to mutate to an alternative allelic state, to recombine with other similar genes, and to control function, i.e., the synthesis of a specific cellular constituent, namely, a specific protein.

The era of "fine-structure" genetics was initiated by the studies of Benzer from 1955 on with a particular gene of bacteriophage T4 (and T2) called the *r*II region. The fantastic resolving power of this particular system is based on the fact that, whereas in one type of bacterial host (B) these mutants simply show a different plaque morphology (the *r* phenotype) that allowed their selection in the first place, in another (K)[1] no infective progeny is produced, and thus no plaques are formed. Therefore if one were to perform a phage cross between two separate *r*II mutants in strain B, but score for recombinants on agar plates covered with a lawn of bacteria of strain K, only recombinants for r^+, the wild (or standard) type, would form visible plaques. This test has a resolving power such that r^+ recombinants occurring with a frequency of 0.0001 per cent can readily be detected. By this and by means of some short-cut methods involving overlapping deletions,[2] Benzer proceeded to map this region. He was able to show that the individual *r*II gene contained a large but not infinite number of individual recombinational loci, which could be arranged in a linear array on the basis of recombination frequency. Thus he had constructed the first fine-structure map of a gene containing a large number of alleles (see Fig. 19-5). How many? It turned out that the lowest frequency of r^+ recombinants actually observed in all his crosses between independently produced (spontaneous or chemically mutagenized) *r*II mutants was about 0.01, even though much lower frequencies could readily have been detected. This number then allows us to estimate the size of the smallest recombinational unit, called the "recon" by Benzer. The total genetic map of T4 covers a distance of about 700 units, where 1 unit corresponds to a recombination frequency (for both recombinant types) of 1 per cent in a standard cross, in which each parent is present in exactly equal amounts. A frequency of 0.01 per cent therefore corresponds to $2 \times 0.01/700 = 3 \times 10^{-5}$ of the total phage chromosome. In terms of DNA, if we assume no nongenetic regions in the molecule and equal probability of recombination throughout its length, this corresponds to $3 \times 10^{-5} \times 2 \times 10^5$ nucleotide pairs = 6 nucleotide pairs. Therefore the "recon" consists of a very small number of nucleotide pairs or perhaps even of an individual nucleotide pair. Thus in terms of fine-structure genetics it is not meaningful any longer to speak of the gene as a discrete unit of recombination.

The Nature
of Mutations

What about the gene as the individual unit of mutation, the unit called the "muton" by Benzer? In terms of the DNA-segment model of the gene one would expect the smallest muton also to be constituted by the individual nucleotide pair. For no matter what detailed mechanism we postulate for the *translation* of the polynucleotide code into a polypeptide code, an alteration in a base, or at most one in a group of two or three bases, might well result in an altered

---

[1] Really K12 (λ), i.e., *E. coli* K12 lysogenic for phage λ.

[2] That is, losses of whole segments of the gene.

protein. Such an alteration would therefore produce a mutant organism distinct in its phenotype and thus constitute a *point mutation*. We might conceive of the following alternatives in terms of a model involving small groups of adjacent deoxynucleotide pairs as code groups for specifying individual amino acids in a

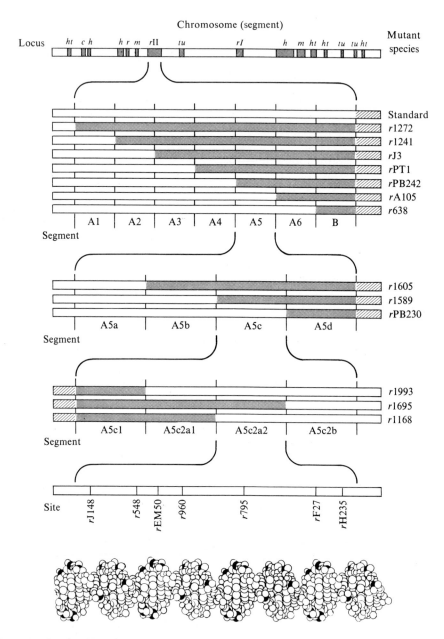

FIGURE 19-5.   Mapping the *r*II Region.

Mapping techniques localize the position of a given mutation in progressively smaller segments of the DNA molecule contained in the T4 phage. The *r*II region represents, to start with, only a few per cent of the entire molecule. The mapping is done by crossing an unknown with known deletions in the *r*II region. The order and spacing of the seven mutational sites in the bottom row are still tentative. Each site probably represents the smallest mutable unit in the DNA molecule, a single base pair. The molecular segment (extreme bottom), estimated to be roughly in proper scale, contains a total of about 40 base pairs.—*From S. Benzer, Sci. Am.,* **206** (*I*): 70 (1962).

protein that constitutes the eventual gene product (see Fig. 19-6). The figure is reasonably self-explanatory except perhaps for the alternative 4. Let us assume, for argument's sake, a *coding ratio* of 3; that is, r, the number of nucleotide pairs[1] in a code group equals that number. Then

$$(x_1y_1z_1)(x_2y_2z_2)\cdots(x_ny_nz_n)(x_{n+1}y_{n+1}z_{n+1})\cdots(x_my_mz_m)$$

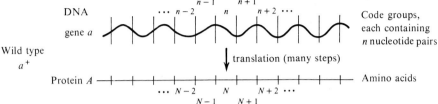

The result is an accumulation of mis-sense
and untranslatable code groups (gibberish)

FIGURE 19-6. Phenotypic Consequences of Point Mutations.

[1] Since normal double-stranded DNA is self-complementary, it does not now matter whether we look at the nucleotide pairs in the duplex or the nucleotides in either one of the component strands. As a corollary, if one strand is really both necessary and sufficient to carry all the genetic information, then the chemical alteration of a single nucleotide in a pair should produce a heterozygote; i.e., its progeny should consist of both the parental and a mutant genotype. This has actually been demonstrated.

can be thought to stand respectively for the nucleotide pairs comprising the first, second, nth, $n + 1$st, and mth code groups of gene a. They can then, by an as yet unspecified mechanism, uniquely determine the sequence of amino acids $aa_1 aa_2 \ldots aa_n aa_{n+1} \ldots aa_m$ in the protein A. Now let us also assume that reading and translation have to start with code group 1 and with nucleotide x_1 at that. What is the consequence if we eliminate one nucleotide (pair) in one of the groups, say, y_n? Well, everything proceeds as before until we reach code group n, but now suddenly, since the translation proceeds continuously in groups of three without interruption, the machine responsible now sees

$$\cdots (x_n z_n x_{n+1})(y_{n+1} z_{n+1} x_{n+2})(y_{n+2} z_{n+2} x_{n+3})(y_{n+3} z_{n+3} x_{n+4}) \cdots (y_{m-1} z_{m-1} x_m) y_m z_m$$

that is, a tape that is completely garbled beyond the point of insertion or deletion. This type of mutation, therefore, corresponds to a *change in phase or reading frame*, producing alterations at code group n and beyond, that are reflected in a continued misreading of the genetic message beyond that point. If the triplets still code, but do so for amino acids differing from those specified originally, we have an accumulation of *missense* or gibberish. If they do not code, we have a similar accumulation of *nonsense*.

Are most of the mutants at independent alleles in the rII region indeed point mutants? If so, they should satisfy the following two criteria: (1) they ought to yield r^+ recombinants when crossed with at least one of two other nonallelic rII mutants which themselves have yielded such recombinants when crossed with each other, and (2) they ought to be capable of "reverting" back to wild type with a measurable frequency, especially when the mutation rate (here from rII $\rightarrow r^+$) is enhanced by appropriate treatments. Indeed most of the rII mutants studied did behave in the predicted manner, although their "reversion index" or frequency appeared to differ widely. Interestingly enough many cases of induced mutations could be shown to fall into just two classes (see Table 19-2A): (1) those

TABLE 19-2A.   Types of Point Mutations

Mutagen, acting on	Base pair	Product	Consequence	Final outcome
5-Bromouracil (BU). When in keto form pairs with A, in enol form pairs with G	A—T	A—BU	BU can pair with G G—BU $\rightarrow$ G—C	Transition AT $\rightarrow$ GC
	G—C	G—BU	BU can pair with A G—BU $\rightarrow$ A—BU $\rightarrow$ AT	Transition GC $\rightarrow$ AT
2-Aminopurine (AP). Normally pairs with T, but can also pair with C	A—T	AP—T	AP now pairs with C AP—T $\rightarrow$ AP—C $\rightarrow$ G—C	Transition AT $\rightarrow$ GC
	G—C	AP—C	AP now pairs with T AP—C $\rightarrow$ AP—T $\rightarrow$ AT	Transition GC $\rightarrow$ AT
Nitrous acid (NA). Deaminates A $\rightarrow$ I, G $\rightarrow$ X, C $\rightarrow$ U	A—T	I—T	I pairs with C IT $\rightarrow$ IC $\rightarrow$ GC	Transition AT $\rightarrow$ GC
	G—C	X—U	Although X pairs like G, U $\simeq$ T; X—U $\rightarrow$ A—U $\rightarrow$ AT	Transition GC $\rightarrow$ AT
Hydroxylamine (HA). Converts cytosine (NH$_2$) to NHOH, which pairs only with A	G—C	G—C$_x$	G—C$_x$ $\rightarrow$ A—C$_x$ $\rightarrow$ AT	Transition GC $\rightarrow$ AT
	A—T	No action		
Acridines (proflavine, acriflavine, quinacrine, etc.). Acts by intercalation	Any		Locally distorts double helix, allowing insertion or removal of one (or small number) base	Produces shifts in reading frame

induced by base substitutions — growth on 5-bromouracil or 2-aminopurine, treatment with hydroxylamine, nitrous acid, or ethyl methane sulfonate (see Chap. 5 for mode of action) could be shown to form an increased number of revertants by the same or a different mutagen in this same group but never by acridine dyes; and conversely, (2) those induced by treatment with acridine dyes, as well as some spontaneous ones, formed revertants under the influence of acridines but never by treatment designed to introduce base substitution. (See Table 19-2B.) The conclusion was therefore reached that the first class involved transitions $A—T \rightleftharpoons G—C$ or $T—A \rightleftharpoons C—G$, and the second class involved insertion or deletion of single nucleotides, i.e., a change in reading frame. Reversions in the first class, then, would entail a second substitution in the same spot, with a resultant return to the *status quo*, for example, $A—T \rightarrow G—C \rightarrow A—T$; reversions in the second class would entail an insertion followed by a deletion or vice versa.

TABLE 19-2B.   Reversion of Mutations (Largely rII) by Mutagens

Mutation originally induced by	BU	AP	NA	HA	Acridines	Likely base pair affected by original mutation
BU	+	+++	+++	−	−	GC (some AT)
AP	+++	+	+++	++	−	AT (some GC)
NA	++	++	+++	+	−	AT or GC
HA	++	+++	+	−	−	GC
Acridines	−	−	±(?)	−	+	Any

CODE:
+++ = virtually quantitative reversion
++ = reversion in majority of cases
+ = reversion in some cases
± = occasional reversion
− = reversion virtually absent

Those mutants which were not point mutants turned out to be actual deletions of whole segments of the genome, varying in length. In other similar systems, such as bacteriophage λ, an analogous deletion (λcb_2) has been studied which leads to a decrease in physical length of DNA by 3μ (from 17.3 to 14.3), corresponding to a decrease in molecular weight of 6×10^6, or the equivalent of 1,000 nucleotide pairs (see Fig. 5-8).

The Unit of Function

Studies with rII Mutants. It became apparent that all mutants could be shown to fall into just two classes, A and B, by the following simple test. Again we infect one host cell simultaneously with two different viruses, either one wild type plus one mutant, or two mutants, but now we use strain K rather than strain B to form this doubly infected complex. Now, remember that the characteristic property of an rII mutant is its very inability to yield any progeny in strain K, presumably because in this host it is incapable of specifying a protein exhibiting normal function, which is essential for phage production. What would we predict? Surely that the configuration wild type/mutant should produce functional protein[1] and therefore normal behavior and produce progeny, whereas the configuration mutant/mutant should fail to do so. But this is not what was found. Some mutant pairs, viz., those of group I, did indeed behave in this way, but a great many, those of group II, yielded progeny, i.e., were capable of mutual *complementation*. The two classes of mutants then are those of classes *A* and *B*, which are defined in the following manner: Each and every class *A* mutant can cooperate with (complement) each and every class *B* mutant with very high efficiency, whereas intraclass complementation does not occur at all or constitutes an exceedingly rare event.[2] This means that we have the following possibilities: $AB/Ab \rightarrow$ progeny; $AB/aB \rightarrow$ progeny; $AB/ab \rightarrow$ progeny; $Ab/aB \rightarrow$ progeny; $aB/Ab \rightarrow$ progeny; aB/aB or $Ab/Ab \rightarrow$ no progeny. Here $AB =$ wild type; aB, mutant of class *A*; Ab, mutant of class *B*. The two classes have been variously referred to as *complementation groups*, or, since the test used is known in genetics as the cis-trans test, as *cistrons*. (Two markers *a* and *b* are said to be cis in the configuration AB/ab, trans in Ab/aB or aB/Ab.) Thus we see that *A* and *B* are indeed dominant over their mutant alleles *a* and *b*. In functional terms the true genetic units must be provided by the two gene segments, or cistrons, *A* and *B*, which, incidentally, occupy distinct but of course adjacent segments in the genetic map. Each cistron then specifies a distinct functional entity, inactive by itself even when normal, fully active when supplemented by its equally inactive normal partner. The gene product of each of the mutant alleles, then, must be one that cannot form a normal functional product in the presence of a standard partner. This makes sense if we postulate that the true functional genetic unit, gene, or cistron, is one that specifies the true structural subunit in protein chemistry: the individual polypeptide chain. Let us assume that a functional protein is made up of groups of *n* separate and distinct polypeptide chain subunits held together by covalent or other bonds; it then requires *n* genes or cistrons for its complete specification. We therefore postulate two polypeptide chains in the present instance. Even if the mutation $A \rightarrow a$ or $B \rightarrow b$ produces a complete absence of the corresponding polypeptide or a completely garbled one, it is evident that in the intracellular pool we shall have available intact standard subunit polypeptides *A* and *B*, just as long as the appropriate standard gene for each is present.

The difference between a cistron and a gene as the unit of function is an evanescent one, e.g., in humans the two genes specifying the α and β chains of hemoglobin are unlinked and may even be located on different chromosomes. The two genes for tryptophan synthetase in *E. coli*, as we shall see in the next section, are very closely linked but distinct. By contrast in *Neurospora*, the analogous enzyme—very similar in function and mechanism, and even molecular weight, to its *E. coli* counterpart — is specified by two cistrons of one and the same gene. In any event many proteins now have been shown, usually by means of the cis-trans test, to be specified by more than one gene or cistron.

---

[1] That is, wild type which can produce protein is dominant over mutant which cannot.

[2] In other systems intraclass complementation can however be shown to occur. It is observed when (1) the functional protein is made up of two or more identical polypeptide subunits and (2) such subunits damaged in different portions of the polypeptide chain can still aggregate to form a more or less functional complex.

Suppression. Examination of apparent reversion to wild type, or prototrophy, in many systems has shown that frequently the true cause of the phenomenon lies, not in a true reversal of the primary genetic event, but in the introduction of an additional mutation(s) elsewhere in the genome. We are dealing with a "pseudo revertant," formed as a consequence of a *suppressor mutation.* Some of the examples found can be explained on the basis of what has already been discussed. Let us return to Fig. 19-6, case 4, and the discussion on page 464 concerning the production of gibberish by an alteration in reading frame. We can ask the question: What will be the consequence of introducing an additional deletion had we started with a deletion, or insertion, had we started with an insertion, close to the site of the first mutagenic event? In the example given we find after removal of, say, y_{n+1},

$$(x_n z_n x_{n+1})(z_{n+1} x_{n+2} y_{n+2})(z_{n+2} x_{n+3} y_{n+3}) \cdots (z_{m-1} x_m y_m) z_m$$

which is still devoid of meaning. But what if we introduce yet another deletion, i.e., number 3 in the set? The product is, if we remove, say, x_n,

$$\cdots (z_n x_{n+1} z_{n+1})(x_{n+2} y_{n+2} z_{n+2})(x_{n+3} y_{n+3} z_{n+3}) \cdots (x_m y_m z_m)$$

and lo and behold, starting with code group $n + 2$ to the end of the chain we are back in phase and produce a perfectly intelligible message. Therefore, providing that the missense produced by the few altered code groups — here code group n has been eliminated and code group $n + 1$ has become $(z_n x_{n+1} z_{n+1})$ — is not too overwhelming, we can see how a new functional protein may emerge as a result of r successive mutational events in series.[1] But we remember that r equals the coding ratio, the number of nucleotide (pairs) in DNA required to specify any one amino acid. This exceedingly ingenious argument and the experimental proof that $r = 3$, employing experiments of this type with acridine-induced mutants of bacteriophage T4, were first advanced by F. H. C. Crick and his collaborators in 1961.

What about *intragenic suppressor mutations* for base substitution or missense mutations, usually now called "second-site reversions"? These also exist: the original mutational event, we remember, produced an inactive or impaired protein with an altered amino acid substituted at a single and defined position in the polypeptide chain. A second, independent mutational event in the same gene will lead to a second amino acid substitution elsewhere. Under certain circumstances this second substitution, although producing an altered protein when present alone, may be beneficial and relieve more or less completely the original impairment of function due to the first substitution. A case in the tryptophan synthetase A protein is known where the substitution of Glu for Gly at one position can be compensated for by a second substitution — which by itself also produces an inactive protein — of Cys for Tyr, 36 amino acids distant.

Extragenic suppression is of at least two distinct types. First is one in which the phenotypic expression of the original mutational alteration is compensated for by the introduction of a *specific* suppressor mutation into the same genome. The second arises as a result of the introduction of a nonspecific, more generalized

---

[1] Really $n \times r$, where n is any small number.

suppressor that affects mutants in more than one gene so as to allow them to form proteins functional to one degree or another. In this latter instance the suppressor mutation and the original mutation need not even have been present in one and the same organism. For instance, the growth of conditionally lethal phage mutants in certain permissive strains and their inability to grow in others is now known to be due to the presence of a suppressor in the genome of the permissive host. The introduction of the same suppressor also permits the synthesis of functionally active host proteins, e.g., alkaline phosphatase, in host mutants ordinarily lacking this capacity. A probable explanation of suppression in molecular terms is deferred to page 500.

Studies on Tryptophan Synthetase of E. coli. The elegant studies by Benzer could only be improved on by a direct correlation with equally sophisticated work on the structure of the protein(s) controlled by the *r*II gene. Unfortunately its function is yet completely unknown and therefore the protein in question has never even been isolated, much less analyzed. Fortunately a formally very similar system has been discovered by Yanofsky and his collaborators as the result of their equally impressive work: the enzyme tryptophan synthetase (TS) and the genes controlling its elaboration in *E. coli.*

The terminal reaction for tryptophan synthesis in this and other organisms catalyzed by TS is that of reaction (1) (see page 418):

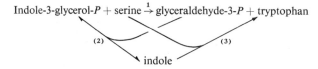

In addition, the standard enzyme, as usually isolated, also catalyzes reactions (2) and (3), yet free indole is not an intermediate in reaction (1). Now this pure enzyme ($M = 105,000$) actually represents an enzyme complex, since it can be dissociated upon chromatography into two protein fractions called A and B. Protein A is of lower molecular weight (29,500) and contains a total of 272 amino acid residues (but no tryptophan) arranged in a single polypeptide chain; protein B accounts for the remainder of the structural units of the complete enzyme. Neither protein A nor protein B catalyzes the overall reaction — Eq. (1) — although a reconstituted enzyme made up of a stoichiometric complex of A and B will again perform this function. However, protein A catalyzes reaction (2), and protein B catalyzes reaction (3) to a slight extent. This provides a means of assaying these components in extracts, but a more convenient measure is presented by simply providing a normal A protein either intracellularly in a complementation test or extracellularly in a test for enzymatic activity.

Colinearity of Maps

By means of these diagnostic tests, by genetic techniques that allow resolution of recombination frequencies at the level of separation corresponding to single nucleotides, and by some elegant fingerprint and sequence work on the A protein, Yanofsky and his group have succeeded in providing unambiguous evidence that the genetic and polypeptide maps are colinear. This statement implies that there exists a precise correlation between polynucleotide sequence in a segment of DNA and amino acid sequence in the polypeptide specified by that polynucleotide. The molecular basis underlying this correlation, i.e., the oligonucleotide sequences corresponding to the various amino acids, constitutes the *genetic code*, whereas its functional counterpart constitutes the mechanism of *translation* of the genetic message. The two maps together with characteristic recombination frequencies and amino acid substitutions corresponding to certain characteristic alleles are shown in Fig. 19-7A. The positions of amino acid replacements in corresponding polypeptide fragments isolated from mutant cells occupy the same relative positions with respect to one another as do the respective mutational sites on the genetic map of the A gene. A number of additional significant conclusions have been drawn from these and related studies. (1) The ratio (genetic) map distance over residue distance is approximately constant and has a value of ≥ 0.01, which means that recombination frequencies lower than this probably always involve replacements of one and the same amino acid. (2) Recombinants between different mutants at one and the same genetic site that produce different amino acid substitutions, e.g., A23 with A46, and A58 with A78, are possible only if the coding units (codons) corresponding to any such pairs differ by more than a single nucleotide. (3) The code is *degenerate*, i.e., a single amino acid can be specified by two or more separate codons. It would be very difficult to explain why out of 22 mutational changes at the first Gly site shown, not a single Gly → Asp or Gly → Cys change could be detected (7 were Gly → Glu and 15 Gly → Arg), but out of 4 such mutants at the third Gly site, 3 corresponded to the first and 1 to the second alternative (see Fig. 19-7B). (4) Effective single-site revertants to apparent wild type, i.e. those producing a fully functional protein, can be of two types: one in which the original amino acid has indeed been restored, another where a new but equivalent amino acid has been substituted. For instance, a mutation in the segment -Gly-Phe-Gly to Glu-Phe-Gly can be restored by the "reversion"-Val-Phe-Gly. A mutant -Val-Phe-Val- is restored to function by either the mutation -Ala-Phe-Val or -Val-Phe-Ala-.

These and related data have been of inestimable value in furnishing clues and confirmatory evidence concerning the code. However, the most convincing hard evidence bearing on both the composition and base sequence of the various codons was provided by straightforward biochemical experiments dealing with protein synthesis in vitro, to be discussed in Chap. 21. Here we shall anticipate to the extent of summarizing certain of the conclusions that bear on the nature of the code itself.

SALIENT FEATURES OF THE GENETIC CODE

Coding Ratio. The coding ratio r is simply defined as the number of nucleotides per codon. We have already mentioned Crick's elegant demonstration of the out-of-phase–into-phase relationships produced by the introduction of three successive mutational events into a particular gene, where the mutations themselves corresponded to different additions or deletions, a single nucleotide or so in length. These experiments strongly suggested 3, or a multiple of 3, as the correct number for r. In theory if we could get a precise estimate of the length of a DNA segment required to specify a particular polypeptide, the coding ratio could be determined directly. No such direct demonstration has yet been possible, but a number of reasonable estimates have been made and suggest that r is certainly less than 10 and probably less than 5. For instance

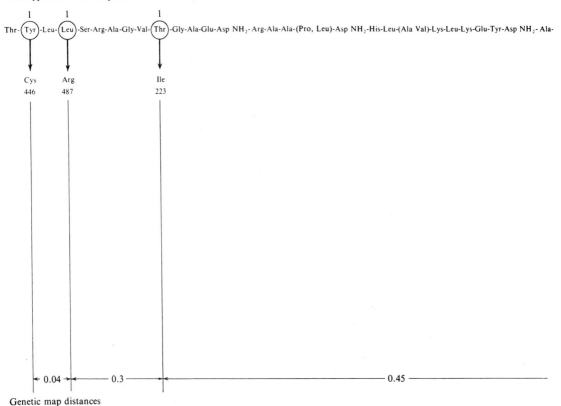

Wild type amino acid sequence

Cys 446
Arg 487
Ile 223

←0.04→←———0.3———→←————————————————0.45————————————————

Genetic map distances

FIGURE 19-7A.   Colinearity of Maps for Tryptophan Synthetase A (or α).—*Adapted from the results of Yanofsky and his collaborators.* [See C. Yanofsky, G. R. Drapeau, J. R. Guest, and B. C. Carlton, *Proc. Natl. Acad. Sci. U.S.*, *57: 296 (1967)*.]

tobacco necrosis satellite virus contains 1,200 nucleotides in its RNA; the protein subunit of its capsid is made up of 400 residues: $r = 3$. Similar numerological exercises can be indulged in for a number of different proteins or groups of proteins. Other lines of evidence are provided by the in vitro system. (1) Trinucleotides are the smallest entities capable of effectively binding specific aminoacyl transfer RNAs to ribosomes; this binding capacity is not improved significantly by extending the chain within limits. (2) A self-consistent set of coding triplets has been derived that accounts admirably for both the amino acid incorporation and binding data in vitro and mutational amino acid substitutions in vivo. (3) Alternating polynucleotides of the type ABABABAB... code for a heteropolymer containing two different amino acids in alternating sequence — this argues for a code in which r is odd, though not necessarily for one in which $r = 3$. (4) Polynucleotides of the type ABCABC... code for precisely *three* different *homo*polypeptides. Finally, the magic number of common amino acids is 20; the number of available nucleotides is 4. Four available letters in code groups of two can specify $4^2 = 16$ amino acids; this is clearly insufficient. Four letters in code groups of three can specify for $4^3 = 64$ amino acids, which is ample. Economy would dictate that this, the minimum number, would be

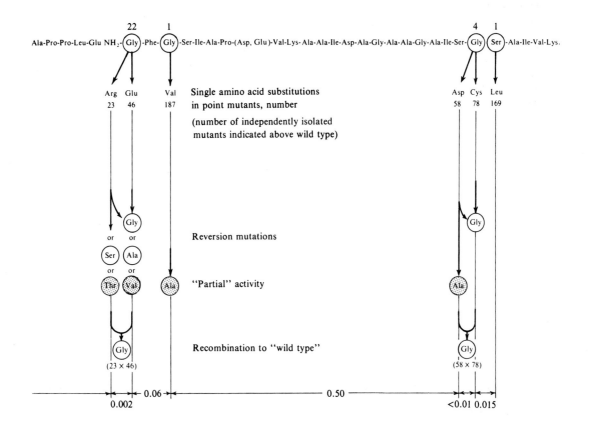

FIGURE 19-7B. Codons Corresponding to Fig. 19-7A.

the actual one. We conclude that the various bits of evidence taken together argue strongly for a coding ratio of 3.

Universality of the Code. The recent demonstration that probably close to all 64 triplets convey some signal in the in vitro system argues strongly for certain universal features of the code throughout living nature. Furthermore, the fact

Amino acid number	Mutation number	Presumed Gly codon	"Mutant" codon	"Revertant" codons	Recombination codon
27	···	GGA/G			
	23		AGA/G (Arg)	GGA/G, ACA/G (Thr), AGU/C (Ser)	
	46		GAA/G (Glu)	GGA/G, GCA/G (Ala), GUA/G (Val)	
6	···	GGU/C			
	58		GAU/C (Asp)	GGU/C, GCU/C (Ala)	
	78		UGU/C (Cys)	GGU/C	
	Genetic cross: 58 × 78				GGU/C

that heterologous in vitro systems consisting of ribosomes from one source plus transfer RNA and amino acid–activating enzymes from a second are capable of at least limited protein synthesis as effective under certain circumstances as is the homologous one again favors universality. There is also the corollary evidence that suggests that identical codon assignments appear to be equally applicable in all systems tested. Finally the protein-synthesizing system from *E. coli* is capable of translating the message carried by the RNA from a plant virus. The self-consistency of such data derived from studies with *E. coli*, other bacteria, viruses, yeast, plant seedlings, rabbit reticulocytes, rat liver, human hemoglobin, etc., is striking. Nevertheless, a word of caution is indicated. Nonuniversal, species-specific features do exist and appear to be localized in the self-recognition of aminoacyl synthetases (activating enzymes) and the various transfer RNAs perhaps involving varying degrees of base modification in the latter.

Degeneracy and Ambiguity. As we shall see, the code is grossly degenerate in the sense that almost all amino acids are coded for by more than one codon.

Degeneracy has obvious biological advantages. For instance, it permits essentially the same complement of enzymes and other proteins to be synthesized by microorganisms varying widely in DNA-base composition. Thus relative invariance in cellular composition that maximizes possible responses to the environment need not be sacrificed to genetic individuality and distinctiveness, or vice versa. Furthermore small "accidental" mutational changes are much less likely to be damaging and are more readily reversed in a degenerate than a nondegenerate code, especially if the degeneracy is such that it leads to the replacement of "equivalent" amino acids (i.e., aliphatic $\leftrightarrow$ aliphatic, acidic $\leftrightarrow$ acidic, basic $\leftrightarrow$ basic, etc.). Therefore degeneracy gives rise to genetic stability.

Under certain circumstances, for example, in the presence of high concentrations of Mg^{+2}, of other cations, especially of the antibiotic streptomycin, or of organic solvents, the code both in vitro and in vivo gives evidence of containing ambiguities. This means that one and the same triplet can code for more than one amino acid. It is believed that suppression may operate by this mechanism: Mutation $X \rightarrow Y$ changes amino acid x to y or to nonsense; suppression permits partial misreading of the code such that x (or an equivalent amino acid x') is again incorporated in the proper spot, at least part of the time. Indeed suppression is rarely completely effective, and suppressed mutants can frequently be shown to contain both types of proteins, one corresponding to the original mutation y and another resembling the normal type with x or x' in the place of y.

Commas and Overlaps. A code is referred to as *commaless* if there are no spacings between adjacent code groups, i.e., in the present case, if each nucleotide in a particular gene of the normal organism actually forms part of a codon. A code is referred to as overlapping if some elements of certain code groups form parts of other code groups:

$$\cdots(XYZ)_n\, a(XYZ)_{n+1}\, ab(XYZ)_{n+2}\cdots \qquad a, ab \text{ are "commas"}$$

$$\cdots W|XY|Z \cdots \qquad \text{code groups } (WXY)(XYZ) \text{ overlap}$$

The evidence so far presented argues compellingly against the presence of either commas or overlap regions in the genetic code, which is therefore commaless and nonoverlapping, at least as far as concerns the structural genes, i.e., those specifying functional polypeptides.[1]

The Nature of the Code. A current version of the actual codons for the 20 common amino acids based principally on studies by Nirenberg and by Khorana and their collaborators is shown in Table 19-3. The base sequences specified are

TABLE 19-3. The Genetic Dictionary

$\dfrac{2nd(Y)\rightarrow}{1st\,(X)\downarrow}$	U	C	A	G	3rd(Z)
U	Phe	*Ser*	Tyr	Cys	U
					C
	Leu*	*Ser*	Ochre	Nonsense	A
	Leu*		Amber	Trp	G
C	*Leu*	*Pro*	His	*Arg*	U
					C
	Leu	*Pro*	Gln	Arg*	A
					G
A	Ile	*Thr*	Asn	Ser	U
					C
	Ile	*Thr*	Lys	Arg*	A
	Met				G
	(Initiate)				
G	*Val*	*Ala*	Asp	*Gly*	U
					C
	Val	*Ala*	Glu	*Gly*	A
	Val or Met				G

Note that in almost all cases a substitution of one pyrimidine, or of one purine for the other (a "transition"), in position Z of an XYZ triplet does not affect the nature of the *aa* specified. In eight cases, indicated by italics, neither does the substitution of *any* purine for any pyrimidine or vice versa ("transversion"), i.e., in these instances the base in position Z appears irrelevant. In at least two instances (Leu, Arg, and perhaps Cys) transitions or transversions in X appear to be allowed. These are marked with an asterisk. Empty space indicates identity with amino acid above.
"Amber" indicates the "amber codon" which does not correspond to any tRNA for nonpermissive strains. In permissive strains containing the SuA mutation, a Ser-tRNA is produced that can recognize this triplet. "Ochre" indicates a similar, suppressible mutation, while "nonsense" indicates a general terminating codon. "Initiate" indicates an initiator codon: matching a Met-tRNA$_{met}$ capable of being formylated to formyl-N-met-tRNA.

written from left to right, i.e., XYZ means $(p)Xp\,YpZ$. This is probably also the direction of read-out. As already mentioned, several characteristic features are immediately apparent: (1) the large proportion of possible triplets assigned to actual coding function and therefore making "sense" and (2) the high degree of degeneracy.

The degeneracy means that many codons may be recognized only partially or may contain alternate "acceptable" bases at one of the terminal positions,

[1] Presumably the whole DNA molecule, and not only those regions concerned in the specification of functional polypeptides, provides some form of genetic message or other, e.g., by specifying various kinds of RNA, and therefore represents the totality of the genetic code. This statement also does not apply to the possible introduction of commas by meaningless or nonsense codons.

especially at the 3′ terminal end and to a lesser extent at the 5′ terminus. This then raises the question of how the codons are to be read and how efficient and accurate these processes are. Presumably the reading involves mutual recognition, by virtue of complementariness, between the codon (really its complementary form) on an RNA messenger (see next section) and an *anticodon* on transfer RNA (see page 493). Within any group of synonyms for the same amino acid, different sets of complementary triplets may be inherently less stable than others. Furthermore, the different tRNAs corresponding may not all be equally available. Both of these, and perhaps other factors as well, can control efficiency and perhaps species specificity. Genetic or environmental factors may control fidelity and allow for a greater or lesser amount of ambiguity with resultant effects on suppression, as we have already seen, and on *polarity*, etc., as we shall see shortly. In line with this there is also some indication that one and the same tRNA can recognize more than one codon.

Finally we may turn our attention to those instances in which the complete structure of tRNA is known, viz., the various tRNAs from yeast, single homogeneous molecular species described on page 144. As suggested there the anticodon-codon sites are for alanine pIpGpC: pGpCpC(U,A); for phenylalanine pOMeGpUpC: pUpUpU(A); for serine pIpGpA : pUpCpC(U,A) and for tyrosine pGpψpA : pUpApC(U).

MESSENGER RNA   *History.* Some species of informational or template RNA, i.e., an RNA molecule capable of specifying polypeptide structure, must be involved in protein synthesis as a direct consequence of the observation that the site of protein synthesis is provided by the ribosomes, a set of cytoplasmic structures, whereas information storage and replication are the province of DNA, which is localized in a separate compartment of even the least differentiated bacterial cell. Furthermore the very stability (chemical and metabolic) of DNA so necessary for its genetic function make it highly improbable that proteins are synthesized on genes directly. This led to the formulation of one of the central dogmas of molecular biology, which states that the flow of information proceeds by the steps DNA → RNA → protein. In this sequence the first arrow does not involve a change of code and is now referred to as *transcription*, whereas the second does involve such a change and requires a code book or dictionary, and is therefore referred to as *translation* proper. In other words the DNA and RNA maps are either identical or complementary, whereas the protein map constitutes only an analogue of either the DNA or the RNA map. The minimal hypothesis which found many adherents prior to 1961 was that ribosomal RNA was itself informational. This meant that each gene would specify a distinct type of ribosome that would then become a stable template and govern the synthesis of a specific protein. The model was supported by the finding that some proportion of the total population of ribosomal RNA appeared to be synthesized quite rapidly, although the bulk was relatively stable metabolically. It was further strengthened by the exciting discovery that the isolated RNA from certain plant viruses was itself infective and thus could act as a carrier of information.

Almost simultaneously, however, a number of facts came to light which in the aggregate made the hypothesis as stated above untenable.

1. Proteins vary widely in size and composition. Yet isolated ribosomes and ribosomal RNAs exhibit remarkable homogeneity in regard to composition, not only for any particular cell population, but even between different species (see Table 5-2). How then can cellular protein composition be governed by the composition of ribosomal RNA?

2. The composition of all the proteins of a cell must in some way be specified by that cell's DNA. The DNA of any one species appears remarkably homogeneous, but it varies from species to species over exceedingly wide limits ($X_A + X_T$ from 0.25 to 0.75). Yet ribosomal RNA, the postulated intermediate which in its aggregate should certainly reflect the composition of the bulk of the DNA, shows no such variation.

3. If new genes are introduced into a bacterial cell by conjugation, the model requires the gradual synthesis of novel ribosomes. This process would result in a parabolic curve if enzyme activity (corresponding to proteins newly synthesized) is plotted against time. Instead what is observed is an eclipse period of 2 min or less during which no protein is apparently synthesized at all followed by active synthesis of the protein at a constant and maximal rate.

4. Soon after the infection of a bacterial cell by a virulent bacteriophage, the former loses its capacity to synthesize characteristic bacterial proteins and instead becomes reprogrammed within a matter of a minute to the synthesis of proteins required for viral replication.

5. The effects of certain genetic alterations, the so-called "operator mutations" (see page 508), are the following. A whole group or block of genes (the operon) is turned on or off simultaneously but only if the mutation is present in the cis configuration. This means the configuration $Oabc/o'$ produces a different effect in the synthesis of proteins A, B, and C than does $o'abc/O$. The first configuration is brought about by introducing o' into a genotype $Oabc$, the second by introducing O into $o'abc$. The change $O \to o'$ may result either in rendering all genes inactive (O^o mutants) or in turning them all on simultaneously in the absence of an externally added inducer (O^c mutants). $Oabc/O^o$ produces functional A, B, and C, but O^oabc/O does not (see page 508). This is easily accounted for if we assume that regulation takes place at the level of transcription and not at that of translation, but this in turn implies the existence of an *unstable* template. The postulate of the existence of such a messenger RNA (mRNA) advanced by Jacob and Monod in 1961 was based primarily on this last point, but it also served to reconcile the others.

Evidence for the Existence of mRNA

1. An unstable RNA is synthesized very rapidly after bacteriophage infection but accounts for only a small fraction (≤ 5 per cent) of the total RNA present. Similar DNA-like RNAs could also be detected in uninfected bacteria and in growing yeast. Alternatively, if extremely short pulses of label are administered, a sizable proportion of the newly synthesized RNA is probably mRNA.

2. The presumed mRNA synthesized in the experiments under (1) hybridizes effectively with its appropriate parent DNA in a highly specific manner, e.g., the mRNA produced after T2 infection hybridizes with homologous phage DNAs but not with heterologous phage or bacterial DNAs, including that of the host.

3. Ribosomes by themselves can be shown to be essentially passive assembly

plants for translation. They are programmed for specific protein synthesis by attachment of a specific messenger to the 30-S (or 40-S in higher organisms) subunit of the active 70-S (or 80-S) ribosome, the transfer RNAs being attached to the 50-S (or 60-S) subunit. Subsequent to T2 infection no new ribosomes are made and preexisting bacterial ribosomes become the site of attachment of the newly synthesized mRNA.

4. Ribosomes with attached "natural" messengers synthesized in vivo can be stripped of practically their whole informational content in vitro. They can then be reprogrammed to synthesize proteins (or rather, to incorporate amino acids) in response to natural messengers. They can also synthesize amino acid homo- and heteropolymers, in response to synthetic messenger RNAs.

5. Viral RNA can function as messenger for the synthesis of virus-specific proteins in vivo even under conditions when the synthesis of all RNAs, including r-RNA, is completely inhibited by Actinomycin D. In selected instances bacteriophage RNA can even code for these proteins in vitro. Also under certain conditions an mRNA can be isolated that is formed subsequent to and duplicates the function of transforming DNA.

6. The biosynthesis of polycistronic messengers has been shown to be specifically elicited by the addition of the appropriate inducers.

7. The half-life of mRNA in different bacteria has been shown by a variety of techniques to be of the order of 90 sec at 37°C. This is a very short time, but longer than the interval currently estimated to be required for the synthesis of a complete polypeptide chain in the same system (≤ 10 sec) by about an order of magnitude which would suggest that an individual messenger can participate not in just one but in several translational cycles.

8. A soluble enzyme that catalyzes the transcription of DNA into complementary RNA has been isolated and extensively purified from a variety of cells. It is described in the next chapter (see page 485).

Some
Properties of mRNA

1. *Half-life.* mRNA molecules must vary greatly in their stability, first of all between microorganisms and higher organisms. This type of variability appears to be related to difference in rate of in vivo protein synthesis, i.e., between *E. coli* and rabbit reticulocytes the rates differ by a factor of about 50 (100 amino acids per sec in the former, 2 amino acids per sec in the latter, both at 37°). mRNAs may also vary in stability even within the same cell. The RNA-containing bacteriophages can function directly as messenger, yet remain inviolate throughout the life cycle of the virus in an infected bacterial cell, a matter of some 30 to 55 min at 37°. Messengers in higher organisms show even greater stability. Once the active cytoplasmic mRNA-Rb-tRNA complex has been formed, it may be turning out proteins continuously perhaps for days, and, under certain circumstances, even in the complete absence of *nuclear* DNA (as in mammalian erythrocytes), and a virtual absence of all RNA turnover.

2. *Size.* Greater care and improved techniques in isolation have led to a continued upward trend in the *s* value (and hence the size) of the entities tentatively identified as mRNA by sedimentation or chromatographic analyses. If, as is now believed, most messengers are themselves *polycistronic* and retain the complete information content of one operon, their size may indeed become quite formidable. For instance for the *His* operon in *E. coli*, which contains the

information for some 15 cistrons, it has been estimated, both from the length of the genetic message and from sedimentation analysis, that the messenger contains some 13×10^3 nucleotides (corresponding to a $M \simeq 4 \times 10^6$), an s value of 30 S, and an extended length of some 30,000 A. Similar evidence is also available for the *Lac* operon.

3. *Complementariness to DNA.* The conclusion has by now become inescapable that, at least in microorganisms, only one of the two strands of the DNA duplex, which may however be required to be present in the double-stranded conformation, is both necessary and sufficient for the specification of mRNA. Thus transcription is *asymmetric* and *strand-selective*.[1] The same holds true of the RNA synthesized in vitro by the DNA-dependent RNA polymerases, provided that DNA is of high molecular weight and retains its native conformation, and provided that care is taken in the isolation of the enzyme.

But asymmetric transcription has an important consequence, especially with regard to mRNAs transcribed from single genes or even operons. There is no reason to suppose, and every reason to doubt, that the base composition of an individual DNA strand in an individual gene or small cluster of genes bears any resemblance in its base composition to the gross global composition of the duplex DNA of the whole organism. Therefore individual mRNA species would not be expected to be DNA-like in their base composition.

Furthermore, all cellular RNAs, and that means the two species of r-RNA and all tRNAs, are complementary to certain specific regions of the homologous DNA. Therefore, not only do there exist specific cistrons for the synthesis of these various RNAs — and hence these particular RNAs themselves constitute final rather than intermediate gene products, in the sense that they do not specify any other molecule — but sequence complementariness is no longer a specific property of mRNA.

Ability to Code for Proteins. One of the characteristics, and indeed a sufficient condition, of mRNA is its ability to code for protein synthesis and amino acid incorporation. For quite some time it was believed that none of the other RNA species, nor DNA, could function in this manner. It now turns out that a crucial determinant is provided in large part by the absence of secondary structure in molecules of this type (correlated no doubt to their complete lack of self-complementariness).

Control of mRNA Formation. It is evident on logical grounds alone that transcription must precede translation in time, at least as far as the initial group of nucleotides transcribed, no matter how small, is concerned. Thus at this level transcription certainly controls translation. What is not certain any longer is whether the two processes are truly independent events in both time and space. One can readily conceive of models in which transcription may come to a halt, or at least the product of transcription be rendered functionally useless,[2] unless the highly reactive unstable mRNA molecule can be immediately integrated into an operational translation machine. Recent experiments in a number of microbial systems and on a number of levels suggest that transcription and

---

[1] Note that nothing is said here to the effect that it must be the same strand for each gene or operon.

[2] Say, by hydrolysis or phosphorolysis, or by interaction with some other cellular component.

translation are indeed tightly coupled in this fashion. For instance, one of the interesting features of microbial RNA synthesis has been the observation that in many strains (the so-called "stringently controlled" species) RNA synthesis in general, and this includes mRNA, appears to be dependent on the simultaneous presence of a full complement of all amino acids. If any one is missing, i.e., not supplied in the medium for an auxotroph requiring that particular amino acid, RNA synthesis ceases. This stringent control is in turn governed by a specific gene (RC^{st}), which can be mapped by standard techniques. Its modification produces so-called relaxed strains (RC^{rel}), which no longer exhibit this tight integration between amino acid supply and RNA synthesis. Also, it is quite likely that induction and repression are exerted at the level of transcription; yet polarity in these processes (see page 508) almost certainly has its roots in translational events.

REFERENCES   See lists following Chaps. 20 and 21, pp. 489 and 509.

20| Biosynthesis of Nucleic Acids

Biosynthesis of the nucleoside polyphosphates, the immediate precursors to the nucleic acids, was detailed in Chap. 18, and the role of nucleic acids as genetic material was developed in Chap. 19. Having this background, we are in a position to consider the mode of assembly of the nucleoside polyphosphates into the nucleic acids. In addition, the chemical inhibition of nucleic acid biosynthesis is discussed briefly.

POLYMERIZATION OF NUCLEOSIDE TRIPHOSPHATES

Biosynthesis of DNA

Since in most cells DNA is the central storehouse of genetic information that determines the biochemical specificity of the cell, and the genetic information is passed intact from parent to progeny on cell division, the central feature of DNA biosynthesis must be that of self-duplication. How may a DNA-directed synthesis of DNA be visualized? The concept of DNA serving as the template for its own reproduction arises naturally from the complementary base pairing between the two strands. Two alternative suggestions concerning the role of DNA as template have been offered. Watson and Crick, on the basis of their structural studies, suggested that each chain of the DNA duplex serves as template for the synthesis of a complementary chain. This model, termed *semi-conservative replication*, predicts that the template DNA molecule is divided equally between newly synthesized molecules after one cycle of replication. On the other hand *conservative replication* is visualized as involving the duplication of only one of the DNA strands, the DNA duplex serving as template, and, subsequently, the newly formed strand serving as template for the formation of its complement. In this case, after one replication cycle, the original DNA molecule would remain intact and the additional molecule would be composed entirely of newly formed strands. The course of DNA replication according to each of these possibilities is indicated schematically in Fig. 20-1.

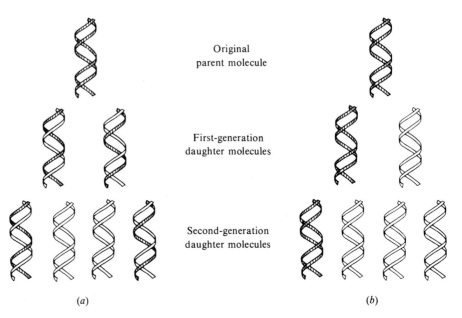

Original
parent molecule

First-generation
daughter molecules

Second-generation
daughter molecules

(a)   (b)

FIGURE 20-1.   Schematic Representation of DNA Replication According to the Semiconservative (a) and Conservative (b) Theories.—*M. Meselson and F. Stahl, Cold Spring Harbor Symp. Quant. Biol.*, **23**: *10 (1958).*

The classic experiment of Meselson and Stahl clearly indicates that, at least in some cases, the essential features of semiconservative replication actually take place in vivo. In this experiment, *E. coli* cultures were grown on a medium containing isotopically pure $N^{15}H_4Cl$ as the only source of nitrogen. Consequently, the DNA synthesized in the course of cell multiplication is "heavy," containing N^{15} rather than N^{14}. Such heavy DNA can be readily distinguished from "light" DNA by ultracentrifugation in a cesium chloride density gradient (see page 126). Cultures grown on $N^{15}H_4Cl$ were abruptly transferred to a medium containing normal (N^{14}) ammonium chloride, and the DNA of these cells was examined in the cesium chloride density gradient as a function of time. Initially, only one band with a density characteristic of the heavy DNA was observed as expected. After one generation of growth in the medium containing N^{14}, the *E. coli* DNA again exhibited a single band in the density gradient; this time the density was at the midpoint between those for the heavy and light species. Hence, after a single replication of the DNA, the product molecules must have contained one strand of the original heavy material and one newly synthesized strand of light material. This result is, of course, precisely that expected on the basis of the semiconservative replication theory. After two generations of growth on N^{14}, the DNA exhibited two equal bands in the density gradient, one with a density equal to that of the light DNA and one with a density equal to that of the light-heavy hybrid observed after one generation of growth. Reference to Fig. 20-1 indicates that this too is the expected result in terms of semiconservative replication.

Although these elegant experiments certainly indicate that for the cases examined the distribution of template material is in accordance with the suggestion of Watson and Crick, they do not prove that the whole template DNA duplex unwinds prior to replication. Indeed, such unwinding at neutral pH appears to be too slow to account for the rate of DNA biosynthesis. Consequently, one may imagine that the unwinding of the template duplex and the winding of the product duplexes may accompany and be aided by enzymatic reactions responsible for polynucleotide formation.

The enzymological aspects of DNA replication are of great interest. The first enzyme that converts deoxynucleoside polyphosphates into polymeric material was discovered in extracts of *E. coli* by A. Kornberg and his associates. This enzyme was termed *DNA polymerase*, or duplicase. The overall reaction catalyzed is indicated below:

$$\begin{matrix} n_1 dATP \cdot Me \\ + \\ n_2 dGTP \cdot Me \\ + \\ n_2 dCTP \cdot Me \\ + \\ n_1 dTTP \cdot Me \end{matrix} \underset{\text{DNA}}{\rightleftharpoons} DNA \begin{bmatrix} dAMP \\ dGMP \\ dCMP \\ dTMP \end{bmatrix}_{2n_1 + 2n_2} + 2(n_1 + n_2)PP_i \cdot Me \qquad (20\text{-}1)$$

The principal features of the reaction catalyzed by this enzyme are the following. (1) The substrates are the deoxynucleoside triphosphates; the diphosphates are not polymerized. All four deoxynucleoside triphosphates are required for reaction, although some exceptions are known; omission of one of these substrates almost completely abolishes formation of polymeric material. (2) The overall reaction is reversible. Pyrophosphate is produced in the polymerization in amounts corresponding to the stoichiometry indicated in Eq. (20-1). Incubation of DNA with high concentrations of pyrophosphate results in a partial depolymerization reaction. (3) The reaction is dependent on the presence of a divalent metal ion, usually magnesium. If the magnesium ion is replaced by a manganese ion, an interesting alteration in specificity is produced. In the presence of magnesium only the deoxynucleoside triphosphates serve as substrates, but in the presence of manganese the corresponding compounds derived from ribose are also utilized. Mixed ribo- and deoxyribonucleic acids may be synthesized in the presence of the latter metal ion. (4) The DNA polymerase reaction is dependent on the presence of a DNA primer. RNA does not substitute for DNA in this capacity. This is a point of great interest and is discussed in detail below. (5) DNA polymerase catalyzes the net synthesis of DNA-like molecules from the triphosphates. Quantities of DNA exceeding those of the primer material by more than twentyfold may be obtained in this reaction.

What are the structural characteristics of the polymeric material produced in this reaction, and what is its relationship to those of the primer? The answers to these questions reflect directly on the role of the DNA primer in this reaction. The primer might either serve as a starting point for the enzyme, and simply catalyze the elongation of the preexisting polynucleotide chains, or more interestingly, the primer might serve as template with the enzyme catalyzing the duplication of the template. The physical properties of the synthetic material argue strongly against the former alternative. Examination in the ultracentrifuge reveals the synthetic material to be polydisperse with sedimentation constants centering about those of the primer. Molecular weights of synthetic and primer DNAs are approximately the same as are the intrinsic viscosities. That the synthetic material is structurally similar to DNA is further established by the demonstration of 3',5'-phosphodiester linkages in dinucleotides obtained from incomplete DNase digests and by the fact that the material is susceptible to DNase digestion. Thus the synthetic material is a DNA and has gross physical characteristics similar to those of the primer.

Further evidence that the primer serves as template for its own replication is derived from base-composition studies. In Table 20-1, the base compositions

TABLE 20-1. Base Composition of Enzymatically Synthesized DNA

DNA	A	T	G	C	$(A+G)/(T+C)$	$(A+T)/(G+C)$
Mycobacterium phlei						
Primer	0.65	0.66	1.35	1.34	1.01	0.49
Product	0.66	0.65	1.34	1.37	0.99	0.48
Escherichia coli						
Primer	1.00	0.97	0.98	1.05	0.98	0.97
Product	1.04	1.00	0.97	0.98	1.01	1.02
Calf thymus						
Primer	1.14	1.05	0.90	0.85	1.05	1.25
Product	1.12	1.08	0.85	0.85	1.02	1.29
Bacteriophage T2						
Primer	1.31	1.32	0.67	0.70*	0.98	1.92
Product	1.33	1.29	0.65	0.70*	1.02	1.90

*Hydroxymethylcytosine.

of several samples of synthetic DNA are compared with those of the primer employed in the reaction. One notes that for all the synthetic products A = T and C = G and that the base compositions of primer and product are remarkably similar.

Clearly, the most elegant way to prove that the structure of the product is identical to that of the primer would be the comparison of base sequences in the two materials. Since the determination of the sequence of long segments of DNA is experimentally too difficult at the present time, one must rely on less direct lines of evidence. A novel approach to this problem has been provided by Kornberg in the form of "nearest-neighbor" analyses. For a nucleic acid containing four bases, there are clearly sixteen possible dinucleotide sequences. A nearest-neighbor analysis involves the determination of the absolute frequency with which each of these dinucleotide sequences appears in the particular DNA of interest. The result of a nearest-neighbor analysis is indicated in Table 20-2.

Three important conclusions may be drawn from extended collections of data of this type. First, all 16 dinucleotide sequences occur, and the frequency with which they occur is a sensitive function of the source of the DNA. Second,

the nearest-neighbor frequencies of product deoxyribonucleic acids are essentially identical to those of the primers, providing further evidence that the primer
serves as template in the DNA polymerase reaction. Finally, the DNA polymerase–catalyzed duplication of DNA yields a product in which the strands

TABLE 20-2. Dinucleotide Frequencies for *M. phlei* DNA Calculated from Radioactivity
Incorporation Experiments

Sequence	Frequency	Sequence	Frequency	Sequence	Frequency	Sequence	Frequency
TpA	0.012	TpT	0.026	TpG	0.063	TpC	0.061
ApA	0.024	ApT	0.031	ApG	0.045	ApC	0.064
CpA	0.063	CpT	0.045	CpG	0.139	CpC	0.090
GpA	0.065	GpT	0.060	GpG	0.090	GpC	0.122

SOURCE: J. Josse, A. D. Kaiser, and A. Kornberg, *J. Biol. Chem.*, **236:** 864 (1961).

are oriented with opposite polarities, as predicted on the basis of the Watson-
Crick model for DNA. The last conclusion is based on the fact that nearest-
neighbor frequencies for certain of the nucleotide pairs are predicted to be
identical on the basis of complementary base pairing; the predicted identities
depend on whether the two strands have similar or opposite polarities. For
example, on the basis of strands of opposite polarity, the frequency of ApG
(0.045) is predicted to be identical to that of CpT (0.045), whereas, on the basis
of strands of similar polarity, the frequency of ApG is predicted to be identical
to that of TpC (0.061). The data clearly support the former alternative. These
concepts are illustrated in Fig. 20-2.

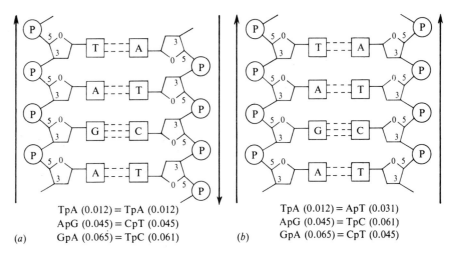

TpA (0.012) = TpA (0.012)	TpA (0.012) = ApT (0.031)
ApG (0.045) = CpT (0.045)	ApG (0.045) = TpC (0.061)
(*a*) GpA (0.065) = TpC (0.061)	(*b*) GpA (0.065) = CpT (0.045)

FIGURE 20-2. Contrast Between a Watson and Crick DNA Model with Strands of Opposite Polarity (*a*) and a
Model with Strands of Similar Polarity (*b*).
The predicted matching nearest-neighbor-sequence frequencies are different. Values in
parentheses are sequence frequencies from the experiment with *M. phlei* DNA. The strands
shown are newly synthesized strands aligned, for ease of comparison, as if they were complementary strands of a DNA double helix.—*J. Josse, A. D. Kaiser, and A. Kornberg, J. Biol.
Chem., 236: 864 (1961)*.

The comparison of base compositions and nearest-neighbor frequencies for primer and product DNA clearly indicates that the primer serves the role of template. However, this conclusion does not prove that the product molecules are identical to those of the primer. Indeed, under in vitro conditions at least, such seems not to be the case. As mentioned above, the physical properties of the product DNA are related but not identical to those of the primer. Furthermore, electron microscopic studies on DNA synthesized, employing a native double-stranded DNA as primer, indicate that the product has a "multiple-hairpin" structure. Thus the enzyme does not copy an entire DNA strand from beginning to end but apparently loops back and recopies material from the strand complementary to that which has already been duplicated. With a partially single-stranded DNA as primer, DNA polymerase serves as a repair enzyme, restoring the double-stranded structure. Further synthesis then results in the formation of multiple-hairpin structures as noted above. These results cast real doubts on the function of this enzyme in the cell. It appears probable that it serves a repair function, although it might function as both a repair and *de novo* synthesis enzyme under intracellular conditions. It seems certain, however, that enzymes having the same general characteristics indicated above must exist in most cells that are capable of catalyzing the precise duplication of DNA.

Biosynthesis of RNA
Several enzymes, differing in their substrate and primer requirements, have been identified that catalyze the polymerization of nucleoside polyphosphates to yield RNA. The first enzyme of this type to be discovered was *polynucleotide phosphorylase*, which was isolated from extracts of *Azotobacter vinelandii* by Grunberg-Manago and Ochoa. This enzyme, which requires a primer, catalyzes the formation of RNA from the nucleoside diphosphates, as indicated below:

$$
\begin{matrix}
n_1 \text{ADP} \\
+ \\
n_2 \text{GDP} \\
+ \\
n_3 \text{CDP} \\
+ \\
n_4 \text{UDP}
\end{matrix}
\xrightleftharpoons{\text{Mg}^{+2}}
\text{RNA}
\begin{bmatrix}
\text{AMP} \\
\text{GMP} \\
\text{CMP} \\
\text{UMP}
\end{bmatrix}_{n_1+n_2+n_3+n_4}
+ (n_1 + n_2 + n_3 + n_4)\text{P}_i
\qquad (20\text{-}2)
$$

The product of the polynucleotide phosphorylase reaction is a linear random polymer of ribonucleotide units linked by 3′,5′-phosphodiester bridges as revealed by chemical and enzymatic degradation. The primary structure of the polymeric product of this reaction is, hence, identical with that of naturally occurring ribonucleic acids.

The biological function of polynucleotide phosphorylase remains obscure. It appears certain that this enzyme is not responsible for synthesis of the various types of cellular RNA, since (1) at the concentrations of nucleoside diphosphates and inorganic phosphate that exist intracellularly, the equilibrium position favors phosphorolysis rather than polymerization, and (2) there is no relationship between primer structure and product structure. Yet as in the case of DNA synthesis, the specific base compositions of cellular ribonucleic acids require a *directed* synthesis. Perhaps polynucleotide phosphorylase serves as a mechanism for the destruction of unnecessary "informational RNA," creating simultaneously the substrates, ribonucleoside diphosphates, for formation of deoxyribonucleosides and subsequent DNA synthesis.

Weiss and his collaborators discovered a particulate enzyme from rat liver that exhibits many characteristics related directly to those of the DNA polymerase reaction. This enzyme, *RNA polymerase* (transcriptase), catalyzes the formation of polymeric material from the nucleoside triphosphates as substrates, with the elimination of pyrophosphate:

$$
\begin{matrix}
n_1 \text{ATP} \cdot \text{Me} \\
+ \\
n_1 \text{UTP} \cdot \text{Me} \\
+ \\
n_2 \text{GTP} \cdot \text{Me} \\
+ \\
n_2 \text{CTP} \cdot \text{Me}
\end{matrix}
\quad \underset{\text{DNA}}{\rightleftharpoons} \quad \text{RNA}
\begin{bmatrix}
\text{AMP} \\
\text{UMP} \\
\text{GMP} \\
\text{CMP}
\end{bmatrix}_{2n_1 + 2n_2}
+ (2n_1 + 2n_2)\text{PP}_i \cdot \text{Me}
\tag{20-3}
$$

Enzymes catalyzing similar reactions have since been isolated from a variety of sources. The polymeric product of these reactions is identical in terms of primary structure to native RNA. This reaction, like those catalyzed by DNA polymerase and polynucleotide phosphorylase, is reversible and is dependent on the presence of a divalent metal ion, ordinarily magnesium. The RNA polymerase reaction requires the presence of all four nucleoside triphosphates. Of particular interest is the requirement for a DNA primer for this reaction. This finding immediately raises the question of the relationship of primer and product structures. The following lines of evidence strongly suggest that the DNA primer serves as a template for RNA synthesis and that the base sequence of the DNA primer is faithfully transcribed into a corresponding sequence in RNA. First, the base ratios of product are nearly identical to those of primer (after substitution of uracil for thymine). When the single-stranded DNA from the virus ϕX174 is employed as primer, the base composition of the product RNA is complementary, as expected, to that of the DNA. Similarly, if the perfectly alternating polymer dAdT — which is formed in the DNA polymerase reaction in the presence of the appropriate triphosphates and in the absence of a primer — is employed as primer, only UMP and AMP are incorporated into the product, the incorporation of each being dependent on the presence of the alternate triphosphate. Second, the nearest-neighbor frequencies of primer and product are essentially identical. In one case, that of perfectly alternating dAdT, the base sequences of the product and primer can be shown, unambiguously, to be perfectly complementary. As shown by a simple nearest-neighbor analysis, the poly rUrA formed in the dAdT-primed reaction is also perfectly alternating. Third, specific complexes between primer DNA and product RNA can be demonstrated by rapid-heating and slow-cooling experiments (see page 140). The existence of such complexes strongly implies complementariness of extended regions of primer and product. Fourth, it has been demonstrated that, following infection of *E. coli* with bacteriophage T4, the RNA synthesized from the T4-DNA can be separated from the bulk bacteria RNA and that mutant (deletion) DNA produces an RNA that lacks a base sequence present in standard type. This result also indicates extensive complementary base pairing. Fifth, all cellular RNA, in the absence of viral infection, is synthesized in vivo from DNA templates. Sixth, actinomycin, a complex molecule which binds tightly to DNA, is a potent inhibitor of RNA synthesis (see below). In summary, RNA polymerase appears to transcribe the base sequence of a template DNA into that of

RNA. As indicated in the following chapter, such transcription is intimately concerned with the problem of informational, or messenger, RNA and the important problem of the DNA-directed assembly of specific polypeptides in general.

The identity of base composition, nearest-neighbor analysis, and the fact that the majority of primer DNA can be complexed with product RNA strongly suggest that in vitro both strands of DNA are transcribed into RNA. Is this also true in vivo? In the test tube, both single-stranded and double-stranded DNA serve as templates for the RNA polymerase reaction. Is this also true in vivo? In answer to the first question, several lines of evidence indicate that only one of the DNA strands is copied in the intact cell. The T4-specific RNA isolated by Bautz and Hall exhibits a noncomplementary base composition consistent with the copying of one strand only. Furthermore, Spiegelman and his collaborators have demonstrated that only one strand of the double-stranded replicating form of ϕX174 DNA is copied, more specifically, the strand that is *complementary* to the original single-stranded material. With bacteriophages it is frequently possible to separate the two strands of DNA physically and to show that the mRNA synthesized shortly after infection is complementary to only one of them. Under appropriate conditions the purified RNA polymerase selects only one of the two strands in double-stranded DNA even in vitro.

In addition to DNA-dependent RNA synthesis, RNA-dependent RNA polymerase (replicase) reactions are also known. The *RNA polymerases* from *M. lysodeikticus* and *Azotobacter* employ either RNA or DNA as primer, and, in each case, the primer appears to function as template. The same thing holds true of the polymerase from *E. coli*, provided the priming RNA is one with a great deal of double-stranded helical structure, such as that of certain animal viruses (*Reovirus*) and that the medium for the reaction includes Mn^{+2}. Once again efficient transcription requires a double-stranded helix, and specificity becomes blurred in the presence of Mn^{+2}. Both in vivo and in vitro RNA polymerization entails growth from the 5′-end as follows:

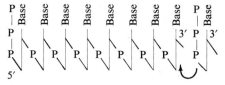

Infection of bacteria with RNA-phages, such as f2, the closely related MS2, and the unrelated Qβ, induces the formation of RNA-dependent RNA polymerases (replicases). These enzymes are responsible for replication of the phage RNA in the host cell. The polymerases induced by MS2 and Qβ appear unique among currently known polynucleotide-forming enzymes in that they are specific for their own RNA as primer. In other words, the enzyme from Qβ does not utilize RNA from MS2, and vice versa. RNAs from other sources also do not prime for these enzymes. Such specificity has obvious merit for phage replication, since the great majority of intracellular RNA encountered by the replicase is that of the host cell. Utilizing the enzyme from Qβ, Spiegelman has reported synthesis of biologically active, i.e., infectious, RNA in vitro. Once again the high specificity and selectivity are only observed in the presence of

Mg^{+2} as divalent metal cofactor and are not maintained in the presence of Mn^{+2}.

The principal types of enzymes responsible for the formation of polynucleotides, including some not specifically discussed above, together with their important properties, are summarized in Table 20-3.

TABLE 20-3. Summary of Some Enzymes That Catalyze Polynucleotide Synthesis

Name	Sources	Substrates	Products	Primer	Function of Primer
DNA polymerase (duplicase)	E. coli, mammalian tissues	All four deoxy-nucleoside triphosphates	DNA* (duplex)	DNA	Template
RNA polymerase (transcriptase)	Microorganisms, animal and plant tissues	All four nucleoside triphosphates	RNA (single-stranded)	DNA†	Template
RNA polymerase (replicase)	Microorganisms (especially virus-infected cells)	All four nucleoside triphosphates	RNA	RNA	Template
Polynucleotide phosphorylase	Microorganisms	One, two, three, or four nucleoside diphosphates	RNA homo-polymers, copolymers	Ribo–oligonucleotides and polynucleotides	Starting point for chain elongation. Also unknown functions
Poly A polymerase‡	Calf thymus Chick embryo	ATP	Poly A	RNA (poly A?)	Probably template

*Following an extended lag period and in the absence of primer, this enzyme will also catalyze the formation of ordered copolymers such as the dAdT copolymer, and the dG : dC homopolymer duplex.
†Some of the RNA polymerases are also primed by RNA under certain conditions.
‡Several enzymes catalyzing reactions of this general type have been identified.

CHEMICAL INHIBITION OF NUCLEIC ACID BIOSYNTHESIS

Interest in the chemical inhibition of the biosynthesis of nucleic acids stems from two principal sources. First, such inhibitors provide sensitive and convenient tools that aid greatly in establishing the interdependence of DNA synthesis, RNA synthesis, and protein synthesis. Second, they are of great interest as antimetabolites in general and, particularly, as antitumor agents. This is based on the fact that nucleic acid synthesis, and the dependent process of protein synthesis, is absolutely required for cell division. The most obvious biochemical difference between bacterial cells and tumor cells compared with the normal somatic cells of an adult animal is that the former types divide much more frequently than the latter. Hence, the antimetabolic function of nucleic acid inhibitors is expected to be more severe toward bacteria and tumor cells than toward the host organism. This partially selective toxicity forms the basis for the use of such agents in chemotherapy.

Most, but not all, chemical inhibitors of nucleic acid synthesis are structural analogues of compounds normally required for these reactions and are, in some cases, very powerful competitive inhibitors of enzymes involved in one or more steps in nucleic acid synthesis. Included in this group are certain compounds related to purines, pyrimidines, glutamine, and folic acid.

Pyrimidine Analogues

Pyrimidine analogues function as inhibitors of nucleic acid synthesis in a manner directly related to that discussed above. The most potent inhibitors of this type, the 5-fluoropyrimidines, particularly 5-fluorodeoxyuridine, specifically inhibit DNA synthesis by preventing the thymidylate synthetase reaction. Incorporation of the 5-fluoropyrimidines into RNA is occasionally noted, with interesting results in producing altered enzymes. These are usually, but not always, less active catalytically than the original. Incorporation into DNA appears not to occur. In contrast, the corresponding chloro, bromo, and iodo derivatives are readily incorporated into DNA, replacing thymine and yielding defective DNA molecules. The bromo derivative is most useful and functions as a potent mutagen (page 461). The distinct behavior of the fluoro, as contrasted to the other halogenated pyrimidines, is apparently a reflection of the fact that the van der Waals radii of the chloro, bromo, and iodo groups are not too different from that of methyl, the 5-substituent in thymine itself. The fluoro group, on the other hand, is very small and more nearly resembles a hydrogen, as in uracil, than the methyl of thymine. Hence the fluorinated, but not the other halogenated, derivatives compete with uracil derivatives in the thymine synthetase reaction and, by the same reasoning, the chloro, bromo, and iodo, but not the fluoro, derivatives act as thymine analogs in the assembly of DNA:

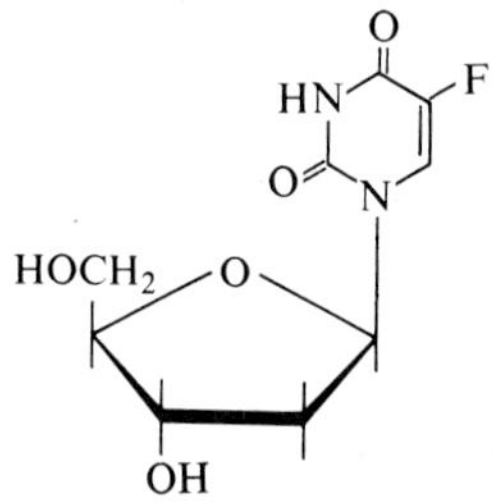

5-Fluorodeoxyuridine

Actinomycin D

Actinomycin D is an antibiotic isolated from *Streptomyces*. It is a complicated molecule structurally, having two short peptide chains that are bound in amide linkage to a dicarboxylic acid derivative of a phenoxazine:

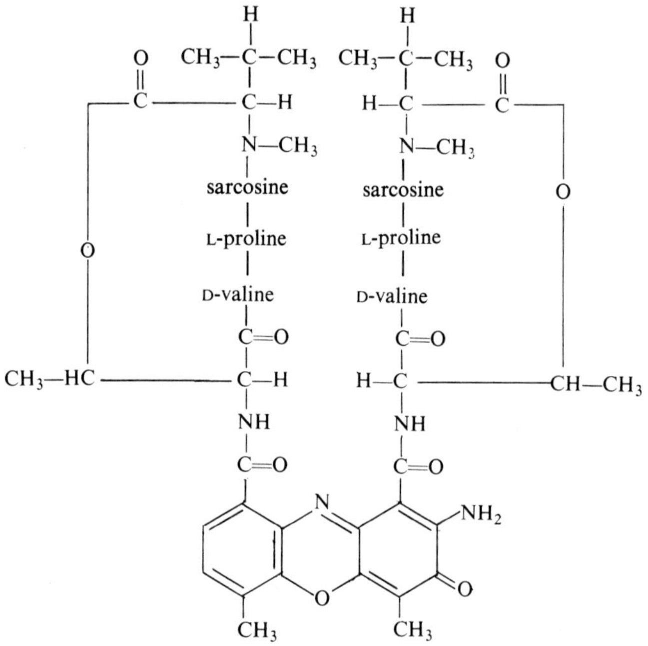

Actinomycin D

In vivo, Actinomycin D at low concentrations inhibits the synthesis of RNA but not of DNA in microorganisms, mammalian tissues, and tumor cells. The mechanism for this inhibition was initially suggested when it was found that this antibiotic binds strongly to DNA but not to RNA. Thus, such binding could quite conceivably render the DNA unsuitable for use as a template for RNA synthesis while permitting DNA synthesis to proceed. If this should be the case, all or most of the RNA synthesis of the cell must be DNA-dependent, since administration of actinomycin almost completely abolishes RNA synthesis. In accord with the DNA-actinomycin concept, DNA-dependent RNA polymerase is very strongly inhibited by actinomycin and, significantly, such inhibition may be partially overcome by the addition of excess DNA. In contrast, DNA polymerase is only slightly subject to actinomycin inhibition, and RNA-dependent RNA polymerase and polynucleotide phosphorylase are insensitive to this material. A hypothesis has been proposed which ascribes actinomycin action to hydrogen bonding with DNA guanines and which places the polypeptide side chains squarely in the major groove of the polymer (see page 122).

REFERENCES   Brockman, R. W., and E. P. Anderson: Biochemistry of Cancer, *Ann. Rev. Biochem.*, **32**: 463 (1963).

Chargaff, E.: "Essays on Nucleic Acids," Elsevier, New York, 1963.

————, and J. N. Davidson (eds.): "The Nucleic Acids," vols. I, II, 1955, and III, 1960, Academic Press, New York.

Cold Spring Harbor Symposium on Quantitative Biology: "Synthesis and Structure of Macromolecules," vol. XXVIII, 1963.

Georgiev, G. P.: The Nature and Biosynthesis of Nuclear Ribonucleic Acids, *Progr. Nucleic Acid Res. in Mol. Biol.*, **6**, 259 (1967).

Grunberg-Manago, M.: Enzymatic Synthesis of Nucleic Acids, *Ann. Rev. Biochem.*, **31**: 301 (1962).

Hershey, A. D.: in D. E. Green (ed.), "Currents in Biochemical Research," p. 1, Interscience, New York (1956).

Karnofsky, D. A., and B. D. Clarkson: Cellular Effects of Anti-cancer Drugs, *Ann. Rev. Pharm.*, **3**: 357 (1963).

Perutz, M. F.: "Proteins and Nucleic Acids: Structure and Function," Elsevier, New York, 1962.

Sinsheimer, R. L.: First Steps Toward a Genetic Chemistry, *Science*, **125**: 1123 (1957).

Stevens, A.: Ribonucleic Acids: Biosynthesis and Degradation, *Ann. Rev. Biochem.*, **32**: 15 (1963).

Taylor, J. H. (ed.): "Molecular Genetics," Academic Press, New York, 1963.

Weissman, C., and S. Ochoa: Replication of Phage RNA, *Progr. Nucleic Acid Res. in Mol. Biol.*, **6**, 353 (1967).

21| Biosynthesis of Proteins

Most of the recent spectacular progress in our understanding of the biochemistry of protein synthesis has been due to the ability to reconstruct most
of its key features in cell-free systems, the time-honored methodological approach
of the biochemist. The first such system was discovered in 1952 by Siekevitz,
then working in Zamecnik's laboratory at Harvard and using the microsomal
fraction of rat liver. Several important discoveries in the next three years similarly
either came from or were simultaneously initiated in Zamecnik's laboratory:
the fact that ribosomes were the portion of the microsomal fraction responsible
for protein synthesis; that the amino acids participating had to be activated by
ATP in a reaction producing PP_i and catalyzed by specific activating enzymes
(amino acyl synthetases or acylases); and that the natural acceptor for these
amino acids, an important intermediate in protein synthesis, was furnished by
a specialized fraction of RNA molecules of low molecular weight, localized in
the cytoplasm, now called transfer RNA (tRNA).

Most of the key experiments have subsequently been performed with just
two systems:

1. A cell-free system from rabbit reticulocytes (immature red cells), first
studied by Schweet in 1958, which has the great advantage of producing, or at
least of completing, the chains of hemoglobin, a well-characterized, soluble
protein, the complete primary structure of which is now known (see page 89).

2. A similar system from *E. coli*, first studied in 1960 by Lamborg and
Zamecnik, and by Tissieres and his associates which has three general advantages: (*a*) it is a great deal more active than most other systems studied; (*b*) under

appropriate conditions it retains many of the features of the in vivo system, including the "flow of information," DNA → RNA → protein, i.e., operationally, the stimulation of amino acid incorporation by addition of DNA, which in turn engenders active RNA synthesis; and most importantly (c) by further treatment the system can be made to respond to the addition of purified oligo- and poly-ribonucleotides ("synthetic" or natural messengers) in a highly specific manner. It was this discovery by Nirenberg and Matthei and shortly thereafter by Ochoa and his collaborators in 1961 which led directly to the cracking of the genetic code. From studies on these systems, and confirmed by many others, a current, generalized picture of protein synthesis would require the following participants (Fig. 21-1):

1. A pool containing adequate amounts of the 20 common amino acids.

2. A minimum of 20 amino acid–activating enzymes plus an adequate supply of ATP.

3. A pool of tRNA molecules consisting of 20 to 50(?) different and specific molecules: as many as there are actual codons, or groups of equivalent codons (synonyms), that specify individual amino acids. This population of tRNAs in the aggregate constitutes the genetic dictionary, the mechanism that brings the polynucleotide into congruence with the polypeptide code.

4. A competent messenger molecule. In the case of the synthesis of a specific polypeptide capable of forming part of a biologically functional protein, this means a polyribonucleotide into which has been transcribed, with complete fidelity, the complete polynucleotide sequence of a particular, genetically active segment of DNA.

5. A pool of active, structurally intact 70-S (80-S in higher organisms) ribosomes, each containing a functional 30-S and 50-S subunit.

6. A minimum of two enzymatic components (transfer factors) concerned with actual polypeptide formation.

7. A pool of GTP, a source of reducing groups (glutathione, mercaptoethanol, etc.), and K^+ and Mg^{+2} ions, all required for process c below.

8. System(s) concerned with chain initiation and, perhaps, release.

These various components participate in a sequential series of reactions summarized in Fig. 21-1, consisting of the following steps, discussed separately below:

a. Activation of amino acids and formation of amino acyl-tRNA molecules;

b. Formation of a competent complex between ribosomes and mRNA;

c. Binding of amino acyl-tRNA to this complex;

d. Initiation of chain growth and formation of peptide bonds in the complex;

e. Release of completed chains from the complex.

Activation and Formation of Amino Acyl-tRNAs

Activating Enzymes (Synthetases). These enzymes appear to be highly specific for individual amino acids and to catalyze the following reactions:

$$\text{Amino acid}_x + \text{ATP} + E_x \underset{}{\overset{Me^{+2}}{\rightleftharpoons}} (\text{amino acyl}_x\ \text{AMP}\cdot E_x) + PP_i \tag{a}$$

$$(\text{Amino acyl}_x\ \text{AMP}\cdot E_x) + \text{tRNA}_x \underset{}{\overset{Me^{+2}}{\rightleftharpoons}} \text{amino acyl}_x\text{-tRNA}_x + E_x + \text{AMP} \tag{b}$$

$$\text{ATP} + \text{amino acid}_x + \text{tRNA}_x \underset{\Delta G^{0\prime} \simeq 0}{\overset{E_x}{\rightleftharpoons}} \text{amino acyl}_x\text{-tRNA}_x + \text{AMP} + PP_i$$

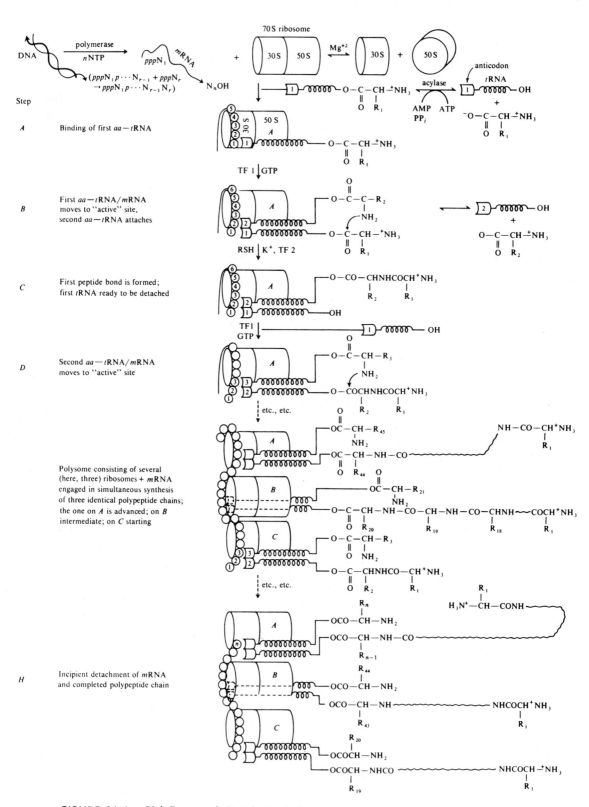

FIGURE 21-1. Unit Processes in Protein Synthesis.

Reaction a is very similar to the first step in the enzymatic activation of acetate and higher fatty acids (see p. 316). Substrate specificity is evident for both partial reactions, with the rejection of inappropriate partners being more stringent in reaction b. This might have been anticipated, since this step involves the mutual recognition of two specific macromolecules. Substitution of one natural amino acid for another in this process has been estimated as occurring 1 time in 10,000. This high degree of selectivity is of the utmost importance in minimizing errors in protein synthesis and maintaining a maximum of fidelity in the translation process. For once the appropriate amino acyl-tRNA has been formed, the only operative code is the polynucleotide one; i.e., there are no additional safeguards assuring the rejection of the wrong amino acids. This is the essence of the "adaptor hypothesis," first proposed by Crick in 1958, which postulates that "adaptor molecules" (now identified as the $tRNA_x$s) intervene between amino acids and the polynucleotide so as to simultaneously bind and interact with, selectively, specific polynucleotide coding units to one portion of the molecule and an appropriate amino acid to another.

The hypothesis also explains two additional experimental facts. On the one hand, for any one polypeptide uniquely specified by a single gene, natural but inappropriate amino acids are very rarely if ever incorporated in the place of other natural amino acids; on the other hand, a number of amino acid analogues (e.g., selenomethionine for methionine, p-fluorophenylalanine or thienylalanine for phenylalanine, 5-hydroxytryptophan or azatryptophan for tryptophan, etc.) are readily incorporated in the place of their natural counterparts. Any amino acid, provided it can only fool the activating enzyme, is inexorably incorporated in the place of its natural analogue.

Transfer RNAs. As the individual entries comprising the genetic dictionary, the transfer RNAs have come in for a considerable share of attention in the course of the past five or six years, culminating in Holley's epochal announcement early in 1965 of the complete structure of one of the $tRNA_{Ala}$ from yeast. To recapitulate some of the general features of tRNA structure (see page 142), they are relatively small, hence "soluble," polyribonucleotide molecules of remarkably uniform size and consisting of some 70 to 80 nucleotide residues. Besides the four common bases they also contain a relatively large proportion of unusual bases, such as pseudouridine and various methylated bases, the modification of which probably took place subsequent to their incorporation into the polymeric structure. In spite of this the molecules show a high degree of sequence complementariness and, hence, especially in the presence of Mg^{+2}, of secondary structure. There may exist as many different species of tRNA as there are meaningful codons, and in certain instances at least (e.g., in the case of leucine), it has been possible to equate particular tRNA fractions with particular coding units, so that a particular fraction serves as a source of activated amino acid in response to one codon rather than another. There appears to be a considerable degree of species specificity but with a kind of mutual complementariness, such that any difference in the structure of any tRNA is compensated for by corresponding alterations of the appropriate activating enzymes. These considerations taken in conjunction with the probable universality of the code, and with the results of experiments involving

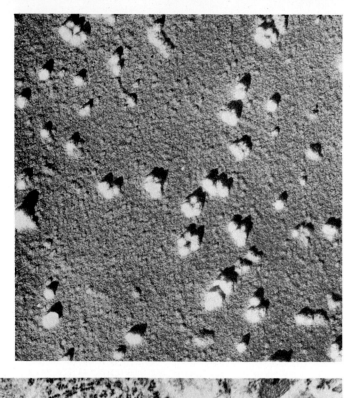

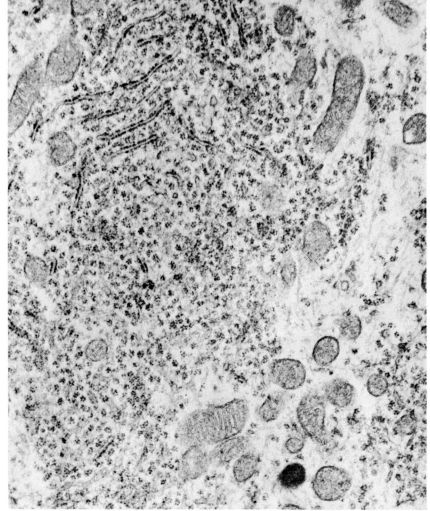

various chemical modifications of different bases, argue strongly in favor of the autonomy and structural distinctiveness of the two recognition sites characteristic of each tRNA molecule: one for mRNA, i.e., the (anti) coding site, the other for the activating enzyme. The recognition at the latter site may involve clusters of the rare bases, and it is this site which may vary from species to species.

In spite of these various strong indications of a high degree of individuality, tRNAs also show additional remarkable similarities of structure and function that may be summarized as follows (see page 142):

pGp···GpTpUpCpGp···pCpCpA

They all share in a terminal 5'-guanylate (occasionally 5'-cytidylate) residue at the tail, in a common pentanucleotide sequence somewhere in the center of the molecule, and in the sequence pCpCpA, i.e., one ending in a free 3'-adenosine residue, at the head. It is at this residue that the attachment of the amino acid takes place, and the aminoacyl-tRNAs are therefore the acyl esters linked to the 2'- (or 3'-, the exact position is not known) hydroxyl of a terminal adenosine.

Formation of a Complex between Rb and mRNA

The Active Complex. The ribosomal particle active in protein synthesis in *E. coli* is one with an s value of 70 S and an overall length of about 180 A made up of two nonidentical subunits of 30 and 50 S that form this specific aggregate in the presence of relatively high concentrations of $Mg^{+2}(\geq 10^{-3}$ M). Each of the two subunits ($M = 9 \times 10^5$ and 1.8×10^6, respectively) contains about one-third protein and two-thirds RNA by weight. The RNA species corresponding to the two subunits have s values of 16 and 23 S each (corresponding to $M \simeq 6 \times 10^5$ and 1.2×10^6), and probably constitute distinct molecular species, not only with respect to size, but also to composition and base sequence.

In systems capable of effective protein synthesis, in vivo or in vitro, these individual 70- or 80-S ribosomes are attached to a more or less fully extended single-stranded mRNA molecule, thus forming linear or rosette-shaped clusters (see Fig. 21-2) or arrays, which have variously been called *polyribosomes*, *polysomes*, or *ergosomes*. During actual protein synthesis the size of these clusters remains remarkably constant, since a single ribosome attaches to one of the terminal ends of the messenger and travels along the mRNA (or at least the two entities shift position relative to one another) away from this end while peptide bonds are formed on the complex. After a certain distance has been

---

FIGURE 21-2. Electron Micrographs of Polysome Structures.
Top: Electron micrograph of a purified and separated fraction of rat brain polysomes. Both clustered and linear pentameters are seen (magnification 63,000×).—*Courtesy of A. Campagnoni and J. Ewing. Bottom*: Cytoplasm of Deiter's neuron from cat brain. In this section of embedded material ribosomes are arrayed along the endoplasmic reticulum as well as in polysomal clusters (magnification 52,500×).—*Courtesy of C. Cotman and S. Hertweck.*

traversed, enough room is made available to allow attachment of a second ribosome, and so on, until the ribosome first to become attached reaches the opposite end of the message, or at least the end of that particular cistron. Upon the resultant attachment and accretion of the last amino acid residue two events take place more or less simultaneously. The completed polypeptide chain becomes detached from the ribosome, and that particle which has been responsible for the process of chain lengthening from residue 1 to residue n either becomes detached from the messenger and reenters the pool of ribosomes or else starts translating the next cistron. Thus on the average the size of the ribosomal cluster is more or less constant and bears some relation to the length of the messenger. Indeed, whereas the polysomes responsible for hemoglobin synthesis (M of polypeptide $= 16 \times 10^3$; 140 aa residues), or those found in normal mammalian cells, consist of clusters with a peak distribution at 5 to 6 particles and s values around 200 S, those formed under the aegis of a very large polycistronic messenger, such as poliovirus RNA, have an average s value of almost 600 S and a peak distribution around 16 to 18 particles per cluster. Similarly serum albumin (575 residues) appears to be specified by an mRNA 6,000 Å long along which cluster 20 ribosomes, and the *lac*- and *his*-messengers are of even larger size. Available data suggest an average length of 30 to 35 amino acids (100 nucleotides) per ribosome as a rough approximation.

Formation of polysomes can be observed, not only with natural mRNA molecules, both in vivo or in vitro, but also with various polyribo- and deoxyribonucleotides, including synthetic homo- and heteropolymers. When these systems are supplied with a pool of appropriate tRNAs acylated by their amino acids (or tRNAs plus free aas plus synthetases plus ATP), transfer and initiation enzymes, GTP, Mg^{+2}, and K^+, active protein or polypeptide synthesis ensues. These are the facts that underlie the observation of polynucleotide-directed polypeptide synthesis already referred to, first reported in 1961 by Nirenberg and Matthei, and by Lengyel, Speyer, and Ochoa, that inexorably led to the breaking of the genetic code.

Results with Synthetic Messengers: Composition of Triplets. The seminal observations were the following. On incubating the partially purified *E. coli* system in the presence of homopolymeric U $(Up)_n$ obtained by the action of polynucleotide phosphorylase on UDP with various amino acid mixtures in which only one of the constituents was labeled, i.e., 19 "cold," 1 "hot," Nirenberg and Matthei found that only phenylalanine appeared to be incorporated. In fact they were able to demonstrate that the highly insoluble product consisted of polyphenylalanine. Thus poly U, and by inference a (p)UpUpU(p) triplet, had "coded" for Phe. The extension of this work — using first a variety of homopolymers and random heterocopolymers all synthesized in vitro by the polynucleotide phosphorylase reaction — rapidly led to the assignment of various coding units, defined by their composition, but not their sequence, and designated as triplets by courtesy only. Thus it was shown that poly C coded for proline and poly A for lysine. With the use of statistical heteropolymers it was possible to relate relative abundance of hypothetical coding units with relative incorporation frequency for instance as follows:

Polymer	Compositional triplet	Relative statistical abundance (calculated)	Relative incorporation frequency* (observed)
UG(5 : 1)	U₃	100	Phe (100)
	U₂G(UUG,UGU,GUU)	20	Cys (20); Val (20)
	UG₂(UGG, GUG, GGU)	4	Gly (4); Trp (5)
	GGG	0.8 (insignificant)	
UA(5 : 1)	U₂A	20	Tyr (25); Ile (20); Leu (14)
	UA₂	4	Lys (3); Asn (7)
AC(5 : 1)	A₃	100	Lys (100)
	A₂C	20	Asn (30); Thr (23); Gln (44)
	AC₂	4	Pro (5)
AU(5 : 1)	A₂U	20	Ile (20); Asn (28)
	UA₂	4	Leu (3); Tyr (3)
CG(5 : 1)	C₃	100	Pro (100)
	C₂G	20	Ala (22); Arg (19)
	CG₂	4	Gly (5)

*Relative to the pure homopolymer (UUU) as (100).

Finally in the hands of Khorana and his collaborators the use of polymers of known sequence, such as ABABAB... and ABCABCABC... led to unambiguous assignments (see page 499).

Direction of
Readout
Earlier work suggested that on relatively short exposure to a labeled amino acid newly synthesized protein molecules show unequal labeling patterns that could be interpreted in terms of the following model (see Fig. 21-3A). Polypeptide chains are initiated at one terminus and grow by the stepwise addition of amino acids one at a time until the other terminus is reached. Therefore at any one moment polypeptides are present at various stages of completion. Now let us add a labeled amino acid at this time. Provided that the duration of the labeling pulse is as short as the period required to synthesize a complete chain, the various chains completed during this pulse incorporate label in direct proportion to the number of times the amino acid appears in the chains yet to be completed. Thus the specific activity of any amino acid in different positions down the length of the chain should be a function of its distance away from the initiating terminus, which can therefore be identified unambiguously.

The model has been tested by several investigators in a number of different systems. For instance Dintzis performed some very elegant experiments (see Fig. 21-3B). He exposed reticulocytes at 15° to H^3-leucine for periods of time varying from 4 to 60 min and found an increase in specific activity of the leucine-containing peptides (seven in the α-chain, eight in the β-chain) rising smoothly as a function of their distance from the N terminus. This effect decreased with length of incubation time.

In all the systems studied, the polypeptide chain is built up by stepwise formation of peptide bonds starting from the N terminus. The time required to complete a polypeptide chain containing some 150 residues in vertebrate systems is of the order of 3 min at 37° and 7 min at 15°. In bacterial systems it is more rapid by about an order of magnitude.

Binding of Amino
Acyl-tRNA to the
mRNA-Rb Complex
Recognition between mRNA and Amino Acyl-tRNA. E. coli ribosomes can be made to bind tRNA specifically involving the actual crucial act of recognition

between the codon on the mRNA and the anticodon or "nodoc" on a charged tRNA[1] by adding to the ribosomes oligo- or polynucleotides. Now poly U induces the binding of phenylalanyl-tRNA specifically, and, as shown by Nirenberg and Leder, so do uridylate oligonucleotides. This exciting observation and its obvious extensions allowed these investigators to obtain answers to the following pivotal qustions in one and the same set of experiments:

1. What is the actual, as distinct from the hypothetical, coding ratio?
2. Are all codons of identical composition and sequence equally effective?
3. What is the actual sequence of bases for various codons?

The answer to question 1 is that the minimal chain length in oligonucleotide messengers required to induce specific binding to tRNA equals 3: $(pU)_3$, $(pA)_3$, and $(pC)_3$ are effective messengers, in this sense, for Phe, Lys, and Pro respectively, and the corresponding $(pN)_2$ are not. (2) The relative effectiveness of the three possible arrangements $pXpYpZ$, $XpYpZp$, and $XpYpZ$, i.e., free

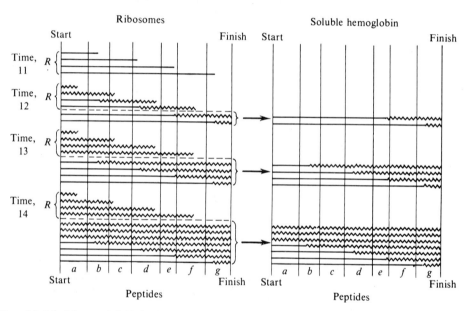

FIGURE 21-3A.   Model of Sequential Chain Growth.
The straight lines represent unlabeled polypeptide chains. The zigzag lines represent radioactively labeled polypeptide chains formed after the addition of a radioactive amino acid at time t_1. The groups of peptides designated R are unfinished bits attached to the ribosomes at each time; the rest, having reached the finish line, are assumed to be present in the soluble hemoglobin. In the ribosomes at time t_2, the top two completely zigzag lines represent peptide chains formed completely from amino acids during the time interval between t_1 and t_2. The middle two lines represent chains that have grown during the time interval but have not reached the finish line and are, therefore, still attached to the ribosomes. The bottom two chains represent those that have crossed the finish line, left the ribosomes, and are to be found mixed with other molecules of soluble hemoglobin.—*H. M. Dintzis and P. M. Knopf, in H. Vogel, V. Bryson, and J. Lampen (eds.). "Informational Macromolecules," Academic Press, New York, 1963.*

---

[1] In the current literature it has become common to refer to the code groups in the mRNA as the primary coding units. This then makes the complementary group on the appropriate tRNA an anticodon. However it is well to remember that in cellular organisms the primary code unquestionably is represented by the DNA base sequence. Thus mRNA codons are complementary and tRNA codons equivalent to the appropriate DNA codons.

3′- (and 2′- OH)(α), free 5′- OH(β) and free OH in both positions (γ), are grossly different, arrangement α being most effective, β being virtually inactive, and γ intermediate in effect. These results suggest the triplets are either read in sequence starting from a free 3′(2′) end (solid lines) or, alternatively, that the

$$\overleftarrow{(p) X_n Y_n Z_n} \quad \overleftarrow{p \cdots} \quad \overleftarrow{p X_3 p \ Y_3 p Z_3} \quad \overleftarrow{p X_2 p \ Y_2 p Z_2} \quad p X_1 p \ Y_1 p Z_1 {-}OH$$

readout starts at the 5′-end but now *requires* 5′-esterified phosphate (dashed line). Recent results tend to favor the latter hypothesis.[1] For instance, poly-nucleotides of the structure A(pA)$_n$pC code for polylysine with a C-terminal asparagine. Hence reading must have progressed from left to right and produced H$_2$N-Lys-(Lys)$_{n/3 - 1}$-Asn-CO$_2$H. (3) Selection of sequence isomers is highly specific and recognition involves polarity; GpUpU induces Val-tRNA binding while UpUpG does not, and in fact produces binding of Leu-tRNA. Together with some of the other lines of evidence already mentioned the current assign-ments summarized in Table 19-3 have been obtained.

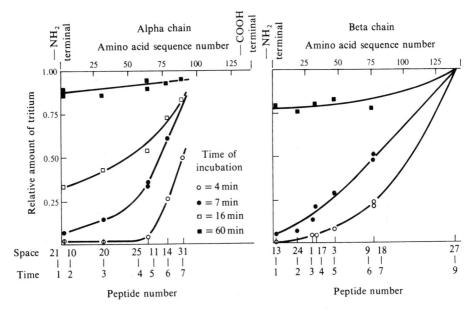

FIGURE 21-3B. Distribution of H^3-leucine Among Tryptic Peptides of Soluble Rabbit Hemoglobin After Various Times of Incubation at 15°.

The peptides are positioned by assuming that the leucines have the same sequence numbers in rabbit and human hemoglobins. If more than one leucine is present in the human peptide, an arithmetic-average sequence number is used to indicate the peptide position. This sequence of peptides along the chains is indicated by their position in "space," starting with the N terminus on the left. After four minutes of exposure to label, only the peptides near the C-terminal end are labeled. After more prolonged exposure, there is a gradient rising from the N-terminal end. This permits the ordering of peptides sequentially during the assembly process—their position in "time."—*H. M. Dintzis and P. M. Knopf, in H. Vogel, V. Bryson, and J. Lampen (eds.), " Informational Macromolecules," Academic Press, New York, 1963.*

---

[1] Since mRNA formation also starts at the 5′-end (the polymerase produces a chain com-mencing with pppX…), it is evident that both transcription and translation start from the same end of the chain.

Miscoding, Ambiguity, Suppression. In view of all these results it is not unlikely that the specific interaction between mRNA and tRNA, which is tantamount to translation at the level of the code, takes place prior to and is indeed independent of the formation of the peptide bond proper. Therefore many of the effects reported concerning incorporation of wrong or ambiguous amino acids probably can be explained by miscoding or incomplete correspondence at this level.

Experiments bearing on the relation between ambiguous coding and suppression are of the greatest interest.[1] We recall the observations that a mutation resulting in a change Gly → Arg resulted in an ineffective A protein (see page 469). Introduction of an unlinked suppressor into the genome produced a cell that produced two different types of A protein. The majority of the molecules still contained Arg instead of Gly, but in a minority the wild type protein was produced; i.e., the reverse change Arg → Gly had taken place.

From Table 19-3, Gly = GpGpU/C, Arg = CpGpU/C. A slight alteration in the structure of the tRNA for Gly, or, as we shall see, in the ribosomes, or even in the intracellular environment, could allow an occasional Gly-tRNA (presumed tRNA triplet = CpCpA/G) instead of the correct Arg-tRNA (triplet = GpCpA/G) to bind to the CpGpU/C triplet of the mRNA.

The intracellular environment also can affect the interaction of ribosomes, mRNA and tRNA. For instance, raising the Mg^{+2} concentration or lowering the temperature increases the extent to which Leu is coded for by poly U. Coincident with this stimulatory effect for Leu there is an inhibitory one for Phe. It would appear then that under certain conditions the specific mRNA-tRNA interaction can be rendered less selective and the degree of ambiguity of certain codons increased. These in vitro effects may have their counterpart in vivo. The inability of phage *r*II mutants to replicate in strain K12 (λ) can be overcome by high concentrations of Mg^{+2}; leucine in excess inhibits the growth of *Aspergillus*, an effect that can be reversed by adding phenylalanine; and even more spectacularly, leucine is lethal to a Phe-, Pro-, and His-requiring strain of *E. coli* K12 when Phe is omitted from the growth medium, but not in the absence of either of the other two amino acids. Finally the action of certain suppressors in permitting the specific synthesis of certain proteins both in vivo and in vitro has been correlated with their ability to permit the ambiguous translation of a nonsense codon in terms of a meaningful amino acid. The reestablishment of proper phasing as the basis of a different type of suppression has already been described on page 467.

Peptide Bond Formation and Chain Elongation

1. There is a single growing polypeptide chain per individual ribosome within a polysomal cluster.

2. Each of these individual particles also carries a minimum of two and a possible maximum of three tRNA molecules. One of these is accounted for by

---

[1] The molecular basis for the amber mutation (see page 460) and its suppressor is the following. The original mutation is, e.g., from Gln (CAG) or Trp (UGG) to the amber nonsense codon UAG. Suppressor A allows the latter to be recognized as a codon for Ser, because of the presence of a novel type of tRNA$_{Ser}$ in strains containing this gene. Similar considerations also obtain for the two other nonsense codons UAA (ochre) and UGA.

the growing chain attached in ester linkage to the 2'-(3')-OH of its terminal adenosine, the other by the free amino acyl-tRNA corresponding to the next residue to be added.

3. The energy required for moving the mRNA relative to the ribosome and positioning the amino acyl-RNA is probably provided by the hydrolysis of GTP.

4. The formation of the peptide bond requires a labile SH- enzyme (transfer factor II or peptide synthetase) and is activated by K^+ ions.

A speculative scheme demonstrating how these various facts may be put together is outlined in Figs. 21-1 and 21-4. The incoming amino acyl-tRNA is

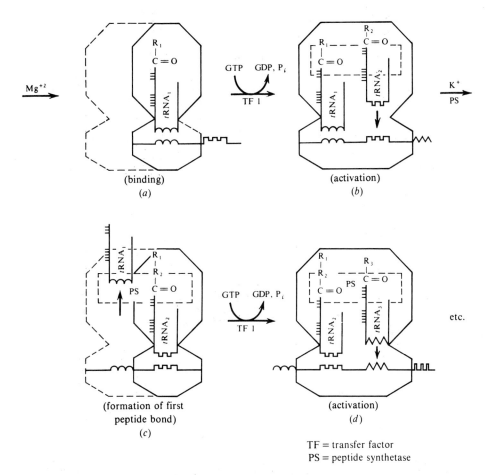

(binding)
(a)

(activation)
(b)

(formation of first
peptide bond)
(c)

(activation)
(d)

etc.

TF = transfer factor
PS = peptide synthetase

FIGURE 21-4. Detailed View of the First Four Steps [(a) Through (d)] in Protein Synthesis (see Fig. 21-1).— *After Schweet, Arlinghaus, Heintz, and Shaeffer; reproduced by permission of Professor R. S. Schweet.*

first aligned on the 50-S ribosomal subunit in such a fashion as to allow maximum and selective recognition between its complementary coding site and the coding site on the mRNA corresponding to the N-terminal amino acid. This amino acyl-tRNA is then primed for polymerization by being moved to the "polymerization site." Simultaneously the mRNA is moved one unit along the ribosome. The energy for these processes is provided by the hydrolysis of one molecule of GTP (in reticulocytes at least, the reaction requires an enzyme, transfer factor I). This movement frees the first, or "recognition site," for positioning of amino acid 2. Peptide bond formation then takes place by attachment of amino acyl residue 1 to the free-NH_2 group of amino acyl-tRNA 2:

$$RHN\!-\!CH(R_1)C \overset{O}{\overset{\|}{}} \underset{\underset{O-tRNA_n:}{}}{} \quad \overset{H}{\underset{H}{N}}\!-\!CH(R_2)\!-\!C \overset{O}{\nearrow}_{O-tRNA_{n+1}}$$

The resulting amino acyl dipeptide-tRNA is thereupon moved into the polymerization site, with an attendant movement of mRNA relative to the ribosome, and amino acyl-$tRNA_3$ can now occupy the recognition site. Peptide formation occurs by attack of the amino group of amino acyl-$tRNA_3$ on the ester carbon of the dipeptidyl-tRNA, which now becomes the carrier of the growing chain, and so forth. We have left open the question of whether the tRNA just freed of its *aa* first occupies an "exit site" or is detached simultaneously with the binding of the incoming amino acyl-tRNA.

Chain Release　　Very little is known concerning the factors, specific or otherwise, that control the release of the completed polypeptide chain from the polysome. One model postulates release to occur when the codon corresponding to the C-terminal residue has passed through the polymerization site and is dependent on the simultaneous removal of the ribosome on which this event took place. This simple picture must certainly be modified in the case of polycistronic messengers, where one or both of the following two mechanisms must be operative. Either there must be a signal that allows a completed polypeptide chain to drop off, which in turn allows the ribosome to commence the translation of the next cistron at a defined starting point and in phase, or else the signal must allow coordinated detachment of both ribosome and polypeptide chain, even though the mRNA continues on and on. In the latter case there must also be another signal at the beginning of the next cistron that tells another ribosome yet to be attached where to resume the translation of the message. Such "end-cistron" – "start-cistron" recognition signals or cistron-dividing elements must certainly exist. What would constitute a suitable candidate for such a chain-terminating element? Current studies suggest that nonsense triplets may well fulfill such a role. In *E. coli* the ochre triplet UpApA may well function this way.

Chain Initiation　　Just as there is a requirement for a signal in the message that spells "terminate," so there is one for the obverse, one that spells "initiate." Recent investigations have led to the startling conclusion that most, if not all, of the proteins of *E. coli* have, at least at the moment of their biosynthesis, the N terminal, i.e., the chain-initiating sequence

formyl$\dashv$NH—Met$\dashv$Ala$\dashv$Ser$\dashv$ · · ·

The formyl group and the Met, Ala, and Ser residues are subsequently removed, to a varying extent, depending on the particular protein produced. A Met codon, specifically one that recognizes N-formyl Met-tRNA is therefore strongly implicated as spelling "initiate." Formylation[1] occurs at the level of a specific methionyl-tRNA by transformylation from N^{10}-formyl FH_4. Thus initiation of translation and, provided that the two processes — which, as we know, started from the same point — are tightly coupled (see page 509), of transcription as well, are all controlled by the availability of an acylated tRNA that is in turn linked to one-carbon metabolism.

CONTROL OF
PROTEIN SYNTHESIS

In this section we discuss certain features of the regulation of protein biosynthesis, turning our attention to both its qualitative and quantitative aspects. That is, we ask the specific question: What are the determinants that control how much of a specific protein is to be synthesized at any one moment of a cell's history? Largely we shall restrict ourselves to results obtained with bacterial systems, since only there has a beginning been made to delineate the factors that define the problem.

Inhibitors of
Protein Synthesis

One of the most useful techniques in this, as in all other branches of biochemistry, has been the discovery of specific inhibitors, i.e., compounds that in this instance interfere with the biosynthetic process at specific points, it is hoped, by a selective and comprehensible mechanism, and therefore permit the dissection of the overall sequence into a number of component steps.

5-Methyltryptophan. Unlike most other amino acid analogues, 5-methyl-tryptophan:

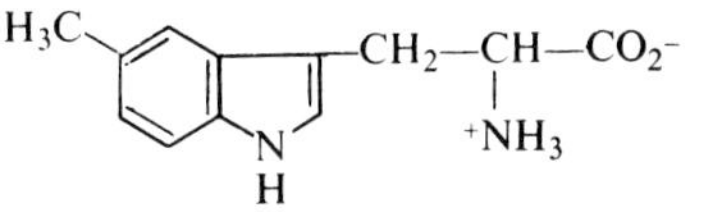

is not incorporated into protein but inhibits competitively the amino acyl synthetase for its parent compound, thus blocking the formation of Trp-tRNA and hence the biosynthesis of all tryptophan-containing polypeptides.

Chloroamphenicol (CAP). Of the various possible optical isomers only the D(−)*threo* form shows significant activity in vivo as an inhibitor of bacterial growth or protein synthesis, or in vitro in the latter process (effective levels 10 to 20 μg/ml):

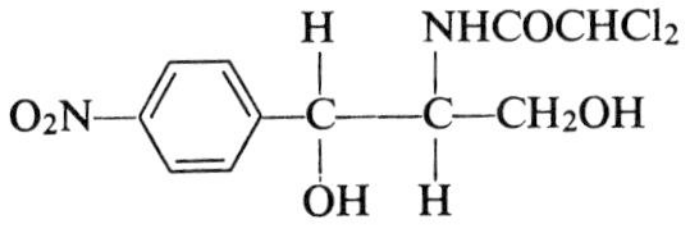

CAP exerts a number of effects on the inhibited cell. Among them is an accumulation of ribosomal precursors. Thus normal protein synthesis is inhibited in a secondary fashion because of the unavailability of functional ribosomes. There is also a more direct, primary effect on protein synthesis that

[1] The requirement for formylation (or acylation in general) of the N-terminal amino acid can be rationalized on the basis of the mechanism presented on page 501. It requires a molecule with $R \neq H$ occupying the "polymerization site." Acylation then renders the reaction forming the first peptide bond ($n = 1$) mechanistically equivalent to all subsequent ones ($n \neq 1$).

requires the compound to be bound to the 50-S subunits of susceptible ribosomes. Such particles are restricted to CAP-sensitive strains of bacteria.

Actidione. Actidione or cycloheximide appears to have a species specificity complementary to that of CAP, since it appears to interfere with cell-free protein synthesis in yeasts, fungi, and all higher organisms in general, yet is relatively ineffective on such systems from bacteria:

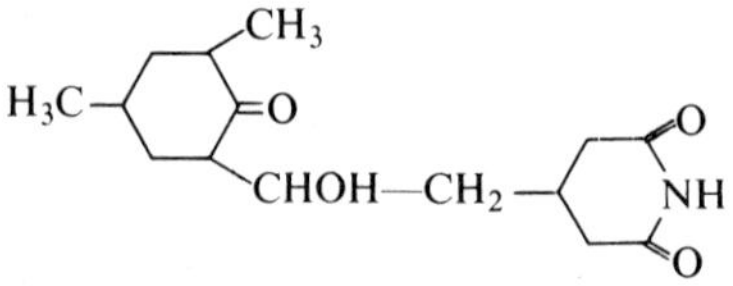

Its mode of action appears quite similar to that of CAP.

Puromycin. Puromycin bears an obvious relationship to the structure of an amino acyl-tRNA. The antibiotic blocks protein synthesis by functioning as an analogue of amino acylated tRNA, specifically by substituting for an incoming amino acyl-tRNA as the acceptor of the carboxyl-activated peptide. The peptidyl puromycins formed in this manner (attack at the N atom shown by arrows) are incapable of further chain growth (no transacylation at the wavy line). Thus puromycin administration leads to the release of peptides of varying chain length but all bearing the appropriate N-terminal amino acid at one end and a puromycin residue instead of a C terminus:

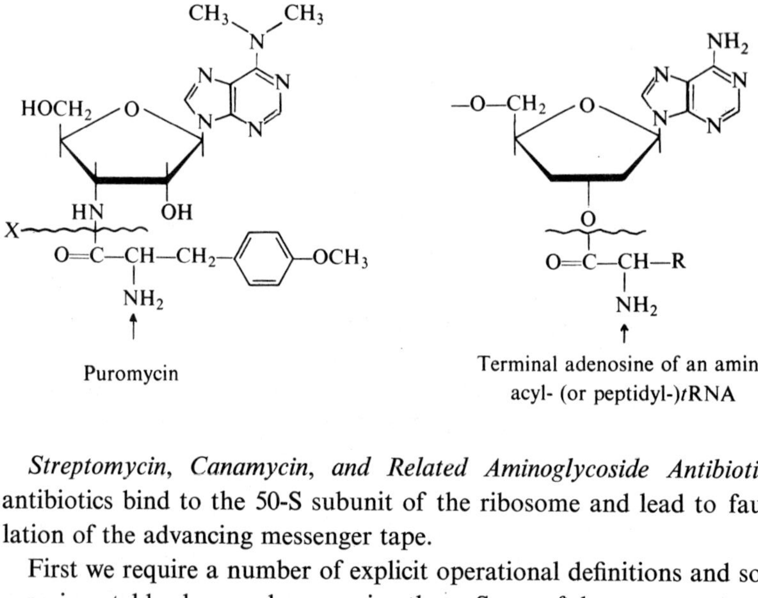

Puromycin

Terminal adenosine of an amino acyl- (or peptidyl-)*t*RNA

Streptomycin, Canamycin, and Related Aminoglycoside Antibiotics. These antibiotics bind to the 50-S subunit of the ribosome and lead to faulty translation of the advancing messenger tape.

First we require a number of explicit operational definitions and some of the experimental background concerning them. Some of these matters were touched on implicitly in Chap. 19.

The Operon. The bacterial chromosome is organized in operons consisting of clusters of genes, the expression of which is regulated jointly and leads to proteins related in function. In the *E. coli-Salmonella* group of bacteria, those responsible for lactose metabolism (*Lac* region), histidine biosynthesis (*His*), galactose metabolism (*Gal*), leucine biosynthesis (*Leu*), isoleucine and valine

Factors and Notions Concerning Control of Protein Synthesis in Bacteria biosynthesis (*Ival*), and arabinose metabolism (*Ara*) have been studied most intensively. The number of genes comprising them vary from three in the case of both the *Gal* and *Lac* operons to nine in the case of the *His* operon. The latter really consists of fifteen cistrons specifying nine enzymes (three enzymes with two cistrons each, one with four cistrons, and five with one cistron apiece) and extending over a total length of 13,000 nucleotides.

Polycistronic mRNA. Apparently the chromosomal unit of transcription is defined, not by the individual cistron or gene, but by the operon as a whole, which is transcribed and produces a polycistronic messenger. Evidence for messengers of appropriate size and complementariness has been obtained in the case of the *His* and *Lac* messengers. Very large polycistronic messengers are also produced either on (in the case of DNA viruses), or directly constituted by (for RNA viruses), the genome of viruses.

The Operator. The actual expression of the various structural genes in the operon is controlled by a small region located at one end of that operon, called the "operator." Mutations in this region affect all the genes of the operon. Operators probably exert their action at the level of transcription, as postulated by Monod and Jacob rather than at the level of translation. An operator maps as follows, where 1 through *n* are the cistrons of the operon and O is the operator region:

Forms of Regulation: Repression versus Induction. Repression is defined as a decrease and induction as an increase in the amount of one or more specific proteins produced as the result of exposing the cell to some regulatory substance. The latter, a small molecule, is frequently identical with or structurally related to the end product, in the case of repression, or the starting material, in the case of induction, of a metabolic sequence. Inducibility or repressibility is also controlled genetically, the genes in question (*regulator genes*) mapping in a position not necessarily linked to the operon comprising the structural gene(s) affected. The regulator gene(s) controls the synthesis of a product — the (*apo*)*repressor* — which then in turn interacts with the operator in either a positive or negative sense (see Fig. 21-5), triggering transcription in the former, blocking it in the latter case. This interaction is in turn regulated by an allosteric interaction with the regulatory small molecule. Thus a "negative" aporepressor may be rendered harmless by an inducer or effective by a corepressor. Induction and derepression are therefore formally and mechanistically equivalent. Induction and repression of enzymes in microorganisms are exceedingly common. Of the six operons listed above, the three concerned with the metabolism of sugars are inducible by their substrates or structural analogues thereto, as might have been expected from the definition given earlier. Those controlling amino acid biosynthesis are repressible by these amino acids.

In general, repression by end products is frequently observed in anabolic pathways for amino acids, vitamins, purines, and pyrimidines; induction is the rule in the case of catabolic sequences involving carbon and energy sources.[1] Regulation can be rationalized on the basis of economy of use in the machinery for protein synthesis: Synthesis of enzymes catalyzing any metabolic sequence is turned on or off, depending on the demands for that specific sequence. Why synthesize proteins unless and until they are needed?

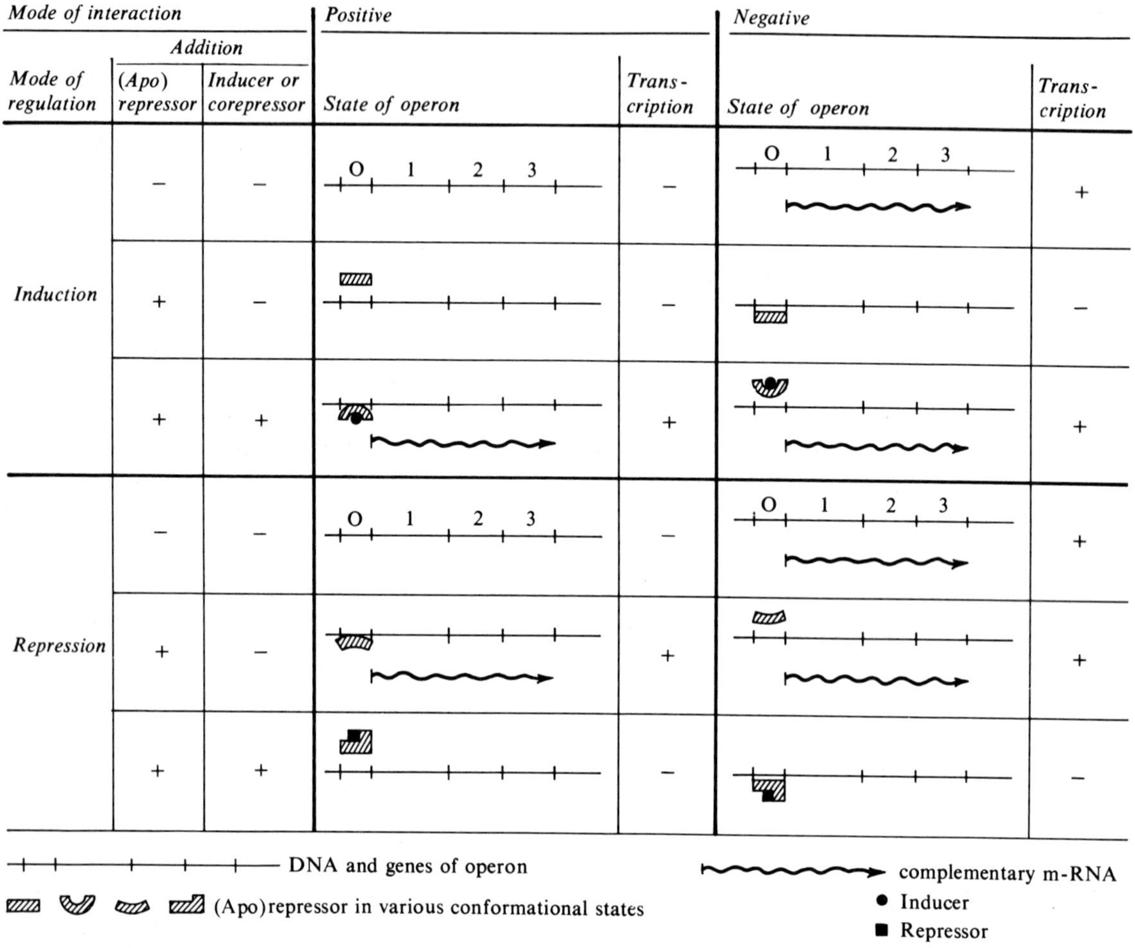

Mode of interaction	Addition		Positive		Negative	
Mode of regulation	(Apo) repressor	Inducer or corepressor	State of operon	Trans-cription	State of operon	Trans-cription
Induction	−	−	O 1 2 3	−	O 1 2 3 (m-RNA)	+
Induction	+	−	(repressor bound)	−	(repressor bound)	−
Induction	+	+	(repressor+inducer, m-RNA)	+	(repressor+inducer, m-RNA)	+
Repression	−	−	O 1 2 3	−	O 1 2 3 (m-RNA)	+
Repression	+	−	(repressor bound, m-RNA)	+	(repressor bound, m-RNA)	+
Repression	+	+	(repressor bound)	−	(repressor bound)	−

├──┼──┼──┼──┼──┤ DNA and genes of operon   ∿∿∿➤ complementary m-RNA

(Apo)repressor in various conformational states   ● Inducer   ■ Repressor

FIGURE 21-5.   Regulation of Genetic Expression.

A particularly instructive example of complex interactions between inductions and repressions to effect close control of the synthesis of various proteins within a group is provided by the enzymes that catalyze the breakdown of mandelic acid (or rather its salt mandelate) in *Pseudomonas*. The following pathway is believed to be involved:

$$\text{Mandelate } (A) \xrightarrow{a} \text{benzoyl formate } (B) \xrightarrow{b} \text{benzaldehyde } (C) \xrightarrow{c} \text{benzoate } (D) \xrightarrow{d} \text{catechol } (E)$$

$$\downarrow e$$
$$\downarrow f$$
$$\text{acetate} + \text{succinate } (I) \xleftarrow{} \xleftarrow{g} \beta\text{-ketoadipate } (G)$$

---

[1] We are reminded of the generalization mentioned in Chap. 11 that pacemaker enzymes in anabolic sequences are frequently inhibited by their end products and that corresponding enzymes in catabolic pathways are sometimes activated by their substrates or products.

First of all the enzymes are sequentially inducible in the sense that the addition of A first induces the synthesis of $a, b, \ldots$, and only as various intermediates, such as D, E, etc., make their appearance does the induction of enzymes d, e, and so forth, commence. Closer attention to detail shows that the enzymes of the pathway are controlled by three operons which we shall call I, II, and III. Operon I controls synthesis of enzymes a, b, and c and is induced by A, the first substrate; it is repressed by D, the immediate product accumulating as a result of its operation, as well as by E and I, the distal products. Operon II controls enzyme d; it is induced by D and repressed by E and I. Finally operon III consists of enzymes e and f and perhaps others. It is induced by E and repressed only by I.

We turn now to the operon that has been studied most intensively, i.e., the *Lac* operon of *E. coli*. It consists of the closely linked genes:

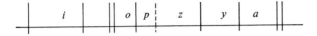

where a controls thiogalactoside transacetylase, y a structure affecting the entry of galactosides into the cell, the permease, and z the β-D-galactosidase itself. A number of constitutive mutants were found that are controlled by a regulator gene called i, which maps outside the *Lac* operon proper, and which were characterized by the production of high levels of enzyme in the absence of inducer. These mutants were therefore designated as i^-, to distinguish them from the standard type i^+, which exhibits low enzyme levels until induced by galactosides. If the cis diploid $z^+ i^+ / i^-$, which contains both allelic forms of the i gene, was constructed by conjugation, transduction, or F-duction, the cell was found to be inducible. Therefore i^+ is dominant over i^-; i.e., i^+ specifies a product lacking in the cell i^-. The product is a cytoplasmic entity, since the trans diploid $z^- i^+ / z^+ i^-$ was also inducible, which implied that the i^+ character controls expression of both chromosomes.

What is the nature of this product, the aporepressor? Recent evidence strongly suggests that it is a protein and that it is capable of binding to DNA, with the o region providing the binding site. Its function is to block transcription, an event that requires for its initiation and regulation the presence of an adjacent region (p for promotor) and takes place upon removal of the repressor, usually by interaction with the inducer. Several different classes of altered repressors are produced by mutation in the i gene: i^- strains either lack the repressor or produce a functionally altered molecule and in consequence produce the three proteins of the operon constitutively; i^s strains produce repressor molecules incapable of effective interaction with inducer, hence the operon is permanently shut off, even when inducer is present; finally i^r strains produce a repressor that requires the presence of inducer before it can bind the operator. Hence, these strains produce the proteins constitutively and are repressed by inducer.

Coordination. For any strain of cells the ratio of the amount of any one enzyme to any other enzyme in the same operon remains constant, regardless of the extent of its induction or repression. This statement implies that the ratio of the amounts of various protein molecules controlled by any individual operon is a constant, though it may differ widely from unity. Therefore the various enzymes are manufactured in constant proportion regardless of the state of induction or repression, which in extreme cases may lead to increases or decreases by a factor of 10^2 or 10^3.

Polarity. Certain mutations in the structural genes of an operon have a dual (pleiotropic) effect. They not only control the structure of the resultant polypeptide, but they also effect a decrease in the amount of all those enzymes controlled by genes located beyond the gene primarily affected and distal from the operator, e.g.,

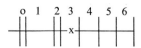

mutation in 3 affects the amount of enzyme produced by 4, 5, and 6. In general mutation in gene n also affects the amounts of gene product controlled by genes $n + 1$ and on. We may, for instance, observe the following levels of amounts of proteins 1 to 6:

	Repressed		Derepressed or induced
Wild type	$10:5:2:1$	$:1:0.5$	$100:50:20:10:10:5$
Polarity mutant 3	$10:5:0:0.5:0.5:0.25$		$100:50:0:5:5:2.5$

Polarity mutations are frequently of the chain-terminating, nonsense type and therefore suppressible. The amount of mRNA produced depends directly on their location within the operon: the farther away from the operator, the greater the proportion transcribed.

Operator Mutations. Originally the operator was defined by the existence of operator constitutive (O^c) mutations, which resemble i^- mutations, in producing elevated levels of all enzymes in the operon in the absence of external inducer. They can however be distinguished from regulator constitutive mutations in four ways: (1) their map position — O^c mutants map at one end but within the operon, whereas i^- mutants map outside; (2) diploids O^c/O^+ are constitutive, whereas i^-/i^+ are inducible; (3) the O^c mutation affects only genes on the same chromosomes, i.e., in the cis configuration; $y^+z^-O^ci^+/y^+z^+O^+i^+$ is constitutive for permease but inducible for galactosidase; (4) all O^c mutations are deletions and, hence, nonsuppressible.

Possible Models. One very plausible and simple model that does account in a consistent manner for almost all the data presented so far is some form of "modulation model" originally formulated by Ames, Hartman, and Martin. It postulates the transcription of the whole operon into a single mRNA, with both transcription and translation of the message commencing at or near the operator and progressing away in a sequential manner from this terminus (promoter?), which also provides the principal attachment site for ribosomes. At any one time many ribosomes are engaged in translation at different stages. When a ribosome reaches the end of the first cistron, it has a choice between falling off the messenger or beginning to translate the next cistron, and these alternatives again present themselves at the end of the next cistron, and so forth. If the ribosome reaches a codon for which the tRNA required is either in short supply or absent entirely, polypeptide formation slows down or ceases entirely, and the progress of the ribosome down the messenger is slowed in a manner analogous to that obtaining at the end of a cistron. As a consequence there is an increased chance that the particle may drop off the messenger before reaching another site capable of chain initiation, succeeding ribosomes may pile up and in turn be bumped off, and the mRNA may be destroyed, starting at its unoccupied end. Induction then makes possible the continued and orderly progression of events outlined above and allows mRNA and protein synthesis to start and continue in a concerted manner, while repression produces the opposite effects. The pertinence of this and other, equally plausible models, formulated on the basis of experiments on a limited number of microbial systems, to higher organisms remains yet to be established.

REFERENCES   Ames, B. N., and R. G. Martin: Biochemical Aspects of Genetics: The Operon, *Ann. Rev. Biochem.*, **33**: 235 (1964).

Anfinsen, C.: "The Molecular Basis of Evolution," Wiley, New York, 1959.

Beckwith, J. R.: Regulation of the Lac Operon, *Science*, **156**: 597 (1967).

Bennett, J. C., and W. J. Dreyer: Genetic Coding for Protein Structure, *Ann. Rev. Biochem.*, **33**: 205 (1964).

Benzer, S.: Genetic Fine Structure, *Harvey Lectures*, **56**: 1 (1961).

Bonner, D. M., and S. E. Mills: "Heredity," 2d ed., Prentice-Hall, Englewood Cliffs, N.J., 1964.

Campbell, P. N.: The Biosynthesis of Proteins, *Progr. Biophys. Mol. Biol.*, **15**: 3 (1965).

Cohn, N. S.: "Elements of Cytology," Harcourt, Brace & World, New York, 1964.

Cold Spring Harbor Symposium on Quantitative Biology, vol. 26: Cellular Regulatory Mechanisms, 1961.

———, vol. 28: Synthesis and Structure of Macromolecules, 1963.

———, vol. 31: The Genetic Code, 1966.

Crick, F. H. C.: The Recent Excitement in the Coding Problem, in J. N. Davidson and W. E. Cohn (eds.), *Progr. in Nucleic Acid Res. and Mol. Biol.*, **1**: 164 (1963).

Freese, E.: Molecular Mechanism of Mutations, in J. H. Taylor (ed.), "Molecular Genetics," vol. 1, p. 207, Academic Press, New York, 1963.

Hayes, W.: "The Genetics of Bacteria and Their Viruses," Wiley, New York, 1964.

Horowitz, N. H., and R. L. Metzenberg: Biochemical Aspects of Genetics, *Ann. Rev. Biochem.*, **34**: 527 (1965).

McElroy, W. D., and B. Glass (eds.): "The Chemical Basis of Heredity," Johns Hopkins Press, Baltimore, 1957.

Moldave, K.: Nucleic Acids and Protein Biosynthesis, *Ann. Rev. Biochem.*, **34**: 419 (1965).

Monod, J., F. Jacob, and F. Gros: Structural and Rate-determining Factors in the Biosynthesis of Adaptive Enzymes, in "The Structure and Biosynthesis of Macromolecules," *Biochem. Soc. Symp. (Cambridge, Eng.)*, vol. 21, 1962.

Nirenberg, M.: Protein Synthesis and the RNA Code, *Harvey Lectures*, **59**: 155 (1964).

Sager, R., and F. J. Ryan: "Cell Heredity," Wiley, New York, 1961.

Schweet, R., R. Arlinghaus, R. Heintz, and J. Shaeffer: Mechanism of Peptide Bond Formation in Protein Synthesis, in "Developmental and Metabolic Control Mechanisms in Neoplasia," 19th Annual M. D. Anderson Symposium on Fundamental Cancer Research, University of Texas Press, Austin, 1966.

——— and R. Heintz, Protein Synthesis, *Ann. Rev. Biochem.*, **35**: 723 (1966).

Singer, M. F., and M. F. Leder: Messenger RNA: An Evaluation, *Ann. Rev. Biochem.*, **35**: 195, (1966).

Stanbury, J. B., J. B. Wyngaarden, and D. S. Frederickson (eds.): "The Metabolic Basis of Inherited Disease," McGraw-Hill, New York, 1960.

Steiner, R. F.: "The Chemical Foundations of Molecular Biology," especially chaps. 1 and 11, Van Nostrand, Princeton, N.J., 1965.

Stent, G. S.: " Molecular Biology of Bacterial Viruses," especially chaps. 8–10, 13, 15, Freeman, San Francisco, 1963.

Thomas, C. A.: Recombination of DNA Molecules, in *Progr. Nucleic Acid Res. in Mol. Biol.*, **5**: 315 (1967).

Watson, J. D.: " Molecular Biology of the Gene," Benjamin, New York, 1965.

Zamenhof, S.: Nucleic Acids and Mutability, in *Progr. Nucleic Acid Res. Mol. Biol.*, **6**: 1 (1967).

INDEX

Index

68 69 70   7 6 5 4 3 2 1